September 17, 1984

I prayed for a daughter. I thought
God wasn't going to answer my prayers.
But now he has.

I love you,
Mom

# Meet the *Southern Living* Foods Staff

*Deborah Garrison and Susan Payne, Assistant Food Editors*

*Jean Wickstrom Liles, Foods Editor*

*Margaret Chason, Associate Foods Editor*

*Susan M. McIntosh and Betsy Fannin, Registered Dietitians*

Southern hospitality has always been a powerful tradition in an area where people enjoy cooking and entertaining in their homes. For years *Southern Living* has played an important role in furthering that tradition as Southern cooks have found our foods pages to be a primary source of irresistible recipes and entertaining ideas.

Not only are our foods pages planned and written with the Southern reader in mind but also the ideas and recipes generally come from these same readers. This type of audience participation enables us to assemble a wide variety of recipes—from traditional Southern foods to cosmopolitan cuisine.

We have a team of food professionals who work diligently to make our foods features special for our audience. A generous measure of "personal touch" goes into all of the articles as each one is planned and written by our foods staff. Our foods editorial staff is guided by Foods Editor Jean Wickstrom Liles, who is assisted by Associate Foods Editor Margaret Chason, Assistant Foods Editors Deborah Garrison and Susan Payne, Registered Dietitians Susan M. McIntosh and Betsy Fannin,

and Editorial Assistant Catherine Garrison. Combined, these professionals bring you the scrumptious stories that appear in the issues of *Southern Living* throughout the year.

Because more and more cooks are experimenting with microwave cooking, a microwave story is included in every month of *Southern Living*. The recipes are developed by our staff and tested several different times in different ovens to perfect the cooking times and techniques.

"Cooking Light" is a new monthly feature that highlights low-calorie and low-sodium versions of the South's favorite foods. These stories show that good food doesn't have to be loaded with calories or salt.

We also find that entertaining is increasingly popular. Our party features are presented as authentically as possible and include menus, recipes, serving suggestions, and preparation tips. When working on an entertainment feature, our editors actually visit in the selected home and spend a great deal of time talking with the host and hostess.

*Catherine Garrison, Editorial Assistant; Lynn Lloyd, Test Kitchens Director*

*Diane Hogan, Peggy Smith, and Fran Tyler, Test Kitchens Staff*

*Laura Nestelroad, Test Kitchens Staff; Karen Parker, Assistant Test Kitchens Director*

Through our regional food stories, readers can travel the South and can take a peek into the kitchens of our "man cooks." Step-by-step photo stories and tips from our kitchens also provide information that is both interesting and practical.

We have a responsibility to our readers to share only the very best recipes. To ensure the quality, each recipe is tested, tasted, and evaluated before publication by our test kitchens staff comprised of Test Kitchens Director Lynn Lloyd, Assistant Test Kitchens Director Karen Parker, Diane Hogan, Laura Nestelroad, Peggy Smith, and Fran Tyler. The three kitchens in which they test the recipes are much like any home kitchen, so that each recipe is tested using the same type equipment and under the same conditions as those of the average homemaker.

Much time is spent in preparing the market order and shopping for the ingredients needed to test an average of 55 to 60 recipes a week. Grocery shopping is done each week at the same kinds of supermarkets where our readers shop. Our recipes utilize ingredients found in a typical Southern kitchen, and when seasonal fruit and vegetables are called for, testing is done while the produce is at its best in terms of flavor and price.

All of our *Southern Living* food photographs serve as an invitation to the reader to enjoy our recipes. Since our aim is to capture a natural look with our food, our photographs reveal its actual appearance. Photo Stylist Beverly Morrow and Senior Foods Photographer Charles Walton work closely with the editors involved to create evocative settings through design and careful selection of props. Our well-equipped photography studio contains an up-to-date display of china, glassware, and table linens.

We also travel throughout the South to photograph regional food stories and entertainment features in Southern settings and in the homes of our readers. These photographs capture the spirit of the events, showing the Southern tradition of people getting together, enjoying good food and good company.

*Beverly Morrow, Photo Stylist; Charles Walton, Senior Foods Photographer*

# Southern Living®
# 1982 ANNUAL RECIPES

*Oxmoor House, Inc., Birmingham*

*Southern Living 1982 Annual Recipes*

*Southern Living*® is a registered trademark of Southern Living,
Inc. *Breakfasts & Brunches*™, *Summer Suppers*®, *Mexican
Food Fest*™, and *Holiday Dinners*™ are trademarks of Southern
Living, Inc.

Library of Congress Catalog Number: 79-88364
ISBN: 0-8487-0537-8

Manufactured in the United States of America
First Printing 1982

Cover: *Our traditional seated dinner begins
with an appetizer of Mushroom Soup (page
286), then offers a classic main course of
Roast Turkey With Rice Dressing (page
286). Refrigerator Rolls (page 287)
accompany side dishes of Sweet Potato
Soufflé (page 286), Creamy Broccoli
Supreme (page 287), and Glazed Carrots
With Grapes (page 287).*

Page i: *Some of the best ways we know to
enjoy pears to the fullest are Pear Preserves
(page 195), Poached Pears in Wine (page
194), Double-Crust Pear Pie (page 194),
and Best Ever Pear Cobbler (page 194).*

Page iv: *To prepare Pork St. Tammany
(page 260), wrap pork tenderloins around a
wild rice and apricot stuffing.*

# Table of Contents

*Sailor Shrimp for Two (page 276)*

*Gourmet Chicken Divan (page 83)*

*Frozen Strawberry Delight (page 112)*

# Our Year at Southern Living

Since its founding sixteen years ago, *Southern Living* has become a Southern tradition in itself. No small part of this tradition is our food section which each year brings to our readers over 1200 new and exciting recipes. Four years ago we initiated a new service to our readers, *Annual Recipes*. *Southern Living* is pleased to present *1982 Annual Recipes*, the fourth edition of this popular collection.

One of the trademarks of a great magazine should be its continuing effort to improve the quality of its product to better serve its readers. In 1982 we instituted some significant changes in our foods section that have brought much positive response from our readers.

We opened the year with our new "Cooking Light" monthly feature which contains low-calorie or low-sodium recipes for the South's favorite foods. It's hardly a secret that more and more people are concerned with calories and

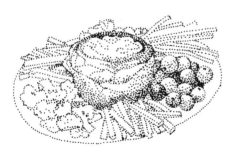

good nutrition. "Cooking Light" specifically addresses these concerns. These features prove you don't have to give up all the foods you love when on a diet. With each "Cooking Light" recipe, the calorie or sodium content per serving is given. Many of these recipes are developed by our foods staff while others are submitted as kitchen-tested favorites from our readers. Along with our recipes you'll find basic information on modifying your own favorite recipes for light cooking.

Also during 1982 we introduced a monthly feature "From Our Kitchen To Yours." Prepared by our test kitchens director, this column is designed to answer the many food and food preparation questions we receive from our readers—from the novice to the experienced cook.

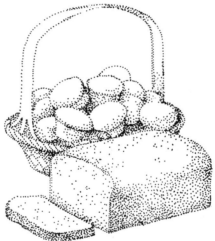

Each year more and more *Southern Living* readers are using microwave ovens on a daily basis. Our monthly "Microwave Cookery" feature has been very popular, particularly for our readers who are time-conscious and energy-conscious. The microwave recipes are developed by our staff and tested several times to perfect cooking times and techniques.

In addition to these special monthly features, you'll discover *1982 Annual Recipes* contains wonderful entertaining ideas for each season, quick and easy dishes for those extra busy days, and recipes for just the two of you. In recognition of the continuing and expanding interest by men in cooking, throughout 1982 we have spotlighted Southern men creating their own sumptuous dishes.

Our food ideas come from the South's best cooks who each month favor us with thousands of their family's favorite recipes. In the past year we have seen an increase in the number of fresh fruit and vegetable recipes submitted to us, which is perhaps indicative of the fact that more and more Southerners are involved with home gardens. Consequently we've given more emphasis to use of the fresh fruits and vegetables that can be grown in our readers' backyards.

*1982 Annual Recipes* brings to you in one handy reference book a collection of the year's recipes. It includes every food article plus 32 color photograph pages packed with ideas for arranging and presenting foods. Throughout the book you will find tips for planning menus, buying food, and preparing and serving recipes for all occasions. To assist you in finding specific recipes, three detailed indexes are included at the end of the book.

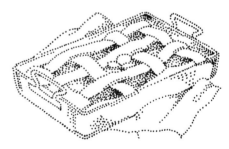

With *1982 Annual Recipes* at hand, enjoy the best of Southern fare throughout the year. We sincerely believe you will find this cookbook a valuable edition to your culinary library. If you'd like to share one of your favorite recipes with our readers, do write us. In the meantime, we hope with this 1982 cookbook you can introduce your family and friends to the most mouth-watering collection of Southern recipes available.

*Jean Wickstrom Liles*

# January

Holiday indulging usually leaves most of us diet conscious, so January is just the month to introduce our new "Cooking Light" column. Designed for calorie-cutting readers, this monthly feature, prepared by one of our staff dietitians, shows how to lighten your diet without sacrificing taste. Since we eat a lot of food here at *Southern Living,* you can imagine how delighted we are to know that we can trim a few calories as we test these dishes! Our first feature presents a tempting menu of Steak Kabobs, Peppered Rice, Spinach-Stuffed Squash, Dressed-Up Fruit, and even Strawberry Puff for dessert. You'll never know the calories are missing.

As long as you're trimming calories, our recipes for dried beans will help trim food costs and serve tasty and nutritious meals as well. Make a main dish from our hearty Beef-and-Bean Supper starring pinto beans or serve our Barbecued Lima Beans for a perky side dish.

# Beans Are Basic, But Oh So Good

With the rising cost of food, especially such high-protein items as meat and fish, now is a good time to reconsider the basic bean. In fact, many people are discovering that dried beans are not only economical, delicious, and versatile, but also very nutritious.

Besides offering significant quantities of protein, a cup of cooked dried beans provides about half the daily iron needs of a man, about a fourth of a woman's needs. Beans also contain very little fat and are a great source of the fiber and bulk necessary for normal digestion. In addition, they are a rich source of several B-complex vitamins.

Then there's the great taste of dried beans, to be enjoyed in dishes like Barbecued Lima Beans, Beef-and-Bean Supper, and Garbanzo Salad.

Dried beans must be soaked before cooking to replace the moisture removed during the drying process. If you remember to plan ahead, the easiest way is to soak the beans overnight. An alternative is the quick-soak method: Boil the beans two minutes, and remove them from the heat; cover and let stand one hour.

Once rehydrated, beans usually cook in one to three hours, depending on the type of bean. Of course, you can cook dried beans without soaking first, but they must cook much longer.

For best results, add a little fat or oil to the beans to reduce the foam that tends to build during cooking. One other important cooking hint—cook beans over very low heat since a rolling boil may cause them to break or burst.

## BEEF-AND-BEAN SUPPER

1 pound dried pinto beans
1 medium onion, chopped
1 clove garlic, minced
2 tablespoons olive oil
1 pound ground beef
1 (28-ounce) can tomatoes, undrained
1 (8-ounce) can tomato sauce
1 teaspoon salt
¼ teaspoon pepper
2 bay leaves

Sort and wash beans; place in a large Dutch oven. Cover with water 2 inches above beans; let soak overnight. Drain beans; cover with water. Cover and bring to a boil; reduce heat, and simmer for 1 hour.

Sauté onion and garlic in oil until tender. Add ground beef; cook, stirring often, until meat is browned. Drain off pan drippings.

Stir ground beef mixture and remaining ingredients into beans. Cover and cook over low heat 2 hours, stirring occasionally. Remove bay leaves. Yield: 10 servings.
*Barbara Bracey,*
*Franklin, Tennessee.*

## BLACK BEANS WITH YELLOW RICE

1 pound dried black beans
1 large green pepper, chopped
1 large onion, chopped
5 cloves garlic, minced
⅓ cup olive oil
½ cup pimiento-stuffed olives, sliced
¼ cup dry white wine
3 tablespoons vinegar
1 bay leaf
1 teaspoon ground oregano
½ teaspoon salt
½ teaspoon pepper
¼ teaspoon ground cumin
Hot cooked yellow rice
Chopped green onion

Sort and wash beans; place in a large Dutch oven. Cover with water 2 inches above beans; let soak overnight.

Sauté green pepper, onion, and garlic in olive oil until tender; stir mixture into beans. Add next 8 ingredients, stirring well. Cover and bring to a boil; reduce heat. Simmer 2 to 3 hours or until desired degree of doneness, adding more water if necessary. Remove and discard bay leaf. Serve over hot cooked yellow rice; top with chopped green onion. Yield: 10 servings.
*Barbara Carson,*
*Hollywood, Florida.*

## BARBECUED LIMA BEANS

1 pound dried lima beans
6 slices bacon
1 cup chopped onion
½ cup chopped green pepper
1 (15-ounce) can tomato sauce with tomato pieces
1 cup commercial barbecue sauce
¾ teaspoon salt

Sort and wash beans; place in a Dutch oven. Cover with water 2 inches above beans; let soak overnight. Cover and bring to a boil; reduce heat, and simmer 1 hour or until beans are tender and all water is absorbed.

Fry bacon in a large skillet until crisp; remove and drain bacon, reserving 2 tablespoons drippings in skillet. Crumble bacon, and set aside.

Sauté onion and green pepper in drippings until tender. Stir in beans, tomato sauce, barbecue sauce, and salt. Spoon bean mixture into a 3-quart casserole.

Bake, uncovered, at 350° for 30 minutes. Sprinkle bacon over beans. Yield: 10 to 12 servings.
*Mrs. W. H. Colley, Jr.,*
*Donelson, Tennessee.*

## GARBANZO SALAD

½ pound dried garbanzo beans
1 (4-ounce) jar diced pimiento
¼ cup chopped fresh parsley
3 green onions, thinly sliced
¼ cup red wine vinegar
2 tablespoons olive oil or vegetable oil
1 teaspoon salt
Dash of pepper
Lettuce leaves

Sort and wash beans; place in a Dutch oven. Cover with water 2 inches above beans; let soak overnight. Drain beans; cover with water. Cover and bring to a boil; reduce heat, and simmer 1 hour or until beans are tender. Drain beans, and let cool.

Combine beans, pimiento, parsley, and green onion; stir well. Combine next 4 ingredients; stir well, and pour over beans. Toss gently; chill several hours or overnight. Serve on lettuce leaves. Yield: 6 to 8 servings.
*Note:* Two (15-ounce) cans garbanzo beans, drained, may be substituted for prepared dried beans.
*Lou Sirois,*
*Auburn, Alabama.*

# Soup's On, Sandwiches Too

A bowl of steaming soup and a plump sandwich—the ideal cold-weather combination. Take your choice of our hearty soups, filled with vegetables, cheese, and meats, and sandwiches made with a variety of breads and tasty fillings.

For our Turkey-Mozzarella Rounds, pocket bread is filled with turkey, cheese, slaw, and tomatoes. Crescent rolls form the wrapping for our hot

Ham-and-Cheese Rolls, while English muffins sport a spicy pizza topping.

Team your choice of sandwiches with our Special Potato Soup; this one includes carrots, celery, and cheese, along with the potatoes. Try Hearty Ham Soup, based on smoked ham hocks, or our version of Italian minestrone, a vegetable soup that will complement any sandwich.

## TURKEY-MOZZARELLA ROUNDS

1 (0.4-ounce) envelope buttermilk salad dressing mix
3 cups coarsely grated cabbage
6 (6-inch) pocket bread rounds
12 slices mozzarella cheese
12 thin slices cooked turkey breast
2 medium tomatoes, chopped

Prepare dressing according to package directions. Combine 1 cup dressing and cabbage; mix well. Reserve remaining dressing for another use.

Cut pocket bread rounds and cheese slices in half. Place a half slice cheese in each pocket bread half; add a turkey slice and another half slice cheese. Spoon about 2 tablespoons cabbage slaw and 2 tablespoons chopped tomato into each sandwich. Serve immediately. Yield: 12 servings.

*Note:* To serve hot, place sandwiches in a 13- x 9- x 2-inch baking pan. Cover with aluminum foil; bake at 350° for 20 minutes or until cheese melts. Add slaw and tomato after heating. *Sue Freesen, Montgomery, Alabama.*

## OPEN-FACE PIZZA SANDWICHES

1 pound ground beef
1 (1.5-ounce) package spaghetti sauce mix
1 (6-ounce) can tomato paste
4 English muffins, split
24 slices pepperoni
¼ pound mozzarella cheese, cut into strips

Cook ground beef until browned, stirring to crumble; drain on paper towels. Return meat to skillet. Add spaghetti sauce mix and tomato paste; stir well. Cook over low heat, stirring occasionally, until mixture is thoroughly heated.

Spoon meat mixture on muffin halves; top each with 3 slices pepperoni. Bake at 350° for 5 to 10 minutes. Top with cheese strips; bake an additional 3 minutes or until cheese melts. Yield: 8 servings. *Elizabeth Kraus, Louisville, Kentucky.*

## HAM-AND-CHEESE ROLLS

1 cup finely chopped cooked ham
¾ cup (3 ounces) finely chopped Swiss cheese
2 green onions, chopped
1½ teaspoons prepared mustard
1 (8-ounce) can refrigerated crescent rolls
1 tablespoon water
1 egg, beaten
½ teaspoon poppy seeds

Combine ham, cheese, onion, and mustard; mix well. Separate rolls into 8 triangles. Place 2 heaping tablespoons ham mixture in center of each triangle. Bring tips of triangle together in center of ham mixture; press edges together to seal. Place on greased baking sheet.

Combine water and egg; brush over rolls. Sprinkle with poppy seeds. Bake at 375° for 12 minutes or until golden. Yield: 8 servings. *Janice C. Hughes, Sulphur, Louisiana.*

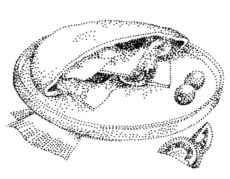

## HOT FRENCH CHEESE SANDWICHES

2 cups (8 ounces) shredded sharp Cheddar cheese
½ cup butter or margarine, softened
2 eggs
⅛ to ¼ teaspoon garlic powder
⅛ to ¼ teaspoon onion powder
16 slices white or rye sandwich bread
Paprika

Combine first 5 ingredients; beat at medium speed of electric mixer until smooth. Spread about 1 tablespoon cheese mixture on each of 8 bread slices. Top with remaining bread slices, and spread remaining cheese mixture on top of the sandwiches; sprinkle with paprika. Bake at 400° about 10 to 12 minutes. Yield: 8 servings.

*Note:* Sandwiches may be frozen. Wrap each unbaked sandwich in freezer-proof wrap; freeze. Thaw sandwiches just before baking.

*Mrs. R. M. Lancaster, Brentwood, Tennessee.*

## SPECIAL POTATO SOUP

2 stalks celery, sliced
1 medium onion, chopped
2 tablespoons butter or margarine, melted
6 medium potatoes, peeled and cubed
2 carrots, sliced
3 cups water
5 chicken-flavored bouillon cubes
¾ teaspoon seasoned salt
½ teaspoon dried whole thyme
½ teaspoon dried whole rosemary, crushed
Dash of garlic powder
Dash of pepper
2 cups milk
1 cup (4 ounces) shredded Longhorn Cheddar cheese

Sauté celery and onion in butter in a large Dutch oven until tender. Add next 9 ingredients; cover and simmer about 20 minutes or until vegetables are tender.

Remove from heat, and mash vegetables with a potato masher. Add milk and cheese; cook, stirring constantly, until cheese is melted. Yield: 10 cups. *Mrs. Bill Anthony, North Little Rock, Arkansas.*

## MARVELOUS VEGETABLE SOUP

1 pound lean beef for stewing, cut into 1-inch cubes
Vegetable oil
4 cups water, divided
4 carrots, sliced
1 (28-ounce) can whole tomatoes, undrained and coarsely chopped
4 potatoes, peeled and cubed
1 large onion, coarsely chopped
1 (10-ounce) package frozen green beans
1 (8-ounce) can whole kernel corn, drained
¼ cup sliced celery
1 large turnip, peeled and cubed
1 teaspoon Worcestershire sauce
1 tablespoon cocktail sauce
1 tablespoon sugar
1 teaspoon salt
¼ teaspoon pepper

Brown beef in hot vegetable oil in a heavy Dutch oven; add 2 cups water. Bring to a boil. Reduce heat; cover and simmer 1½ hours.

Add carrots and remaining 2 cups water; bring to a boil. Reduce heat; cover and simmer 15 minutes. Add remaining ingredients; cover and simmer an additional 30 minutes, stirring occasionally. Yield: about 3 quarts.

*Dorsella Utter, Louisville, Kentucky.*

## MINESTRONE

2 (10½-ounce) cans beef bouillon
½ cup tomato sauce
1 large potato, peeled and diced
1 cup chopped celery
½ cup scraped, sliced carrot
½ cup chopped onion
½ cup chopped cabbage
½ cup frozen green beans
2 tablespoons chopped green pepper
1 clove garlic, crushed
¼ teaspoon pepper
½ teaspoon paprika
⅓ cup frozen English peas
½ cup spaghetti, broken into small pieces
Grated Parmesan cheese (optional)

Dilute bouillon according to label directions. Stir in tomato sauce; bring to a boil. Stir in next 10 ingredients. Bring to a boil; cover and simmer 1 hour.

Return to a boil. Add peas and spaghetti; simmer 15 minutes. Sprinkle with Parmesan cheese before serving, if desired. Yield: 6 cups.

*Charlotte Watkins,*
*Lakeland, Florida.*

## HEARTY HAM SOUP

1½ to 1¾ pounds smoked ham hocks
8 cups water
1 clove garlic, minced
8 whole peppercorns
5 whole cloves
1 teaspoon salt
3 large carrots, scraped and sliced
2 large potatoes, peeled and cubed
½ medium head cabbage, coarsely
    chopped
½ cup chopped onion
8 (¾-inch-thick) slices rye bread, toasted
Grated Parmesan cheese
8 (1-ounce) slices Swiss cheese, cut into
    ¼-inch strips

Combine first 6 ingredients in a large Dutch oven. Bring to a boil. Reduce heat; cover and simmer 1 hour or until ham is tender. Remove ham hocks; cut ham from bones, and coarsely chop. Return ham to liquid; add carrots. Bring to a boil. Reduce heat; cover and simmer 10 minutes. Add potatoes, cabbage, and onion. Bring to a boil. Reduce heat; cover and simmer an additional 30 minutes or until vegetables are tender.

Ladle soup into 8 serving dishes; top each with a bread slice. Sprinkle with Parmesan cheese, and top with Swiss cheese. Broil 2 to 3 minutes or until cheese melts; serve immediately. Yield: 8 cups. *Mrs. F. G. Moore, Jr.,*
*Winchester, Tennessee.*

## Cooking Light

# Lighten Your Diet Deliciously

Does Italian food really have to be fattening? How about dessert? Do you give up the foods you love when on a diet? If you, or someone in your family, are counting calories or trying to cut down on salt, then "Cooking Light" is for you.

Each month "Cooking Light" will feature low-calorie or low-sodium recipes developed by the foods staff at *Southern Living,* as well as kitchen-tested favorites from our readers. We'll include casseroles, desserts, potato dishes, low-sodium menus, and much more. We will also offer basic information on how you can modify your own recipes.

You may be surprised to see rice, a starchy food usually avoided by dieters, in our first "Cooking Light" menu. When seasoned without butter or margarine, rice can be flavorful and filling, yet relatively low in calories. Such is the case with our Peppered Rice, which accompanies an oven-broiled beef kabob.

For the Steak Kabobs, lean chunks of sirloin are marinated overnight in a blend of low-calorie commercial salad dressing and seasonings, then threaded onto skewers with fresh vegetables.

Add color to the menu with Spinach-Stuffed Squash and Dressed-Up Fruit. And finally, dessert—the naturally sweet flavor of fruit makes Strawberry Puff a delicious finale to this surprisingly low-calorie meal.

**Steak Kabobs**
**Peppered Rice**
**Spinach-Stuffed Squash**
**Dressed-Up Fruit**
**Strawberry Puff**

## STEAK KABOBS

2 pounds lean boneless sirloin steak, cut
    into 1½-inch cubes
¾ cup Italian reduced-calorie dressing
3 tablespoons soy sauce
¼ teaspoon garlic powder
16 large mushrooms
16 cherry tomatoes
1 large green pepper, cut into 1-inch
    cubes

Trim all visible fat from meat. Combine dressing, soy sauce, and garlic powder; pour over meat. Cover and marinate overnight in the refrigerator.

Remove meat from marinade, reserving marinade. Alternate meat and vegetables on skewers. Brush with marinade. Broil 4 inches from heat 5 minutes on each side, brushing frequently with marinade. Yield: 8 servings (about 215 calories per serving).

## PEPPERED RICE

2½ cups water
1 beef-flavored bouillon cube
1¼ cups uncooked regular rice
¼ teaspoon garlic powder
¼ teaspoon pepper
1½ tablespoons chopped fresh parsley

Combine water and bouillon cube in a medium saucepan; bring water to a boil, stirring to dissolve cube. Stir in rice, garlic powder, and pepper. Reduce heat; cover and simmer 20 to 25 minutes or until rice is tender and water is absorbed. Remove from heat. Add parsley and toss. Yield: 8 servings (about 105 calories per serving).

## SPINACH-STUFFED SQUASH

8 medium-size yellow squash
1 chicken-flavored bouillon cube
1 (10-ounce) package frozen chopped
    spinach
¼ cup low-fat cottage cheese
1 tablespoon Parmesan cheese
1 large egg, beaten
¼ teaspoon seasoned salt
¼ teaspoon onion salt
¼ teaspoon coarsely ground black pepper
3 tablespoons dry breadcrumbs
Paprika
Vegetable cooking spray

Wash squash thoroughly. Drop in boiling water with bouillon cube; cover and simmer 8 to 10 minutes or until tender but still firm. Drain and cool slightly; trim off stems. Cut squash in half lengthwise. Scoop out pulp, leaving firm shells; mash pulp.

Cook spinach according to package directions; drain well, and add to squash pulp. Add cottage cheese, and mix well. Stir in next 5 ingredients; spoon into squash shells.

Sprinkle squash with breadcrumbs and paprika. Place on a baking sheet sprayed with cooking spray; cover with foil, and bake at 325° for 30 minutes. Yield: 8 servings (about 55 calories per serving).

## DRESSED-UP FRUIT

1 tablespoon all-purpose flour
¼ cup sugar
1 egg, beaten
2 tablespoons vinegar
¾ cup orange juice
2 tablespoons lemon juice
¼ cup water
3 medium apples, unpeeled
3 medium oranges, peeled
1 (15-ounce) can unsweetened pineapple slices, drained
Lettuce leaves

Combine flour and sugar in a small saucepan; mix well. Stir in egg. Add vinegar and orange juice, stirring until mixture is smooth. Cook over low heat, stirring constantly, until thickened and bubbly. Chill thoroughly.

Combine lemon juice and water; set aside. Cut apples and oranges into ¼- to ½-inch slices; place in a medium bowl. Pour lemon juice mixture over fruit; toss gently. Add pineapple slices. Cover and chill at least 1 hour.

Drain fruit mixture, and arrange on lettuce leaves. Serve with chilled dressing. Yield: 8 servings (about 62 calories per serving, plus 31 calories per tablespoon of dressing).

## STRAWBERRY PUFF

1 (16-ounce) package frozen whole strawberries, partially thawed
2 egg whites
¼ cup sugar
1 tablespoon lemon juice
1 cup frozen whipped topping, thawed
½ (16-ounce) package frozen whole strawberries, partially thawed

Combine first 4 ingredients in a large mixing bowl. Beat at high speed of electric mixer 10 to 12 minutes or until stiff peaks form. Add whipped topping; beat until smooth. Spoon into individual serving dishes, and freeze until firm.

Crush remaining strawberries with a fork. Spoon over dessert. Yield: 8 servings (about 110 calories per serving).

*Note:* Whipped evaporated skim milk may be used instead of frozen whipped topping. To prepare, stir ½ teaspoon unflavored gelatin into ½ cup evaporated skim milk, and chill in freezer until ice crystals form around edges.

Add 2 tablespoons sugar, and whip until soft peaks form. Add to strawberry mixture, and continue recipe as above. (Saves about 4 calories per serving.)

# Pour A Steaming Cup Of Cocoa

Topped with marshmallows or a dollop of whipped cream, a piping mug of cocoa will melt away winter's chill. Hot cocoa is perfect with breakfast on a cold, brisk morning and equally delightful with a midnight snack.

Teri Isenhour's Quick Hot Cocoa provides a warm-up in a hurry. For Mrs. Randy Throneberry's Special Hot Chocolate, you'll use your blender to combine candy-coated chocolate, molasses, ginger, and hot milk.

## SPECIAL HOT CHOCOLATE

2 cups milk
½ cup candy-coated chocolate pieces
2 tablespoons molasses
¼ teaspoon ground ginger
Whipped cream

Heat milk in a heavy saucepan to boiling point (212°). Combine candy, molasses, and ginger in container of electric blender; add milk. Blend on high speed about 1 minute or until smooth. Serve in mugs; top with whipped cream. Serve immediately. Yield: about 2½ cups.
*Mrs. Randy Throneberry, Shelbyville, Tennessee.*

## QUICK HOT COCOA

2 teaspoons cocoa
2 teaspoons sugar
¼ cup water
¾ cup milk
Miniature marshmallows (optional)

Combine first 3 ingredients in a small saucepan, and bring to a boil. Boil 3 minutes, stirring constantly. Stir in milk; heat to boiling point (212°). Top with marshmallows, if desired. Serve immediately. Yield: 1 cup. *Teri Isenhour, Charlotte, North Carolina.*

# It's Peak Season For Frozen Vegetables

Winter means that your favorite vegetables may be unavailable or in short supply, but the frozen food section of your supermarket can probably supply whatever taste you're craving.

Many frozen vegetables are less expensive than their fresh counterparts, and you pay only for edible weight. Since they're processed at the peak of ripeness, frozen vegetables often give you more nutrients than fresh vegetables that may have been sitting too long before preparation. Also, frozen foods can usually be cooked right from the freezer, minimizing preparation time.

You can have our Italian Broccoli Casserole mixed up in minutes and ready for the oven. For Shrimp and Vegetables, both the sauce and topping are included in the package of frozen vegetables. With preparation this simple, don't be surprised to find yourself reaching into the freezer at the peak of the fresh-vegetable season.

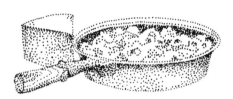

## HASH BROWN SKILLET BREAKFAST

6 slices bacon
1 (12-ounce) package frozen hash brown potatoes with onion, red pepper, and green pepper
6 eggs, beaten
¼ cup milk
½ teaspoon salt
Dash of pepper
1 cup (4 ounces) shredded sharp Cheddar cheese

Cook bacon in a 10-inch skillet until crisp; remove from pan and drain well, reserving drippings in pan. Crumble bacon, and set aside.

Heat drippings in skillet; add frozen potatoes. Cook over low heat until underside is crisp and lightly browned.

Combine eggs, milk, salt, and pepper; stir well, and pour over potatoes. Top with cheese, and sprinkle with reserved bacon. Cover and cook over low heat 10 minutes. Cut into wedges to serve. Yield: 6 servings. *LaMae Swearingen, Nevada, Missouri.*

## VEGETABLE-BURGER SOUP

½ pound ground beef
1 (16-ounce) can stewed tomatoes, undrained
1 (8-ounce) can tomato sauce
2 cups water
1 (10-ounce) package frozen mixed vegetables
¼ cup commercial onion soup mix
1 teaspoon sugar (optional)

Cook beef in a heavy 3-quart saucepan until browned, stirring to crumble; drain off drippings. Stir in remaining ingredients, and bring to a boil. Cover and reduce heat; simmer 30 minutes, stirring occasionally. Yield: about 8 cups.
*Tracie Mark,*
*Homewood, Alabama.*

## ITALIAN BROCCOLI CASSEROLE

2 (10-ounce) packages frozen chopped broccoli
2 eggs, beaten
1 (11-ounce) can Cheddar cheese soup, undiluted
½ teaspoon dried whole oregano, crushed
1 (16-ounce) can stewed tomatoes, drained
3 tablespoons grated Parmesan cheese

Cook broccoli according to package directions, omitting salt; drain well.
Combine eggs, soup, and oregano; mix well. Stir in tomatoes and broccoli. Spoon mixture into a lightly greased 10- x 6- x 2-inch baking dish; sprinkle with Parmesan cheese. Bake, uncovered, at 350° for 30 minutes or until bubbly. Yield: 6 servings. *Mrs. Bill Hodges,*
*Guntersville, Alabama.*

## SHRIMP AND VEGETABLES

½ pound shrimp, peeled and deveined
2 tablespoons butter or margarine, melted
1 (10-ounce) package frozen San Francisco-style vegetables with sauce and topping
1 tablespoon water
¼ teaspoon grated lemon rind
Soy sauce (optional)

Sauté shrimp in butter in a large skillet until shrimp begin to turn pink. Add vegetables and water; set topping package aside. Bring mixture to a boil over medium heat, separating vegetables with a fork. Cover; reduce heat, and simmer 5 minutes.
Stir in lemon rind, and sprinkle with vegetable topping. Serve with soy sauce, if desired. Yield: 4 servings.
*Ella Brown,*
*Proctor, Arkansas.*

# Brownies From Your Own Mix

If you enjoy the convenience of a brownie mix but folks around your house love chewy, homemade brownies, this brownie mix is just right for you. The recipe is from Mrs. E. T. Williams of Baton Rouge and will produce five batches she guarantees will be "soft and fudgelike inside."

## BROWNIE MIX

4 cups all-purpose flour
1 tablespoon plus 1 teaspoon baking powder
1 tablespoon salt
8 cups sugar
2½ cups cocoa
2 cups shortening

Combine first 5 ingredients; stir well. Cut in shortening with pastry blender until mixture resembles coarse meal. Place in an airtight container; store in a cool, dry place or in refrigerator for up to 6 weeks. Yield: 16 cups.

*Quick and Easy Brownies:*

3 cups Brownie Mix
3 eggs, beaten
1½ teaspoons vanilla extract
½ cup chopped pecans

Combine all ingredients, stirring until well mixed. Spoon into a greased and floured 8-inch square pan. Bake at 350° for 35 to 40 minutes. Cut into squares. Yield: 16 brownies.
*Mrs. E. T. Williams,*
*Baton Rouge, Louisiana.*

# Enchiladas, Hot And Saucy

If you like your enchiladas hot and saucy, this recipe from Thelma Moore of Alexandria, Louisiana, is just what you may be looking for. She wraps the fried tortillas around an onion-flavored meat filling, then bakes them in a cheese sauce that's spicy with green chiles.
These enchiladas also offer the convenience of advance preparation; just store in the refrigerator until time to bake.

## HOT AND SAUCY ENCHILADAS

1 pound ground beef
1 medium onion, chopped
1½ dozen frozen corn tortillas, thawed
Vegetable oil
1 (10¾-ounce) can cream of chicken soup, undiluted
1 (5.33-ounce) can evaporated milk
1 (8-ounce) package American process cheese slices
1 (4-ounce) can chopped green chiles, drained
1 (0.56-ounce) package green onion dip mix
1 teaspoon garlic salt
½ cup (2 ounces) shredded Cheddar cheese

Combine ground beef and onion in a large skillet; cook until meat is browned, stirring to crumble. Drain well.
Fry tortillas, one at a time, in ¼ inch of hot oil; cook about 5 seconds on each side or just until softened. Drain well on paper towels. Spoon meat mixture evenly in center of each tortilla, and roll them up. Place tortillas, seam side down, in a jellyroll pan.
Combine remaining ingredients except Cheddar cheese in a small saucepan; cook over medium heat until the slices of American cheese melt. Pour evenly over enchiladas, and sprinkle with Cheddar cheese. Bake at 350° for 20 minutes or until bubbly. Yield: 6 to 9 servings.
*Note:* May be prepared ahead and stored in refrigerator. When ready to serve, bake as directed above.
*Thelma Moore,*
*Alexandria, Louisiana.*

# Cabbage: The Winner By A Head

Our readers have shared with us some wonderful new ways to prepare fresh cabbage. There's a delicious version of cabbage rolls filled with ground beef and rice, two versions of cabbage baked with a cheesy sauce, and a convenient overnight coleslaw.
Besides its versatility, cabbage is packed with minerals and the vitamins A and C. In fact, the United Fresh Fruit and Vegetable Association points out that cabbage is so high in vitamin C that, ounce for ounce, it ranks right along with orange juice.

In selecting a head of cabbage, choose one that is firm and heavy for its size. Cabbage leaves should be fresh, crisp, and free from bruises.

## BEEF STUFFED CABBAGE ROLLS

1 pound ground beef
⅓ cup uncooked regular rice
1 egg, beaten
2½ teaspoons salt, divided
¼ teaspoon pepper, divided
6 large cabbage leaves
1 medium onion, thinly sliced
2 tablespoons butter or margarine, melted
1 (10¾-ounce) can tomato soup, undiluted
1¼ cups water
½ cup chopped celery
1 teaspoon minced fresh parsley
3 tablespoons lemon juice
1 teaspoon sugar

Combine ground beef, rice, egg, 1½ teaspoons salt, and ⅛ teaspoon pepper; stir well.

Cook cabbage leaves in boiling salted water 5 to 8 minutes or until just tender; drain. Place equal portions of meat mixture in center of each cabbage leaf; fold ends over, and fasten with wooden picks.

Sauté onion in butter in a large skillet until tender but not brown. Add tomato soup and remaining ingredients, stirring well; simmer 10 minutes.

Place cabbage rolls in tomato mixture; cover and simmer 1½ to 2 hours. Yield: 6 servings. *Mrs. S. Korzun, Holiday, Florida.*

## SMOTHERED CABBAGE WEDGES

1 medium cabbage
½ cup finely chopped green pepper
¼ cup finely chopped onion
¼ cup butter or margarine
¼ cup all-purpose flour
2 cups milk
½ teaspoon salt
⅛ teaspoon pepper
½ cup mayonnaise or salad dressing
¾ cup (3 ounces) shredded medium Cheddar cheese
3 tablespoons chili sauce

Cut cabbage into 8 wedges, removing core; cover and cook 10 minutes in a small amount of lightly salted boiling water. Drain well; place cabbage wedges in a 13- x 9- x 2-inch baking dish.

Sauté green pepper and onion in butter until tender. Add flour and cook 1 minute, stirring constantly. Gradually

add milk; cook over medium heat, stirring constantly, until thickened and bubbly. Stir in salt and pepper. Pour sauce over cabbage. Bake at 375° for 20 minutes.

Combine mayonnaise, cheese, and chili sauce; mix well. Spoon sauce over cabbage wedges, and bake 5 additional minutes. Yield: 8 servings.
*Opal M. Rogers, Tempe, Arizona.*

## CHEESE SCALLOPED CABBAGE

1 medium cabbage, cored and cut into small wedges
½ cup butter or margarine
¼ cup all-purpose flour
2 cups milk
½ teaspoon salt
¼ teaspoon pepper
Dash of ground nutmeg
2 cups (8 ounces) shredded medium Cheddar cheese
1 cup soft breadcrumbs

Cook cabbage in a small amount of boiling water until tender; drain well.

Melt butter in a heavy saucepan over low heat; add flour and cook 1 minute, stirring constantly. Gradually add milk; cook over medium heat, stirring constantly, until thickened and bubbly. Stir in salt, pepper, and nutmeg. Remove from heat; add the shredded cheese, stirring until melted.

Place half the cabbage in a greased 2½-quart casserole; top with half of cheese sauce. Repeat layers; top with breadcrumbs. Bake at 350° for 30 to 35 minutes. Yield: 8 servings.
*Jeanne Lee Smith, Louisville, Kentucky.*

## OVERNIGHT CABBAGE SLAW

1 medium cabbage, shredded
1 small onion, grated
1 medium-size green pepper, finely chopped
8 pimiento-stuffed olives, sliced
¾ cup sugar
¾ cup vinegar
½ cup vegetable oil
1 teaspoon celery seeds
1 teaspoon dry mustard
1 teaspoon salt
⅛ teaspoon pepper

Combine cabbage, onion, green pepper, and olives in a large bowl; sprinkle with sugar.

Combine remaining ingredients in a medium saucepan; boil 3 minutes. Pour

over vegetables, stirring well. Chill overnight. Yield: 8 to 10 servings.
*Faye Beard, Lipscomb, Alabama.*

# Another Way To Enjoy Turkey

Finding new ways to use up all the leftover turkey the holidays leave behind is sometimes a problem. Hortense Callaway of Tallahassee, Florida, solves the dilemma by using her turkey leftovers in a fabulous Lattice-Topped Turkey Pie. Even the crust is easy to make, she explains. "It's made from canned crescent dinner rolls cut into strips and woven into a lattice design."

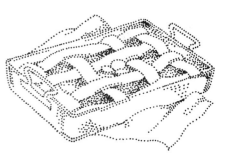

## LATTICE-TOPPED TURKEY PIE

2 cups chopped cooked turkey
1 (10-ounce) package frozen English peas
1 cup (4 ounces) shredded sharp Cheddar cheese
1 cup diced celery
½ cup soft breadcrumbs
¼ cup chopped onion
¼ teaspoon salt
⅛ teaspoon pepper
1 cup mayonnaise
3 dashes hot sauce
1 (8-ounce) can crescent dinner rolls
2 teaspoons sesame seeds
Radish slices (optional)
Fresh parsley sprigs (optional)

Combine first 10 ingredients; mix well. Spoon into a 12- x 8- x 2-inch baking dish.

Separate crescent dough into 2 rectangles; press perforations to seal. Cut into 4 long strips and 4 short strips. Arrange strips in lattice design across top of casserole. Sprinkle with sesame seeds. Bake at 350° for 35 minutes. Garnish with radish slices and parsley, if desired. Yield: 6 servings.
*Hortense Callaway, Tallahassee, Florida.*

# Bake A Lucky Almond Cake

Start a fun tradition at your home on New Year's Eve with this Almond Legend Cake. Somewhere inside is hidden a single, whole almond. Judy Cunningham of Roanoke, Virginia, says her family enjoys slicing the cake to see who'll get the piece with the almond. That person, according to legend, will enjoy good fortune during the coming year.

### ALMOND LEGEND CAKE

1 (2½-ounce) package slivered almonds, chopped
⅓ cup butter or margarine, softened
⅓ cup shortening
1½ cups sugar, divided
3 eggs, separated
1 teaspoon grated lemon rind
2 tablespoons lemon juice
1 teaspoon vanilla extract
1 teaspoon almond extract
2⅓ cups all-purpose flour
2 teaspoons baking powder
¼ teaspoon soda
¾ teaspoon salt
¾ cup milk
½ teaspoon cream of tartar
1 whole almond
Apricot Glaze

Sprinkle chopped almonds into a well-greased 9-inch Bundt pan; set aside.

Cream butter and shortening; gradually add 1¼ cups sugar, beating until light and fluffy. Add egg yolks, and beat well. Add lemon rind, juice, and flavorings; beat well.

Combine flour, baking powder, soda, and salt; stir well. Add dry ingredients to creamed mixture alternately with milk, beginning and ending with flour mixture, beating well after each addition. Set batter aside.

Beat egg whites (at room temperature) with cream of tartar until foamy. Gradually add remaining ¼ cup sugar, beating until stiff peaks form; fold egg white mixture into reserved batter.

Pour batter into prepared Bundt pan. Press whole almond just below surface of batter. Bake at 300° for 1 hour and 20 minutes or until cake tests done. Cool cake 10 minutes in pan on a wire rack. Loosen edges of cake, if necessary. Invert cake on serving plate. Cool completely. Drizzle Apricot Glaze over cake. Yield: one 9-inch cake.

*A drizzle of apricot-rum glaze and a surprise lucky almond make Almond Legend Cake perfect for a New Year's party.*

*Apricot Glaze:*

½ cup apricot preserves
2 teaspoons rum or orange juice

Strain preserves through a sieve. Add rum; stir well. Yield: about ½ cup.

*Judy Cunningham,*
*Roanoke, Virginia.*

# Avocados With A Texas Flair

These recipes, all from the Lone Star State, prove Texans know how to make the most of a favorite fruit—the avocado. You can dice them into salads, mash them for sandwich fillings and dips, or slice them onto your favorite Mexican-flavored pie. Mrs. Bob Joe of Austin even threads chunks of avocado onto skewers along with cheese, bacon, tomato, and chicken.

Fresh avocados in supermarkets are generally too firm for eating right away and should be allowed to soften several days at room temperature on a countertop or in a fruit bowl. To test for softness, cradle the avocado between the palms of your hands, and press gently. If it yields to gentle pressure, it's ready to eat and will be easy to cut.

You can hurry the ripening process a little by putting avocados in a brown paper bag. This facilitates softening by confining and concentrating the gases the fruit gives off. Once the fruit is soft, it can be stored in the refrigerator up to about 10 days.

## MEXICAN SALAD SUPPER

1 pound ground beef
1 (15½-ounce) can kidney beans, drained
1 medium head lettuce, shredded
2 medium avocados, peeled and chopped
2 large tomatoes, chopped
1 small onion, chopped
1 medium-size green pepper, chopped
1 cup sliced fresh mushrooms
1 cup chopped celery
1 carrot, scraped and thinly sliced
4 cups (16 ounces) shredded Cheddar
    cheese
1 (8-ounce) bottle commercial French or
    Catalina dressing
1 (8-ounce) package tortilla chips,
    crumbled

Cook ground beef until browned, stirring to crumble; drain and cool slightly. Combine meat with remaining ingredients, except tortilla chips, tossing well. Add tortilla chips, and serve immediately. Yield: 12 to 15 servings.

*Jan Dreasher,*
*Lubbock, Texas.*

## CHILI-TAMALE PIE

1 (25-ounce) can chili with beans
1 (14½-ounce) can tamales, cut into thirds
1 medium onion, chopped
1 or 2 jalapeño peppers, seeded and
    finely chopped
1 cup crushed corn chips
1 cup (4 ounces) shredded Cheddar cheese
1 avocado, peeled and sliced

Combine first 4 ingredients in a lightly greased 1¾-quart casserole. Bake at 400° for 25 minutes or until bubbly. Combine corn chips and cheese; sprinkle over top of casserole. Bake 5 additional minutes or until cheese melts. Top with avocado. Yield: 6 servings.

*Mrs. W. C. Olsen,*
*Bastrop, Texas.*

## MEXICAN CHEESE PIE

6 (6-inch) flour tortillas
1 small onion, sliced and separated
    into rings
1 large tomato, peeled and chopped
1 (4-ounce) can diced green chiles,
    drained
1 cup (4 ounces) shredded Cheddar cheese
3 tablespoons all-purpose flour
½ teaspoon baking powder
½ teaspoon salt
½ cup milk
3 eggs, beaten
1 medium avocado, peeled and sliced
Commercial taco sauce

Line bottom and sides of a well-greased 9-inch quiche dish with tortillas. Top with onion, tomato, green chiles, and cheese.

Combine flour, baking powder, salt, milk, and eggs, stirring until smooth. Pour mixture into quiche dish. Bake at 350° for 40 to 45 minutes. Top with avocado. Serve with taco sauce. Yield: 6 servings.

*Becky Holzhaus,*
*Castroville, Texas.*

## CHICKEN-AVOCADO KABOBS

2 slices bacon, cut in half
¾ cup all-purpose flour
¼ teaspoon salt
⅛ teaspoon pepper
1 pound skinned and boned chicken
    breasts, cut into 8 equal pieces
1 egg, beaten
Vegetable oil
1 small avocado, peeled and cut into 8
    pieces
Lemon or lime juice
4 cherry tomatoes
¼ pound Monterey Jack cheese, cut
    into 4 equal pieces

Fry bacon until transparent; drain and set aside.

Combine flour, salt, and pepper, stirring well. Dip chicken into egg, and dredge in flour mixture. Fry chicken in deep hot oil (375°) until golden brown. Drain on paper towels.

Dip avocado into lemon juice, and set aside.

Alternate chicken, avocado, tomato, bacon, and cheese on skewers. Broil 6 inches from heat, turning several times, until cheese begins to melt. Yield: 2 to 4 servings.         *Mrs. Bob Joe,*
*Austin, Texas.*

## GUACAMOLE SANDWICHES

3 avocados, peeled and quartered
1 small tomato, peeled and quartered
½ cup cottage cheese
2 tablespoons lemon juice
1½ teaspoons garlic salt
6 (8-inch) flour tortillas
12 ounces Cheddar cheese
1 cup bean sprouts
1 cup alfalfa sprouts
Commercial taco sauce (optional)
Crushed tortilla chips (optional)

Combine first 5 ingredients in container of an electric blender. Blend mixture until smooth, and set aside.

Place tortillas on a lightly greased baking sheet. Cut cheese into twelve 2- x 5-inch slices; place 2 slices on surface of each tortilla. Broil 6 inches from heat just until cheese melts.

Spoon ⅓ cup avocado mixture on each tortilla; top with bean and alfalfa sprouts. Fold tortillas in half; serve with taco sauce and crushed tortilla chips, if desired. Yield: 6 servings.

*Jan K. Sliwa,*
*Temple, Texas.*

## AVOCADO SALAD

½ large head iceberg lettuce, torn
10 cherry tomatoes, halved
1 large avocado, peeled and chopped
3 pitted ripe olives, thinly sliced
⅓ cup commercial Thousand Island
    dressing
1 teaspoon chili powder

Combine lettuce, tomatoes, avocado, and olives, tossing gently. Stir together dressing and chili powder; serve over salad. Yield: 6 servings.

*Mary Thielman,*
*San Marcos, Texas.*

## ZIPPY AVOCADO DIP

2 ripe avocados, peeled and coarsely
    chopped
2 tablespoons picante sauce
2 teaspoons lemon or lime juice
1 teaspoon chopped onion
⅛ teaspoon seasoned salt

Combine all ingredients in container of electric blender. Blend and chill. Serve with corn chips. Yield: about 1½ cups.

*Note:* Avocado seed may be placed in dip to prevent the mixture from darkening.         *Jean Westmoreland,*
*Manvel, Texas.*

*Tip: Read labels to learn the weight, quality, and size of food products. Don't be afraid to experiment with new brands. Store brands can be equally good in quality and nutritional value, yet lower in price. Lower grades of canned fruits and vegetables are as nutritious as higher grades. Whenever possible, buy most foods by weight or cost per serving rather than by volume or package size.*

# Try Apricots Anytime

Although the season for fresh apricots is short (June through August), you can enjoy this vitamin A-rich fruit in canned and dried form throughout the year.

Try apricots in breads, side dishes, and desserts for a pleasant change of pace this winter.

Fran Collier's recipe for Delicious Baked Apricots may be served as a side dish with pork, or it can double as a delightful warm dessert when topped with whipped cream.

## SAUSAGE-APRICOT BREAKFAST DISH

2 cups buttermilk pancake mix
1 cup milk
2 eggs, beaten
¼ cup vegetable oil
1 (17-ounce) can apricot halves
1 (8-ounce) package brown-and-serve
   sausage links
Additional apricot halves, sliced (optional)
Apricot Fruit Syrup

Combine first 4 ingredients, stirring well (batter will be lumpy); pour into a well-greased 13- x 9- x 2-inch baking dish. Set aside.

Drain apricot halves, reserving ½ cup syrup; set aside. Cut each sausage link in half; arrange sausage and apricot halves on top of batter.

Bake at 350° for 30 minutes. Cut into squares; garnish with additional apricot slices, if desired. Serve with Apricot Fruit Syrup. Yield: 6 servings.

*Apricot Fruit Syrup:*

¼ cup sugar
1 tablespoon cornstarch
½ cup reserved apricot syrup
¾ cup maple or maple-flavored syrup
1 tablespoon butter or margarine

Combine sugar and cornstarch in a small saucepan; stir well. Stir in apricot syrup. Cook over medium heat, stirring constantly, until thickened and bubbly.

Add maple syrup and butter, stirring until the butter melts and mixture is well blended. Serve hot. Yield: about 1¼ cups. *Mrs. R. P. Hotaling, Martinez, Georgia.*

## TASTY APRICOT-NUT LOAF

1 cup dried apricots, chopped
¾ cup boiling water
⅓ cup butter, softened
1 cup sugar
2 eggs
½ cup light corn syrup
1 cup chopped pecans
3 cups all-purpose flour
1 tablespoon baking powder
½ teaspoon salt

Combine apricots and boiling water in a small bowl; set aside to soak 15 minutes.

Cream butter and sugar; beat in eggs and corn syrup. Stir in apricots (including liquid); add pecans, and mix well. Combine remaining ingredients; gradually add to batter, stirring just until all ingredients are moistened.

Spoon batter into a well-greased 9- x 5- x 3-inch loafpan. Bake at 350° for 1 hour and 15 to 25 minutes or until a wooden pick inserted in center comes out clean. Cool 10 minutes in pan on a wire rack. Remove from pan; serve warm or cold. Yield: 1 loaf.

*Joanne Champagne, Covington, Louisiana.*

## APRICOT FREEZE

1 (17-ounce) can apricot halves, undrained
   and chopped
1 (8¼-ounce) can crushed pineapple,
   undrained
3 medium bananas, mashed
1 (6-ounce) can frozen orange juice
   concentrate, thawed and undiluted
1 teaspoon lemon juice
¼ cup sugar
Whipped cream (optional)

Combine first 6 ingredients in a large bowl, mixing well. Spoon mixture into paper-lined muffin pans, filling three-fourths full. Freeze overnight. Let stand at room temperature 5 minutes before serving. Garnish with whipped cream, if desired. Yield: about 18 servings.

*Betty J. Moore, Belton, Texas.*

## DELICIOUS BAKED APRICOTS

4 (17-ounce) cans apricot halves, drained
1½ cups butter or margarine, melted
1 cup firmly packed light brown sugar
1 cup firmly packed dark brown sugar
1 (16-ounce) package round buttery
   crackers, crushed
Whipped cream (optional)

Place half of apricots and half of butter in a 13- x 9- x 3-inch baking dish. Combine sugar; sprinkle half over apricots. Cover with half of cracker crumbs. Layer remaining apricots and sugar in dish. Combine remaining cracker crumbs and butter; sprinkle over top. Bake at 300° for 50 to 60 minutes. Serve warm. Top with whipped cream, if desired. Yield: 15 servings. *Fran Collier, Jacksonville, Florida.*

# Microwave Cookery

# Homemade Chili In An Hour

If you think homemade chili requires hours of slow cooking, then you may not have thought of using the microwave. Our test kitchens experimented with chili and discovered excellent results by microwaving on HIGH power at the beginning of the cooking time and then reducing to MEDIUM (50% power) to develop and enhance the flavor. These four recipes all cook in less than 55 minutes, and we think you'll agree they taste like old-fashioned chili that simmered for many hours.

Each recipe gives a time range to allow for the difference in wattage of microwave ovens. To avoid overcooking, check for doneness at the lower end of the range. (This is more critical when cooking at HIGH power than at MEDIUM.)

Here are some pointers for converting your conventional chili recipes to microwave cooking.

—To accommodate less evaporation, the amount of liquid should be reduced. Add the liquid last and only enough to bring the mixture to desired consistency. Then, if necessary, add more liquid during microwaving. Seasonings should also be reduced since there is less liquid to dilute them. More can be added after tasting, if desired.

—To ensure doneness, vegetables such as onions and green peppers should be partially microwaved before adding seasonings and liquid. If you're using ground meat, brown it with the vegetables; then drain off excess drippings. Lean stew meat should be cooked with the liquid ingredients to avoid toughness.

—Cook vegetables and ground meat at HIGH; then add liquid and seasonings, and continue to microwave at HIGH for 10 minutes. Reduce power to MEDIUM, and cook an additional 30 to 35 minutes.

—If your recipe calls for dried beans, you may want to substitute canned beans. Microwaving leaves dried beans less tender and saves little or no time.

## BASIC CHILI

1 pound ground beef
1 medium onion, coarsely chopped
1 green pepper, coarsely chopped
1 clove garlic, minced
1 (16-ounce) can tomatoes, undrained
1 (16-ounce) can kidney beans, drained
1 (6-ounce) can tomato paste
½ cup water
2 tablespoons chili powder
½ teaspoon ground cumin
½ teaspoon salt
¼ teaspoon pepper

Combine beef, onion, and pepper in a 3-quart casserole, stirring to crumble beef. Cover with casserole lid or heavy-duty plastic wrap. Microwave at HIGH for 6 to 9 minutes or until beef is browned; drain well.

Add remaining ingredients, mixing well. Cover and microwave at HIGH for 10 minutes; stir. Cover and microwave at MEDIUM (50% power) for 30 to 35 minutes. Yield: 7 cups.

## CHEESE-TOPPED CHILI

1 pound ground beef
1 medium onion, coarsely chopped
1 green pepper, coarsely chopped
1 stalk celery, coarsely chopped
1 clove garlic, minced
1 (16-ounce) can stewed tomatoes, undrained
1 (6-ounce) can tomato paste
¾ cup beef broth
2 teaspoons chili powder
½ teaspoon dried whole oregano
½ teaspoon salt
½ teaspoon pepper
1 bay leaf
1½ cups (6 ounces) shredded sharp
  Cheddar cheese

Combine first 5 ingredients in a 3-quart casserole, stirring to crumble beef. Cover with casserole lid or heavy-duty plastic wrap. Microwave at HIGH for 6 to 9 minutes or until the beef is browned; drain well.

Add remaining ingredients, except cheese; mix well. Cover and microwave

at HIGH for 10 minutes; stir. Cover and microwave at MEDIUM (50% power) for 30 to 35 minutes. Spoon into serving bowls, and immediately sprinkle with cheese. Yield: 7 cups.

## BEEFY SAUSAGE CHILI

½ pound ground beef
½ pound hot bulk pork sausage
1 medium onion, sliced and separated
  into rings
1 cup chopped celery
2 (10¾-ounce) cans tomato soup, undiluted
1 (16-ounce) can kidney beans, drained
½ cup water
1 teaspoon chili powder
½ teaspoon dried whole oregano
¼ teaspoon red pepper

Combine first 4 ingredients in a 3-quart casserole, stirring to crumble meat. Cover with casserole lid or heavy-duty plastic wrap. Microwave at HIGH for 6 to 9 minutes or until meat is browned; drain well.

Add remaining ingredients, mixing well. Cover and microwave at HIGH for 10 minutes; stir. Cover and microwave at MEDIUM (50% power) for 30 to 35 minutes. Yield: 6 cups.

## CHILI WITH RICE

1 pound ground beef
½ pound Italian sausage, cut into ½-inch
  pieces
1 medium onion, coarsely chopped
1 green pepper, coarsely chopped
1 clove garlic, minced
2 (16-ounce) cans stewed tomatoes,
  undrained
1 (16-ounce) can kidney beans, drained
1 (8-ounce) can tomato sauce
2 teaspoons chili powder
½ teaspoon salt
½ teaspoon red pepper
¼ teaspoon ground cumin
½ cup uncooked regular rice

Combine first 5 ingredients in a 3-quart casserole, stirring to crumble beef. Cover with casserole lid or heavy-duty plastic wrap. Microwave at HIGH for 8 to 10 minutes or until the meat is browned; drain well.

Add remaining ingredients, except rice. Cover and microwave at HIGH for 10 minutes; stir. Cover and microwave at MEDIUM (50% power) for 10 minutes. Stir in rice; cover and microwave at MEDIUM for 15 to 20 minutes or until rice is done. Yield: 9 cups.

# Pork: A Year-Round Favorite

Pork is a year-round favorite—whether it be in the form of chops, roasts, ribs, or ground meat. Everyone has favorite ways to prepare this versatile meat, and this group of recipes includes some of the most popular: ribs baked in a tangy barbecue sauce, sweet-and-sour pork, a boneless roast filled with a savory breadcrumb stuffing.

A word about preparation: To preserve its delicate flavor and juiciness, cook pork until well done but avoid overcooking. For best results, use a meat thermometer to ensure that the larger cuts of meat are thoroughly cooked. The meat is done when the thermometer registers 170°.

## BARBECUED PORK SHOULDER

1 (3½- to 4-pound) pork shoulder
  roast
1 cup catsup
½ cup firmly packed brown sugar
2 teaspoons salt
1 teaspoon pepper
1 to 2 tablespoons chili powder
¼ cup plus 2 tablespoons vinegar
2 tablespoons lemon juice
¼ cup Worcestershire sauce
2 teaspoons prepared mustard
Hamburger buns (optional)

Cover roast with lightly salted water in a large Dutch oven. Cover and cook over medium heat 2 to 2½ hours or until the meat is tender. Drain, and slice thinly; place in a shallow 2-quart baking dish.

Combine next 9 ingredients, stirring well. Spoon sauce over sliced roast, turning slices to coat. Bake at 300° for 45 minutes. Serve on buns, if desired. Yield: 6 servings.          *Brentz Moore,*
*Kenton, Tennessee.*

*Tip: Properly canned foods have been sterilized and won't spoil as long as the container remains airtight. However, most canned foods have a "shelf life" of approximately one year—they then may begin to slowly lose flavor and nutrients. If you use large amounts of canned foods, date them at time of purchase and use the oldest first.*

## STUFFED PORK ROAST

1 (4- to 5-pound) boneless pork shoulder
   roast or pork loin roast
Salt, pepper, and poultry seasoning to
   taste
4 cups soft breadcrumbs
1 cup chopped celery
¾ cup chopped onion
1 teaspoon ground sage
1 teaspoon salt
¼ teaspoon pepper
½ cup butter or margarine, melted

Cut a wide, deep pocket in roast.
Season roast on all sides with salt, pepper,
and poultry seasoning. Combine remaining
ingredients and stuff into
pocket. Secure roast with metal skewers.
Bake at 325° about 35 to 40 minutes
per pound or until thermometer
registers 170°. Yield: 8 to 10 servings.
*Mrs. Leslie McIver,*
*Holly Springs, North Carolina.*

## SWEET-AND-SOUR PORK

1 (20-ounce) can pineapple chunks
1½ pounds boneless pork shoulder, cut
   into 2-inch strips
3 tablespoons vegetable oil
½ cup water
¼ cup firmly packed light brown sugar
2 tablespoons cornstarch
½ teaspoon salt
¼ cup cider vinegar
2 tablespoons soy sauce
1 small green pepper, cut into strips
1 small onion, thinly sliced
Hot cooked rice

Drain pineapple, reserving juice; set
both aside.
Brown pork in oil in a large skillet;
stir in water. Cover and simmer 1 hour
or until tender. Combine sugar, cornstarch,
and salt in a medium bowl; stir
in reserved pineapple juice, vinegar,
and soy sauce. Add to pork and cook,
stirring constantly, until smooth and
thickened. Add pineapple, green pepper,
and onion; toss lightly, and cook 2
to 3 minutes. Serve over rice. Yield: 4
to 6 servings. *Dorothy L. Anderson,*
*Manor, Texas.*

*Tip: Fresh meat, poultry, and fish
should be loosely wrapped and refrigerated;
use in a few days. Loosely
wrap fresh ground meat, liver, and kidneys;
use in one or two days. Wieners,
bacon, and sliced sandwich meats can
be stored in original wrappings in the
refrigerator.*

## BARBECUED SPARERIBS

3 pounds spareribs
½ cup chopped onion
1 clove garlic, minced
¼ cup butter or margarine
2 (8-ounce) cans tomato sauce
⅓ cup water
¼ cup Worcestershire sauce
2 tablespoons lemon juice
2 tablespoons vinegar
2 teaspoons chili powder
2 teaspoons salt
4 drops hot sauce

Place spareribs in shallow baking pan.
Bake, uncovered, at 325° for 1½ hours.
Drain off pan drippings.
Sauté onion and garlic in butter in a
medium saucepan. Add remaining ingredients;
bring to a boil. Pour over
ribs, and bake 45 to 60 minutes or until
tender, basting occasionally. Yield: 6
servings. *Karol Stephenson,*
*Washington, Georgia.*

## PORK CHOPS JARDINIERE

4 (½-inch-thick) pork chops
1 tablespoon vegetable oil
2 chicken-flavored bouillon cubes
1½ cups boiling water
1 to 1¼ teaspoons salt
½ teaspoon sugar
½ teaspoon pepper
2 medium stalks celery, chopped
1 medium carrot, scraped and chopped
1 tablespoon all-purpose flour
Mashed potatoes (optional)

Brown pork chops on both sides in
hot oil in a large skillet; drain.
Dissolve bouillon cubes in boiling
water. Stir in next 6 ingredients; pour
over pork chops. Bring to a boil; cover
and simmer 1 hour or until tender.
Serve over mashed potatoes, if desired.
Yield: 4 servings. *Alda Reynolds,*
*Lincolnton, North Carolina.*

## SAUSAGE CASSEROLE

1 large onion, finely chopped
1 pound bulk pork sausage
1 (4-ounce) package (2 envelopes) chicken
   noodle soup mix
½ cup uncooked regular rice
4½ cups water
1 (4-ounce) package slivered almonds
   (optional)

Brown onion and sausage in a large
skillet, stirring to crumble sausage;
drain. Add soup mix, rice, water, and
almonds, if desired; mix well, and simmer
7 minutes. Spoon into a greased
2½-quart casserole; bake at 400° for 30
minutes. Yield: 5 to 6 servings.
*Joan Prescott,*
*Savannah, Georgia.*

## HAM BALLS WITH SPICED
## CHERRY SAUCE

2 cups ground cooked ham
⅓ cup dry breadcrumbs
¼ cup milk
1 egg, beaten
⅛ teaspoon pepper
¼ cup vegetable oil
¼ cup hot water
1 cup cherry preserves
2½ tablespoons lemon juice
¾ teaspoon ground cinnamon
¼ teaspoon ground cloves

Combine first 5 ingredients, mixing
well. Shape into 1½-inch balls. Heat
vegetable oil in a skillet over medium
heat; add ham balls, and cook until
browned.
Drain off drippings, and add ¼ cup
hot water to the skillet. Cover and simmer
15 to 20 minutes or until done.
Combine cherry preserves, lemon
juice, cinnamon, and cloves in a small
saucepan. Place over low heat, and
cook until mixture comes to a low boil,
stirring occasionally.
Place ham balls in a chafing dish or
on a warm platter, and cover with
sauce. Yield: 4 to 6 servings.
*Mrs. A. Stancill,*
*Bel Air, Maryland.*

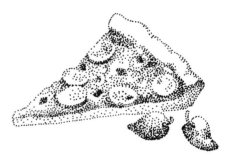

# Slice Into Tostada Pizza

If you like both pizza and Mexican
food, you'll love Betty Wise's Tostada
Pizza. The Duncanville, Texas, reader
starts with an easy biscuit mix crust,
then adds refried beans, ground beef,
chiles, lettuce, tomatoes, onion, and
cheese.

## TOSTADA PIZZA

2 tablespoons yellow cornmeal
2 cups biscuit mix
½ cup cold water
1 pound ground beef
¾ cup water
3 tablespoons chopped, seeded
  canned green chiles
1 (1.25-ounce) package taco seasoning mix
1 (16-ounce) can refried beans
2 cups (8 ounces) shredded sharp process
  American cheese, divided
3 cups shredded iceberg lettuce
1 large tomato, chopped
½ cup chopped onion
Taco sauce

Sprinkle a well-greased 12-inch pizza pan with cornmeal.

Combine biscuit mix and ½ cup water in a medium bowl; stir vigorously with a fork until a soft dough is formed. Turn out on a floured surface; knead lightly about 5 times. Roll dough into a 14-inch circle. Fit dough into pizza pan; crimp edges. Bake at 425° for 10 to 12 minutes.

Cook ground beef in a medium skillet until browned; drain. Add ¾ cup water, chiles, and taco mix, stirring well. Bring to a boil; reduce heat and simmer, uncovered, 10 minutes or until thickened.

Spread beans evenly over pizza crust, leaving a ½-inch border around edges. Spoon meat mixture over beans. Bake at 425° for 8 to 10 minutes. Sprinkle top with 1 cup cheese; bake an additional 2 minutes or until cheese melts. Top with lettuce, tomato, onion, and remaining cheese. Cut into wedges; serve with taco sauce. Yield: one 12-inch pizza.
*Betty Wise,*
*Duncanville, Texas.*

# Take A Little Thyme

Thyme, known as "the poor man's herb" because it's so easy to grow, rates as a best seller in supermarkets. Southerners enjoy thyme's sweet but pungent taste and trust the herb to flavor even their most renowned dishes—from soups and stews to vegetable, poultry, and seafood specialties.

Like any herb, store thyme in an airtight container away from light and heat to preserve its potency; if space permits, your freezer provides ideal storage. The herb stays free flowing and will be ready to spice up your meals.

## CREAMY BROCCOLI SOUP

1 (10¾-ounce) can cream of potato soup,
  undiluted
1 (10¾-ounce) can cream of celery soup,
  undiluted
1¼ cups milk
1 teaspoon Dijon mustard
½ teaspoon dried whole thyme
¼ teaspoon dry mustard
¼ teaspoon dried whole basil (optional)
1 (10-ounce) package frozen chopped
  broccoli

Heat soup in a 2-quart saucepan; gradually add milk, stirring until smooth.

Add remaining ingredients; cook over low heat 40 minutes, stirring mixture occasionally. Yield: about 5 cups.
*Susan A. Houston,*
*Tucker, Georgia.*

## BEEF STEW WITH PARSLEY DUMPLINGS

⅓ cup all-purpose flour
2½ teaspoons salt
¼ teaspoon pepper
3 pounds lean beef for stewing, cut into
  1-inch cubes
¼ cup butter or margarine
3 cups water
½ cup chopped celery tops
1½ teaspoons dried whole thyme
4 whole cloves
2 sprigs fresh parsley
1 bay leaf
1 pound boiling onions
1 pound carrots, scraped and cut in half
  crosswise
1½ pounds small new potatoes
2 medium turnips, peeled and
  quartered
2 stalks celery, cut into 1-inch pieces
¼ cup water
3 tablespoons all-purpose flour
½ cup milk
1 egg
2 tablespoons chopped fresh parsley
2 cups biscuit mix

Combine ⅓ cup flour, salt, and pepper; dredge meat in flour mixture, and brown in butter in an 8-quart Dutch oven. Stir in next 6 ingredients; bring to a boil. Reduce heat; cover and simmer 2 hours, stirring occasionally.

Add onions, carrots, and potatoes; cover and cook over medium heat 20 minutes. Stir in turnips and celery; cover and cook 20 minutes.

Combine ¼ cup water and 3 tablespoons flour, stirring until smooth. Stir flour mixture into stew; cook until mixture is thickened.

Combine milk, egg, and 2 tablespoons parsley; stir well. Add milk mixture to biscuit mix, and stir just until all ingredients are moistened. Drop by tablespoonfuls onto stew. Cook, uncovered, over low heat 10 minutes. Cover and cook 10 additional minutes. Yield: 10 to 12 servings.
*Lilly B. Smith,*
*Richmond, Virginia.*

## FANCY FOWL

4 whole chicken breasts, split, skinned,
  and boned
3 thin slices cooked ham, cut into
  julienne strips
1 cup (4 ounces) shredded Gruyère or
  Swiss cheese
Salt
White pepper
Dried whole thyme
1 cup all-purpose flour
¼ cup butter or margarine
3 tablespoons chopped shallots or green
  onion
2 cups sliced fresh mushrooms
1 cup dry white wine
1 cup whipping cream
2 tablespoons tomato paste
Hot cooked rice

Place each chicken breast on a sheet of waxed paper; flatten to ¼-inch thickness, using a meat mallet or rolling pin.

Place 4 to 5 strips of ham horizontally across each chicken breast; sprinkle cheese evenly over chicken. Sprinkle with salt, pepper, and thyme. Fold long sides of chicken to center; fold in sides of chicken to center, and secure with wooden picks. Dredge chicken in flour.

Melt butter in large skillet; add chicken and sauté, turning gently, until tender. Transfer chicken to an ovenproof dish, reserving drippings in pan; keep chicken warm in oven.

Add shallots and mushrooms to reserved pan drippings; sauté until shallots are browned. Combine wine, whipping cream, and tomato paste, stirring until smooth; add to mushroom mixture. Cook over low heat 10 to 15 minutes or until thickened, stirring constantly. Pour mixture over chicken, and serve with rice. Yield: 8 servings.
*Ted J. Kleisner,*
*Savannah, Georgia.*

*Tip: Immediately before using fresh mushrooms, wipe them clean or quickly rinse them in a colander; never immerse mushrooms in water.*

## Spice Up The Day With Gingerbread

Remember the last time you had homemade gingerbread? If it's been so long you can't remember, it's time to try one of these three recipes and enjoy again its spicy, old-fashioned goodness.

All have a flavor to match what grandma used to bake.

### MOCHA GINGERBREAD

1 (14.5-ounce) package gingerbread mix
1 cup lukewarm coffee
1 egg, beaten
½ cup chopped pecans
Orange Cream Frosting
Grated orange rind

Combine gingerbread mix, coffee, and egg in an ungreased 8-inch square pan. Stir with a fork about 2 minutes or until batter is of uniform color and consistency. Stir in pecans. Bake at 350° for 30 to 35 minutes or until wooden pick inserted in center comes out clean. Cool. Frost with Orange Cream Frosting. Garnish with orange rind. Yield: 9 servings.

*Orange Cream Frosting:*

2 (3-ounce) packages cream cheese, softened
½ teaspoon grated orange rind
2 tablespoons orange juice
1 cup sifted powdered sugar

Beat cream cheese; add rind and juice. Gradually add sugar, beating until light and fluffy. Yield: ½ cup.
*Mrs. Harvey Kidd, Hernando, Mississippi.*

### GINGERBREAD LOAF

½ cup butter or margarine, softened
1 cup firmly packed brown sugar
2 eggs
2 cups all-purpose flour
1 teaspoon soda
1 teaspoon ground cinnamon
1 teaspoon ground cloves
1 teaspoon ground ginger
½ cup boiling water
½ cup molasses
Hard sauce (recipe follows)

Cream butter; gradually add sugar, beating well. Add eggs, beating well. Combine dry ingredients; add to creamed mixture alternately with water and molasses, beginning and ending with flour mixture, and beating well after each addition. Pour into a greased and floured 9- x 5- x 3-inch loafpan; bake at 350° for 55 to 60 minutes or until a wooden pick inserted in the center comes out clean. Serve warm with hard sauce. Yield: 1 loaf.

*Hard Sauce:*

½ cup butter or margarine, softened
1 cup sifted powdered sugar
1 teaspoon vanilla extract

Combine all ingredients; beat on medium speed of electric mixer until smooth. Yield: 1 cup. *Heather Riggins, Nashville, Tennessee.*

### OLD-FASHIONED GINGERBREAD

½ cup butter or margarine, softened
½ cup sugar
1 egg
1 cup molasses
2½ cups all-purpose flour
1½ teaspoons soda
½ teaspoon salt
1 teaspoon ground cinnamon
1 teaspoon ground cloves
1 teaspoon ground ginger
1 cup hot water

Cream butter; gradually add sugar, mixing well. Add egg and molasses, mixing well.
Combine dry ingredients; add to the creamed mixture alternately with hot water, beginning and ending with the flour mixture, and beating well after each addition. Pour batter into a lightly greased and floured 9-inch square pan. Bake at 350° for 35 to 40 minutes or until a wooden pick inserted in the center comes out clean. Yield: 9 servings.
*Evelyn Howell, Orange, Texas.*

## Oyster Lover Invents A New Trick

Dr. D. P. Hightower of York, Alabama, has developed a recipe for those who love raw oysters but also enjoy the crunchiness of fried oysters. He first breads the oysters, then freezes them until firm. Quick-frying crisps the crackercrumb coating but only thaws the oyster. Your "fried raw" oysters will be a hit with any oyster lover.

### FRIED RAW OYSTERS

½ cup fine cracker crumbs
⅛ teaspoon salt
¼ teaspoon pepper
1 (12-ounce) can fresh Select oysters, drained
Vegetable oil

Combine cracker crumbs, salt, and pepper; dredge oysters in crumbs. Place on a baking sheet, and freeze until firm.
Heat 1 inch of oil to 350°. Fry frozen oysters in oil until golden brown; drain on paper towels. Yield: 4 servings.
*Dr. D. P. Hightower, York, Alabama.*

## Spaghetti With A Special Sauce

Tender strips of sautéed veal, green peppers, mushrooms, and tomatoes all add up to a delicious spaghetti sauce sent to us by Ann Marcuccilli of Louisville. Spoon this special sauce over a platter of hot cooked spaghetti, pass the Parmesan cheese, and enjoy.

### SPAGHETTI WITH VEAL AND PEPPERS

2 pounds boneless veal cutlets, cut into thin strips
¼ cup all-purpose flour
¼ cup olive oil
2 medium-size green peppers, chopped
1 (4-ounce) can sliced mushrooms, drained
2 (28-ounce) cans tomatoes, undrained
2 (8-ounce) cans tomato sauce
1 teaspoon dried whole basil
1 teaspoon dried whole oregano
1 teaspoon garlic powder
Hot cooked spaghetti
Grated Parmesan cheese

Dredge veal in flour; sauté in oil in a Dutch oven until no longer pink. Add green pepper and cook, stirring occasionally, until tender. Stir in next 6 ingredients. Cover and simmer 1 hour.
Serve sauce over spaghetti; sprinkle with Parmesan cheese. Yield: about 8 servings.
*Ann Marcuccilli, Louisville, Kentucky.*

# February

When cold winter winds howl, it's time to keep kitchens warm for rising yeast bread. The beckoning aroma of rising dough and bread baking saturated *Southern Living* kitchens as our home economists shaped one basic dough into Cheese Crescents, Orange Rolls, Cinnamon Loaf, Sesame Buns, Filled Coffee Ring, Braided Loaf, and Cloverleaf Rolls. We loved the variety of golden-crusted goodies this single dough yields; we think you will too.

Of course, we couldn't let February slip by without offering some sweet ideas for that special someone—create your own greeting or design on our Valentine Sugar Cookies or indulge your loved one with a batch of our rich Chocolate Fudge.

And if you are dreaming of warmer days and fresh seafood by the shore, our Shrimp Destin is just for you. This dish has become first choice with our food staff for a special company entrée.

# Catch A Little Sunshine With Carrots

Many folks think that the best way to eat a fresh carrot is crispy cold and raw. Along with the crunch, they are enjoying a low-calorie food that's high in fiber and rich in vitamin A—good for your eyes, as we all know.

Carrots are often added to the pot with a roast and potatoes or shredded into salads. But you don't have to stop there. Ever tried Fried Carrot Balls? Or a Festive Carrot Ring filled with English peas? Carrot-Bran Cupcakes with cream cheese frosting make a perfect snack or dessert. You'll want to try all these delicious ways to enjoy the colorful, nutritious carrot.

There's an abundant supply of fresh carrots available throughout the year. Select carrots that are firm and smooth; those with cracks tend to be overgrown and tough. The darker the orange color, the greater the content of vitamin A. Use baby carrots when you can—they're especially tender and delicious.

Carrots may be kept fresh in the refrigerator for up to four weeks. Remove the leafy tops as soon as possible, since they draw moisture and valuable nutrients from the root.

## FESTIVE CARROT RING

2 cups cooked, mashed carrots (about 1½ pounds)
1 cup fine, dry breadcrumbs
1 cup milk
¾ cup (3 ounces) shredded sharp Cheddar cheese
⅓ cup butter, melted
1 small onion, grated
1 teaspoon salt
¼ teaspoon pepper
⅛ teaspoon red pepper
3 eggs
1 (10-ounce) package frozen English peas or lima beans
Leaf lettuce

Combine first 9 ingredients in a large mixing bowl; mix well, and set aside. Beat eggs with electric mixer at high speed until frothy and thickened (about 1 minute); gently fold eggs into carrot mixture.

Spoon mixture into a well-greased 1½-quart ring mold. Bake at 350° for 45 minutes. Remove from oven; cool on wire rack 20 minutes.

Cook peas according to package directions; drain well. Invert carrot ring onto lettuce-lined platter; fill center with cooked peas. Yield: 8 to 10 servings.
*Mrs. T. A. Jones,*
*Mount Airy, North Carolina.*

## FRIED CARROT BALLS

2 tablespoons butter or margarine
2 tablespoons all-purpose flour
⅔ cup milk
½ teaspoon salt
⅛ teaspoon pepper
3 cups finely chopped cooked carrots
2 tablespoons chopped fresh parsley
1 tablespoon minced onion
1 tablespoon sugar
1 cup all-purpose flour
3 eggs
3 tablespoons whipping cream
2 cups soft breadcrumbs
Vegetable oil

Melt butter in a heavy saucepan over low heat; add 2 tablespoons flour, stirring until smooth. Cook 1 minute, stirring constantly. Gradually add milk; cook over medium heat, stirring constantly, until thickened and bubbly. Stir in salt and pepper.

Combine white sauce, carrots, parsley, onion, and sugar; mix well. Shape into 1½-inch balls; dredge each in remaining flour. Combine eggs and whipping cream; mix well. Dip carrot balls in egg mixture; coat well with breadcrumbs. Fry in deep hot oil (375°) until golden. Drain on paper towels. Yield: about 2½ dozen.
*Connie Weathers,*
*Dalton, Georgia.*

## SUNSHINE CARROTS

1 pound baby carrots, scraped
1 teaspoon sugar
1 teaspoon cornstarch
¼ teaspoon salt
¼ teaspoon ground ginger
¼ cup orange juice
1 tablespoon butter or margarine

Cook carrots in a small amount of salted water 20 minutes or until tender. Drain well.

Combine next 5 ingredients in a small saucepan; cook over low heat, stirring constantly, about 5 minutes or until thickened. Add butter, stirring well. Pour over carrots; stir gently to coat well. Yield: 3 to 4 servings.
*Nelda Hase,*
*Gainesville, Georgia.*

## CARROT-BRAN CUPCAKES

1 cup all-purpose flour
½ cup firmly packed brown sugar
⅓ cup sugar
1½ cups 100% wheat bran cereal, crushed
½ cup raisins
⅓ cup chopped pecans or walnuts
2 teaspooons baking powder
2 teaspoons ground cinnamon
¼ teaspoon salt
1½ cups shredded carrots
½ cup vegetable oil
1 egg
¼ cup milk
Orange-Cream Cheese Frosting

Combine first 9 ingredients in a large bowl; make a well in center of mixture, and set aside. Combine carrots, oil, egg, and milk; add to dry ingredients, stirring just until moistened. Spoon batter into paper-lined muffin pans, filling two-thirds full. Bake at 400° for 20 minutes. Cool and frost with Orange-Cream Cheese Frosting. Yield: about 1½ dozen.

*Orange-Cream Cheese Frosting:*

1 (3-ounce) package cream cheese, softened
¾ cup sifted powdered sugar
1 teaspoon grated orange rind
1 teaspoon orange juice

Beat cream cheese well; gradually add sugar, beating until light and fluffy. Stir in rind and juice. Yield: enough frosting for 1½ dozen cupcakes.
*Connie Weathers,*
*Dalton, Georgia.*

# Breads From One Basic Dough

Yeast bread was probably discovered by accident, the result of a microorganism falling into a batch of dough and causing it to rise dramatically—surprising an ancient baker. A mystique still surrounds leavened bread and gives it a reputation for being difficult to bake.

But we've developed an easy dough recipe that you can use to make bread in many shapes and flavors. It's quick to mix, simple to work with, requires little kneading, and will keep in the refrigerator for up to five days. You'll get a tempting yeast flavor and aroma, and a soft, even texture beneath a golden crust.

Our test kitchen home economists had fun inventing different ways to use the dough. One spread it with butter and cheese and rolled it into crescents. Another shaped sesame seed buns. A sweet roll fan drenched spiral rolls with frosting, while someone else laced the dough into an impressive braided loaf.

Even a novice baker can turn out beautiful breads with this simple dough; just follow directions precisely, and be aware of the basic techniques.

## Techniques of Breadmaking

**Dissolving the yeast**—In our basic dough recipe, we dissolve the yeast in warm water (105° to 115°) before adding any other ingredients. Water that is too hot will kill the yeast, while water too cool will make the bread slow to rise.

**Kneading the dough**—Ideal proportions of ingredients make our dough require very little kneading. Once the dough has risen, turn it out onto a lightly floured surface. With lightly floured hands, lift the edge of the dough that is farthest from you and fold it toward you. Using the heels of both hands, press down into the dough and away from you. Give the dough a quarter turn. Fold the dough toward you again, and repeat the process until the dough is smooth and elastic and loses its stickiness.

**Rising**—The ideal rising temperature for good yeast breads is 85°. A gas oven with a pilot light or an electric oven containing a large pan of hot water should provide this temperature, as well as a draft-free environment.

Place the dough in a greased bowl, turning it to coat the top surface. Cover the bowl with plastic wrap.

Rising is complete when the dough has doubled in bulk. To test for this, lightly press a finger ½ inch into the dough. If the indention remains, the dough is ready.

Punch the dough down in the center with your fist, and fold the edges to the center. Turn the dough over, and place on a lightly floured surface.

To make the dough ahead of time, let it rise in the refrigerator. It will take about eight hours to rise at this cooler temperature, and it will keep there for up to five days. Punch the dough down each day.

**Shaping**—Divide the dough according to your particular recipe, and shape the portion you will be using into a ball. (Store excess dough in the refrigerator until needed.) Cover and let rest 5 to 10 minutes. This allows the gluten in the dough to relax, making the dough less elastic and easier to handle.

Directions for shaping rolls, buns, loaves, and crescents are given in the following recipes. After the shaped dough has doubled in size, lightly press a finger against the edge of the loaf. If the indention remains, it has risen enough.

**Baking**—Preheat the oven. When minimum baking time is up, tap the top crust with your finger. If bread sounds hollow, it is done. Remove bread from pans immediately; cool on wire racks. Wrap bread with foil or plastic wrap to store.

### BASIC ROLL DOUGH

1 package dry yeast
1 cup warm water (105° to 115°)
3 tablespoons sugar
2 tablespoons shortening
1 egg
¾ teaspoon salt
3 to 3½ cups all-purpose flour, divided

Dissolve yeast in warm water in a large bowl. Add sugar, shortening, egg, salt, and half the flour; beat at low speed of electric mixer until smooth. Stir in enough of remaining flour to make a soft dough.

Place dough in a greased bowl, turning to grease top. Cover and let rise in a warm place (85°), free from drafts, 1 hour or until doubled in bulk, or cover and refrigerate up to 5 days.

Punch dough down; turn out onto a lightly floured surface, and knead 4 or 5 times. Shape and bake as directed.

### ORANGE ROLLS

1 recipe Basic Roll Dough
¼ cup butter or margarine, softened
½ cup sugar, divided
2 tablespoons grated orange rind
¼ cup butter or margarine
¼ cup commercial sour cream
1 tablespoon orange juice

Roll dough into a 14- x 9-inch rectangle on a lightly floured surface. Combine softened butter, 2 tablespoons sugar, and orange rind; spread over dough, leaving a ½-inch margin. Roll up jellyroll fashion, starting at long side; pinch long edge (do not seal ends). Cut roll into 1½-inch slices. Place slices, cut side down, ½ inch apart in greased 9-inch square pan.

Cover and let rise in a warm place (85°), free from drafts, about 40 minutes or until doubled in bulk. Bake at 400° for 20 to 25 minutes or until browned. Remove from pan while hot.

Combine remaining sugar, butter, sour cream, and juice in a saucepan; cook over medium heat, stirring constantly, until thoroughly heated. (Do not boil.) Pour over warm rolls. Yield: 9 rolls.

### SESAME BUNS

1 recipe Basic Roll Dough
1 egg white
1 tablespoon water
1 tablespoon plus 1 teaspoon sesame seeds

Divide dough into 8 equal pieces. Roll each into a ball, and place on greased baking sheets; press down lightly with fingertips to resemble a bun.

Cover and let rise in a warm place (85°), free from drafts, about 30 minutes or until doubled in bulk. Combine egg white and water, beating until frothy; gently brush over buns. Sprinkle buns with sesame seeds. Bake at 400° for 15 to 20 minutes or until brown. Yield: 8 buns.

### BRAIDED LOAF

1 recipe Basic Roll Dough
1 egg white
1 tablespoon water

Divide dough into thirds. Shape each third into a 12-inch rope. Place ropes on a greased baking sheet (do not stretch); pinch ends together at one end to seal. Braid ropes; pinch ends to seal.

Cover and let rise in a warm place (85°), free from drafts, about 30 minutes or until doubled in bulk. Combine egg white and water, and beat until frothy; gently brush over loaf. Bake at 350° for 25 to 30 minutes or until bread sounds hollow when tapped. Yield: 1 loaf.

**Braided Loaf**—*Divide dough into 3 parts, and shape each into a rope. Place ropes on a greased baking sheet; pinch ends together at one end. Braid ropes together; pinch loose ends to seal.*

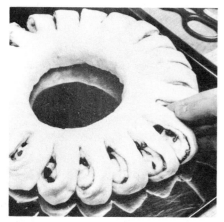

**Filled Coffee Ring**—*Roll dough into a rectangle, and add filling; roll up jellyroll fashion, starting at long side. Place on greased cookie sheet, and shape into ring; pinch ends to seal. Cut two-thirds of way through dough at 1-inch intervals. Turn each slice on its side, overlapping slices.*

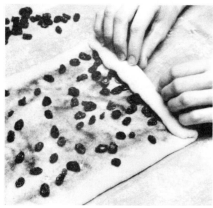

**Cinnamon Loaf**—*Roll dough into a rectangle, and add filling; roll up dough jellyroll fashion, starting at short side. Pinch seam and ends to seal, and place in a greased loafpan.*

**Cheese Crescents**—*Roll the dough into a circle. Brush with butter, and sprinkle with cheese. Cut into wedges. Roll wedges tightly, beginning at wide end. Seal points, and place rolls on greased baking sheets; curve rolls into crescent shape.*

## FILLED COFFEE RING

1 recipe Basic Roll Dough
2 tablespoons butter or margarine, melted
½ cup raisins
½ cup chopped pecans
⅓ cup sugar
1 teaspoon ground cinnamon
1 cup sifted powdered sugar
1½ tablespoons milk

Roll dough into a 21- x 7-inch rectangle on a lightly floured surface. Brush butter evenly over dough, leaving a 1-inch margin. Combine raisins, chopped pecans, ⅓ cup sugar, and cinnamon; sprinkle mixture evenly over the dough, leaving a 1-inch margin.

Roll up dough, jellyroll fashion, beginning at long side; pinch edges to seal. Place roll on a large, greased baking sheet, seam side down; shape into a ring, and pinch ends together to seal.

Using kitchen shears, make cuts in dough every inch around ring, cutting two-thirds of the way through roll at each cut. Gently turn each piece of dough on its side, slightly overlapping slices. Cover, and let rise in a warm place (85°), free from drafts, for 45 minutes or until doubled in bulk. Bake at 375° for 20 to 25 minutes or until golden brown. Transfer to a wire rack. Combine powdered sugar and milk; drizzle over bread while warm. Yield: 1 coffee cake.

## CINNAMON LOAF

½ recipe Basic Roll Dough
2 tablespoons butter or margarine, melted
1 tablespoon plus 1 teaspoon sugar
1 teaspoon ground cinnamon
⅓ cup raisins
1 cup sifted powdered sugar
1 to 1½ tablespoons milk
¼ cup chopped pecans

Roll dough into a 15- x 7-inch rectangle on a lightly floured surface; brush with melted butter. Combine 1 tablespoon plus 1 teaspoon sugar and cinnamon; sprinkle over dough. Sprinkle raisins over dough. Roll up jellyroll fashion, starting at short side. Pinch seams and ends together. Place roll, seam side down, in a greased 8½- x 4½- x 3-inch loafpan.

Cover, and let rise in a warm place (85°), free from drafts, about 40 minutes or until doubled in bulk. Bake at 350° for 25 to 30 minutes or until loaf sounds hollow. Remove from pan to a wire rack; cool. Combine powdered sugar and milk, stirring until smooth. Drizzle over loaf, and sprinkle with pecans. Yield: 1 loaf.

## CHEESE CRESCENTS

½ recipe Basic Roll Dough
2 tablespoons butter or margarine, melted
¼ cup grated Parmesan cheese
Butter or margarine, melted

Roll dough into a 12-inch circle on a lightly floured surface. Brush with 2 tablespoons melted butter, and sprinkle with Parmesan cheese. Cut into 12 wedges; roll each wedge tightly, beginning at the wide end. Seal points, and place rolls on a greased baking sheet.

Cover rolls, and let rise in a warm place (85°), free from drafts, about 30 minutes or until doubled in bulk. Bake at 400° for 8 to 10 minutes or until browned. Brush rolls with melted butter. Yield: 1 dozen.

## CLOVERLEAF ROLLS

1 recipe Basic Roll Dough
¼ cup butter or margarine, melted

Lightly grease muffin pans. Shape dough into 1-inch balls; place 3 balls in each muffin cup. Cover and let rise in a warm place (85°), free from drafts, for 40 minutes or until doubled in bulk. Bake at 400° for 12 to 15 minutes or until golden; brush with melted butter. Yield: 2 dozen.

**Cooking Light**

# It's Italian And It's Light

Italian spaghetti and garlic bread are usually flatly refused by a dedicated dieter—the hundreds of calories hidden in saucy pasta and toasted bread are certainly taboo on a low-calorie diet. However, calorie counters can indulge in this month's light Italian menu without a worry. Each of these recipes has been stripped of extra calories in our test kitchens and given our stamp of approval for flavor and appeal.

Our menu features one entrée based on chicken, a popular ingredient in light cooking because of its low-fat content. In Chicken and Spinach Noodles, chicken is combined with peas, mushrooms, Parmesan cheese, and colorful spinach noodles for an attractive, low-calorie dish. Skim milk replaces cream in the sauce—another way to reduce fat and calories.

Removing much of the fat from the cooking process and from the food itself is essential to light cooking. In the form of oil, butter, or margarine, fat provides about 100 calories per tablespoon. For our alternative entrée, Meaty Spaghetti, lean ground chuck is browned and then drained thoroughly; even the pan is wiped clean before proceeding with the recipe.

Our Italian Vegetable Salad is prepared without the oil and sugar common in many marinated salads. The combination of vinegar, spices, and fresh vegetables makes a perfect accompaniment to either of our entrées.

What Italian meal would be complete without garlic bread, usually spread with lots of butter? Our light Garlic Bread is sliced thin, sprinkled with garlic powder for flavor, and baked. At only 40 calories per slice, it's sure to be a favorite with other menus as well.

In true Italian tradition, end your meal with fruit. Fresh pears are poached in spiced unsweetened orange juice; then the cooking juices are thickened into a delicious orange sauce to serve over the pears. It's the perfect finale to a menu that says Italian can be light.

**Chicken and Spinach Noodles
or
Meaty Spaghetti
Italian Vegetable Salad
Garlic Bread
Poached Pears in Orange Sauce**

## CHICKEN AND SPINACH NOODLES

**2 whole chicken breasts, skinned
Water
1 tablespoon salt
8 ounces uncooked spinach noodles
¾ cup cooked English peas
1 (2½-ounce) jar sliced mushrooms, drained
1 (4-ounce) jar sliced pimiento, drained
2 egg yolks
1 cup skim milk
½ cup freshly grated Parmesan cheese
Freshly ground black pepper**

Place chicken and 1 cup water in a saucepan; cover and cook until tender. Drain and remove chicken from bone; cut chicken into strips and set aside.

Bring 3 quarts water and salt to a boil in a large Dutch oven. Gradually stir in noodles; return water to a boil. Boil 14 to 15 minutes; drain and return to

Dutch oven. Add chicken, peas, mushrooms, and pimiento.

Beat egg yolks and milk with a fork until foamy; gradually add to noodles in Dutch oven, stirring well. Add Parmesan cheese and pepper; cook mixture over medium-high heat, stirring gently, until thickened. Yield: 8 servings (about 242 calories per serving).

## MEATY SPAGHETTI

**1½ pounds lean ground chuck
1 medium onion, chopped
1 cup chopped celery
½ cup chopped green pepper
2 cloves garlic, minced
1 (15-ounce) can tomato sauce
1 (6-ounce) can tomato paste
¾ cup water
1 (4-ounce) can stems and pieces mushrooms, undrained
1½ teaspoons dried whole oregano
½ teaspoon salt
½ teaspoon pepper
1 (12-ounce) package thin spaghetti**

Cook ground chuck in a Dutch oven over medium heat, stirring to crumble, until meat is browned. Drain meat in a colander, and pat dry with a paper towel. Wipe pan drippings from pan with a paper towel.

Return meat to Dutch oven; add onion, celery, green pepper, and garlic. Cook over low heat, stirring frequently, 5 minutes. Add next 7 ingredients, and stir well; bring mixture to a boil. Reduce heat; cover and simmer 1½ hours, stirring occasionally.

Cook spaghetti according to package directions; drain. Spoon meat sauce over spaghetti. Yield: 8 servings (about 330 calories per serving).

## ITALIAN VEGETABLE SALAD

**6 medium ripe tomatoes, cut into wedges
1 green pepper, cut into strips
1 medium onion, sliced and separated into rings
1 cucumber, cut into ¼-inch slices
¾ cup white wine vinegar
¼ cup water
1½ teaspoons mustard seeds
1½ teaspoons celery salt
½ teaspoon salt
¼ teaspoon black pepper
Dash of red pepper
Lettuce leaves**

Combine vegetables, and set aside.
Combine vinegar, water, and seasonings in a saucepan, mixing well. Bring

to a boil; cook 1 minute, stirring constantly. Pour hot mixture over vegetables, tossing gently.

Cover salad, and chill well. Serve on lettuce leaves. Yield: 8 servings (about 35 calories per serving).

## GARLIC BREAD

**8 (½-inch) slices Italian bread
⅛ to ¼ teaspoon garlic powder**

Place bread slices on an ungreased cookie sheet; bake at 400° for 10 to 15 minutes. Remove from oven; turn slices over, and sprinkle with garlic powder. Bake an additional 2 minutes or until golden brown. Yield: 8 servings (about 40 calories per serving).

## POACHED PEARS IN ORANGE SAUCE

**8 pears
1¼ cups orange juice
½ teaspoon grated lemon rind
2 tablespoons lemon juice
½ teaspoon ground cinnamon
3 whole cloves
1½ teaspoons cornstarch
¼ cup cold water
Orange rind strips**

Peel pears; remove core, leaving stem end intact.

Combine next 5 ingredients in a Dutch oven; bring to a boil. Place pears, stem end up, in the Dutch oven; spoon juices over pears. Reduce heat; cover and simmer 10 to 15 minutes or until tender. Remove pears with slotted spoon; set aside.

Combine cornstarch and water; stir well. Pour cornstarch mixture into pan juices; cook over low heat, stirring constantly, until thickened. Pour orange sauce over pears; garnish each with a strip of orange rind. Yield: 8 servings (about 123 calories per serving).

# Sweeten Valentine Day

Valentine Day is a time for sweets. Creamy Chocolate Fudge will win someone's heart; so will a jar full of specially frosted sugar cookies.

## CHOCOLATE FUDGE

2½ cups sugar
1 (5.33-ounce) can evaporated milk
2 (1-ounce) squares unsweetened chocolate
2 tablespoons light corn syrup
Dash of salt
2 tablespoons butter
1 teaspoon vanilla extract
1 cup chopped pecans or walnuts

Combine first 5 ingredients in a Dutch oven. Cook over low heat, stirring constantly, until sugar is dissolved.

Continue to cook, stirring, until mixture reaches soft ball stage (236°). Remove from heat; add butter and vanilla (do not stir). Cool to lukewarm (110°).

Add pecans; beat with a wooden spoon until mixture is thick and begins to lose its gloss (2 to 3 minutes). Pour into a buttered 8-inch square pan. Mark warm fudge into 1⅓-inch squares. Cool and cut. Yield: 3 dozen.     *Helen Dill, Oklahoma City, Oklahoma.*

## VALENTINE SUGAR COOKIES

¾ cup shortening
1 cup sugar
2 eggs
1 teaspoon vanilla extract
2½ cups all-purpose flour
1 teaspoon baking powder
½ teaspoon salt
Decorator frosting (recipe follows)

Cream shortening; gradually add sugar, beating until fluffy. Add eggs and vanilla; mix well. Combine dry ingredients; add to creamed mixture, mixing well. Divide dough in half; wrap in waxed paper, and chill at least 1 hour.

Roll half of dough to ¼-inch thickness on a lightly floured surface; keep remaining dough chilled. Cut dough with a heart-shaped cookie cutter. Place on lightly greased cookie sheets; bake at 350° for 12 minutes or until edges are lightly browned. Cool cookies on a wire rack. Repeat with remaining dough. Frost with decorator frosting. Yield: 3 dozen.

*Decorator Frosting:*

¼ cup plus 2 tablespoons butter or margarine, softened
1 (16-ounce) package powdered sugar, sifted
¼ cup milk
1 teaspoon vanilla extract
Red food coloring (optional)

Cream butter; gradually add sugar, beating until well blended. Add milk and vanilla, mixing until smooth. Stir in food coloring, if desired. Yield: frosting for 3 dozen cookies.

*Mary Ann Ferguson, Union City, Tennessee.*

# Microwave Cookery

# Frozen Vegetables, Ready In Minutes

Frozen vegetables are quick and easy to cook conventionally, but microwaving multiplies their advantages. In the microwave, vegetables cook still faster, and more nutrients are preserved because most of the cooking liquid is actually natural water of the vegetable. Since little if any water is added, your vegetables have a brighter color and more full-bodied flavor.

You can microwave vegetables right in the box. Simply remove the outside wrapping (wax contained in wrappings of some brands can melt onto your hands), and place the box in a flat baking dish. (Use a paper platter if you want to eliminate dishwashing.) Prick the box several times with a fork to let steam escape, and microwave according to the time specified in the recipe. Watch out for steam as you open the box.

To cook solid-pack frozen vegetables in a microwave-safe dish, remove them from the box and place them, icy side up, in the dish. Add 1 tablespoon of water for each box you're cooking; cover with the glass lid made for the dish or with heavy-duty plastic wrap. Cooking times in a dish are often the same as in the box, but can be a minute or two longer.

Always cook loose-pack vegetables in a dish, and add 2 tablespoons of water per 16-ounce package since they contain fewer ice crystals.

Here are some other pointers:

—Whether you're cooking vegetables in the box or in a dish, they will probably need stirring or breaking up halfway through the cooking time. To do so, simply untuck the box lid, or remove the glass lid or plastic wrap.

—If you're cooking more than one box at a time, rearrange the boxes halfway through the cooking time.

—To avoid drying the vegetables, add salt after the initial cooking period.

—If any package of frozen vegetables contains foil, the vegetables must be removed from the package and microwaved in a baking dish.

*Note:* The time range given in each recipe allows for the difference in wattage of microwave ovens. To prevent overcooking, always check for doneness at the lower end of the range.

## GREEN BEANS AMANDINE

2 (10-ounce) packages frozen cut green beans
3 tablespoons butter or margarine
⅓ cup minced onion
⅓ cup sliced almonds
¾ teaspoon salt

Remove wrappers from boxes; place boxes in a flat baking dish, and pierce with a fork. Microwave at HIGH for 12 to 15 minutes or until done, rearranging boxes once. Drain and set aside.

Place butter in a 1-quart casserole. Microwave at HIGH for 20 to 25 seconds or until melted. Stir in onion and almonds; cover with heavy-duty plastic wrap, and microwave at HIGH for 4 to 6 minutes or until almonds are browned and onion is tender. Stir in beans and salt. Cover; microwave at HIGH for 2 to 3 minutes or until thoroughly heated. Yield: 6 to 8 servings.

## BROCCOLI AU GRATIN

2 (10-ounce) packages frozen broccoli spears
2 tablespoons butter or margarine
2 tablespoons all-purpose flour
¼ teaspoon salt
Dash of pepper
1 cup milk
1 cup (4 ounces) shredded Cheddar cheese

Remove wrappers from boxes; place boxes in a flat baking dish, and pierce with a fork. Microwave at HIGH for 10 to 12 minutes or until done, rearranging boxes once. Drain broccoli, and set aside.

Place butter in a 4-cup glass measure. Microwave at HIGH for 20 seconds or until melted. Add flour, salt, and pepper; stir until smooth. Gradually add milk, stirring well. Microwave at HIGH for 2 minutes; stir until smooth. Microwave at HIGH for 1 to 2½ minutes, stirring at 1-minute intervals, until thickened and bubbly. Add cheese, stirring until melted. Arrange broccoli on serving platter; top with sauce. Serve immediately. Yield: 4 to 6 servings.

## MEXI-CORN

1 (10-ounce) package frozen cut corn
2 tablespoons butter or margarine
¼ cup chopped green pepper
¼ cup chopped onion
½ teaspoon salt
1 small tomato, peeled and chopped
⅛ teaspoon dried whole oregano

Remove wrapper from box; place box in a flat baking dish, and pierce with a fork. Microwave at HIGH for 4 to 6 minutes or until done, turning once. Drain, if necessary, and set aside.

Place butter in a 1-quart casserole. Microwave at HIGH for 20 seconds or until melted. Stir in green pepper and onion. Cover with heavy-duty plastic wrap, and microwave at HIGH for 2 to 3 minutes or until vegetables are tender.

Stir in corn and remaining ingredients. Cover and microwave at HIGH for 1 to 2 minutes or until thoroughly heated. Yield: 3 to 4 servings.

## CHEESY SQUASH CASSEROLE

2 (10-ounce) packages frozen sliced yellow
    squash
4 slices bacon
⅔ cup chopped onion
2 eggs, beaten
1 cup (4 ounces) shredded process
    American cheese
½ teaspoon salt
¼ teaspoon pepper
1 tablespoon Worcestershire sauce

Remove wrappers from boxes; place boxes in a flat baking dish, and pierce with a fork. Microwave at HIGH for 9 to 12 minutes or until done, rearranging boxes once. Drain, if necessary, and set squash aside.

Place bacon on a bacon rack in a 12- x 8- x 2-inch baking dish; cover with paper towels. Microwave at HIGH for 3 to 4 minutes or until the bacon is done; drain and crumble bacon, reserving

drippings in baking dish. Set bacon aside. Stir onion into reserved drippings. Cover with heavy-duty plastic wrap, and microwave at HIGH for 1 to 2 minutes or until onion is tender.

Combine squash, bacon, onion, and remaining ingredients in a round 1-quart casserole; stir well. Cover with heavy-duty plastic wrap, and microwave at MEDIUM (50% power) for 10 to 13 minutes or until casserole is almost set, turning twice. Let sit 2 to 3 minutes. Continue microwaving briefly if casserole is not set. Yield: 6 servings.

# Cooking For Two Made Easy

If you're cooking for two and like to avoid recipes that yield lots of leftovers, here are some new ideas for you. We've included recipes for everything from soup to baked apples; they're all quick to fix and sized just for two.

## CREAM OF POTATO SOUP

1 tablespoon plus 1 teaspoon butter or
    margarine
2 tablespoons all-purpose flour
2 cups milk
1 cup peeled, diced cooked potatoes
¼ to ½ teaspoon salt
Pepper to taste

Melt butter in a heavy saucepan over low heat; add flour, stirring until smooth. Cook 1 minute, stirring constantly. Gradually add milk; cook over medium heat, stirring constantly, until thickened and bubbly. Stir in potatoes, salt, and pepper; cook 5 minutes or until thoroughly heated. Yield: about 2½ cups.                    *Ava Merchant,*
*West Columbia, South Carolina.*

## HURRY-UP MEAT LOAF

¾ pound ground beef
1 (8-ounce) can tomato sauce, divided
½ cup soft breadcrumbs
1 egg, slightly beaten
1 tablespoon dried minced onion flakes
½ teaspoon salt
⅛ teaspoon pepper
1 tablespoon brown sugar
2 teaspoons dried parsley flakes
½ teaspoon Worcestershire sauce

Combine ground beef, ½ cup tomato sauce, breadcrumbs, egg, onion flakes, salt, and pepper; mix well. Shape meat mixture into 4 individual loaves; place in a lightly greased 11- x 7- x 1½-inch baking pan. Bake loaves at 450° for 30 minutes.

Combine remaining tomato sauce, brown sugar, parsley flakes, and Worcestershire sauce; mix well. Pour over loaves, and bake an additional 5 minutes. Yield: 2 servings.
*Marilyn Mollenkamp,*
*Atlanta, Georgia.*

## HERBED SOLE FILLETS

¼ cup butter or margarine
1 tablespoon vegetable oil
⅛ teaspoon onion salt
⅛ teaspoon dried whole oregano
⅛ teaspoon dried parsley flakes
⅛ teaspoon dried whole tarragon
⅛ teaspoon pepper
⅛ teaspoon minced garlic
2 fillets of sole
1½ tablespoons dry sherry

Melt butter in a large heavy skillet; add next 7 ingredients, and sauté over medium heat 1 minute. Reduce heat to low; add fish. Cook fish 3 minutes; turn and cook an additional 2 or 3 minutes or until fish flakes easily when tested with a fork (do not overcook). Remove fish with a slotted turner; place on a heated platter, and keep warm.

Pour sherry into skillet; cook over high heat 30 to 45 seconds. Pour sherry mixture over fish; serve immediately. Yield: 2 servings.        *Ethel Evans,*
*St. Petersburg, Florida.*

## GREEN BEANS WITH MUSHROOMS

1 tablespoon minced onion
1 tablespoon vegetable oil
1 (8-ounce) can cut green beans, drained
1 tablespoon diced pimiento
1 teaspoon chopped fresh parsley
1 (4-ounce) can mushroom pieces and
    stems, drained
⅛ teaspoon salt
⅛ teaspoon pepper

Sauté onion in oil in a medium skillet until transparent. Stir in remaining ingredients; cover and cook over medium heat 10 minutes or until thoroughly heated. Yield: 2 servings.
*Mrs. L. R. Koenig,*
*Charleston, South Carolina.*

## SWEET-AND-SOUR BEETS

¼ cup sugar
1 teaspoon cornstarch
2 tablespoons water
2 tablespoons vinegar
1 tablespoon vegetable oil
1 (16-ounce) can sliced beets, drained
⅛ teaspoon salt
Dash of pepper

Combine sugar and cornstarch in a saucepan; stir well. Gradually add water, stirring until smooth. Stir in vinegar and oil; cook over medium heat, stirring constantly, until thickened. Add beets, salt, and pepper; cook over medium heat about 10 minutes or until thoroughly heated. Yield: 2 servings.
*Ann F. Caffi,*
*Arlington, Virginia.*

## EASY BAKED APPLES

2 medium-size baking apples
¼ cup honey
½ teaspoon lemon juice

Core apples; peel top third of each. Place apples in a shallow baking dish; add water to cover bottom of dish.

Combine honey and lemon juice; mix well. Fill center of apples with honey mixture, spreading mixture over peeled portion of apples. Bake at 350° for 45 minutes or until tender, basting occasionally with pan juices. Yield: 2 servings.
*Kaye B. Hirst,*
*Salisbury, North Carolina.*

# Have You Tried Cooking In Paper?

Wrapping food before exposing it to direct heat is an ancient cooking technique. Cabbage leaves, grape leaves, banana leaves, corn husks, and aluminum foil are just a few of the wrappers used over the years to help retain moisture and steam food as it bakes. Another kind of wrapper that is fun to work with is parchment—a type of paper specially prepared for cooking. Preparing foods in parchment is called cooking in papillote, and the result is definitely dramatic to serve.

Mrs. Rodger Giles of Augusta, Georgia, fills pieces of parchment with sole, mushroom sauce, shrimp, and crabmeat. As it bakes, some of the steam evaporates through the paper. However, the bag will rise and puff up as the heating process progresses.

When preparing food in papillote, remember that making and sealing the paper bags can be tricky, so follow directions very carefully. Also, we recommend using only cooking parchment for papillote; some other types of paper may flame when exposed to heat.

## SOLE IN PAPILLOTE

3 cups water
½ teaspoon liquid crab boil
½ pound medium shrimp
5 tablespoons butter or margarine, divided
¼ pound fresh mushrooms, sliced
½ cup chopped green onion
3 tablespoons all-purpose flour
1 cup half-and-half
½ cup dry white wine
2 tablespoons chopped pimiento
Dash of salt
Dash of pepper
Dash of paprika
Olive oil
4 large sole fillets
½ pound fresh crabmeat
1 egg, beaten
3 tablespoons all-purpose flour

Cut eight 12- x 10¾-inch pieces of parchment paper; cut each into a large heart shape. Set aside.

Combine water and crab boil; bring to a boil. Add shrimp; reduce heat, and simmer 3 to 5 minutes. Drain well; rinse with cold water. Chill. Peel and devein shrimp; set aside.

Melt 2 tablespoons butter in a heavy skillet; add mushrooms and onion. Sauté until onion is tender; set aside.

Melt remaining 3 tablespoons butter in a heavy saucepan over low heat; add 3 tablespoons flour, stirring until smooth. Cook 1 minute, stirring constantly. Gradually add half-and-half and wine; cook over medium heat, stirring constantly, until thickened and bubbly. Stir in mushroom mixture, pimiento, and seasonings.

Lightly brush one side of 4 paper hearts with olive oil. Place 1 sole fillet in center of each; top with one-fourth each of the shrimp, crabmeat, and mushroom sauce. Combine egg and 3 tablespoons flour, stirring until smooth; brush a small amount along the edges of each of the paper hearts.

Place another paper heart over top of seafood, sealing edges to bottom heart with flour and egg mixture. Fold paper edges over to seal securely. Carefully place parchment bags on baking sheet; bake at 425° for 15 minutes or until bags are puffed and lightly browned. Cut an opening in bags before serving. Yield: 4 servings. *Mrs. Rodger Giles,*
*Augusta, Georgia.*

# Enjoy The Richness Of Buttermilk

As far as Southern cooks are concerned, buttermilk is a staple. Here it adds rich flavor to griddle cakes, yeast rolls, and a lemon pie.

## BUTTERMILK REFRIGERATOR ROLLS

1 package dry yeast
½ cup warm water (105° to 115°)
½ cup shortening, melted
4½ cups all-purpose flour
¼ cup sugar
1 tablespoon plus 1 teaspoon baking powder
1 teaspoon salt
½ teaspoon soda
2 cups buttermilk

Dissolve yeast in warm water in a large mixing bowl; let stand 5 minutes. Stir in melted shortening.

Combine dry ingredients in a small bowl. Add dry ingredients and buttermilk to yeast mixture; mix well. Turn dough out on a well-floured surface; knead gently until dough can be handled. Shape dough into a ball; place in a greased bowl, turning to grease top. Cover dough, and refrigerate until needed (dough will keep 1 week).

Shape dough into rolls, as desired; place on lightly greased baking sheets. Bake at 400° for 8 to 10 minutes or until lightly browned. Yield: about 2 dozen.
*Mrs. Larry Doskocil,*
*Lott, Texas.*

## BUTTERMILK GRIDDLE CAKES

2 cups all-purpose flour
3 tablespoons sugar
2 teaspoons baking powder
1 teaspoon salt
½ teaspoon soda
1 egg
1½ cups buttermilk
3 tablespoons shortening, melted
Maple syrup (recipe follows)

Combine dry ingredients. Combine egg and buttermilk; slowly stir into dry ingredients. Add shortening, mixing lightly.

Drop mixture by heaping tablespoonfuls onto a hot, lightly greased griddle. Turn pancakes when tops are covered with bubbles and edges are brown. Serve hot with maple syrup. Yield: 4 to 6 servings.

*Maple Syrup:*

**2 cups water**
**4 cups sugar**
**2 teaspoons imitation maple flavoring**

Heat water to boiling in a medium saucepan; add sugar and reduce heat. Stir until sugar is dissolved (do not let mixture boil). Remove from heat, and add maple flavoring. Serve warm. Store in refrigerator. Yield: 4 cups.
*Ansel L. Todd,*
*Royston, Georgia.*

## BUTTERMILK LEMON PIE

**3 eggs**
**1½ cups sugar**
**½ cup buttermilk**
**3 tablespoons butter or margarine, melted**
**1 tablespoon all-purpose flour**
**2 tablespoons lemon juice**
**1 teaspoon lemon extract**
**1 unbaked 9-inch pastry shell**

Beat eggs; add next 6 ingredients, and mix well. Pour into pastry shell.

Bake at 425° for 10 minutes; place foil over edges of crust, and bake 5 to 10 minutes longer or until set. Let cool on a wire rack. Yield: one 9-inch pie.
*Mrs. Raymond Simpson,*
*Cleveland, Tennessee.*

## WILLIAMSBURG ORANGE CAKE

**2½ cups all-purpose flour**
**1½ cups sugar**
**1½ teaspoons soda**
**¼ teaspoon salt**
**1½ cups buttermilk**
**½ cup butter or margarine, softened**
**¼ cup shortening**
**3 eggs**
**1½ teaspoons vanilla extract**
**1 tablespoon grated orange rind**
**1 cup golden raisins, chopped**
**½ cup finely chopped pecans**
**Williamsburg Butter Frosting**

Combine first 10 ingredients in a large mixing bowl; beat with an electric mixer for 30 seconds on low speed. Beat 3 minutes on high speed. Stir in chopped raisins and pecans.

Pour batter into a greased and floured 13- x 9- x 2-inch baking pan. Bake at 350° for 45 to 55 minutes; cool. Frost with Williamsburg Butter Frosting. Yield: one 13- x 9- x 2-inch cake.

*Williamsburg Butter Frosting:*

**⅓ cup butter or margarine, softened**
**3 cups sifted powdered sugar**
**1 tablespoon grated orange rind**
**3 to 4 tablespoons orange juice or orange-flavored liqueur**

Cream butter and sugar until fluffy. Add orange rind and juice; beat until smooth. Yield: frosting for one 13- x 9- x 2-inch cake.
*Margie L. Warthan,*
*Avery, Texas.*

# Salads For The Winter Table

With winter's fresh produce and a little help from the freezer and grocery shelf, you can make your winter salads every bit as appealing and delicious as the salads of spring and summer.

## WINTER FRUIT SALAD

**1½ tablespoons sugar**
**2¼ teaspoons all-purpose flour**
**¼ teaspoon dry mustard**
**⅛ teaspoon salt**
**Dash of red pepper**
**1 egg yolk, slightly beaten**
**½ cup milk**
**2¼ teaspoons butter**
**1 tablespoon vinegar**
**4 Delicious apples, cored and chopped**
**1 (8-ounce) can crushed pineapple, drained**
**¾ cup chopped pecans**
**Lettuce leaves**

Combine first 5 ingredients in the top of a double boiler; stir in egg yolk and milk. Add butter. Bring water to a boil; reduce heat to low, and cook until butter is melted, stirring constantly. Gradually add vinegar; cook, stirring constantly, until mixture is thickened and smooth. Cool completely.

Combine apples, pineapple, and pecans; stir dressing into fruit. Chill. Serve on lettuce leaves. Yield: 6 to 8 servings.
*Mrs. Ralph Dillon,*
*Boone, North Carolina.*

## SWEDISH VEGETABLE SALAD

**2 (10-ounce) packages frozen English peas and carrots**
**1 (9-ounce) package frozen French-style green beans**
**1½ cups diced raw cauliflower**
**1 (14-ounce) can artichoke hearts, drained and quartered**
**½ cup chopped onion**
**½ cup chopped celery**
**¾ cup mayonnaise**
**¼ cup chili sauce**
**1 teaspoon dried dillweed**
**1 teaspoon salt**
**⅛ teaspoon pepper**
**1 teaspoon lemon juice**

Cook frozen vegetables according to package directions; drain well and cool. Combine cooked vegetables, cauliflower, artichoke hearts, onion, and celery in a large bowl; toss gently.

Combine remaining ingredients, mixing well. Pour over vegetables, and toss gently. Cover and chill overnight. Yield: 8 to 10 servings.
*Jan Wisland,*
*St. Louis, Missouri.*

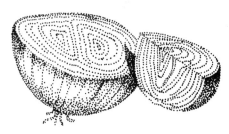

## ORIENTAL SPINACH SALAD

**1 pound spinach, torn**
**1 (5½-ounce) package fresh bean sprouts or 1 (14-ounce) can bean sprouts, drained**
**1 (8-ounce) can sliced water chestnuts, drained**
**6 slices bacon, cooked and crumbled**
**3 hard-cooked eggs, sliced**
**Dressing (recipe follows)**

Combine first 5 ingredients in a large salad bowl; toss lightly. Serve with dressing. Yield: 8 to 10 servings.

*Dressing:*

**1 cup vegetable oil**
**½ cup sugar**
**⅓ cup catsup**
**¼ cup vinegar**
**1 tablespoon Worcestershire sauce**
**1 medium onion, chopped**

Combine all ingredients in container of electric blender, and process well. Yield: about 2½ cups. *Patricia Street,*
*Bedford, Texas.*

## BROCCOLI SALAD

2 (10-ounce) packages frozen chopped
   broccoli
1 cup chopped celery
⅓ cup chopped onion
1 (2-ounce) jar diced pimiento, drained
⅓ cup mayonnaise
⅓ cup plain yogurt
1 teaspoon seasoned salt
¼ teaspoon pepper

Thaw broccoli; drain well on paper towels. Combine broccoli, celery, onion, and pimiento.

Combine mayonnaise, yogurt, seasoned salt, and pepper; stir well. Pour mayonnaise mixture over vegetables, and stir well. Cover and chill for 2 hours. Yield: about 6 to 8 servings.

*Mrs. Gene Coleman,*
*Whispering Pines, North Carolina.*

## CRUNCHY MACARONI SALAD

1 (8-ounce) package elbow macaroni
1 cup chopped celery
¼ cup chopped fresh parsley
⅓ cup chopped green pepper
6 green onions, sliced
⅔ cup diced Cheddar cheese
1 (2-ounce) jar diced pimiento, drained
½ cup mayonnaise
½ cup commercial sour cream
1 tablespoon red wine vinegar
¼ to ½ teaspoon seasoned salt
¼ teaspoon pepper
Lettuce leaves

Cook macaroni according to package directions; drain and let cool. Add next 6 ingredients, and stir gently.

Combine next 5 ingredients; mix well. Pour the dressing over macaroni mixture, and stir gently. Cover and chill at least 2 hours; serve salad on lettuce leaves. Yield: 12 servings.

*Mrs. W. B. Shepard, Jr.,*
*Albuquerque, New Mexico.*

## INDIVIDUAL MEAT LOAVES

2 pounds ground beef
1 cup round buttery cracker crumbs
1 egg, beaten
½ cup finely chopped green pepper
½ cup finely chopped onion
½ cup evaporated milk
1 teaspoon salt
¼ teaspoon pepper
1 teaspoon seasoned meat tenderizer
1¼ cups catsup, divided
3 tablespoons dark corn syrup

Combine first 9 ingredients and ¼ cup catsup; mix well. Shape mixture into 6 loaves, and wrap individually in freezer paper or aluminum foil. Freeze. To serve, thaw in refrigerator; bake at 350° for 35 minutes. Combine corn syrup and remaining 1 cup catsup; brush on tops of meat loaves. Bake 10 minutes longer. Yield: 6 servings.

*Mary H. Gillian,*
*Cartersville, Virginia.*

## SLOPPY JOES

3 pounds ground beef
1 medium onion, finely chopped
1 cup finely chopped celery
1 (10¾-ounce) can tomato soup,
   undiluted
1 cup catsup
1 teaspoon salt
⅛ teaspoon pepper
8 hamburger buns, halved
Shredded Cheddar cheese

Brown meat in a large skillet. Add onion and celery; cook until tender. Drain off drippings. Stir in tomato soup, catsup, salt, and pepper; simmer 30 minutes.

Freeze in a plastic freezer container. To serve, thaw in refrigerator, and heat in a saucepan. Spoon over warm bun halves, and sprinkle with cheese. Yield: 16 servings.

*Nell Little,*
*Jonesboro, Tennessee.*

## FREEZER SLAW

1 large cabbage
½ green pepper
6 large carrots
1 teaspoon salt
2 cups sugar
1 teaspoon dry mustard
½ cup water
1 cup vinegar
1 teaspoon celery seeds

Shred cabbage, green pepper, and carrots. Sprinkle with salt, and let stand 1 hour. Drain if water accumulates.

Combine remaining ingredients in a saucepan. Bring to a boil; boil 3 minutes. Cool. Pour over cabbage mixture, and let stand 3 minutes. Stir well. Freeze in plastic freezer bags or containers. To serve, thaw in refrigerator. Yield: about 10 servings.

*Mrs. Ken Keller,*
*Alcoa, Tennessee.*

## STRAWBERRY FROST

½ cup butter
1 cup all-purpose flour
¼ cup firmly packed brown sugar
½ cup finely chopped pecans
2 egg whites
1 (10-ounce) package frozen sliced
   strawberries, slightly thawed
⅔ cup sugar
2 tablespoons lemon juice
1 cup whipping cream
Whole fresh strawberries (optional)

Melt butter in a 13- x 9- x 2-inch baking pan. Add flour, brown sugar, and pecans; mix well. Pat out evenly in pan. Bake at 350° for 10 minutes. Stir and bake 10 minutes longer. Cool; remove one-third of crumbs for topping. Pat remaining crumbs smoothly in pan.

Combine egg whites, sliced strawberries, sugar, and lemon juice. Beat on high speed of electric mixer for 15 minutes. Beat whipping cream until light and fluffy; fold into strawberry mixture. Spread mixture over crust in pan, and sprinkle with remaining crumbs.

Cover tightly with aluminum foil, and freeze. Cut into squares, and garnish with whole strawberries, if desired. Yield: 12 to 16 servings.

*Mrs. W. G. Greenlee,*
*Inverness, Florida.*

# Freezing Ahead Is Easy–And Smart

Wouldn't it be nice to be able to go to the freezer and take out a whole meal that's already prepared? These recipes let you do just that. You can make a meal out of our Individual Meat Loaves and Freezer Slaw, with Strawberry Frost for dessert. For a more casual meal, try our Sloppy Joes.

# Fry Potatoes To Perfection

Fried potatoes seem a perfect match for everything from hamburgers and hot dogs to steaks. Our recipes give them a new look and an even more delicious flavor by varying the way they are sliced and seasoned. You'll see for yourself when you try our thin and crispy Homemade Potato Chips. Or try our Oven-Fried Potatoes—they're a welcome alternative to stove-top frying.

Selecting quality potatoes is the first step in producing good fries. Purchase potatoes that are firm, clean, and smooth. Avoid those with wrinkled or withered skins. A green color on the skin indicates the potato is sunburned and will have a bitter flavor.

## OVEN-FRIED POTATOES

3 medium potatoes
¼ cup vegetable oil
1 tablespoon grated Parmesan cheese
½ teaspoon salt
¼ teaspoon garlic powder
¼ teaspoon paprika
¼ teaspoon pepper

Scrub potatoes, and cut each into ⅛-inch wedges. Place wedges, slightly overlapping, in a single layer in a 13- x 9- x 2-inch baking pan.

Combine remaining ingredients, stirring well. Brush potatoes with half of oil mixture. Bake, uncovered, at 375° for 45 minutes, basting occasionally with remaining seasoned oil mixture. Yield: 4 to 6 servings. *Sara Sellers, New Providence, New Jersey.*

## ALMOND-FRIED POTATOES

2 tablespoons finely chopped onion
⅓ cup sliced almonds
¼ cup butter or margarine
4¼ cups cubed cooked potatoes
¾ teaspoon salt
¼ teaspoon pepper
¼ cup whipping cream

Sauté onion and almonds in butter until almonds are golden brown. Add potatoes, salt, and pepper, mixing well. Stir in cream. Cook over low heat until potatoes are brown, turning as necessary. Yield: 4 to 6 servings.
*Jodie McCoy, Tulsa, Oklahoma.*

## HOMEMADE POTATO CHIPS

4 medium potatoes, peeled
Vegetable oil
Imitation butter-flavored salt

Slice potatoes into very thin slices; place in ice water until slicing is completed. Drain potatoes well; pat dry.

Heat 1 inch of oil to 375° in a large skillet. Fry potatoes, a small amount at a time, 2 minutes or until golden; drain well on paper towels. Sprinkle with salt. Yield: 6 to 8 servings. *Joy M. Hall, Lucedale, Mississippi.*

## SOUTHERN-FRIED POTATOES

1 small onion, chopped
½ cup vegetable oil
3 medium potatoes, peeled and cut into 1½-inch cubes
½ teaspoon salt
⅛ teaspoon pepper

Sauté onion in oil in a heavy 10-inch cast-iron skillet until transparent; add potatoes. Fry until potatoes are tender and golden, turning as necessary. Sprinkle with salt and pepper. Yield: 4 servings. *Audrey Donahew, Garland, Texas.*

## FRIED POTATO PATTIES

4 medium potatoes, peeled and shredded
1 small onion, finely chopped
1 egg, beaten
1 tablespoon all-purpose flour
1 teaspoon salt
¼ teaspoon pepper
⅛ teaspoon red pepper
Vegetable oil

Squeeze potatoes between paper towels to remove excess moisture. Combine all ingredients except vegetable oil, mixing well. Drop ¼ cup of potato mixture at a time into ⅛ inch hot oil (375°); press into 3-inch rounds with the back of a fork. Fry until golden brown, turning once, if necessary. Drain well. Yield: 6 servings. *Mrs. Roy Carlisle, Columbus, Georgia.*

## HERB-FRIED POTATOES

3 tablespoons butter or margarine
3 large potatoes, peeled and cut into thin strips
2 tablespoons chopped fresh parsley
1 teaspoon dried whole oregano
½ teaspoon instant minced onion
½ teaspoon salt
¼ teaspoon pepper

Melt butter in a 10-inch skillet. Add potatoes; cover and cook over medium heat 10 minutes or until tender. Turn potatoes; cook, uncovered, 5 minutes.

Combine remaining ingredients; sprinkle over potatoes. Cook potatoes, uncovered, 5 additional minutes, turning occasionally to brown all sides. Remove potatoes from skillet, and drain well on paper towels. Yield: 4 servings.
*Reba B. Wilson, Jasper, Alabama.*

*Tip: When browning food in a skillet, dry the food first on paper towels.*

# Pork Chops Make Meaty Meals

Everybody knows how good pork chops can taste. And they can taste even better by enhancing their flavor with sauces and seasonings.

When selecting fresh pork chops, look for those that have a delicate rose or grayish pink color. Remember to store the meat in the coldest part of the refrigerator and prepare it within one or two days after purchase. For freezer storage, the pork chops should be securely wrapped and frozen for a maximum period of three to six months.

## PEPPERED PORK CHOP CASSEROLE

6 (½-inch-thick) pork chops
Salt and pepper to taste
2 medium-size green peppers, cut into ¼-inch rings
1½ cups uncooked regular rice
2 (8-ounce) cans tomato sauce
1 cup water
½ cup chopped onion
1 teaspoon salt
¼ teaspoon pepper

Sprinkle pork chops with salt and pepper, and arrange in a lightly greased 13- x 9- x 2-inch baking dish. Top each pork chop with one green pepper ring; spoon rice into and around rings.

Chop remaining green pepper rings; stir in remaining ingredients, and pour mixture over rice. Cover and bake at 350° for 55 to 60 minutes or until done. Yield: 6 servings. *Cindy Murphy, Cleveland, Tennessee.*

## ORANGE-GLAZED PORK CHOPS

4 (¾-inch-thick) pork chops
Salt and pepper to taste
All-purpose flour
1 tablespoon vegetable oil
½ cup orange juice
2 tablespoons orange marmalade
2 tablespoons brown sugar
1 tablespoon vinegar

Sprinkle pork chops lightly with salt and pepper; dredge in flour.

Heat oil in a heavy skillet; brown pork chops on both sides. Combine remaining ingredients, mixing well; pour over pork chops. Reduce heat; cover and simmer 40 to 45 minutes. Yield: 4 servings. *Mrs. Russell Spear, Hilliard, Florida.*

## APPLE-CRUMB STUFFED PORK CHOPS

**4 (1-inch-thick) pork chops, cut with pockets**
**Apple-Crumb Stuffing**
**Salt and pepper to taste**
**1 tablespoon butter or margarine**
**3 tablespoons water**

Stuff pockets of pork chops with Apple-Crumb Stuffing, and secure with wooden picks. Sprinkle pork chops with salt and pepper.

Melt butter in a large, heavy skillet; brown pork chops on both sides. Add water; reduce heat. Cover and simmer 50 to 55 minutes or until pork chops are tender. Yield: 4 servings.

*Apple-Crumb Stuffing:*

**1 cup soft breadcrumbs**
**½ cup diced apple**
**3 tablespoons minced onion**
**3 tablespoons raisins, chopped**
**½ teaspoon salt**
**½ teaspoon sugar**
**Pinch of pepper**
**Pinch of ground sage**
**1½ tablespoons butter or margarine, melted**

Combine all ingredients; mix well. Yield: about 1¾ cups.
*Mrs. Sidney I. McGrath,*
*Hopkinsville, Kentucky.*

## PORK CHOPS RISOTTI

**¾ cup uncooked brown rice**
**1 (10½-ounce) can beef broth, undiluted**
**¼ cup water**
**2 medium carrots, scraped and diagonally sliced**
**½ cup thinly sliced onion**
**½ cup Sauterne or other dry white wine**
**½ teaspoon salt**
**Dash of pepper**
**¼ teaspoon ground marjoram**
**⅛ teaspoon ground oregano**
**1 tablespoon vegetable oil**
**4 (½-inch-thick) pork chops**

Combine rice, broth, and water in a heavy saucepan; bring to a boil. Reduce heat; cover and simmer 50 minutes or until rice is done. Add carrots, onion, wine, and seasonings; mix thoroughly. Spoon rice mixture into a lightly greased 12- x 8- x 2-inch baking dish; set aside.

Heat oil in a skillet; brown pork chops on both sides. Drain well; arrange on top of rice mixture. Cover and bake at 350° for 1 hour. Yield: 4 servings. *Mrs. Ralph E. Chase,*
*Hendersonville, North Carolina.*

## OVEN-BARBECUED PORK CHOPS

**2 cups soy sauce**
**1 cup water**
**½ cup firmly packed brown sugar**
**1 tablespoon molasses**
**1 teaspoon salt**
**6 (¾- to 1-inch-thick) pork chops**
**1 tablespoon dry mustard**
**½ cup firmly packed brown sugar**
**⅓ cup water**
**1 (14-ounce) bottle catsup**
**1 (12-ounce) bottle chili sauce**

Combine first 5 ingredients in a large shallow container; mix well. Add pork chops, and turn once to coat; cover container, and marinate overnight.

Remove pork chops from marinade, reserving marinade for use with other meat recipes. Place pork chops in a 13- x 9- x 2-inch baking pan. Cover and bake at 350° for 1½ hours.

Combine remaining ingredients in a heavy saucepan; bring to a boil, stirring constantly. Pour over pork chops; bake, uncovered, an additional 20 to 25 minutes. Yield: 6 servings.

*Note:* Any remaining sauce may be stored in the refrigerator and used later with either chicken or beef.
*Mina DeKraker,*
*Holland, Michigan.*

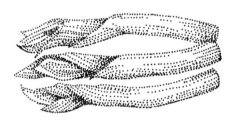

# Take A Close Look At Leeks

If you've never prepared fresh leeks, take a closer look next time you spot them in the produce section of your supermarket. This mild-tasting member of the onion family looks like an overgrown green onion and has thick, rope-like roots.

Sliced leeks add zesty flavor to soups and stews, but they can also be cooked whole and served as a side dish. Mrs. John Armstrong of Farwell, Texas, glazes whole leeks in a brown sugar and butter sauce; she likes to serve them with pork, a beef roast, or steak.

Some supermarkets carry leeks year-round, but they are most plentiful October through May. To prepare leeks, cut off the roots, and remove the tough outer leaves. Trim off all but an inch or two of the green tops. Be sure to wash leeks thoroughly to remove any dirt trapped between the leaves.

## GLAZED LEEKS

**6 medium leeks**
**2 tablespoons butter or margarine**
**2 tablespoons brown sugar**

Remove roots, tough outer leaves, and tops from leeks; wash leeks thoroughly. Place leeks in a large heavy skillet; cover and cook in a small amount of boiling salted water 8 to 10 minutes or until tender. Drain; remove leeks from skillet, and set aside.

Combine butter and sugar in skillet; cook over low heat, stirring constantly, until sugar dissolves. Return leeks to skillet and cook over low heat, turning frequently, until golden. Yield: 3 servings. *Mrs. John R. Armstrong,*
*Farwell, Texas.*

## DILLY LEEK COMBO

**¼ cup butter or margarine**
**3 medium carrots, scraped and thinly sliced**
**3 stalks celery, thinly sliced**
**2 large leeks, thinly sliced**
**1 small onion, chopped**
**1 (10-ounce) package frozen English peas**
**½ pound fresh mushrooms, sliced**
**2 tablespoons chopped fresh parsley**
**1 teaspoon dried whole dillweed**
**½ teaspoon salt**
**¼ teaspoon pepper**

Melt butter in a large skillet over high heat; add carrots. Reduce heat to low; cover and cook 5 minutes. Add celery, leeks, and onion; sauté until vegetables are tender. Add peas, stirring to separate. Add mushrooms, parsley, and dillweed; cover and simmer 5 minutes. Add salt and pepper; stir well. Yield: 6 to 8 servings. *Ginger McVay,*
*Miami, Florida.*

Right: *Dried-bean dishes are not only delicious and economical, they're also very nutritious. Take your pick of Barbecued Lima Beans, Garbanzo Salad, and Black Beans With Yellow Rice (recipes on page 2).*

Page 28: *The variety of fillings, toppings, and shapes makes it hard to believe all these yeast breads started from the same dough: Sesame Buns (page 17), Cloverleaf Rolls (page 18), Cheese Crescents (page 18), and Cinnamon Loaf (page 18).*

# Harvest Some Shrimp Specialties

Shrimp is the South's favorite shellfish. And no wonder. The delicate pink flesh retains its fresh ocean flavor no matter how you prepare it—fried, broiled, or sautéed in a buttery sauce.

Quick and delicious is the way to describe Shrimp Destin from Frances Ponder of Cullman, Alabama: The shrimp are sautéed with scallions and garlic, then served atop toasted French bread. If fried shrimp is your favorite, try dipping the shrimp in our fluffy beer batter; the result is light, crisp, and golden. If you like shrimp in an Oriental setting, try our Shrimp Chow Mein.

When shopping for shrimp, look for a firm texture and a fresh smell. Cook them within a day or two of purchase, or freeze them; raw shrimp in their shells will maintain quality during freezing better than cooked shrimp. When you cook them, the most important thing to remember is to avoid overcooking. Shrimp cook in minutes; prolonged heat will dry and toughen them.

*Shrimp Destin is especially easy to prepare; simply sauté the shrimp with garlic and scallions, and serve over toasted French rolls.*

## GOLDEN FRIED SHRIMP

¼ cup all-purpose flour
¼ cup cornstarch
⅛ teaspoon salt
¼ cup beer
1 egg yolk
2 tablespoons melted butter or margarine
1 pound large shrimp, peeled and deveined
Vegetable oil

Combine flour, cornstarch, and salt in a small bowl. Add beer, egg yolk, and butter; beat until smooth.

Dip shrimp into batter; deep fry in hot vegetable oil (375°) until golden brown. Yield: 4 servings.

*Lilly B. Smith,*
*Richmond, Virginia.*

*Tip: New cast-iron cookware should always be seasoned before using. Rub the interior of the utensil with oil or shortening, and place in a 250° or 300° oven for several hours. Wipe off oily film, and store. If scouring is necessary after using the utensil, reseason the surface immediately to prevent rusting.*

*If utensils are to be stored for any length of time between use, rub a light film of oil over interior. Wipe off film before using, and wash in clear water.*

## LEMON-GARLIC BROILED SHRIMP

2 pounds medium shrimp, peeled and deveined
2 cloves garlic, halved
¼ cup butter or margarine
3 tablespoons lemon juice
½ teaspoon salt
Coarsely ground black pepper
3 drops hot sauce
1 tablespoon Worcestershire sauce
3 tablespoons chopped fresh parsley

Place shrimp in a single layer in a 15- x 10- x 1-inch jellyroll pan, and set aside.

Sauté garlic in butter until garlic is brown; remove and discard garlic. Add next 5 ingredients, stirring well; pour mixture over shrimp.

Broil shrimp 4 inches from heat for 8 to 10 minutes, basting once. Sprinkle with parsley; serve immediately. Yield: 6 servings.

*Peggy Kettell,*
*Spanish Fort, Alabama.*

## SHRIMP DESTIN

¼ cup chopped scallions or green onion
2 teaspoons minced garlic
1 cup butter or margarine
2 pounds large shrimp, peeled and deveined
1 teaspoon lemon juice
1 tablespoon white wine
½ teaspoon salt
Coarsely ground black pepper
1 teaspoon dried whole dillweed
1 teaspoon chopped fresh parsley
3 French rolls, split lengthwise and toasted

Sauté scallions and garlic in butter until scallions are tender. Add shrimp, lemon juice, white wine, salt, and pepper; cook over medium heat about 5 minutes, stirring occasionally. Stir in dillweed and parsley. Spoon shrimp mixture over the toasted rolls, and serve immediately. Yield: 6 servings.

*Frances Ponder,*
*Cullman, Alabama.*

## SHRIMP CHOW MEIN

1 cup chopped onion
1½ cups chopped celery
2 tablespoons butter or margarine
1 (14-ounce) can bean sprouts, drained
1 (2½-ounce) can sliced mushrooms,
    drained
½ cup chicken broth
¼ cup soy sauce
½ teaspoon brown sugar
Salt and pepper to taste
2 pounds medium shrimp, peeled and
    deveined
3 tablespoons water
3 tablespoons cornstarch
Hot cooked rice or chow mein noodles

Sauté onion and celery in butter until onion is tender. Add next 6 ingredients, stirring well; simmer 5 minutes. Add shrimp; simmer 5 minutes, stirring often. Combine water and cornstarch, stirring until smooth; add to shrimp mixture. Cook over low heat, stirring constantly, until thickened and bubbly. Serve over hot cooked rice or chow mein noodles. Yield: 6 to 8 servings.
*Mrs. Charles R. Simms,*
*Palestine, Illinois.*

# Six Choices For Chicken

Any way you prepare it, chicken is a family favorite. And it makes sense to take advantage of chicken's low cost and versatility. Ranging from savory chicken pie to creamed chicken served over rice, these will both satisfy your family and please the pocketbook.

## TOMATO-BAKED CHICKEN

1 (2½- to 3-pound) broiler-fryer, cut into
    serving-size pieces
Salt and pepper
2 tablespoons vegetable oil
½ cup chopped onion
1 clove garlic, pressed
1 (16-ounce) can whole tomatoes,
    undrained and quartered
¼ cup grated Parmesan cheese
3 tablespoons all-purpose flour
½ cup commercial sour cream

Sprinkle chicken with salt and pepper; sauté in oil until brown. Remove chicken from skillet, and set aside. Sauté onion and garlic in drippings until onion is tender. Stir in tomatoes; bring to a boil.

Place chicken in a 13- x 9- x 2-inch baking dish. Pour tomato mixture over chicken. Cover and bake at 350° for 1 hour or until done. Remove chicken to a serving platter, reserving the drippings; sprinkle chicken with Parmesan cheese.

Combine flour, sour cream, and drippings in a saucepan; mix well. Cook over low heat, stirring constantly, until mixture thickens. Spoon sauce over chicken. Yield: 4 to 6 servings.
*Gwen Granderson,*
*Kingsland, Arkansas.*

## CHICKEN AND PINEAPPLE

2 chicken legs
2 chicken thighs
2 whole chicken breasts, split
½ cup all-purpose flour
⅓ cup vegetable oil
1 teaspoon salt
¼ teaspoon pepper
1 (20-ounce) can sliced pineapple
1 cup sugar
2 tablespoons cornstarch
¾ cup cider vinegar
1 tablespoon soy sauce
¼ teaspoon ground ginger
1 chicken-flavored bouillon cube
1 large green pepper, sliced into ¼-inch
    rings
Hot cooked rice (optional)

Dredge chicken pieces in flour, coating well; brown in hot oil over medium heat. Place chicken in a 13- x 9- x 2-inch baking pan; sprinkle with salt and pepper. Set aside.

Drain pineapple, reserving juice. Add enough water to pineapple juice to make 1¼ cups liquid. Combine sugar and cornstarch in a saucepan; add pineapple juice mixture, vinegar, soy sauce, ginger, and bouillon cube. Bring sauce to a boil; reduce heat and simmer 2 minutes, stirring constantly. Pour sauce over chicken.

Bake, uncovered, at 350° for 30 minutes. Place pineapple and green pepper slices over chicken; bake an additional 30 minutes. Serve with rice, if desired. Yield: 4 to 6 servings.
*Louise Denmon,*
*Silsbee, Texas.*

*Tip: Use baking soda on a damp cloth to shine up your kitchen appliances.*

## PEANUT BUTTER-MARMALADE CHICKEN

1 teaspoon salt
¼ teaspoon pepper
⅛ teaspoon ground ginger
2 whole chicken breasts, split and skinned
⅓ cup peanut butter
⅓ cup orange marmalade
3 tablespoons orange juice
1 tablespoon lemon juice
1 cup round buttery cracker crumbs
¼ cup vegetable oil

Combine salt, pepper, and ginger; rub into chicken. Combine peanut butter, marmalade, orange juice, and lemon juice. Dip chicken in peanut butter mixture; coat well with cracker crumbs.

Pour oil into a 13- x 9- x 2-inch baking dish; arrange chicken in dish. Bake at 350° for 30 minutes. Turn chicken, and cook 30 additional minutes or until done. Yield: 4 servings.
*Bonnie Baumgardner,*
*Sylva, North Carolina.*

## CHICKEN-VEGETABLE POT PIE

1 (2½- to 3-pound) broiler-fryer
3 teaspoons salt, divided
1 teaspoon pepper, divided
4 to 5 medium potatoes, pared
5 stalks celery
½ pound carrots, scraped
1 (17-ounce) can English peas, drained
½ cup butter or margarine
⅔ cup all-purpose flour
1 cup milk
1 chicken-flavored bouillon cube
Pastry for a double-crust 9-inch pie

Place chicken, 1 teaspoon salt, ½ teaspoon pepper, and water to cover in a Dutch oven. Bring to a boil; cover and simmer 1 hour or until tender. Remove chicken from broth; cool. Remove chicken from bone, and cut into bite-size pieces.

Cut potatoes, celery, and carrots into 1-inch chunks. Place in broth; simmer until tender. Drain vegetables, reserving 3 cups broth. Combine chicken, potatoes, celery, carrots, and peas; spoon into a 13- x 9- x 2-inch pan.

Melt butter in a heavy saucepan over low heat; add flour, stirring until smooth. Cook 1 minute, stirring constantly. Gradually stir in milk, 3 cups chicken broth, and bouillon cube; cook over medium heat, stirring constantly, until thickened and bubbly. Stir in remaining 2 teaspoons salt and ½ teaspoon pepper. Pour sauce evenly over chicken-vegetable mixture.

Prepare pastry; roll to fit a 13- x 9- x 2-inch pan. Place crust over chicken mixture; cut 4 to 6 small slits in crust to allow steam to escape. Bake at 400° for 45 to 55 minutes or until crust is golden brown. Yield: 6 to 8 servings.

*Mrs. Bob Whitmire,*
*Burleson, Texas.*

## CHICKEN PIE

1 (2½- to 3-pound) broiler-fryer
1 stalk celery, cut into large pieces
Salt
½ cup margarine, melted
1 cup all-purpose flour
1 tablespoon baking powder
¼ teaspoon salt
½ teaspoon pepper
1 cup milk
1 (10¾-ounce) can cream of celery soup, undiluted

Combine chicken, celery, salt to taste, and water to cover in a Dutch oven. Bring to a boil; cover and simmer 1 hour or until chicken is tender. Remove chicken from Dutch oven, reserving 1¼ cups chicken broth.

Remove chicken from bone; dice meat. Place in a lightly greased 11- x 7- x 2-inch baking dish. Drizzle with melted margarine.

Combine flour, baking powder, ¼ teaspoon salt, pepper, and milk; beat until smooth. Pour over chicken.

Combine cream of celery soup and reserved chicken broth in a small saucepan; bring soup mixture to a boil over medium heat. Pour over chicken mixture. Bake at 425° about 50 minutes or until top is golden brown. Yield: about 6 servings.

*Fay Newsom,*
*Madison, North Carolina.*

## CREAMED CHICKEN OVER CONFETTI RICE SQUARES

3 cups cooked regular rice
1 cup (4 ounces) shredded Swiss cheese
½ cup chopped fresh parsley
⅓ cup chopped onion
⅓ cup chopped pimiento
1 teaspoon salt
3 eggs, beaten
1½ cups milk
2 tablespoons butter or margarine
3 tablespoons all-purpose flour
2 cups milk
½ teaspoon salt
¼ teaspoon ground marjoram
3 cups cubed cooked chicken
Paprika

Combine first 8 ingredients; spoon into a buttered 8-inch baking dish. Bake at 325° for 1 hour or until a knife inserted in center comes out clean.

Melt butter in a heavy saucepan over low heat; add flour, and stir until smooth. Cook 1 minute, stirring constantly. Gradually add milk; cook over medium heat, stirring constantly until thickened and bubbly. Stir in salt and marjoram. Stir in chicken; sprinkle with paprika. Cut rice into squares. Spoon creamed chicken over rice squares. Yield: 4 to 6 servings.

*Mrs. James Barden,*
*Suffolk, Virginia.*

# Hot Sandwiches For Chilly Days

Lighten up lunch or liven up supper with one of these hot and saucy sandwiches. Add a serving of coleslaw, potato salad, or a choice of relishes, and enjoy an easy but nourishing meal.

Our hearty Open-Face Chili Burgers are festively topped with lettuce, olives, onion rings, and chiles. The ground beef is simmered with onion in a taco-flavored tomato sauce. And if you'd like an idea for leftover sliced chicken, try our Saucy Chick-Wiches.

## OPEN-FACE CHILI BURGERS

1½ pounds ground beef
½ cup chopped onion
1 (8-ounce) can tomato sauce
1 (1¼-ounce) package taco seasoning mix
6 hamburger buns
12 slices tomato
1 cup (4 ounces) shredded Cheddar cheese
¾ cup shredded lettuce
¼ cup chopped stuffed olives
1 small onion, cut into rings and separated
1½ tablespoons chopped red and green chiles

Brown meat and onion in a large skillet; drain. Stir in tomato sauce and taco seasoning; simmer 5 minutes.

Split and toast hamburger buns; spread with meat mixture. Place tomato slice on each sandwich, and sprinkle with cheese; bake at 400° for 4 minutes or until cheese melts. Top with lettuce, olives, onion, and chiles. Yield: 12 servings.

*Dorothy Cox,*
*Snyder, Texas.*

## BARBECUED BEEF SANDWICHES

1½ pounds ground beef
¾ cup finely chopped celery
¾ cup finely chopped onion
½ cup finely chopped green pepper
1 (8-ounce) can tomato sauce
¼ cup catsup
2 tablespoons brown sugar
2 tablespoons barbecue sauce
2 tablespoons vinegar
1 tablespoon prepared mustard
1 tablespoon Worcestershire sauce
1½ teaspoons salt
¼ teaspoon pepper
8 to 10 hamburger buns

Brown meat in a large skillet; drain. Add celery, onion, and green pepper; cook 5 minutes or until onion is tender. Add next 9 ingredients; cover and simmer 1 hour. Serve on hamburger buns. Yield: 8 to 10 servings. *Sherry Smith,*
*Afton, Tennessee.*

## EASY SLOPPY JOES

1 pound ground beef
1 medium onion, chopped
1 teaspoon salt
¼ teaspoon pepper
1 (10¾-ounce) can chicken gumbo soup, undiluted
1½ tablespoons catsup
1 tablespoon prepared mustard
6 to 8 hamburger buns

Combine meat, onion, salt, and pepper in a large skillet; cook until meat is lightly browned. Drain off drippings. Stir in soup, catsup, and mustard; simmer mixture 15 minutes. Serve on buns. Yield: 6 to 8 servings. *Gayle Hurdle,*
*Carthage, Mississippi.*

## SAUCY CHICK-WICHES

4 slices cooked chicken
4 slices bread, toasted and buttered
8 slices tomato
4 slices process American cheese
1 (10½-ounce) can chicken gravy

Arrange chicken on toast; top with tomato slices. Broil 4 inches from heat for 3 minutes or until hot. Top with cheese, and broil until melted. Heat gravy, and spoon over sandwiches. Yield: 4 servings. *Melody Fowler,*
*Devine, Texas.*

*Tip: Rub hands with parsley to remove any odor.*

# Revive Menus With Onions

Onions are combined so often in other dishes we tend to forget they make a delicious side dish on their own. Filled with a flavorful stuffing or baked with cheese, the onion deserves center stage. Mrs. Walter L. Reese, Jr., of Birmingham shares an especially easy way to prepare onions in the microwave oven.

When selecting onions, consider all the flavor possibilities. The large Spanish or Bermuda onion and the small white onion are usually mild in flavor, while Globe types, such as the red, brown, and small yellow onion, are stronger.

### CREOLE ONIONS

2 large Spanish onions, thinly sliced
½ teaspoon salt
¼ teaspoon pepper
½ cup tomato puree
¼ cup dry white wine
¼ cup water
¼ teaspoon dried whole thyme
2 slices bacon
¼ cup chopped green pepper
1 clove garlic, minced

Place onion in a lightly greased 2-quart casserole. Sprinkle with salt and pepper.

Combine tomato puree, wine, water, and thyme; stir well, and pour over sliced onion in casserole.

Fry bacon until crisp; drain, reserving pan drippings. Crumble bacon, and sprinkle over onion.

Sauté green pepper and garlic in reserved drippings until tender; spoon over onion. Cover and bake at 375° for 30 to 35 minutes. Yield: 4 to 6 servings.
*Jodie McCoy,*
*Tulsa, Oklahoma.*

### CHEESE ONION BAKE

6 medium onions, thinly sliced
¼ cup butter or margarine
¼ cup all-purpose flour
2 cups milk
2 cups (8 ounces) shredded Cheddar
   cheese
½ teaspoon salt

Place onion in a lightly greased 2-quart casserole; set aside.

Melt butter in a heavy saucepan over low heat; add flour, stirring until smooth. Cook 1 minute, stirring constantly. Gradually add milk; cook over medium heat, stirring constantly, until thickened and bubbly. Add cheese and salt, stirring until cheese melts and sauce is smooth.

Pour cheese sauce over onion. Bake, uncovered, at 350° about 1 hour. Yield: 8 servings.
*Mildred Clute,*
*Marquez, Texas.*

### SHERRIED CHEESE ONIONS

24 to 26 small boiling onions
2 teaspoons salt
2 tablespoons butter or margarine
2 tablespoons all-purpose flour
1½ cups milk
½ cup (2 ounces) shredded mild Cheddar
   cheese
1½ tablespoons dry sherry

Peel onions; place in a large saucepan. Add several inches of water; sprinkle with salt, and bring to a boil. Reduce heat, and cook 10 to 15 minutes or until tender. Drain well, and place onions in an 8-inch square baking dish.

Melt butter in a heavy saucepan over low heat; add flour, stirring until smooth. Cook 1 minute, stirring constantly. Gradually add milk; cook over medium heat, stirring constantly, until thickened and bubbly. Add cheese, stirring until cheese melts and sauce is smooth. Stir in sherry, and pour sauce over onions. Bake at 350° for 20 minutes. Yield: 6 to 8 servings.
*Pamela Nordyke,*
*San Angelo, Texas.*

### MICRO-BAKED ONIONS

4 medium onions
1 tablespoon plus 1 teaspoon butter or
   margarine
2 tablespoons grated Parmesan cheese
Paprika

Peel onions, and cut a thin slice from top of each. Reserve tops for use in another recipe.

Arrange onions, cut side up, in a shallow 2-quart microwave-safe casserole. Top each onion with 1 teaspoon butter and ½ tablespoon cheese; sprinkle with paprika. Cover casserole with heavy-duty plastic wrap. Microwave at HIGH for 10 to 12 minutes, giving dish one half-turn after 5 or 6 minutes. Yield: 4 servings.
*Mrs. Walter L. Reese, Jr.,*
*Birmingham, Alabama.*

### STUFFED BAKED ONIONS

6 large Vidalia or Bermuda onions
1 (6-ounce) package cornbread stuffing
   mix
2 cups (8 ounces) shredded sharp
   Cheddar cheese

Peel onions, and cut a small slice from top and bottom. Slice each onion into 6 wedges, cutting to within ½ inch of bottom. Set aside.

Prepare stuffing mix according to package directions; cool. Stir in cheese.

Fill onions with stuffing mixture; wrap each onion in aluminum foil. Place onions in a 13- x 9- x 2-inch baking pan. Bake at 350° for 45 minutes or until tender. Yield: 6 servings.
*Mrs. Harry Lay, Jr.,*
*Fairmount, Georgia.*

# Roll Up A Quick Snack

Would you like a lunch or snack idea that's easy to make and fun to serve? Try this tasty Pepperoni and Cheese Loaf sent to us from Kathy Chaney of Charleston, West Virginia. She starts with frozen bread dough, rolls it into a circle, and spreads it with pepperoni and mozzarella cheese. Then it's rolled into a loaf and baked until golden brown.

Sound simple? It is—and you'll find it equally versatile. "I substitute different luncheon meats and cheeses to suit my cravings," says Kathy. We think it will satisfy your cravings too.

### PEPPERONI AND CHEESE LOAF

1 (1-pound) loaf frozen bread dough
1 egg, beaten
½ cup grated Parmesan cheese
2 (3½-ounce) packages sliced pepperoni
2 cups (8 ounces) shredded mozzarella
   cheese
½ teaspoon dried whole oregano

Thaw dough, and allow to rise according to package directions. Divide dough in half, and set one portion aside.

Turn out remaining portion of dough on a lightly floured surface. Roll dough into a 10-inch circle. Combine egg and Parmesan cheese, stirring well; spread half of egg mixture over circle, leaving a ½-inch margin at edges. Layer half of pepperoni and half of mozzarella cheese over egg mixture, and sprinkle with half of oregano.

Roll up dough jellyroll fashion. Seal edges, and fold under ends. Transfer loaf, seam side down, to an ungreased baking sheet. Repeat procedure with remaining ingredients. Bake at 375° for 30 minutes. Cut into slices to serve. Yield: 6 to 8 servings. *Kathy Chaney, Charleston, West Virginia.*

## No Crust, No Fuss

Can you spare 10 minutes to make a pie? Sure you can, because with no crust to prepare, these two pies are a cinch. A few minutes to measure and mix, and the pies are ready to bake.

Crustless Brownie Pie is a chocolate lover's dream. Served with a scoop of vanilla ice cream or a dollop of whipped cream, this fudgy dessert can be prepared fast enough to satisfy a chocolate craving almost as soon as it hits.

Eggs, milk, sugar, and coconut are combined in Coconut Custard Pie, also crustless. Baked and then chilled before serving, this delightfully easy pie is a variation on two old Southern favorites, egg custard and coconut pie.

### COCONUT CUSTARD PIE

½ cup all-purpose flour
½ cup sugar
2 cups milk
4 eggs
¼ cup butter or margarine, melted
1 tablespoon vanilla extract
¼ teaspoon salt
1½ cups flaked coconut

Combine first 7 ingredients in container of electric blender, and process 10 seconds. Stir in coconut. Pour into a buttered 9-inch deep-dish pieplate. Bake at 350° for 40 minutes or until set. (Pie will puff, then fall slightly.) Cool; chill thoroughly. Yield: one 9-inch pie. *Rebecca Solomon, Charlotte, North Carolina.*

### CRUSTLESS BROWNIE PIE

1 cup sugar
½ cup all-purpose flour
¼ cup cocoa
½ cup butter or margarine, softened
2 eggs
1 teaspoon vanilla extract
Pinch of salt
½ cup chopped pecans or walnuts
Whipped cream or ice cream

Combine first 7 ingredients; beat 4 minutes at medium speed of electric mixer. Stir in nuts. Spread batter evenly in a buttered 9-inch pieplate. Bake at 325° for 35 to 40 minutes or until wooden pick inserted in center comes out clean. (Pie will puff, then fall slightly.) Serve with whipped cream or ice cream. Yield: one 9-inch pie. *Susie Timmons, Winston-Salem, North Carolina.*

## Broccoli–Enjoy It Crisp Or Tender

If you need a green vegetable to round out the menu, think of broccoli. Its bright green color is welcome on any menu, and broccoli is just as delicious served raw in a salad, stir-fried and crispy in an Oriental dish, or baked until tender in a quiche.

You'll want to try Donna Field's Easy Broccoli Quiche; it's simple and surprising. Just fill a pieplate with chopped broccoli, green pepper, onion, and cheese; then top with a blend of eggs and biscuit mix. This custardy mixture forms its own crust as it bakes.

### CHICKEN-BROCCOLI STIR-FRY

1 large whole chicken breast
2 teaspoons cornstarch
½ to 1 teaspoon freshly grated gingerroot
¼ cup soy sauce
2 tablespoons vegetable oil
1 cup diagonally sliced fresh broccoli
1 medium onion, thinly sliced
½ pound fresh mushrooms, quartered
Hot cooked rice or chow mein noodles

Place chicken in a medium saucepan, and cover with water. Bring to a boil; cover and reduce heat. Simmer 15 minutes or until chicken is tender. Drain, reserving ½ cup broth. Bone chicken, and chop meat.

Combine cornstarch, gingerroot, and soy sauce; stir well. Add the chicken; mix well, and let marinate in refrigerator 30 minutes.

Pour oil around top of a large skillet or wok, coating sides; allow to heat at medium-high (325°) for 2 minutes. Add broccoli and reserved broth; cover and cook 2 minutes. Reduce heat to medium (275°). Stir in chicken and marinade. Add onion, and stir-fry 1 minute. Add mushrooms; stir-fry 1 to 2 minutes or until tender. Serve over hot cooked rice or chow mein noodles. Yield: 4 servings. *Doris Garton, Shenandoah, Virginia.*

### BROCCOLI-CHICKEN CASSEROLE

1 (3-pound) broiler-fryer
1 (1-pound) bunch fresh broccoli
1 (10¾-ounce) can cream of chicken soup, undiluted
½ cup mayonnaise
½ teaspoon lemon juice
½ cup fine, dry breadcrumbs
2 tablespoons butter or margarine, melted
¼ cup (1 ounce) shredded sharp Cheddar cheese

Place chicken in a Dutch oven, and cover with water. Bring to a boil; cover and reduce heat. Simmer 1 hour or until tender. Remove chicken, and let cool. (Reserve broth for use in another recipe.) Bone chicken, and chop meat; set aside.

Trim off large leaves of broccoli. Remove tough ends of lower stalks, and wash broccoli thoroughly. Separate into spears. Cook broccoli, covered, in a small amount of boiling water for 10 minutes or until crisp-tender; drain and set aside. Combine soup, mayonnaise, and lemon juice; stir well. Set aside.

Arrange broccoli in a lightly greased 12- x 8- x 2-inch baking dish; top with chicken and soup mixture. Combine breadcrumbs and butter, stirring well; sprinkle over top of casserole. Bake at 350° for 20 minutes. Sprinkle cheese over top of casserole; return to oven 5 minutes or until cheese melts. Yield: 8 servings. *Mrs. G. L. Bellamy, Texas City, Texas.*

*Tip: When food boils over in the oven, sprinkle the burned surface with a little salt. This will stop smoke and odor from forming and make the spot easier to clean. Also, rubbing damp salt on dishes in which food has been baked will remove brown spots.*

## EASY BROCCOLI QUICHE

2 cups finely chopped fresh broccoli
½ cup chopped green pepper
⅓ cup chopped onion
1 cup (4 ounces) shredded Colby cheese
1 cup milk
½ cup biscuit mix
3 eggs
¼ teaspoon salt
¼ teaspoon pepper

Cook broccoli, covered, in a small amount of boiling water 10 minutes; drain. Place broccoli in a lightly greased 9-inch pieplate; sprinkle with green pepper, onion, and cheese. Set aside.

Combine remaining ingredients in container of electric blender; blend 15 seconds or until smooth. Pour over broccoli mixture; bake at 375° for 25 to 30 minutes or until set. Let stand 5 minutes before serving. Yield: 6 servings.
*Donna Field,*
*Blackwell, Oklahoma.*

## BROCCOLI SUPREME

3 cups chopped fresh broccoli
1½ cups sliced fresh mushrooms
1 large onion, chopped
¼ cup butter or margarine, divided
2 tablespoons all-purpose flour
1 cup milk
½ teaspoon salt
¼ teaspoon pepper
1 cup (4 ounces) shredded Cheddar cheese
Hot cooked rice
Soy sauce

Cook broccoli, covered, in a small amount of boiling salted water 5 minutes; drain and set aside.

Sauté mushrooms and onion in 2 tablespoons butter until onion is tender; set aside.

Melt 2 tablespoons butter in a heavy saucepan over low heat; add flour, stirring until smooth. Cook 1 minute, stirring constantly. Gradually add milk; cook over medium heat, stirring constantly, until thickened and bubbly. Remove from heat. Add salt, pepper, and cheese; stir until cheese melts. Stir in mushroom mixture.

Place broccoli in a lightly greased 1½-quart casserole. Top with sauce, and bake at 350° for 25 minutes. Serve broccoli over rice; sprinkle with soy sauce. Yield: 6 servings. *Wanda Raper,*
*Marietta, Georgia.*

## BROCCOLI WITH SESAME SEEDS

1 (1½-pound) bunch fresh broccoli
1 tablespoon sesame seeds
3 tablespoons vegetable oil
3 cloves garlic, finely chopped
½ cup sliced water chestnuts
3 tablespoons dry white wine
3 tablespoons water
2 tablespoons soy sauce
½ teaspoon salt
½ teaspoon sugar

Trim off large leaves of broccoli. Remove tough ends of lower stalks, and wash broccoli thoroughly. Remove flowerets from stems, and set aside; slice stems thinly, and set aside.

Allow wok to heat at medium-high (325°) for 2 minutes. Spoon sesame seeds into wok; cook, stirring constantly, until seeds are toasted. Remove seeds from wok, and set aside.

Pour oil around top of wok, coating sides; allow to heat at high (375°) for 2 minutes. Add garlic; cook, stirring constantly, 15 seconds. Add sliced broccoli stalks, and stir-fry 4 to 5 minutes.

Reduce heat to medium-high (325°). Stir in broccoli flowerets, water chestnuts, wine, water, soy sauce, salt, and sugar; mix well. Cover and cook 3 to 4 minutes. Remove to serving dish, and sprinkle with the sesame seeds. Yield: 6 servings. *Mrs. Ralph E. Chase,*
*Hendersonville, North Carolina.*

## FRESH BROCCOLI SALAD

1 (1-pound) bunch fresh broccoli
½ cup grated Parmesan cheese
½ cup pickle relish
½ cup mayonnaise
½ cup chopped fresh mushrooms
3 hard-cooked eggs, chopped
2 tablespoons chopped onion

Trim off large leaves of broccoli. Remove tough ends of lower stalks, and wash broccoli thoroughly; cut flowerets and stems into bite-size pieces.

Add remaining ingredients, tossing gently. Chill at least 3 hours. Yield: about 8 servings. *Gwen Louer,*
*Roswell, Georgia.*

# Pack A Lunch To Go

Running out of ideas for nutritious, enjoyable, and packable lunches? Our readers offer some exciting new suggestions that even the kids will love.

To lessen your morning work load, you can make and freeze several lunches ahead of time. Just pull a sandwich from the freezer in the morning, and by lunchtime it'll be perfect for eating. However, avoid freezing sandwiches made with mayonnaise; spread the bread with cream cheese, butter, or margarine instead.

Even our Refreshing Fruit Slush can be frozen in individual plastic containers that will fit in a lunchbox. By noon the punch should be thawed, but still cold and slushy.

## HAM-CHEESE CHIPS

1 cup finely crushed potato chips
½ cup (2 ounces) shredded Cheddar cheese
2 (4½-ounce) cans deviled ham
1 cup all-purpose flour
¼ teaspoon red pepper

Combine all ingredients; mix well. Shape mixture into a 9-inch roll; chill well. Cut into ¼-inch-thick slices, and place on lightly greased cookie sheets. Bake at 425° for 10 to 12 minutes. Cool on wire rack, and store in an airtight container. Yield: about 3 dozen.
*Mrs. Bill Hodges,*
*Guntersville, Alabama.*

## HOMEMADE CHICKEN SOUP

2 stalks celery, cut into 3-inch pieces
1 large carrot, cut into 3-inch pieces
1 large leek, cut into 3-inch pieces
6 sprigs fresh parsley
1 bay leaf
2 whole cloves
1 large onion
9 cups water
1 (5- to 6-pound) baking hen
1 tablespoon salt
8 whole peppercorns
1 cup scraped, diced carrots
½ cup diced celery
½ cup diced onion
⅓ cup uncooked regular rice
1 (10-ounce) package frozen English peas
½ teaspoon salt
¼ teaspoon pepper
Chopped fresh parsley (optional)

Combine first 5 ingredients in a cheesecloth bag. Insert cloves into onion. Combine water, baking hen, vegetable bag, clove-studded onion, 1 tablespoon salt, and peppercorns in a large Dutch oven; cover and simmer 2 to 2½ hours or until hen is tender.

Remove chicken from broth; bone and chop chicken. Set aside 3 to 4 cups chopped chicken; reserve remaining chicken for use in other recipes.

Strain broth, and discard vegetables. Skim off excess fat. Stir in diced carrots, celery, onion, and rice; simmer 10 minutes. Add 3 to 4 cups chicken, peas, ½ teaspoon salt, and pepper; continue to cook 10 minutes or until rice is tender. Sprinkle with parsley, if desired. Yield: about 14 cups.

*Mrs. H. G. Drawdy,*
*Spindale, North Carolina.*

## PIMIENTO CHEESE SPREAD

4 cups (1 pound) shredded extra-sharp Cheddar cheese
1 (4-ounce) jar diced pimiento, drained
¾ cup chopped pecans
½ cup mayonnaise
12 pimiento-stuffed olives, diced
2 tablespoons dry sherry
1 tablespoon olive juice
1 teaspoon sugar
½ teaspoon pepper
½ teaspoon hot sauce

Combine all ingredients, and stir well. Chill. Yield: about 4 cups.

*Aileen Wright,*
*Nashville, Tennessee.*

## CREAM CHEESE-OLIVE SPREAD

2 (3-ounce) packages cream cheese, softened
2 tablespoons mayonnaise
⅛ teaspoon pepper
4 small green onions, finely chopped
½ cup chopped pimiento-stuffed olives

Combine cream cheese, mayonnaise, and pepper; beat until smooth. Stir in onion and olives. Mixture may be used to stuff celery or tomatoes or as a sandwich spread. Yield: about 1¼ cups.

*Barbara McCumber,*
*Florence, Mississippi.*

*Tip: Shred Cheddar or Swiss cheese and freeze; whenever you need some for cooking, just measure.*

## PINEAPPLE-CREAM CHEESE SPREAD

1 (8-ounce) package cream cheese, softened
¼ cup diced pineapple
2 tablespoons finely chopped pecans
1 teaspoon vanilla extract

Combine all ingredients; stir well. Serve on date-nut or whole wheat bread. Yield: about 1 cup.

*Auberrie Flakes,*
*Birmingham, Alabama.*

## CALICO SALAD

2 (16-ounce) cans mixed vegetables, drained
1 (15-ounce) can kidney beans, drained
1 medium-size green pepper, chopped
1 small onion, chopped
½ cup chopped celery
¾ cup sugar
1 tablespoon all-purpose flour
1 tablespoon dry mustard
½ teaspoon salt
½ cup vinegar

Combine vegetables in a large bowl, and toss lightly.

Combine sugar, flour, mustard, and salt in a small saucepan. Gradually add vinegar; cook over medium heat, stirring constantly, until mixture is smooth and thickened. Pour hot marinade over vegetables; stir gently. Cover and chill overnight. Yield: 8 to 10 servings.

*Mary Dishon,*
*Stanford, Kentucky.*

## CHOCOLATE-CHOCOLATE CHIP COOKIES

1 cup butter or margarine, softened
1 cup sugar
½ cup firmly packed brown sugar
2 tablespoons half-and-half
1 teaspoon vanilla extract
1¾ cups all-purpose flour
⅓ cup cocoa
¼ teaspoon soda
1 cup chopped pecans
1 (6-ounce) package semisweet chocolate morsels

Cream butter; gradually add sugar, beating until light and fluffy. Add half-and-half and vanilla.

Combine flour, cocoa, and soda; add to creamed mixture, beating just until blended. Stir in chopped pecans and chocolate morsels.

Drop dough by heaping teaspoonfuls 1½ inches apart on ungreased cookie

sheets. Bake at 350° for 10 to 12 minutes (do not overbake). Cool slightly on cookie sheet before removing to rack. Yield: 6 dozen.

*Janet M. Filer,*
*Arlington, Virginia.*

## REFRESHING FRUIT SLUSH

1 (46-ounce) can fruit juicy red Hawaiian punch
1½ cups orange juice
¼ cup lemon juice
1 (10-ounce) package frozen strawberries, thawed
2 (12-ounce) cans lemon-lime carbonated beverage

Combine all ingredients; stir well. Freeze mixture overnight or until firm. Remove from freezer 1 hour before serving (mixture should be slushy). Yield: about 3 quarts.

*Shirley Thrasher,*
*St. Petersburg, Florida.*

# Make Your Next Sandwich Puffy

Run out of sandwich ideas? Try this unusual open-face version. It starts with a simple chicken or turkey salad mixture spread over toasted bread and ends with an airy topping of stiffly beaten egg whites and cheese.

## PUFFED CHICKEN SANDWICHES

1⅔ cups finely chopped cooked chicken or turkey
½ cup minced celery
⅓ cup mayonnaise
1½ tablespoons lemon juice
Salt and pepper to taste
6 slices whole wheat bread
Softened butter or margarine
3 egg whites
¾ cup (3 ounces) shredded Cheddar cheese

Combine first 5 ingredients in a small mixing bowl; mix well. Toast one side of bread. Lightly butter untoasted sides; spread chicken mixture over butter. Beat egg whites (at room temperature) until stiff peaks form; fold in cheese. Spread over chicken mixture. Bake at 450° for 10 minutes or until golden brown. Serve immediately. Yield: 6 servings.

*Florence Mangin,*
*Green Bay, Wisconsin.*

# Help Yourself To A Texas Bread

Hushpuppies made with potatoes? Mrs. Ted Robertson of Canton, Texas, says that Wampus Bread, her unusual variation of that Southern favorite, is great not only with fish but other meats as well. Discover another delicious use of potatoes in Lexie Freeman's Feathery Light Potato Rolls. Also included in this collection of Texas recipes are some fruit and nut breads. Either fresh or frozen cranberries can be used to make Raisin-Cranberry Bread.

## QUICK MONKEY BREAD

½ cup chopped pecans
½ cup sugar
1 teaspoon ground cinnamon
3 (10-ounce) cans refrigerated buttermilk biscuits
1 cup firmly packed brown sugar
½ cup butter or margarine, melted

Sprinkle chopped pecans evenly in the bottom of a well-greased 10-inch Bundt pan. Set aside.

Combine sugar and cinnamon. Cut biscuits into quarters; roll each piece in sugar mixture, and layer in pan.

Combine brown sugar and butter; pour over dough. Bake at 350° for 30 to 40 minutes. Cool bread 10 minutes in pan; invert onto serving platter. Yield: one 10-inch coffee cake.

*Judy Richardson,*
*Pearland, Texas.*

## SPICY ZUCCHINI BREAD

3 cups all-purpose flour
1 teaspoon baking powder
1 teaspoon soda
1 teaspoon ground cinnamon
1 teaspoon ground nutmeg
1 cup chopped pecans or walnuts
¾ cup vegetable oil
3 eggs
2 cups sugar
2 teaspoons vanilla extract
3 cups unpeeled shredded zucchini

Combine first 6 ingredients in a mixing bowl; make a well in center of mixture. Combine oil, eggs, sugar, and vanilla; mix well. Stir in shredded zucchini. Add mixture to dry ingredients, stirring just until moistened.

Spoon mixture into 2 greased and floured 8½- x 4½- x 3-inch loafpans. Bake at 350° for 1 hour. Cool loaves 10 minutes in pans; remove to wire rack, and cool completely. Yield: 2 loaves.

*Mrs. Ellis D. Weathermon,*
*Comanche, Texas.*

## FEATHERY LIGHT POTATO ROLLS

1 (2-ounce) package instant potato flakes or 1½ cups mashed potatoes
1 cup milk
⅔ cup shortening
½ cup sugar
1 teaspoon salt
1 package dry yeast
½ cup lukewarm water (105° to 115°)
2 eggs
7½ cups all-purpose flour
Melted butter or margarine

Prepare instant potatoes according to package directions.

Scald milk; remove from heat and add shortening, potatoes, sugar, and salt. Stir until shortening is melted; cool mixture to lukewarm.

Dissolve yeast in water in a large bowl; let stand 5 minutes. Add milk mixture and eggs, beating well. Gradually beat in 2 cups flour; add remaining flour to form a moderately stiff dough, beating well after each addition.

Turn dough onto a lightly floured surface; knead until smooth and elastic (about 7 minutes). Place in a well-greased bowl, turning to grease top. Cover and let rise in a warm place (85°), free from drafts, 1½ hours or until doubled in bulk.

Punch dough down. Shape into 1½-inch balls; arrange in a lightly greased jellyroll pan. Cover and let rise in a warm place, free from drafts, 1 hour or until doubled in bulk. Bake at 350° for 20 to 25 minutes; brush tops with melted butter. Yield: about 8 dozen rolls.

*Lexie Freeman,*
*Fort Worth, Texas.*

## RAISIN-CRANBERRY BREAD

2 cups all-purpose flour
1 cup sugar
1½ teaspoons baking powder
½ teaspoon soda
½ teaspoon salt
¼ cup butter or margarine
1 teaspoon grated orange rind
¾ cup orange juice
1 egg, beaten
1½ cups raisins
1½ cups fresh cranberries, chopped

Combine first 5 ingredients; cut in the butter until mixture resembles coarse crumbs. Combine orange rind, orange juice, and egg; add to dry ingredients, and stir just until moistened. Fold in raisins and cranberries.

Spoon batter into a greased and floured 9- x 5- x 3-inch loafpan. Bake at 350° for 1 hour and 10 minutes or until wooden pick inserted in center comes out clean. Remove from pan; cool on wire rack. Yield: 1 loaf.

*Mrs. Gary L. Jones,*
*Austin, Texas.*

## WAMPUS BREAD

2 cups cornmeal
1 cup all-purpose flour
1 tablespoon baking powder
1 teaspoon sugar
1 teaspoon salt
1 cup minced onion
1 cup peeled shredded potato
1 cup evaporated milk
Vegetable oil

Combine first 5 ingredients, mixing well; stir in onion, potato, and milk. Drop by tablespoonfuls into hot oil (375°). Cook until golden brown (3 to 5 minutes), turning once. Drain on paper towels. Yield: about 1½ dozen.

*Mrs. Ted Robertson,*
*Canton, Texas.*

## CHERRY NUT BREAD

2½ cups all-purpose flour
1 cup buttermilk
1 cup chopped pecans or walnuts
½ cup sugar
½ cup firmly packed brown sugar
2 eggs, beaten
¼ cup shortening
¼ cup maraschino cherry juice
1 tablespoon baking powder
½ teaspoon salt
½ teaspoon soda
½ cup chopped drained maraschino cherries

Combine all ingredients, except cherries, in a mixing bowl. Blend on low speed of electric mixer 15 seconds; increase to medium speed, and blend 30 seconds. Stir in cherries.

Pour batter into a greased and floured 9- x 5- x 3-inch loafpan. Bake at 350° for 1 hour and 10 to 15 minutes or until wooden pick inserted in center comes out clean. Cool 10 minutes in pan; remove to wire rack, and cool bread completely. Yield: 1 loaf.

*Judy Irwin,*
*Mabank, Texas.*

# March

Along with the promise of spring, March brings an abundance of tender, fresh spinach. In this chapter we offer some new ideas for spinach lovers, like cheese-sprinkled Cream of Spinach Soup and Florentine-Style Eggs.

Southerners' thoughts turn to entertaining as the weather warms, so we traveled to Vicksburg, Mississippi, to bring you more mouth-watering recipes for our *Breakfasts & Brunches* special section. Our featured hostess begins her brunch in traditional Southern style by greeting guests on the front porch with a tray of refreshing Mint Juleps. We share this recipe and other entertaining ideas on the pages to follow.

And speaking of Southern traditions, take a look at our collection of some of the South's most popular desserts of the past. Old-Fashioned Buttermilk Pound Cake, Fresh Coconut Cake, Black Bottom Pie, and Banana Pudding are sure to bring back some sweet memories.

# Try Our Fresh Ideas For Spinach

Since fresh spinach is most available during the winter and spring, that's the perfect time to try some of our new spinach dishes. We recommend a recipe that was a favorite with our test kitchen staff—Cream of Spinach Soup; it's rich in spinach flavor and color and is topped with a few croutons and a sprinkling of Parmesan cheese. Serve either Miniature Spinach Quiche or Layered Spinach Supreme as a tasty appetizer or party food, and try stir-frying the vegetable with soy sauce and onion for a delicious Chinese Spinach side dish.

You'll need to wash spinach several times since sand tends to cling to its crisp, curly leaves. To make the job easier, dissolve a little salt in the first wash water, or use warm water if the spinach is to be cooked. Continue washing with clean, cold water until sand no longer settles to the bottom of the sink. Drain and pat the leaves dry if the spinach is to be used raw.

The trick in preparing fresh spinach is to guard against overcooking. Cooking it quickly preserves its color and quality as well as valuable nutrients (vitamin A, vitamin C, and iron). You won't have to add extra water to the pan—the water that clings to the leaves after the spinach has been washed and drained provides sufficient moisture to steam it.

## MINIATURE SPINACH QUICHE

1 (10¾-ounce) can cream of mushroom soup, undiluted
1 (8-ounce) package cream cheese, softened
4 eggs, slightly beaten
1 cup firmly packed finely chopped fresh spinach
¾ cup (3 ounces) shredded Swiss cheese
½ cup finely chopped cooked ham
¼ cup finely chopped green onion
½ teaspoon hot sauce
Crêpes (recipe follows)

Combine soup and cream cheese; beat well. Add next 6 ingredients; stir well, and set aside.

Lightly oil sixteen 2½- x 1¼-inch muffin tins; line muffin tins with crêpes (spotted side up). Spoon 3 tablespoons spinach filling into crêpe cups. Bake at 375° for 10 minutes; cover with aluminum foil, and bake an additional 20 minutes. Carefully remove crêpe cups from muffin tins; cool 5 minutes on wire racks. Yield: 16 appetizers.

*Crêpes:*

1 cup all-purpose flour
¼ teaspoon salt
2 eggs
½ cup milk
½ cup water
2 tablespoons butter or margarine, melted
Vegetable oil

Combine flour, salt, and eggs; mix well. Add milk, water, and butter; beat until smooth. Refrigerate batter at least 2 hours. (This allows flour particles to swell and soften so the crêpes will be light in texture.)

Brush the bottom of a 6-inch crêpe pan or heavy skillet with vegetable oil; place pan over medium heat until oil is just hot, not smoking.

Pour 2 to 3 tablespoons batter into pan; quickly tilt pan in all directions so batter covers the pan in a thin film. Cook about 1 minute.

Lift edge of crêpe to test for doneness. Crêpe is ready for flipping when it can be shaken loose from pan. Flip the crêpe, and cook about 30 seconds on the other side. (This side is rarely more than spotty brown and is the side on which the filling is placed.) Place on a towel to cool. Stack between layers of waxed paper to prevent sticking. Yield: 16 crêpes.
*Sandra Russell,*
*Gainesville, Florida.*

## FLORENTINE-STYLE EGGS

1½ pounds fresh spinach
1 tablespoon butter or margarine
⅛ teaspoon salt
⅛ teaspoon pepper
2 to 3 tablespoons butter or margarine
8 eggs
8 slices bread, toasted
1 tablespoon anchovy paste, divided
2 tablespoons grated Parmesan cheese, divided

Remove stems from spinach; wash leaves thoroughly in lukewarm water. Place in Dutch oven (do not add water). Add butter, salt, and pepper; cover and cook over high heat 3 to 5 minutes. Drain spinach well; chop and set aside.

Melt butter in a heavy skillet, and heat until hot enough to sizzle a drop of water. Break each egg into a saucer; carefully slip each egg, one at a time, into skillet. Cook eggs over low heat until whites are firm and yolks are soft, or cook to desired degree of doneness.

Spread each bread slice with an equal amount of spinach; top each with 1 egg.

Spread a small amount of anchovy paste over each egg, and sprinkle with Parmesan. Bake at 350° for 10 minutes. Yield: 4 servings.      *Mrs. Charles R. Simms,*
*Palestine, Illinois.*

## LAYERED SPINACH SUPREME

1 pound fresh spinach
1 cup biscuit mix
2 eggs
¼ cup milk
¼ cup finely chopped onion
2 eggs, beaten
1 cup diced Monterey Jack cheese
½ cup grated Parmesan cheese
1 small clove garlic, minced

Remove stems from spinach; wash leaves thoroughly in lukewarm water. Place in Dutch oven (do not add water); cover and cook over high heat 3 to 5 minutes. Drain spinach well; chop and set aside.

Combine biscuit mix, 2 eggs, milk, and onion; mix well. Pat mixture into a greased 12- x 8- x 2-inch baking dish.

Combine spinach and remaining ingredients, stirring well. Spoon over mixture in baking dish. Bake at 375° for 30 minutes. Let stand 5 minutes before cutting. Yield: 8 servings.

*Note:* Baked spinach may be cut into 2-inch squares for 24 appetizer servings.
*Mrs. Paul Caldwell,*
*Tuscaloosa, Alabama.*

## CREAM OF SPINACH SOUP

1 large onion, finely chopped
3 tablespoons butter or margarine
1 pound fresh spinach, washed and drained
1 medium potato, peeled and quartered
¼ cup finely chopped ham
2 beef-flavored bouillon cubes
½ teaspoon salt
¼ teaspoon pepper
1 clove garlic, minced
4 cups hot water
½ cup milk
Croutons (optional)
Parmesan cheese (optional)

Sauté onion in butter in a large Dutch oven. Add next 8 ingredients; bring to a boil. Cover; reduce heat and simmer 10 to 15 minutes or until potato is tender, stirring occasionally.

Spoon half of spinach mixture into container of electric blender; process until smooth. Repeat procedure with remaining spinach mixture.

Pour spinach mixture back into Dutch oven; stir in milk. Cook over low heat,

stirring constantly, until heated. Ladle into bowls; add croutons and sprinkle with Parmesan cheese, if desired. Yield: 6½ cups.      *Mrs. John J. O'Neill,*
*Welaka, Florida.*

## CHINESE SPINACH

**1 pound fresh spinach**
**2 tablespoons vegetable oil**
**2 tablespoons soy sauce**
**½ teaspoon sugar**
**2 tablespoons finely chopped onion**
**1 (8-ounce) can sliced water chestnuts, drained**
**2 tablespoons chopped pimiento (optional)**

Remove stems from spinach. Wash leaves thoroughly in lukewarm water; tear into bite-size pieces. Place spinach in Dutch oven (do not add water); cover and cook over high heat 3 minutes. Drain spinach well.

Heat oil, soy sauce, and sugar in a large skillet. Add spinach and onion; stir-fry 2 to 3 minutes. Remove from heat; stir in water chestnuts and pimiento, if desired. Yield: 4 to 6 servings.      *Mrs. R. M. Lancaster,*
*Brentwood, Tennessee.*

# What To Do With All That Ham

If you wonder what to do with all those leftovers once you've baked a ham, take a look at these tasty ways our readers keep ham a favorite at their house—even the second or third time around. They toss sliced or diced bits of ham into hearty main dishes, grind and roll it into appetizer ham balls, and fry it as fritters. And if you thought stroganoff was just for beef, try our ham version; it's a snap to mix up with the aid of a few canned ingredients.

When you shop for ham, you may be confused by the many types and sizes available. Most hams have been cured (pumped with a salt-and-sugar solution for flavor) and/or smoked. The label on the ham should identify the type of processing, as well as whether or not the ham has been cooked.

Ham labeled "fully cooked" does not require further heating and may be eaten cold. Those who prefer to heat it find that an internal temperature of 140° brings out the most flavor. Ham marked "cook before eating" must be cooked to

an internal temperature of 160°. If the wrapping does not indicate whether or not the ham has been cooked, it's wise to assume that it needs cooking.

You'll find ham available either boneless or bone-in. Bone-in hams are marketed whole, in halves, in butt or shank portions, or as center-cut slices. The butt half generally has a higher proportion of meat to bone and is more expensive than the shank portion.

Boneless hams slice easier and have little or no waste; they are often the best buy, even though the price is higher. Boneless hams are sold whole or as halves, slices, quarters, or pieces.

Canned hams are always boneless and are fully cooked during the canning process. A small amount of unflavored gelatin is added to canned hams before sealing to absorb the natural juices as the ham cooks during processing; this causes the jelled substance that is common in canned hams.

Cured hams will keep in the refrigerator up to one week, whether cooked or uncooked. Refrigerate canned hams both before and after opening unless otherwise marked; unopened, they will keep up to one year unless the label says otherwise.

Freezing is generally not recommended for ham because of flavor and texture changes, but these changes are minimal if the ham is frozen less than two months in an airtight container. Canned hams should never be frozen because expansion during freezing may damage the seams of the can.

## APPETIZER HAM BALLS

**6 cups ground cooked ham**
**¾ cup regular oats, uncooked**
**2 eggs, slightly beaten**
**1 tablespoon brown sugar**
**⅛ teaspoon ground cloves**
**Vegetable oil**
**15 to 20 whole cloves**
**⅓ cup firmly packed brown sugar**
**2 tablespoons cornstarch**
**1 cup cold water**
**2 cups pineapple juice**
**¼ cup lemon juice**

Combine first 5 ingredients, mixing well; shape into 1-inch balls. Fry in a small amount of hot oil over medium heat until brown. Drain on paper towels.

Tie whole cloves in cheesecloth, and set aside.

Combine ⅓ cup brown sugar and cornstarch in a large saucepan. Gradually add water, stirring until smooth.

Add pineapple juice and lemon juice; cook, stirring constantly, until smooth and thickened. Add meatballs and whole cloves; simmer over low heat 30 minutes, stirring occasionally. Remove cheesecloth bag. Yield: about 4½ dozen.      *Cathy Darling,*
*Grafton, West Virginia.*

## PARTY HAM TURNOVERS

**¾ cup ground cooked ham**
**2 tablespoons chili sauce or catsup**
**1 to 1½ teaspoons prepared mustard**
**½ teaspoon Worcestershire sauce**
**Dash of hot sauce**
**Cream Cheese Pastry**

Combine first 5 ingredients; mix well, and set aside.

Roll pastry to ⅛-inch thickness on a lightly floured surface; cut with a 2¾-inch biscuit cutter. Place 1 teaspoonful ham mixture in center of each circle, and fold pastry in half. Moisten edges with water, and press with a fork to seal. Prick tops with fork.

Place turnovers on ungreased baking sheets, and bake at 400° for 15 to 20 minutes or until lightly browned. Yield: about 2 dozen.

*Cream Cheese Pastry:*

**1 (3-ounce) package cream cheese, softened**
**½ cup butter or margarine, softened**
**1 cup all-purpose flour**

Combine cream cheese and butter in a small bowl; stir until smooth. Add flour; mixing well. Shape dough into a ball; chill for 1 hour. Yield: enough pastry for 2 dozen turnovers.
*Jodie McCoy,*
*Tulsa, Oklahoma.*

## HAM FRITTERS

**⅔ cup all-purpose flour**
**1 teaspoon baking powder**
**2 eggs, slightly beaten**
**⅓ cup milk**
**2 cups ground cooked ham**
**1 (8-ounce) can crushed pineapple, well drained**
**Vegetable oil**

Combine flour and baking powder in a large mixing bowl. Stir in eggs. Gradually add milk, stirring until smooth. Stir in ham and pineapple. Spoon ¼ cupfuls into a small amount of hot oil; brown on both sides. Drain well on paper towels. Yield: 8 servings.
*Janis Moyer,*
*Farmersville, Texas.*

## UPSIDE-DOWN HAM LOAF

½ cup firmly packed brown sugar
¼ teaspoon ground cloves
4 cups ground cooked ham
1 pound ground lean pork
¾ cup cornflake crumbs
2 eggs
1 cup milk
3 tablespoons finely chopped green pepper
½ teaspoon salt
Plum Sauce

Combine brown sugar and cloves; pat in bottom of a 9- x 5- x 3-inch loafpan. Combine meats, cornflake crumbs, eggs, milk, green pepper, and salt; mix well. Spoon mixture into loafpan. Bake at 350° for 1 hour. Invert on platter; serve hot with Plum Sauce. Yield: 8 servings.

*Plum Sauce:*

1 (16-ounce) can prune plums
2 tablespoons lemon juice
1 (1-inch) stick cinnamon
¼ teaspoon salt
1 tablespoon cornstarch
3 tablespoons cold water
Pinch of ground allspice

Drain plums, reserving juice; pit plums, and set aside. Combine plum juice, lemon juice, cinnamon stick, and salt in a saucepan; bring to a boil. Dissolve cornstarch in cold water; add to juice mixture, stirring until smooth.
Stir in allspice. Bring to a boil; cook over medium heat, stirring constantly, until thickened and bubbly (about 1 minute). Remove from heat; stir in plums. Remove cinnamon stick. Yield: 1⅔ cups. *Sarah Watson, Knoxville, Tennessee.*

## QUICK HAM-BROCCOLI CASSEROLE

¼ cup chopped onion
1 (10-ounce) package frozen chopped broccoli, thawed and drained
2 tablespoons butter or margarine
1 (10¾-ounce) can cream of chicken soup, undiluted
2 cups chopped cooked ham
1 cup uncooked instant rice
½ cup process cheese spread
¼ cup milk
½ teaspoon Worcestershire sauce

Sauté onion and broccoli in butter in a large skillet until onion is tender. Remove from heat. Stir in remaining ingredients. Spoon mixture into a lightly greased 1½-quart casserole. Bake at 350° for 25 to 30 minutes or until bubbly. Yield: 6 servings. *Dorothy Grant, Pensacola, Florida.*

## HAM STROGANOFF

1 pound cooked ham, cut into strips
½ cup chopped onion
2 tablespoons butter or margarine
1 (10¾-ounce) can cream of mushroom soup, undiluted
1 (4-ounce) can sliced mushrooms, undrained
1 (8-ounce) carton commercial sour cream
Hot cooked noodles

Sauté ham and onion in butter until onion is tender. Stir in soup and mushrooms; cook over medium heat 5 minutes, stirring occasionally. Stir in sour cream, and cook just until thoroughly heated. Serve over hot noodles. Yield: 6 servings. *Mrs. Richard L. Winstead, Groves, Texas.*

## OPEN-FACE HAM SANDWICHES

1 (8-ounce) package cream cheese, softened
½ cup butter or margarine, softened
½ cup grated Parmesan cheese
1 teaspoon paprika
½ teaspoon dried whole oregano
½ teaspoon garlic powder
4 English muffins, split
8 slices cooked ham (about ¾ pound)
8 slices tomato
Fresh parsley sprigs

Combine cream cheese and butter; stir until smooth. Stir in cheese, paprika, oregano, and garlic powder. Spread two-thirds of mixture evenly over cut surface of English muffins; top each with a ham and tomato slice. Spoon remaining cheese mixture on center of each tomato slice. Place on a baking sheet, and broil until golden brown. Arrange sandwiches on platter, and garnish with parsley. Yield: 8 servings. *Mrs. Harry A. Smith, Corbin, Kentucky.*

## HAM-RICE TOSS

3 cups cooked regular rice, chilled
1 cup diced cooked ham
½ cup chopped green pepper
⅓ cup sliced celery
1 tablespoon minced onion
½ cup commercial Italian salad dressing
Lettuce leaves
2 tomatoes, cut into wedges

Combine first 6 ingredients, stirring well. Chill well. Serve on lettuce leaves, and garnish with tomato wedges. Yield: 4 to 6 servings. *Mrs. H. J. Sherrer, Bay City, Texas.*

## CREAMED HAM AND EGGS

1 tablespoon butter or margarine
¾ cup sliced fresh mushrooms
1 clove garlic, minced
1 (10¾-ounce) can cream of mushroom soup, undiluted
¼ cup plus 2 tablespoons milk
¼ cup dry sherry
1 cup cubed cooked ham
3 hard-cooked eggs, sliced
Toast cups or patty shells

Melt butter in a large skillet; add mushrooms and garlic, and cook until tender. Stir in soup, milk, sherry, and ham; simmer 5 minutes. Gently stir in eggs. Serve in toast cups. Yield: 4 servings. *Mrs. J. Wells, Fairfax, Virginia.*

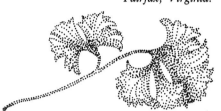

## HAM-AND-CORN CHOWDER

2 cups diced cooked ham
1 cup chopped celery
½ cup chopped onion
½ cup butter or margarine
3 (10-ounce) packages frozen cream-style corn, thawed
1 cup milk
½ teaspoon onion salt
½ teaspoon celery salt
½ teaspoon pepper
Chopped fresh parsley (optional)

Sauté ham, celery, and onion in butter in a Dutch oven. Stir in next 5 ingredients, and bring to a boil. Reduce heat, and simmer 20 minutes. Garnish with parsley, if desired. Yield: about 6 cups. *Florence L. Costello, Chattanooga, Tennessee.*

## HEARTY HAM SALAD

3 cups diced cooked ham
1½ cups (6 ounces) shredded Cheddar cheese
2 cups diced apples, unpeeled
1 cup diced celery
½ teaspoon lemon-pepper seasoning
¾ to 1 cup mayonnaise
Lettuce leaves (optional)

Combine all ingredients except lettuce; mix well. Chill 2 to 3 hours before serving. Serve on lettuce leaves, if desired. Yield: 6 to 8 servings.
*Mrs. William S. Bell, Chattanooga, Tennessee.*

# BREAKFASTS&BRUNCHES™

## Morning-Fresh Ideas For Brunch And Breakfast

How do you usually begin your day—with breakfast in bed, a casual brunch on the terrace, or a quick snack on-the-run? Or perhaps you're one of many Southerners who've found that a brunch is the ideal way to entertain.

With this in mind, we share our annual *Breakfasts & Brunches* special section, a collection of recipes and menus suitable for however you want to enjoy the first meal of the day.

Our ideas for morning beverages range from zesty Eye-Opener Bloody Marys to creamy Peanut Butter Shake, while the side dishes we've included can turn a plain breakfast into a tantalizing buffet. Jalapeño Hominy, Sausage-Rice Casserole, and Orange-Glazed Apples are just a sampling.

We've even thought about garnishes, an essential part of any successful meal. Take an omelet, for example, add an Aztec mushroom or a tomato rose, and you'll double its appeal. These are just two of several garnishes we help you learn to make.

And if you and your friends are calorie conscious, we've tailored a menu just for you, dishes so delicious you'd never guess they're low in calories.

For Sara and Freddy Abraham of Vicksburg, Mississippi, a lavish brunch is the way they choose to celebrate the city's homes tour, the Vicksburg Pilgrimage. It's an event their friends look forward to every spring.

Entertaining is a natural part of the Abrahams' life, and they accomplish it with elegance and ease. When asked why brunch was a favorite way to entertain, Sara answered, "Because it usually requires less fanfare and is more relaxed than a formal dinner party." Speaking from a practical standpoint, Freddy

added, "There's plenty of time to clean up in the afternoon, so the guests can stay longer. No one needs to rush home."

Icy-cold mint juleps await guests as they arrive at Flowers Hill, the Abrahams' gracious home. For those preferring a tamer beverage, Wine Cooler is a refreshing alternative. Green Onion Teasers and Brie Appetizer Round are Sara's hors d'oeuvre choices, prepared in advance so she can be on hand to offer a warm welcome.

"Planning and thinking things out far in advance is the key to giving successful parties. I have a list for everything," explains Sara. And for the most part, all of her brunch recipes can be made ahead and reheated at the last minute.

When the weather permits, Sara sets up the buffet around the pool. No single dish steals the show, for Oysters Johnny Reb, Creole Eggs, and Spinach Surprise are all outstanding. The eggs are especially attractive, spooned over the cheesy Cornmeal Puff. Completing the menu are slices of smoked sausage to tuck in golden-brown biscuits.

For dessert, there's Chocolate Coffee, Cinnamon-Topped Sour Cream Pound Cake, and some of the most exquisite Caramel Tarts we've ever tasted. These wonderful pastries are made with a homemade caramel syrup and topped with fluffy meringue before baking.

**Mint Juleps        Wine Cooler**
**Brie Appetizer Round**
**Green Onion Teasers**
**Creole Eggs        Cornmeal Puff**
**Oysters Johnny Reb**
**Spinach Surprise**
**Southern Sausage and Biscuits**
**Cinnamon-Topped Sour Cream**
**Pound Cake**
**Caramel Tarts        Chocolate Coffee**

## MINT JULEPS

1 cup sugar
1¾ cups water
15 fresh mint sprigs, finely chopped
2 quarts bourbon
Shaved ice
20 fresh mint sprigs

Combine first 4 ingredients in a glass container; stir until sugar is dissolved. Cover and let stand 4 to 6 hours.

Strain mixture into a large pitcher, discarding chopped mint. To serve, fill glasses with shaved ice; add bourbon mixture, and garnish with mint sprigs. Yield: about 20 servings.

## WINE COOLER

2 (25.4-ounce) bottles Sauterne or other dry white wine
1½ cups sugar
½ cup brandy
½ cup lemon juice
1 (25.4-ounce) bottle champagne, chilled

Combine Sauterne and sugar, stirring until sugar dissolves. Stir in brandy and lemon juice. Cover and let stand overnight at room temperature.

Pour mixture into an ice-filled punch bowl. Add champagne, stirring slightly. Yield: about 11 cups.

## BRIE APPETIZER ROUND

1 (2½-pound) round fully ripened Brie
⅔ cup coarsely chopped pecans
2 to 3 tablespoons brown sugar

Remove rind from top of cheese, cutting to within ¼ inch of outside edges. Place cheese on an ungreased baking sheet, and arrange pecans over top. Sprinkle with sugar.

Broil 8 inches from heat for 3 to 5 minutes or until sugar and cheese are bubbly. Serve with crackers. Yield: one cheese round.

## GREEN ONION TEASERS

1 pound bacon, cooked and crumbled
2 bunches green onions, sliced
Dash of pepper
¾ cup mayonnaise
1 (1-pound) loaf sandwich bread, crusts
 removed

Combine first 4 ingredients, mixing well. Cut each slice of bread into 4 triangles, and toast on both sides. Spread about 1 teaspoon green onion mixture on each triangle. Yield: about 5½ dozen.

## CREOLE EGGS

1 large onion, chopped
⅓ cup chopped green onion
½ cup chopped celery
2 medium-size green peppers, chopped
¼ cup butter or margarine
1 (28-ounce) can whole tomatoes,
 undrained
½ teaspoon salt
1½ teaspoons chili powder
½ teaspoon pepper
1 cup thick white sauce (recipe follows)
12 hard-cooked eggs, thinly sliced
¼ cup fine, dry breadcrumbs
¼ cup grated Parmesan cheese
Tomato roses (page 51)

Sauté onion, celery, and green pepper in butter in a large skillet until tender. Stir in tomatoes, salt, chili powder, and pepper. Bring mixture to a boil; reduce heat. Cover and simmer, stirring occasionally, until thick (about 20 minutes).

Combine tomato mixture, white sauce, and eggs; stir well. Spoon into a lightly greased 2-quart casserole. Combine the breadcrumbs and cheese; sprinkle over casserole. Bake at 350° for 20 minutes or until hot and bubbly. Garnish with tomato roses. Serve over Cornmeal Puff. Yield: 10 to 12 servings.

*Thick White Sauce:*

3 tablespoons butter or margarine
¼ cup all-purpose flour
1 cup milk
¼ teaspoon salt

Melt butter in a heavy saucepan over low heat; add flour, stirring until smooth. Cook 1 minute, stirring constantly. Gradually add milk; cook over medium heat, stirring constantly, until thickened and bubbly. Stir in salt. Yield: about 1 cup.

*Note:* Recipe may be doubled.

## CORNMEAL PUFF

1 cup cornmeal
1½ teaspoons salt
4 cups milk
1 cup whipping cream
1 cup (4 ounces) shredded Swiss cheese,
 divided
Fresh parsley sprigs

Combine cornmeal and salt in a medium saucepan; stir in milk. Bring to a boil; reduce heat and simmer, stirring occasionally, until thickened (about 4 minutes). Gradually add whipping cream, stirring until smooth.

Spoon half of cornmeal mixture into a lightly greased 8-inch square baking dish. Sprinkle ½ cup cheese over top. Spoon remaining cornmeal mixture over cheese. Bake at 350° for 35 minutes. Sprinkle remaining cheese over casserole; bake 5 additional minutes. Garnish with parsley. Yield: 10 to 12 servings.

*Note:* Recipe may be doubled.

## OYSTERS JOHNNY REB

2 quarts oysters, drained
Salt and pepper
Hot sauce
½ cup finely chopped fresh parsley
½ cup finely chopped shallots
1 tablespoon Worcestershire sauce
2 tablespoons lemon juice
½ cup melted butter
2 cups cracker crumbs
Paprika
¾ cup half-and-half
Fresh parsley sprigs
Lemon slices

Layer half of oysters in a lightly greased shallow 2-quart baking dish; season to taste with salt, pepper, and hot sauce. Sprinkle with half of next 6 ingredients. Repeat layers, and lightly sprinkle with paprika.

Make evenly spaced indentations in casserole; fill each with half-and-half, being careful not to moisten all of crumb topping. Bake at 375° about 30 minutes or until bubbly. Garnish with parsley and lemon slices. Yield: 10 to 12 servings.

*Note:* Recipe may be doubled.

## SPINACH SURPRISE

4 (10-ounce) packages frozen spinach
¼ cup chopped onion
¼ cup butter or margarine
¼ cup all-purpose flour
1 cup evaporated milk
2 (6-ounce) rolls process cheese food with
 jalapeño peppers, cubed
2 teaspoons Worcestershire sauce
½ to 1 teaspoon pepper
1½ teaspoons celery salt
1½ teaspoons garlic salt
⅛ teaspoon red pepper (optional)
½ cup fine, dry breadcrumbs
2 tablespoons butter or margarine,
 melted
Lemon slices
Fresh parsley sprigs

Cook spinach according to package directions; drain well, reserving 1 cup of liquid. Set aside.

Sauté onion in ¼ cup butter in a heavy saucepan over low heat until tender. Add flour, stirring until smooth. Cook 1 minute, stirring constantly. Gradually add reserved spinach liquid and milk; cook over medium heat, stirring constantly, until thickened and bubbly. Add cheese, Worcestershire sauce, and seasonings; stir until cheese melts.

Stir spinach into sauce, and pour into a lightly greased 10- x 6- x 2-inch baking dish. Combine breadcrumbs and 2 tablespoons melted butter, mixing well; sprinkle over spinach mixture. Bake at 350° for 30 minutes. Garnish with lemon slices and parsley. Yield: 10 servings.

*Note:* Recipe may be doubled.

## SOUTHERN SAUSAGE AND BISCUITS

**2 cups all-purpose flour**
**1 tablespoon plus 1 teaspoon baking powder**
**1 tablespoon sugar**
**½ teaspoon salt**
**½ cup shortening**
**⅔ cup milk**
**1 egg, beaten**
**1 pound smoked sausage, cut into ¼-inch slices**

Combine flour, baking powder, sugar, and salt; stir well. Cut in shortening with pastry blender until mixture resembles coarse meal.

Combine milk and egg; mix well. Add to flour mixture, stirring until dry ingredients are moistened. Turn dough out on a heavily floured surface, and lightly knead 4 or 5 times.

Roll dough to ⅜-inch thickness, and cut with a 1½-inch biscuit cutter. Place on ungreased baking sheets, and bake at 450° for 10 to 12 minutes.

Arrange sausage slices in a 15- x 10- x 1-inch baking pan. Bake at 350° for 10 minutes or until hot. Drain well. Serve with biscuits. Yield: 4½ dozen.

## CINNAMON-TOPPED SOUR CREAM POUND CAKE

**1 cup butter or margarine, softened**
**2 cups sugar**
**2 eggs**
**2 cups all-purpose flour**
**1 teaspoon baking powder**
**½ teaspoon salt**
**1 (8-ounce) carton commercial sour cream**
**1 teaspoon vanilla extract**
**½ cup sliced almonds, toasted**
**½ teaspoon ground cinnamon**
**2 teaspoons sugar**

Cream butter; gradually add 2 cups sugar, beating until light and fluffy. Add eggs, one at a time, beating 30 seconds after each addition.

Combine flour, baking powder, and salt; add a third of dry ingredients to creamed mixture, stirring with a spoon until blended. Add half of sour cream, stirring until blended. Repeat procedure, ending with flour mixture. Stir in vanilla.

Combine almonds, cinnamon, and remaining 2 teaspoons sugar; sprinkle a third of mixture in a well-greased and floured 10-inch Bundt pan. Pour in half of batter, and sprinkle with another third of almond mixture. Pour remaining batter into pan, and top with remaining almond mixture. Bake at 350° for 50 to 60 minutes. Cool 1 hour before removing from pan. Yield: one 10-inch cake.

## CARAMEL TARTS

**1½ cups milk**
**1 cup sugar, divided**
**¼ cup cornstarch**
**3 eggs, separated**
**½ cup caramel syrup (recipe follows)**
**2 tablespoons butter or margarine**
**1 teaspoon vanilla extract**
**8 baked 3-inch tart shells**
**Pinch of cream of tartar**
**¼ teaspoon cornstarch**

Scald milk in a heavy 3-quart saucepan. Combine ¾ cup sugar and ¼ cup cornstarch; add to hot milk, stirring well. Beat egg yolks; gradually stir in about one-fourth of hot mixture. Add egg mixture to remaining hot mixture, stirring constantly.

Add caramel syrup and butter to milk mixture; cook over low heat, stirring constantly, until smooth and thickened (about 10 minutes). Remove from heat, and stir in vanilla; set aside to cool. Spoon cooled custard into tart shells.

Combine egg whites (at room temperature) and cream of tartar; beat until foamy. Combine ¼ cup sugar and ¼ teaspoon cornstarch; add to egg whites, 1 tablespoon at a time, beating until stiff peaks form. Spread meringue over cooled tarts, sealing to edge of shells.

Bake at 350° for 5 to 7 minutes or until meringue is golden brown. Cool completely before serving. Yield: 8 tarts.

*Note:* Do not double recipe; repeat it to serve larger crowds.

*Caramel Syrup:*

**2 cups sugar**
**¾ cup boiling water**

Sprinkle 1 cup sugar in a 10-inch heavy cast-iron skillet; place over medium heat, stirring constantly with a wooden spoon until sugar is melted and becomes a light golden brown. Gradually add remaining sugar, and repeat process. Gradually add boiling water, stirring to make a smooth syrup. Yield: 1½ cups.

*Note:* Caramel syrup may be poured into an airtight container and stored at room temperature for use in other recipes.

## CHOCOLATE COFFEE

**1½ to 2 teaspoons Kahlúa or other coffee-flavored liqueur**
**1 commercial chocolate liqueur cup**
**½ cup hot coffee**
**Sweetened whipped cream**
**Chocolate shavings**

Pour Kahlúa into chocolate liqueur cup; place in demitasse cup. Fill demitasse cup with coffee; top with whipped cream, and sprinkle with chocolate shavings. Yield: one 4-ounce serving.

*Note:* Squares of milk chocolate candy may be substituted for commercial chocolate liqueur cups. Place 2 (1-inch) candy squares in each demitasse cup; add Kahlúa and coffee.

*Tip: Get in the habit of grocery shopping with a list. Watch newspapers for advertised "specials"; then plan a week's menus around bargains in foods the family enjoys.*

# Wake Up Your Breakfast With The Unusual

Pan-fried quail, sautéed crabmeat, and grilled steaks sound like entrées offered at an elegant dinner. But with our recipes, you'll be preparing these dishes for breakfast or brunch instead.

Mrs. George Limbaugh of Childersburg, Alabama, wife and mother in a family of hunters, says her Fried Quail delights her sportsmen. The secret to her success with quail is steaming them after frying to make the game birds tender and moist. Although she occasionally serves quail as a dinner entrée, she prefers preparing them for a hearty breakfast. Along with homemade biscuits and milk gravy, scrambled eggs, and buttery grits, her fried quail makes breakfast the family's favorite meal.

Chicken livers sautéed with onion and mushrooms provide a delicious filling for Chicken Liver Omelet. And be sure to try Crabmeat and Eggs New Orleans. A bed of crabmeat is topped with poached eggs and a brandy white sauce.

## STEAK BRUNCH GRILL

3 tablespoons butter or margarine, melted
2 tablespoons lemon juice
4 (4-ounce) cubed beef steaks
4 slices bacon, cut crosswise into halves
4 (½-inch-thick) slices tomato
Salt and pepper

Combine butter and lemon juice; stir well, and set aside.

Place steaks on broiler rack; brush with half of butter mixture. Broil steaks 6 inches from heating element for 8 minutes. Turn steaks, and brush with remaining butter mixture. Place bacon on broiler rack. Broil steaks and bacon 3 minutes. Place tomato on broiler rack; broil meats and tomato 1 to 2 minutes. Sprinkle tomato with salt and pepper.

To serve, layer steak, tomato, and 2 slices bacon. Yield: 4 servings.
*Mrs. H. L. Bennett,*
*Dunedin, Florida.*

## CORNED BEEF BRUNCH BAKE

½ cup chopped onion
½ cup finely chopped celery
½ cup chopped green pepper
2 tablespoons butter or margarine
12 slices white bread, crusts removed
12 ounces cooked, sliced corned beef
1 cup (4 ounces) shredded Cheddar cheese
3 eggs, beaten
1½ cups milk
1 teaspoon salt
Dash of pepper

Sauté onion, celery, and green pepper in butter in a small skillet until tender.

Arrange 6 bread slices in a lightly greased 12- x 8- x 2-inch baking dish; place an equal amount of corned beef on each. Spoon an equal amount of onion mixture over corned beef slices; sprinkle with cheese. Top with remaining slices of bread.

Combine eggs, milk, salt, and pepper; mix well, and gently pour over bread slices. Bake at 350° for 40 minutes. Yield: 6 servings. *Mrs. Lyn Renwick,*
*Charlotte, North Carolina.*

## CHEESY CHICKEN ROLLUPS

1 tablespoon minced onion
1 teaspoon minced green pepper
1 tablespoon butter or margarine
1 (5-ounce) can chicken, drained
1½ cups (6 ounces) shredded sharp Cheddar cheese, divided
½ cup commercial sour cream
1 teaspoon hot sauce
¼ teaspoon pepper
1 (10-ounce) can buttermilk biscuits
1 (10¾-ounce) can cream of chicken soup, undiluted
⅔ cup milk

Sauté onion and green pepper in butter in a medium skillet until tender. Drain, if necessary. Stir in chicken, 1 cup cheese, sour cream, hot sauce, and pepper.

Roll each biscuit to ¼- to ⅛-inch thickness; spread each biscuit with

about 2 tablespoons chicken mixture. Roll up biscuits, jellyroll fashion, pinching edges to seal.

Place rolls in a lightly greased 10- x 6- x 2-inch baking dish. Bake at 450° for 10 to 12 minutes.

Combine soup and milk in a medium saucepan; mix well, and cook until thoroughly heated. Pour soup mixture over rollups; sprinkle with remaining ½ cup cheese. Bake at 450° for 2 to 3 minutes or until cheese melts. Yield: 5 servings. *Mrs. E. Lamar McMath,*
*Jacksonville, Florida.*

## CHICKEN LIVER OMELET

2 tablespoons chopped onion
2 tablespoons butter or margarine
¼ cup sliced fresh mushrooms
¾ cup chicken livers, diced
⅛ teaspoon pepper
2½ tablespoons Chablis or other dry white wine
1½ teaspoons all-purpose flour
1½ teaspoons chopped fresh parsley
6 eggs
3 tablespoons whipping cream
¼ teaspoon salt
¼ teaspoon pepper
3 tablespoons butter

Sauté onion in 2 tablespoons butter until crisp-tender. Add mushrooms, chicken livers, and pepper; cook 3 to 5 minutes or until chicken livers are done. Remove from heat; stir in wine, flour, and parsley.

Combine eggs, cream, salt, and pepper; beat well. Heat a 10-inch omelet pan or heavy skillet until it is hot enough to sizzle a drop of water. Add butter; rotate pan to coat bottom.

Pour egg mixture into pan all at once. Shake pan vigorously (or use spatula to lift cooked portion) so uncooked portion flows underneath. Slide pan back and forth over heat to keep mixture in motion.

Spoon chicken liver filling over half of omelet when eggs are set and top is still moist and creamy. Fold unfilled side over filling. Serve omelet immediately. Yield: 3 servings. *Darlene Steel,*
*Nashville, Arkansas.*

## ENGLISH MUFFIN DELIGHT

1½ cups diced cooked chicken
1 (8-ounce) package frozen cooked small
   shrimp, thawed and drained
½ cup finely chopped celery
½ cup mayonnaise
¼ teaspoon salt
⅛ teaspoon pepper
6 English muffins, split and toasted
12 slices process American cheese

Combine first 6 ingredients; mix well.
Top each muffin half with 2 tablespoons chicken and shrimp mixture.
Bake at 350° for 10 minutes. Top each with a slice of cheese; return to oven just until cheese melts. Yield: 12 servings.
*Mrs. Larry E. Elliott,*
*Winston-Salem, North Carolina.*

## CRABMEAT AND EGGS
## NEW ORLEANS

1 pound fresh crabmeat, drained and
   flaked
¼ cup butter
½ teaspoon salt
½ teaspoon white pepper
12 poached eggs
Spicy Cream Sauce
Chopped fresh parsley (optional)

Sauté crabmeat in butter in a large skillet about 5 minutes, stirring frequently. Stir in salt and pepper.
Spoon a small amount of crabmeat onto 6 individual dishes. Top each serving with 2 poached eggs; spoon remaining crabmeat over eggs.
Spoon Spicy Cream Sauce over eggs. Sprinkle with chopped parsley, if desired. Yield: 6 servings.

*Spicy Cream Sauce:*
¼ cup butter
3 tablespoons all-purpose flour
1½ cups milk
⅛ teaspoon hot sauce
½ teaspoon salt
¼ teaspoon ground nutmeg
3 tablespoons brandy

Melt butter in a heavy saucepan over low heat; add flour, stirring until smooth. Cook 1 minute, stirring constantly. Gradually add milk; cook over

For English Muffin Delight, a chicken and shrimp combination and a slice of cheese top toasted English muffins.

medium heat, stirring constantly, until thickened and bubbly. Stir in remaining ingredients. Yield: 1½ cups.
*Cher Haile,*
*Atlanta, Georgia.*

## FRIED QUAIL

8 quail, cleaned
Salt and pepper
1 cup all-purpose flour
Vegetable oil
½ cup water
¼ cup all-purpose flour
2 cups milk
¼ teaspoon salt
⅛ teaspoon pepper

Sprinkle quail with salt and pepper; dredge in 1 cup flour, coating well. Heat ¼ inch of oil in a skillet; add quail, and cook over medium heat 10 minutes or until golden brown, turning occasionally. Remove quail from skillet.
Pour off all but ½ cup oil from skillet. Add water and quail; cover and cook over medium heat 15 minutes. Remove quail to serving platter. Drain off drippings, reserving ¼ cup in skillet.
Add ¼ cup flour to reserved drippings; cook over low heat, stirring until smooth. Cook 1 minute, stirring constantly. Gradually add milk; cook over medium heat, stirring constantly, until thickened and bubbly. Stir in ¼ teaspoon salt and ⅛ teaspoon pepper. Serve gravy with quail. Yield: 4 servings.
*Mrs. George Limbaugh,*
*Childersburg, Alabama.*

*Tip: Always turn saucepan and skillet handles toward the back of the range to prevent accidents.*

# Feast On French Toast And Crêpes

For that special brunch with friends or just a leisurely weekend breakfast with the family, French toast or filled crêpes are always a good choice. Our readers have added their own personal touch to these favorites, and the results are not to be missed.

A few tips: Try our Oven-Baked French Toast; just set your timer, and prepare the rest of breakfast while the toast is baking. For homemade crêpes, make them well in advance and refrigerate or freeze until needed. Layer crêpes between waxed paper, and store in an airtight container.

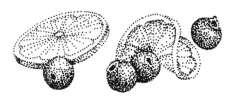

## LEMON CREPES WITH FRUIT FILLING

2 cups frozen blueberries, thawed
⅓ cup sugar
2½ cups cream-style cottage cheese, drained
1 cup sifted powdered sugar
1½ teaspoons vanilla extract
Lemon Crêpes
1½ cups whipping cream
⅓ cup sifted powdered sugar
2 cups canned, sliced, drained peaches

Combine blueberries and ⅓ cup sugar; stir gently, and set aside.

Combine next 3 ingredients in container of electric blender; process until mixture is smooth.

Fill each crêpe with about 2 tablespoons cottage cheese mixture and 1 tablespoon blueberries. Roll up and place seam side up on serving dish.

Beat whipping cream until foamy; gradually add ⅓ cup powdered sugar, beating until soft peaks form. Top each crêpe with a dollop of whipped cream; garnish with peach slices and remaining blueberries. Yield: 16 servings.

*Lemon Crêpes:*

¼ cup margarine, melted
½ cup cold water
¼ cup plus 2 tablespoons milk
2 eggs
2 egg yolks
¾ cup all-purpose flour
1 tablespoon sugar
¼ teaspoon salt
1 teaspoon grated lemon rind
¼ teaspoon lemon extract
Vegetable oil

Combine first 10 ingredients in container of electric blender; process 1 minute. Scrape down sides of the blender container with rubber spatula; process an additional 15 seconds. Refrigerate batter 1 hour. (This allows the flour particles to swell and soften so crêpes are light in texture.)

Brush the bottom of a 6-inch crêpe pan with oil; place pan over medium heat until oil is just hot, not smoking.

Pour 2 tablespoons batter into pan; quickly tilt pan in all directions so batter covers the pan in a thin film. Cook about 1 minute.

Lift edge of crêpe to test for doneness. Crêpe is ready for flipping when it can be shaken loose from pan. Flip crêpe, and cook about 30 seconds on other side. (This side is rarely more than spotty brown.) Place on a towel to cool. Stack crêpes between layers of waxed paper to prevent sticking. Yield: 16 crêpes.

*Sue Sandidge,*
*Spring, Texas.*

## HAM-AND-EGG CREPES WITH MUSHROOM SAUCE

1¼ cups finely chopped cooked ham
2 tablespoons butter or margarine
8 eggs
½ cup milk
¼ cup water
½ teaspoon pepper
Crêpes (recipe follows)
Mushroom Sauce

Sauté ham in butter in a large skillet about 5 minutes or until ham is lightly browned.

Combine eggs, milk, water, and pepper; beat well. Add egg mixture to ham. Cook, stirring occasionally, until eggs are firm but still moist.

Spoon ¼ cup egg mixture in center of each crêpe; fold sides of crêpe over filling. Place crêpes, seam side down, in a lightly greased 13- x 9- x 2-inch baking dish, tucking ends under. Pour Mushroom Sauce evenly over crêpes. Cover and bake at 350° for 10 to 15 minutes or until crêpes are thoroughly heated. Yield: 6 servings.

*Crêpes:*

3 eggs
1½ cups milk
1⅓ cups all-purpose flour
½ teaspoon salt
1½ tablespoons vegetable oil
Additional vegetable oil

Combine first 5 ingredients in container of an electric blender; process 1 minute. Scrape down sides of blender with rubber spatula; process an additional 15 seconds. Refrigerate batter 1 hour. (This allows flour particles to swell and soften so crêpes are light in texture.)

Brush the bottom of a 10-inch crêpe pan or nonstick skillet with vegetable oil; place pan over medium heat until oil is just hot, not smoking.

Pour about 3 tablespoons batter into pan; quickly tilt pan in all directions so batter covers pan in a thin film. Cook about 1 minute.

Lift edge of crêpe to test for doneness; crêpe is ready for flipping when it can be shaken loose from the pan. Flip the crêpe, and cook about 30 seconds on the other side. (This side is rarely more than spotty brown.) Place crêpes on a towel to cool. Stack between layers of waxed paper to prevent sticking. Yield: about 12 crêpes.

*Mushroom Sauce:*

½ pound fresh mushrooms, sliced
2 tablespoons chopped onion
3 tablespoons butter or margarine
1 tablespoon all-purpose flour
⅓ cup milk
1 teaspoon prepared mustard
½ teaspoon salt
⅛ teaspoon pepper
⅛ teaspoon ground nutmeg
1 (8-ounce) carton commercial sour cream
2 tablespoons chopped fresh parsley

Sauté mushrooms and onion in butter in a large skillet 3 to 5 minutes or until onion is tender. Add flour, stirring until vegetables are coated. Cook 1 minute, stirring constantly. Gradually add milk; cook over medium heat, stirring constantly, until thickened and bubbly. Stir in mustard, salt, pepper, and nutmeg. Add sour cream and parsley; cook, stirring constantly, until sauce is thoroughly heated. Yield: about 2 cups.

*Connie Scopes,*
*Metairie, Louisiana.*

## BAKED TOAST AMANDINE

**½ cup butter or margarine, melted and divided**
**7 eggs, beaten**
**½ cup milk**
**¼ cup liquid brown sugar**
**1 (16-ounce) loaf French bread, cut into ¾-inch slices**
**Almond Syrup**

Divide ¼ cup butter evenly into two 15- x 10- x 1-inch jellyroll pans; spread to sides of pan, and set aside.

Combine remaining butter and next 3 ingredients in a large mixing bowl; mix well. Dip slices of bread, one at a time, in egg mixture, coating well. Arrange in prepared pans; bake at 450° for 20 minutes, turning once, until golden. Serve with Almond Syrup. Yield: 8 servings.

*Almond Syrup:*

**½ cup sliced almonds**
**2 tablespoons butter or margarine**
**1½ cups liquid brown sugar**
**½ teaspoon almond extract**

Sauté almonds in butter in a small saucepan over medium heat until golden. Stir in sugar and almond extract; serve warm. Yield: about 2 cups.

*Charlotte Farmer,*
*Richmond, Virginia.*

## WAFFLED FRENCH TOAST

**¾ cup milk**
**2 eggs**
**1 tablespoon butter or margarine, melted**
**1 tablespoon sugar**
**¼ teaspoon salt**
**6 slices day-old bread**

Combine first 5 ingredients in a shallow bowl, beating well. Dip bread slices, one at a time, into egg mixture, coating well; drain. Bake in preheated oiled waffle iron 2 minutes or until browned. Yield: 3 servings.

*Freda Carver,*
*Sebree, Kentucky.*

## FRENCH TOAST WITH ORANGE SAUCE

**3 eggs**
**½ cup half-and-half**
**1 tablespoon grated orange rind**
**⅓ cup orange juice**
**⅛ teaspoon ground nutmeg**
**Dash of salt**
**About ¼ cup butter or margarine, divided**
**8 slices bread**
**Orange Sauce**

Combine eggs, half-and-half, orange rind, juice, nutmeg, and salt in a shallow bowl; beat well.

Melt 2 tablespoons butter in a large skillet; dip 4 bread slices, one at a time, into egg mixture, coating well. Let drain; arrange in skillet, and cook 4 minutes on each side or until browned. Repeat procedure with remaining bread slices, adding additional butter to skillet as needed. Serve toast hot with Orange Sauce. Yield: 4 servings.

*Orange Sauce:*

**1 cup firmly packed brown sugar**
**2 teaspoons grated orange rind**
**½ cup orange juice**

Combine all ingredients in a small saucepan, stirring well. Bring to a boil. Reduce heat; simmer until thickened (about 5 minutes), stirring frequently. Yield: 1¼ cups.

*Delana Pearce,*
*Mulberry, Florida.*

*Tip: To use a griddle or frying pan, preheat on medium or medium-high heat before adding the food. It is properly preheated when a few drops of water spatter when they hit the surface. Add food and reduce heat so that it cooks without spattering and smoking.*

## OVEN-BAKED FRENCH TOAST

**¼ cup butter or margarine, melted**
**2 tablespoons honey**
**½ teaspoon ground cinnamon**
**3 eggs**
**½ cup orange juice**
**⅛ teaspoon salt**
**6 slices whole wheat bread**
**Honey**

Combine butter and 2 tablespoons honey in a 13- x 9- x 2-inch pan, spreading to sides of pan; sprinkle with cinnamon. Combine eggs, juice, and salt in a shallow bowl; mix well. Dip bread slices, one at a time, into egg mixture, coating well; let drain, and arrange on top of honey mixture. Bake at 400° for 20 minutes or until browned. Invert to serve. Serve with additional honey. Yield: 3 servings.

*Susan E. Scarr,*
*Marietta, Georgia.*

# Beverages To Suit Your Brunch

Whether you are planning the simplest of morning repasts or an elaborate formal brunch, choosing a beverage to complement the food is an important part of planning. Following is a wide range of morning beverage ideas that we hope you'll enjoy.

Included is a version of the classic brunch offering, Eye-Opener Bloody Marys. Another bracing beverage choice is our Lemon Cooler, featuring refreshing lemonade and brandy.

## SPEEDY BREAKFAST NOG

**3 cups pineapple juice, chilled**
**2 eggs**
**2 tablespoons honey**

Combine all ingredients in container of electric blender; process until smooth and frothy. Yield: about 3 cups.

*Mrs. B. W. Zeagler,*
*Baytown, Texas.*

## ORANGE SPICED NOG

6 eggs
½ to ¾ cup sugar
¼ teaspoon ground cinnamon
½ teaspoon ground nutmeg
1 cup evaporated milk, chilled
1 cup milk
1 cup orange juice
Grated orange rind
Ground nutmeg

Beat eggs in a large bowl until light and fluffy. Add sugar, cinnamon, and nutmeg, beating constantly. Stir in milk and orange juice, blending well. Ladle into individual serving glasses; sprinkle with orange rind and a dash of nutmeg. Yield: 6 cups. *Mrs. Bernie Benigno, Gulfport, Mississippi.*

## ORANGE-BANANA FLIP

2 large oranges, peeled, sectioned, and seeded
1 large banana, peeled and sliced
1 cup cold milk
¼ cup sugar
⅛ teaspoon salt
5 to 6 ice cubes

Combine all ingredients in container of electric blender; process until smooth. Yield: 1 quart. *Mrs. H. J. Sherrer, Bay City, Texas.*

## LEMON COOLER

1 (6-ounce) can frozen lemonade concentrate, thawed and undiluted
1½ cups vanilla ice cream
¼ to ½ cup brandy
8 ice cubes
Lemon slices (optional)

Combine first 4 ingredients in container of electric blender; blend until smooth and frothy. Garnish each serving with a lemon slice, if desired. Yield: about 3 cups. *Sandra Benton, Potomac, Maryland.*

## SPARKLING GRAPE PUNCH

2 cups sugar
4 cups water
2 cups orange juice
4 cups grape juice
4 (33.8-ounce) bottles ginger ale

Combine sugar and water in a medium saucepan, stirring well; bring to a boil. Boil 3 minutes, stirring often. Cool. Stir in orange juice and grape juice; chill. Stir in ginger ale before serving. Yield: about 1½ gallons. *Freda Lovelace, Wytheville, Virginia.*

## PEANUT BUTTER SHAKE

2 cups milk
1 pint vanilla ice cream
¼ cup creamy peanut butter

Combine all ingredients in container of electric blender; process until smooth. Serve at once. Yield: about 4 cups. *Bertha Fowler, Woodruff, South Carolina.*

## EYE-OPENER BLOODY MARYS

1 quart tomato juice
1 quart tomato cocktail
½ teaspoon salt
⅛ teaspoon pepper
Dash of hot sauce
Dash of Worcestershire sauce
Dash of celery salt
1½ cups vodka
Ice cubes (optional)
Celery stalks

Combine first 7 ingredients, mixing well; chill overnight. Stir vodka into tomato juice mixture; pour over ice cubes, if desired. Garnish with celery stalks. Yield: 9½ cups. *Karen Sue Woodall, Mercedes, Texas.*

*Tip: Keep celery fresh and crisp by wrapping in paper towels; place in plastic bag in refrigerator. The towels absorb excess moisture.*

## Cooking Light

# A Light Brunch Brightens Your Morning

While it's fun to entertain with brunch, dieting guests shy away from the delicious but often calorie-rich morning favorites. So what can you serve to those weight-watching friends for a light but appealing brunch? A poached egg on top of dry toast? You can do a lot better than that, and this kitchen-tested menu shows you how.

Calorie counters will relax when offered refreshing Orange Slush as a welcoming appetizer. Follow this with a choice of entrées: Swiss-Zucchini Quiche or Creamed Chicken; a choice of vegetables: Herbed Tomatoes or Light Asparagus Vinaigrette. End the meal with our naturally sweet Spiced Fruit Dessert.

Swiss-Zucchini Quiche claims a unique rice crust as its special calorie-saving attraction. The amount of fat in the filling is reduced by using evaporated skim milk instead of the usual half-and-half. You'll also limit fat and calories by sautéing the fresh vegetables in a skillet sprayed with vegetable cooking spray instead of coated with butter or oil.

Stir chopped chicken and vegetables into a flavorful white sauce for our second entrée choice. The white sauce starts with a reduced amount of margarine for the roux and calls for skim milk instead of cream. It's best to use a tub margarine that lists one of the following oils as the first ingredient on the package label: safflower, soybean, corn, cottonseed, or sesame. Although the calories are the same as in other margarines, the concentration of saturated fats is lower or absent. Saturated fats increase blood cholesterol, one of the prime risk factors of heart disease.

We're suggesting two vegetable choices (one served hot and one served cold). Fresh vegetables such as asparagus, broccoli, summer squash, lettuce, and celery are excellent diet choices. Prepared without oil, butter, or margarine, these vegetables are low in calories but are filling since they're high in dietary fiber.

Fruit spiced with cinnamon and cloves makes a refreshing finale for our light brunch. Select canned fruit packed in water or unsweetened fruit juice. When fruit is packed in heavy syrup the fruit absorbs the extra sucrose, or sugar, and it is impossible to drain or even rinse it all away.

**Orange Slush**
**Swiss-Zucchini Quiche**
**or**
**Creamed Chicken**
**Herbed Tomatoes**
**or**
**Light Asparagus Vinaigrette**
**Spiced Fruit Dessert**
**Coffee or Tea**

## ORANGE SLUSH

**2 cups unsweetened orange juice**
**½ cup instant nonfat dry milk powder**
**¼ teaspoon vanilla extract**
**8 ice cubes**

Combine all ingredients in container of electric blender; process until mixture is frothy. Serve immediately. Yield: about 4 cups or 6 servings (about 72 calories per serving).

## SWISS-ZUCCHINI QUICHE

**1½ cups (⅛-inch-thick slices) zucchini**
**Vegetable cooking spray**
**¼ pound fresh mushrooms, sliced**
**1 small onion, chopped**
**3 eggs, beaten**
**½ cup evaporated skim milk**
**¼ cup water**
**½ teaspoon salt**
**¼ teaspoon pepper**
**¾ cup (3 ounces) shredded Swiss cheese, divided**
**Rice-Cheese Shell**

Cook zucchini in a small amount of unsalted boiling water 3 minutes; drain and press gently to remove excess water.

Spray a small skillet with cooking spray. Sauté mushrooms and onion in skillet over low heat until vegetables are tender but not brown; set aside.

Combine eggs, milk, water, salt, and pepper; mix well. Add zucchini, mushroom mixture, and ½ cup cheese; stir well. Pour zucchini mixture into Rice-Cheese Shell; top with remaining ¼ cup cheese. Bake at 375° for 40 minutes or until set. Yield: 6 servings (about 197 calories per serving).

*Rice-Cheese Shell:*

**Vegetable cooking spray**
**1½ cups cooked regular rice**
**1 egg, beaten**
**¼ cup (1 ounce) shredded Swiss cheese**

Spray a 10-inch pieplate with vegetable cooking spray.

Combine remaining ingredients; stir well. Press mixture into pieplate; bake at 350° for 5 minutes. Press rice mixture back up sides of pieplate with the back of a spoon, if necessary. Yield: one 10-inch shell.

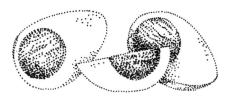

## CREAMED CHICKEN

**3 small chicken breast halves, skinned**
**Vegetable cooking spray**
**1 tablespoon plus 1 teaspoon margarine, divided**
**½ cup sliced fresh mushrooms**
**¼ cup chopped green pepper**
**1 tablespoon chopped celery**
**1 tablespoon minced onion**
**2 tablespoons all-purpose flour**
**1 cup skim milk**
**1 hard-cooked egg, thinly sliced**
**2 tablespoons diced pimiento**
**½ teaspoon salt**
**⅛ teaspoon pepper**
**3 English muffins, split and toasted**
**Paprika**

Cook chicken in unsalted boiling water 30 minutes; drain. Remove chicken from bone; coarsely chop, and set aside.

Spray a medium skillet with cooking spray; add 1 teaspoon margarine. Sauté mushrooms, green pepper, celery, and onion over low heat until vegetables are tender but not brown. Remove vegetables from skillet; drain and set aside.

Melt 1 tablespoon margarine in skillet over low heat; add flour, stirring until smooth. Cook 1 minute, stirring constantly. Gradually add milk; cook over medium heat, stirring constantly, until thickened and bubbly. Add chicken, sautéed vegetables, egg, pimiento, salt, and pepper; stir gently.

Spoon mixture over English muffins; sprinkle with paprika. Yield: 6 servings (about 197 calories per serving).

## HERBED TOMATOES

**6 medium tomatoes**
**Salt**
**¼ cup plus 2 tablespoons fine, dry breadcrumbs**
**1 clove garlic, minced**
**3 tablespoons chopped onion**
**1½ teaspoons chopped fresh parsley**
**¾ teaspoon celery seeds**
**⅛ teaspoon dried whole basil**
**⅛ to ¼ teaspoon pepper**
**Chopped fresh parsley**

Wash tomatoes thoroughly. Cut tops from tomatoes; scoop out pulp, leaving shells intact. Chop pulp, and set aside. Sprinkle salt in tomatoes; invert to drain.

Combine tomato pulp and next 7 ingredients; stir well. Fill tomato shells with breadcrumb mixture; sprinkle with additional parsley. Bake at 350° for 10 to 15 minutes. Yield: 6 servings (about 57 calories per serving).

*Tip: Wash or chop vegetables and open cans before you begin preparing any recipe. It is also a good idea to have most ingredients measured before beginning to cook.*

## LIGHT ASPARAGUS VINAIGRETTE

2 (10-ounce) packages frozen asparagus
   spears
½ cup vinegar
½ cup water
2 tablespoons chopped fresh parsley
2 tablespoons chopped fresh chives
2 tablespoons Dijon mustard
½ teaspoon dried whole tarragon
½ pound fresh spinach leaves
2 medium tomatoes, cut into wedges

Cook asparagus according to package directions; drain and place asparagus in a shallow container.

Combine next 6 ingredients; mix well. Pour dressing over asparagus; chill for 3 to 5 hours.

Place asparagus on spinach leaves; pour dressing over salad. Garnish with tomatoes. Yield: 6 servings (about 51 calories per serving).

## SPICED FRUIT DESSERT

1 orange
1 (15¼-ounce) can pineapple chunks in
   unsweetened juice
2 (16-ounce) cans pear halves in
   unsweetened juice, drained
1 (16-ounce) can apricot halves in extra
   light syrup, drained
2 (2-inch) sticks cinnamon
6 whole cloves

Peel orange, reserving rind; divide orange into sections, removing membrane. Drain pineapple, reserving juice. Combine orange sections, pineapple, pears, and apricots in a large bowl; set aside.

Combine rind, pineapple juice, cinnamon, and cloves in a small saucepan; simmer 5 minutes. Strain juice, and pour over fruit; cover and chill dessert several hours. Yield: 6 servings (about 116 calories per serving).

*Tip: Organize your spice shelf and save much time by keeping the spices in alphabetical order. Store all spices in tightly covered containers to retain flavor and fragrance.*

# These Side Dishes Are Worth Noticing

If you want your guests to remember your brunch as extra special, fill in the menu with side dishes that are just as appetizing as the entrée. Liven up hominy with hot jalapeño peppers and Cheddar cheese—the unexpected sharp flavor goes well with egg or meat entrées. Or combine rice, carrots, and onion with sausage for our easy and delicious Sausage-Rice Casserole.

For an unusual fruit side dish, coat chunks of banana in pancake batter and fry until golden brown. A sprinkle of powdered sugar makes Banana Boats attractive and slightly sweet.

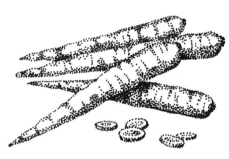

## SAUSAGE-RICE CASSEROLE

1 cup uncooked regular rice
2 cups scraped, chopped carrots
1 large onion, chopped
1 cup chopped celery
½ cup chopped green pepper
1 (14½-ounce) can chicken broth
¼ cup water
1 pound bulk pork sausage
Aztec mushroom (page 51)
Fresh parsley sprigs (optional)

Spread rice evenly in a lightly greased 3-quart casserole. Spoon vegetables over rice. Pour chicken broth and water over vegetables.

Cook sausage until browned; drain well. Spoon sausage over vegetables. Cover and bake at 350° for 30 minutes. Remove from oven, and stir well; cover and bake an additional 30 minutes. Garnish with Aztec mushroom and parsley, if desired. Yield: 8 to 10 servings.
*Mrs. Kenneth Olson,*
*Dunnellon, Florida.*

## BAKED PEACHES AND SAUSAGE

1 pound mild bulk pork sausage
1 (29-ounce) can peach halves
¼ cup firmly packed brown sugar
½ teaspoon ground cinnamon
¼ teaspoon ground cloves

Cook sausage until browned, stirring to crumble. Drain well on paper towels, and set aside.

Drain peach halves, reserving ¼ cup juice. Place peaches, cut side up, in a well-greased 10- x 6- x 2-inch glass baking dish; add reserved juice. Combine brown sugar and spices, stirring well; sprinkle over peach halves.

Bake at 450° for 15 minutes; remove from oven, and sprinkle cooked sausage evenly over top. Return to oven, and bake 15 minutes. Yield: 6 servings.
*Kay Castleman,*
*Nashville, Tennessee.*

## HASH BROWN CHEESE BAKE

1 (32-ounce) package frozen shredded
   hash brown potatoes, thawed
2 (10¾-ounce) cans potato soup, undiluted
2 (8-ounce) cartons commercial sour
   cream
2 cups (8 ounces) shredded sharp
   Cheddar cheese
1 cup grated Parmesan cheese

Combine all ingredients, stirring well; spoon into a greased 13- x 9- x 2-inch baking dish. Bake at 350° for 40 minutes. Yield: 12 to 15 servings.
*Mrs. Dennis Long,*
*Monmouth, Illinois.*

## BANANA BOATS

1 cup pancake mix
1 tablespoon sugar
1 egg
⅔ cup milk
6 medium-size firm bananas
Vegetable oil
Powdered sugar

Combine first 4 ingredients; stir until mixture is blended, and set aside.

Peel bananas and cut into 1½-inch pieces; dip into batter. Drop coated pieces into hot oil (375°). Fry until golden, turning once. Drain on paper towels; sprinkle with powdered sugar. Serve hot. Yield: 10 to 12 servings.

*T. O. Davis,*
*Waynesboro, Mississippi.*

### JALAPENO HOMINY

3 (29-ounce) cans hominy, drained
1 (10¾-ounce) can cream of mushroom
  soup, undiluted
1 (10½-ounce) can cream of asparagus
  soup, undiluted
4 cups (16 ounces) shredded Cheddar
  cheese
1 (4-ounce) jar diced pimiento, drained
3 to 5 jalapeño peppers, seeded and finely
  chopped

Combine all ingredients in a large mixing bowl; stir well. Spoon into a 3-quart casserole. Bake, uncovered, at 350° for 20 minutes or until mixture is bubbly. Yield: 20 servings. *Jan Norris,*
*Houston, Texas.*

### ORANGE-GLAZED APPLES

2 (20-ounce) cans sliced apples, drained
¼ cup butter or margarine
1½ cups sugar
2 tablespoons grated orange rind
½ cup orange juice
¼ cup all-purpose flour
Whipped cream (optional)
Strip of orange rind (optional)

Place apples in a 1½-quart baking dish; set aside. Melt butter in a small saucepan; stir in next 4 ingredients. Cook over medium heat until mixture thickens, stirring occasionally. Pour over apples, and bake at 375° for 30 minutes. Garnish with whipped cream and a strip of orange rind, if desired. Serve warm. Yield: 6 to 8 servings.

*Marie W. Harris,*
*Sevierville, Tennessee.*

*Tip: A clean toothbrush is a handy gadget to aid in the removal of all bits of grated rind from a grater.*

# Garnish The Morning In Style

Whether the entrée you've chosen for your brunch is simple or elaborate, an attractive garnish will add a great deal of eye appeal. Here are several garnishes that are simple to make from fresh fruit and vegetables, even butter; be sure to choose one that will complement the food in color, texture, size, and taste.

**Tomato rose:** With a sharp paring knife, cut a thin slice from the top of the tomato (not stem end); discard. Begin at top, and peel a paper-thin continuous strip about ¾ inch wide from

the entire tomato. Last portion of strip cut will be the smallest. Begin at first portion cut to shape the strip into a rose shape. With flesh side inward, coil the strip tightly at first to form the center of the rose, gradually letting it become looser to form the outer petals.

**Aztec mushroom:** The only tool needed to make this impressive garnish is a small paring knife with a sharp

point. Select firm, white mushrooms; and before starting, rub the entire mushroom with lemon juice to keep it from turning brown.

Holding the stem of mushroom in one hand and the blade of the knife loosely in the other hand, press the point of the blade into the center of the mushroom

cap, with the flat surface of the blade against the mushroom. Make four other indentations around the center of the cap. Move the knife slightly down the side of the cap, still keeping the point toward the center of the mushroom top. Make indentations all around the mushroom in even rows, continuing around the cap until you reach the bottom edge. Use very gentle pressure as you approach the edge because the cap is more likely to break there.

**Fluted lemon slices:** Using a citrus stripper, cut thin strips of peel from a lemon, tip to tip, at equally spaced intervals. Slice the lemon, and remove any seeds with the tip of a knife.

**Frosted grapes:** Place green or purple grapes on a wire rack (individually or in bunches). Beat one or more egg whites just until frothy. Using a soft pastry brush, paint the grapes with the beaten white. While grapes are still wet, sprinkle with granulated sugar to create a frosted look, and allow to dry in a cool place. Don't refrigerate the frosted grapes because the moisture in the refrigerator will melt the sugar.

**Butter curls:** Begin with a slightly softened stick of butter or margarine.

Pull a hook-shaped butter curler over the length of the butter stick to make a smooth, round curl. To avoid a last-minute job the day of the brunch, curl the butter a day or two in advance, and refrigerate or freeze the curls.

# Applause For Favorite Southern Desserts

Traditional desserts have a way of coming back for encores time and again. Lauded for their sweet concoctions, generations of Southern cooks have made desserts the focus of attention at county fairs and covered dish suppers. The best have been passed down to us—old favorites like banana pudding, coconut cake, and buttermilk pie. But let's not forget chocolaty black bottom pie, laced with a sip of Irish whiskey, and buttermilk pound cake.

We applaud these old Southern standbys and hope you'll make one the finale to your next meal.

## OLD-FASHIONED BUTTERMILK POUND CAKE

½ cup butter or margarine, softened
½ cup shortening
2 cups sugar
4 eggs
½ teaspoon soda
1 cup buttermilk
3 cups all-purpose flour
⅛ teaspoon salt
2 teaspoons lemon extract
1 teaspoon almond extract

Cream butter and shortening; gradually add sugar, beating until light and fluffy. Add eggs, one at a time, beating well after each addition.

Dissolve soda in buttermilk. Combine flour and salt; add to creamed mixture alternately with buttermilk, beginning and ending with flour mixture. Mix well after each addition. Stir in lemon and almond flavorings.

Pour batter into a greased and floured 10-inch tube pan. Bake at 350° for 1 hour and 5 minutes or until a wooden pick inserted in center comes out clean. Cool cake in pan 10 to 15 minutes; remove from pan, and cool completely. Yield: one 10-inch cake.

*Mrs. R. A. Dibrell,*
*Dallas, Texas.*

*Tip: Always measure accurately. Level dry ingredients in a cup with a knife edge or a spoon handle. Measure liquids in a cup so that the fluid is level with the top of the measuring line. Measure solid shortening by packing it firmly in a graduated measuring cup.*

*Old-Fashioned Buttermilk Pound Cake combines lemon and almond extracts for a favorite cake that calls for seconds.*

## FRESH COCONUT CAKE

¾ cup shortening
1½ cups sugar
3 eggs
2¼ cups sifted cake flour
2½ teaspoons baking powder
½ teaspoon salt
¾ cup milk
1 teaspoon vanilla extract
Custard filling (recipe follows)
Snow Peak Frosting
2 cups grated fresh coconut

Cream shortening, and gradually add sugar; beat until light and fluffy. Add eggs, one at a time, beating well after each addition.

Combine flour, baking powder, and salt; add to creamed mixture alternately with milk, beginning and ending with flour mixture. Stir in vanilla.

Pour batter into 2 greased and floured 9-inch round cakepans. Bake at 375° for 20 to 25 minutes or until wooden pick inserted in center comes out clean. Cool in pans 10 minutes; remove from pans, and cool completely.

Split cake layers in half horizontally to make 4 layers.

Spread custard filling between layers; spread top and sides with Snow Peak Frosting, and sprinkle with coconut. Yield: one 4-layer cake.

*Custard Filling:*

2 cups milk
4 egg yolks
½ cup sugar
⅓ cup cornstarch
3 tablespoons orange-flavored liqueur or 1 teaspoon orange flavoring
1 cup grated fresh coconut

Combine first 4 ingredients in a heavy saucepan; stir with a wire whisk until well blended. Cook over medium heat, stirring constantly, until thickened and smooth. Stir in liqueur. Chill mixture thoroughly. Stir in coconut. Yield: about 2¾ cups.

*Snow Peak Frosting:*

1¼ cups light corn syrup
2 egg whites
Dash of salt
1 teaspoon vanilla extract

Bring syrup to a boil.

Combine egg whites and salt in a large mixing bowl. Beat egg whites (at room temperature) until soft peaks form; continue to beat, slowly adding syrup. Add vanilla; continue beating until stiff peaks form and frosting is thick enough to spread. Yield: enough for one 4-layer cake.       *Kay Kelly,*
*Pelham, Alabama.*

## BLACK BOTTOM PIE

14 gingersnaps, crushed
¼ cup plus 1 tablespoon butter or margarine, melted
½ cup sugar
1½ teaspoons cornstarch
4 eggs, separated
2 cups milk
1½ (1-ounce) squares unsweetened chocolate
1 teaspoon vanilla extract
1 envelope unflavored gelatin
2 tablespoons cold water
¼ teaspoon cream of tartar
½ cup sugar
2 teaspoons Irish whiskey or bourbon
½ cup whipping cream, whipped
Chocolate shavings (optional)

Combine cookie crumbs and butter, mixing well. Press mixture firmly into a 9-inch pieplate. Bake at 375° for 8 minutes. Let cool.

Combine ½ cup sugar and cornstarch in top of double boiler. Beat egg yolks; combine egg yolks and milk, mixing well. Gradually stir into dry ingredients. Bring water in bottom of double boiler to a boil. Reduce heat to low; cook mixture, stirring constantly, until slightly thickened or until custard coats a spoon. Remove from heat.

Remove 1 cup custard; add chocolate to it, stirring until melted. Cool slightly. Add vanilla, and pour into prepared crust. Chill until slightly set.

Dissolve gelatin in cold water; add to remaining hot custard, stirring constantly. Cool. Beat egg whites (at room temperature) until frothy; add cream of tartar and ½ cup sugar. Beat until stiff peaks form. Add Irish whiskey; beat

until blended. Fold into plain custard. Spoon over chocolate custard; chill until set. Top with whipped cream; garnish with chocolate shavings, if desired. Yield: one 9-inch pie.
*Edna Earle Moore,*
*Hueytown, Alabama.*

## BURNT CARAMEL PIE

1½ cups sugar, divided
1½ cups evaporated milk, scalded
3 tablespoons all-purpose flour
3 eggs, separated
1 tablespoon butter or margarine
1 teaspoon vanilla extract
Salt
1 baked 9-inch pastry shell
¼ cup plus 2 tablespoons sugar

Sprinkle ¾ cup sugar evenly in a 10-inch cast-iron skillet; place over medium heat. Caramelize sugar by constantly stirring with a wooden spoon. Remove sugar from heat; gradually add the milk, stirring constantly.

Combine ¾ cup sugar and flour; add to caramelized sugar mixture.

Beat egg yolks. Gradually stir about one-fourth of hot mixture into yolks; add to remaining hot mixture, stirring constantly. Return to low heat; cook, stirring constantly, until smooth and thickened. Add butter, vanilla, and pinch of salt, stirring well. Spoon custard into pastry shell, and set aside.

Add a pinch of salt to egg whites, and beat (at room temperature) until foamy. Gradually add remaining sugar, 1 tablespoon at a time, beating until stiff peaks form. Spread meringue over custard, sealing to edge of pastry. Bake at 425° for 10 minutes or until meringue is golden brown. Cool pie completely before serving. Yield: one 9-inch pie.
*Mrs. Joe Brogdon,*
*Texarkana, Texas.*

*To caramelize sugar for Burnt Caramel Pie, stir sugar in a cast-iron skillet over medium heat until light brown and melted.*

## BUTTERMILK PIE

½ cup butter or margarine, softened
2 cups sugar
3 tablespoons all-purpose flour
3 eggs
1 cup buttermilk
1 teaspoon vanilla extract
1 unbaked 9-inch pastry shell

Cream butter; gradually add sugar, beating well. Add flour, and beat until smooth. Add eggs; beat until combined. Stir in buttermilk and vanilla; beat well. Pour filling into pastry shell. Bake at 400° for 5 minutes; reduce oven temperature to 350°, and bake an additional 45 minutes or until set. Yield: one 9-inch pie.
*Pamela Nordyke,*
*San Angelo, Texas.*

## BANANA PUDDING

3½ tablespoons all-purpose flour
1⅓ cups sugar
Dash of salt
3 eggs, separated
3 cups milk
2 teaspoons vanilla extract, divided
1 (12-ounce) package vanilla wafers
6 medium bananas
¼ cup plus 2 tablespoons sugar

Combine flour, 1⅓ cups sugar, and salt in a heavy saucepan. Beat egg yolks; combine egg yolks and milk, mixing well. Stir into dry ingredients; cook over medium heat, stirring constantly, until smooth and thickened. Remove from heat; stir in 1 teaspoon vanilla.

Layer one-third of the vanilla wafers in a 4-quart baking dish. Slice 2 bananas; layer over wafers. Pour one-third of the filling over bananas. Repeat layers twice.

Beat egg whites (at room temperature) until foamy. Gradually add remaining sugar, 1 tablespoon at a time, beating until stiff peaks form. Add 1 teaspoon vanilla, and beat until blended. Spread meringue over filling, sealing to edge of dish. Bake at 425° for 10 to 12 minutes or until golden brown. Yield: 10 servings.   *Mrs. Julian Moats,*
*Birmingham, Alabama.*

*Tip: For ingredients listed in recipes: If the direction comes before the ingredient—for example, sifted flour— first sift the flour, then measure. If the direction comes after the ingredient—for example, pecans, chopped—first measure pecans, then chop.*

# Salads Ready When You Are

If you're planning a company meal, chances are you'll have several dishes that require last-minute attention. At least you won't have to worry about the salad if you've chosen a make-ahead recipe, such as the marinated vegetable and congealed fruit salads we offer.

Our Marinated English Pea Salad is crunchy with bean sprouts and celery, bright with pimiento. Three-Layer Mold offers a variety of fruit and flavors in three layers. And for a colorful addition to your menu, try Frozen Peach Salad.

## CAULIFLOWER-BROCCOLI TOSS

1 large head cauliflower
1 bunch fresh broccoli
1 bunch green onions, chopped
¾ to 1 cup mayonnaise
½ (1.4-ounce) package buttermilk salad
  dressing mix
2 tablespoons sugar
2 tablespoons vinegar

Remove outer green leaves of cauliflower, and break into flowerets; wash thoroughly. Set aside.

Trim off large leaves of broccoli. Remove stalks, separate into flowerets, and wash thoroughly. Reserve stalks for use in other recipes.

Combine cauliflower, broccoli, and onion; toss gently. Combine remaining ingredients; mix well and pour over vegetables, tossing gently. Cover and chill overnight. Yield: 6 to 8 servings.
*Deanne Anthony,*
*Poteau, Oklahoma.*

## MARINATED ENGLISH PEA SALAD

2 (17-ounce) cans English peas, drained
1 (16-ounce) can bean sprouts, drained
1 (4-ounce) jar whole pimientos, drained
  and chopped
4 stalks celery, finely chopped
1 medium onion, finely chopped
¾ cup vegetable oil
¾ cup vinegar
¾ cup sugar
1 teaspoon dried whole basil
1 teaspoon garlic powder
1 teaspoon salt
Lettuce leaves (optional)

Combine the first 5 ingredients, tossing lightly.

Combine vegetable oil, vinegar, sugar, and seasonings in a jar. Cover tightly, and shake vigorously; pour over vegetables. Cover and chill 8 to 10 hours or overnight. Serve in a lettuce-lined bowl, if desired. Yield: 8 servings.
*Dee Yates,*
*Greensboro, North Carolina.*

## PINEAPPLE-PEAR DELIGHT

1 (8-ounce) can crushed pineapple
1 (16-ounce) can pear halves
1 (6-ounce) package lime-flavored gelatin
2 cups boiling water
2 (3-ounce) packages cream cheese,
  softened
2 tablespoons mayonnaise

Drain pineapple and pears, reserving juice; add enough water to juice to make 2 cups liquid, and set aside. Dissolve gelatin in boiling water; stir in the reserved liquid.

Combine cream cheese and mayonnaise, mixing well. Dice pears. Stir pears and pineapple into cream cheese mixture; stir cheese mixture into gelatin mixture. Pour into a lightly oiled 8-cup mold, and chill until firm. Yield: 10 to 12 servings.
*Aileen D. Lorberg,*
*Cape Girardeau, Missouri.*

## FROZEN PEACH SALAD

1 (3-ounce) package cream cheese,
  softened
2 tablespoons mayonnaise
1 cup whipping cream
1⅔ cups miniature marshmallows
1 (16-ounce) can peach slices, drained
1 (20-ounce) can pineapple chunks,
  drained
½ cup sliced maraschino cherries
½ cup chopped pecans
Lettuce leaves

Combine cream cheese and mayonnaise; beat until smooth. Beat whipping cream until soft peaks form; add cream cheese mixture, and beat until blended. Fold in remaining ingredients except lettuce; spoon into a 12- x 8- x 2-inch dish. Freeze until firm. Cut into squares; serve on lettuce leaves. Yield: 12 servings.
*Marie H. Webb,*
*Roanoke, Virginia.*

*Tip: For salad success be sure lettuce is cold, crisp, and dry. Tear, don't cut, lettuce into bite-size pieces. Add the dressing just before serving.*

## THREE-LAYER MOLD

1 (3-ounce) package cherry-flavored
  gelatin
1 cup boiling water
1 (16½-ounce) can pitted dark sweet
  cherries, undrained
1 (3-ounce) package lemon-flavored gelatin
1 cup boiling water
1 (3-ounce) package cream cheese,
  softened
1 cup milk
1 (3-ounce) package lime-flavored gelatin
1 cup boiling water
1 (20-ounce) can crushed pineapple,
  undrained

Dissolve cherry gelatin in 1 cup boiling water. Add cherries, and pour into a lightly oiled 10-cup mold. Chill until set.

Dissolve lemon gelatin in 1 cup boiling water; set aside. Beat cream cheese with electric mixer; add milk, and mix well. Add lemon gelatin to cream cheese mixture, mixing well. Spoon over cherry layer; chill until set.

Dissolve lime gelatin in 1 cup boiling water. Chill until the consistency of unbeaten egg white. Stir in pineapple. Spoon mixture over lemon layer; chill until firm. Yield: 16 to 18 servings.
*Mrs. Edward Kunuty,*
*Palm Beach Gardens, Florida.*

# Spice Up Your Meals With Mustard

A hot dog isn't a hot dog without mustard. But if you limit your use of mustard to hot dogs and sandwiches, you're missing the flavor this versatile spice can lend to meats, salads, and sauces.

Enjoy tangy mustard in its many forms. For Jezebel Sauce, a whole can of dry mustard is blended with prepared horseradish, apple jelly, and pineapple preserves to make a pungent sauce especially good with beef or pork. Be sure to use it sparingly—it's hot! Whole mustard seeds are tossed into Tangy Cabbage Salad, and commercially prepared mustard adds zest to Honey Chicken.

If you'd like to make your own mustard, we've included Zesty Homemade Mustard, which gets its nippy flavor from a mixture of dry mustard and tarragon vinegar. It's great as a sandwich spread, but don't neglect to experiment with it in cooking, too.

## HONEY CHICKEN

½ cup butter or margarine, melted
½ cup honey
¼ cup prepared mustard
2 tablespoons lemon juice
1 (2- to 3-pound) broiler-fryer, cut up
Salt and pepper

Combine butter, honey, mustard, and lemon juice; stir well. Lightly sprinkle chicken with salt and pepper; place chicken, meaty side down, in a lightly greased 13- x 9- x 2-inch baking pan. Pour honey mixture over chicken; cover and refrigerate 3 to 4 hours.

Remove from refrigerator; bake, covered, at 350° for 30 minutes. Remove cover, and turn chicken pieces; bake 30 minutes longer or until done, basting occasionally with pan drippings. Yield: 4 to 5 servings. *Susan Erickson, State University, Arkansas.*

## GRECIAN POTATO SALAD

6 medium potatoes
2 medium onions, chopped
¾ cup chopped celery
¾ cup mayonnaise
¼ cup chopped dill pickle
2 hard-cooked eggs, chopped
Juice of 1 lemon
⅛ teaspoon black pepper
⅛ teaspoon red pepper
About 2 cups torn lettuce
½ teaspoon dried whole oregano
Dressing (recipe follows)
Assorted garnishes

Cook potatoes in boiling water about 20 minutes or until tender; drain and cool. Peel potatoes, and cut into ½-inch cubes. Combine potatoes and next 8 ingredients; toss lightly. Chill thoroughly.

Arrange lettuce on a large serving platter; spoon potato salad over lettuce. Sprinkle with oregano. Pour dressing over salad. Serve salad with several of the following garnishes: sliced feta cheese, radish roses, carrot curls, green pepper rings, pitted ripe olives, green onions, tomato wedges, sliced avocado, sliced pepperoni, anchovy fillets, cubed cooked ham, and whole or chopped shrimp. Yield: about 8 to 10 servings.

*Dressing:*

½ cup peanut oil
½ cup vinegar
Juice of 1 lemon
1 teaspoon salt
1 tablespoon Dijon mustard
¾ teaspoon freshly ground pepper
¼ teaspoon dry mustard
1 small clove garlic, crushed

Combine all ingredients in a jar. Cover tightly, and shake vigorously. Chill several hours. Yield: about 1 cup. *Katharyn B. Riley, Kingsport, Tennessee.*

## TANGY CABBAGE SALAD

1 medium head cabbage, shredded
2 large onions, chopped
2 green peppers, chopped
2 carrots, shredded
2 cups vinegar
1½ cups sugar
2 tablespoons mustard seeds
2 tablespoons celery seeds

Combine vegetables in a large bowl.
Combine remaining ingredients in a saucepan; bring to a boil, stirring occasionally. Pour over vegetables, and toss. Chill well. Yield: about 12 servings.
*Mrs. Fred C. Powers, Newport, Arkansas.*

## JEZEBEL SAUCE

1 (18-ounce) jar pineapple preserves
1 (18-ounce) jar apple jelly
1 (1.12-ounce) can dry mustard
1 (5-ounce) jar prepared horseradish
1 tablespoon cracked peppercorns

Combine all ingredients; stir well. Pour sauce into airtight containers; store in refrigerator. Serve sauce over cream cheese with crackers as an appetizer or with pork or beef. Yield: 3⅔ cups. *Mrs. Harvey T. Kidd, Hernando, Mississippi.*

## ZESTY HOMEMADE MUSTARD

½ cup dry mustard
⅓ cup tarragon vinegar
¼ cup sugar
2 tablespoons plus 2 teaspoons butter or margarine
¼ teaspoon salt
2 eggs, beaten

Sprinkle mustard in the top of a double boiler; add vinegar. Do not stir; cover and let stand overnight.

Add sugar, butter, and salt to mustard mixture. Cook over boiling water until butter melts, stirring occasionally. Gradually stir about one-fourth of hot mixture into eggs; add to remaining hot mixture. Reduce heat to low; cook, stirring constantly and rapidly, until mixture is thickened.

Cool mixture, and pour into airtight container; store in refrigerator up to one month. Yield: about 1 cup.
*Note:* Recipe may be doubled.
*Mrs. William Fisher, Punta Gorda, Florida.*

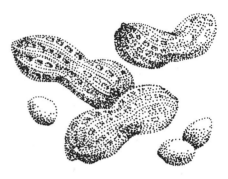

# Do More With Peanut Butter

Everyone knows that peanut butter makes a great sandwich, especially when teamed with jelly or jam. But don't limit your peanut butter to plain slices of bread. Try a different approach with our French toast-style Peanut Butter Breakfast Sandwich.

Another way to enjoy this protein-rich food is in Peanut Butter-Honey Muffins. And if you've never mixed a little peanut butter with vanilla ice cream, then Peanutty Ice Cream Pie will be a special treat—delicious and easy to prepare.

## PEANUT BUTTER BREAKFAST SANDWICH

½ cup crunchy peanut butter
¼ cup honey
8 slices white bread
2 eggs, beaten
½ cup milk
2 tablespoons butter or margarine

Combine peanut butter and honey; mix well. Spread peanut butter mixture evenly over 4 slices of bread. Place remaining bread slices over peanut butter mixture to make a sandwich.

Combine eggs and milk in a shallow pan; place each sandwich in egg mixture, turning to coat evenly.

Melt butter in a 9-inch square pan. Arrange sandwiches in pan. Bake at 400° for 20 minutes; turn sandwiches, and bake 20 more minutes. Yield: 4 servings. *Geraldine B. Johnson, Bossier City, Louisiana.*

## PEANUTTY ICE CREAM PIE

1¼ cups graham cracker crumbs
¼ cup sugar
¼ cup butter or margarine, softened
½ cup light corn syrup
⅓ cup peanut butter
1 quart vanilla ice cream, divided and softened
⅔ cup chopped unsalted dry-roasted peanuts, divided

Combine cracker crumbs and sugar; cut in butter. Press crumb mixture firmly into a 9-inch pieplate. Bake at 375° for 8 minutes; cool completely.

Combine corn syrup and peanut butter; mix well, and set aside.

Spread half of softened ice cream over bottom of crust. Drizzle half of peanut butter mixture over ice cream. Sprinkle with half the peanuts. Repeat layers. Freeze until very firm (at least 4 hours). Let stand at room temperature about 5 to 10 minutes before slicing. Yield: one 9-inch pie. *Joyce Whitley, Statesville, North Carolina.*

## PEANUT BUTTER COOKIES

1 cup shortening
1 cup sugar
1 cup firmly packed brown sugar
2 eggs
2 tablespoons water
3 cups all-purpose flour
1½ teaspoons soda
¼ teaspoon salt
1 cup crunchy peanut butter

Cream shortening; gradually add sugar, beating until light and fluffy. Add eggs and water, beating well.

Combine dry ingredients; add to creamed mixture, beating well. Stir in peanut butter. Shape into 1-inch balls; place 3 inches apart on ungreased cookie sheets. Dip a fork in flour, and flatten cookies to ¼-inch thickness in a crisscross pattern. Bake at 375° for 10 to 12 minutes. Remove to wire racks, and cool completely. Yield: about 8 dozen. *Mrs. Russell Rehkemper, Tampa, Florida.*

## PEANUT BUTTER-CHOCOLATE CANDY SQUARES

1 cup butter or margarine
1 cup peanut butter
1 (16-ounce) package powdered sugar, sifted
1½ cups graham cracker crumbs
1 (12-ounce) package semisweet chocolate morsels, melted

Melt butter in a medium saucepan. Remove from heat, and stir in next 3 ingredients; mix well. Press mixture into a 13- x 9- x 2-inch ungreased baking pan; spread melted chocolate morsels evenly over top. Chill 30 minutes. Cut into 1½-inch squares. Yield: about 4 dozen. *Darlene Dakin, Drakesboro, Kentucky.*

## PEANUT BUTTER-HONEY MUFFINS

1 cup all-purpose flour
1 cup quick-cooking whole wheat cereal
1½ teaspoons baking powder
¼ teaspoon salt
¾ cup milk
⅓ cup honey
¼ cup vegetable oil
⅓ cup crunchy peanut butter
1 egg, beaten

Combine first 4 ingredients in a large bowl; make a well in center of mixture. Combine milk, honey, oil, peanut butter, and egg; add to dry ingredients, stirring just until moistened. Spoon batter into greased muffin pans, filling two-thirds full. Bake at 400° for 20 to 25 minutes. Yield: 1 dozen. *Bobby McVey, Hutchinson, Kansas.*

# Enjoy Cherries Now

Although fresh cherries aren't available until late May, you can enjoy these plump berries anytime—canned, frozen, or in prepared pie filling.

For cherry pie, start with one that turned out so well in our test kitchens that we call it Prize-Winning Cherry Pie. The flavor of a few ounces of grenadine syrup changes an ordinary pie into a delectable creation; a tender, flaky double-crust pastry encloses this goodness.

Surprise Cherry Squares were another favorite with our test kitchen staff because they're so easy to make and remind everyone of cherry-flavored doughnuts. Inside each cakelike square is a dollop of rich cherry pie filling.

Sweet red wine complements the flavor of dark cherries in Elegant Cherry-Wine Salad. Cherry-Orange Salad features a refreshing combination of cherries, mandarin orange slices, green grapes, and miniature marshmallows.

## CHERRY-ORANGE SALAD

¼ cup frozen orange juice concentrate, thawed
2 eggs, beaten
¼ cup sugar
½ cup whipping cream, whipped
2 (17-ounce) jars light or dark sweet cherries, drained and pitted
1 (11-ounce) can mandarin oranges, drained
2 cups miniature marshmallows
2 cups green grapes

Combine orange juice, eggs, and sugar in a small saucepan. Cook over low heat, stirring constantly, until thickened. Cool.

Fold whipped cream into orange juice mixture. Add remaining ingredients, stirring gently until coated. Chill 1 hour. Yield: 8 to 10 servings. *Kay Baker, Laurel, Florida.*

## ELEGANT CHERRY-WINE SALAD

2 (16½-ounce) cans pitted dark sweet cherries
2 (3-ounce) packages cherry-flavored gelatin
1 envelope unflavored gelatin
2 cups boiling water
½ cup port or other sweet red wine
¼ cup lemon juice

Drain cherries, reserving 1⅓ cups liquid. Cut cherries in half; set aside.

Dissolve gelatin in boiling water; let cool slightly. Stir in reserved cherry liquid, port, and lemon juice; chill until the consistency of unbeaten egg white. Fold in cherries. Pour gelatin mixture into a lightly oiled 6-cup ring mold. Chill until firm. Yield: 8 to 10 servings. *Audrey Bledsoe, Smyrna, Georgia.*

## CHERRY UPSIDE-DOWN CAKE

1 cup butter or margarine, divided
2 cups sugar, divided
1 (16-ounce) can pitted tart cherries, drained
1 cup chopped pecans
2 eggs
2½ cups all-purpose flour
1 tablespoon baking powder
¼ teaspoon salt
⅔ cup milk
1 teaspoon vanilla extract
Whipped cream (optional)
Fresh cherries (optional)
Pecan halves (optional)

Melt ⅓ cup butter in a 10-inch cast-iron skillet. Spread ½ cup sugar evenly over butter; continue cooking over low heat until sugar is dissolved. Arrange cherries and chopped pecans in skillet; remove from heat, and set aside.

Cream remaining ⅔ cup butter; gradually add remaining 1½ cups sugar, beating until light and fluffy. Add eggs, one at a time, beating well after each addition.

Combine flour, baking powder, and salt; stir well and add to creamed mixture alternately with milk, beginning and ending with flour mixture. Stir in vanilla.

Spoon batter evenly over cherries and pecans in skillet. Bake at 350° for 50 minutes or until cake tests done. Cool in skillet 10 minutes; invert cake onto a plate. Cool cake completely. Top with whipped cream and garnish with cherries and pecan halves, if desired. Yield: one 10-inch cake. *Mrs. E. T. Williams, Baton Rouge, Louisiana.*

## PRIZE-WINNING CHERRY PIE

1 cup sugar
3 tablespoons cornstarch
¼ teaspoon salt
⅔ cup grenadine syrup
½ teaspoon red food coloring (optional)
2 (16-ounce) packages frozen cherries, thawed
½ teaspoon cherry extract
2 tablespoons butter or margarine
Flaky Double-Crust Pastry
2 teaspoons milk

Combine sugar, cornstarch, and salt in a medium saucepan; stir mixture to remove lumps. Stir grenadine syrup into sugar mixture; add food coloring, if desired. Cook over medium heat until smooth, stirring constantly. Add cherries; simmer until liquid is transparent (about 4 minutes), stirring gently once or twice. Add cherry extract and butter, stirring until butter is melted; cool.

Line a 9-inch deep-dish pieplate with half of pastry (dough is very fragile). Pour cooled cherry mixture into pastry shell.

Cover with top crust. Trim edges of pastry; seal and crimp edges. Cut slits in top of crust for steam to escape. Brush top of pastry lightly with milk. Bake at 400° for 55 minutes or until golden brown. Cool pie before serving. Yield: one 9-inch pie.

*Flaky Double-Crust Pastry:*

3 cups all-purpose flour
¾ teaspoon salt
1 cup shortening
¾ cup half-and-half

Combine flour and salt in bowl; cut in shortening with pastry blender until mixture resembles coarse meal. Sprinkle half-and-half evenly over surface; stir with a fork until all dry ingredients are moistened. Shape dough into a ball; chill. Roll dough to ⅛-inch thickness on a lightly floured surface. Yield: pastry for one double-crust 9-inch pie.

## SURPRISE CHERRY SQUARES

1 cup butter or margarine, softened
1½ cups sugar
4 eggs, beaten
2 cups all-purpose flour
1 teaspoon vanilla extract
1 teaspoon lemon extract
1 (21-ounce) can cherry pie filling

Cream butter; gradually add sugar, beating until light and fluffy. Add eggs, one at a time, beating well after each addition. Gradually add flour, beating well. Stir in flavorings. Pour the batter into a lightly greased 15- x 10- x 1-inch jellyroll pan, spreading evenly.

Lightly cut through batter with a small knife to mark off 24 squares. Spoon about 1 tablespoon pie filling in center of each square. Bake at 350° for 45 minutes or until lightly browned (batter will puff up around filling while baking).

Cool cake in pan 10 minutes. Cut into squares, and remove from pan. Yield: 2 dozen. *Sue Turnbow, Baker, Louisiana.*

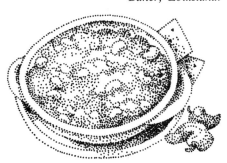

# Talk Of Spicy Chili

When the subject of chili comes up, the talk never ends, for there seem to be as many varieties of the spicy red as there are cooks.

Mrs. J. A. Satterfield of Fort Worth cooks fine egg noodles with her chili, while Mrs. R. A. Dibrell of Dallas adds hominy and cheese. A Corsicana reader, Mrs. Gary Ferguson, starts with a chuck blade steak for Chuck Wagon Chili and sprinkles the spicy result with chopped onion and shredded cheese.

## CHUCK WAGON CHILI

1 (2-pound) boneless chuck blade steak, cut into ½-inch cubes
2 tablespoons vegetable oil
1 cup chopped onion, divided
1 large green pepper, diced
2 cloves garlic, crushed
1 (28-ounce) can whole tomatoes, undrained and chopped
1 (6-ounce) can tomato paste
1 cup water
3 tablespoons chili powder
1 tablespoon salt
1 teaspoon dried whole oregano
½ teaspoon pepper
½ cup (2 ounces) shredded Monterey Jack cheese

Brown meat in oil in a Dutch oven. Remove meat, reserving drippings. Sauté ¾ cup onion, green pepper, and garlic in reserved drippings until tender. Add meat and next 7 ingredients, mixing well. Bring to a boil. Reduce heat; cover and simmer 1½ hours, stirring occasionally. Place in serving bowls; sprinkle with remaining onion and cheese. Yield: about 9 cups. *Mrs. Gary Ferguson, Corsicana, Texas.*

## CHILI WITH NOODLES

3 pounds ground beef
1 medium onion, chopped
2 (1.25-ounce) packages chili seasoning mix
1 (5-ounce) package fine egg noodles
1 (46-ounce) can tomato juice
2 (15½-ounce) cans chili beans
1 tablespoon Worcestershire sauce
½ teaspoon garlic salt
½ teaspoon onion salt
¼ teaspoon pepper

Combine ground beef, onion, and chili seasoning mix in a Dutch oven; cook until beef is browned, stirring to crumble meat. Drain off drippings. Add remaining ingredients, mixing well. Cook over low heat 1 hour, stirring occasionally. Yield: about 12 cups. *Mrs. J. A. Satterfield, Fort Worth, Texas.*

*Tip: During the week, keep a shopping list handy to write down items as you need them. This will eliminate unnecessary trips to the store. Before your weekly shopping trip, make a complete shopping list. If the list is arranged according to the layout of the store, you will save time and steps.*

## CHILI HOMINY BAKE

1 pound ground beef
½ cup chopped onion
2 tablespoons all-purpose flour
1 teaspoon salt
1 teaspoon chili powder
1 (14½-ounce) can hominy, undrained
1 (16-ounce) can tomatoes, undrained and
  chopped
¼ cup (1 ounce) shredded Cheddar cheese
  (optional)

Combine ground beef and onion; cook until beef is browned, stirring to crumble meat. Drain off drippings.

Add remaining ingredients except cheese; stir well. Spoon mixture into a greased 2-quart casserole. Bake, uncovered, at 350° for 25 minutes; sprinkle chili with shredded Cheddar cheese, if desired, and bake 5 additional minutes. Yield: 4 servings. *Mrs. R. A. Dibrell, Dallas, Texas.*

## QUICK AND SIMPLE CHILI

1 pound ground beef
1 cup chopped onion
1 clove garlic, crushed
2 (8-ounce) cans tomato sauce
Salt and pepper to taste
¼ cup chili powder
2 cups water

Combine ground beef, onion, and garlic in a large saucepan; cook until beef is browned, stirring to crumble meat. Drain off drippings. Add the remaining ingredients, and simmer 45 minutes to 1 hour. Yield: about 6 cups. *Becky Reynolds, Rio Vista, Texas.*

## MEATY CHILI

3 pounds ground beef
1 medium onion, chopped
3 small cloves garlic, minced
1 (15-ounce) can tomato sauce
5½ cups water
¼ cup plus 2 tablespoons chili powder
1 tablespoon paprika
1 tablespoon cumin seeds
1 teaspoon salt

Combine ground beef, onion, and garlic in a Dutch oven; cook until beef is browned, stirring to crumble meat. Drain off drippings. Add remaining ingredients, mixing well. Cook over low heat 3 to 4 hours, stirring occasionally. Yield: about 9½ cups. *Judy Irwin, Mabank, Texas.*

# For Perfectly Poached Eggs

As the star of Eggs Benedict and numerous other out-of-the-ordinary dishes, poached eggs make everyday meals a savory delight.

If you've avoided poaching eggs because you thought they were too hard to make, you're in for a pleasant surprise. Several types of equipment now on the market make egg poaching easier for today's cook.

Poacher cups, designed to be set in a skillet or in electric covered egg cookers, create pretty, evenly shaped eggs. To cook eggs in poacher cups in a pan or skillet, use a pastry brush to coat the cups with oil or margarine. Set the poacher cups in a skillet of boiling water. The water level should be just below the bottom of the poacher. Reduce the heat to simmer, and cook 3 to 5 minutes or to desired doneness. Lift the poacher cups from the hot skillet with a fork. Loosen cooked eggs with a spatula and slide onto toasted bread or muffins.

It must be noted that the eggs cooked in poacher cups and in covered egg cookers are not true poached eggs. They actually are steamed. Traditional poached eggs are cooked directly in hot liquid.

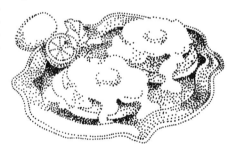

## BASIC POACHED EGGS

Fill a saucepan with 1½ inches of salted water, and heat to boiling. You may want to use nonaluminum cookware since eggs leave a dark deposit on aluminum surfaces. (To poach four eggs at a time, use a deep 10-inch skillet.) When the water boils, lower the heat to simmer. Break the eggs, one at a time, into a custard cup. Hold the lip of the cup close to the water, and gently slip the egg into the pan or skillet. Simmer until eggs reach desired degree of doneness. Do not allow the water to boil since eggs cooked at high temperatures will have tough whites and mealy yolks. Remove the egg with a slotted spoon or pancake turner, and drain well over paper towels.

For neatly cooked poached eggs, use only fresh, cold eggs. The whites of older eggs will coagulate in shreds on contact with hot liquid. Refrigerator-cold eggs will cook in neater form than those at room temperature.

For perfectly round eggs, set a greased metal ring in the bottom of the pan. A tuna can with both ends removed can be used. Slide the egg into the center of the ring. When the egg white sets, remove the ring and continue to cook.

## FRENCH-STYLE POACHED EGGS

French-style poached eggs should be cooked one at a time. Add 1 tablespoon of vinegar to salted water, and bring to a boil. (The vinegar helps to set the egg white.) Break the egg into a custard cup. Hold the cup in one hand, and swirl the boiling water with a spoon in the other hand to form a deep whirlpool in the center of the pan. Slip the egg into the center of the whirlpool, and reduce the heat to simmer. As the egg spins, the white will wrap around the yolk and create an oval shape with the white completely surrounding the yolk. Continue to cook to desired doneness.

## SERVING SUGGESTIONS

■ Although most poached egg recipes call for salted, simmering water, a variety of liquids may be used to tempt the adventurous cook. Milk, soup, tomato juice, broth, vegetable cocktail juice, or wine may be substituted.

■ To keep poached eggs hot before serving time, let them rest in a bowl of hot water until time to serve. Drain well to avoid a soggy underpinning if the egg is to be served on toast or a muffin.

■ Don't reserve poached egg dishes for morning meals only. Try poached eggs atop codfish cakes smothered with cheese sauce or in a nest of finely chopped spinach capped with white sauce and sprinkled with cheese. Experiment with poached eggs on rice or noodles, and serve with leftover gravy or mushroom, onion, or tomato sauce. A cream sauce seasoned with herbs, onion, celery, or green pepper can spice up any poached egg dish.

*Tip: Do not wash eggs before storing; washing removes the coating that prevents the entrance of bacteria. Wash just before using, if desired.*

# Appetizers To Warm The Party

Most parties would not be complete without an array of dips or spreads. If you've been relying on cold appetizers, try serving some of these appealing hot dips at your next gathering.

If it's seafood you're interested in, offer Oven-Baked Crab Dip or Hot Clam Dip. Vegetable lovers will go for Cheesy Spinach Dip and Broccoli-Garlic Dip. For something unusual, serve Meaty Cheese Dip. It's a spicy mixture of ground beef, tomatoes and green chiles, and chili seasoning mix. Kept in a chafing dish, this dip will be just the right temperature to enjoy with assorted crackers or corn chips.

## MEATY CHEESE DIP

½ pound ground beef
1 clove garlic, minced
2 pounds process cheese spread, cut into 1-inch cubes
1 (10-ounce) can tomatoes and green chiles, undrained and chopped
2 tablespoons chili seasoning mix

Cook ground beef and garlic until meat is browned, stirring to crumble meat. Drain well, and set aside.

Place cheese and tomatoes and green chiles in top of double boiler; bring water to a boil. Reduce heat to low; cook until cheese is melted, stirring constantly. Stir in ground beef and chili seasoning mix. Serve warm with corn chips or assorted crackers. Yield: about 4½ cups.
*Deanne Anthony,*
*Poteau, Oklahoma.*

## HOT CLAM DIP

2 (8-ounce) packages cream cheese, softened
1 (6½-ounce) can minced clams, undrained
1 teaspoon Creole seasoning
½ clove garlic, crushed
Juice of 1 lemon
Paprika

Combine all ingredients except paprika in a medium saucepan; cook over low heat, stirring constantly, until mixture is smooth and well heated. Sprinkle with paprika. Serve warm with crackers. Yield: about 2½ cups.
*Joanne Champagne,*
*Covington, Louisiana.*

## OVEN-BAKED CRAB DIP

2 (8-ounce) packages cream cheese, softened
⅓ cup mayonnaise
1 tablespoon powdered sugar
1 tablespoon Chablis or other dry white wine
½ teaspoon onion juice
½ teaspoon prepared mustard
¼ teaspoon garlic salt
¼ teaspoon salt
1 (6-ounce) can crabmeat, drained and flaked
Chopped fresh parsley

Combine first 8 ingredients; mix well. Gently stir in crabmeat. Spoon crabmeat mixture into a lightly greased 1-quart baking dish. Bake at 375° for 15 minutes. Sprinkle with parsley. Serve warm with crackers. Yield: about 2¾ cups.
*Grace Bravos,*
*Timonium, Maryland.*

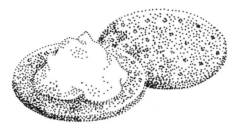

## BROCCOLI-GARLIC DIP

1 (10-ounce) package frozen chopped broccoli
1 (6-ounce) roll process cheese food with garlic, cubed
1 (10¾-ounce) can cream of mushroom soup, undiluted
½ cup chopped almonds, toasted

Cook broccoli according to package directions, omitting salt; drain and press well to remove liquid.

Combine cheese and soup in a heavy saucepan; place over low heat, stirring frequently, until cheese melts. Stir in broccoli and almonds. Serve warm with crackers. Yield: about 2 cups.
*Patricia Pashby,*
*Memphis, Tennessee.*

## CHEESY SPINACH DIP

1 (10-ounce) package frozen chopped spinach
1 tablespoon butter or margarine
1 tablespoon all-purpose flour
1 cup (4 ounces) shredded Cheddar cheese
½ cup commercial sour cream
½ teaspoon onion salt
¼ teaspoon lemon juice
⅛ teaspoon pepper

Cook spinach according to package directions, omitting salt; drain and press well to remove liquid.

Melt butter in a heavy saucepan over low heat; add flour, stirring until smooth. Cook 1 minute, stirring constantly. Add spinach and remaining ingredients; stir well. Serve warm with crackers. Yield: about 2 cups.
*Heather Riggins,*
*Nashville, Tennessee.*

# Get Out The Skillet For A Texas Supper

When a Chinese neighbor prepared weekly Saturday night suppers for Mary Ann Owens' family 20 years ago, a favorite with everyone was a skillet dish of pineapple and pork in a sweet-and-sour sauce. Mary Ann, who now lives in Houston, still serves Pineapple Pork to her family; she spoons the Oriental-style dish over fluffy white rice and completes the meal with a fresh green salad.

The nice thing about Pineapple Pork and our other skillet dishes is that all it takes is the addition of a simple salad or cooked vegetable to make a satisfying, nutritious meal.

For Skillet Company Chicken, chicken breasts are simmered in a mixture of carbonated beverage and chopped vegetables. Stir in sour cream if you like, but if you're cutting calories, just serve the chicken with the vegetables and juices from the skillet.

## BEEFY BEANS

1 pound ground beef
2 cups chopped celery
½ cup chopped onion
1 (16-ounce) can whole tomatoes
2 (16-ounce) cans pork and beans
½ cup catsup
⅓ cup firmly packed brown sugar
¼ cup Worcestershire sauce
1 tablespoon lemon juice
¼ teaspoon salt
¼ teaspoon pepper

Combine ground beef, celery, and onion in a large skillet; cook until meat is browned and vegetables are tender. Drain mixture well. Stir in remaining ingredients; cover and simmer 30 minutes. Yield: 6 servings. *Ruby Bonelli,*
*Pearland, Texas.*

## GROUND BEEF SKILLET DINNER

1 pound ground beef
1 cup chopped onion
1 cup chopped green pepper
3 cups tomato juice
1 (5-ounce) package egg noodles
1 to 1½ teaspoons salt
1 teaspoon celery salt
2 teaspoons Worcestershire sauce
⅛ teaspoon pepper
1 (8-ounce) carton commercial sour cream

Cook ground beef, onion, and green pepper over medium heat in a skillet until meat is browned, stirring to crumble meat. Drain well.

Stir in remaining ingredients except sour cream; cover and simmer 20 to 25 minutes. Stir in sour cream, and cook until thoroughly heated (do not boil). Yield: 4 to 6 servings. *Margot Foster, Hubbard, Texas.*

## QUICK SAUCY HAMBURGERS

1½ pounds ground beef
2 tablespoons dry onion soup mix
¼ teaspoon salt
⅛ teaspoon pepper
2 tablespoons all-purpose flour
1 tablespoon vegetable oil
1 tablespoon chopped onion
1 tablespoon chopped green pepper
1 clove garlic, minced
1 (8-ounce) can tomato sauce
¼ cup catsup
1 teaspoon Worcestershire sauce
Dash of hot sauce
1 bay leaf
½ teaspoon chili powder
6 hamburger buns, split and toasted
  (optional)

Combine first 4 ingredients, and shape into 6 balls; roll in flour, and flatten slightly. Heat oil in a large skillet; add patties, and brown on both sides. Remove hamburger patties, and set aside; drain off pan drippings, reserving 1 tablespoon in skillet.

Add onion, green pepper, and garlic to pan drippings; cook until tender. Stir in next 6 ingredients. Add patties; cover and simmer 15 minutes. Turn patties; cover and continue to cook 10 minutes. Remove bay leaf; serve patties with buns, if desired. Yield: 6 servings.

*Jodell Wright, Houston, Texas.*

## SKILLET COMPANY CHICKEN

3 whole chicken breasts, skinned and split
Salt and pepper
¼ cup butter or margarine
4 green onions, chopped
1 medium-size green pepper, chopped
½ cup chopped celery
½ pound fresh mushrooms, sliced
1 (12-ounce) can or 1½ cups lemon-lime carbonated beverage
¼ teaspoon rosemary, crushed
1 (8-ounce) carton commercial sour cream
  (optional)
Paprika
Hot cooked rice

Sprinkle chicken with salt and pepper. Sauté chicken in butter in a large skillet over medium heat until browned. Remove chicken; set aside.

Add vegetables to pan drippings; cook until tender. Add lemon-lime beverage and rosemary. Return chicken to skillet; cover and cook over low heat 20 to 30 minutes or until tender. Remove chicken to serving platter; keep warm.

Add sour cream to vegetable mixture, if desired. Cook over low heat, stirring, until heated (do not boil). Spoon mixture over chicken; then sprinkle with paprika, and serve with rice. Yield: 6 servings. *Mrs. F. W. Armstrong, Dallas, Texas.*

## PINEAPPLE PORK

1 (20-ounce) can pineapple chunks
1 tablespoon vegetable oil
1½ pounds boneless pork, trimmed of fat and cut into 1-inch cubes
1 medium onion, chopped
¼ cup firmly packed brown sugar
2 tablespoons cornstarch
½ teaspoon salt
½ cup water
⅓ cup vinegar
2 tablespoons catsup
1 tablespoon soy sauce
1 green pepper, cut into 1-inch pieces
Hot cooked rice

Drain pineapple, reserving juice.

Heat oil in a large skillet; add pork, and cook until lightly browned. Add onion, and cook until tender. Combine sugar, cornstarch, and salt in a small bowl. Add water, stirring until smooth. Stir in pineapple juice, vinegar, catsup, and soy sauce. Add mixture to pork, stirring constantly; cook until thickened. Cover and simmer 1 hour. Stir in pineapple and green pepper; cover and cook 3 minutes. Serve with rice. Yield: 4 to 6 servings. *Mary Ann Owens, Houston, Texas.*

## PORK RISOTTO

2 pounds pork shoulder blade steaks (¾ inch thick)
1 tablespoon vegetable oil
1 teaspoon salt
¼ cup water
1 (10¾-ounce) can chicken broth
1 cup uncooked regular rice
½ cup chopped onion
1 cup water
1 (10-ounce) package frozen English peas

Brown steaks on both sides in hot oil in a 10-inch skillet. Sprinkle steaks with salt, and add ¼ cup water. Cover; simmer 45 minutes. Remove steaks from skillet.

Stir broth, rice, onion, and 1 cup water into drippings; add steaks. Cover and simmer 20 to 25 minutes or until liquid is absorbed. Stir in peas; cook mixture 5 to 8 minutes or until peas are thoroughly heated. Yield: 6 servings.

*Carolyn Look, El Paso, Texas.*

## CURRIED HAM AND PEACHES

1 (16-ounce) can peach halves
1 tablespoon butter or margarine
4 slices cooked ham (about ¾ pound)
1 teaspoon curry powder
2 tablespoons brown sugar
1 tablespoon butter or margarine

Drain peach halves, reserving syrup. Set aside.

Melt 1 tablespoon butter in a large skillet. Brown ham in butter; remove and set aside. Add peach syrup and curry powder to pan drippings. Place peach halves, cut side down, in syrup mixture; cook over medium heat 2 minutes. Turn peaches; fill cavities with brown sugar, and dot with remaining butter. Return ham to skillet; cover and cook 3 minutes. Yield: 4 servings.

*Mary Ann Lewis, Houston, Texas.*

Right: *Open-Face Ham Sandwiches and Ham-Rice Toss will keep ham in demand at your house, even as a leftover (recipes on page 40).*

Page 64: *Enjoy the fine flavor of fresh spinach in Cream of Spinach Soup (page 38) and in colorful Chinese Spinach (page 39).*

Far left: *Blueberries and peaches lend flavor and color to Lemon Crêpes With Fruit Filling (page 46).*

Left: *Plan your next brunch around Crabmeat and Eggs New Orleans (page 45); here, this spectacular entrée is garnished with sugar-frosted grapes (page 51), orange slices, and fresh mint leaves.*

Below: *Before serving, drench each slice of Baked Toast Amandine (page 47) with warm almond syrup.*

# Make The Bread Whole Grain

You can help improve your family's nutrition by baking whole grain breads. The wonderful flavor of a homemade loaf or muffin will convert even the staunchest of white-bread fans.

Bread becomes whole grain when white flour is replaced with whole wheat or rye. Or you can stir unprocessed bran or granola into the dough to achieve a full, fiber-rich texture. In addition to dietary fiber, whole grain breads also provide trace vitamins and minerals not present in regular white bread.

Several of our readers have found delicious ways to increase their family's intake of fiber. Mrs. Ralph Dillon of Boone, North Carolina, treats her children to a wholesome breakfast of toasted Whole Wheat Quick Bread. Spread with peanut butter and served with milk and fruit, it's a complete, nutritious meal.

## RYE SANDWICH BREAD

About 2¼ cups all-purpose flour, divided
1 cup rye flour
1 package dry yeast
1 tablespoon grated orange rind
1 teaspoon anise seeds
1 teaspoon salt
1 cup water
¼ cup molasses
1 tablespoon vegetable oil
Melted butter or margarine (optional)

Combine 1 cup all-purpose flour, rye flour, yeast, rind, anise seeds, and salt in a large mixing bowl; stir well. Combine water, molasses, and oil in a small saucepan; heat mixture to 130°, stirring occasionally.

Gradually add hot liquid mixture to dry ingredients, beating at low speed of electric mixer 30 seconds. Beat 3 additional minutes at high speed. Gradually add enough of remaining flour to form a moderately stiff dough, beating well after each addition.

Turn dough out onto a lightly floured surface, and knead until smooth and elastic (about 8 minutes). Shape into a ball, and place in a well-greased bowl; turn to grease top. Cover and let rise in a warm place (85°), free from drafts, 1½ hours or until doubled in bulk.

Punch dough down; let rest 10 minutes. Shape into a ball, and place in a well-greased 1½-quart oven-proof bowl. Let rise about 1 hour or until doubled in bulk.

Brush top with melted butter, if soft crust is desired. Bake at 350° for 35 to 40 minutes or until loaf sounds hollow when tapped. Transfer loaf to a wire rack to cool. Yield: 1 loaf.

*Doris Amonette,*
*Mount Clemens, Michigan.*

## WHOLE WHEAT QUICK BREAD

2 cups whole wheat flour
½ cup firmly packed brown sugar
1 teaspoon baking powder
1 teaspoon soda
¾ teaspoon salt
1 egg, beaten
1½ cups buttermilk
½ cup raisins
½ cup chopped pecans or walnuts

Combine first 5 ingredients in a large mixing bowl; stir well. Add egg and buttermilk, and mix well. Stir in raisins and pecans. Spoon into a greased and floured 8- x 4- x 3-inch loafpan; bake at 350° about 55 minutes or until a wooden pick inserted in center comes out clean. Yield: 1 loaf.       *Mrs. Ralph Dillon,*
*Boone, North Carolina.*

## WHOLE WHEAT HONEY BREAD

2½ cups warm water (105° to 115°)
⅓ cup instant nonfat dry milk powder
⅓ cup shortening
¼ cup honey
2 packages dry yeast
1 tablespoon salt
3½ cups whole wheat flour
About 3½ cups all-purpose flour

Combine first 6 ingredients in a large mixing bowl; let stand 5 minutes. Add whole wheat flour; mix with electric mixer at low speed until blended. Increase speed to medium, and beat 3 minutes. Gradually add remaining flour.

Turn dough out onto a heavily floured surface (dough will be sticky), and knead until smooth and elastic. Cover and let rest in a warm place (85°), free from drafts, 15 minutes. (Dough will be soft.)

Divide dough in half; place each half in a greased 9- x 5- x 3-inch loafpan. Cover and let rise in a warm place (85°), free from drafts, about 1½ hours or until doubled in bulk. Bake at 375° for 40 to 45 minutes or until loaves sound hollow when tapped. Transfer loaves to wire racks to cool. Yield: 2 loaves.       *Teri Isenhour,*
*Charlotte, North Carolina.*

## BEST EVER NUT CRUNCH MUFFINS

1½ cups unbleached all-purpose flour
½ cup sugar
¼ cup cornmeal
¼ cup wheat germ
2 tablespoons baking powder
½ teaspoon salt
1½ cups unprocessed bran
½ cup granola
2 cups buttermilk
1½ tablespoons crunchy peanut butter
2½ tablespoons vegetable oil
2 eggs, beaten

Combine the first 6 ingredients in a large mixing bowl; set mixture aside.

Combine bran, granola, and buttermilk; mix well, and soak 5 minutes. Add peanut butter, vegetable oil, and eggs, mixing well.

Make a well in center of dry ingredients; pour in liquid ingredients. Stir just until moistened.

Fill greased muffin pans two-thirds full. Bake at 400° for 25 minutes. Remove from pan immediately. Yield: about 2 dozen.       *Kim Chutter,*
*San Antonio, Texas.*

*Tip: Have your oven thermostat professionally checked at least once a year. Another way to occasionally check oven temperature is to prepare a cake mix according to package directions; the cake should cook the entire recommended time and test done (a wooden pick inserted in the center should come out clean).*

*You'll forget about the salt when you sit down to Roasted Rock Cornish Hens, Squash Sauté, Low-Sodium Refrigerator Rolls, and a salad with Lemon-Herb Salad Dressing.*

## Cooking Light

# Go Light On The Salt

If you've been told you have hypertension (high blood pressure), eating less sodium will help keep your blood pressure under control. And even if your blood pressure is normal, eating less sodium is a positive step toward healthier nutrition. To help you get started, we've put together an entire kitchen-tested low-sodium menu.

Roasted Rock Cornish Hens is the focus of our menu. Note that unsalted margarine is used to baste the hens during roasting, while herbs are the seasoning for the Low-Sodium Stuffing.

The vegetable of the day is Squash Sauté, a combination of fresh zucchini and yellow squash. While fresh vegetables contain little sodium, salt is generally added to frozen vegetables packaged in a sauce and most canned

vegetables. Also, many people season vegetables with generous amounts of salt, or they use other salty seasonings, such as bouillon cubes, bacon drippings, salt pork, or salted butter or margarine.

The seasonings for our low-sodium squash dish are unsalted margarine, garlic, and oregano—a pleasing blend that's also good with other vegetables.

Fresh vegetables are also our choice for a salad, again taking advantage of their low-sodium quality. But since commercial salad dressings are generally forbidden to a sodium watcher, we suggest our salt-free Lemon-Herb Salad Dressing for the tossed greens. It's a flavorful combination of safflower oil and several herbs, including garlic, oregano, and basil.

Even our dinner rolls are prepared without salt. The rolls are so low in sodium that they could be enjoyed on even the strictest of low-sodium diets. Instead of spreading the hot rolls with salted butter or margarine, choose the unsalted kind. Better still, try Herbed Unsalted Butter for a change—you'll find it delicious not only for rolls, but also as a seasoning for cooked vegetables.

**Roasted Rock Cornish Hens**
**Green Salad**
**Lemon-Herb Salad Dressing**
**Squash Sauté**
**Low-Sodium Refrigerator Rolls**
**Herbed Unsalted Butter**
**Nutty Pumpkin Pie**

### ROASTED ROCK CORNISH HENS

**4 (1½-pound) Cornish hens**
**Low-Sodium Stuffing**
**2 tablespoons unsalted margarine, melted**
**Green grapes (optional)**

Remove giblets from hens, and reserve for another use. Rinse hens with cold water, and pat dry. Lift wingtips up and over back so they are tucked under hen.

Stuff hens lightly with Low-Sodium Stuffing. Close cavities, and secure with wooden picks; truss. Tie leg ends together with string or cord.

Brush hens with half of the unsalted margarine, and place breast side up in a 13- x 9- x 2-inch baking pan. Cover tightly with foil, and bake at 350° for 1 hour. Uncover and bake at 400° for 15 additional minutes, basting often with remaining margarine. Split hens before serving; garnish with green grapes, if desired. Yield: 8 servings (about 142 milligrams sodium per serving).

*Low-Sodium Stuffing:*
**½ cup finely chopped onion**
**1 teaspoon finely chopped green pepper**
**1 clove garlic, minced**
**2 tablespoons unsalted margarine**
**3 cups low-sodium breadcrumbs**
**1 tablespoon minced fresh parsley**
**2 eggs, well beaten**
**½ cup water**
**½ teaspoon butter flavoring**
**1½ teaspoons ground savory**
**½ teaspoon dried whole thyme**
**¼ teaspoon dried whole marjoram**
**¼ teaspoon pepper**

Sauté onion, green pepper, and garlic in unsalted margarine until tender. Combine vegetables with remaining ingredients, mixing well. Yield: enough stuffing for 4 Cornish hens.
*Mrs. Earl L. Faulkenberry,*
*Lancaster, South Carolina.*

*Tip: Always try to use a meat thermometer when roasting. This can usually prevent overcooking. Get in the habit of using a minute timer for precise cooking. Do follow your recipes; they were meant as a guide.*

## LEMON-HERB SALAD DRESSING

1 cup safflower oil
⅓ cup fresh lemon juice
1 small clove garlic, minced
¼ teaspoon pepper
¼ teaspoon dried whole oregano
¼ teaspoon dried whole basil
¼ teaspoon dried whole tarragon

Combine all ingredients in a jar. Cover tightly, and shake vigorously. Chill several hours. Serve dressing over salad greens. Yield: 1⅓ cups (less than 1 milligram sodium per tablespoon).
*Mildred Carkern,*
*Jackson, Mississippi.*

## SQUASH SAUTE

1 pound zucchini, sliced
1 pound yellow squash, sliced
2 cloves garlic, minced
¼ cup unsalted margarine
½ teaspoon dried whole oregano
⅛ teaspoon pepper
1 tomato, cut into 8 wedges

Sauté squash and garlic in margarine until crisp-tender; stir in the seasonings. Add tomato wedges, and cook just until heated. Yield: 8 servings (about 2 milligrams sodium per serving).
*Mrs. J. Fishback,*
*Cookeville, Tennessee.*

## LOW-SODIUM REFRIGERATOR ROLLS

2 packages dry yeast
¼ cup warm water (105° to 115°)
1 tablespoon sugar
1 cup boiling water
¾ cup shortening
¾ cup cold water
¼ cup sugar
2 eggs, beaten
6 cups all-purpose flour
Melted unsalted margarine

Dissolve yeast in warm water; add 1 tablespoon sugar, and set aside. Pour boiling water over shortening in a large bowl, stirring to melt shortening. Stir in cold water and ¼ cup sugar; add eggs and yeast mixture, mixing well. Gradually add flour, mixing well. Cover and chill 24 hours.

Turn dough out onto a lightly floured surface, and knead 2 to 3 minutes. Shape dough into 1½-inch balls; dip in melted margarine, and place on greased baking sheets. Let rise in a warm place (85°), free from drafts, 1 hour or until doubled in bulk.

Bake rolls at 400° for 20 to 25 minutes or until lightly browned. Yield: about 3 dozen (about 4 milligrams sodium per roll).

## HERBED UNSALTED BUTTER

½ cup unsalted butter or margarine, softened
1 teaspoon chopped chives
½ teaspoon dried dillweed
½ teaspoon chopped fresh parsley
¾ teaspoon lemon juice
Dash of hot sauce

Combine all ingredients, and beat until light and fluffy. Store in a covered container in refrigerator until ready to use. Serve with rolls, or use on vegetables. Yield: about ½ cup (less than 1 milligram sodium per serving).
*Linda Harbour,*
*Birmingham, Alabama.*

## NUTTY PUMPKIN PIE

1 package unflavored gelatin
¼ cup cold water
1½ cups canned pumpkin
¾ cup sugar
2 tablespoons unsalted margarine
1 teaspoon grated orange rind
2 tablespoons orange juice
1 teaspoon ground cinnamon
½ teaspoon ground nutmeg
Sesame Pastry Shell
½ cup chopped pecans

Soften gelatin in water; let stand 5 minutes.

Combine gelatin and next 7 ingredients in a heavy saucepan, mixing well; cook over medium heat, stirring constantly, 3 to 4 minutes or until mixture is thoroughly heated. Pour into pastry shell, and sprinkle pecans on top. Chill until firm. Yield: 8 servings (about 2 milligrams sodium per serving).

*Sesame Pastry Shell:*

1 cup all-purpose flour
¼ teaspoon grated lemon rind
⅛ teaspoon ground mace
½ to 1 teaspoon sesame seeds
⅓ cup shortening
2 tablespoons cold water

Combine flour, lemon rind, mace, and sesame seeds; cut in shortening with pastry blender until mixture resembles coarse meal. Sprinkle cold water evenly over surface, and stir with a fork until all dry ingredients are moistened. Shape dough into a ball; chill.

Roll dough to ⅛-inch thickness on a lightly floured surface. Fit pastry into a 9-inch pieplate, and flute edges as desired. Bake at 475° for 8 to 10 minutes or until golden. Yield: one 9-inch pastry shell.
*Kathleen Stone,*
*Houston, Texas.*

# Microwave Cookery

# Entrées In 25 Minutes Or Less

Although the main dish is the most important part of any meal, it doesn't have to be the most time consuming to prepare. All the entrées included here microwave in 25 minutes or less—much less in the case of Saucy Sole, which takes only about 5 minutes. Even the Mock Filet Mignon Patties require just 23 minutes of microwaving.

Without question, a microwave oven dramatically reduces cooking time, but that's only part of the story of meal preparation. Getting a dish ready to microwave takes time, too. With some recipes, even this time can be reduced. The key is doing some of the preparation in advance. For example, flatten the chicken breasts for Chicken and Spinach Rollups as soon as you buy them rather than waiting until close to mealtime.

Also, learn to use cooking time for making sauces, toppings, and any other preparation that can be done simultaneously. With Veal, Italian Style, you can easily mix up the Italian Tomato Sauce while the veal is cooking.

With all of our microwave entrées, a time range is given in each recipe to allow for the difference in wattage of microwave ovens. To prevent overcooking, always check for doneness at the lower end of the range. Here are two other pointers on microwaving.

—Whenever a meat or chicken dish needs to be covered during microwaving, waxed paper works best. Use heavy-duty plastic wrap to cover vegetables or fish.

—Don't be tempted to increase the amount of seasonings called for in a microwave recipe. You can easily overdo it because there's usually less liquid to reduce their flavor; you can always add more after tasting.

## MOCK FILET MIGNON PATTIES

**6 slices bacon**
**1 pound lean ground beef**
**2 tablespoons fine, dry breadcrumbs**
**1 tablespoon dried parsley flakes**
**¼ teaspoon salt**
**¼ teaspoon garlic salt**
**⅛ teaspoon pepper**
**1 teaspoon soy sauce**
**1 (2½-ounce) jar sliced mushrooms,**
**  drained**
**1 medium onion, thinly sliced**
**⅓ cup chopped green pepper**

Place bacon on a bacon rack in a 12- x 8- x 2-inch baking dish; cover with paper towels. Microwave at HIGH for 5½ to 7½ minutes or until bacon is done; crumble bacon, and set aside.

Combine ground beef and next 5 ingredients; mix well. Shape mixture into 8 patties about ¼ inch thick. Place one-fourth of bacon on center of each of 4 patties; top with remaining patties, and press edges to seal.

Place patties in a 12- x 8- x 2-inch baking dish. Cover with waxed paper, and microwave at HIGH for 2½ minutes. Turn patties over; cover and microwave 1½ to 3 additional minutes or until desired degree of doneness.

Remove patties to serving platter; cover and let stand. Drain off all but 2 tablepoons drippings from baking dish; add remaining ingredients to dish. Cover with heavy-duty plastic wrap, and microwave at HIGH for 8 to 10 minutes or until vegetables are tender. Spoon over patties. Yield: 4 servings.

## VEAL, ITALIAN STYLE

**4 (¼-inch-thick) veal cutlets**
**¼ cup all-purpose flour**
**½ teaspoon salt**
**⅛ teaspoon pepper**
**1 egg**
**2 tablespoons milk**
**⅔ cup fine, dry breadcrumbs**
**½ teaspoon paprika**
**2 tablespoons olive oil**
**Italian Tomato Sauce**
**¾ cup (3 ounces) shredded mozzarella**
**  cheese**
**1 tablespoon grated Parmesan cheese**
**2 teaspoons chopped fresh parsley**

Remove and discard any excess fat from cutlets. Place cutlets on waxed paper, and flatten to ⅛-inch thickness with a meat mallet or rolling pin.

Combine flour, salt, and pepper; stir well. Combine egg and milk, beating well. Combine breadcrumbs and paprika, stirring well. Dredge cutlets in

flour mixture; then dip in egg mixture, and thoroughly coat with breadcrumb mixture.

Pour oil into a 12- x 8- x 2-inch baking dish; arrange cutlets in dish. Cover with waxed paper, and microwave at MEDIUM (50% power) for 14 to 16 minutes or until done.

Spoon Italian Tomato Sauce over cutlets; sprinkle with mozzarella cheese, and top with Parmesan. Microwave, uncovered, at MEDIUM for 2 to 3 minutes or until cheese melts. Sprinkle with parsley. Yield: 4 servings.

*Italian Tomato Sauce:*

**¼ cup chopped onion**
**1 tablespoon olive oil**
**1 (8-ounce) can tomato sauce**
**½ teaspoon dried whole basil**

Combine onion and oil in a 1-quart casserole. Cover with heavy-duty plastic wrap, and microwave at HIGH for 1 to 2 minutes or until onion is tender. Stir in tomato sauce and basil. Microwave, uncovered, at HIGH for 3 to 4 minutes or until sauce is thickened. Yield: about 1 cup.

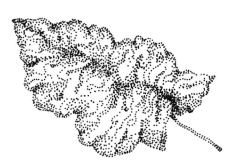

## CHICKEN AND SPINACH ROLLUPS

**1 (10-ounce) package frozen chopped**
**  spinach, thawed**
**1 tablespoon butter or margarine**
**½ cup seasoned dry breadcrumbs**
**½ cup finely chopped onion**
**1 egg, beaten**
**2 tablespoons grated Parmesan cheese**
**¼ teaspoon garlic powder**
**¼ teaspoon pepper**
**1 teaspoon lemon juice**
**3 whole chicken breasts, split, boned, and**
**  skinned**
**1 egg, beaten**
**⅓ cup seasoned dry breadcrumbs**

Place spinach on paper towels, and squeeze until barely moist.

Place butter in a medium bowl; microwave at HIGH for 30 seconds or until butter melts. Add spinach and next 7 ingredients, stirring well; set aside.

Place chicken breasts on waxed paper. Flatten to ¼-inch thickness, using a meat mallet or rolling pin. Top each with an equal amount of spinach mixture, and spread evenly. Roll up each, and secure with a wooden pick; dip in egg, and coat with remaining breadcrumbs.

Place rolls, seam side down, in a 12- x 8- x 2-inch baking dish. Cover with waxed paper, and microwave at HIGH for 9 to 12 minutes or until done; rotate dish after 4 minutes, and rearrange rolls so uncooked portions are to outside of dish. Yield: 6 servings.

## SAUCY SOLE

**¼ cup fine, dry breadcrumbs**
**¼ cup chopped green onion**
**2 tablespoons chopped green pepper**
**1 (6½-ounce) can crabmeat, drained,**
**  rinsed, and flaked**
**1 egg, beaten**
**1 teaspoon lemon juice**
**⅛ teaspoon paprika**
**6 sole fillets (about 1 pound)**
**2 tablespoons butter or margarine**
**Sour Cream Sauce**
**Chopped fresh parsley**

Combine first 7 ingredients, mixing well. Divide crabmeat mixture among fillets, spreading evenly. Roll up each fillet, and secure with a wooden pick; arrange in an 8-inch square baking dish.

Place butter in a 1-cup glass measure, and microwave at HIGH 30 seconds or until butter melts; brush over fillets. Cover with heavy-duty plastic wrap, and microwave at HIGH 3½ to 5½ minutes; rotate dish once during microwaving. Remove fillets to serving dish; top with Sour Cream Sauce, and garnish with parsley. Yield: 6 servings.

*Sour Cream Sauce:*

**1 (8-ounce) carton commercial sour**
**  cream**
**1 teaspoon dry mustard**
**½ teaspoon salt**

Combine all ingredients, stirring well. Yield: 1 cup.

*Tip: It's a good idea to learn as much as you can about the metric system of measuring since these measurements are now appearing on some foods. To give you an idea of some new measurements: 1 cup flour equals 140 grams; 1 cup butter equals 200 grams; and 1 cup sugar equals 190 grams.*

# April

Y ou'll find our pretty, make-ahead mousses in this chapter to be as light and airy as April itself. Chilled Caviar Mousse makes a dainty appetizer spread, while our satiny dessert mousses are flavored with peppermint, apricot, strawberry, and chocolate. We loved testing these creamy creations; cool-tasting Peppermint Candy Mousse became our favorite.

If you're tired of scrambling or frying eggs, try one of our fancy egg dishes like puffy Rolled Mushroom Omelet, Baked Eggs in Spinach Nests, or Eggs in Brandied Cream Sauce. All of these are impressive enough to serve anytime of the day.

Southerners love fried foods no matter what the season, so we scouted out recipes for crispy appetizers to add variety to frying. French-Fried Pickles was a new idea to some of us and a spicy treat you'll want to try if you've never tasted them. Along with these, we offer some recipes for frying crunchy servings of cauliflower, potato skins, cheese, mushrooms, and zucchini.

# Let The Eggs Be Special

What's your favorite way to enjoy eggs? Scrambled and served with a mound of hot grits and strips of bacon on the side? Or perhaps your choice is fried or poached eggs accompanied by hot buttered biscuits. But there's no need to stop there—not with the almost limitless number of ways to present this nutritious food, including main dishes just right for lunch, supper, or the fanciest brunch.

A basic rule in egg cookery is to always cook them at moderate to low temperature. If cooked at high heat or for too long at low heat, eggs become dry and rubbery. Another rule: Always store eggs, large end up, in their original container in the refrigerator. Under these conditions, eggs will stay fresh for up to four or five weeks.

## ROLLED MUSHROOM OMELET

**1 pound bacon**
**1 pound fresh mushrooms, finely chopped**
**1 (0.87-ounce) package white sauce mix**
**1 cup milk**
**12 eggs, separated**
**1 cup (4 ounces) shredded Swiss cheese**

Rub bottom and sides of a 15- x 10- x 1-inch jellyroll pan with vegetable oil. Line with waxed paper, allowing paper to extend beyond ends of pan; rub waxed paper with oil.

Cook bacon, reserving ¼ cup drippings. Set bacon aside, and keep warm. Sauté mushrooms in reserved bacon drippings; drain well, and keep warm.

Prepare white sauce mix according to package directions, using 1 cup milk. Slightly beat egg yolks; gradually stir about one-fourth of white sauce into yolks, and mix well. Add yolk mixture to remaining white sauce; cook over medium heat, stirring constantly, until smooth and thickened.

Beat egg whites (at room temperature) until stiff peaks form. Fold one-third of egg whites into yolk mixture; carefully fold in remaining egg whites.

Pour egg mixture into jellyroll pan, spreading evenly. Bake on center rack of oven at 450° for 12 to 15 minutes or until omelet is puffed and firm to the touch (do not overcook).

Quickly invert jellyroll pan onto waxed paper with long side nearest you; remove pan, and carefully peel waxed paper from omelet. Spoon mushrooms over surface, spreading to edge; sprinkle with cheese. Starting at long side, carefully roll omelet jellyroll fashion; use the waxed paper to help support the omelet while you roll. Carefully slide omelet onto a large serving platter, seam side down; garnish with bacon slices. Yield: 6 servings.

*Mrs. W. A. Ellis,*
*Talbott, Tennessee.*

## TEXAS BRUNCH

**3 tablespoons butter or margarine**
**3 tablespoons all-purpose flour**
**2 cups milk**
**¼ teaspoon salt**
**⅛ teaspoon pepper**
**6 hard-cooked eggs, chopped**
**½ cup mayonnaise or salad dressing**
**Buttermilk Cornbread**
**Chopped green onion**
**Crumbled cooked bacon**
**Shredded Cheddar cheese**

Melt butter in a heavy saucepan over low heat; add flour, stirring until smooth. Cook 1 minute, stirring constantly. Gradually add milk; cook until thickened and bubbly, stirring constantly. Add next 4 ingredients, mixing well; cook, stirring constantly, just until thoroughly heated.

To serve, slice cornbread squares in half horizontally; spoon on egg mixture, and sprinkle with onion, bacon, and cheese. Yield: 9 servings.

*Buttermilk Cornbread:*

**1 cup yellow cornmeal**
**⅓ cup all-purpose flour**
**1 teaspoon baking powder**
**½ teaspoon salt**
**¼ teaspoon soda**
**1 egg, beaten**
**1 cup buttermilk**

Combine dry ingredients; add egg and buttermilk, mixing well. Pour batter into a well-greased 8-inch square pan. Bake at 400° for 20 minutes or until lightly browned. Cut cornbread into squares. Yield: 9 servings.

*Mrs. N. A. Gilcrease,*
*Corsicana, Texas.*

*Tip: For perfect hard-cooked eggs, place eggs in a saucepan and cover with water; bring to a boil, lower heat to simmer, and cook 14 minutes. Pour off hot water and add cold water; shells will come off easily.*

## EGGS IN BRANDIED CREAM SAUCE

**4 poached eggs**
**2 English muffins, halved and toasted**
**Brandied Cream Sauce**
**1 cup (4 ounces) shredded Cheddar cheese**
**Paprika**

Place 1 poached egg on each toasted muffin half. Cover with Brandied Cream Sauce; top with the shredded cheese, and sprinkle with paprika. Serve immediately. Yield: 2 servings.

*Brandied Cream Sauce:*

**2 tablespoons butter or margarine**
**2 tablespoons all-purpose flour**
**¾ cup evaporated milk**
**¼ cup chicken broth**
**2 tablespoons brandy**

Melt butter in a heavy saucepan over low heat, and stir in flour; cook 1 minute, stirring constantly. Gradually add milk and broth; cook over medium heat, stirring constantly, until thickened and bubbly. Stir in brandy. Yield: about 1 cup.

*E. Secrust,*
*Plantation, Florida.*

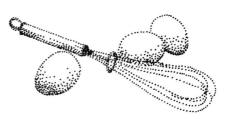

## BAKED EGGS IN SPINACH NESTS

**1 (10-ounce) package frozen chopped spinach**
**2 tablespoons butter or margarine**
**1 tablespoon finely chopped onion**
**2 tablespoons all-purpose flour**
**1 teaspoon chicken-flavored bouillon granules**
**1½ cups milk**
**¼ teaspoon salt**
**⅛ teaspoon ground nutmeg**
**2 eggs**
**½ cup (2 ounces) shredded Cheddar cheese**
**Grated Parmesan cheese**

Cook spinach according to package directions, omitting the salt. Drain thoroughly, and set aside.

Melt butter in a heavy saucepan over low heat; add onion, and sauté until tender. Stir in flour and bouillon granules; cook 1 minute, stirring constantly. Gradually add milk; cook over medium heat, stirring constantly, until thickened and bubbly. Stir in salt and nutmeg.

Stir spinach into white sauce; spoon equal portions into 2 (10-ounce) custard cups or ramekins, spreading sides slightly higher. Break an egg into each cup. Bake at 350° for 25 to 30 minutes or until eggs are set. Sprinkle with Cheddar cheese and Parmesan 5 minutes before baking time is complete. Yield: 2 servings.

*Mrs. H. R. McCarney,*
*Seaford, Virginia.*

## Spring Blossoms With Satiny Mousses

Ever see anything quite as appealing as our pretty mousses? Filled with airy lightness and creamy coolness, each mouthful is sheer delight.

For most people, a mousse generally brings dessert to mind, and the choices we offer include peppermint, chocolate, and apricot. But there's another side to mousse. Our delicately flavored Roquefort Mousse is served with crackers as an appetizer. A plus of the recipes offered here is that all can be fully prepared a day ahead and require only minimum last-minute attention.

Traditionally, mousses have relied on beaten egg whites, whipped cream, or a combination of both for their smooth texture and airy lightness, with gelatin added for firmness. That's not necessarily the case with today's versions. Our Caviar Mousse, for example, contains gelatin but no beaten egg whites or whipped cream; its smoothness is owed to sour cream. On the other hand, Blender Chocolate Mousse doesn't use gelatin; it depends on a generous amount of chocolate for firmness.

The perfect mousse is not difficult to prepare, but every step in its creation must be carried out with care and precision. In some mousses, such as Peppermint Candy Mousse and Roquefort Mousse, egg yolks are used to make a custard base. The key to success here is keeping the heat low and stirring the mixture constantly until smooth and thickened. The custard must be cooled before the beaten egg whites and whipped cream are folded in; otherwise, the entire mixture will collapse.

When egg whites or whipping cream are ingredients, they should be beaten until stiff enough to thicken the mousse. For maximum volume, let the egg whites reach room temperature; then beat until they peak and become stiff, but not dry. Whipping cream reaches maximum volume when beaten in a chilled bowl with a chilled whisk or beaters.

Your completed mousse can be simply presented or as elaborately garnished as those we offer. Among a few ideas for some finishing touches are chocolate curls or chocolate leaves, dollops of whipped cream, mandarin orange slices, fresh mint leaves, and toasted almonds.

### CAVIAR MOUSSE

1 envelope unflavored gelatin
2 tablespoons cold water
½ cup boiling water
2 (8-ounce) cartons commercial sour cream
1 (3½-ounce) jar black or red caviar
2 tablespoons mayonnaise
2 tablespoons lemon juice
Dash of hot sauce

Soften gelatin in cold water; add boiling water, stirring until gelatin is dissolved. Stir in remaining ingredients; spoon into a lightly oiled 4-cup mold. Cover and chill several hours or until set. Serve with crackers. Yield: 4 cups.

*Mrs. D. R. Heun,*
*Louisville, Kentucky.*

### ROQUEFORT MOUSSE

6 egg yolks
2 cups whipping cream, divided
2 envelopes unflavored gelatin
½ cup cold water
4 (3-ounce) packages Roquefort cheese
Dash of salt
4 egg whites

Combine egg yolks and ½ cup whipping cream in top of double boiler; bring water to a boil. Reduce heat to low; cook, stirring constantly, until thickened. Remove from heat.

Soften gelatin in cold water. Add gelatin mixture, Roquefort cheese, and salt to egg yolk mixture; beat with electric mixer until mixture is smooth. Let cool completely.

Beat egg whites (at room temperature) until stiff peaks form. Pour remaining whipping cream into a chilled bowl, and beat until soft peaks form. Fold beaten egg whites and whipped cream into Roquefort mixture.

Pour mixture into a lightly oiled 5-cup mold. Cover and refrigerate several hours or until set. Serve with crackers. Yield: 4½ cups.

*Rex Lyons,*
*Midway, Kentucky.*

### BLENDER CHOCOLATE MOUSSE

⅓ cup hot coffee
1 (6-ounce) package semisweet chocolate morsels
4 eggs, separated
2 tablespoons crème de cacao
Whipped cream
Sliced toasted almonds

Combine coffee and chocolate morsels in container of electric blender; process until smooth. Add egg yolks and crème de cacao; process 1 minute.

Beat egg whites (at room temperature) until stiff peaks form; fold in chocolate mixture. Spoon into stemmed glasses or individual serving dishes; chill until set. Top with whipped cream and almonds. Yield: 6 to 8 servings.

*Joy M. Hall,*
*Lucedale, Mississippi.*

### PEPPERMINT CANDY MOUSSE

1 envelope unflavored gelatin
1 cup milk
2 eggs, separated
⅓ cup sugar
1 cup whipping cream
¾ cup finely crushed soft-type peppermint sticks
Additional whipped cream (optional)
Chocolate leaves or chocolate curls (optional)
Mint leaves (optional)

Combine gelatin and milk in a heavy saucepan, and let stand 5 minutes; stir in egg yolks. Cook over medium heat, stirring constantly, until smooth and thickened. Remove from heat, and let cool.

Beat egg whites (at room temperature) until foamy; gradually add sugar, 1 tablespoon at a time, beating until stiff peaks form. Fold into milk mixture.

Pour whipping cream in a large chilled bowl, and beat until stiff peaks form; fold in egg white mixture and candy. Spoon into a lightly oiled 5-cup mold, and chill until set. Garnish with whipped cream, chocolate leaves, and mint leaves, if desired. Yield: 6 to 8 servings. *Mrs. Thomas Lee Adams,*
*Kingsport, Tennessee.*

## APRICOT MOUSSE

3 (17-ounce) cans apricot halves
¼ cup apricot preserves
2 tablespoons apricot brandy
2 tablespoons lemon juice
3 envelopes unflavored gelatin
½ cup water
½ cup sugar
2 cups whipping cream
Additional whipped cream (optional)
Mandarin orange slices (optional)

Drain apricots, reserving syrup. Press apricots and preserves through a food mill or sieve. Combine apricot puree, brandy, and lemon juice; stir well, and set aside.

Sprinkle gelatin over water, and let stand 5 minutes. Combine reserved apricot syrup and sugar in a medium saucepan; bring to a boil, stirring constantly, until sugar dissolves. Remove from heat; add gelatin mixture, stirring until gelatin is dissolved.

Combine apricot puree and gelatin mixture in a large bowl, stirring well. Chill until partially set; beat at medium speed of electric mixer for 10 seconds.

Pour whipping cream into a chilled bowl, and beat until stiff peaks form; fold into apricot mixture. Spoon into a lightly oiled 12-cup mold, and chill until set. Garnish with whipped cream and orange slices, if desired. Yield: 16 servings. *Mrs. W. J. Scherffius, Mountain Home, Arkansas.*

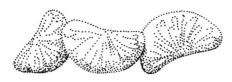

## FRESH STRAWBERRY MOUSSE

1 pint strawberries
1 (3-ounce) package strawberry-flavored gelatin
¼ cup sugar
2 cups whipping cream

Mash strawberries; drain, reserving juice. Set pulp aside. Add enough water to juice to make 1½ cups liquid.

Bring juice mixture to a boil. Add gelatin, stirring until dissolved; chill until consistency of unbeaten egg white.

Combine strawberry pulp and sugar, stirring well; stir into gelatin mixture. Pour whipping cream into a chilled bowl, and beat until soft peaks form; fold into strawberry mixture. Spoon into a lightly oiled 7-cup mold. Chill until set. Yield: 10 to 12 servings.
*Wilda B. Bell, Chattanooga, Tennessee.*

# Bake A Catch Of Fish Fillets

Fish fillets are a pleasure to prepare and eat, thanks to simple preparation and the absence of bones. And as these recipes show, a deft use of seasonings will enhance the delicate flavor of baked fish.

Baked Snapper and Stuffing calls for red snapper fillets to be baked with an herbed breadcrumb mixture and topped with grated onion and tomato slices.

An onion-green pepper sauce is served over fried snapper fillets for Company Red Snapper. Sautéed artichoke hearts are an added touch. For Southern Baked Fish, slices of lime are placed over fillets and baked. While this recipe calls for perch, other types of fish, such as trout and bass, should work just as well.

One thing to remember when preparing fish: Bake it only until the flesh can be easily flaked with a fork; overcooking makes it tough and dry. Properly prepared fish is moist, tender, and delicately flavored. It's best to eat fish within a day or two after it has been purchased—or caught.

## BAKED SNAPPER AND STUFFING

1 cup soft breadcrumbs
¼ cup butter or margarine, melted
1 teaspoon dried parsley flakes
1 teaspoon onion juice or 1 small onion, chopped
1 teaspoon lemon juice
¼ teaspoon salt
¼ to ½ teaspoon pepper
2 (¾-pound) red snapper fillets
Salt and pepper
1 tablespoon butter or margarine
1 small onion, grated
2 to 3 tomato slices
1 tablespoon soft breadcrumbs

Combine first 7 ingredients; stir well. Place 1 fillet, skin side down, in a greased 13- x 9- x 2-inch baking dish. Spoon stuffing along center of fillet; top with remaining fish, skin side up. Sprinkle fish with salt and pepper; dot with 1 tablespoon butter. Spoon onion over fish; add tomato, and sprinkle with breadcrumbs.

Bake at 350° for 35 to 45 minutes or until fillets flake easily when tested with a fork. Yield: 4 servings.
*Mary Mostoller, Tallahassee, Florida.*

## COMPANY RED SNAPPER

1 egg, beaten
½ cup milk
6 red snapper fillets (about 3 pounds)
1 cup all-purpose flour
½ cup vegetable oil
2 (14-ounce) cans artichoke hearts, drained
¼ cup butter or margarine
Onion Sauce

Combine egg and milk; beat well. Dip fish in egg mixture, and dredge in flour. Fry in hot oil (375°) until golden. Do not overcook. Drain on paper towels.

Sauté artichoke hearts in butter 5 minutes; drain well. Arrange fish and artichoke hearts in a lightly greased 12- x 8- x 2-inch baking dish. Serve Onion Sauce over fish. Yield: 6 servings.

*Onion Sauce:*

1 cup finely chopped onion
⅓ cup finely chopped green pepper
2 tablespoons finely chopped celery
½ cup butter or margarine
1½ tablespoons lemon juice
Dash of Worcestershire sauce
⅛ teaspoon salt
⅛ teaspoon pepper

Sauté onion, green pepper, and celery in butter until tender and transparent; drain. Add remaining ingredients; stir well. Yield: about 1½ cups.
*Mrs. Carlton James, New Orleans, Louisiana.*

## GREEK FISH WITH VEGETABLE SAUCE

½ cup chicken broth
1 cup chopped onion
1 (16-ounce) can whole tomatoes, undrained and chopped
½ cup chopped green pepper
½ cup chopped fresh parsley
1 clove garlic, crushed
½ teaspoon dried whole oregano
½ teaspoon salt
3 pounds fresh fish fillets
Pepper
Ground mace
Parsley sprigs (optional)
Lemon wedges (optional)

Place broth and onion in a medium saucepan, and bring to a boil. Reduce heat; cover and simmer until tender. Remove from heat; stir in next 6 ingredients. Set aside.

Place fish in a single layer on a lightly greased 15- x 10- x 1-inch jellyroll pan;

spoon vegetable mixture over fish. Sprinkle lightly with pepper and mace; bake, uncovered, at 350° for 30 minutes or until fish flakes easily when tested with a fork. Garnish with parsley sprigs and lemon wedges, if desired. Yield: 6 servings. *Charlene Keebler, Savannah, Georgia.*

## SOUTHERN BAKED FISH

**2 pounds perch fillets**
**2 tablespoons butter or margarine, melted**
**2 limes, thinly sliced**
**1 teaspoon paprika**

Place fillets, skin side down, in a greased 13- x 9- x 2-inch baking dish; brush with butter. Arrange limes over fillets; sprinkle with paprika.

Bake at 350° for 30 minutes or until fish flakes easily when tested with a fork. Yield: 6 servings.

*Mrs. James K. Powell, North Myrtle Beach, South Carolina.*

# No-Fuss Cooking For Two

How do you halve an egg? What can you do with one-third of a can of soup? If you cook for two people and find dividing recipes as frustrating as wrestling with leftovers, then *Southern Living's Cookbook for Two* was designed just for you. It's packed with no-fuss menus and recipes that make small-scale cooking a pleasure.

Here we offer a sample of those meals for two, a pair of menus from the chapter on "Special Dinners." The meal highlighting Barbecued Shrimp defines "ease of preparation," since everything can be made in advance. Like all the other menus, this one's complete right down to a suggested wine.

Chilled Gazpacho teases appetites to sample the other dishes. The nutritious main course features Fruit-Glazed Pork Chops With Rice and Fresh Spinach Salad, while Lemon Poached Pears end the meal with elegance and ease. For those who like to cook in larger quantities when it's just as simple, and reserve a portion for a busy day to come, this menu and others include recipes with double-batch instructions.

**Gazpacho**
**Fruit-Glazed Pork Chops With Rice**
**Fresh Spinach Salad**
**Commercial Breadsticks**
**Lemon Poached Pears**
**White Zinfandel**

## GAZPACHO

**1 (10¾-ounce) can tomato soup, undiluted**
**1½ cups tomato juice**
**1¼ cups water**
**½ to 1 cup chopped cucumber**
**½ to 1 cup chopped tomatoes**
**½ cup chopped green pepper**
**½ cup chopped Spanish onion**
**1 tablespoon commercial Italian dressing**
**2 tablespoons olive oil**
**2 tablespoons wine vinegar**
**1 tablespoon lemon or lime juice**
**1 clove garlic, minced**
**¼ teaspoon salt**
**¼ teaspoon pepper**
**¼ teaspoon hot sauce**
**⅛ teaspoon garlic salt**
**Dash of Worcestershire sauce**
**Cucumber slices (optional)**

Combine all ingredients except cucumber slices in a large bowl; chill at least 6 hours. Mix well before serving. Garnish with cucumber slices, if desired. Yield: about 6 servings.

*Note:* Store remaining gazpacho in an airtight container in the refrigerator.

## FRUIT-GLAZED PORK CHOPS WITH RICE

**4 (1¼-inch-thick) butterfly pork chops**
**¾ cup (4 ounces) mixed dried fruit, peaches, apricots, apples, prunes**
**1 (1-ounce) package golden raisins**
**1½ cups orange juice**
**½ cup cream sherry**
**½ teaspoon dry mustard**
**¼ teaspoon ground ginger**
**1 tablespoon cornstarch**
**2 tablespoons cold water**
**Hot cooked rice**

Place pork chops on rack in broiler pan. Broil at moderate temperature 3 to 5 inches from heat until done, about 20 to 25 minutes, turning once.

Combine dried fruit, raisins, orange juice, sherry, mustard, and ginger in a medium saucepan. Bring to a boil. Cover; reduce heat, and simmer 10 to 15 minutes or until fruit is tender and plump.

Combine cornstarch and cold water in small bowl. Stir into fruit mixture. Cook over medium heat, stirring constantly, until mixture is thickened and bubbly. Cook 1 minute longer. Serve pork chops over hot rice and spoon sauce over or around broiled chops, as desired. Yield: 4 servings.

*To freeze:* Place remaining cooked chops and sauce in a moisture-vapor proof freezer container. Seal, label, and date.

*To reheat:* Place frozen chops and sauce in a baking dish. Add 2 tablespoons water. Bake, covered, at 375° for 30 to 45 minutes or until thoroughly heated.

## FRESH SPINACH SALAD

**⅓ pound fresh spinach**
**¼ cup sliced water chestnuts**
**3 slices bacon, cooked and crumbled**
**⅓ cup vegetable oil**
**¼ cup sugar**
**⅛ teaspoon dry mustard**
**⅛ teaspoon onion juice**
**¼ teaspoon salt**
**3 tablespoons cider vinegar**
**Salt and pepper**
**Sieved egg yolk**

Remove stems from spinach; wash leaves thoroughly, and pat dry. Tear into bite-size pieces. Combine spinach, water chestnuts, and bacon in a large bowl; set aside.

Combine oil, sugar, mustard, onion juice, and salt in container of an electric blender; blend well. Remove lid; slowly add vinegar while blender is running.

Toss spinach mixture with dressing until well coated. Season to taste with salt and pepper, and garnish with sieved egg yolk. Yield: 2 servings.

*Tip: Remember that deep green, yellow, and orange fruit and vegetables are good sources of vitamin A. Sources of vitamin C are citrus fruit, deep green vegetables, and potatoes.*

## LEMON POACHED PEARS

2 fresh, ripe winter pears
1 cup water
¼ cup sugar
2 teaspoons lemon juice
½ teaspoon vanilla extract
¼ cup sliced almonds, toasted
Grated semisweet chocolate

Peel pears and core from blossom end, leaving stems intact. Combine water, sugar, lemon juice, and vanilla in a medium saucepan. Bring to a boil. Boil 5 minutes; add pears. Cover and simmer gently 12 to 15 minutes, or until pears are tender, basting occasionally with syrup. Cool pears in syrup.

To serve, place each pear in an individual dessert dish; sprinkle with toasted almonds and grated chocolate. Yield: 2 servings.

**Barbecued Shrimp**
**Savory Green Salad**
**Commercial French Bread**
**Coffee Pecan Pie**
**Chardonnay**

## BARBECUED SHRIMP

1¼ to 1½ pounds fresh shrimp, unpeeled
3 stalks celery with leaves, coarsely
    chopped
1 clove garlic, chopped
2 lemons, cut in half
½ cup butter or margarine, cut
    into cubes
2 tablespoons cracked black pepper
1 tablespoon Worcestershire sauce
1½ teaspoons salt
½ teaspoon hot sauce
Lemon wedges

Wash shrimp thoroughly and place in a large, shallow pan. Add celery and garlic. Squeeze juice from 2 lemons over top. Dot shrimp with butter, and sprinkle with remaining ingredients except lemon wedges.

Place shrimp under broiler until butter melts and shrimp start to turn pink (about 5 minutes), stirring several times. When all shrimp are slightly pink, reduce temperature to 350° and bake for 15 to 20 minutes or until done, stirring often. Do not overcook or shrimp will become mushy. Taste for doneness. Garnish with lemon wedges. Yield: 2 generous servings.

*Note:* Flavor improves if shrimp are cooked ahead of time and reheated, but do not overcook.

## SAVORY GREEN SALAD

2 tablespoons vegetable oil
1½ tablespoons wine vinegar
1 clove garlic, crushed
¼ teaspoon salt
¼ teaspoon pepper
¼ teaspoon dried whole thyme
1 small tomato, chopped
½ cup chopped green onion
½ cup chopped fresh parsley
3 cups torn lettuce
½ cup croutons

Combine first 6 ingredients, and let stand several hours to allow flavors to blend. Add tomato, onion, and parsley; mix until well coated. Add lettuce, and toss well. Sprinkle with croutons just before serving. Yield: 2 servings.

## COFFEE PECAN PIE

1 egg, separated
¼ teaspoon salt
¼ cup sugar
1½ cups finely chopped pecans
1 tablespoon instant coffee granules
¼ cup boiling water
2¼ cups miniature marshmallows
½ teaspoon almond extract
2 cups whipping cream, divided
Grated chocolate

Combine egg white (at room temperature) and salt; beat until stiff but not dry. Gradually beat in sugar; fold in pecans. Spread into a well-greased 8-inch piepan. Prick with fork. Bake at 400° for 12 minutes; cool.

Dissolve coffee in boiling water, and add marshmallows; place over medium heat until marshmallows melt. Beat egg yolk; slowly add marshmallow mixture to yolk, beating constantly. Beat until mixture begins to set, and stir in almond extract.

Whip 1 cup whipping cream; fold into filling. Spoon into crust; chill. Whip remaining cream, and spread over top. Garnish with grated chocolate. Yield: one 8-inch pie.

# Always Time For These Breads

Canned biscuits, frozen yeast bread dough, and biscuit mix are the key to these easy-to-prepare bread recipes. Our hot Caramel Bread, for instance, calls for frozen bread dough. You simply let the dough thaw, cut it into small pieces, and coat a layer of the dough with a brown sugar-vanilla pudding mixture. Top with remaining dough, let rise, and bake. Serve this irresistible sweet bread as a breakfast coffee cake or as dessert.

Easy Cheese Bread is made with a biscuit mix, while Breakaway Vegetable Bread gets a shortcut from canned biscuits. Both are assembled in just a matter of minutes.

## EASY CHEESE BREAD

3¾ cups biscuit mix
2 cups (8 ounces) shredded sharp
    Cheddar cheese
2 tablespoons poppy seeds
⅛ teaspoon ground red pepper
1¼ cups milk
1 egg, beaten

Combine first 4 ingredients; stir well. Combine milk and egg; add to cheese mixture, and stir 2 minutes.

Pour batter into a greased 9- x 5- x 3-inch loafpan. Bake at 350° for 55 to 60 minutes. Remove from pan, and cool slightly. Yield: 1 loaf.

*Mrs. John L. Paul,*
*Columbia, South Carolina.*

## BREAKAWAY VEGETABLE BREAD

3 (10-ounce) cans refrigerated buttermilk
    biscuits
½ cup margarine, melted
½ pound bacon, cooked and crumbled
½ cup (2 ounces) grated Parmesan cheese
1 small onion, finely chopped
1 small green pepper, finely chopped

Cut biscuits into quarters; dip each piece in margarine, and layer one-third in a lightly greased 10-inch Bundt pan. Sprinkle with half of bacon, Parmesan cheese, onion, and green pepper. Repeat layers until all ingredients are used, ending with biscuits. Bake at 350° for 40 to 45 minutes or until done. Yield: one 10-inch loaf. *Marilyn Fields,*
*Pryor, Oklahoma.*

## QUICK POPPY SEED LOAF

1 (18-ounce) package butter pecan
    cake mix
1 (3¾-ounce) package French vanilla
    instant pudding and pie filling
1 cup hot water
½ cup vegetable oil
4 eggs
1 cup chopped pecans
1 tablespoon poppy seeds

Combine first 5 ingredients in a large
mixing bowl; beat well. Stir in pecans
and poppy seeds.

Pour batter into a greased 9- x 5- x
3-inch loafpan. Bake at 350° for 1 hour
and 5 minutes or until a wooden pick
inserted in center comes out clean. Cool
in pan 10 minutes; remove from pan,
and cool on a wire rack. Yield: 1 loaf.
*Margie Hinson,*
*Mount Pleasant, Tennessee.*

## CARAMEL BREAD

1 pound frozen yeast bread dough,
    thawed
½ cup firmly packed brown sugar
¼ cup butter or margarine, melted
1 (3¾-ounce) package vanilla instant
    pudding and pie filling
2 tablespoons milk
¼ teaspoon ground cinnamon
Melted butter or margarine

Cut bread dough into ½-inch pieces.
Arrange half of pieces in a greased 9-
inch square baking pan. Combine next 5
ingredients; mix well. Spoon over
dough. Top with remaining dough
pieces. Brush dough with melted butter.
Cover; let rise in a warm place (85°),
free from drafts, 1 hour or until dough
has doubled in bulk.

Bake at 350° for 25 minutes. Serve
immediately. Yield: 9 servings.
*Ro Ann North,*
*Fort Smith, Arkansas.*

## ORANGE-NUT BREAD

3 cups biscuit mix
⅔ cup sugar
1 tablespoon grated orange rind
¾ cup orange juice
3 eggs
¾ cup chopped pecans
Orange Glaze

Combine first 5 ingredients in a mixing bowl; beat on low speed of electric
mixer 30 seconds. Beat on high speed 3
minutes. Stir in pecans.

Spoon batter into a 9- x 5- x 3-inch
loafpan. Bake at 350° for 55 minutes.
Cool in pan 10 minutes; turn out on a
wire rack. Cool. Drizzle bread with Orange Glaze. Yield: one loaf.

*Orange Glaze:*

2 tablespoons butter or margarine, melted
½ cup sifted powdered sugar
½ teaspoon grated orange rind
1½ teaspoons orange juice

Combine all ingredients; mix well.
Yield: about ¼ cup.
*Mrs. E. W. Hanley,*
*Macon, Georgia.*

# Considered Cauliflower Lately?

There are more ways to prepare cauliflower than tossed in a green salad or
covered in cheese sauce. Try some of
these fresh ideas, and spruce up a plain
meal or do justice to a fancy one.

Irene Haverland bakes Cauliflower
Soufflé, a splendid side dish that's light,
airy, and delicate. Another reader
cooks Creamy Cauliflower Soup. First
cooked in bouillon, the cauliflower is
blended in a food processor and heated
in white sauce. If your preference leans
toward raw vegetables, try stirring the
flowerets into a crunchy salad filled with
radishes and water chestnuts.

## CRUNCHY CAULIFLOWER SALAD

1 medium head cauliflower
1 cup sliced radishes
½ cup sliced green onion
1 (8-ounce) can sliced water chestnuts,
    drained
¾ cup commercial sour cream
¾ cup mayonnaise
2 tablespoons caraway seeds
1 (0.37-ounce) package buttermilk salad
    dressing mix

Wash the cauliflower, and break into
flowerets. Combine cauliflower and next
3 ingredients in a medium mixing bowl;
toss gently.

Stir together remaining ingredients;
pour over vegetables, and stir well.
Spoon into serving bowl; cover and chill
before serving. Yield: 6 to 8 servings.
*Cindy Freeman,*
*St. Simons Island, Georgia.*

*For a special crunchy salad, mix cauliflower flowerets, radishes, onion, water chestnuts, and caraway seeds with a sour cream dressing.*

## CAULIFLOWER SOUFFLE

1 small head cauliflower
½ cup butter or margarine
¼ cup plus 2 tablespoons all-purpose
  flour
1½ cups milk
4 eggs, separated
1 (3-ounce) package cream cheese, cubed
  and softened
½ teaspoon salt
¼ teaspoon white pepper
⅛ teaspoon ground thyme

Wash the cauliflower, and break into flowerets. Cook, covered, in a small amount of boiling salted water 10 minutes or until tender. Drain well; place cauliflower in container of electric blender or food processor, process until smooth, and set aside.

Melt butter in a heavy saucepan over low heat; add flour, stirring until smooth. Cook 1 minute, stirring constantly. Gradually add milk; cook over medium heat, stirring constantly, until the mixture is thickened and bubbly.

Beat egg yolks until thick and lemon colored. Gradually stir about one-fourth of hot white sauce into yolks; add to remaining white sauce, stirring constantly. Add cream cheese, stirring until melted. Add cauliflower, salt, pepper, and thyme; stir well.

Beat egg whites (at room temperature) until stiff but not dry. Gently fold into cauliflower mixture. Spoon into a 2-quart soufflé dish. Bake at 350° for 45 to 50 minutes or until golden brown. Serve immediately. Yield: 6 to 8 servings.
*Irene Haverland,*
*Deepwater, Missouri.*

## CREAMY CAULIFLOWER SOUP

1 medium head cauliflower, quartered
4 cups water
1 small onion, chopped
4 chicken-flavored bouillon cubes
¼ cup butter or margarine
¼ cup all-purpose flour
2 cups skim milk
½ teaspoon salt
¼ teaspoon ground nutmeg
¼ teaspoon pepper
Shredded Cheddar cheese

Wash the cauliflower, and break into flowerets. Combine water, onion, and bouillon cubes in a large saucepan; bring to a boil. Add cauliflower; cover and cook 10 to 15 minutes or until tender.

Spoon half of cauliflower mixture into container of electric blender or food

processor; process until smooth. Repeat with remaining mixture.

Melt butter in a heavy saucepan over low heat; add flour, stirring until smooth. Cook 1 minute, stirring constantly. Gradually add milk; cook over medium heat, stirring constantly, until thickened and bubbly. Stir in salt, nutmeg, and pepper.

Return cauliflower mixture to large saucepan; stir in white sauce. Cook over low heat, stirring constantly, until well heated. Serve immediately, sprinkling each serving with cheese. Yield: about 5½ cups.
*Gloria Pedersen,*
*Brandon, Mississippi.*

## Microwave Cookery

# Ham Takes To The Microwave

In the microwave, ham cooks in a matter of minutes and yields the same juicy tenderness you've enjoyed from the conventional oven. Our recipe called Ham With Raisin Sauce tells you how to cook a ham in the microwave, and fresh from our test kitchens come some tempting ways to finish off the leftovers.

The following guidelines will ensure good results with microwaved ham.

—When buying a whole or half ham for microwaving, choose the boneless, fully cooked type; this kind cooks more quickly and evenly than other types. We recommend a cooking time of 8 to 10 minutes per pound, with the time range allowing for the difference in wattage of microwave ovens. Turn the ham over approximately halfway through the cooking period.

—The upper, cut edge of a ham cooks faster than the center, so shield this area with a narrow strip of aluminum foil; this will reduce energy received and slow the cooking process. Before shielding, however, check the manufacturer's directions with your oven; some older models can be damaged by the use of foil.

Make sure the shield is at least 3 inches from the top of the oven and 1 inch from the walls. Fold the foil smoothly over the cut edge of the ham; if not smooth or if it touches the walls,

it may cause an arc (spark of electricity). If an arc occurs, flatten the foil and continue microwaving.

—To seal in juices and prevent spattering, cover the entire ham and dish with heavy-duty plastic wrap.

—Cook a whole or half ham, slices, and loaves on MEDIUM (50% power) or MEDIUM HIGH (70% power). Sugar used in curing ham attracts microwaves and can cause overcooking or uneven cooking when microwaved at HIGH. Recipes that mix chopped ham with other ingredients can generally be cooked on HIGH.

—When microwaving a ham loaf, our test kitchens staff suggests shaping it into a round loaf so there will be no corners to overcook.

## HAM WITH RAISIN SAUCE

1 (4- to 5-pound) boneless ham, fully
  cooked
2 tablespoons cornstarch
½ cup water
1 cup sugar
1 cup raisins
2 tablespoons butter or margarine
2 tablespoons vinegar
Dash of Worcestershire sauce
½ teaspoon salt
¼ teaspoon ground cloves

Place ham in a 12- x 8- x 2-inch glass baking dish. Shield upper, cut edge of ham with a 1½-inch-wide strip of foil. Cover the entire dish with heavy-duty plastic wrap. Microwave at MEDIUM (50% power) for 8 to 10 minutes per pound or until thoroughly heated, turning ham over after about half of cooking time has elapsed. (Rearrange foil strip when ham is turned.) Let stand for 10 minutes before serving.

Place cornstarch in a 4-cup glass measure; add a small amount of the water, stirring until cornstarch is dissolved. Stir in remaining water and all other ingredients. Microwave at HIGH for 5 to 6 minutes or until clear and thickened, stirring every 2 minutes. Serve sauce with ham. Yield: 12 to 15 servings.

*Tip: Check foods closely as you are shopping to be sure they are not spoiled before you purchase them. Do not buy cans that are badly dented, leaking, or bulging at the ends. Do not select presealed packages which have broken seals.*

## HAM TETRAZZINI

¼ cup butter or margarine
1 medium-size green pepper, chopped
1 tablespoon all-purpose flour
1 cup milk
1½ cups diced cooked ham
1 (10¾-ounce) can cream of mushroom
  soup, undiluted
1 (2-ounce) jar diced pimiento, undrained
1 small clove garlic, minced
¼ cup dry sherry
1 (4½-ounce) jar sliced mushrooms,
  drained
⅓ cup grated Parmesan cheese
3 cups (12 ounces) shredded process
  American cheese, divided
1 (12-ounce) package spaghetti, cooked
  and drained
½ cup sliced almonds

Place butter in a 2-quart glass mixing bowl, and microwave at HIGH for 30 seconds or until melted. Add green pepper, and cover with heavy-duty plastic wrap; microwave at HIGH for 2 minutes or until crisp-tender. Add flour, stirring until smooth; gradually add milk, stirring well. Microwave at HIGH for 2 minutes, and stir until smooth. Microwave at HIGH for 1 to 2½ minutes, stirring at 1-minute intervals, until thickened.

Stir next 7 ingredients and 2 cups American cheese into sauce. Cover and microwave at HIGH for 4 minutes or until hot; stir well.

Spread half of spaghetti in a lightly greased 12- x 8- x 2-inch baking dish; spread evenly with half of ham mixture. Repeat layers and top with remaining cheese; sprinkle with almonds. Cover and microwave at MEDIUM HIGH (70% power) for 6 to 8 minutes or until thoroughly heated, giving dish one half-turn after 4 minutes. Let stand before serving. Yield: 6 to 8 servings.

## CHEESY HAM TOWERS

2 tablespoons butter or margarine
2 tablespoons all-purpose flour
1 cup milk
½ teaspoon chicken-flavored bouillon
  granules
½ teaspoon prepared mustard
½ teaspoon Worcestershire sauce
½ cup (2 ounces) shredded process
  American cheese
1 cup cubed cooked ham
2 tablespoons sliced pitted ripe olives
1 tablespoon chopped pimiento
1 tablespoon minced fresh parsley
4 baked patty shells

Place butter in a 4-cup glass measure; microwave at HIGH for 30 seconds or until melted. Add flour, stirring until smooth; gradually add milk, stirring well. Microwave at HIGH for 2 minutes, and stir until smooth. Microwave at HIGH for 1 to 1½ minutes or until thickened and bubbly, stirring after 1 minute.

Stir in next 8 ingredients. Microwave at HIGH for 1 to 1½ minutes or until thoroughly heated. Spoon filling into patty shells. Yield: 4 servings.

## CRANBERRY-HAM LOAF

1 pound ground cooked ham
1 pound ground fresh lean pork
2 eggs, slightly beaten
1 cup cracker crumbs
½ teaspoon onion powder
¼ teaspoon salt
¼ teaspoon seasoned pepper
¼ cup firmly packed brown sugar
1 teaspoon dry mustard
1½ tablespoons vinegar
1 (8-ounce) can whole-berry cranberry
  sauce
Fresh parsley sprigs

Combine first 7 ingredients, mixing well; press into a 10-inch pieplate, and cover with waxed paper. Microwave at MEDIUM HIGH (70% power) for 6 minutes. Rotate dish one half-turn; microwave at MEDIUM HIGH for 6 minutes. Drain well.

Combine brown sugar, mustard, and vinegar; mix well, and spoon over meat loaf. Cover and microwave at MEDIUM HIGH for 6 to 8 minutes or until loaf is firm to the touch. Drain off drippings.

Top loaf with cranberry sauce, and microwave at MEDIUM HIGH for 2 to 3 minutes. Let stand 5 minutes before serving. Garnish with parsley. Cut into wedges to serve. Yield: 6 to 8 servings.

# Fry The Best Appetizers

Have you ever wondered how to make fried mushrooms or potato skins similar to those served in your favorite restaurant? Appetizers like these are easy to make—just heat up the oil, and in a matter of minutes your guests will be nibbling on crumb-coated bits of melted cheese, crunchy cauliflowerets, or even crispy zucchini.

Fried dill pickles may be a novelty to you, as they were for us. On a recent trip to Mississippi, we discovered they are a popular appetizer and snack in many restaurants and homes. Janice Jones, of Jackson, agreed to share her spicy-hot version; she cuts the pickles into thin crosswise slices, then batters and fries them until golden. A word of caution—these appetizers are so tempting you may find yourself making them a meal.

## FRIED CHEESE BITES

6 ounces Gruyère cheese, cut into 1-inch
  cubes
2 eggs, well beaten
¾ cup all-purpose flour
1½ cups fine, dry breadcrumbs
Vegetable oil

Dip cheese cubes into egg; dredge in flour, and dip again in egg. Roll cubes in breadcrumbs, pressing firmly so crumbs adhere; place on waxed paper, and chill 30 minutes.

Deep fry cubes in hot oil (375°) until golden brown. Drain on paper towels; serve immediately. Yield: about 1½ dozen appetizer servings.

*Audrey Bledsoe,*
*Smyrna, Georgia.*

## FRENCH-FRIED PICKLES

1 quart dill pickles, thinly sliced
1¾ cups all-purpose flour, divided
2 teaspoons red pepper
2 teaspoons paprika
2 teaspoons pepper
2 teaspoons garlic salt
1 teaspoon salt
3 dashes of hot sauce
1 cup beer
Vegetable oil

Dredge sliced pickles in 1 cup flour; set aside. Combine remaining ¾ cup flour and dry ingredients; add hot sauce and beer, mixing well. Dip dredged pickles into batter. Deep fry in hot oil (375°) until pickles float to surface and are golden brown. Drain on paper towels; serve immediately. Yield: about 2½ dozen appetizer servings.

*Janice Jones,*
*Jackson, Mississippi.*

## CHEESY POTATO SKINS

3 medium baking potatoes
Vegetable oil
Seasoned salt
1 cup (4 ounces) shredded Cheddar cheese
6 slices bacon, cooked and crumbled
Commercial sour cream

Scrub potatoes thoroughly, and rub skins with oil; bake at 400° for 1 hour or until done.

Allow potatoes to cool to touch. Cut in half lengthwise; carefully scoop out pulp, leaving ¼- to ⅛-inch shell. (Pulp may be used for mashed potatoes or reserved for another recipe.) Cut shells in half crosswise, and deep fry in hot oil (375°) for 2 minutes or until lightly browned. Drain on paper towels. Place skins on a baking sheet; sprinkle with salt, cheese, and bacon. Place under broiler until cheese melts. Serve with sour cream. Yield: 1 dozen appetizer servings.
*Merry Eisele,*
*Birmingham, Alabama.*

## GOLDEN FRIED CAULIFLOWER

1 medium head cauliflower
¾ cup all-purpose flour
1 teaspoon salt
¼ teaspoon pepper
2 eggs, beaten
Vegetable oil

Wash cauliflower, and break into flowerets. Cook, covered, in a small amount of boiling salted water 5 to 8 minutes or until crisp-tender; drain.

Combine flour, salt, and pepper; stir well. Dredge each floweret in flour mixture; dip in egg. Deep fry in hot oil (375°) until golden brown. Serve immediately. Yield: about 2 dozen appetizer servings.
*Dr. W. H. Pinkston,*
*Knoxville, Tennessee.*

## FRENCH-FRIED MUSHROOMS

1 egg
½ cup milk
⅓ cup all-purpose flour
½ teaspoon salt
20 medium-size fresh mushrooms
1 cup cornflake crumbs
Vegetable oil
Seasoned salt

Combine egg and milk, beating well. Stir together flour and salt. Dredge mushrooms in flour mixture, and dip in egg mixture; roll in cornflake crumbs.

Deep fry in hot oil (375°) until golden brown. Drain on paper towels, and sprinkle with salt. Serve immediately. Yield: 20 appetizer servings.
*Mary Mostoller,*
*Tallahassee, Florida.*

## ZUCCHINI FRENCH FRIES

2 eggs
1 tablespoon water
¼ cup plus 2 tablespoons all-purpose flour
2 medium zucchini, cut into 1-inch slices
Peanut oil
Salt

Combine egg and water; beat well. Add flour and beat until smooth. Dip zucchini in batter, and deep fry in hot oil (375°) until golden brown. Drain on paper towels; sprinkle with salt. Serve immediately. Yield: about 2½ dozen appetizer servings.
*John N. Riggins,*
*Nashville, Tennessee.*

<br>

# Cooking Light

# Salads That Slenderize Your Menu

Losing weight usually means eating lots of salads. Mrs. J. E. Sutphin of Newport, Virginia, avoids monotony by creating some exciting low-calorie main dish salads for lunch and sometimes for dinner. Chicken-Fruit Salad is one of her favorites, and she even serves it to company. Made with lean chicken and reduced-calorie mayonnaise, it's filling and tasty as well as light.

What calorie-counter hasn't relied on tuna salads? Well, it's time you try a delicious version of this popular dieter's food—Tuna Chef Salad. Water-packed tuna, instead of tuna packed in oil, and canned asparagus spears are topped with a yogurt-based curry dressing.

Try each of our light main dish salads, and then come up with some of your own. Start with fresh vegetables—those bulky foods that are filling yet very low in calories. Include celery, cucumbers, summer squash, green pepper, mushrooms, broccoli, and cauliflower. And try different kinds of lettuce for variety, remembering that the darker green leaves have more nutrients. What about using a bed of fresh spinach instead of lettuce for a change?

Top the vegetables with strips of broiled steak, chicken, turkey, lean ham, canned seafood, cheese, or eggs—but don't go overboard. Many of us tend to eat more protein than we actually need, and proteins do contribute calories. It's a good idea to buy a set of kitchen scales so you'll know just how much you're eating. Include only 2 to 3 ounces of the protein food to make a satisfying, nutritious main dish salad.

While fresh salads are great for dieters, regular salad dressings can send the calorie count straight up. About 1 tablespoon of most commercial dressings is about 60 calories—that's about the same as in a whole pound of lettuce. And mayonnaise is even higher, scaling in at 100 calories per tablespoon.

So instead of pouring on lots of calories, try our light versions of Thousand Island, creamy cucumber, and French—they're made with cottage cheese, plain yogurt, and tomato juice instead of oil. And at only 5 to 13 calories per tablespoon, they're delightful alternatives to commercial dressings.

## TUNA CHEF SALAD

Lettuce leaves
1 (14½-ounce) can asparagus spears, drained and chilled
2 (7-ounce) cans water-packed tuna, drained and chilled
Curry Dressing
3 hard-cooked eggs, sliced
Paprika

Place lettuce leaves on a serving platter. Arrange asparagus spears on lettuce; top with tuna. Spoon Curry Dressing over tuna. Arrange egg slices on top, and sprinkle lightly with paprika. Yield: 4 servings (about 240 calories per serving).

*Curry Dressing:*

1 (8-ounce) carton plain low-fat yogurt
½ teaspoon curry powder
¼ teaspoon salt
⅛ teaspoon ground ginger
Dash of red pepper

Combine all ingredients; mix well. Chill. Yield: about 1 cup.
*Kathleen Stone,*
*Houston, Texas.*

## CHICKEN-FRUIT SALAD

3 whole chicken breasts, skinned
1 (15¼-ounce) can pineapple chunks in
    unsweetened juice
1 medium apple, unpeeled
1 cup seedless grapes, halved
¼ cup reduced-calorie mayonnaise
Lettuce leaves

Place chicken in 1½ cups water in a Dutch oven; cover and cook 15 to 20 minutes until tender. Drain and remove chicken from bone; coarsely chop, and set aside.

Drain pineapple, and reserve juice. Coarsely chop apple; dip in pineapple juice to prevent browning. Combine chicken, pineapple, apple, grapes, and mayonnaise; mix well. Cover and chill 2 hours. Serve on lettuce leaves. Yield: 6 servings (about 237 calories per serving).               *Mrs. J. E. Sutphin,*
*Newport, Virginia.*

## MIRACLE FRENCH DRESSING

½ teaspoon unflavored gelatin
1 tablespoon cold water
¼ cup boiling water
½ cup tomato juice
3 to 4 tablespoons vinegar
1 tablespoon sugar
1 teaspoon Worcestershire sauce
½ teaspoon salt
¼ teaspoon dry mustard
⅛ teaspoon garlic powder
Dash of pepper

Dissolve gelatin in cold water, stirring well. Add boiling water; stir gelatin well, and set aside.

Combine remaining ingredients in container of electric blender; process on low speed. Add gelatin mixture; continue to process until smooth (about 1 minute). Chill thoroughly. Stir well before serving. Yield: 1 cup (about 5 calories per tablespoon).     *Dana Thomas,*
*Birmingham, Alabama.*

## SPECIAL THOUSAND ISLAND DRESSING

1 cup low-fat cottage cheese
¼ cup chili sauce
¼ cup plus 2 tablespoons skim milk
1 teaspoon paprika
½ teaspoon salt
2 hard-cooked eggs, chopped
2 tablespoons finely chopped celery
2 tablespoons finely chopped green pepper
1 tablespoon sweet pickle relish
1 tablespoon finely chopped onion

Combine first 5 ingredients in container of electric blender; blend until smooth. Stir in remaining ingredients. Chill before serving. Yield: 2⅛ cups (about 13 calories per tablespoon).

## CREAMY CUCUMBER SALAD DRESSING

1 medium cucumber, peeled and sliced
1 (12-ounce) carton low-fat cottage cheese
2 tablespoons prepared horseradish
½ teaspoon dried whole dillweed

Combine all ingredients in container of electric blender; process until smooth. Store in an airtight container in refrigerator. Yield: about 2 cups (about 8 calories per tablespoon).
*M. B. Burnham,*
*Port Orange, Florida.*

# Stuff Eggs With Variety

Deviled eggs are great for garnishing main dishes and for taking to covered-dish meals, but they can easily become humdrum. So instead of stuffing eggs with your usual filling, try some of these fancy variations.

Eggs Deluxe takes the basic egg yolk-and-mayonnaise mixture and adds deviled ham, green pepper, and Cheddar cheese. This dish is served cold, but stuffed eggs can also be enjoyed hot from the oven. In Creamed Deviled Eggs, they're baked in a cheesy sauce, while Saucy Deviled Eggs are baked in a tomato sauce.

## DEVIL'S ISLAND EGGS

6 hard-cooked eggs
2 slices bacon, cooked and crumbled
⅓ cup commercial Thousand Island
    dressing
24 pimiento strips

Slice eggs in half lengthwise, and carefully remove yolks. Mash yolks; add bacon and dressing, mixing well. Stuff whites with yolk mixture. Garnish each egg half with 2 pimiento strips. Yield: 6 to 8 servings.     *Bobbie McGuire,*
*Norris, South Carolina.*

## EGGS DELUXE

6 hard-cooked eggs
3 tablespoons mayonnaise or salad
    dressing
1 (2¼-ounce) can deviled ham
3 tablespoons finely chopped green pepper
¼ cup (1 ounce) shredded Cheddar cheese
Paprika

Slice eggs in half lengthwise, and carefully remove yolks. Mash yolks, and add mayonnaise; mix well. Stir in deviled ham and green pepper. Stuff whites with mixture; sprinkle with cheese and paprika. Yield: 6 servings.
*Mary H. Gilliam,*
*Cartersville, Virginia.*

## CREAMED DEVILED EGGS

6 hard-cooked eggs
1 tablespoon mayonnaise
1 tablespoon butter or margarine,
    softened
1 tablespoon vinegar
1 (2¼-ounce) can deviled ham
1 teaspoon prepared mustard
⅛ teaspoon ground turmeric
Cheesy Cream Sauce
2 to 3 tablespoons chopped fresh
    parsley

Slice eggs in half lengthwise, and carefully remove yolks. Mash yolks, and add mayonnaise; mix well. Stir in next 5 ingredients. Stuff whites with yolk mixture, and arrange in a lightly greased 1½-quart shallow baking dish.

Pour Cheesy Cream Sauce over eggs, and bake at 350° for 15 minutes. Sprinkle with parsley. Yield: 6 servings.

*Cheesy Cream Sauce:*

2 tablespoons butter or margarine
2 tablespoons all-purpose flour
1 beef-flavored bouillon cube
½ cup hot water
½ cup milk
Dash of pepper
Dash of paprika
½ cup (2 ounces) shredded process
    American cheese

Melt butter in a heavy saucepan over low heat, and stir in flour. Cook 1 minute, stirring constantly. Dissolve bouillon cube in hot water; add milk, stirring well.

Gradually add liquid to flour mixture; cook over medium heat, stirring constantly, until thickened and bubbly. Add pepper, paprika, and cheese; stir until cheese melts. Yield: 1 cup.
*Ann Elsie Schmetzer,*
*Madisonville, Kentucky.*

## SAUCY DEVILED EGGS

6 hard-cooked eggs
¼ cup mayonnaise
2 tablespoons chopped onion
1 teaspoon vinegar
1 teaspoon prepared mustard
⅛ teaspoon salt
Dash of pepper
Paprika
2 (8-ounce) cans tomato sauce
½ cup water
½ cup chopped onion
½ teaspoon salt
½ teaspoon paprika
6 slices bacon, cooked and crumbled
½ cup buttered breadcrumbs
Buttered toast points

Slice eggs in half lengthwise, and carefully remove yolks. Mash yolks, and add mayonnaise; mix well. Stir in next 5 ingredients. Stuff whites with yolk mixture, and sprinkle with paprika.

Combine next 5 ingredients in a shallow 1-quart casserole dish, stirring well. Arrange eggs in dish. Sprinkle eggs with bacon, and top with breadcrumbs. Bake at 450° for 15 minutes. Serve over buttered toast points. Yield: 6 servings.
*Mrs. Robert Borig,*
*Baltimore, Maryland.*

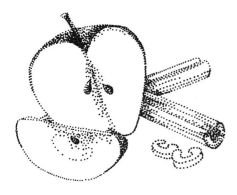

# Chilled Fruit Salads Welcome Spring

Fruit salads are a favorite year-round, but when spring arrives, the thought of a refreshing congealed or frozen fruit salad is even more appealing.

These congealed salads include a version of Waldorf Salad based on apple cider. Pineapple-Buttermilk Salad, fluffy and apricot-colored, will make a colorful addition to any lunch or dinner. Besides our frozen treats like creamy Frozen Banana Salad, we've also included Old-Fashioned Fruit Salad—a traditional fruit salad that will complement any menu.

## CONGEALED WALDORF SALAD

2 cups apple cider, divided
1 (3-ounce) package lemon-flavored gelatin
1 large apple, unpeeled and finely chopped
¼ cup finely chopped celery
¼ cup finely chopped pecans
Lettuce leaves
Mayonnaise

Bring 1 cup cider to a boil; add gelatin, and stir until dissolved. Stir in remaining cider. Chill until consistency of unbeaten egg white. Fold in apple, celery, and pecans. Pour into a 4-cup mold, and chill until set. Unmold on a lettuce-lined plate, and top with a dollop of mayonnaise. Yield: 6 servings.
*Sherry Phillips,*
*Knoxville, Tennessee.*

## FROZEN APPLE-CREAM SALAD

1 (8-ounce) can crushed pineapple
½ cup sugar
3 eggs, slightly beaten
⅓ cup lemon juice
¼ teaspoon salt
2 cups applesauce
1 (8-ounce) carton commercial sour cream
1 cup diced celery
½ cup shredded carrots
½ cup chopped walnuts

Drain pineapple, reserving juice; set pineapple aside. Combine pineapple juice, sugar, eggs, lemon juice, and salt in a medium saucepan; cook over low heat until smooth and thickened, stirring constantly. Let cool. Stir in pineapple and remaining ingredients.

Spoon mixture into a 12- x 8- x 2-inch dish. Freeze until firm. Cut into squares to serve. Yield: 12 servings.
*Mrs. J. W. Hopkins,*
*Abilene, Texas.*

## OLD-FASHIONED FRUIT SALAD

1 (15-ounce) can pineapple chunks
½ cup sugar
3 apples, unpeeled and chopped
3 oranges, peeled, seeded, and sectioned
3 bananas, sliced
1 cup miniature marshmallows
1 cup chopped pecans or walnuts
1 cup grapes, halved

Drain pineapple, reserving ¼ cup juice. Combine reserved juice and sugar; stir well, and set aside.

Combine remaining ingredients. Pour pineapple juice mixture over salad; toss gently. Chill at least 1 hour. Yield: 12 servings.
*Roxie Mosley,*
*Annville, Kentucky.*

## FROZEN BANANA SALAD

2 (8-ounce) cartons commercial sour cream
1 (20-ounce) can crushed pineapple, undrained
2 bananas, mashed
¾ cup sugar
½ cup chopped pecans or walnuts
2 tablespoons chopped maraschino cherries
¼ teaspoon salt

Combine all ingredients; stir until well blended. Pour into an oiled 5-cup mold; freeze several hours or overnight. Unmold salad; let stand at room temperature 15 minutes before serving. Yield: 10 servings.
*Mrs. H. G. Drawdy,*
*Spindale, North Carolina.*

## PINEAPPLE-BUTTERMILK SALAD

1 (20-ounce) can crushed pineapple, undrained
2 tablespoons sugar
1 (6-ounce) package orange-flavored gelatin
2 cups buttermilk
1 (8-ounce) container frozen whipped topping, thawed
1 cup chopped pecans

Combine pineapple and sugar in a saucepan; bring to a boil, stirring occasionally. Remove from heat; add gelatin, stirring until dissolved. Cool. Add buttermilk, and stir until combined. Fold in whipped topping and pecans. Spoon into a 12- x 8- x 2-inch dish, and chill until firm. Cut salad into squares to serve. Yield: 8 servings.
*Mrs. Robert H. Kirk,*
*Winchester, Virginia.*

*Right: For Texas Brunch (page 70), hard-cooked eggs are gently heated in a creamy sauce and spooned over slices of buttermilk cornbread. The final touch is a colorful topping of shredded cheese, crumbled bacon, and bits of green onion.*

*Page 82: Savor squash in this colorful array of dishes: Stuffed Pattypan Squash (page 103), Zucchini Salad (page 104), and Yellow Squash Puffs (page 103).*

# Chicken Gets A Classic Touch

A family meal of chicken may likely center around fried chicken or a favorite casserole, but when it's time to entertain, you'll want to try a chicken recipe with a gourmet touch. Our readers are ready with suggestions that range from versions of classic chicken dishes like Oven Chicken Kiev, Gourmet Chicken Divan, and Chicken Cordon Bleu to surprises like Stuffed Chicken Thighs.

We especially recommend Gourmet Chicken Divan, made with fresh steamed broccoli, mushrooms, and a sour cream sauce. It's as attractive to serve as it is delicious. Company Creamed Chicken is another perfect choice for a special meal: chicken in a savory cream sauce served in patty shells and topped with melted cheese and toasted almonds.

## SUPREMES DE VOLAILLE A BLANC
### (Chicken Breasts in Cream Sauce)

4 whole chicken breasts, split, boned, and skinned
1 cup all-purpose flour
1 teaspoon salt
¼ teaspoon white pepper
2 tablespoons butter or margarine
2 tablespoons vegetable oil
1 cup whipping cream
½ cup chicken broth
½ cup dry white wine
Minced parsley

Place each chicken breast half on a sheet of waxed paper. Flatten chicken to ¼-inch thickness, using a meat mallet or rolling pin.

Combine flour, salt, and pepper; stir well. Dredge chicken in flour mixture, and let stand 20 minutes. Reserve 2 tablespoons flour mixture.

Heat butter and oil in a heavy skillet. Cook chicken in butter mixture over medium heat 5 to 7 minutes on each side or until golden brown. Remove chicken to a warmed serving platter.

Combine whipping cream, broth, and wine; set aside. Stir reserved flour mixture into pan drippings. Cook 1 minute, stirring constantly. Gradually add cream mixture; cook over medium heat, stirring constantly, until thickened and bubbly. Pour sauce through a sieve over chicken. Sprinkle with parsley. Yield: 8 servings. *Bobbie J. Davis, Dallas, Texas.*

## CHICKEN CORDON BLEU

4 whole chicken breasts, split, boned, and skinned
8 (1-ounce) slices cooked ham
8 (1-ounce) slices Swiss cheese
3 tablespoons minced fresh parsley
¼ teaspoon pepper
1 egg, beaten
½ cup Italian breadcrumbs
¼ cup butter or margarine
1 (10¾-ounce) can mushroom soup, undiluted
1 (8-ounce) carton commercial sour cream
⅓ cup dry sherry
1 (4-ounce) can sliced mushrooms, drained

Place each chicken breast half on a sheet of waxed paper; flatten to ¼-inch thickness, using a meat mallet or rolling pin. Place one slice of ham and one slice of cheese in the center of each chicken piece. Sprinkle evenly with parsley and pepper. Roll up lengthwise, and secure with wooden picks.

Dip each chicken breast in egg; coat well with breadcrumbs.

Melt butter in a heavy skillet; brown chicken on all sides. Remove chicken to a 12- x 8- x 2-inch baking dish, reserving drippings in skillet.

Add remaining ingredients to reserved drippings, and stir well. Pour sauce over chicken; bake, uncovered, at 350° for 40 to 45 minutes. Yield: 8 servings. *Janet M. Filer, Arlington, Virginia.*

## OVEN CHICKEN KIEV

3 tablespoons butter, softened
1 teaspoon minced fresh parsley
¼ teaspoon garlic salt
3 whole chicken breasts, split, boned, and skinned
2 tablespoons vegetable oil
1 cup cracker crumbs
⅛ to ¼ teaspoon seasoned salt
⅓ cup evaporated milk
Fresh parsley sprigs (optional)

Combine first 3 ingredients; mix well, and shape into a stick (like butter). Cover and freeze about 45 minutes or until firm.

Place each chicken breast half on a sheet of waxed paper; flatten chicken to ¼-inch thickness, using a meat mallet or rolling pin.

Cut butter mixture into 6 portions; place a piece in center of each chicken breast half. Fold long sides of chicken over butter; fold ends over, and secure with wooden picks.

Spread oil in a 13- x 9- x 2-inch pan and set aside.

Combine cracker crumbs and seasoned salt. Dip each chicken piece into milk, and coat with cracker crumbs.

Place chicken, seam side up, in prepared pan; bake at 425° for 15 minutes; carefully turn each piece. Bake an additional 5 to 10 minutes (do not overbake). Place chicken on a heated platter; garnish with parsley, if desired. Yield: 6 servings. *Mrs. John Woods, Memphis, Tennessee.*

## GOURMET CHICKEN DIVAN

⅓ cup all-purpose flour
Freshly ground pepper to taste
2 whole chicken breasts, split, boned, and skinned
⅓ cup butter or margarine
1⅓ cups chicken broth
½ teaspoon dried whole basil
1 pound fresh broccoli
2 tablespoons butter or margarine
¼ pound fresh mushrooms, sliced
1 (8-ounce) carton commercial sour cream
2 tablespoons grated Parmesan cheese

Combine flour and pepper; dredge chicken in flour. Melt ⅓ cup butter in a large skillet; brown chicken in butter on both sides. Remove chicken from skillet; drain on paper towels.

Add broth to skillet; cook over low heat 5 minutes, stirring to loosen brown particles. Return chicken to skillet, and sprinkle with basil. Cover and simmer 30 minutes.

Trim off large leaves of broccoli. Remove tough ends of lower stalks, and wash broccoli thoroughly. Make lengthwise slits in thick stalks. Arrange broccoli in steaming rack with stalks to center of rack. Steam 10 minutes or until crisp-tender; set aside.

Melt 2 tablespoons butter in a small skillet; add the sliced mushrooms, and sauté 2 minutes.

Place broccoli in a buttered 13- x 9- x 2-inch baking pan. Remove chicken from skillet with a slotted turner, reserving pan drippings; arrange chicken on broccoli. Spoon mushrooms over chicken.

Stir sour cream into reserved pan drippings; cook over low heat until thoroughly heated (do not boil). Pour sauce over chicken; sprinkle with cheese. Place pan 6 inches from broiler element; broil 3 to 5 minutes or until top is golden brown. Yield: 4 servings. *Chris Adkins, Austin, Texas.*

## ITALIAN BAKED CHICKEN

½ cup butter or margarine
½ cup commercial Italian salad dressing
¼ cup lemon juice
¼ cup Worcestershire sauce
2 cloves garlic, crushed
2 whole chicken breasts, split
Salt and pepper

Combine first 5 ingredients in a medium saucepan; cook over medium heat until butter melts.

Place chicken in a 12- x 8- x 2-inch baking dish. Sprinkle with salt and pepper; pour sauce over chicken. Bake, uncovered, at 325° for 1 hour or until tender. Yield: 4 servings.

*Mrs. Farmer L. Burns,*
*New Orleans, Louisiana.*

## COMPANY CREAMED CHICKEN

1 cup diced celery
1 medium onion, chopped
2 tablespoons chopped green pepper
¼ cup plus 2 tablespoons butter or margarine, divided
¼ cup plus 2 tablespoons all-purpose flour
3 cups milk
1 (10¾-ounce) can cream of mushroom soup, undiluted
4 cups diced cooked chicken
1 (4-ounce) can sliced mushrooms, drained
2 tablespoons chopped pimiento
1 cup grated Parmesan cheese
1 (2¼-ounce) package sliced almonds, toasted
12 baked patty shells

Sauté celery, onion, and green pepper in 1 tablespoon butter in a large saucepan until tender.

Melt remaining butter in a heavy saucepan over low heat; add flour, and stir until smooth. Cook 1 minute, stirring constantly. Gradually add milk; cook over medium heat, stirring constantly, until thickened and bubbly. Add soup, stirring until smooth. Stir in chicken, mushrooms, pimiento, and sautéed vegetables. Spoon mixture into a lightly greased 12- x 8- x 2-inch baking dish; sprinkle with the cheese and almonds. Bake at 350° for 30 to 40 minutes or until bubbly. Serve in patty shells. Yield: 12 servings.

*Anne Twining,*
*Princess Anne, Maryland.*

## STUFFED CHICKEN THIGHS

12 chicken thighs, skinned and boned
¾ cup finely chopped dried beef
¾ cup (3 ounces) shredded Cheddar cheese
1 whole pimiento, sliced into 12 strips
12 slices bacon
2 eggs, well beaten
2 tablespoons lemon juice
1 cup fine, dry breadcrumbs
2 teaspoons lemon-pepper seasoning
⅓ cup vegetable oil
3 tablespoons lemon juice

Place each chicken thigh on a sheet of waxed paper; flatten to ¼-inch thickness, using a meat mallet or rolling pin.

Place 1 tablespoon each of dried beef and cheese in center of each chicken thigh; top each with a slice of pimiento. Fold long sides of chicken over stuffing; fold ends over, and wrap each with a slice of bacon. Secure with wooden picks.

Combine eggs and lemon juice. Dip each chicken thigh in egg mixture. Combine the breadcrumbs and lemon-pepper seasoning; dredge each thigh in breadcrumb mixture. Heat oil in a large skillet, and cook chicken until golden on all sides. Transfer to a shallow baking pan; sprinkle with lemon juice. Bake, uncovered, at 350° for 45 minutes or until done. Yield: 12 servings.

*Lee Ann Ray,*
*Pilot Point, Texas.*

# Whirl Sauces In The Blender

Some folks think that a sauce isn't a sauce unless it's meticulously cooked in a double boiler, stirred carefully, and watched closely. But some of our readers have experimented with electric blender sauces, and they've discovered that a smooth and creamy sauce can be just a push-button away.

For béarnaise and hollandaise, two popular meat or vegetable sauces, the basic ingredients are combined and blended briefly. Then the melted butter is added in a slow and steady stream while blending constantly. If your blender has a two-sectioned lid, remove the smaller one so you can pour in the butter while leaving the larger section in place. That way you'll avoid splashes during blending.

For our Herbed Mayonnaise, the blender produces a puree of fresh and

dried herbs and mayonnaise. Honey-Lime Sauce is a smooth emulsion of vegetable oil, limeade, honey, and poppy seeds; enjoy this delicious blend on fruit salads.

## QUICK BEARNAISE SAUCE

4 egg yolks
1 tablespoon plus 1 teaspoon tarragon vinegar
1 tablespoon plus 1 teaspoon lemon juice
¼ teaspoon salt
¼ teaspoon dried whole tarragon, crushed
Pinch of dry mustard
Pinch of white pepper
½ cup butter, melted

Combine first 7 ingredients in container of electric blender; blend on high speed 3 seconds.

Turn blender to low speed; add butter to yolk mixture in a slow, steady stream. Turn blender to high speed, and blend until thick. Serve over meat or vegetables. Yield: about 1 cup.

*Charles Walton,*
*Birmingham, Alabama.*

## SEAFOOD SAUCE

¾ cup catsup
¼ cup whipping cream
2 tablespoons Worcestershire sauce
1 tablespoon lemon juice
½ teaspoon finely chopped fresh or frozen chives
½ teaspoon hot sauce
Pinch of soda

Combine all ingredients in container of electric blender; blend on low speed 1 minute or until smooth. Refrigerate 2 to 3 hours. Yield: about 1 cup.

*Jan Johnson,*
*Louisville, Kentucky.*

## BLENDER HOLLANDAISE SAUCE

3 egg yolks
1 tablespoon lemon juice
⅛ teaspoon salt
Dash of pepper
½ cup butter or margarine, melted

Combine first 4 ingredients in container of electric blender; blend until thick and lemon colored. Add butter in a slow, steady stream; continue to blend until thick. Serve over vegetables, seafood, or chicken. Yield: about ⅔ cup.

*Judy Woodall,*
*Duncanville, Texas.*

## HERBED MAYONNAISE

1½ cups mayonnaise
2 tablespoons finely chopped fresh parsley
1 tablespoon finely chopped fresh or
   frozen chives
1 teaspoon dried whole tarragon
¼ teaspoon dried dillweed

Combine all ingredients in container of electric blender; blend on low speed 1 minute or until smooth. Chill thoroughly. Serve with raw vegetables or on beef, poultry, or ham sandwiches. Yield: about 1⅓ cups.

*Ruth E. Cunliffe,*
*Lake Placid, Florida.*

## HONEY-LIME SAUCE

1 (6-ounce) can frozen limeade
   concentrate, thawed and undiluted
¾ cup vegetable oil
½ cup honey
2 teaspoons poppy seeds

Combine all ingredients in container of electric blender; blend 15 seconds or until smooth. Serve over fruit. Yield: 2 cups.

*Bertha Fowler,*
*Woodruff, South Carolina.*

# Everyone Loves A Pie

Single, double, or graham cracker crust, fruit or creamy custard filling, hot from the oven or frozen from the freezer—no matter how you bake or serve it, everyone loves a pie.

If your family's favorite is custard, serve them our Coconut Cream Pie; its coconut flavor is enhanced with coconut extract in the filling and meringue. Cottage Cheese Pie has a cheesecake-like texture and a cinnamon topping. And for a cool after-dinner refresher, enjoy our Frozen Lemon Cream Pie.

## DOUBLE-CRUST PINEAPPLE PIE

Double-crust pastry (recipe follows)
1 (15¼-ounce) can crushed pineapple
¾ cup sugar
2½ tablespoons cornstarch
3 tablespoons butter or margarine
2 teaspoons lemon rind
2 tablespoons lemon juice

Roll half of pastry to ⅛-inch thickness, and fit into a 9-inch pieplate.

Drain pineapple, reserving ½ cup pineapple juice. Combine sugar and cornstarch in a saucepan; stir well. Add reserved pineapple juice; cook over medium heat, stirring constantly, until thickened. Remove from heat. Add pineapple, butter, lemon rind, and juice; stir until butter melts.

Pour into pastry-lined pieplate. Cover with top crust, and slit in several places to allow steam to escape; seal and flute edges. Bake at 425° for 20 to 30 minutes. Yield: one 9-inch pie.

*Double-Crust Pastry:*

2 cups all-purpose flour
½ teaspoon salt
⅔ cup shortening
5 to 6 tablespoons cold water

Combine flour and salt; cut in shortening with pastry blender until mixture resembles coarse meal. Sprinkle cold water evenly over surface; stir with a fork until all dry ingredients are moistened. Shape dough into a ball; chill. Yield: pastry for one double-crust 9-inch pie.

*Edith M. Seeley,*
*London, Kentucky.*

## COCONUT CREAM PIE

1 cup sugar
¼ cup cornstarch
¼ teaspoon salt
2 cups milk
3 eggs, separated
2 tablespoons butter or margarine
1 (3½-ounce) can flaked coconut
1½ teaspoons coconut extract,
   divided
Pastry (recipe follows)
¼ teaspoon cream of tartar
¼ cup plus 2 tablespoons sugar

Combine first 3 ingredients in the top of a double boiler; stir in milk. Cook over boiling water, stirring constantly, until very thick and smooth (approximately 25 minutes).

Beat egg yolks until thick and lemon colored. Gradually stir about one-fourth of hot mixture into yolks; add to remaining hot mixture, stirring constantly. Cook, stirring constantly, until mixture thickens (about 4 minutes). Remove from heat, and gently stir in butter, coconut, and 1 teaspoon extract. Pour into baked pastry shell.

Combine egg whites (at room temperature) and cream of tartar; beat until foamy. Gradually add remaining sugar, 1 tablespoonful at a time, beating until stiff peaks form. Beat in remaining extract. Spread meringue over hot filling, sealing to edge of pastry. Bake at 350° for 12 to 15 minutes or until golden brown. Cool to room temperature; chill. Yield: one 9-inch pie.

*Pastry:*

1 cup all-purpose flour
½ teaspoon salt
⅓ cup plus 1 tablespoon shortening
2 to 3 tablespoons cold water
1 egg white

Combine flour and salt; cut in shortening with pastry blender until mixture resembles coarse meal. With a fork, stir in enough cold water (1 tablespoonful at a time) to moisten dry ingredients. Shape dough into a ball.

Roll out dough to ⅛-inch thickness on a lightly floured surface. Place in a 9-inch pieplate; trim off excess pastry around edges. Fold edges under and flute; brush with egg white. Prick bottom and sides of shell with a fork. Bake at 425° for 12 to 15 minutes or until golden brown. Yield: one 9-inch pastry shell.

*Peggy McEwen,*
*Columbiana, Alabama.*

## COTTAGE CHEESE PIE

½ cup plus 1 tablespoon sugar, divided
3 eggs
½ cup half-and-half
2 tablespoons all-purpose flour
2 teaspoons lemon juice
⅛ teaspoon salt
2 cups cream-style cottage cheese
1 unbaked 9-inch pastry shell
1 tablespoon sugar
½ teaspoon ground cinnamon

Combine ½ cup sugar and eggs in a container of an electric blender; process 15 to 20 seconds or until well blended. Add half-and-half, flour, lemon juice, and salt; process 15 to 20 seconds or until smooth. Add cottage cheese; process on medium speed until smooth. Pour into pastry shell.

Bake at 350° for 40 to 45 minutes or until set. Combine remaining sugar and cinnamon; sprinkle over pie while warm. Yield: one 9-inch pie.

*Betty Chason,*
*Tallahassee, Florida.*

*Tip: Pans used for pastry never need greasing. The pastry shell or crumb crust will not stick to the sides.*

## CHOCO-PECAN PIE

½ cup chopped pecans
2 tablespoons plus 1 teaspoon bourbon
3 eggs, well beaten
1 cup sugar
¾ cup light corn syrup
¼ cup butter or margarine, melted
¼ teaspoon salt
1 teaspoon vanilla extract
½ cup semisweet chocolate morsels
1 unbaked 9-inch pastry shell

Combine pecans and bourbon; set aside. Combine next 6 ingredients, mixing well. Stir in chocolate morsels and pecan mixture. Pour mixture into pastry shell. Bake at 375° for 55 to 60 minutes or until set. Yield: one 9-inch pie.

*Mrs. W. P. Chambers,*
*Louisville, Kentucky.*

## FROZEN LEMON CREAM PIE

⅓ cup butter or margarine, melted
1¼ cups graham cracker crumbs
¾ cup sugar, divided
2 eggs, separated
2¼ teaspoons grated lemon rind
¼ cup lemon juice
¾ cup whipping cream, whipped

Combine butter, graham cracker crumbs, and ¼ cup sugar, mixing well. Press mixture into bottom and sides of a 9-inch pieplate, reserving 1 tablespoon.

Beat egg whites (at room temperature) until foamy. Gradually add remaining sugar, 2 tablespoons at a time, beating until stiff peaks form; set aside.

Beat yolks until thick and lemon colored. Add lemon rind and juice; beat until smooth. Fold yolk mixture and whipped cream into egg whites. Spoon into crumb crust; freeze until firm. Remove pie from freezer; sprinkle reserved crumb mixture over top. Let stand 5 to 10 minutes before serving. Yield: one 9-inch pie.

*Mrs. Bernie Benigno,*
*Gulfport, Mississippi.*

# Recipe Ideas From The Kitchen Shelf

Armed with a can opener, a can of meat or seafood, and a few kitchen staples, our readers have met the challenge of what to fix in a hurry with foods on hand. Starting with canned corned beef, deviled ham, tuna, and salmon, they produce delicious results that range from appetizer snacks to entrées.

Goldie Bertch of Hope Mills, North Carolina, gets a lot of mileage from canned corned beef, serving it in the form of baked squares accompanied by cooked cabbage—all topped with a sauce. Tiny bow twists made from biscuit mix are filled with deviled ham to make unique appetizers; you'll want to prepare and freeze a batch for your next party. On the seafood side, try puffy Salmon Quiche or Quick Creole Gumbo made with canned crabmeat and shrimp.

Several points to keep in mind when cooking with canned meats or seafood:

—The liquid in a can of shrimp is seasoned with salt, so try to avoid adding more salt to the recipe.

—Commercially canned meat and seafood are usually sealed in the can and then cooked. This means it may be eaten directly from the can without reheating. Once a can is opened, the contents should be wrapped in plastic wrap or placed in an airtight container and refrigerated.

—Always check cans for signs of leakage, swelling, or bulging, as this indicates the food is spoiled and the contents of the can should be discarded.

## CORNED BEEF SQUARES AND CABBAGE

2 (12-ounce) cans corned beef, crumbled
1 cup milk
1 cup cracker crumbs
2 eggs, beaten
½ cup onion, coarsely chopped
1 tablespoon prepared horseradish
1 teaspoon prepared mustard
1 medium head cabbage
1 (10¾-ounce) can cream of mushroom soup, undiluted
⅔ cup milk
1 teaspoon dillseeds
1 teaspoon mustard seeds

Combine first 7 ingredients, mixing well. Spoon into a greased 9-inch square pan; bake at 350° for 30 minutes.

Cut cabbage into 9 wedges; cover and cook 10 minutes in a small amount of boiling salted water. Drain cabbage well.

Combine soup, milk, dill seeds, and mustard seeds in a small saucepan; cook over medium heat, stirring constantly, until mixture comes to a boil. Remove from heat. Cut corned beef mixture into 9 squares. Carefully arrange the cabbage wedges and corned beef squares on a serving platter; pour soup mixture over top. Yield: 9 servings.

*Goldie Bertch,*
*Hope Mills, North Carolina.*

## MOLDED CORNED BEEF SALAD

1 (3-ounce) package lemon-flavored gelatin
1½ cups boiling water
1 cup mayonnaise
1 (12-ounce) can corned beef, shredded
2 hard-cooked eggs, finely chopped
1 cup finely chopped celery
½ cup finely chopped onion
½ cup finely chopped green pepper
Lettuce leaves (optional)
Egg slices (optional)
Pitted ripe olives (optional)

Dissolve gelatin in boiling water. Add mayonnaise, stirring until smooth; chill until consistency of unbeaten egg white. Fold in next 5 ingredients; spoon into a 9-inch square pan. Chill until firm. Cut into squares, and serve on lettuce leaves, if desired; garnish with egg and olive slices, if desired. Yield: 9 servings.

*Kay Baker,*
*Laurel, Florida.*

## DEVILED HAM TWISTS

3 (4½-ounce) cans deviled ham
¼ cup minced pimiento-stuffed olives
3 tablespoons chopped onion
3 tablespoons chopped walnuts or pecans
6 (2-inch-square) saltine crackers, finely crushed
¼ to ½ teaspoon red pepper
¾ cup milk
2¾ cups biscuit mix
Paprika (optional)

Combine first 6 ingredients; stir well, and set aside.

Stir milk into biscuit mix; beat until dough is stiff (about 20 strokes). Divide dough in half. Roll half of dough into a 12-inch square on a floured surface. Spread half of ham mixture on half of square; fold dough over ham mixture to form a 12- x 6-inch rectangle.

Cut dough into 2- x 1-inch rectangles; gently twist to form a bow. Place bows on ungreased baking sheets; sprinkle with paprika, if desired. Repeat procedure with remaining dough and ham mixture. Bake at 400° for 12 to 15 minutes; serve hot. Yield: about 6 dozen.

*Note:* Twists may be frozen before baking. Freeze on baking sheets, and place in freezer-proof containers. To bake, place twists on baking sheets; thaw completely before baking.

*Mrs. John Rucker,*
*Louisville, Kentucky.*

## QUICK CREOLE GUMBO

3 tablespoons butter or margarine
3 tablespoons all-purpose flour
½ cup chopped onion
1 clove garlic, minced
1 (16-ounce) can whole tomatoes, undrained and chopped
1½ cups water
½ cup chopped green pepper
1 teaspoon pepper
¼ teaspoon hot sauce
1 (4¼-ounce) can shrimp, drained
1 (6½-ounce) can crabmeat, drained and flaked
Hot cooked rice
Gumbo filé

Melt butter in a Dutch oven; add flour and cook over medium heat, stirring constantly, until roux is the color of a copper penny (about 10 minutes). Stir in onion and garlic; cook until tender.

Add tomatoes, water, green pepper, pepper, and hot sauce to roux mixture; stirring well. Bring to a boil; reduce heat and simmer, covered, 20 minutes.

Stir in shrimp and crabmeat; cook just until thoroughly heated. Serve over rice. Add a small amount of filé to each serving. Yield: about 5 cups.

*Heather Riggins,*
*Nashville, Tennessee.*

## SEAFOOD SANDWICH SPREAD

1 (3-ounce) package cream cheese, softened
½ to 1 cup relish sandwich spread
1 (4½-ounce) can broken or tiny shrimp, drained
1 (3¾-ounce) can salmon, drained and flaked
1 (3½-ounce) can tuna, drained and flaked
1 tablespoon commercial sour cream
1 tablespoon mayonnaise
1 teaspoon dried shredded green onion
1 teaspoon minced fresh chives
Dash of garlic powder

Beat cream cheese until fluffy. Add remaining ingredients, stirring well. Serve on bread. Yield: about 2½ cups.

*Mrs. H. Mark Webber,*
*New Port Richey, Florida.*

## CREAMY TUNA SALAD

2 envelopes unflavored gelatin
1 cup cold water
1 (10¾-ounce) can tomato soup, undiluted
1 tablespoon sugar
½ teaspoon salt
¼ teaspoon pepper
2 (3-ounce) packages cream cheese, softened
1 cup mayonnaise
1 (9¼-ounce) can tuna, drained and flaked
1 cup diced celery
¼ cup chopped green pepper
¼ cup finely chopped onion
Lettuce leaves (optional)
Cherry tomatoes (optional)

Soften gelatin in water; set aside. Heat soup in a medium saucepan. Stir in softened gelatin mixture, sugar, salt, and pepper; remove from heat.

Combine cream cheese and mayonnaise; add to soup mixture, stirring well. Stir in next 4 ingredients. Spoon into an oiled 5-cup mold; chill until firm. Unmold on lettuce-lined serving plate, and garnish with cherry tomatoes, if desired. Yield: 6 to 8 servings.

*Mrs. H. S. Wright,*
*Leesville, South Carolina.*

## SALMON QUICHE

Pastry for 9-inch pie shell
1 small onion, chopped
½ cup chopped fresh mushrooms
1 tablespoon chopped fresh parsley
½ cup mayonnaise
1 (7¾-ounce) can salmon, drained and flaked
¼ cup half-and-half
⅛ teaspoon salt
¼ teaspoon pepper
¼ teaspoon garlic salt
1 teaspoon prepared horseradish
1 teaspoon Worcestershire sauce
3 eggs, beaten
1 cup (4 ounces) shredded Swiss cheese, divided

Line a 9-inch quiche dish or pieplate with pastry; trim excess pastry around edges and flute. Prick bottom and sides of quiche shell with a fork; bake at 425° for 10 to 12 minutes. Let cool on rack.

Combine remaining ingredients, except cheese, stirring well; set aside. Sprinkle ½ cup cheese into pastry shell; top with salmon mixture. Bake at 375° for 50 minutes. Sprinkle remaining cheese over quiche, and bake 5 additional minutes. Yield: one 9-inch quiche.

*Cynthia Stewart Neely,*
*Charlotte, North Carolina.*

# Pound For Pound, These Cakes Are The Best

With a pound each of flour, butter, sugar, and eggs, great-grandmother lovingly baked her family's favorite dessert: pound cake. Our recipes don't call for a pound of every ingredient, but these cakes do capture the simplicity and goodness of the old-fashioned version. At the same time they reflect new tastes with the delightful additions of chocolate, coconut, lemon, and other flavorings.

To bake a successful pound cake, follow these suggestions from our test kitchens staff:

—Measure ingredients accurately with standard measuring cups and spoons; don't estimate.

—Combine ingredients according to recipe directions. For example, a critical step in preparing a pound cake batter is creaming the butter or shortening and sugar until light and fluffy. This procedure should take from 5 to 7 minutes using an electric mixer.

—When adding the dry ingredients, mix or stir until the batter is smooth, but do not overbeat.

## COCONUT POUND CAKE

1 cup butter, softened
3 cups sugar
6 eggs
3 cups all-purpose flour
¼ teaspoon soda
¼ teaspoon salt
1 (8-ounce) carton commercial sour cream
1 cup frozen coconut, thawed
1 teaspoon vanilla extract
1 teaspoon coconut extract

Cream butter; gradually add sugar, beating until mixture is light and fluffy. Add eggs, one at a time, beating well after each addition.

Combine flour, soda, and salt; mix well. Add to creamed mixture alternately with sour cream, beginning and ending with flour mixture. Stir in coconut and flavorings.

Pour batter into a greased and floured 10-inch tube pan. Bake at 350° for 1 hour and 10 to 15 minutes or until a wooden pick inserted in center comes out clean. Cool in pan 10 to 15 minutes; remove from pan, and cool completely. Yield: one 10-inch cake.

*Mrs. Gary W. Taylor,*
*Afton, Virginia.*

## CHOCOLATE POUND CAKE

½ cup shortening
1 cup margarine, softened
3 cups sugar
5 eggs
3 cups all-purpose flour
½ teaspoon baking powder
½ teaspoon salt
½ cup cocoa
1¼ cups milk
1 teaspoon vanilla extract
Creamy Chocolate Glaze
Chopped pecans

Cream shortening and margarine; gradually add sugar, beating until light and fluffy. Add eggs, one at a time, beating well after each addition.

Combine flour, baking powder, salt, and cocoa; mix well. Add to creamed mixture alternately with milk, beginning and ending with flour mixture. Stir in vanilla extract.

Pour batter into a greased and floured 10-inch tube pan; bake at 350° for 1 hour and 15 minutes or until a wooden pick inserted in center comes out clean. Cool in pan 10 to 15 minutes; invert onto serving plate. Spoon Creamy Chocolate Glaze over top of warm cake, allowing it to drizzle down sides. Sprinkle with chopped pecans. Yield: one 10-inch cake.

*Creamy Chocolate Glaze:*

2¼ cups sifted powdered sugar
3 tablespoons cocoa
¼ cup margarine, softened
3 to 4 tablespoons milk

Combine sugar and cocoa, mixing well. Add remaining ingredients; beat until smooth. Yield: about 2 cups.

*Mary Griffin,*
*Birmingham, Alabama.*

## PRALINE POUND CAKE

1 cup butter, softened
½ cup shortening
1 (16-ounce) package dark brown sugar
5 eggs
3 cups all-purpose flour, divided
½ teaspoon baking powder
¼ teaspoon soda
¾ cup milk
2 cups chopped pecans
2 teaspoons vanilla extract

Cream butter and shortening; gradually add sugar, beating until light and fluffy. Add eggs, one at a time, beating well after each addition.

Combine 2½ cups flour, baking powder, and soda; stir well. Add to creamed mixture alternately with milk, beginning and ending with flour mixture. Dredge pecans in remaining ½ cup flour. Stir pecans and vanilla into batter.

Pour batter into a greased and floured 10-inch tube pan. Bake at 350° for 1 hour and 15 minutes or until a wooden pick inserted in center comes out clean. Cool in pan 10 to 15 minutes; remove from pan, and let cool. Yield: one 10-inch cake.

*Mrs. J. Russell Buchanan,*
*Monroe, Louisiana.*

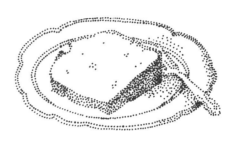

## OLD-FASHIONED POUND CAKE

2 cups butter, softened
2 cups sugar
8 eggs
3¼ cups all-purpose flour
½ teaspoon salt
2 teaspoons vanilla extract
1 teaspoon almond extract

Cream butter; gradually add sugar, beating until mixture is light and fluffy. Add eggs, one at a time, beating well after each addition.

Combine flour and salt, stirring well; add to creamed mixture. Stir in vanilla and almond flavorings.

Pour batter into a greased and floured 10-inch tube pan. Bake at 350° for 1 hour or until a wooden pick inserted in center comes out clean. Cool in pan 10 to 15 minutes; remove from pan, and cool on a rack. Yield: one 10-inch cake. *Mrs. Bud Holtum,*
*Charlotte, North Carolina.*

## LEMON POUND CAKE

1½ cups butter or margarine, softened
3 cups sugar
8 eggs
3 cups all-purpose flour
1 tablespoon plus 1½ teaspoons lemon juice
1 tablespoon plus 1½ teaspoons lemon extract

Cream butter; gradually add sugar, beating until light and fluffy. Add eggs, one at a time, beating well after each addition. Add flour, mixing well. Stir in lemon juice and lemon extract.

Pour batter into a greased and floured 10-inch tube pan. Bake at 350° for 1 hour and 15 minutes or until a wooden pick inserted in center comes out clean. Cool in pan 10 to 15 minutes; remove from pan, and cool completely. Yield: one 10-inch cake.

*Dorothy Pearce,*
*Portland, Texas.*

# Go Mexican With A Main Dish

Add a bit of spice to your menus by serving main dishes that feature tortillas, green chiles, refried beans, and cheese. These hearty, Mexican-style creations are easily made with convenient ingredients appearing on most supermarket shelves.

Packaged tortillas and bottled taco sauce are real time-savers when you prepare Easy Chicken Enchiladas. Canned refried beans combine with ground beef and canned salsa to make one of our favorites, Cheesy Beef-and-Bean Bake. And nothing could be easier than Chile-Cheese Casserole topped with commercial picante sauce.

## CRUSTY BEEF CASSEROLE

1 pound ground beef
¼ cup chopped onion
1 clove garlic, crushed
2 (8-ounce) cans tomato sauce
2 tablespoons chili powder
1 cup (4 ounces) shredded Cheddar cheese
1 (16-ounce) can pinto beans, undrained
1 (6-ounce) package cornbread mix

Cook ground beef, onion, and garlic in a large skillet until meat is browned, stirring to crumble. Drain off pan drippings; stir in tomato sauce and chili powder. Spoon meat mixture into a lightly greased 12- x 8- x 2-inch baking dish. Top with cheese; spoon beans over cheese.

Prepare cornbread mix according to package directions; pour over beans. Bake at 400° for 25 minutes or until cornbread is golden. Yield: 6 servings.

*Sally Pedigo,*
*Dallas, Texas.*

## CHEESY BEEF-AND-BEAN BAKE

1½ pounds ground beef
4 (7-ounce) cans green chili salsa, divided
1 (16-ounce) can refried beans
1 cup (4 ounces) shredded Monterey Jack cheese
½ teaspoon ground cumin
¼ teaspoon garlic powder
8 (8-inch) flour tortillas
3 cups (12 ounces) shredded Colby or Cheddar cheese
4 green onions, chopped
2 large tomatoes, peeled and chopped
Shredded lettuce
Commercial sour cream (optional)

Cook ground beef in a large skillet until browned, stirring to crumble; drain off pan drippings. Add 2 cans chili salsa; bring to a boil. Reduce heat to low, and cook 10 minutes or until liquid has completely evaporated.

Combine refried beans, Monterey Jack cheese, cumin, and garlic powder. Spread a small amount of bean mixture on each tortilla; top with a small amount of meat mixture. Roll up each tortilla; place seam side down in a lightly greased 13- x 9- x 2-inch baking dish. Pour remaining 2 cans chili salsa over tortillas; sprinkle with remaining cheese. Top with onion and tomato. Bake at 350° for 30 minutes or until bubbly. Serve with lettuce and sour cream, if desired. Yield: 6 to 8 servings.

*Jan Moses,*
*Greensboro, North Carolina.*

## SKILLET ENCHILADAS

1 pound ground beef
½ cup chopped onion
1 (10¾-ounce) can cream of mushroom soup, undiluted
1 (10-ounce) can mild enchilada sauce
⅓ cup milk
2 tablespoons chopped green chiles
8 (8-inch) flour tortillas
Vegetable oil
2½ cups (10 ounces) shredded sharp process American cheese, divided
½ cup chopped ripe olives

Cook ground beef and onion in a large skillet until meat is browned, stirring to crumble. Drain off pan drippings. Stir in soup, enchilada sauce, milk, and chiles. Cook over low heat 15 minutes or until thickened, stirring occasionally. Remove from heat, and set aside.

Fry tortillas, one at a time, in ¼ inch hot oil (375°) for 5 seconds on each side or just until softened. Drain tortillas on paper towels.

Sprinkle each tortilla with ¼ cup cheese and 1 tablespoon olives; roll up tightly. Place tortillas, seam side down, in meat sauce in skillet. Cover and simmer until thoroughly heated (about 5 minutes). Sprinkle with remaining cheese; cover and cook an additional minute or until cheese melts. Yield: 4 servings.

*Susan Erickson,*
*Pocahontas, Arkansas.*

## CHICKEN TORTILLA BAKE

1 cup chopped fresh mushrooms
1 medium onion, chopped
2 tablespoons vegetable oil
6 cups chopped cooked chicken
1 (10¾-ounce) can cream of mushroom soup, undiluted
1 (10¾-ounce) can cream of chicken soup, undiluted
1 (4-ounce) can chopped green chiles, undrained
¼ cup chicken broth
¼ teaspoon salt
¼ teaspoon pepper
⅛ teaspoon garlic powder
4 frozen corn tortillas, thawed
1 cup (4 ounces) shredded Cheddar cheese
1 cup (4 ounces) shredded Monterey Jack cheese

Sauté mushrooms and onion in oil until tender. Remove from heat; stir in remaining ingredients, except the tortillas and cheese.

Tear each tortilla into 4 pieces. Layer half of the tortillas, chicken mixture, and cheese in a lightly greased 12- x 8- x 2-inch baking dish. Repeat layers. Bake at 350° for 30 minutes or until bubbly. Yield: 8 servings.

*Anne Nelson,*
*Richardson, Texas.*

## EASY CHICKEN ENCHILADAS

2 cups chopped cooked chicken
2 (8-ounce) jars taco sauce
1 tablespoon chicken-flavored bouillon granules
2 cups half-and-half
10 to 12 (8-inch) flour tortillas
2 cups (8 ounces) shredded Monterey Jack cheese
Fresh parsley sprigs (optional)
Jalapeño peppers (optional)

Combine chicken and taco sauce in a large saucepan; cook over low heat 15 minutes, stirring often.

Dissolve bouillon in half-and-half in a large skillet over low heat (do not boil).

Cook tortillas, one at a time, in an ungreased skillet about 10 seconds on each side or until softened. Dip each tortilla into half-and-half mixture.

Spoon 1 heaping tablespoon chicken mixture in center of each tortilla; roll up tightly, and place seam side down in a lightly greased 13- x 9- x 2-inch baking dish. Pour remaining half-and-half mixture over tortillas; sprinkle with cheese. Bake at 350° for 30 minutes. Garnish with parsley and jalapeño peppers, if desired. Yield: 8 servings.

*Rinnie Ashcraft,*
*Louisville, Kentucky.*

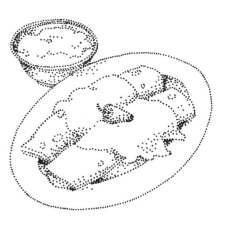

## SPICY MEXICAN CHICKEN

½ cup all-purpose flour
2 teaspoons salt, divided
1 teaspoon pepper
1 (3- to 3½-pound) broiler-fryer, cut up
¼ cup vegetable oil
¼ cup butter or margarine
1½ cups chopped onion
¾ cup chopped green pepper
3 cloves garlic, minced
1 (14½-ounce) can whole tomatoes, undrained and chopped
1 (10-ounce) can tomatoes with green chiles, undrained and chopped
1 (10-ounce) package frozen whole kernel corn, partially thawed
2 tablespoons chili powder
1 teaspoon cumin seeds

Combine flour, 1 teaspoon salt, and pepper; mix well. Dredge chicken in flour mixture; heat oil and butter in a heavy skillet. Brown chicken on all sides, and transfer to a 13- x 9- x 2-inch baking dish.

Add onion, green pepper, and garlic to pan drippings; sauté until tender. Add remaining ingredients; stir well and pour over chicken. Cover and bake at 325° for 1 hour or until chicken is tender. Yield: 6 servings.

*Margaret Paul,*
*Lafayette, Louisiana.*

## CHILE-CHEESE CASSEROLE

1 (4-ounce) can whole green chiles, drained
1½ cups (6 ounces) shredded Cheddar cheese
1½ cups (6 ounces) shredded Monterey Jack cheese
6 eggs, beaten
1 (5.33-ounce) can evaporated milk
3 tablespoons all-purpose flour
1 (8-ounce) can tomato sauce
¼ cup commercial picante sauce

Cut chiles in half lengthwise, and discard seeds; then cut into thin strips. Arrange strips in a lightly greased 11- x 7- x 2-inch baking dish; top with cheese.

Combine eggs, milk, and flour; stir well, and pour over cheese. Bake mixture at 300° for 30 minutes.

Combine tomato sauce and picante sauce; mix well, and pour over egg mixture. Bake 15 additional minutes. Let stand 5 minutes before serving; cut into squares to serve. Yield: 6 servings.
*Carol Lane,*
*Waco, Texas.*

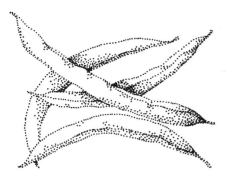

## Bring Out The Flavor Of Green Beans

Helping to string or snap green beans seems to be a routine part of childhood. So is remembering the delicious aroma as they simmered with ham hocks or bacon drippings on the stove's back burner. Our readers have other good ideas for green beans, such as cooking them until crisp-tender with chives and tarragon or baking them with sour cream. Mary Rose Metzcus of Miami Lakes, Florida, simmers green beans with cumin seeds in a tangy tomato sauce.

Be sure to purchase beans with long, straight pods that snap readily when broken. Store fresh beans in the refrigerator in a moisture-proof container, and use them as soon as possible.

## GREEN BEANS WITH HERBS

2 pounds fresh green beans
1 cup water
¼ cup butter or margarine
2 teaspoons chopped chives
½ teaspoon sugar
¾ teaspoon salt
½ to 1 teaspoon dried whole tarragon
⅛ teaspoon pepper

Remove strings from beans; wash and cut into 1½-inch pieces. Combine beans and remaining ingredients in a large saucepan; cover and cook over low heat 12 minutes or until crisp-tender. Yield: 8 servings.
*Elizabeth Grimes,*
*Fremont, North Carolina.*

## CUMIN GREEN BEANS

1 pound fresh green beans
6 slices bacon
1 medium onion, chopped
1 clove garlic, minced
1 (15-ounce) can tomato sauce
1 tablespoon cumin seeds
1 teaspoon sugar

Remove strings from beans; wash and cut into 1-inch pieces. Cook beans, covered, in a small amount of boiling salted water 15 to 20 minutes or until tender. Drain and set aside.

Cook bacon in a large skillet until crisp; remove bacon, reserving drippings. Crumble bacon and set aside. Sauté onion and garlic in bacon drippings until tender. Stir in beans, bacon, and remaining ingredients; reduce and simmer, uncovered, 10 to 15 minutes. Yield: 4 servings.
*Mary Rose Metzcus,*
*Miami Lakes, Florida.*

## GREEN BEANS WITH SOUR CREAM

1½ pounds fresh green beans
1 small clove garlic, crushed
¼ cup butter or margarine
2 tablespoons soft breadcrumbs
½ cup chopped fresh parsley
Pepper to taste
1 (8-ounce) carton commercial sour cream

Remove strings from beans; wash and cut into 1-inch pieces. Cook beans, covered, in a small amount of boiling salted water 15 to 20 minutes or until tender. Drain and set aside.

Sauté garlic in butter in a small skillet until tender; add breadcrumbs and cook, stirring occasionally, until browned. Add breadcrumb mixture, parsley, pepper, and sour cream to green beans. Spoon mixture into a lightly greased 1½-quart casserole. Bake at 350° for 15 minutes. Yield: 6 servings.
*Anna Hoosack,*
*Knob Noster, Missouri.*

## SWEET-AND-SOUR GREEN BEANS

1¼ pounds fresh green beans
4 slices bacon
1 small onion, chopped
¾ cup sugar
½ cup vinegar

Remove strings from beans; wash and cut into 1-inch pieces. Set aside.

Cook bacon in a large skillet until crisp; remove bacon, reserving drippings. Crumble bacon and set aside.

Sauté onion in bacon drippings until tender. Add sugar, stirring until dissolved. Stir in bacon, beans, and vinegar. Cover and bring to a boil; reduce heat, and simmer 25 minutes or until beans are tender. Yield: 6 servings.
*Kay Baker,*
*Laurel, Florida.*

## He Grills A Family Favorite

A Vicksburg, Mississippi, surgeon and father of four, Dr. Briggs Hopson has little time to spend in the kitchen. Even so, his family and friends consider him an exceptionally good cook. According to his wife, Pat, "Briggs loves to experiment with food, and the children and I look forward to sampling his new creations."

"This is my favorite recipe," Dr. Hopson says of his Grilled Beef Eye of Round. "I prepare it for special occasions and then use the leftovers for sandwiches." Using a metal skewer, he makes small holes in a beef eye of round and fills each with a peppercorn. The roast is placed in a plastic bag with a zip seal to marinate in a tangy sauce. "These bags work great because the marinade can reach all sides of the meat at one time. Plus, they make it easy to lift and turn the meat whenever needed."

Sometimes Dr. Hopson uses the microwave oven to reduce preparation time in his recipes. For Crabmeat and

Mushrooms on Toast Points, he saves time by microwaving the mushroom caps while preparing the crabmeat mixture. This flavorful seafood dish is topped with bacon and shredded Colby cheese.

Dr. Hopson's specialties are followed by recipes from other men who also enjoy cooking.

## GRILLED BEEF EYE OF ROUND

1 (3- to 3½-pound) beef eye of round
Whole black peppercorns
¼ teaspoon garlic salt
¼ teaspoon seasoned pepper
1⅓ cups commercial low-calorie Italian dressing
¾ cup Madeira wine
2 tablespoons Worcestershire sauce
Fresh parsley sprigs (optional)

Using a metal skewer, make 1-inch-deep holes spaced ¾ inch apart around entire roast; insert a peppercorn in each hole. Rub surface of roast with smooth edge of skewer to close holes. Rub garlic salt and seasoned pepper over surface of the meat.

Place roast in plastic bag with zip seal. Combine next 3 ingredients, and pour over meat; close bag. Marinate in refrigerator 12 to 24 hours, turning bag several times. Remove roast from bag; pour marinade in a small saucepan, and set aside.

Loosely wrap roast in a double thickness of heavy-duty aluminum foil. Place roast on gas grill; cook over medium heat to desired degree of doneness (30 minutes per pound for rare). Let roast stand at room temperature 15 minutes before carving; cut into ¼-inch-thick slices. Garnish with parsley, if desired.

Heat reserved marinade to boiling point; serve with roast. Yield: about 6 servings.

*Note:* Roast may marinate in a large, shallow container, rather than a plastic bag. If desired, roast may be cooked over an electric grill according to the manufacturer's directions.

*Tip: When grilling steak, turn only once. Always use tongs to turn steak; a fork will pierce the meat and allow juices to escape. To prevent steak from curling while grilling, score or slit the fat along the edge at about 1½-inch intervals before placing on the grill.*

## CRABMEAT AND MUSHROOMS ON TOAST POINTS

4 slices bacon, cut in half
1 pound fresh mushrooms
2 tablespoons butter or margarine, melted
½ teaspoon Worcestershire sauce
¼ teaspoon hot sauce
1 pound fresh lump crabmeat, drained and flaked
2 tablespoons mayonnaise
2 tablespoons fine, dry breadcrumbs
1 tablespoon chopped fresh parsley
Juice of 1 lemon
1 cup (4 ounces) shredded natural Colby cheese
Toast points

Cook bacon until transparent (not crisp); drain and set aside.

Clean mushrooms with damp paper towels. Remove mushroom stems, and reserve for use in another recipe. Place mushroom caps in a 12- x 8- x 2-inch baking dish. Combine butter, Worcestershire sauce, and hot sauce; stir well, and drizzle over mushroom caps. Bake at 350° for 15 minutes. Remove mushroom caps with a slotted spoon; drain off excess liquid. Return mushroom caps to baking dish; set aside.

Combine the crabmeat, mayonnaise, breadcrumbs, parsley, and lemon juice; spoon over mushroom caps. Sprinkle with cheese; arrange bacon over top. Bake at 350° for 15 to 20 minutes or until bacon is done. Serve on toast points. Yield: 6 servings.

*Note:* To cook mushroom caps in a microwave oven, place in a 12- x 8- x 2-inch baking dish. Drizzle butter mixture over caps. Cover with heavy-duty plastic wrap. Microwave at HIGH 6 to 8 minutes, rearranging after 3 minutes. Complete recipe as described above.

## SAUTEED JULIENNE CARROTS

1 tablespoon butter or margarine
1 tablespoon olive oil
3 to 4 medium carrots, cut into thin lengthwise strips
1 small green pepper, cut into thin lengthwise strips
½ teaspoon salt
Pinch of pepper
Dillweed or seeds to taste
Pinch of sugar

Melt butter in a large skillet; add oil. Add remaining ingredients; cook, stirring occasionally, 5 minutes or until carrots are crisp-tender. Yield: 4 servings.
*Bruce Whitehouse,*
*Hockessin, Delaware.*

## CHERRY COBBLER

2 (16-ounce) cans pitted tart red cherries
3 tablespoons cornstarch
¾ cup sugar
3 tablespoons butter or margarine
1 tablespoon grated lemon rind
¼ teaspoon almond extract
1 cup all-purpose flour
¾ cup sugar
1 teaspoon baking powder
¼ teaspoon salt
½ cup milk
¼ cup shortening
1 teaspoon vanilla extract
1 egg
Vanilla ice cream (optional)

Drain cherries, reserving 1 cup liquid. Combine cornstarch, ¾ cup sugar, and reserved cherry liquid in a medium saucepan; cook over medium heat, stirring constantly, until smooth and thickened. Remove from heat and add butter, lemon rind, and almond extract; stir until butter melts. Gently stir in cherries; pour into a lightly greased 12- x 8- x 2-inch baking dish. Set aside.

Combine flour, ¾ cup sugar, baking powder, and salt; stir gently. Add milk, shortening, and vanilla; beat 2 minutes on medium speed of electric mixer. Add egg; beat 2 minutes. Spoon batter evenly over cherry mixture; bake at 350° for 35 to 40 minutes or until done. Serve warm cobbler with ice cream, if desired. Yield: 8 servings.
*Dr. W. H. Pinkston,*
*Knoxville, Tennessee.*

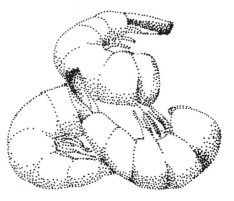

## SEAFOOD SAUCE DELIGHT

⅓ cup chili sauce
2 tablespoons lemon juice
1½ tablespoons prepared horseradish
1 teaspoon grated onion
1 teaspoon Worcestershire sauce
⅛ teaspoon hot sauce

Combine all ingredients, stirring until smooth. Cover and chill at least 2 hours. Yield: about ½ cup.
*Roy Carlisle,*
*Columbus, Georgia.*

## PERFECT CUSTARD PIE

**4 eggs, slightly beaten**
**½ cup sugar**
**¼ teaspoon salt**
**1 teaspoon vanilla extract**
**½ teaspoon almond extract**
**2 cups milk, scalded**
**1 unbaked 9-inch pastry shell**
**Ground nutmeg (optional)**

Combine eggs, sugar, salt, and flavorings; beat until blended. Gradually stir in scalded milk. Pour into pastry shell; sprinkle with nutmeg, if desired.

Bake at 400° for 15 minutes; reduce temperature to 350°, and bake 15 to 20 additional minutes or until knife inserted in center comes out clean. Cool to room temperature; chill before serving. Yield: one 9-inch pie.

*Gene Warner,*
*Macon, Georgia.*

# Easter Bread

According to legend, breads similar to this rich, sweet loaf were baked for Greek Easter celebrations. Since it's similar to a coffee cake, you can enjoy Trinity Feast Bread loaves for breakfast or brunch. Just slice and serve bread with butter.

### TRINITY FEAST BREAD

**2 packages dry yeast**
**5 to 6 cups all-purpose flour, divided**
**¾ cup sugar**
**¼ teaspoon salt**
**¾ cup half-and-half**
**¼ cup water**
**½ cup butter or margarine**
**4 eggs, beaten**
**1 tablespoon grated lemon rind**
**2 teaspoons vanilla extract**
**1 egg white**
**1 tablespoon water**
**Powdered sugar glaze (recipe follows)**
**Decorator candies**

Combine yeast, 1½ cups flour, sugar, and salt in a large bowl; stir well.

Combine half-and-half, ¼ cup water, and butter in a small saucepan; place over low heat until very warm (120° to 130°). Gradually add cream mixture to flour mixture, stirring well; beat at medium speed of electric mixer 2 minutes. Add eggs, lemon rind, and vanilla; beat well. Gradually add 1 cup flour; beat at

high speed 2 additional minutes. Stir in enough remaining flour (2½ to 3½ cups) to make a soft dough.

Turn dough out onto a lightly floured surface, and knead until smooth and elastic (about 8 to 10 minutes). Place dough in a well-greased bowl, turning to grease top. Cover and let rise in a warm place (85°), free from drafts, 1 hour or until doubled in bulk.

Punch dough down; turn out on a lightly floured surface. Divide dough in half; shape each portion into a ball. Divide 1 ball of dough into 3 equal portions, and shape each into a smooth round ball; place in a 3-leaf clover design on a greased baking sheet. Repeat procedure with remaining dough. Cover; let rise in a warm place (85°), free from drafts, 1 hour or until doubled in bulk.

Combine egg white and 1 tablespoon water, mixing well; gently brush over each loaf. Bake at 350° for 20 minutes. Cover loaves loosely with aluminum foil; continue to bake at 350° for 20 minutes or until loaves sound hollow when tapped. Cool loaves on wire racks. Drizzle with powdered sugar glaze and sprinkle with decorator candies. Yield: 2 loaves.

*Powdered Sugar Glaze:*

**1 cup sifted powdered sugar**
**½ teaspoon vanilla extract**
**1½ tablespoons milk**

Combine all ingredients, mixing well. Yield: about ½ cup.

# Try Your Hand With Artichokes

If you've been shying away from the thick-leaved artichoke, then you're missing a delicious food that makes an elegant dish for almost any special occasion. And since the peak season for artichokes is during April and May, that is the perfect time to experiment with them.

Select heavy, compact artichokes that yield slightly to pressure. While brown-tipped leaves may look unappealing, they don't necessarily mean inferior quality; artichokes are easily bruised or discolored by frost, but the fine flavor remains.

To prepare the artichoke for boiling, the stem end, top, and leaves are

trimmed. The center cone and fuzzy choke should be removed after the artichoke cooks.

In this featured recipe, artichokes are parboiled, then filled with a cheesy ham stuffing before baking. While enjoying the stuffing, you can also break off the outer leaves and pull the fleshy part of the artichoke leaf through your teeth. Be sure to eat the heart (near the base), too; it's the most prized part of this vegetable.

### STUFFED ARTICHOKES

**5 artichokes**
**Lemon wedge**
**1 clove garlic**
**2 cups chopped cooked ham**
**1 cup cubed Swiss cheese**
**½ cup mayonnaise**
**⅓ cup chopped green pepper**
**¼ cup finely chopped onion**
**2 teaspoons lemon juice**
**½ teaspoon salt**

Wash artichokes by plunging up and down in cold water. Cut off the stem end, and trim about ½ inch from top of each artichoke. Remove any loose bottom leaves. With scissors, trim away about a fourth of each outer leaf. Rub top and edges of leaves with a lemon wedge to prevent discoloration.

Place artichokes and garlic in 2 inches water in a large Dutch oven. Cover and heat to boiling; reduce heat, and simmer 20 minutes. Spread leaves apart; then scrape out the fuzzy thistle center (choke) with a spoon.

Combine remaining ingredients; stir well. Spoon ham mixture into center of each artichoke. Place artichokes in a 2-quart shallow casserole with about ½ inch of water. Cover and bake at 375° for 35 minutes or until leaves pull out easily. Yield: 5 servings.

*Florence L. Costello,*
*Chattanooga, Tennessee.*

# Let Lamb Lead The Menu

With lamb available year-round and at prices comparable to beef, consider making it the focus of your menus. Take a look at these delectable choices.

Pineapple and celery seeds flavor the stuffing for our version of roast leg of lamb. After baking, it comes to the table glazed with red currant jelly—all tender, juicy, and so delicious. To save time in preparation, have the butcher bone the leg of lamb rather than doing it yourself.

Lamb chops get special treatment in Gourmet Lamb Chops Dijonaise. After marinating the chops in a brandied sauce, they are spread with a mustard-breadcrumb topping and sprinkled with rosemary before broiling.

## STUFFED LEG OF LAMB

1 (7-pound) leg of lamb, boned
1½ tablespoons butter or margarine
2 slices soft bread, crumbled
½ teaspoon celery seeds
¼ teaspoon salt
¼ teaspoon pepper
1 (8-ounce) can crushed pineapple, drained
2 cloves garlic, sliced
1 tablespoon margarine, softened
¼ teaspoon ground ginger
1 tablespoon lemon juice
About ¼ cup red currant jelly

Place lamb, fat side up, in an open roasting pan. Melt 1½ tablespoons butter in a small skillet, and add crumbled bread; cook until brown, stirring constantly. Stir in celery seeds, salt, pepper, and pineapple. Pack mixture into pocket of lamb. Fasten open edges together with skewers.

Make several small slits on outside of lamb, and stuff with garlic slices. Rub outside of lamb with softened margarine, and sprinkle with ginger and lemon juice.

Bake at 325° for 2 hours and 15 minutes. Glaze roast with currant jelly, and bake an additional 15 minutes. Let stand 10 minutes before carving. Make gravy from pan drippings, if desired, and serve with roast. Yield: 6 to 8 servings.
*Helen L. Berman,*
*Dover, Delaware.*

## LAMB SHANKS MILANAISE

4 lamb shanks
¼ cup plus 2 tablespoons all-purpose flour
¼ teaspoon pepper
¼ cup plus 2 tablespoons vegetable oil
1 cup white wine
¼ cup chicken broth
1 clove garlic, minced
1 tablespoon dried parsley
Grated rind of 1 lemon

Trim lamb shanks of excess fat; rinse and pat dry. Combine flour and pepper; dredge lamb in flour mixture.

Heat oil in an electric skillet or large Dutch oven; add lamb, and cook over medium heat until browned. Drain oil from skillet. Add wine to lamb; cook, uncovered, 5 minutes. Add broth, and reduce heat. Cover and simmer 1 hour and 15 minutes or until lamb is tender. If mixture becomes too thick, add additional broth.

Combine garlic, parsley, and lemon rind; sprinkle over lamb the last 5 minutes of cooking. Yield: 2 to 4 servings.
*Ernestine Donaldson,*
*De Funiak Springs, Florida.*

## GOURMET LAMB CHOPS DIJONAISE

4 (¾-inch-thick) loin lamb chops
1 clove garlic
½ cup olive oil
½ cup brandy
1 tablespoon dried whole rosemary
1 teaspoon seasoned pepper
1 tablespoon garlic powder
2 cloves garlic, minced
2 tablespoons Italian breadcrumbs
1 tablespoon margarine, melted
½ cup Dijon mustard, divided
1 tablespoon dried whole rosemary
Mint jelly

Rub lamb chops with garlic clove, and place chops in a shallow dish. Combine next 6 ingredients, stirring well; pour over chops. Cover and marinate in refrigerator at least 8 hours, turning chops several times.

Remove chops from marinade, and place on broiler pan. Combine breadcrumbs, margarine, and ¼ cup Dijon mustard; mix well, and spread evenly on top of chops. Sprinkle lamb chops with 1 tablespoon rosemary.

Broil 11 inches from heat 10 minutes. Remove from oven, and brush top of chops with remaining Dijon mustard. Return to oven, and broil an additional 10 minutes. Remove from oven, and allow to stand 5 minutes. Serve with mint jelly. Yield: 2 to 4 servings.
*Mrs. W. Rodger Giles,*
*Augusta, Georgia.*

*Tip: Freeze small portions of leftover meat or fowl till you have enough for a pot pie, curry, or rice casserole.*

## CURRIED LAMB WITH RICE

2 tablespoons margarine
½ pound boneless lamb, cut into 1-inch cubes
⅔ cup diced onion
1 cup water
1 tablespoon all-purpose flour
¼ teaspoon curry powder
1 teaspoon salt
Dash of pepper
Hot cooked rice
Paprika
Fresh parsley sprigs

Melt margarine in a skillet; add lamb and onion. Sauté over medium heat until lamb is brown. Reduce heat, and add water; cover and simmer 1 hour.

Stir flour and seasonings into lamb mixture; cook, stirring constantly, until thickened. Serve over hot rice. Garnish with paprika and sprigs of parsley. Yield: 2 servings. *Edith E. Rumford,*
*Fort Lawn, South Carolina.*

# Salad Dressings To Brag About

One of these creamy homemade salad dressings can turn a simple tossed salad into a "creation." Caesar Salad Dressing proved to be a real favorite with our test kitchens staff. Get out your blender, and whirl up this mixture of eggs, anchovies, celery, onion, garlic, seasonings, and oil in a matter of seconds. Another favorite was Celery Seed Salad Dressing flavored with onion, ground celery seed, and dry mustard.

## AVOCADO FRUIT SALAD DRESSING

1 ripe avocado, peeled and chopped
½ cup whipping cream
3 tablespoons powdered sugar
2 tablespoons lemon juice
¼ teaspoon salt
⅛ teaspoon ground ginger
½ cup whipping cream, whipped

Combine first 6 ingredients in container of electric blender; process until smooth. Fold in whipped cream; serve dressing over fruit salad. Store in refrigerator. Yield: about 2 cups.
*Evelyn Weisman,*
*Kingsville, Texas.*

## BLUE CHEESE SALAD DRESSING

1 (8-ounce) carton commercial sour cream
1 cup mayonnaise
¼ cup red wine vinegar
3 ounces blue cheese, crumbled
2 tablespoons chopped green onion
2 tablespoons chopped fresh parsley
1 teaspoon lemon juice

Combine all ingredients, stirring well. Chill before serving; serve dressing over salad greens. Store in refrigerator. Yield: about 2½ cups.
*Jeanne H. Minetree,*
*Dinwiddie, Virginia.*

## CAESAR SALAD DRESSING

3 eggs
1 stalk celery, coarsely chopped
½ cup coarsely chopped onion
1 (2-ounce) can anchovies, drained
2 cloves garlic
2 tablespoons prepared mustard
1 tablespoon lemon juice
1 teaspoon monosodium glutamate
1 teaspoon pepper
½ teaspoon sugar
2 cups vegetable oil

Combine all ingredients, except oil, in container of electric blender; process until smooth. Add oil, ¼ cup at a time, processing after each addition. Chill before serving; serve dressing over salad greens. Store in refrigerator. Yield: about 3½ cups.
*Meta Davis,*
*St. Charles, Missouri.*

## CELERY SEED SALAD DRESSING

1 cup vegetable oil
⅔ cup sugar
¼ cup tarragon wine vinegar
¼ cup cider vinegar
3 tablespoons coarsely chopped onion
1 tablespoon paprika
1 tablespoon ground celery seeds
1½ teaspoons salt
½ teaspoon dry mustard

Combine all ingredients in container of electric blender; process mixture until smooth. Chill before serving; serve dressing over salad greens. Yield: about 2 cups.
*Mrs. John R. Armstrong,*
*Farwell, Texas.*

## SWEET FRENCH DRESSING

1 (22-ounce) bottle catsup
1½ cups sugar
1 (10¾-ounce) can tomato soup, undiluted
1 cup cider vinegar
1 cup vegetable oil
1 clove garlic, crushed
1 teaspoon paprika
1 teaspoon salt
1 teaspoon dry mustard
1 teaspoon Worcestershire sauce

Combine all ingredients in container of electric blender; process until smooth. Chill before serving; serve dressing over salad greens. Yield: about 6½ cups.
*Mrs. Thomas R. Cherry,*
*Birmingham, Alabama.*

## CREAMY FRUIT SALAD DRESSING

⅔ cup sugar
2 tablespoons all-purpose flour
2 tablespoons vegetable oil
1 cup pineapple juice
2 eggs
2 tablespoons lemon juice
¼ cup orange juice
1 cup whipping cream, whipped

Combine sugar and flour in top of double boiler, stirring well; stir in oil and pineapple juice. Bring water to a boil; cook, stirring constantly, until thickened.

Beat eggs; gradually stir in lemon and orange juice. Gradually stir about one-fourth of hot mixture into egg mixture; add to remaining hot mixture, stirring constantly. Place over boiling water; cook, stirring constantly, 2 to 3 minutes or until smooth and thickened. Remove from heat; cool. Fold in whipped cream; serve over fruit salad. Store in refrigerator. Yield: about 3 cups.
*Mrs. Earl L. Faulkenberry,*
*Lancaster, South Carolina.*

# Yeast Biscuits To Freeze

Nothing whets an appetite like the aroma of steaming, hot yeast biscuits fresh from the oven. Delightfully sweet and tender, Southern Raised Biscuits are as tasty as they are easy to make. If you can resist eating them immediately, freeze a batch for later use. Just bake the biscuits 5 minutes, cool, and freeze.

## SOUTHERN RAISED BISCUITS

2 packages dry yeast
¼ cup warm water (105° to 115°)
2 cups buttermilk
5 cups all-purpose flour
⅓ cup sugar
1 tablespoon baking powder
1 teaspoon soda
1¼ teaspoons salt
1 cup shortening

Combine yeast and warm water; let stand 5 minutes or until bubbly. Add buttermilk to yeast mixture, and set aside.

Combine dry ingredients in a large bowl; cut in shortening until mixture resembles coarse meal. Add buttermilk mixture, mixing with a fork until dry ingredients are moistened. Turn dough out on a floured surface, and knead lightly 3 or 4 times.

Roll dough to ½-inch thickness; cut with a 2¾-inch biscuit cutter, and place on lightly greased baking sheets. Cover and let rise 1 hour.

Bake at 450° for 10 to 12 minutes. Yield: about 2 dozen.

*Note:* Biscuits can be made ahead and frozen. To freeze, bake only 5 minutes; cool. Wrap in aluminum foil; freeze. To serve, place biscuits on lightly greased baking sheets and thaw. Bake at 450° for 7 to 10 minutes.
*Mrs. W. P. Chambers,*
*Louisville, Kentucky.*

# It's Easy To Slice A Pineapple

When your mouth waters for pineapple or when a recipe calls for this exotic fruit, a fresh one is a delightful change from the canned version. You'll be tempted to use fresh pineapple more often if you know how to choose one and also how to cut it easily.

When selecting fresh pineapple at the market, it's helpful to know that the fruit has been examined and picked at the peak of ripeness before leaving the plantation. The shells may be either golden or green, but the pineapple meat will be juicy and sweet.

Fragrance is one of the best signs of sweetness; you should sniff the fruit to be sure it smells fresh, with a faint pineapple scent. Choose a pineapple that is plump and heavy for its size, with a green, leafy crown.

The sooner fresh pineapple is eaten, the better. If you must store it, keep it in a plastic bag in the refrigerator. One important cooking hint—fresh pineapple contains an enzyme that prevents gelatin mixtures from setting. So if you're making anything congealed, use either canned pineapple or simmer the fresh fruit for several minutes to deactivate the enzyme.

If you have never cut a fresh pineapple before or find it difficult to do, here are some tips for slicing into the golden

fruit. To achieve the results shown here, have a large heavy knife and a smaller thin-blade knife on hand. For cutting neatly along curved edges, you'll find it helpful to use a grapefruit knife.

Bear in mind that the core of the fruit is tough and fibrous and is usually cut away and discarded. Also, you must make your cut far enough inside the shell of the pineapple to remove the eyes (similar to those found in a potato). The edible portion that remains will be about half of the whole fruit.

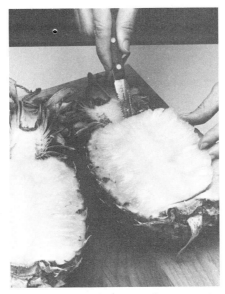

To hollow the whole fruit, start by cutting off the crown and a slice from the bottom of the pineapple. Insert knife close to the skin, and cut completely around the outside edge using a sawing motion.

One easy way to slice pineapple is to cut it in half from the bottom through the crown. Remove the meat from the skin with a curved knife.

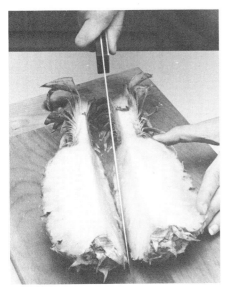

Another method is to slice the pineapple in half and then into quarters. With a curved knife, remove the core and separate the meat from the skin. Then cut the meat crosswise into strips.

# Vegetables Enjoy A Touch Of Herbs

Ever tried seasoning yellow squash with a bay leaf and dash of basil? How about adding parsley and thyme to potatoes? Good cooks know that the flavor of vegetables is enhanced with careful use of herbs.

If you're a novice with herb cookery, start with these ideas and then experiment on your own. Be sure to use just enough seasoning to enhance the natural flavor of food—not to disguise or change it. So start with a little, and then gradually increase the amount until you get the flavor you want. Combine several different herbs if you like, but use only one if it's very strong.

Always store herbs in a cool, dry place—never above the range or in any other warm area. To test for freshness, crush a small amount; if you're unable to detect a distinct aroma, the seasoning ability has weakened and the entire container should be replaced.

When fresh herbs are available, substitute them for dried; but remember the flavor of fresh herbs is less intense, so use three times more of the fresh than is recommended for dry.

### BROCCOLI PUFF

1 (10-ounce) package frozen chopped broccoli
½ cup chopped onion
2 tablespoons butter or margarine
1 (10¾-ounce) can cream of mushroom soup, undiluted
2 cups cooked rice
1 teaspoon Worcestershire sauce
¼ teaspoon dried whole thyme
4 eggs, separated
2 cups (8 ounces) shredded Cheddar cheese

Cook broccoli according to package directions; drain and set aside.

Sauté onion in butter until tender but not brown; stir in broccoli and next 4 ingredients. Spoon broccoli mixture into a buttered shallow 2-quart casserole. Bake at 400° for 20 minutes.

Beat egg yolks until thick and lemon colored; add cheese, stirring well.

Beat egg whites (at room temperature) until soft peaks form; fold egg whites into cheese mixture. Spread egg mixture over top of casserole; bake an additional 15 minutes or until top is puffed and golden brown. Yield: 6 to 8 servings.          Mrs. W. H. Burnside, Newport, North Carolina.

## GREEN BEANS WITH BASIL

1 pound fresh green beans
½ teaspoon salt
½ cup chopped onion
¼ cup chopped celery
2 tablespoons butter or margarine
1 clove garlic, minced
½ teaspoon dried whole rosemary
½ teaspoon dried whole basil
2 (¼-inch) onion slices

Remove strings from beans; cut beans into 1-inch pieces. Wash thoroughly.

Place beans, salt, and about 1 cup water in a medium saucepan; bring to a boil. Reduce heat; cover and simmer 10 minutes. Add remaining ingredients except onion slices; cover and continue to cook 10 to 15 minutes or until tender. Separate onion slices into rings; place on top of beans. Yield: 4 servings.
*Mrs. James L. Twilley,*
*Macon, Georgia.*

## SAUTEED EGGPLANT AND ZUCCHINI

2 medium onions, thinly sliced
1 medium-size green pepper, cut into strips
2 cloves garlic, minced
⅓ cup vegetable oil
1 small eggplant, peeled and cubed
3 small zucchini (about ½ pound), sliced
1 teaspoon sugar
1 teaspoon dried whole oregano
½ teaspoon salt
½ teaspoon pepper
4 medium tomatoes, peeled and sliced

Sauté onion, green pepper, and garlic in oil 3 to 5 minutes. Stir in eggplant and zucchini; cook until vegetables are crisp-tender. Sprinkle vegetables with sugar and seasonings; stir well. Top with tomato slices; cook just until thoroughly heated. Yield: 10 to 12 servings.
*L. K. Klomfar,*
*Gulfport, Florida.*

## CRISPY OVEN POTATOES

¼ cup butter or margarine, melted
1 tablespoon grated onion
1 tablespoon chopped fresh parsley
½ teaspoon dried whole thyme
½ teaspoon salt
⅛ teaspoon pepper
4 large unpeeled potatoes, thinly sliced
1½ cups (6 ounces) shredded Cheddar cheese

Combine first 6 ingredients. Layer potatoes in a lightly greased 13- x 9- x

2-inch baking dish, brushing each layer with butter mixture. Bake at 425° for 40 minutes or until potatoes are tender; sprinkle with cheese.

Bake an additional 5 minutes or until cheese melts. Yield: about 6 servings.
*Joan B. Piercy,*
*Memphis, Tennessee.*

## SKILLET SUMMER SQUASH

2 tablespoons vegetable oil
1 small onion, sliced
4 medium-size yellow squash, cut into ¼-inch-thick slices
½ teaspoon dried whole basil, crushed
½ teaspoon salt
¼ teaspoon freshly ground pepper
1 bay leaf

Heat oil in a skillet over medium heat. Add onion; sauté until tender but not brown. Add remaining ingredients. Reduce heat; cover and simmer 15 minutes. Yield: 4 servings.
*Catherine Green,*
*Kansas City, Kansas.*

# English Muffins Take A New Shape

If you shy away from making English muffins because each has to be individually shaped, we've found a recipe to solve that dilemma—English Muffin Loaf. It's shaped in a regular loafpan and bakes up crusty outside with the typical rugged texture of English muffins inside.

## ENGLISH MUFFIN LOAF

About 3 cups all-purpose flour
1 package dry yeast
1 tablespoon sugar
¾ teaspoon salt
1¼ cups warm water (105° to 115°)
Cornmeal

Combine 1 cup flour, yeast, sugar, and salt in a large mixing bowl; add water, and beat on low speed of electric mixer 3 minutes. Stir in enough remaining flour to make a very soft dough. Shape dough into a ball; place in a well-greased bowl, turning to grease top.

Cover and let rise in a warm place (85°), free from drafts, 1 hour or until doubled in bulk.

Punch dough down; shape into an 8- x 4-inch loaf. Grease a 9- x 5- x 3-inch loafpan; sprinkle bottom and sides with cornmeal. Place dough in pan; sprinkle with cornmeal.

Cover and let rise in a warm place (85°), free from drafts, 30 minutes or until doubled in bulk. Bake at 400° for 35 to 40 minutes. Yield: 1 loaf.
*Carol Forcum,*
*Marion, Illinois.*

# Barbecue Straight From The Oven

Forget the grill and charcoal. With an oven, some good cuts of meat, and these recipes, you can have that tender, juicy, sauce-dripping barbecue you're longing for.

Even if you think the one and only way to prepare ribs is on the grill, just try Easy Barbecued Spareribs. It's hard to believe something this easy can taste so good. The sauce flavors the ribs as they bake.

Another favorite, Barbecued Beef Roast, features an eye-of-round roast basted with a tangy sauce. Old South Barbecued Chicken is cooked with a spicy, catsup-based sauce and served over noodles or rice.

## BARBECUED BEEF ROAST

1 (4- to 5-pound) eye-of-round roast
½ teaspoon salt
½ teaspoon pepper
½ teaspoon garlic salt
½ teaspoon meat tenderizer
1 cup water
¾ cup peeled chopped tomato
¼ cup vinegar
¼ cup catsup
2 tablespoons chopped onion
1 clove garlic, minced
2 stalks celery, sliced
1 tablespoon Worcestershire sauce
1 teaspoon lemon juice
¼ cup butter or margarine
1 cup commercial barbecue sauce

Rub roast on all sides with salt, pepper, garlic salt, and meat tenderizer; place roast in a 13- x 9- x 2-inch baking pan, and set aside.

Combine next 9 ingredients in a large saucepan; bring to a boil. Reduce heat; simmer 15 minutes. Stir butter and barbecue sauce into liquid.

Pour half the sauce mixture over roast; bake at 300° for 2½ hours, basting frequently with pan drippings and half of remaining sauce.

Thinly slice roast, and serve with remaining sauce. Yield: 16 to 18 servings. *Billie Taylor, Afton, Virginia.*

## PORK ROAST BARBECUE

1 (4- to 5-pound) pork loin roast
1½ cups water
1 cup vinegar
½ cup catsup
½ cup Worcestershire sauce
1 medium onion, chopped
3 tablespoons dry mustard
3 tablespoons brown sugar
1½ teaspoons salt
¼ teaspoon crushed red pepper
¼ teaspoon pepper

Place roast, fat side up, in a 13- x 9- x 2-inch baking pan. Insert meat thermometer (not touching bone or fat).

Combine remaining ingredients; mix well, and pour over roast. Bake, uncovered, at 325° for 2½ to 3 hours or until thermometer reaches 170°, basting roast frequently.

Let stand 10 to 15 minutes; serve with any remaining sauce. Yield: 8 to 10 servings. *Kathy Plowman, Concord, North Carolina.*

## EASY BARBECUED SPARERIBS

3 pounds spareribs
1 (14-ounce) bottle catsup
1¼ cups water
¼ cup vinegar
3 tablespoons brown sugar
1 tablespoon dry mustard
3 tablespoons Worcestershire sauce
2 teaspoons chili powder
Pinch of ground cloves
Pinch of garlic powder

Cut ribs into serving-size pieces; place in a 13- x 9- x 2-inch baking pan. Bake at 400° for 30 minutes.

Combine remaining ingredients; mix well. Spoon over ribs. Reduce heat to 350°; bake an additional 1½ hours or until tender, basting occasionally. Yield: 3 to 4 servings. *Gail Thomas, White Hall, Maryland.*

## OLD SOUTH BARBECUED CHICKEN

1 (2½- to 3-pound) broiler-fryer, cut up
Salt
½ cup all-purpose flour
⅓ cup vegetable oil
1 medium onion, diced
½ cup chopped celery
1 cup catsup
1 cup water
¼ cup lemon juice
3 tablespoons Worcestershire sauce
2 tablespoons brown sugar
2 tablespoons vinegar
1 small hot pepper
Cooked rice or noodles

Sprinkle chicken with salt. Dredge chicken in flour, and brown in hot oil in a Dutch oven. Remove chicken from Dutch oven. Drain off excess oil.

Combine remaining ingredients except rice in Dutch oven; add chicken. Cover and bake at 350° for 1 hour. Remove hot pepper and discard. Serve over rice or noodles. Yield: 4 servings. *Mrs. J. O. Branson, Thomasville, North Carolina.*

## BARBECUED CHICKEN

1 cup all-purpose flour
2 teaspoons paprika
1 teaspoon salt
¼ teaspoon pepper
1 (2½- to 3-pound) broiler-fryer, cut up
¼ cup butter or margarine, melted
½ cup catsup
¼ cup water
½ medium onion, thinly sliced
1 tablespoon sugar
1 tablespoon vinegar
1 tablespoon Worcestershire sauce
1 teaspoon salt
½ teaspoon chili powder
¼ teaspoon pepper

Combine first 4 ingredients; mix well. Dredge chicken in flour mixture. Pour butter into a 13- x 9- x 2-inch baking pan. Arrange chicken in pan, skin side down. Bake at 350° for 30 minutes.

Combine remaining ingredients in a medium saucepan; mix well. Bring mixture to a boil; reduce heat, and simmer 15 minutes.

Remove chicken from oven, and turn; spoon sauce over chicken. Bake an additional 30 minutes. Yield: 4 servings. *Sue-Sue Hartstern, Louisville, Kentucky.*

# Celery To Suit Your Fancy

Whether you prefer the crisp, fresh texture of raw celery or the savory taste of cooked celery, you'll find recipes here to suit your fancy. Cooked celery fans will love Buttered Celery Amandine, celery simmered in a wine sauce with sautéed almonds. And for those who prefer their celery raw, there's Overnight Alfalfa-Celery Salad with the extra crunch of water chestnuts and alfalfa sprouts.

For dishes that use raw celery, select pale-green, thick, brittle stalks since the dark-green, narrow stalks tend to be stringy. Be sure to save the celery leaves: The outer leaves can serve as seasoning in soups, stuffings, and other cooked dishes. The inner leaves add a nice flavor to tossed salads.

## OVERNIGHT ALFALFA-CELERY SALAD

½ pound alfalfa sprouts
1½ cups chopped green onion
2 cups chopped celery
1 (8-ounce) can sliced water chestnuts, drained
1 (10-ounce) package frozen English peas, thawed
2 cups mayonnaise
2 teaspoons sugar
½ teaspoon salt
½ teaspoon pepper
1 cup (4 ounces) shredded mozzarella cheese
½ cup grated Parmesan cheese
Tomato wedges
Dried parsley flakes

Layer alfalfa sprouts, green onion, celery, water chestnuts, and peas in a 4-quart bowl. Combine mayonnaise, sugar, salt, and pepper; mix well. Spread over top, sealing to edge of bowl. Combine cheese, and sprinkle over top. Cover tightly, and chill 24 hours.

At serving time, arrange tomato wedges around edge of bowl; sprinkle the salad with parsley flakes. Yield: 10 to 12 servings. *Mrs. John R. Armstrong, Farwell, Texas.*

*Tip: Brush a small amount of oil on a grater before shredding cheese for easier cleaning.*

## BUTTERED CELERY AMANDINE

1 chicken-flavored bouillon cube
¼ cup boiling water
2 tablespoons butter or margarine, divided
½ cup slivered almonds
4 cups diagonally sliced celery (¼-inch slices)
2 teaspoons instant minced onion
½ teaspoon salt
⅛ teaspoon garlic powder
2 tablespoons dry white wine
1 teaspoon chopped fresh parsley

Dissolve bouillon cube in boiling water; set aside.

Melt 1 tablespoon butter in a heavy saucepan; add slivered almonds, and sauté until golden.

Melt remaining butter in a saucepan; add celery, bouillon, onion, salt, and garlic powder. Cover and cook over low heat 12 minutes; stir in wine and almonds. Cover and cook an additional 3 minutes. Spoon into serving dish; sprinkle with parsley. Yield: 6 servings.

*Mrs. Harland J. Stone,*
*Ocala, Florida.*

## CREAMY CELERY CASSEROLE

½ cup water
½ teaspoon salt
4 cups sliced celery (½-inch slices)
¼ cup chopped pimiento-stuffed olives
¼ cup butter or margarine
¼ cup all-purpose flour
1½ cups milk
¼ cup slivered almonds, toasted
1 cup soft breadcrumbs
Sliced pimiento-stuffed olives
Fresh parsley sprigs

Combine first 3 ingredients in a medium saucepan. Bring to a boil. Reduce heat; cover and simmer 15 minutes or until celery is tender. Drain, reserving ½ cup liquid. Combine cooked celery and olives; toss lightly. Spoon into a greased 1-quart casserole. Set aside.

Melt ¼ cup butter in a heavy saucepan over low heat; gradually blend in flour and cook 1 minute, stirring constantly. Combine reserved liquid and milk; gradually add to flour mixture, stirring constantly. Cook over medium heat, stirring constantly, until thickened and bubbly. Stir in slivered almonds. Pour sauce over celery mixture.

Sprinkle breadcrumbs over casserole. Bake at 350° for 20 minutes. Garnish the casserole with sliced olives and parsley. Yield: 6 servings.

*Harriette G. Simpkins,*
*Nashville, Tennessee.*

## BAKED CELERY

3 tablespoons butter or margarine
3 tablespoons all-purpose flour
1½ cups milk
⅜ teaspoon salt
¼ teaspoon pepper
6 cups sliced celery (½-inch slices)
½ cup chopped, blanched almonds, toasted
½ cup (2 ounces) shredded process American cheese
½ cup fine, dry buttered breadcrumbs

Melt butter in a heavy saucepan over low heat; add flour, stirring until smooth. Cook 1 minute, stirring constantly. Gradually add milk; cook over medium heat, stirring constantly, until sauce is thickened and bubbly.

Add salt, pepper, celery, and almonds; stir well. Pour mixture into a lightly greased 10- x 6- x 2-inch baking dish. Sprinkle with cheese, and top with buttered breadcrumbs. Bake at 375° for 25 minutes. Yield: 8 servings.

*Grace Owens,*
*Pride, Louisiana.*

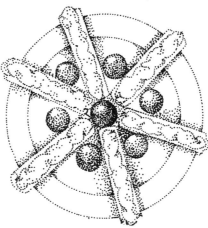

## STUFFED CELERY

2 (8-ounce) packages cream cheese, softened
½ cup butter or margarine, softened
½ cup commercial sour cream
2 tablespoons minced capers
1 teaspoon anchovy paste
1 teaspoon minced onion
1 teaspoon dry mustard
¼ teaspoon salt
Dash of pepper
1 bunch celery, cut into 4-inch pieces
Paprika
Cherry tomatoes (optional)

Combine first 9 ingredients, beating well. Stuff celery pieces with cream cheese mixture. Sprinkle with paprika; garnish with cherry tomatoes, if desired. Chill. Yield: about 1½ dozen.

*Charlotte Pierce,*
*Greensburg, Kentucky.*

# Add Crunch With Snow Peas

If the thought of fresh vegetables and beef sizzling in a wok makes you feel adventurous, try tossing in some snow peas for extra crunch and a bright-green color. Our Beef and Snow Pea Stir-Fry calls for using the entire pod; the tiny, tender peas within the pod add a sweet taste. Look for these crisp, flat, edible pea pods in the produce section of your market from May through September.

## BEEF AND SNOW PEA STIR-FRY

2 pounds boneless round steak
½ pound fresh snow peas
2 tablespoons vegetable oil
3 stalks celery, diagonally sliced
2 carrots, diagonally sliced
1 large onion, coarsely chopped
1 small zucchini, diagonally sliced
1 (8-ounce) can sliced water chestnuts, drained
1 (3½-ounce) jar sliced mushrooms, drained
2 tablespoons cornstarch
1 tablespoon sugar
⅔ cup water
½ cup soy sauce
Hot cooked rice

Partially freeze steak; slice across grain into 3- x ¼-inch strips, and set aside. Wash snow peas; trim ends, and remove strings. Set aside.

Place oil in a preheated wok, coating sides; heat at medium high (325°) 2 minutes. Add beef; stir-fry until browned. Remove beef, and set aside. Stir in vegetables. Cover and reduce heat to low (225°); cook 3 minutes or until crisp-tender. Stir in beef.

Combine cornstarch, sugar, water, and soy sauce; add to meat mixture. Cook, stirring constantly, until thickened; serve over rice. Yield: 8 servings.

*Note:* One 6-ounce package of frozen Chinese pea pods, thawed and drained, can be substituted for fresh snow peas.

*Janice S. Elder,*
*Spartanburg, South Carolina.*

*Tip: Experiment with new cooking methods. Oriental stir-fry cooking is not only intriguing as a change-of-pace menu idea, it's more energy efficient and nutritious than boiling or steaming. Cut foods into small pieces so that they can cook quickly.*

# May

Juicy strawberries sparkle like ruby-colored jewels on produce stands in May. And for Southerners, it's the end of months of anticipating this sweet fruit flavor. While the berries are plump and flavor-rich, use them in our recipes for pie, sherbet, and fresh fruit salad; or save them with our freezer preserves.

Now is the time for enjoying fresh salads, and we found some recipes with spectacular appeal—they're all served in natural, edible shells. You'll want to try our Summertime Melon Salad; a mixture of fruit is mounded into scalloped-edged cantalopes. And our recipe for Avocado-Stuffed Tomatoes makes a pretty vegetable dish; a filling of avocado and bacon is spooned into tomato shells.

But the star of our recipe testing for this month had to be Southern-Style Collards. We all raced for second helpings (and some for thirds!) of the ham broth-seasoned greens, especially when we learned that each serving contained only 60 calories! Check our "Cooking Light" section in this chapter and see how collards and other vegetables can be prepared with the same Southern flavor and fewer calories.

# Desserts With A Splash Of Spirits

How many bottles of liqueurs or cordials have you tucked away and half-forgotten after tasting them just once? What we suggest you do is get them out and experiment. Take that leftover crème de menthe and stir it into a sauce for ice cream, or lace fresh strawberries with the forgotten kirsch. Once you begin, you'll soon discover all kinds of deliciously simple dessert possibilities.

Soaked in a little Cointreau or other orange-flavored liqueur, fresh blueberries are delightful when topped with a generous dollop of whipped cream and brought to the table in stemmed glasses. Or use your Cointreau in a raspberry sauce for spooning over strawberries.

Kirsch also does wonders for fruit. With a little of this cherry-flavored brandy and a can of cherry pie filling, our Quick Cherries Jubilee is just minutes away—even quicker with the microwave method we've also included.

When something richer than a fruit dessert is in order, stir generous portions of crème de cacao and brandy into vanilla ice cream. Our After Dinner-Drink Dessert is for those who prefer something to sip after dinner.

## BLUEBERRIES AND COINTREAU

2 cups fresh blueberries, rinsed and
    drained
¼ cup Cointreau or other orange-flavored
    liqueur
½ cup whipping cream
3 tablespoons powdered sugar

Place ½ cup blueberries in each of 4 stemmed glasses; pour about 1 tablespoon Cointreau over each serving. Beat whipping cream until foamy; gradually add powdered sugar, beating until soft peaks form. Top each serving of blueberries with a dollop of whipped cream. Yield: 4 servings.

## QUICK CHERRIES JUBILEE

1 (21-ounce) can cherry pie filling
¼ cup kirsch or other cherry-flavored
    brandy
Vanilla ice cream

Pour pie filling into a small saucepan; cook over medium heat until bubbly. Transfer to a small chafing dish or flambé pan, and keep warm.

Rapidly heat kirsch in a small saucepan to produce fumes (do not boil). Pour over cherries, and ignite with a long match; stir until flames die down. Serve immediately over ice cream. Yield: 8 servings.

*Note:* To prepare recipe in microwave oven, pour cherry pie filling into a glass bowl. Microwave at HIGH for 3 to 4 minutes or until bubbly; stir well after 1½ minutes. Pour kirsch into a glass measuring cup; microwave at HIGH for 15 seconds, and proceed as directed above.

## CHOCOLATE-MINT DESSERT

1 (5.5-ounce) can chocolate syrup
2 tablespoons green crème de menthe
Brownies
Vanilla or chocolate-mint ice cream

Combine chocolate syrup and crème de menthe, stirring well. Serve warm or cold over brownies topped with ice cream. Yield: about ⅔ cup sauce.

## GOLDEN DREAM

4 scoops vanilla ice cream (about 1 cup)
2 tablespoons Galliano
½ cup orange juice
Grated orange rind (optional)

Combine first 3 ingredients in container of electric blender; process until smooth (add additional ice cream for a thicker beverage). Garnish each serving with grated orange rind, if desired. Yield: 1½ cups. *John N. Riggins, Nashville, Tennessee.*

## STRAWBERRIES AND CREAM

1 quart fresh strawberries, hulled
¼ cup firmly packed brown sugar
⅓ cup kirsch or other cherry-flavored
    brandy
1 cup whipping cream

Combine strawberries, sugar, and kirsch; mix gently. Cover and chill overnight. Drain berries, reserving 3 tablespoons liquid.

Beat whipping cream until foamy; then gradually add reserved liquid, beating until soft peaks form. Top each serving of strawberries with a dollop of whipped cream mixture. Yield: 6 to 8 servings. *John Floyd, Birmingham, Alabama.*

## RUBY STRAWBERRIES

1 (10-ounce) package frozen raspberries,
    thawed
½ cup sugar, divided
1 tablespoon lemon juice
1 tablespoon Cointreau or other
    orange-flavored liqueur
1 quart fresh strawberries, hulled
⅓ cup slivered almonds, toasted

Press raspberries through a food mill or sieve; discard seeds. Combine raspberry liquid, ¼ cup sugar, lemon juice, and Cointreau; stir well.

Combine strawberries and remaining sugar; toss gently. Pour raspberry sauce over strawberries, and chill 3 to 4 hours. Top each serving with almonds. Yield: 6 to 8 servings.
*Mrs. W. J. Scherffius,
Mountain Home, Arkansas.*

## AFTER DINNER-DRINK DESSERT

½ gallon vanilla ice cream,
    softened
¼ cup brandy
¼ cup crème de cacao
Chocolate curls or chocolate shavings
    (optional)

Combine first 3 ingredients, mixing well. Pour into shallow container, and freeze until firm. Spoon into sherbet glasses; garnish with chocolate curls, if desired. Yield: 10 servings.
*Mrs. W. D. Schmitt,
Montrose, Alabama.*

# Serve Salads In A Natural Shell

The arrival of spring and summer means planning menus around colorful fresh fruit and vegetable salads that do justice to the flavor and colors of the season. And what more natural way to serve salads than in shells made from the fruit and vegetables themselves.

Set your summer luncheon table with beautifully carved cantaloupe shells filled with a refreshing assortment of melon balls and other fresh fruit. As a perfect final touch, garnish the salad with whole strawberries and mint leaves.

Serve fresh ripe avocado halves filled with a fruited chicken salad. Guests will enjoy scooping out the smooth, creamy avocado along with a salad of chicken, oranges, apples, and nuts in a mayonnaise dressing.

Tomatoes may be the most popular shell for salads, and no wonder since their color and flavor combine with just about any filling. And we offer you a choice of several delicious possibilities.

## FRUITED CHICKEN-AVOCADO SALAD

2 cups diced cooked chicken
1 large apple, unpeeled and chopped
1 large orange, peeled, seeded, and sectioned
½ cup coarsely chopped walnuts
⅓ cup mayonnaise
¼ cup orange juice
½ teaspoon salt
3 large ripe avocados, halved
2 tablespoons lemon juice
Lettuce leaves
Orange slices (optional)

Combine first 4 ingredients; set aside. Combine mayonnaise, orange juice, and salt; mix until smooth. Add mayonnaise mixture to chicken mixture; toss gently. Chill at least 2 hours.

Sprinkle each avocado half with 1 teaspoon lemon juice. Spoon chicken mixture into avocado halves; serve on lettuce leaves. Garnish with orange slices, if desired. Yield: 6 servings.
*Mrs. G. E. Hull,*
*Arlington, Texas.*

## AVOCADO-STUFFED TOMATOES

6 medium tomatoes
Salt
2 medium avocados
2 teaspoons lemon juice
1 medium onion, finely chopped
1 to 2 canned whole green chiles, seeded and finely chopped
3 slices bacon, cooked and crumbled
Lettuce leaves

Slice off top of each tomato; scoop out pulp, leaving shells intact. Reserve pulp. Sprinkle inside of each tomato shell with ⅛ teaspoon salt; invert on paper towels.

Chop reserved pulp. Peel, seed, and mash avocados; combine with chopped pulp and next 3 ingredients. Stir well. Fill tomato shells with avocado mixture; sprinkle with bacon. Serve tomatoes on lettuce leaves. Yield: 6 servings.
*Doris Garton,*
*Shenandoah, Virginia.*

## ARTICHOKE-STUFFED TOMATO SALAD

6 large tomatoes
Salt
2 (14-ounce) cans artichoke hearts, drained and chopped
½ cup chopped celery
½ cup chopped green onion and tops
½ to ¾ cup mayonnaise
⅛ teaspoon pepper
8 slices bacon, cooked and crumbled
Lettuce leaves

Slice off top of each tomato; scoop out pulp, leaving shells intact. Reserve pulp for use in other recipes. Sprinkle inside of each tomato shell with ⅛ teaspoon salt. Invert on paper towels. Cover and chill.

Combine next 5 ingredients; stir well. Chill until serving time.

Spoon artichoke mixture into tomato shells; sprinkle with bacon. Serve on lettuce leaves. Yield: 6 servings.
*Kathy A. Murtiashaw,*
*Columbia, South Carolina.*

## ORIENTAL-STUFFED TOMATO SALAD

1 (16-ounce) can bean sprouts, drained
⅓ cup chopped green onion
⅓ cup sliced celery
1 small green pepper, cut into thin strips
⅓ cup vegetable oil
1 tablespoon sugar
2 tablespoons cider vinegar
2 tablespoons soy sauce
¼ teaspoon salt
⅛ teaspoon pepper
8 medium tomatoes
Salt
Salad dressing or mayonnaise
Lettuce leaves

Combine first 4 ingredients; mix well. Combine oil, sugar, vinegar, soy sauce, ¼ teaspoon salt, and pepper; mix well, and pour over vegetables. Cover and chill 3 hours.

Cut tops from tomatoes; scoop out pulp, leaving shells intact. Reserve pulp. Sprinkle inside of each shell with ⅛ teaspoon salt; invert on paper towels.

Coarsely chop reserved pulp; toss with marinated vegetables. Spoon vegetable mixture into tomato shells; top with salad dressing. Serve on lettuce leaves. Yield: 8 servings.
*Mrs. Jack Corzine,*
*St. Louis, Missouri.*

## SUMMERTIME MELON SALAD

1 (6-ounce) can frozen lemonade concentrate, thawed and undiluted
¼ cup orange marmalade
2 tablespoons Triple Sec or other orange-flavored liqueur
3 cups assorted melon balls (cantaloupe, honeydew, and watermelon)
1 cup halved fresh strawberries
1 (15½-ounce) can pineapple chunks, drained
1 (11-ounce) can mandarin oranges, drained
4 cantaloupes, halved and seeded
Mint leaves (optional)
Whole strawberries (optional)

Combine lemonade concentrate, marmalade, and Triple Sec; mix well. Combine melon balls, strawberries, pineapple, and oranges in a large bowl; pour lemonade mixture over fruit, stirring gently. Cover and chill at least 2 hours.

Spoon fruit mixture into cantaloupe halves; garnish with mint leaves and whole strawberries, if desired. Yield: 8 servings.
*Nell Wallace,*
*Cadiz, Kentucky.*

# Crisp Salads From The Garden

With these salad recipes you can take advantage of the garden-fresh goodness of raw vegetables and keep your distance from the stove. Our recipes—Frozen Coleslaw, Spinach Salad, Simple Carrot Salad, and Creamy Cauliflower Salad—all enjoy a crisp texture that comes from raw vegetables.

## SIMPLE CARROT SALAD

1 (8¼-ounce) can crushed pineapple
1½ cups shredded carrots (about 6 medium)
¼ cup flaked coconut
1 tablespoon sugar
2 tablespoons mayonnaise

Drain pineapple, reserving ¼ cup juice. Combine pineapple, carrots, coconut, and sugar; mix well.

Combine mayonnaise and reserved juice; beat with a wire wisk until smooth. Pour over carrot mixture; mix well and chill. Yield: 4 to 6 servings.
*Reba B. Wilson,*
*Jasper, Alabama.*

## SPINACH SALAD

1 bunch fresh spinach, torn into bite-size
   pieces
½ pound fresh bean sprouts
1 (8-ounce) can sliced water chestnuts,
   drained
2 large tomatoes, cut into wedges
2 hard-cooked eggs, sliced
3 to 4 slices bacon, cooked and crumbled
Dressing (recipe follows)

Combine vegetables, eggs, and bacon
in a large bowl; toss well. Serve with
dressing. Yield: 10 servings.

*Dressing:*
1 medium onion, grated
1 cup vegetable oil
⅓ cup catsup
⅓ cup sugar
¼ cup vinegar

Combine all ingredients in a jar.
Cover tightly, and shake vigorously.
Chill several hours. Yield: about 2 cups.
*Debbie Thomas,*
*Birmingham, Alabama.*

## CREAMY STUFFED CELERY

3 stalks celery
1 (3-ounce) package cream cheese,
   softened
1 tablespoon finely chopped
   pimiento-stuffed olives
1 tablespoon finely chopped onion
1 tablespoon finely chopped sweet pickle
1 tablespoon finely chopped pecans
1½ teaspoons mayonnaise

Wash celery, and cut into 3-inch
pieces. Combine remaining ingredients,
mixing well. Stuff the celery pieces with
cream cheese mixture. Yield: 9 celery
pieces. *Johnabeth Frost,*
*Vinita, Oklahoma.*

## CREAMY CAULIFLOWER SALAD

1 medium head cauliflower, broken into
   flowerets
1 bunch green onions, sliced
1 cup sliced radishes
1 cup mayonnaise
1 (0.7-ounce) package garlic cheese
   dressing
2 teaspoons caraway seeds

Combine first 3 ingredients in a medium bowl. Combine remaining ingredients, and pour over vegetables; toss
lightly to coat. Cover; refrigerate overnight. Yield: 6 to 8 servings.

*Patti Brown,*
*Carrollton, Georgia.*

## FROZEN COLESLAW

1 large head cabbage, shredded
1 green pepper, chopped
1 large carrot, shredded
1 teaspoon salt
1 cup vinegar
1 cup sugar
¼ cup water
1 teaspoon dry mustard
1 teaspoon celery seeds

Combine vegetables; sprinkle with
salt, and let stand 1 hour. Drain mixture if water accumulates.

Combine remaining ingredients in a
saucepan. Bring to a boil; boil 1 minute. Cool. Pour over cabbage mixture;
stir well. Freeze in plastic freezer bags
or containers. To serve, thaw in refrigerator. Yield: 8 to 10 servings.
*Mrs. Varden Hiner,*
*Abilene, Texas.*

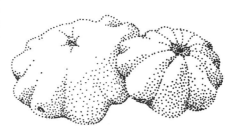

# Summer Squash: So Versatile, So Delicious

Backyard gardens and farmers' markets show a seasonal trend: Everyone
seems to be growing squash. If you
aren't, maybe you'll be lucky enough to
have a friend share some.

The sculptural forms of summer
squash delight cooks and inspire a multitude of ways to prepare these versatile
vegetables: bright and curvy yellow
squash; long, slender zucchini; and the
disc-shaped, scallop-edged pattypan.

Our recipes have it tossed in a salad,
simmered in soup, and fried into fritters. We even shred squash and stuff it
into a tomato shell, or use the whole
vegetable itself as a container for a tasty
filling.

Since the summer types of squash are
picked before maturity, the skin and
seeds are tender and edible; discarding
these portions is discarding nutrients
and fiber. Before use, scrub squash
under running water, and slice away the
stem and blossom ends. Peel only if the
skin is especially tough. Store up to one
week in the refrigerator.

## FIESTA SQUASH

1 medium onion, chopped
1 medium-size green pepper, chopped
2 tablespoons butter or margarine
1½ pounds yellow squash, cut into ¼-inch
   slices
1 teaspoon salt
⅛ teaspoon pepper
1 teaspoon lemon juice

Sauté onion and green pepper in butter in a large skillet until tender. Stir in
remaining ingredients. Cover and cook
over low heat 8 to 10 minutes or until
squash is just tender. Yield: 4 servings.
*Mrs. E. T. Williams,*
*Baton Rouge, Louisiana.*

## SQUASH-STUFFED TOMATOES

8 medium tomatoes
Salt and pepper
2 tablespoons vegetable oil
1 pound zucchini, shredded
1 pound yellow squash, shredded
2 teaspoons salt
1 large red onion, minced
1 clove garlic, minced
2 tablespoons butter or margarine
2 tablespoons olive oil
1 cup whipping cream
⅛ teaspoon pepper
½ cup (2 ounces) shredded Gruyère or
   Swiss cheese
¼ cup grated Parmesan cheese

Wash tomatoes thoroughly. Cut tops
from tomatoes; scoop out pulp, leaving
shells intact. Reserve pulp for use in
other recipes. Sprinkle cavity of each
tomato with salt and pepper, and brush
with vegetable oil. Place tomatoes, cut
side up, on a baking sheet. Bake at 325°
for 10 minutes. Invert tomato shells on
paper towels, and let drain for at least
30 minutes.

Place zucchini and yellow squash in a
colander; sprinkle with 2 teaspoons salt,
and toss gently. Let drain 30 minutes,
stirring occasionally.

Sauté onion and garlic in butter and
olive oil in a large skillet until onion is
tender. Add squash mixture; cook 3 to
5 minutes, stirring frequently. Stir in
cream and ⅛ teaspoon pepper; cook
over low heat until cream is absorbed.
Remove from heat; stir in Gruyère
cheese.

Spoon squash mixture into tomatoes;
sprinkle with Parmesan cheese. Broil 5
inches from heat about 3 to 4 minutes
or just until cheese is lightly browned.
Serve immediately. Yield: 8 servings.
*Carol Laster,*
*Birmingham, Alabama.*

## MEXICAN SQUASH

1 medium onion, chopped
2 cloves garlic, minced
2 tablespoons vegetable oil
1½ pounds yellow squash, cut into ½-inch slices
1½ cups peeled and coarsely chopped tomatoes
1 to 2 teaspoons cumin seeds
¾ teaspoon salt
2 or 3 hot peppers, seeded and chopped (optional)

Sauté onion and garlic in hot oil until tender; add squash, tomatoes, cumin seeds, and salt. Cook over low heat 15 minutes, stirring often. Add peppers, if desired; cook an additional 15 minutes or until squash is tender. Yield: 6 servings. *Mrs. Parke LaGourgue Cory, Neosho, Missouri.*

## YELLOW SQUASH PUFFS

¾ pound yellow squash, sliced
1 egg, beaten
⅓ cup all-purpose flour
⅓ cup cornmeal
1 teaspoon baking powder
½ teaspoon salt
1 medium onion, grated
Vegetable oil

Cook squash, covered, in boiling water 10 to 15 minutes or until tender. Drain; mash enough squash to measure 1 cup; reserve any remaining squash for use in other recipes.
Combine 1 cup mashed squash and egg; stir well.
Combine flour, cornmeal, baking powder, and salt; stir well. Add squash mixture and onion; stir until blended.
Drop squash mixture by level tablespoonfuls into hot oil. Cook until golden brown, turning once. Drain well on paper towels. Yield: about 2 dozen. *B. A. McGuire, Norris, South Carolina.*

## STUFFED PATTYPAN SQUASH

6 medium pattypan squash
2 eggs, well beaten
1 (7-ounce) can whole kernel corn, drained
1 (2-ounce) jar diced pimiento, drained
2 tablespoons chopped green onion
1 teaspoon seasoned salt
¼ teaspoon white pepper
½ cup (2 ounces) shredded sharp process American cheese
Cherry tomatoes
Fresh parsley sprigs

Wash squash thoroughly. Drop in boiling salted water; reduce heat and cook, covered, 15 minutes or until tender but firm. Drain and allow to cool to touch.
Place squash, flat side down, on a smooth surface; scoop out pulp, leaving a ¼-inch shell. Chop pulp and combine with next 6 ingredients, stirring well.
Spoon stuffing mixture into shells. Place squash in a shallow baking pan; pour in enough water to cover bottom of pan to prevent sticking. Bake at 350° for 25 minutes. Remove from oven. Sprinkle cheese over squash; bake 5 minutes or until cheese melts. Arrange squash on a platter with tomatoes and parsley. Yield: 6 servings.
*Lorine Kramer, Needville, Texas.*

## PATTYPAN-ZUCCHINI SKILLET

1 medium onion, sliced and separated into rings
½ cup chopped green pepper
2 tablespoons butter or margarine
1 tablespoon sugar
1 tablespoon all-purpose flour
½ teaspoon salt
¼ teaspoon pepper
⅛ teaspoon garlic powder
1 medium pattypan squash, cubed
1 medium zucchini, sliced
3 medium tomatoes, quartered

Sauté onion and green pepper in butter until tender. Stir in sugar, flour, salt, pepper, and garlic powder. Add squash; cook over medium heat 4 minutes; add tomatoes, and cook until squash is crisp-tender. Yield: 6 servings.

## ZUCCHINI PARMESAN

3 slices bacon
1 small onion, chopped
2 large zucchini, cut into ¼-inch slices
Salt and pepper
¼ cup grated Parmesan cheese

Fry bacon in a large skillet until crisp; remove from pan and drain well, reserving 2 tablespoons bacon drippings. Crumble bacon, and set aside.
Sauté onion in bacon drippings until tender. Layer bacon, zucchini, salt, pepper, and cheese over onion in skillet. Cover and cook over low heat 15 minutes. Yield: 4 to 6 servings.
*Mrs. R. L. Bryant, Franklin, Virginia.*

## CHEESY ZUCCHINI PIE

Pastry for 9-inch pie
1 tablespoon Dijon mustard
¼ cup butter or margarine
2 large zucchini, thinly sliced
1 cup chopped onion
½ cup chopped fresh parsley
¼ to ½ teaspoon dried whole basil
¼ teaspoon garlic powder
¼ teaspoon ground oregano
2 eggs, beaten
2 cups (8 ounces) shredded mozzarella cheese

Line a 9-inch pieplate with pastry; trim excess pastry around edges. Prick bottom and sides of shell with a fork, and bake at 425° for 6 to 8 minutes. Let cool on wire rack. Spread mustard evenly over bottom of pastry shell.
Melt butter in a large skillet. Add zucchini and onion; cook over low heat 10 minutes, stirring occasionally. Stir in parsley, basil, garlic powder, and oregano; cover and simmer 5 to 7 minutes. Combine eggs and mozzarella cheese; stir into zucchini mixture. Pour mixture into pastry shell.
Bake at 375° for 50 minutes or until a knife inserted about an inch from center comes out clean. Let stand 10 minutes before serving. Yield: one 9-inch pie.
*Marian A. Kraus, Falls Church, Virginia.*

## ZUCCHINI SQUARES

1 cup biscuit mix
4 eggs, beaten
½ cup vegetable oil
½ cup grated Parmesan cheese
½ cup chopped onion
2 tablespoons chopped fresh parsley
1 clove garlic, minced
½ teaspoon seasoning salt
½ teaspoon dried whole oregano
Dash of pepper
2 medium zucchini, thinly sliced

Combine all ingredients except zucchini; beat well. Stir in zucchini. Pour mixture into a greased 13- x 9- x 2-inch baking pan. Bake at 350° for 35 minutes or until golden brown. Let stand 10 minutes; cut into squares to serve. Yield: 12 servings. *Mrs. Melburn Snell, Apollo, Pennsylvania.*

*Tip: Chopped onions have the best flavor if they are browned in shortening before being added to casserole dishes.*

## ZUCCHINI SOUP

1 pound bulk Italian sausage
2 cups diagonally sliced celery (cut ½ inch thick)
2 pounds zucchini, cut into ½-inch slices
1 cup chopped onion
2 (28-ounce) cans tomatoes, undrained
1 teaspoon Italian seasoning
1 teaspoon salt
1 teaspoon sugar
1 teaspoon dried whole oregano
½ teaspoon garlic powder
2 green peppers, cut into ½-inch pieces

Brown sausage in a large Dutch oven, stirring to crumble; drain off pan drippings. Add celery; cook 10 minutes, stirring occasionally. Add next 8 ingredients; simmer 20 minutes. Add green pepper; cover and cook 10 minutes. Yield: about 16 cups. *Frances House, Coral Springs, Florida.*

## ZUCCHINI SALAD

2 small zucchini, thinly sliced
2 medium tomatoes, cut into wedges
1 medium-size green pepper, cut into thin strips
1 small onion, chopped
¼ cup vegetable oil
¼ cup wine vinegar
2 tablespoons chopped fresh parsley
2 cloves garlic, minced
½ teaspoon salt
¼ teaspoon pepper
Lettuce leaves

Combine zucchini, tomato, green pepper, and onion; toss lightly. Combine next 6 ingredients; mix well, and pour over vegetables. Cover and refrigerate several hours. Drain and spoon into a lettuce-lined bowl. Yield: 6 servings. *Irene Murry, Herculaneum, Missouri.*

# Bake A Batch Of Sweet And Spicy Muffins

If you want a homemade bread that's quick-as-a-wink and delicious any time of day, bake a batch of muffins. Try Banana Surprise Muffins—the surprise is a sweet spoonful of marmalade between layers of tender banana-flavored muffin. Our cakelike Tea Muffins are a

*It's no trouble to mix up Bite-Size Applesauce Muffins or almond-flavored Cherry Muffins, and they'll disappear in as little time as it took to make them.*

little different—the tops don't rise to the usual muffin shape.

Bite-Size Applesauce Muffins are miniature apple-flavored treats. Susan Silver mixes hers in a food processor for added convenience. Just be sure not to over-beat the batter.

## BITE-SIZE APPLESAUCE MUFFINS

½ cup butter or margarine, softened
½ cup sugar
2 eggs
¾ cup applesauce
1¾ cups all-purpose flour
1 tablespoon baking powder
½ teaspoon salt
¼ cup butter or margarine, melted
¼ cup sugar
⅛ teaspoon ground cinnamon

Cream ½ cup butter; gradually add ½ cup sugar, beating until light and fluffy. Add eggs, one at a time, beating well after each addition. Stir in applesauce. Combine flour, baking powder, and salt; add to creamed mixture, and stir just until moistened.

Spoon batter into lightly greased miniature muffin pans, filling two-thirds full. Bake at 425° for 15 minutes or until done. Remove from pan immediately, and dip muffin tops in melted butter. Combine ¼ cup sugar and cinnamon; sprinkle sugar mixture over top of each muffin. Yield: about 3½ dozen. *Susan Silver, Stone Mountain, Georgia.*

*Tip: Always measure ingredients accurately. For liquids, use a glass measuring cup; this allows you to see that you are measuring correctly. Use metal or plastic dry measuring cups for solids; fill cups to overflowing, and level off with a knife or metal spatula.*

## CHERRY MUFFINS

2 cups all-purpose flour
¼ cup sugar
¼ cup chopped maraschino cherries
1 tablespoon baking powder
1 teaspoon salt
¾ cup milk
¼ cup vegetable oil
3 tablespoons maraschino cherry juice
1 egg, beaten
2 tablespoons chopped almonds
2 tablespoons sugar

Combine first 5 ingredients in a large bowl; make a well in center of mixture. Combine milk, oil, cherry juice, and egg; add to dry ingredients, stirring just until moistened. Spoon into greased muffin pans, filling two-thirds full.

Combine almonds and 2 tablespoons sugar; sprinkle over muffins. Bake at 375° for 25 to 30 minutes. Yield: 1 dozen.                *Vicki L. Bryant,*
*Jacksonville, Florida.*

## BANANA SURPRISE MUFFINS

1¾ cups all-purpose flour
⅓ cup sugar
2 teaspoons baking powder
¾ teaspoon salt
¼ teaspoon soda
1 egg, beaten
⅓ cup vegetable oil
1 cup mashed ripe banana
¼ cup jelly or marmalade

Combine first 5 ingredients in a large bowl; make a well in center of mixture. Add egg, oil, and banana, stirring just until moistened. Spoon into greased muffin pans, filling one-third full. Spoon 1 teaspoon jelly in center of each muffin cup; spoon remaining batter over jelly, filling each cup two-thirds full. Bake at 400° for 18 to 20 minutes or until done. Yield: 1 dozen.        *Jeannine Allen,*
*McAllen, Texas.*

## LAST-MINUTE GINGERBREAD MUFFINS

1 cup shortening
1 cup sugar
1 cup dark molasses
4 eggs
2 teaspoons soda
1 cup buttermilk
4 cups all-purpose flour
1 tablespoon plus 1 teaspoon ground ginger
1 teaspoon ground allspice
½ teaspoon ground nutmeg

Cream shortening; gradually add sugar, beating until light and fluffy. Stir in molasses. Add eggs, one at a time, beating well after each addition. Dissolve soda in buttermilk.

Combine flour and spices; add to creamed mixture alternately with buttermilk, beating well after each addition. Cover and store in refrigerator until ready to bake. (Batter can be kept in refrigerator up to 3 weeks.)

To bake, spoon batter into greased muffin pans, filling two-thirds full. Bake at 350° for 20 minutes. Yield: about 3 dozen.               *Janie King,*
*San Antonio, Texas.*

## TEA MUFFINS

½ cup butter or margarine, softened
¾ cup sugar
1 egg
2 cups all-purpose flour
2 teaspoons baking powder
1 teaspoon ground cinnamon
½ teaspoon salt
1 cup milk
¼ cup firmly packed brown sugar
2 tablespoons finely chopped walnuts

Cream butter and gradually add sugar, beating until mixture is light and fluffy. Add egg; beat until blended.

Combine flour, baking powder, cinnamon, and salt; add to creamed mixture alternately with milk, beginning and ending with flour mixture. Spoon into greased muffin pans, filling half full.

Combine brown sugar and walnuts; sprinkle over batter. Bake at 350° for 20 minutes. Yield: about 2 dozen.
*Martha Hoover,*
*Huntsville, Texas.*

# Sizzling Specialties From The Grill

Nothing signals the welcome arrival of warm weather like the tantalizing aroma of meat sizzling on an outdoor grill. Imagine, for example, golden chicken flavored with honey and soy sauce, or pork chops glazed with pineapple preserves, or chunks of beef, marinated in a seasoned lemon juice mixture, threaded on skewers with fresh vegetables for a tasty meal-on-a-stick.

Our Poor Boy Fillets are a delightful new version of the hamburger patty. A rectangle of ground beef is spread with Parmesan cheese and mushrooms, rolled into a log shape, and sliced into patties. Each patty is circled with a strip of bacon before grilling.

## MARINATED BEEF KABOBS

½ cup lemon juice
¼ cup Worcestershire sauce
1 cup vegetable oil
¾ cup soy sauce
¼ cup prepared mustard
2 cloves garlic, minced
3 pounds sirloin tip, cut into 1½-inch cubes
2 large green peppers, cut into 1½-inch pieces
½ pound fresh mushroom caps
12 cherry tomatoes
12 small onions
Hot cooked rice (optional)

Combine first 6 ingredients; stir well. Add meat. Cover and marinate 12 hours in refrigerator, turning meat occasionally.

Remove meat from marinade, reserving marinade. Alternate meat and vegetables on skewers. Grill over medium coals 15 to 20 minutes or until desired degree of doneness, basting with marinade. Serve with rice, if desired. Yield: 12 servings.           *Anne Ringer,*
*Warner Robins, Georgia.*

## TENDERIZED FLANK STEAK

1 (2-pound) flank steak
¼ cup vegetable oil
¼ cup red wine vinegar
¼ cup lemon juice
½ teaspoon sugar
½ teaspoon salt
½ teaspoon dried whole thyme
½ teaspoon pepper

Score surface of steak with a knife. Place steak in a shallow baking dish. Combine remaining ingredients, stirring well. Pour over steak; cover and marinate about 12 hours in the refrigerator, turning steak occasionally.

Remove steak from marinade. Grill 5 inches from hot coals about 8 minutes on each side.

To serve, slice across grain into thin slices. Yield: 6 servings.
*DeLea Lonadier,*
*Montgomery, Louisiana.*

## POOR BOY FILLETS

1 pound ground beef
1 (4-ounce) can mushroom stems and
    pieces, drained
3 tablespoons finely chopped
    pimiento-stuffed olives
2 tablespoons finely chopped green pepper
2 tablespoons finely chopped onion
¼ cup grated Parmesan cheese
½ teaspoon salt
½ teaspoon lemon pepper seasoning
6 slices bacon

Shape ground beef into a 12- x 7½-inch rectangle on a sheet of waxed paper. Sprinkle next 7 ingredients evenly over beef. Begin at short end, and roll jellyroll fashion, lifting waxed paper to help support ground beef as you roll. Carefully slide roll onto a cookie sheet, seam side down. Smooth and shape beef roll with your hands. Refrigerate 2 to 3 hours.

Cook bacon until transparent (not crisp); drain. Cut beef roll into 1½-inch-thick slices. Wrap a slice of bacon around edges of each fillet, and secure with a wooden pick.

Grill fillets 4 to 5 inches from hot coals 8 minutes on each side or until desired degree of doneness. Yield: 6 servings.                    *D. Brown,*
*Austin, Texas.*

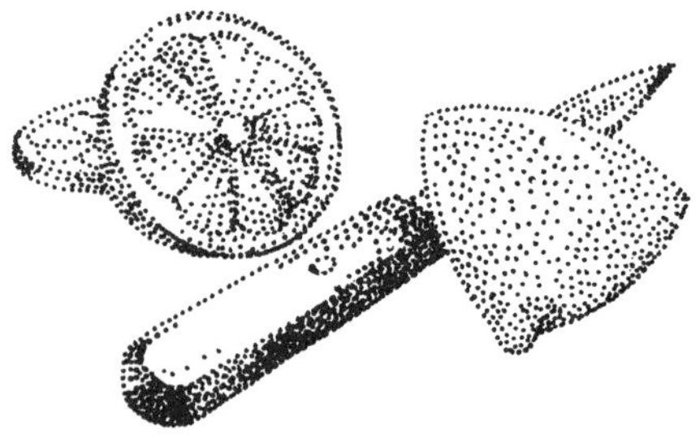

## TANGY BARBECUED SPARERIBS

3 pounds spareribs
1 large onion, finely chopped
2 cloves garlic, finely chopped
2 tablespoons vegetable oil
1 (12-ounce) bottle chili sauce
½ cup lemon juice
¼ cup molasses
¼ cup dark rum
3 tablespoons Dijon mustard
1 tablespoon Worcestershire sauce

Cut ribs into serving-size pieces (3 to 4 ribs per person); place in a large Dutch oven. Add enough water to cover ribs; cover and simmer 40 minutes. Drain ribs, and place in a shallow baking dish. Set ribs aside.

Sauté onion and garlic in oil in a medium saucepan until onion is tender. Stir in next 6 ingredients; reduce heat,

and simmer 25 minutes. Pour barbecue sauce over ribs; cover and marinate overnight in refrigerator.

Place ribs, bone side down, on grill over slow coals. Grill 20 minutes; turn meaty side down, and cook 10 to 15 minutes. Brush ribs with sauce, and let cook 5 to 10 additional minutes on each side. Yield: 4 to 5 servings.
*Mrs. Edward Lea,*
*Raleigh, North Carolina.*

## PINEAPPLE-CURRY GLAZED CHOPS

1 cup pineapple preserves
¼ cup firmly packed light brown sugar
¼ cup dill pickle juice
⅛ teaspoon coarsely ground black pepper
½ teaspoon dried parsley flakes
1 teaspoon curry powder
6 (1-inch-thick) pork chops

Combine first 6 ingredients, stirring well. Place chops on grill 4 to 5 inches from heat. Grill over slow coals 30 to 45 minutes or until chops are no longer pink, turning and basting occasionally with sauce. Yield: 6 servings.
*Martha Ann Rabon,*
*Stapleton, Alabama.*

## BARBECUED CHICKEN

½ cup honey
½ cup soy sauce
½ teaspoon ground ginger
¼ teaspoon seasoned pepper
1 teaspoon garlic powder
2 teaspoons dry mustard
1 teaspoon grated lemon rind
2 tablespoons lemon juice
1 (3- to 3½-pound) broiler-fryer, cut into
    serving-size pieces

Combine first 8 ingredients, stirring well. Place chicken, skin side down, on grill. Grill over medium coals 50 to 60 minutes or until tender, turning chicken about every 10 minutes. Brush with sauce during last 20 minutes. Yield: 4 to 6 servings.     *Mary Ann Bealefeld,*
*Reisterstown, Maryland.*

*Tip: Roll lemons, oranges, and grape-fruits on a counter before cutting to soften; you will get more juice.*

Cooking Light

# Lighten Up The Calories In Vegetables

Believe it or not, fried green tomatoes don't have to be greasy—that is, if they're prepared the "Cooking Light" way. Our Oven-Fried Green Tomatoes are baked; not a drop of high-calorie oil is used. A high oven temperature makes the cornmeal coating crispy, and the result is a Southern vegetable favorite that's approved for dieters.

Speaking of Southern favorites, let's not forget the familiar pot of black-eyed peas or collard greens. Although both are nutritious, fiber-rich vegetables, dieters must beware of the usual seasonings, such as ham hock, bacon, or salt pork. In this month's feature, we show you how to capture the Southern flavor while leaving the extra calories behind. Boil the ham hock in water first—then refrigerate the broth so every particle of hardened fat can be removed. What's left is a flavorful pot liquor that can be used to cook almost any vegetable.

Try this procedure with beef and poultry bones, too. Remember that the fat-free broth will contain salt if you use a cured or salted meat as the base—so be careful about adding any more salt while cooking your vegetables.

Broccoli in a light cheese sauce? Melinda Hoffman of Rocky Mount, North Carolina, cuts calories from the sauce by substituting skim milk, reduced-fat cheese, and diet margarine—all adding up to a savings of 15 to 20 calories per tablespoon. If you don't have diet margarine on hand, you can start the sauce by using half as much regular margarine instead.

Finally, it's a good idea to cook your vegetables only until tender, since overcooking causes loss of nutrients. Use as little liquid as possible, and always cover the pan with a tight-fitting lid.

## DILLED GREEN BEANS

1 pound fresh green beans
1 cup water
¼ cup chopped green pepper
2 tablespoons chopped onion
1 beef-flavored bouillon cube
¼ to ½ teaspoon dillseeds

Remove strings from beans; wash and cut into 1½-inch pieces.

Combine beans and remaining ingredients in a saucepan. Bring to a boil; cover and cook over medium heat 10 to 12 minutes or until tender. Yield: about 4 servings (about 36 calories per ¾-cup serving).

*Betty Minick,*
*Brooklet, Georgia.*

## BROCCOLI WITH CHEESE SAUCE

**2 pounds fresh broccoli**
**2 tablespoons diet margarine**
**2 tablespoons all-purpose flour**
**1 cup skim milk**
**2 slices low-fat process American cheese, torn into small pieces**
**¼ teaspoon salt**
**⅛ teaspoon white pepper**

Trim off large leaves of broccoli, and remove tough ends of lower stalks. Wash broccoli thoroughly, and separate into spears. Cook broccoli, covered, in a small amount of boiling salted water 10 minutes or until crisp-tender. Drain well, and keep warm.

Melt margarine in a heavy saucepan over low heat; add flour, stirring until smooth. Cook 1 minute, stirring constantly. Gradually add milk; cook over medium heat, stirring constantly with a wire whisk, until thickened and bubbly. Add cheese, salt, and pepper; stir until cheese melts. Serve sauce over broccoli. Yield: 8 servings (about 24 calories per serving plus 20 calories per tablespoon of sauce).

*Note:* One tablespoon regular margarine may be substituted for 2 tablespoons diet margarine. The flour-and-margarine mixture will be dry.

*Melinda Hoffman,*
*Rocky Mount, North Carolina.*

## CARROTS IN ORANGE SAUCE

**⅔ cup unsweetened orange juice**
**½ teaspoon cornstarch**
**3 cups (1 pound) diagonally sliced carrots**
**¼ teaspoon ground cinnamon**

Combine orange juice and cornstarch in a medium saucepan. Add carrots and cinnamon; cover and cook over low heat 15 to 20 minutes or until carrots are done. Yield: 4 servings (about 61 calories per ¾-cup serving).

*Lucy Wagner,*
*Charlotte, North Carolina.*

## SOUTHERN-STYLE COLLARDS

**About ¾ pound ham hocks**
**1 quart water**
**1 bunch (about 5 pounds) collard greens**
**1 to 1½ teaspoons salt**

Wash ham hocks, and place in a Dutch oven. Add water, and bring to a boil. Reduce heat; simmer, uncovered, 30 to 45 minutes or until meat is tender. Remove ham hocks and discard, or reserve any meat for use in other recipes. Strain broth, and chill until fat rises to the surface and hardens. Remove fat and discard.

Check leaves of collards carefully; remove pulpy stems and discolored spots on leaves. Wash leaves thoroughly; drain well and chop. Place collards, broth, and salt in a large Dutch oven; bring to a boil. Reduce heat; cover and simmer about 30 to 45 minutes or until collards are tender. Yield: 10 servings (about 60 calories per 1-cup serving).

## CREOLE EGGPLANT

**1 medium eggplant, peeled and cubed**
**1 medium-size green pepper, chopped**
**1 medium onion, chopped**
**2 cloves garlic, minced**
**1 (8-ounce) can tomato sauce**
**½ teaspoon dried whole dillweed**
**¼ teaspoon dried whole rosemary, crushed**
**¼ teaspoon dried whole thyme**

Combine all ingredients in a skillet. Cover and cook over low heat 15 to 20 minutes or until tender, stirring occasionally. Yield: 6 servings (about 38 calories per ⅔-cup serving). *Ruth Taylor,*
*Pompano Beach, Florida.*

## SOUTHERN-STYLE BLACK-EYED PEAS

**About ¾ pound ham hocks**
**1 quart water**
**4 cups shelled fresh black-eyed peas**
**1 medium onion, minced**
**½ teaspoon salt**
**¼ teaspoon pepper**

Wash ham hocks, and place in a 3-quart Dutch oven; add water, and bring to a boil. Reduce heat; simmer, uncovered, 30 to 45 minutes or until meat is tender. Remove ham hocks and discard, or reserve any meat for use in other recipes. Strain broth, and chill until fat rises to the surface and hardens. Remove fat and discard.

Place broth, peas, onion, salt, and pepper in a 3-quart Dutch oven; bring to a boil. Reduce heat; cover and simmer 30 minutes or until peas are tender. Add more water, if necessary. Yield: 7 servings (about 106 calories per ½-cup serving).

## SQUASH BAKE

**2 small yellow squash, sliced**
**1 medium zucchini, sliced**
**1 large tomato, peeled and cut into wedges**
**1 small onion, sliced and separated into rings**
**1 teaspoon dried whole basil**
**Vegetable cooking spray**
**2 tablespoons grated Parmesan cheese**

Combine vegetables and basil in a 1¾-quart casserole sprayed with cooking spray; toss lightly. Sprinkle with cheese. Cover and bake at 350° for 25 to 30 minutes or until done. Yield: 6 servings (about 35 calories per serving).

*Mrs. R. J. Spitzer,*
*Pinson, Alabama.*

## OVEN-FRIED GREEN TOMATOES

**½ cup cornmeal**
**½ teaspoon salt**
**¼ teaspoon pepper**
**1 egg**
**1 tablespoon water**
**3 medium-size green tomatoes, cut into ¼-inch slices**
**Vegetable cooking spray**

Combine cornmeal, salt, and pepper; set aside. Combine egg and water; beat well. Dip tomatoes in egg mixture; dredge in cornmeal mixture. Lightly coat a 15- x 10- x 1-inch baking pan with cooking spray. Place tomatoes in a single layer in pan. Bake at 450° for 30 to 40 minutes or until golden brown, turning once. Yield: 6 servings (about 64 calories per serving).

*Note:* Yellow squash may be substituted for tomatoes.

# Timbales Taste Like A Party

Planning a party? Timbale shells with tasty fillings may be just the appetizer you're looking for. You can make the timbale shells right in your own kitchen. All you need are timbale irons, available at most kitchen shops or department stores, a pan of hot oil, and a few helpful tips.

To ensure a crisp pastry, preheat the iron in hot oil before dipping into batter. Be careful not to cover the top of the iron with batter so that they'll be perfectly formed and easily removed when done. You can make the shells up to a week in advance and store in airtight containers. When it's party time, just add the filling. The amount of filling needed will depend on the size and number of timbales you have made.

Spoon Cheesy Mexicali Appetizer into timbales to make a snappy south-of-the-border snack. Teamed with Hamburger Stroganoff, timbales are hearty enough to offer as a main dish. For a large gathering, you can keep these fillings warm in a chafing dish, and let guests serve themselves. As a dessert, fill the pastry shells with Peach Almond Cream—a delicate mixture of pudding, whipped cream, and peaches.

*Dip hot timbale irons into batter; then fry in hot oil until the shell is crisp and golden brown.*

### TIMBALE SHELLS

1 cup all-purpose flour
1 cup milk
1 egg
1 tablespoon sugar
½ teaspoon vanilla extract
¼ teaspoon salt
Vegetable oil

Combine first 6 ingredients; beat at low speed of an electric mixer until smooth. Cover and chill 30 minutes or overnight.

Heat 2 to 3 inches oil to 370° in a medium saucepan. Heat timbale iron in hot oil 1 minute. Drain excess oil from iron; dip into batter (do not coat top of iron with batter). Immediately return iron to hot oil. Cook about 30 seconds or until timbale is crisp and brown; lift iron slowly up and down to release. (Push timbale gently with a fork, if necessary.) Drain upside down on paper towels.

Reheat iron 1 minute, and repeat procedure for each shell, stirring batter occasionally. Yield: 2 dozen 3-inch shells.

### HAMBURGER STROGANOFF

1 pound ground beef
½ cup chopped onion
1 small clove garlic, minced
1 (3-ounce) jar sliced mushrooms, drained
2 tablespoons butter or margarine
2 tablespoons all-purpose flour
1 (8-ounce) carton commercial sour cream
¼ cup plus 1 tablespoon commercial chili sauce
1 teaspoon salt
½ teaspoon Worcestershire sauce
¼ teaspoon pepper

Cook ground beef in a large heavy skillet until browned; drain off pan drippings. Stir onion, garlic, mushrooms, and butter into beef. Add flour, and stir until blended. Stir in remaining ingredients; cook just until thoroughly heated. Spoon into timbale shells. Yield: 2 cups. *Mrs. C. D. Marshall, Culpeper, Virginia.*

### CHEESY MEXICALI APPETIZER

¾ pound ground beef
3 tablespoons butter or margarine
1 medium onion, chopped
½ cup chopped green pepper
2 tablespoons all-purpose flour
1 cup milk
2 cups (about 14 ounces) cubed process American cheese
1 (16-ounce) can whole tomatoes, drained and chopped
1 canned jalapeño pepper, seeded and chopped
⅛ teaspoon red pepper
2 egg yolks

Cook beef until browned; drain well.

Melt butter in top of a double boiler over boiling water. Sauté onion and green pepper in butter until tender. Add flour and cook 1 minute, stirring constantly. Gradually add milk; cook over medium heat, stirring constantly, until thickened and bubbly.

Add cheese to sauce, stirring until cheese is melted and smooth. Stir in ground beef, tomatoes, jalapeño, and red pepper. Beat egg yolks until thick and lemon colored. Gradually stir about one-fourth of hot mixture into yolks; add yolks to remaining hot mixture, stirring constantly. Spoon into timbale shells. Yield: about 5 cups.

*Mrs. Tom Levens, Abilene, Texas.*

### CHICKEN CHUTNEY SALAD

⅔ cup mayonnaise
½ teaspoon grated lime rind
2 tablespoons lime juice
2 tablespoons chutney
½ teaspoon curry powder
¼ teaspoon salt
2 cups diced cooked chicken
1 (8¼-ounce) can crushed pineapple, drained
1 cup chopped celery
½ cup thinly sliced green onion
¼ cup chopped salted peanuts

Combine first 6 ingredients; stir well, and set aside.

Combine remaining ingredients; pour dressing over top. Toss gently; chill 1 to 2 hours. Spoon into timbale shells. Yield: about 4½ cups. *Kay Castleman, Nashville, Tennessee.*

### PEACH ALMOND CREAM

1 (3¾-ounce) package instant vanilla pudding mix
1½ cups milk
¼ teaspoon almond extract
½ cup whipping cream, whipped
¾ cup diced canned peaches, chilled

Prepare pudding mix according to package directions, using 1½ cups milk. Fold in remaining ingredients; spoon into timbale shells. Yield: 2½ cups.

*Mrs. E. F. Bastable, Chevy Chase, Maryland.*

*Tip: Mix liquid from canned fruit in a jar as you acquire it; use it in a gelatin dessert or as a punch drink.*

# From Our Kitchen To Yours

We do a lot of cooking at *Southern Living*. Every recipe that appears in our magazine is carefully tested in one of three home-style kitchens by our staff of home economists. "From Our Kitchen to Yours" is our way of sharing what we've learned while preparing about 3,000 recipes a year.

## Outdoor Cooking

When warm weather arrives, you'll want to do more and more cooking outdoors. Try some of these helpful tips for your next cookout.

■ Successful grilling starts with a good fire. If you're using a charcoal fire, spread the briquets in a single layer with tongs, making sure the edges of the coals touch.

When we're testing our recipes on the grill, we always check the temperature of the coals before adding the food. Here's the easy method we use: Hold your hand at cooking height, palm-side down above the coals. If you can leave your hand in position 2 to 3 seconds, the fire is hot; 4 seconds, medium; and 5 seconds, low. To lower the temperature, raise the grid or spread the coals. To raise the temperature, tap ash away from the coals or push them together. If more coals are needed, add them to the outer edges of the hot coals. Be sure the edges are touching.

■ While the briquets are heating, assemble all the grilling equipment you'll need on a large tray. Be sure to include a pair of long-handled tongs for turning meats. (Never use a fork; it pierces the meat, and flavorful juices are lost.) Also include gloves or mitts, a spatula, a small long-handled cotton dishmop for basting, a drip pan to catch meat juices, a water-mist bottle for extinguishing flare-ups, and the food, seasonings, and basting sauces. Running back to the kitchen at the last minute to grab a forgotten item could mean the difference between perfection and a charred disaster.

■ Basting the food as it grills adds flavor, but you must add the basting sauce at the correct time. With some sauces, you'll want to baste every 10 to 15 minutes. Our home economists add sauces containing sugar, honey, or other ingredients that burn easily only during the final 15 to 30 minutes of cooking time. This prevents a heavy, charred coating from forming on the food. For quick, no-fuss basting sauces, we recommend trying commercial Italian dressing or teriyaki sauce.

■ As we grill, we always keep careful notes on each recipe. Since many outdoor chefs enjoy experimenting as they cook instead of following a recipe, we think it's a good idea to record your own observations in a notebook. Put down the type of food, the weight or amount, added extras such as a marinade or seasonings, temperature of the fire, and cooking time. Be sure to note the flavor, tenderness, and appearance of the food. That way you can duplicate the successful results.

## Some Other Tips

**Strawberries**—May is the month for strawberries. Although we buy most of our groceries several days ahead, we wait until the last minute to buy strawberries. That way they'll always look and taste fresh. Never buy berries more than a day or two before using them. Wash them thoroughly, but don't remove the caps before washing. The caps prevent water from soaking into the berries, which can make them soggy and dilute their flavor.

**Time saver**—Do you get tired of dirtying the food processor or grater when a recipe calls for only a half cup of shredded cheese? Then do what we do. Shred an entire pound of cheese at one time; use what's needed, and freeze the rest. Put the shredded cheese in a freezer bag, label it with the type of cheese and the date, and store in the freezer. When your recipe calls for shredded cheese, just take out the bag and measure the amount you need. You're already a step ahead.

**Cleanup**—Do fish and onion odors seem to linger on your hands for days? Try rubbing your hands with a little vinegar, lemon juice, or fresh parsley. Then wash your hands in soapy water.

# Keeping The Cookie Jar Full

If keeping the cookie jar full is a seemingly endless task at your house, here are a few tempting new selections to try.

As you might expect, our Ambrosia Cookies are full of coconut. Chewy Cheesecake Cookies are light in color and have a delicate cream cheese taste. Debbie Thomas' Jumbo Chocolate Chip Cookies may be too big to fit in your cookie jar, but try them anyway for the great taste.

Remember that underbaked cookies tend to have a chewy consistency; overbaking causes them to become hard and dry with dark, crisp edges. Once the cookies have baked the minimum amount of time, test for doneness by lightly touching the center of a cookie. If only a slight imprint remains, the cookies are done. Use a wide spatula to remove the cookies, and place them on a rack to cool.

### CHEWY CHEESECAKE COOKIES

½ cup butter, softened
1 (3-ounce) package cream cheese, softened
1 cup sugar
1 cup all-purpose flour
½ cup chopped pecans

Cream butter and cream cheese; gradually add sugar, beating until light and fluffy. Add flour, and beat well. Stir in chopped pecans.

Shape dough into 1-inch balls; place 2 inches apart on ungreased cookie sheets. Dip bottom of a glass in water, and gently press each cookie until 2 inches in diameter. Bake at 375° for 12 to 13 minutes. Cool 2 to 3 minutes on cookie sheets before removing to cooling rack. Yield: 2½ dozen.

*Jan Wisland,*
*St. Louis, Missouri.*

### OATMEAL-DATE COOKIES

1 cup shortening
⅔ cup sugar
⅔ cup firmly packed brown sugar
2 eggs
1 teaspoon vanilla extract
1½ cups all-purpose flour
1 teaspoon salt
1 teaspoon soda
1 cup regular oats, uncooked
1 (8-ounce) package chopped dates

Cream shortening; gradually add sugar, beating well. Add eggs and vanilla; beat well. Combine flour, salt, and soda; add to creamed mixture, mixing well. Stir in oats and dates.

Drop dough by rounded teaspoonfuls onto lightly greased cookie sheets. Bake at 350° for 10 to 12 minutes (centers will be slightly soft). Remove from cookie sheets while warm; complete cooling on wire racks. Yield: about 5½ dozen.

*Mrs. Bill Murphy,*
*Big Spring, Texas.*

## AMBROSIA COOKIES

½ cup butter or margarine, softened
½ cup shortening
1 cup firmly packed brown sugar
1 cup sugar
2 eggs
1 tablespoon grated orange rind
2 cups all-purpose flour
1 teaspoon baking powder
½ teaspoon salt
½ teaspoon soda
3 tablespoons orange juice
1½ cups regular oats, uncooked
3 cups flaked coconut

Cream butter and shortening; gradually add sugar, beating until light and fluffy. Add eggs and orange rind, and beat well.

Combine next 4 ingredients; add to creamed mixture alternately with orange juice, beginning and ending with dry ingredients. Stir in oats and coconut. Chill dough at least 1 hour.

Drop dough by heaping teaspoonfuls onto ungreased cookie sheets. Bake at 375° for 12 minutes. Cool on wire racks. Yield: about 8 dozen.
*Mrs. J. A. Satterfield,*
*Fort Worth, Texas.*

## JUMBO CHOCOLATE CHIP COOKIES

½ cup butter or margarine, softened
½ cup shortening
1 cup firmly packed brown sugar
½ cup sugar
2 eggs
2 teaspoons vanilla extract
2½ cups all-purpose flour
1 teaspoon soda
½ teaspoon salt
1 (12-ounce) package semisweet chocolate morsels
1 cup chopped pecans

Cream butter and shortening; gradually add sugar, beating until light and fluffy. Add eggs and vanilla, beating well. Combine flour, soda, and salt; add to creamed mixture, beating well. Stir in chocolate morsels and pecans.

Drop dough by scant one-fourth cupfuls onto ungreased cookie sheets. Bake at 375° for 10 to 12 minutes. Cool slightly on cookie sheets; remove to wire racks. Yield: 2 dozen.
*Debbie Thomas,*
*Birmingham, Alabama.*

# Four Ideas For Ground Beef

These four hearty entrées make you appreciate ground beef for being such a reliable standby. You'll stretch your food budget and satisfy a hungry family when you serve these ground beef creations, which range from dressed-up burgers to Old-Fashioned Meat Pie.

## HAMBURGER STROGANOFF

1 pound ground beef
4 slices bacon, chopped
½ cup chopped onion
1 (10¾-ounce) can cream of mushroom soup, undiluted
½ teaspoon salt
¼ teaspoon paprika
1 (8-ounce) carton commercial sour cream
Hot cooked noodles

Combine ground beef, bacon, and onion in a skillet; cook over medium heat until meat is browned. Drain off pan drippings.

Add soup, salt, and paprika to skillet; mix well. Continue cooking 15 to 20 minutes, stirring occasionally. Stir in sour cream; heat thoroughly, but do not boil. Serve over hot cooked noodles. Yield: 4 to 6 servings.
*Mrs. Roy McKnight,*
*Abbeville, Alabama.*

## SUPER SUPPER BURGERS

1½ pounds ground beef
1 egg
¼ cup grated carrot
¼ cup dry breadcrumbs
1 onion, chopped
1 tablespoon Worcestershire sauce
1 tablespoon dried parsley flakes
1 teaspoon salt
½ teaspoon rubbed sage or poultry seasoning
¼ teaspoon pepper
1 (10¾-ounce) can tomato soup, undiluted and divided
2 tablespoons vegetable oil
1 teaspoon vinegar

Combine first 10 ingredients in a large mixing bowl; mix well. Add ¼ cup tomato soup; mix well. Shape mixture into 6 patties. Brown patties on both sides in hot oil in a large skillet. Drain off pan drippings.

Combine vinegar and remaining soup; stir well. Pour over burgers, and bring to a boil. Reduce heat; cover and simmer 25 minutes. Remove cover, and simmer 5 additional minutes, spooning soup over burgers occasionally. Yield: 6 servings.
*Mrs. J. M. Hamilton,*
*Fort Mill, South Carolina.*

## OLD-FASHIONED MEAT PIE

1 pound ground beef
2 (8-ounce) cans tomato sauce with onion, divided
1 egg
¼ cup dry breadcrumbs
1 teaspoon salt
1 (10-ounce) package frozen mixed vegetables, thawed
½ teaspoon whole thyme leaves
½ teaspoon pepper
1 (12-ounce) package frozen hash brown potatoes, thawed
2 tablespoons vegetable oil
1 tablespoon butter or margarine, melted
6 slices American cheese, cut into ½-inch strips

Combine ground beef, 2 tablespoons tomato sauce, egg, breadcrumbs, and salt in a large mixing bowl; mix well. Shape into 1-inch meatballs. Brown meatballs in a large skillet; drain off pan drippings. Add remaining tomato sauce, mixed vegetables, thyme, and pepper to skillet; simmer 5 minutes.

Press potatoes firmly into a lightly greased 12- x 8- x 2-inch baking dish; drizzle with oil and butter. Broil until lightly browned.

Spoon meatball mixture over potatoes. Arrange cheese on top of meat mixture in lattice pattern. Bake at 375° for 20 minutes. Yield: 6 to 8 servings.
*Mrs. M. Griffith,*
*Jonesboro, Arkansas.*

## MEATBALLS ESPANOL

1 pound ground beef
1 cup soft breadcrumbs
¼ cup finely chopped onion
¼ cup chopped celery
1 egg
1½ teaspoons Worcestershire sauce
1 teaspoon garlic salt
¼ teaspoon pepper
1 (16-ounce) can stewed tomatoes
2½ cups thinly sliced zucchini
½ teaspoon dried whole oregano
½ teaspoon dried whole basil
1 teaspoon garlic salt
½ teaspoon sugar
1 tablespoon cornstarch
1 cup beef broth
Hot cooked rice

Combine first 8 ingredients in a large mixing bowl, and mix well. Shape mixture into 1½-inch balls. Arrange meatballs in a greased 9-inch square baking pan. Bake at 375° for 20 minutes.

Combine tomatoes, zucchini, oregano, basil, 1 teaspoon garlic salt, and sugar in a large skillet; mix well. Combine cornstarch and beef broth; mix well, and stir into tomato mixture. Simmer about 5 minutes, stirring constantly, until thickened and bubbly. Pour over meatballs; bake 10 minutes longer. Serve over hot cooked rice. Yield: 6 servings. *Mrs. J. C. Graham, Athens, Texas.*

# Slice Cucumbers A New Way

Don't put yourself in a pickle over how to use all those cucumbers pouring into your local market. If you're short of ideas on what to do with a cucumber, try these inventive new ways our readers have devised to enjoy this crisp green vegetable.

How about fresh Cucumber Sauce for seafood? Our test kitchens staff loved this blend with shrimp and agreed it would complement other delicacies from the sea equally well. Our Cucumber Salad Mold captures the cucumber's cool, fresh taste and pale-green color in a rich and creamy gelatin base.

Whenever you need an attractive garnish, don't forget the cucumber. Score the edges of an unpeeled cucumber with the tines of a fork; then slice the vegetable into thin, fluted rounds. Float them atop soup or use them to crown a salad or garnish a dinner plate.

### CUCUMBER SALAD MOLD

**5 large cucumbers**
**3 envelopes unflavored gelatin**
**¾ cup water**
**1 (8-ounce) carton commercial sour cream**
**1 cup mayonnaise**
**1 tablespoon grated onion**
**1½ teaspoons salt**
**1 teaspoon sugar**
**½ cup whipping cream**
**Leaf lettuce**
**Cucumber slices**

Peel cucumbers, and cut in half lengthwise; scoop out seeds. Coarsely chop cucumbers, and place in container of an electric blender; process until smooth. Set aside 4 cups puree.

Sprinkle gelatin over water in a saucepan, and let stand 5 minutes; cook over medium heat until gelatin is dissolved, stirring constantly and scraping sides occasionally.

Combine sour cream, mayonnaise, onion, salt, and sugar; stir in 4 cups cucumber puree and gelatin. Beat whipping cream until thickened but not stiff; stir into cucumber mixture. Pour mixture into a lightly oiled 6-cup mold; chill until firm. Unmold on lettuce, and garnish with cucumber slices. Yield: 12 servings. *Eunice M. Davies, Sarasota, Florida.*

### MARINATED CUCUMBER SALAD

**2 medium cucumbers, thinly sliced**
**1 medium onion, cut into rings**
**2 cups thinly sliced carrots**
**½ cup sliced celery**
**1 cup vinegar**
**¼ cup vegetable oil**
**¾ cup sugar**
**1 teaspoon celery seeds**
**1 teaspoon salt**
**¼ teaspoon pepper**
**Leaf lettuce**

Combine first 4 ingredients in a large shallow dish; set aside.

Combine next 6 ingredients, mixing well; pour over vegetables, tossing lightly. Cover and chill 8 to 10 hours. Drain and serve in a lettuce-lined bowl. Yield: 6 servings. *Mary Linda Brooks, Hayes, Virginia.*

### MARINATED CUCUMBERS AND ARTICHOKES

**1 medium cucumber, peeled and thinly sliced**
**1 (14-ounce) can artichoke hearts, drained and sliced in halves**
**¾ cup vegetable oil**
**½ cup vinegar**
**1 tablespoon instant minced onion**
**½ teaspoon dry mustard**
**½ teaspoon garlic salt**
**½ teaspoon dried whole basil**
**⅛ teaspoon pepper**

Combine cucumber and artichokes in a medium bowl. Combine remaining ingredients, and pour over cucumber mixture; toss lightly. Cover and refrigerate overnight. Yield: 4 to 6 servings. *Kathy A. Murtiashaw, Columbia, South Carolina.*

### CUCUMBER SAUCE

**½ cup peeled, chopped cucumber**
**½ cup mayonnaise**
**½ cup commercial sour cream**
**1 tablespoon chopped fresh chives**
**½ teaspoon chopped fresh parsley**
**¼ teaspoon salt**
**¼ teaspoon dried dillweed**

Combine all ingredients; mix well and chill. Serve with seafood. Yield: about 1½ cups. *Gladys C. White, Winter Haven, Florida.*

# Savor A Citrus Favorite

The fresh flavor of citrus fruit and juice adds a special touch to meals. You'll enjoy this flavor to the fullest in our lemony cupcakes, orange-flavored pudding, and refreshing grapefruit aspic.

Remember to select firm, well-rounded fruit that is heavy for its size. If possible, store citrus in the refrigerator. This will prolong its keeping time.

### ORANGE PUDDING

**2 eggs, separated**
**¼ cup sugar**
**¼ teaspoon salt**
**2 tablespoons all-purpose flour**
**2 tablespoons butter or margarine, softened**
**1 tablespoon orange rind**
**¼ cup orange juice**
**1 tablespoon lemon juice**
**¼ cup sugar**
**1 cup milk**

Beat egg whites (at room temperature) until frothy; add ¼ cup sugar and salt; continue beating until soft peaks form. Set aside.

Beat egg yolks until lemon colored; add flour, butter, orange rind, juice, and ¼ cup sugar. Gradually beat in milk. Fold egg white mixture into yolk mixture. Spoon into six 6-ounce buttered custard cups. Place in a pan of hot water; bake at 350° for 35 to 40 minutes or until a knife inserted in center comes out clean. Chill. Yield: 6 servings. *Varniece Warren, Hermitage, Arkansas.*

## LEMON MOIST CUPCAKES

¾ cup butter or margarine, softened
1 cup sugar
2 eggs
2 cups self-rising flour
½ cup milk
1 teaspoon vanilla extract
1 cup sugar
Grated rind of 1 lemon
Grated rind of 1 orange
Juice of 2 lemons
Juice of 2 oranges

Combine butter and 1 cup sugar in a large mixing bowl, creaming until light and fluffy. Add eggs, beating well. Stir in flour. Add milk and vanilla, mixing just until blended.

Spoon batter into paper-lined muffin pans, filling each cup half full. Bake at 350° for 20 to 25 minutes.

Combine remaining ingredients, stirring until blended. Spoon glaze over warm cupcakes. Yield: about 2 dozen.
*Mrs. Lyman Clayborn,*
*Kinston, North Carolina.*

## GRAPEFRUIT ASPIC

1 (3-ounce) package lemon- or
   lime-flavored gelatin
1 tablespoon sugar
¾ cup boiling water
1 cup unsweetened grapefruit juice
2 medium grapefruit, peeled, seeded, and
   sectioned
¾ cup sliced almonds
Lettuce leaves

Dissolve gelatin and sugar in boiling water; stir in grapefruit juice. Chill until consistency of unbeaten egg white.

Chop grapefruit sections; drain. Stir grapefruit and almonds into thickened gelatin. Pour mixture into lightly oiled ⅓-cup molds. Chill until firm. Serve on lettuce leaves. Yield: 8 servings.
*Mrs. E. C. Holloway,*
*Murfreesboro, Tennessee.*

# Bring On The Strawberries

When the first strawberries of the season appear, Mary Davis of Hueytown, Alabama, makes Chilled Strawberry Pie. She starts with an unusual shell of egg whites, cracker crumbs, and nuts,

and then folds sliced strawberries into sweetened whipped cream for the filling. Additional berries on top of the pie make a colorful garnish.

Another way to enjoy fresh strawberries is in Lilly Pegourie's easy-to-make refrigerator ice cream. Lilly likes to keep a container of Frozen Strawberry Delight on hand through the summer— it's perfect for unexpected guests.

## FROZEN STRAWBERRY DELIGHT

4 cups strawberries
1 (14-ounce) can sweetened condensed
   milk
1 (8-ounce) container frozen whipped
   topping, thawed
1 (8¼-ounce) can crushed pineapple,
   drained
¼ cup lemon juice

Puree strawberries in container of an electric blender; set aside.

Combine condensed milk and whipped topping; stir until well blended. Stir in strawberry puree, pineapple, and lemon juice. Spoon mixture into a 13- x 9- x 2-inch pan; freeze until firm. Let stand at room temperature 15 minutes before serving. Yield: 10 to 12 servings.
*Lilly Pegourie,*
*Louisville, Kentucky.*

## HAWAIIAN FRUIT DISH

6 cups watermelon balls
4 cups strawberries
4 cups honeydew balls
1 fresh pineapple, cut into chunks
½ pound seedless grapes
2 bananas, peeled and sliced
2 large oranges, peeled and sectioned
½ to 1 cup light rum

Combine fruit in a large shallow bowl. Add rum, tossing gently. Cover and chill at least 1 hour. Yield: 15 to 18 servings.
*Margie Hinson,*
*Mount Pleasant, Tennessee.*

## CHILLED STRAWBERRY PIE

3 egg whites
1 cup sugar
1 teaspoon vanilla extract
1 cup round buttery cracker crumbs
1 cup chopped pecans
1 cup whipping cream
2 tablespoons powdered sugar
2 cups strawberries, sliced
Whole strawberries (optional)

Beat egg whites (at room temperature) until soft peaks form. Gradually add sugar and vanilla, and beat until stiff peaks form. Fold in cracker crumbs and pecans. Spread mixture in a buttered 10-inch pieplate, spreading sides slightly higher. Bake at 350° for 30 minutes or until lightly browned. Cool pie shell completely.

Beat whipping cream until foamy; gradually add powdered sugar, beating until soft peaks form. Fold in strawberries. Spread mixture evenly in pie shell. Garnish with whole strawberries, if desired. Chill pie at least 4 hours before serving. Yield: one 10-inch pie.
*Mary Davis,*
*Hueytown, Alabama.*

## STRAWBERRY SHERBET

4 cups strawberries, mashed
2 cups sugar
2 cups buttermilk

Combine strawberries and sugar; beat well with electric mixer. Stir in buttermilk; pour into an 8-inch square pan. Freeze mixture until slushy; beat well with an electric mixer. Return to freezer, and freeze until firm. Yield: 1 quart.
*Barbara Harden,*
*Savannah, Georgia.*

## SMOOTHIE STRAWBERRY POPSICLES

1 cup sliced strawberries
½ cup sliced peaches
½ cup sliced bananas
½ cup orange sections
1½ cups pineapple-coconut juice

Combine fruit in container of food processor or electric blender; process until smooth. Combine fruit mixture and juice, stirring well.

Pour mixture into eight 5-ounce paper drink cups. Partially freeze; add popsicle sticks, and freeze until firm. To serve, let popsicles stand 5 to 10 minutes at room temperature. Yield: 8 servings.
*Judy Woodall,*
*Duncanville, Texas.*

## FREEZER STRAWBERRY PRESERVES

3 cups crushed strawberries
5 cups sugar
¾ cup water
1 (1¾-ounce) package powdered fruit
   pectin

Combine strawberries and sugar; let stand 20 minutes, stirring occasionally.

Combine water and fruit pectin in a small saucepan. Bring pectin mixture to a boil; boil 1 minute, stirring constantly. Add pectin mixture to fruit, and stir 3 minutes. Immediately spoon preserves into freezer containers, leaving ½-inch headspace. Cover at once with lids. Let stand at room temperature 24 hours; freeze. To serve, thaw preserves. Yield: about 6 cups.

*Note:* Preserves may be stored in the refrigerator 3 weeks. *Susan Erickson, Pocahontas, Arkansas.*

## FRESH STRAWBERRY MILKSHAKE

1½ cups strawberries
1 cup milk
1 cup vanilla ice cream
1 tablespoon honey
1 teaspoon lemon juice

Combine all ingredients in container of electric blender; process until smooth. Yield: about 3½ cups.

*Arline Newton, Lincoln, Nebraska.*

# These Salads Are Ready To Go

If you need a special salad to take to a spring picnic or a family reunion, one of our carry-alongs should be just right. Marinated Vegetable Toss, Bean Sprout Salad, and Colorful Fruit Salad are all easy to take with you since they don't contain ingredients that require constant refrigeration.

## MARINATED VEGETABLE TOSS

1 (1½-pound) bunch broccoli
1 medium head cauliflower
2 carrots, scraped and sliced
4 large fresh mushrooms, sliced
1 (4½-ounce) jar pimiento-stuffed olives, drained
1 (3.2-ounce) can ripe olives, drained
1 (8-ounce) bottle commercial Italian salad dressing

Trim off large leaves of broccoli. Remove tough ends of lower stalks, and wash broccoli thoroughly. Cut into bite-size pieces.

Wash cauliflower thoroughly, and remove green leaves. Separate cauliflower into flowerets, slicing large flowerets into bite-size pieces.

Cook broccoli, cauliflower, and carrots in boiling water 3 minutes. Plunge vegetables immediately into ice water. Drain well when cool.

Combine cooked vegetables and the remaining ingredients, tossing gently. Cover and chill at least 3 hours before serving. Yield: 12 servings. *Sue Greer, Waco, Texas.*

## BEAN SPROUT SALAD

1 cup vinegar
1 cup sugar
3 tablespoons vegetable oil
1 tablespoon soy sauce
½ teaspoon salt
1 (16-ounce) can French-style green beans, drained
1 (14-ounce) can bean sprouts, drained
½ cup chopped celery
½ cup chopped onion
¼ cup chopped pimiento

Combine first 5 ingredients in a medium saucepan; bring to a boil, stirring occasionally. Cool.

Combine vegetables, tossing lightly. Pour vinegar mixture over vegetables, stirring gently to blend well. Cover and refrigerate 24 hours. Yield: 6 servings.

*Janet G. Comegys, Doraville, Georgia.*

## COLORFUL FRUIT SALAD

1 (21-ounce) can apricot pie filling
1 (16-ounce) can sliced peaches, drained
1 (15¼-ounce) can pineapple chunks, drained
1 (11-ounce) can mandarin oranges, drained
4 bananas, peeled and sliced
1 cup maraschino cherries (optional)

Combine all ingredients; toss gently. Cover and chill. Yield: 8 to 10 servings.

*Marcene Measures, Lubbock, Texas.*

# For Supper, A One-Dish Meal

There are so many times when a one-dish dinner solves the problem of what to have for supper. With chicken, pork, and ground beef for starters, you can come up with a satisfying—and good—meal-in-a-dish. We suggest a bubbling-hot chicken pie, a pork chop and potato combination, and a spicy, cheesy enchilada casserole.

## SOUR CREAM ENCHILADA CASSEROLE

1 cup water
¼ cup plus 2 tablespoons picante sauce, divided
12 corn tortillas
2 pounds ground beef
1 onion, chopped
1 to 1½ teaspoons salt
⅛ teaspoon pepper
2 teaspoons ground cumin
1 tablespoon chili powder
1 teaspoon garlic powder
¾ cup ripe olives, sliced
½ cup butter or margarine
2 tablespoons all-purpose flour
1½ cups milk
1 (16-ounce) carton commercial sour cream
2 cups (8 ounces) shredded Cheddar cheese

Combine water and 2 tablespoons picante sauce in a large shallow dish. Place tortillas in picante sauce mixture; let stand 5 minutes. Drain.

Cook ground beef and onion in a heavy skillet until brown; drain off drippings. Stir in salt, pepper, cumin, chili powder, garlic powder, olives, and ¼ cup picante sauce; simmer meat mixture 5 minutes.

Melt butter in a heavy saucepan over low heat; add flour, stirring until smooth. Cook 1 minute, stirring constantly. Gradually stir in milk; cook over medium heat, stirring constantly, until thickened and bubbly. Remove from heat, and add sour cream; stir until well blended.

Place half of tortillas in a 13- x 9- x 2-inch baking dish. Pour half of sour cream sauce over tortillas; spoon half of meat mixture evenly over sauce. Sprinkle half of cheese over meat mixture. Repeat layers with remaining ingredients. Bake at 375° for 25 minutes. Yield: about 8 servings.

*Mrs. Hubert Watson, Caldwell, Texas.*

## CHICKEN POT PIE

1 cup chopped onion
1 cup chopped celery
1 cup chopped carrot
⅓ cup butter or margarine
½ cup all-purpose flour
2 cups chicken broth
1 cup half-and-half
1 teaspoon salt
¼ teaspoon pepper
4 cups chopped cooked chicken
Basic Pastry
Fresh parsley sprigs (optional)

Sauté onion, celery, and carrot in butter for 10 minutes. Add flour to sautéed mixture, stirring well; cook 1 minute, stirring constantly.

Combine broth and half-and-half; gradually stir into vegetable mixture. Cook over medium heat, stirring constantly, until thickened and bubbly. Stir in salt and pepper. Add chopped chicken, stirring well.

Pour chicken mixture into a greased shallow 2-quart casserole. Top with pastry; cut slits to allow steam to escape. Decorate with pastry cutouts, if desired. Bake at 400° for 40 minutes or until crust is golden brown. Garnish with parsley, if desired. Yield: about 6 servings.

*Basic Pastry:*

1 cup all-purpose flour
½ teaspoon salt
⅓ cup plus 1 tablespoon shortening
2 to 3 tablespoons cold water

Combine flour and salt in bowl; cut in shortening with pastry blender until mixture resembles coarse meal. Sprinkle cold water evenly over surface; stir with a fork until all dry ingredients are moistened. Shape into a ball; chill. Roll pastry to fit casserole dish. Yield: enough pastry for 9-inch pie.
*Janet Eubanks,*
*Paris, Arkansas.*

## PORK CHOPS AND POTATO SCALLOP

1 (10¾-ounce) can cream of mushroom
  soup, undiluted
½ cup commercial sour cream
¼ cup water
½ teaspoon dried dillweed
4 cups thinly sliced potatoes
4 pork chops
Salt and pepper to taste
Vegetable oil
Fresh parsley sprigs (optional)

Combine mushroom soup, sour cream, water, and dillweed in a small bowl; blend well. Alternate layers of potatoes and soup mixture in a lightly greased 2-quart casserole. Cover; bake at 375° for 45 minutes.

Sprinkle pork chops with salt and pepper; brown on both sides in a small amount of oil in a large skillet. Drain on paper towels. Place chops on top of potatoes; cover and bake an additional 30 minutes. Garnish with parsley, if desired. Yield: 4 servings. *Rita Bufkin, Mansfield, Louisiana.*

# Crackling Good Cornbread

When L. E. Sellers of Chipley, Florida, saw a *Southern Living* recipe for Cowboy Cornbread, he decided to try his own variation as an experiment. By substituting some old-fashioned cracklings for the cooked bacon called for originally, he came up with a crackling cornbread much like the one his mother used to make when he was a boy.

We think you'll find that the combination of cracklings with onion, cheese, and corn makes Crackling Cowboy Cornbread especially delicious.

## CRACKLING COWBOY CORNBREAD

1½ cups cornmeal
½ cup all-purpose flour
½ teaspoon soda
½ teaspoon salt
1 cup milk
2 eggs, beaten
2 tablespoons vegetable oil
2 cups (8 ounces) shredded Cheddar
  cheese
1 (8-ounce) can cream-style corn
1 small onion, chopped
2 cups cracklings
2 tablespoons chopped pimiento

Combine first 4 ingredients; mix well. Add milk, eggs, and vegetable oil; stir well. Stir in the remaining ingredients. Pour into a greased 10-inch cast-iron skillet. Bake at 350° for 30 to 35 minutes or until lightly browned. Yield: 8 servings.
*L. E. Sellers,*
*Chipley, Florida.*

# A Quick Nut Treat

If you're a peanut brittle fan, this version offers a bonus—a luscious chocolate topping. Just sprinkle peanuts in the pan, top with the hot candy mixture, and dot chocolate morsels over the top. When the morsels have melted, spread the chocolate evenly over the top to a smooth finish, and get ready to enjoy.

## QUICK CHOCOLATE BRITTLE

½ cup raw peanuts
¾ cup firmly packed brown sugar
½ cup butter or margarine
1 (6-ounce) package semisweet chocolate
  morsels

Lightly grease a 9-inch square pan; sprinkle peanuts into pan, and set aside.

Combine brown sugar and butter in a medium saucepan; cook over low heat, stirring constantly, until mixture reaches soft crack stage (about 270°). Immediately pour over peanuts, spreading to sides of pan; sprinkle chocolate morsels over top. Cover with aluminum foil, and let stand 2 minutes.

Remove foil, and spread melted chocolate evenly over top; chill until firm. Remove candy from pan, and break into pieces. Yield: about 1 pound.
*Charlotte A. Pierce,*
*Greensburg, Kentucky.*

Right: *Cantaloupe halves are scalloped and filled with an assortment of fresh fruit in a lemon-flavored dressing for Summertime Melon Salad (page 101).*

Page 118: *French-Fried Okra is probably everybody's favorite, but you'll also enjoy it with a medley of vegetables in Plantation Okra (recipes on page 126).*

Above: *Fancy Fruit Tart (page 128) looks and tastes delicious, but fresh fruit keeps the calorie count at a minimum.*

Right: *Try this trio of lighter-than-air dessert mousses. Clockwise: Blender Chocolate Mousse (page 71), Peppermint Candy Mousse (page 71), and Apricot Mousse (page 72).*

Far right: *Cordials and liqueurs make the most of fruit and ice cream in these simple, delicious desserts. Clockwise: Ruby Strawberries, After Dinner-Drink Dessert, Chocolate-Mint Dessert, Strawberries and Cream, and Golden Dream (recipes on page 100).*

# The Casserole Advantage

The advantages of serving a main-dish casserole are many. Casseroles are usually quick to assemble, easy to serve, and most can be prepared hours or even a day ahead—left in the refrigerator and heated shortly before serving time. And with any of these recipes featured here, all you need to complete the meal are a salad and dessert.

## LAYERED GRECIAN BAKE

1½ pounds ground beef
½ cup chopped onion
½ cup dry breadcrumbs
1 egg, slightly beaten
1¼ teaspoons salt
1 teaspoon dried whole basil
¼ teaspoon pepper
2 (8-ounce) cans tomato sauce with cheese
1 small eggplant, peeled and cut into ½-inch slices
1 cup (4 ounces) shredded Cheddar cheese
½ cup commercial sour cream

Combine first 7 ingredients; stir in 1 can tomato sauce. Divide meat mixture in half; spread one-half in an 8-inch square baking dish. Place eggplant slices on top of meat mixture. Combine cheese and sour cream; spread over eggplant. Top with remaining meat mixture, spreading evenly. Bake at 350° for 1 hour; drain and discard excess drippings. Pour 1 can tomato sauce over meat. Bake 15 minutes longer. Yield: 6 servings. *Mrs. Bill Guthrie, Mount Sterling, Kentucky.*

## LASAGNA

1 pound ground beef
2 tablespoons vegetable oil
1 (28-ounce) can whole tomatoes, coarsely chopped
2 (6-ounce) cans tomato paste
2 teaspoons salt
1 teaspoon Italian seasoning
¼ teaspoon pepper
¼ teaspoon crushed red pepper
⅛ teaspoon garlic powder
1 (8-ounce) package lasagna noodles
1 cup (4 ounces) shredded mozzarella cheese
1 cup ricotta or small curd cottage cheese
¼ cup grated Parmesan cheese
3 to 4 slices mozzarella cheese, halved diagonally

Brown ground beef in oil in a large skillet, stirring to crumble; drain off pan drippings. Stir tomatoes, tomato paste, and seasonings into meat. Bring to a boil; reduce heat and simmer 40 minutes, stirring occasionally.

Cook noodles according to package directions; drain.

Place half of noodles in a lightly greased 12- x 8- x 2-inch baking dish, slightly overlapping lengthwise edges. Spoon one-third of meat mixture over noodles; add half of shredded mozzarella, ricotta, and Parmesan cheese. Repeat layers, and spoon on remaining meat mixture. Arrange mozzarella slices on top. Bake at 350° for 30 minutes. Yield: 6 to 8 servings. *Lou Harper, Edmonton, Kentucky.*

## GOLDEN HAM CASSEROLE

2 cups cubed potatoes
1 cup sliced carrots
1 cup chopped celery
2 cups cubed cooked ham
2 tablespoons chopped green pepper
2 teaspoons chopped onion
¼ cup plus 3 tablespoons butter or margarine, divided
3 tablespoons all-purpose flour
1½ cups milk
½ cup (2 ounces) shredded Cheddar cheese
½ teaspoon salt
⅛ teaspoon pepper
½ cup soft breadcrumbs

Cook potatoes, carrots, and celery in a small amount of boiling unsalted water until crisp-tender; drain and set aside.

Sauté ham, green pepper, and onion in 3 tablespoons butter in a medium skillet until ham is golden brown. Place ham mixture and cooked vegetables in a deep, greased 2-quart casserole.

Melt ¼ cup butter in a heavy saucepan over low heat; add flour, stirring until smooth. Cook 1 minute, stirring constantly. Gradually stir in milk; cook over medium heat, stirring constantly, until thickened and bubbly. Stir in cheese, salt, and pepper; cook over low heat until cheese melts and mixture is slightly thickened. Pour cheese sauce over ham and vegetables; sprinkle with breadcrumbs. Bake at 375° for 25 to 30 minutes. Yield: 4 to 6 servings. *Annie Knight, Chesnee, South Carolina.*

## TUNA CASSEROLE

3 tablespoons chopped onion
3 tablespoons chopped green pepper
1 tablespoon vegetable oil
1 (10¾-ounce) can tomato soup, undiluted
1 teaspoon chili powder
½ teaspoon salt
1 teaspoon Worcestershire sauce
1½ cups cooked noodles
1¼ cups (5 ounces) shredded sharp Cheddar cheese, divided
1 (6¾-ounce) can tuna, drained and flaked

Sauté onion and green pepper in oil in a medium saucepan. Add soup, chili powder, salt, and Worcestershire sauce; simmer 5 minutes. Add noodles, 1 cup cheese, and tuna. Spoon into a greased 1-quart casserole, and bake at 350° for 30 minutes. Sprinkle with remaining cheese while still hot. Yield: 4 to 5 servings. *Jane McGuire, Roanoke, Virginia.*

# Fruit Accents The Entrée

Add pineapple to chicken, peaches to ham, apples to sausage, and you've got a perfect meat and fruit combo. With these recipes, fruit adds its natural juiciness and a touch of sweetness to the meat. Smother ham steaks with a medley of fruit; bake them covered with a sauce of butter, brown sugar, and curry powder. Sauté apple rings, and serve them atop sausage. And enjoy the sweet-and-sour flavor of Pineapple Chicken Bake made with crushed pineapple.

## HAM CROQUETTES

2 cups ground ham
½ cup soft breadcrumbs
¼ cup milk
1 egg, beaten
1 (16-ounce) can sliced peaches, drained
1 tablespoon brown sugar

Combine first 4 ingredients; mix well. Shape mixture into 4 rolls. Place rolls in a greased 12- x 8- x 2-inch baking dish. Bake at 350° for 40 minutes.

Remove from oven. Arrange peaches around rolls; sprinkle peaches with brown sugar. Bake an additional 10 minutes. Yield: 4 servings. *Mrs. William S. Bell, Chattanooga, Tennessee.*

## CURRIED HAM STEAK

2 (½-inch-thick) smoked ham steaks
1 (17-ounce) can apricot halves, drained
1 (16-ounce) can pear halves, drained
1 (15¼-ounce) can pineapple slices, drained
¼ cup raisins
¼ cup butter or margarine
¼ cup firmly packed brown sugar
1 tablespoon curry powder

Place ham steaks in a 13- x 9- x 2-inch baking dish. Arrange fruit evenly over ham.

Melt butter in a small saucepan, and stir in brown sugar and curry. Pour sauce over fruit. Bake at 350° for 30 minutes or until thoroughly heated. Yield: 6 servings. *Mrs. C. D. Marshall, Culpeper, Virginia.*

## PINEAPPLE SWEET-AND-SOUR PORK

1 pound boneless pork shoulder, cut into ½-inch cubes
2 tablespoons vegetable oil
1 cup beef broth
Pepper to taste
1 (20-ounce) can pineapple chunks
¼ cup sugar
¼ cup vinegar
2 teaspoons soy sauce
3 tablespoons cornstarch
1 large green pepper, cut into strips
1 small onion, sliced and separated into rings
Hot cooked rice

Brown pork in oil in a large skillet; add beef broth and pepper. Cover and simmer 30 minutes. Remove from heat. Drain pineapple, reserving juice. Combine pineapple juice, sugar, vinegar, soy sauce, and cornstarch; stir until sugar and cornstarch dissolve. Add to pork, stirring until combined.

Add vegetables; cook over low heat 10 minutes, stirring constantly. Serve over rice. Yield: 4 servings.
*Debra Leckie, Shreveport, Louisiana.*

## APPLES ON SAUSAGE PATTIES

1 (16-ounce) package bulk pork sausage
2 medium cooking apples
3 tablespoons sugar
¼ teaspoon ground cinnamon
2 tablespoons butter or margarine
2 tablespoons chopped fresh parsley (optional)

Shape sausage into 6 patties 3½ inches in diameter and about ½ inch thick. Cook patties over medium heat until done, turning once. Place on serving dish, and keep warm.

Core apples; remove a ¼-inch slice from both ends and discard. Cut remainder of each apple into 3 rings. Combine sugar and cinnamon, mixing well. Dredge apple rings in cinnamon mixture.

Melt butter in a skillet; add apple rings, and cook over medium heat until browned, turning often. Sprinkle any remaining cinnamon mixture over apples as they cook. Place an apple ring on top of each sausage patty; sprinkle with chopped parsley, if desired. Serve immediately. Yield: 6 servings.
*Kay Castleman, Nashville, Tennessee.*

## PINEAPPLE CHICKEN BAKE

2 whole chicken breasts, split, boned, and skinned
2 tablespoons butter or margarine, melted
½ teaspoon salt
¼ teaspoon pepper
1 cup firmly packed brown sugar
1 (8-ounce) can crushed pineapple, drained
¼ cup lemon juice
2 tablespoons prepared mustard
1 teaspoon Worcestershire sauce
Dash of soy sauce
Hot cooked rice

Brush chicken with butter; sprinkle with salt and pepper. Place chicken in a 12- x 8- x 2-inch baking dish. Bake, uncovered, at 375° for 30 minutes.

Combine next 6 ingredients, stirring well. Spoon glaze over chicken. Bake an additional 20 minutes, basting occasionally. Serve over rice. Yield: 4 servings.
*Adrian Palmer, Chattanooga, Tennessee.*

*Tip: Keep butter, margarine, and fat drippings tightly covered in the refrigerator. Vegetable shortening can be kept covered at room temperature. Homemade salad dressing should be kept in the refrigerator; mayonnaise and commercial salad dressings should be refrigerated after opening. Foods mixed with mayonnaise, such as potato salad or egg salad, should be refrigerated and used within a couple of days.*

# Roll Up The Berries In A Cake

You can find lots of fresh strawberries in the spring—so it's a perfect time to try Carol Horn's delectable Strawberry Roll. All you need is an angel food cake mix, a quart of fresh strawberries, and some sweetened whipping cream. You can substitute other fresh fruit when strawberries aren't available.

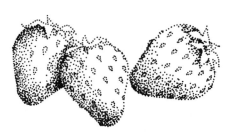

## STRAWBERRY ROLL

Vegetable oil
1 (14.5-ounce) package white angel food cake mix
Powdered sugar
1 quart strawberries, sliced
¼ cup sugar
2 cups whipping cream
3 tablespoons powdered sugar
Whole strawberries

Grease a 17- x 11½- x 1-inch jellyroll pan with vegetable oil, and line with waxed paper. Grease waxed paper with vegetable oil; set aside.

Prepare cake mix according to package directions; spread batter in prepared pan. Bake at 375° for 10 to 12 minutes or until firm to touch (do not overbake).

Sift powdered sugar in a 17- x 11½-inch rectangle on a linen towel. When cake is done, immediately loosen from sides of pan, and turn out on powdered sugar. Peel off waxed paper. Starting at narrow end, roll up cake and towel together; cool on a wire rack 20 minutes, seam side down.

Combine sliced strawberries and sugar; set aside. Beat whipping cream until foamy; gradually add 3 tablespoons powdered sugar, beating until soft peaks form.

Drain strawberries. Unroll cake and remove towel. Spread cake with half of whipped cream. Top with berries; reroll. Place on serving plate, seam side down; spread remaining whipped cream on all sides. Garnish with whole strawberries. Chill before serving. Yield: 10 to 12 servings.
*Carol Horn, Huntsville, Alabama.*

# Refreshing Beverages Keep You Cool

For your next get-together, bring out your punch bowl and treat your friends to new thirst-quenching flavors with the hospitality of the South. Whether the base is fruit juice, alcohol, or ice cream, punch is the perfect answer for crowd-size entertaining.

To spruce up any punch bowl, add a fruit-filled ice ring made from the same ingredients you use in the punch. (If you use only water for the ice ring, it will dilute the punch as it melts.) Just follow these easy instructions for preparing the ice ring.

Lightly spray a ring mold or Bundt pan with vegetable cooking spray. Pour fruit juice about ¼ to ½ inch deep in the mold. Arrange assorted sliced fruit (oranges, limes, lemons) and whole fruit (cherries, strawberries) in the bottom of the mold. Freeze until firm. Next, place assorted fruit up the sides of the mold. Fill the mold about half full with fruit juice or water; then freeze until firm. Finally, fill the mold with additional fruit juice or water, and freeze until firm. (By freezing the mold in steps, the fruit will freeze in place and won't shift.)

Before serving the punch, let the mold sit at room temperature a few minutes or run cold water over the bottom until the ring unmolds. Place the ice ring in the punch bowl, add the punch, and you're ready to serve your guests.

### FALSE-KICK PUNCH

2 (46-ounce) cans pineapple juice
½ cup sugar
1 tablespoon almond extract
2 (33.8-ounce) bottles ginger ale, chilled

Combine pineapple juice, sugar, and almond extract; stir until sugar dissolves. Chill. To serve, combine chilled mixture and ginger ale, and serve over ice. Yield: about 1¼ gallons.
*Mrs. E. Lamar McMath,*
*Jacksonville, Florida.*

### SANGRIA

6 oranges, thinly sliced
3 lemons, thinly sliced
1 lime, thinly sliced
1½ cups sugar
1 cup brandy
1 gallon burgundy or other dry red wine

Arrange fruit slices in bottom of a large punch bowl; sprinkle with sugar. Pour brandy over fruit; cover and let stand at least 1 hour. Add wine; mix well. Let stand at least 1 hour. Serve over ice. Yield: 4¼ quarts.
*Mrs. Jesse Look,*
*El Paso, Texas.*

### BUDGET CITRUS PUNCH

¼ cup citric acid
2 quarts boiling water
5 cups sugar
5 quarts cold water
1 (46-ounce) can pineapple juice, chilled
1 (6-ounce) can frozen orange juice concentrate, thawed and undiluted

Combine citric acid and boiling water in a ceramic heatproof container; stir until citric acid dissolves. Let mixture stand 24 hours.

Combine sugar and cold water; stir until sugar is dissolved. Add citric acid mixture, pineapple juice, and orange juice; stir well. Serve over ice. Yield: about 8½ quarts. *Evelyn Scott,*
*Birmingham, Alabama.*

### ORANGE-MINT PUNCH

2 cups sugar
2½ cups water
¼ cup dried mint leaves
1 (12-ounce) can frozen orange juice concentrate, thawed and undiluted
⅓ cup lemon juice
6 cups cold water

Combine sugar and 2½ cups water in a medium saucepan; bring to a boil, and boil 10 minutes. Stir in mint leaves; steep 1 hour. Strain.

Stir in remaining ingredients. Serve over crushed ice. Yield: about 2½ quarts. *Mrs. Ed Lee Niles,*
*Marshall, North Carolina.*

### RICH-AND-CREAMY COFFEE PUNCH

1 gallon strong hot coffee
1¼ cups sugar
2 cups whipping cream, whipped
1 pint vanilla ice cream, softened
1 pint chocolate ice cream, softened

Combine coffee and sugar, stirring until sugar dissolves; chill well. Fold in whipped cream and ice cream just before serving. Yield: about 5 quarts.
*Mildred Sherrer,*
*Bay City, Texas.*

# What's New About Yogurt?

Yogurt, that light, refreshing dairy product, used to be considered mainly diet food. But more and more cooks across the South are adding yogurt to baked goods, salad dressings, and desserts. Our Yogurt-Cheese Pie, for example, is a creamy cheesecake-like dessert topped with a peach glaze. Or enjoy yogurt in mint-flavored Yogurt-Cucumber Salad.

Dieters can trim extra calories by substituting yogurt for sour cream. If a recipe calls for heating the yogurt, be sure to cook at low temperatures for short periods of time to prevent separation. Adding a little flour or cornstarch helps to stabilize heated yogurt.

### YOGURT-CHEESE PIE

1 tablespoon cornstarch
1 tablespoon orange juice
1 (8-ounce) package cream cheese, softened
½ cup sugar
2 eggs
1 teaspoon grated lemon rind
½ teaspoon vanilla extract
1 (8-ounce) carton lemon yogurt
1 (9-inch) graham cracker crust
1 teaspoon cornstarch
½ teaspoon ground cinnamon
1 (8¾-ounce) can sliced peaches

Dissolve 1 tablespoon cornstarch in orange juice; set aside. Beat cream cheese at medium speed of electric mixer until light and fluffy. Add sugar, eggs, orange juice, lemon rind, and vanilla; beat well. Fold in yogurt. Pour into graham cracker crust. Bake at 350° for 1 hour or until pie is set in center. Turn oven off, and leave pie in oven 30 minutes longer.

Combine 1 teaspoon cornstarch and cinnamon in a heavy saucepan. Drain peaches, reserving syrup; add enough water to syrup to measure ½ cup. Stir syrup into cornstarch mixture. Cook over medium heat until mixture is thickened and translucent. Arrange peach slices on top of pie. Pour glaze over peaches and pie. Chill 1 hour before serving. Yield: one 9-inch pie.
*Jeaune L. Smith,*
*Louisville, Kentucky.*

## CREME DE MENTHE SALAD

1 (3-ounce) package lime-flavored gelatin
¾ cup boiling water
1 (8¼-ounce) can crushed pineapple
2 tablespoons crème de menthe
1 (8-ounce) carton commercial sour
 cream, divided
1 (16-ounce) can pear halves, drained and
 diced
½ cup plain yogurt
1 teaspoon lime juice
Lime slices (optional)

Dissolve gelatin in boiling water. Drain pineapple, reserving juice. Combine pineapple juice, crème de menthe, and enough water to measure ¾ cup; stir into gelatin mixture. Chill until consistency of unbeaten egg white.

Fold ½ cup sour cream, pears, and pineapple into gelatin. Pour into a lightly oiled 4-cup mold. Chill until firm.

Combine yogurt, the remaining sour cream, and lime juice; mix well. Unmold salad; serve with dressing. Garnish with lime slices, if desired. Yield: 6 to 8 servings.
*Kay Baker,*
*Laurel, Florida.*

## YOGURT-CUCUMBER SALAD

4 cucumbers
1½ teaspoons salt
2 (8-ounce) cartons plain yogurt
2 tablespoons lemon juice
1 clove garlic, minced
1 teaspoon dried whole dillweed
2 teaspoons chopped fresh mint or ½
 teaspoon mint flakes

Peel cucumbers, and quarter lengthwise; cut crosswise into thin slices. Spread cucumber slices in a large shallow dish. Sprinkle with salt, and let stand 15 minutes. Drain well.

Combine remaining ingredients except mint; add cucumber slices, and mix well. Sprinkle with mint. Yield: 8 servings.
*Debra Leckie,*
*Shreveport, Louisiana.*

# Here's A Centerpiece You Can Eat

An attractive centerpiece and a refreshing appetizer all in one? This Fresh Vegetable Party Tray is simple to make, involves no cooking, and can be made well ahead of party time. You simply cut out a portion of a head of cabbage, fill it with dip (we use a Green Goddess salad dressing), and arrange assorted fresh vegetables around it.

By varying the vegetables according to the season, you can serve this appetizer any time of year.

## FRESH VEGETABLE PARTY TRAY

1 large leafy head cabbage
2 to 3 medium-size yellow squash, sliced
2 to 3 medium cucumbers, sliced
5 carrots, cut into 3-inch sticks
3 to 4 celery stalks, cut into 3-inch sticks
1 small head cauliflower, separated into
 flowerets
Radish roses
1 (8-ounce) bottle Green Goddess salad
 dressing, chilled

Wash cabbage, and remove leaves that are damaged or bruised. Trim core so cabbage stands level. Cut a 3-inch-deep square in cabbage, leaving a 1-inch-thick shell. Lift square out to form a well. (Reserve the cabbage center for use in other recipes.)

Place cabbage on a large serving plate, and carefully fold back outer leaves to lay flat on plate. Arrange vegetables around cabbage. Fill cabbage with salad dressing just before serving. Yield: 8 to 10 appetizer servings.

# Microwave Cookery

# Microwaves Speed Fancy Morning Dishes

With the help of your microwave oven, the entrée for a special breakfast or brunch can be showy, yet simple to prepare. Here are some suggestions to highlight your menu.

Microwaved eggs cook faster and fluffier than conventionally prepared eggs. Try our Golden Vegetable Omelet, and you'll be tempted to discard your omelet pan. This high-rising combination of beaten egg whites, yolks, sour cream, and mayonnaise cooks in a pieplate.

When preparing Breakfast Sandwiches, be sure to pierce the egg yolk with a wooden pick before microwaving; this releases excess steam, which would otherwise burst the yolk. A close watch on cooking time is also essential; if you microwave an egg until the white is set, the yolk tends to become tough. Standing time allows the white to cook completely without hardening the yolk.

If your favorite choice for a special breakfast is quiche, you'll want to try our savory Crab Quiche. Whether cooked conventionally or in a microwave, quiche also requires about 10 minutes standing time. The center of a microwaved quiche will be slightly soft at the end of the cooking cycle, but should continue to cook if left standing. Stop microwaving when a knife inserted off-center comes out clean; avoid cooking until the center is set.

For a meatier main dish, try Oriental Sausage and Rice Casserole. Sausage, like ground beef, should be placed in a covered casserole and stirred once during microwaving. The cooked, drained sausage is added to a wild rice mixture to complete the casserole.

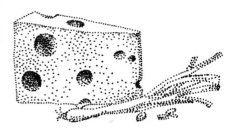

## CRAB QUICHE

1 cup (4 ounces) shredded Swiss cheese
Microwaved quiche pastry (recipe follows)
1 (6-ounce) package frozen crabmeat,
 thawed and drained
⅓ cup chopped green onion
4 eggs, beaten
1¾ cups half-and-half
½ teaspoon salt
½ teaspoon grated lemon rind
Dash of dry mustard
Dash of pepper

Sprinkle cheese in bottom of pastry shell; top with crabmeat and onion. Combine eggs, half-and-half, salt, lemon rind, dry mustard, and pepper; mix well, and pour into quiche shell.

Microwave at MEDIUM HIGH (70% power) for 8 to 11 minutes. Give dish one half-turn; microwave at MEDIUM HIGH for 9 to 16 minutes or until knife inserted off-center comes out clean (center will be slightly soft). Let stand 10 minutes before serving. Yield: one 9½-inch quiche.

*Microwaved Quiche Pastry:*

**1 cup all-purpose flour**
**½ teaspoon salt**
**⅓ cup plus 1 tablespoon shortening**
**2 to 3 tablespoons cold water**
**3 to 4 drops yellow food coloring**
**(optional)**

Combine flour and salt; cut in shortening with pastry blender until mixture resembles coarse meal. Combine water and food coloring if extra color is desired (pastry will not brown in microwave oven). Sprinkle water evenly over flour mixture; stir with a fork until all ingredients are moistened. Shape dough into a ball.

Place dough on a lightly floured surface, and roll it into a circle 2 inches larger than inverted 9½-inch quiche dish. Fit pastry loosely into dish. Trim edges, and fold under to form a standing rim; flute.

Place a piece of heavy-duty plastic wrap over pastry; cover with dried beans or peas. Microwave at HIGH for 6½ to 8½ minutes or until pastry is opaque and bottom is dry. Yield: pastry for one 9½-inch quiche.

## GOLDEN VEGETABLE OMELET

**2 tablespoons butter or margarine, divided**
**¼ cup chopped green pepper**
**¼ cup chopped onion**
**1 tablespoon chopped pimiento**
**3 eggs, separated**
**2 tablespoons commercial sour cream**
**2 tablespoons mayonnaise**
**Dash of salt**
**Dash of pepper**

Place 1 tablespoon butter, green pepper, onion, and pimiento in a 1-quart casserole; cover with heavy-duty plastic wrap, and microwave at HIGH for 3 to 3½ minutes. Set aside.

Beat egg whites (at room temperature) until stiff peaks form. Combine yolks, sour cream, mayonnaise, salt, and pepper; beat well. Gently fold egg whites into yolk mixture.

Place remaining tablespoon butter in a 9-inch pieplate. Microwave at HIGH for 45 seconds to 1 minute or until melted (tip to coat plate). Pour egg mixture into pieplate. Microwave at MEDIUM (50% power) for 5 minutes or until partially set; lift edges with a spatula so uncooked portion spreads evenly. Microwave at MEDIUM for 3 to 5½ minutes or until center is almost set. Spread vegetable mixture over half of omelet. Loosen omelet with spatula, and fold in half. Gently slide omelet onto a serving plate. Yield: 2 servings.

## BREAKFAST SANDWICHES

**8 slices bacon**
**4 eggs**
**4 slices bread, toasted**
**4 slices tomato**
**Cheese sauce (recipe follows)**

Place bacon on a microwave bacon rack; cover with paper towels. Microwave at HIGH for 6½ to 8 minutes or until crisp. Crumble, and set aside.

Gently break 1 egg into each of four 6-ounce microwave custard cups; pierce each yolk with a wooden pick. Cover cups with heavy-duty plastic wrap, and arrange in a circle on a microwave-safe platter. Microwave at MEDIUM (50% power) for 1 minute 15 seconds to 1½ minutes or until eggs are almost set (eggs will be soft and moist). Let stand 2 to 3 minutes to complete cooking.

Sprinkle toast with bacon and top with a slice of tomato. Remove eggs from custard cups with a slotted spoon, and place 1 egg on each slice of tomato. Top with cheese sauce. Serve immediately. Yield: 2 to 4 servings.

*Cheese Sauce:*

**2 tablespoons butter or margarine**
**2 tablespoons all-purpose flour**
**¼ teaspoon salt**
**1 cup milk**
**¾ cup (3 ounces) shredded sharp Cheddar cheese**

Place butter in a 2-cup glass measure; microwave at HIGH for 45 seconds to 1 minute or until butter is melted. Blend in flour and salt; stir well. Microwave at HIGH for 2 to 2½ minutes; stir well. Add milk; microwave at HIGH for 2½ to 3 minutes, stirring at 1-minute intervals, until thickened. Add cheese, stirring until melted. Yield: about 1 cup.

## ORIENTAL SAUSAGE AND RICE CASSEROLE

**1 pound bulk pork sausage**
**1 medium onion, chopped**
**1 medium-size green pepper, chopped**
**1 (6-ounce) package long grain and wild rice mix**
**1 (8-ounce) can sliced water chestnuts, drained**
**2 (4-ounce) cans sliced mushrooms, drained**
**3 cups chicken broth**
**1 tablespoon soy sauce**

Crumble sausage into a 2-quart casserole; add onion and green pepper. Cover with waxed paper; microwave at HIGH for 5 to 7 minutes or until sausage is done and vegetables are tender, stirring once. Remove sausage mixture from casserole, and drain on paper towels; set mixture aside.

Combine remaining ingredients in casserole; cover with heavy-duty plastic wrap, and microwave at HIGH for 6 to 7 minutes. Stir well; cover and microwave at MEDIUM (50% power) for 30 to 35 minutes. Stir in sausage mixture; cover and microwave at MEDIUM for 15 to 20 minutes or until rice is tender and all liquid is absorbed. Yield: 6 to 8 servings.

# Sausage Spices These Main Dishes

Sausage—hot or mild—spices up these three hearty dishes: a make-ahead breakfast casserole, a noodle casserole, and a cheesy casserole featuring ground beef, corn, and chili.

Unless the recipe specifies hot sausage, we used mild sausage for testing. However, if you prefer a spicier dish, substitute a hot version.

## SAUSAGE AND NOODLE CASSEROLE

**1 pound bulk pork sausage**
**½ cup chopped onion**
**¼ cup chopped green pepper**
**1 (10¾-ounce) can cream of chicken soup, undiluted**
**1⅓ cups water**
**1 (8-ounce) package egg noodles, cooked and drained**
**Salt and pepper to taste**
**½ cup canned French-fried onion rings, crushed**

Crumble sausage in a large skillet; add onion and green pepper. Cook over medium heat until meat is browned and vegetables are tender, stirring occasionally. Drain well.

Combine soup and water. Add meat mixture, noodles, salt, and pepper; mix well. Spoon mixture into a greased 2-quart baking dish. Sprinkle with onion rings. Bake at 350° for 30 minutes or until bubbly. Yield: 4 to 6 servings.

*Mrs. Max E. Ayer,*
*Elizabethton, Tennessee.*

## CHEESY SAUSAGE CASSEROLE

1½ pounds ground beef
1 pound hot bulk pork sausage
1 large onion, chopped
1 large green pepper, chopped
1 hot pepper, chopped (optional)
Salt and pepper to taste
1 (17-ounce) can cream-style corn
1 (15-ounce) can chili with beans
3 tablespoons chili powder
2 (8-ounce) cans tomato sauce
2 cups (8 ounces) shredded Cheddar
   cheese
1 (12-ounce) package wide egg noodles,
   cooked and drained

Crumble ground beef and sausage in a large skillet; add onion, green pepper, hot pepper, if desired, salt, and pepper. Cook over medium heat until meat is browned and onion is tender. Drain off drippings. Stir in remaining ingredients, mixing well. Spoon into a lightly greased 3-quart casserole. Bake at 350° for 25 to 30 minutes or until bubbly. Yield: 12 servings. *Gayle Hurdle, Carthage, Mississippi.*

### BRUNCH CASSEROLE

1 pound bulk pork sausage
1 (8-ounce) can refrigerated crescent
   dinner rolls
2 cups (8 ounces) shredded mozzarella
   cheese
4 eggs, beaten
¾ cup milk
¼ teaspoon salt
⅛ teaspoon pepper

Crumble sausage in a medium skillet; cook over medium heat until brown, stirring occasionally. Drain well. Line bottom of a buttered 13- x 9- x 2-inch baking dish with crescent rolls, firmly pressing perforations to seal. Sprinkle with sausage and cheese.

Combine remaining ingredients; beat well, and pour over sausage. Bake at 425° for 15 minutes or until set. Let stand 5 minutes; cut into squares, and serve immediately. Yield: 6 to 8 servings. *Billie G. Costigan, Mount Sterling, Kentucky.*

# There's Chocolate In The Cinnamon Rolls

If you like cinnamon rolls, Chocolate Sticky Buns are a cocoa-flavored variation you don't want to miss. The yeast rolls are filled with cocoa, sugar, and cinnamon and baked with a chocolate-nut glaze on the bottom of the pan.

### CHOCOLATE STICKY BUNS

1 package dry yeast
⅓ cup warm water (105° to 115°)
⅓ cup sugar
1 teaspoon salt
½ cup butter or margarine
¾ cup milk, scalded
About 3½ cups all-purpose flour, divided
1 egg, beaten
½ cup butter
1 cup firmly packed brown sugar
¼ cup light corn syrup
3 tablespoons cocoa
1 cup chopped pecans
1 cup sugar
2 tablespoons cocoa
2 teaspoons ground cinnamon
¼ cup butter or margarine, melted

Dissolve yeast in warm water; set aside. Combine ⅓ cup sugar, salt, ½ cup butter, and scalded milk in a mixing bowl; stir until butter melts. Cool to 105° to 115°. Stir in 1½ cups flour, egg, and yeast mixture. Beat on medium speed of electric mixer 2½ minutes. Stir in enough remaining flour to make a soft dough.

Place dough in a greased bowl, turning to grease top. Cover and let rise in a warm place (85°), free from drafts, about 1 hour or until doubled in bulk.

Melt ½ cup butter in a small saucepan. Add brown sugar, corn syrup, and 3 tablespoons cocoa; bring to a boil and cook, stirring constantly, 1 minute. Pour sugar mixture evenly into two greased 9-inch cakepans. Sprinkle pecans over sugar mixture. Set aside.

Combine 1 cup sugar, 2 tablespoons cocoa, and cinnamon; set aside.

Punch dough down, and divide in half. Roll each half into a 14- x 9-inch rectangle; brush with melted butter; sprinkle half of cocoa-cinnamon mixture over each dough rectangle. Starting at widest end, roll up each strip in jellyroll fashion; pinch edges together to seal.

Cut each roll into 1-inch slices. Place 9 slices in each prepared cakepan. Cover and let rise in a warm place (85°), free from drafts, about 1 hour or until doubled in bulk.

Bake at 375° for 25 minutes. Invert pans on serving plates; serve warm. Yield: 1½ dozen.
*Mrs. Robert W. Caldwell, Birmingham, Alabama.*

# Fruit Served In Style

Cindi Rawlins of Dunwoody, Georgia, has some simple, but refreshing suggestions to perk up a fruit cup. Champagne adds sparkle to her Champagne Fruit Compote, a mixture of oranges, green grapes, and pineapple chunks. For Raspberry Prunes, pitted prunes are marinated in white wine, then combined with orange slices and a colorful puree of raspberries. Serve either fruit cup in long-stemmed glasses for an elegant look.

### CHAMPAGNE FRUIT COMPOTE

4 oranges, peeled, seeded, and sectioned
1½ cups seedless green grapes, halved
1 (20-ounce) can pineapple chunks,
   drained
¼ cup sifted powdered sugar
1 teaspoon grated orange or lemon rind
1 (25.4-ounce) bottle champagne, chilled
Orange wedges (optional)

Combine fruit in a large bowl; stir in sugar and orange rind. Chill. Stir in champagne. Serve in stemmed glasses. Garnish with orange wedges, if desired. Yield: 6 to 8 servings. *Cindi Rawlins, Dunwoody, Georgia.*

### RASPBERRY PRUNES

1 (12-ounce) package pitted prunes
1 cup Chablis or other dry white wine
1 (10-ounce) package frozen raspberries,
   thawed
1 medium orange, peeled and thinly sliced
Whipped cream or plain yogurt (optional)

Combine prunes and wine; cover and let stand at room temperature 8 hours.

Process raspberries in food mill or container of electric blender; strain, discarding seeds. Cut orange slices in half, and discard seeds.

Add raspberry pulp and orange slices to prune mixture; stir gently. Cover and chill 2 to 3 hours. Serve in stemmed glasses; top with whipped cream or yogurt, if desired. Yield: 8 servings.

# June

When Southern tables groan with bountiful harvests in June, fresh vegetable dinners are a seasonal treat. Our recipes for an all-vegetable meal were tasted carefully for light seasonings that wouldn't overpower the flavor of tender, fresh produce. Try some of our savory selections like Cheesy Stuffed Squash, Seasoned Baked Corn on the Cob, or Green Chile Cornbread.

Fresh okra surely won't be overlooked in harvesting or on the kitchen table; Southerners agree it's a summer favorite. We feature a variety of ways it's most enjoyed across the South in our recipes for Three-Seafood Jambalaya, crispy French-Fried Okra, and Mixed Vegetable Medley.

And since June is the month to honor brides and graduates with showers, teas, and receptions, we offer some finger food recipes in this chapter to suit the occasion. Cheese Straws, Glazed Pecans, Cherry Pecan Cookies, and Party Fruit Punch make a light, refreshing combination for any party.

# Summer Comes Up Okra

For the majority of Southerners, fresh okra means a platterful of the crispy-fried slices waiting to be enjoyed. This treat doesn't have to be just anticipated anymore, thanks to the abundance of fresh okra that summer brings to backyard gardens, produce stands, and supermarkets across the South.

There are probably as many versions of fried okra as there are Southern cooks. One recipe you'll want to sample is from Fannie B. Scott of Clio, Alabama. She coats the slices with buttermilk and dredges them in flour before frying. Or make the most of okra's delicate flavor by combining it with other vegetables. Tomatoes are a natural companion, as Plantation Okra and Okra Pilaf deliciously illustrate.

It's helpful when buying okra to know that 1 pound of the fresh pods will yield about 2 cups of slices. If you can't use the okra immediately, wash it, shake dry, and place in a covered container in the refrigerator. Stored in this manner, the okra should keep well for three to five days.

A word about preparation: Be sure to cook okra quickly, as overcooking results in a gummy texture. Also, don't cook or serve it in copper, brass, or iron utensils; if you do, the okra will turn an unappealing brown color. In recipes that call for frozen okra, substitute fresh okra as follows: For a 10-ounce package of frozen, use 1¼ cups sliced, uncooked fresh okra.

## MIXED VEGETABLE MEDLEY

3 tablespoons vegetable oil
1¼ cups sliced okra
1 (8-ounce) can whole kernel corn, undrained
1 medium onion, chopped
1 medium-size green pepper, chopped
1 (6-ounce) can tomato paste
⅔ cup water
1 teaspoon salt
¼ teaspoon pepper
5 to 6 drops hot sauce
2 hot peppers (optional)

Heat oil in a heavy Dutch oven, and stir in remaining ingredients. Bring to a boil; cover and reduce heat. Simmer 45 minutes, stirring occasionally. Remove hot peppers before serving. Yield: about 6 cups.
*Jill Rorux,*
*Dallas, Texas.*

## THREE-SEAFOOD JAMBALAYA

2 slices bacon, cut into 1-inch pieces
1 medium onion, chopped
1 medium-size green pepper, chopped
2½ cups peeled, coarsely chopped tomatoes
2½ cups sliced okra
1 bay leaf
1½ teaspoons ground cumin
½ teaspoon dried whole thyme
¼ teaspoon ground oregano
1 tablespoon salt
¼ teaspoon hot sauce
4 cups water
1 cup uncooked regular rice
1¼ pounds medium shrimp, peeled and deveined
1 pint oysters
1 (6½-ounce) can crabmeat, drained and flaked

Cook bacon in a Dutch oven over medium heat until limp. Add onion and green pepper; cook, stirring constantly, until vegetables are tender. Add tomatoes, okra, herbs, salt, and hot sauce. Reduce heat; cover and simmer 20 minutes, stirring often.

Add water and rice to vegetable mixture; bring to a boil. Reduce heat; cover and simmer 15 minutes; add shrimp, oysters, and crabmeat. Cook an additional 10 minutes. Remove bay leaf before serving. Yield: 6 servings.
*Mrs. Jack Corzine,*
*St. Louis, Missouri.*

## OKRA PILAF

3 slices bacon, diced
2 teaspoons vegetable oil
2 cups thinly sliced okra
1 cup chopped green pepper
1 cup chopped onion
1 cup uncooked regular rice
2 cups chicken broth
1 teaspoon salt
1 (16-ounce) can whole tomatoes, drained and chopped

Cook bacon in a Dutch oven over medium heat until limp. Add oil and okra; sauté until lightly browned. Add green pepper and onion; cook, stirring constantly, until tender.

Stir rice, chicken broth, and salt into vegetable mixture. Bring to a boil, stirring once. Cover, reduce heat, and simmer 20 minutes or until liquid is absorbed. Add tomatoes, stirring lightly. Yield: 6 to 8 servings.
*DeLea Lonadier,*
*Montgomery, Louisiana.*

## PLANTATION OKRA

1 (16-ounce) can whole tomatoes, undrained
1½ cups (½ pound) sliced okra
1 (7-ounce) can whole kernel corn with sweet peppers, undrained
½ cup chopped onion
½ cup sliced celery
½ teaspoon salt
¼ teaspoon pepper

Coarsely chop tomatoes. Combine all ingredients in a heavy skillet, and bring to a boil. Reduce heat; cover and simmer 15 to 20 minutes or until okra is tender. Yield: 6 servings.
*Maxine Dillingham,*
*Fredonia, Kentucky.*

## FRENCH-FRIED OKRA

1 pound okra
½ teaspoon salt
1½ cups buttermilk
2 cups self-rising flour
Vegetable oil

Wash okra, and drain well. Remove tip and stem end; cut okra into 1-inch slices. Sprinkle okra with salt; add buttermilk, stirring until well coated. Let stand 15 minutes; drain okra well, and dredge in flour.

Deep fry okra in hot oil (375°) until golden brown. Drain on paper towels. Yield: 6 servings.
*Fannie B. Scott,*
*Clio, Alabama.*

# Cook Your Own At The Coast

Some of the most beautiful beaches and coastal vacation areas are right here in the South. And along with the scenery comes a wonderful array of seafood harvested daily by area fishermen. So if you spend your next coastal vacation in accommodations with kitchen facilities, take advantage of the local seafood bounty and try a little down-home coastal cooking instead of dining out every meal.

That's not to say you should spend your vacation in the kitchen. There are many seafood dishes that are quick and easy to prepare—many on the grill—and compared to dining out, these dishes are usually a bargain.

Finding the seafood can be an adventure in itself. Walk the docks where the fishing boats come in and you'll soon find out which fish are in season. In fact, many commercial fishermen will sell dressed fish right off their boat. Seafood markets can usually provide you with the day's catch of anything in season, and any of the local people should be able to direct you to the best places to shop. Also, the shrimp and oysters sold from small trucks along the main streets and thoroughfares are often competitively priced.

## Preparing the Catch

Charcoal grilling gives **fish** a wonderful flavor. It's as easy as grilling hamburgers and costs little more. Fillets, steaks, chunks, and even whole fish can be grilled to perfection.

The secret to keeping fish from falling apart during grilling is to clamp it in a hinged wire grill coated with vegetable cooking spray. Cook the fish slowly (4 to 6 inches above a bed of glowing coals), turning frequently. Baste often with a lemon-butter mixture (and a touch of garlic or paprika, if you wish) to prevent drying. The fish is done when it is opaque throughout, slightly browned, and flakes easily when tested with a fork.

**Shrimp** are a seafood favorite, and the easiest way to prepare them is to boil a few pounds; they will keep for two to three days in the refrigerator. Although they are referred to as "boiled" shrimp, the water should only simmer after the shrimp are added. Cook, covered, 3 to 4 minutes or until the largest shrimp are opaque throughout. Beer, crab boil, lemon wedges, and herbs can be added to the water for extra flavor. Enjoy them hot or cold with your favorite sauce. Or if you're grilling, stick wooden picks through a few cooked and peeled shrimp, dip in barbecue sauce, and heat on the grill.

**Crabs** are cooked the same as shrimp, using the same seasonings; just simmer longer (12 to 15 minutes). But with crab, you'll need a good nutcracker and a pick to get to all the meat.

**Oysters** are available fresh daily in the shell and shucked. Lovers of raw oysters usually prefer them on the half shell; but for frying, it's convenient to buy them shucked by the pint. For a quick treat all will enjoy, try them baked: Drain the liquid from oysters on the half shell, add a 1-inch strip of bacon and a dab of barbecue sauce to each. Bake on medium heat (325°) until the oysters are firm and the bacon crisp.

# Side Dishes Spark A Cookout

Make your next cookout really sizzle by serving one or more of these side dishes along with your favorite grilled meat. Some are light, others hearty, but all go well with grilled chicken, beef, pork, or fish.

Grilled Parmesan Corn won a spot on the cookout menus of our foods staff as soon as it was tested. Fresh ears of corn are spread with a mixture of Parmesan cheese, butter, and parsley. For a salad selection, choose Zesty Slaw; pimiento-stuffed olives add bits of color and flavor to this tasty coleslaw.

When preparing a side dish for a large crowd, consider Crowd-Pleasing Baked Beans, which yields around 20 servings.

## CROWD-PLEASING BAKED BEANS

2 pounds dried Great Northern beans
1 cup firmly packed brown sugar
½ cup molasses
1 tablespoon plus 1 teaspoon dry mustard
1 tablespoon salt
1 large onion, chopped
1½ pounds slab bacon, cut into 1-inch squares

Sort and wash beans; place in a Dutch oven. Cover with water 2 inches above beans; let soak overnight. Cover and bring to a boil; reduce heat, and simmer 45 minutes. Drain, reserving liquid. Add enough water to bean liquid to make 1¾ cups; set aside.

Combine brown sugar, molasses, mustard, and salt; stir well. Layer half of beans, brown sugar mixture, onion, and bacon in a 4½-quart casserole. Top with remaining beans. Pour reserved bean liquid over top. Cover and bake at 300° for 5 hours. Yield: 20 to 22 servings. *Jenneth Pollard, Florence, Mississippi.*

## GRILLED PARMESAN CORN

8 ears fresh corn
½ cup butter or margarine, softened
½ cup grated Parmesan cheese
1 tablespoon finely chopped fresh parsley
¼ teaspoon salt

Remove husks and silks from corn just before cooking. Combine remaining ingredients, stirring well. Spread butter mixture on corn, and place each ear on a piece of aluminum foil; wrap tightly.

Grill corn over medium coals 20 to 30 minutes, turning several times. Yield: 8 servings. *Bobbie McGuire, Norris, South Carolina.*

## EASY DEVILED EGGS

6 hard-cooked eggs
¼ cup mayonnaise
1 tablespoon sweet pickle relish
1 teaspoon vinegar
½ teaspoon Worcestershire sauce
¼ teaspoon salt
¼ teaspoon dry mustard
Paprika

Slice eggs in half lengthwise, and carefully remove yolks. Mash yolks with mayonnaise. Add remaining ingredients except paprika. Stir well. Stuff egg whites with yolk mixture. Garnish eggs with paprika. Yield: 6 to 8 servings. *Mrs. Ronald Nichols, Winchester, Virginia.*

## ZESTY SLAW

1 large cabbage, finely shredded
1 large onion, chopped
1 large green pepper, chopped
1 cup pimiento-stuffed olives, chopped
1 cup vinegar
1 cup olive oil
½ cup dill pickle relish
1 teaspoon sugar
1 teaspoon celery seeds
1 teaspoon garlic salt
½ teaspoon salt
1 teaspoon pepper

Combine all ingredients in a large bowl; stir well. Cover and chill at least 1 hour before serving. Yield: 12 servings. *Patricia Pashby, Memphis, Tennessee.*

## HERBED CHERRY TOMATOES

1½ pints cherry tomatoes
½ cup soft breadcrumbs
¼ cup plus 2 tablespoons minced onion
¼ cup plus 2 tablespoons minced fresh
   parsley
2 tablespoons olive oil
1 large clove garlic, minced
½ teaspoon dried whole thyme
¼ teaspoon salt
⅛ teaspoon pepper

Place tomatoes in an 8-inch baking dish. Combine remaining ingredients, stirring well; spoon over tomatoes. Bake at 425° for 6 to 8 minutes. Yield: 6 servings. *Mrs. James E. Krachey, Guymon, Oklahoma.*

## Cooking Light

# Indulge In A Light Dessert

While the looks and taste of these desserts say "fattening," they're not. That's because only the unwanted calories have been trimmed—none of the flavor. Take our Strawberry-Lemon Mousse, for example. With just 153 calories per half-cup serving, you get a smooth, lemony mousse topped with luscious strawberries.

Baked Vanilla Custard is much like standard baked custard. But here, skim milk replaces whole milk, and the recipe calls for only a small amount of sugar.

Carol Neff of Buckhannon, West Virginia, sent us a recipe for a refreshing frozen dessert that's just right for a hot summer day. Her Pineapple-Orange Bars are made with instant nonfat dry milk powder and crushed pineapple packed in its own juice. Also, the graham cracker crust calls for less margarine than usual, a calorie-cutting technique that works well with other crumb crusts.

If you need a company-perfect dessert, try our Fancy Fruit Tart with its topping of fresh peaches, strawberries, grapes, and blueberries in a cornstarch-thickened glaze. Substitute other fresh fruit if you like; if fresh isn't available, use unsweetened canned or frozen fruit.

Speaking of fruit, don't overlook the virtues of fresh fruit. It's not only naturally sweet, but also high in fiber, quite

filling, and relatively low in calories, ranging from about 60 for a single orange to 100 for a single banana.

Even cholesterol watchers will find that some of our desserts are right in keeping with their diet, including our Orange-Banana Pops, Strawberry-Lemon Mousse, and Pineapple-Orange Bars. That's because they call for skim milk and only the whites of eggs. The Layered Lemon Pudding, however, is made with whipped topping mix and whole eggs, which are restricted on a low-cholesterol diet. Also note that whole eggs are used in the recipes for Baked Vanilla Custard and Fancy Fruit Tart.

Have fun treating yourself to these tasty desserts, keeping one thing in mind: With any of our light recipes, you must divide the final product evenly into the number of servings specified; otherwise the calorie calculations given will not be correct.

## FANCY FRUIT TART

1 cup all-purpose flour
¼ cup cornstarch
¼ cup sugar
⅓ cup margarine
1 egg, beaten
Vegetable cooking spray
1 cup sliced fresh strawberries
1 cup sliced fresh peaches
½ cup seedless green grapes, halved
¼ cup fresh blueberries
Citrus Glaze

Combine flour, cornstarch, and sugar; cut in margarine with pastry blender until mixture resembles coarse meal. Add egg, and stir with a fork until all ingredients are moistened.

Spray a 14½- x 12-inch baking sheet with cooking spray. Shape dough into a ball, and place directly on baking sheet. Roll pastry into a 10½-inch circle; trim edges. Bake at 400° for 8 to 10 minutes or until lightly browned. Cool on baking sheet 10 minutes; then carefully remove to wire rack to complete cooling.

Place pastry on a serving platter, and arrange fruit attractively over top; spoon Citrus Glaze evenly over fruit. Refrigerate tart at least 1 hour before serving. Yield: 10 servings (about 170 calories per serving).

*Citrus Glaze:*

1 tablespoon cornstarch
¼ cup water
¾ cup unsweetened orange juice
¼ teaspoon grated lemon rind
1 tablespoon lemon juice

Combine first 3 ingredients in a small saucepan. Bring to a boil; cook over medium heat 1 minute, stirring constantly. Remove from heat; stir in lemon rind and juice. Cover; let cool. Yield: about 1 cup glaze.

## LAYERED LEMON PUDDING

2 eggs, beaten
¼ cup sugar
1 tablespoon grated lemon rind
¼ cup lemon juice
1 tablespoon margarine
1 (1.25-ounce) envelope whipped
   topping mix
½ cup skim milk
½ teaspoon vanilla extract
Lemon twists

Combine first 5 ingredients in a small saucepan; cook over low heat until thickened. Cool slightly. Spoon 1 tablespoon into each of 5 dessert cups; set aside remaining lemon mixture.

Combine whipped topping mix, milk, and vanilla; beat 2 minutes at high speed of electric mixer. Spoon 3 tablespoons whipped topping over lemon layer in each dessert cup.

Gently fold remaining whipped topping into remaining lemon mixture; spoon evenly into dessert cups. Cover and chill. Garnish each serving with a lemon twist. Yield: 5 servings (about 142 calories per ½-cup serving).
*Betty Jane Morrison, Lakewood, Colorado.*

## STRAWBERRY-LEMON MOUSSE

¾ cup sugar
½ cup cornstarch
3 cups skim milk
1½ teaspoons grated lemon rind
½ cup lemon juice
4 egg whites
¼ cup sugar
2½ cups sliced strawberries, chilled

Combine ¾ cup sugar and cornstarch in a medium saucepan; gradually stir in milk. Cook over medium heat, stirring constantly, until smooth and thickened. Remove from heat, and stir in lemon rind and juice; cool, stirring mixture occasionally.

Beat egg whites (at room temperature) until foamy. Gradually add ¼ cup sugar, 1 tablespoon at a time, beating until soft peaks form. Fold into lemon mixture. Spoon ½-cup portions into individual serving dishes, and chill until firm. Top each serving with ¼ cup sliced strawberries. Yield: 10 servings (about 153 calories per serving).

## PINEAPPLE-ORANGE BARS

⅔ cup plus 2 tablespoons graham cracker crumbs, divided
2 tablespoons margarine, softened
½ cup instant nonfat dry milk powder
½ cup unsweetened orange juice, chilled
1 egg white
1 tablespoon lemon juice
¼ cup sugar
1 (8-ounce) can crushed pineapple in unsweetened juice, drained

Combine ⅔ cup graham cracker crumbs and margarine, mixing well. Press into an 8-inch square pan; set aside.

Combine next 4 ingredients; beat at high speed of electric mixer for 3 minutes. Add sugar, and beat an additional 3 minutes; fold in pineapple, and spoon into prepared pan. Sprinkle remaining graham cracker crumbs on top.

Freeze 8 hours or overnight. Let stand at room temperature 15 minutes before serving. Yield: 9 servings (about 92 calories per serving).     *Carol Neff, Buckhannon, West Virginia.*

## ORANGE-BANANA POPS

3 medium bananas, mashed (about 2 cups)
1 cup unsweetened orange juice
¼ cup water
2 tablespoons sugar
1 teaspoon lime or lemon juice

Combine all ingredients, mixing well. Pour mixture into 6 (5-ounce) paper drink cups. Partially freeze, then insert a wooden stick or wooden spoon into center of each cup, and freeze until firm. To serve, let pops stand at room temperature 5 minutes; tear off cups. Yield: 6 servings (about 86 calories per serving).     *Jan Hughes, Batesville, Arkansas.*

## BAKED VANILLA CUSTARD

3 eggs, slightly beaten
¼ cup sugar
¼ teaspoon salt
½ to 1 teaspoon vanilla extract
2 cups skim milk, scalded
Ground nutmeg (optional)

Combine first 4 ingredients, beating well; gradually add milk, stirring constantly. Pour into 6 (6-ounce) custard cups. Sprinkle with nutmeg, if desired.

Place custard cups in a 13- x 9- x 2-inch baking pan; pour hot water into pan to a depth of 1 inch. Bake at 325° for 40 to 45 minutes or until knife inserted halfway between center and edges of custard comes out clean. Remove cups from water; cool. Chill thoroughly. Yield: 6 servings (about 101 calories per serving).     *Debra Rich, Vancouver, Washington.*

# Bread Tastes Fresh From The Freezer

When you're baking bread, why not bake a lot? Store the excess in the freezer, and you can pull out a fresh loaf or a supply of breakfast muffins at a moment's notice.

The key to maintaining freshness of frozen breads is proper storage. Wrap the bread tightly in foil as soon as it cools; press excess air from the package, and get it to the freezer as soon as possible. Serving-size portions are the most convenient to work with; be sure to label each package with the name and date. Bread will stay fresh in the freezer from two to three months; it's safe to eat after that time, but you will lose flavor and freshness.

When ready to serve, thaw the bread at room temperature in the original package; this will take from one to three hours, depending on the size of the bread. If you want to serve the bread for breakfast, remove it from the freezer the night before. Reheat bread, still in the wrapper, according to recipe directions. The foil retains moisture in the bread, but you can remove the wrapping the last 5 minutes of heating to obtain a crisper crust, if desired.

## BEST-EVER BEER BREAD

½ cup water
1 (12-ounce) can beer
3 tablespoons vegetable oil
5 to 6 cups all-purpose flour, divided
2 packages dry yeast
3 tablespoons sugar
1½ teaspoons salt

Combine water, beer, and oil in a saucepan; heat to 120° to 130°. Set aside.

Combine 2 cups flour, yeast, sugar, and salt in a large mixing bowl; add beer mixture, and beat 5 minutes at medium speed of an electric mixer. Stir in enough remaining flour to make a soft dough.

Turn dough out on a floured surface; knead until smooth and elastic (about 8 to 10 minutes).

Place dough in a greased bowl, turning to grease top. Cover and let rise in a warm place (85°), free from drafts, 1 hour or until doubled in bulk.

Punch dough down, and divide in half. Shape each half into a loaf; place in 2 greased 9- x 5- x 3-inch loafpans. Cover and let rise in a warm place, free from drafts, 45 minutes or until doubled in bulk. Bake at 375° for 30 to 35 minutes or until loaves sound hollow when tapped. Yield: 2 loaves.

*Note:* Wrap any leftovers in foil and freeze. To reheat, thaw to room temperature and bake in unopened foil at 350° for 30 minutes or until hot.
*Carol Forcum, Marion, Illinois.*

## OATMEAL MUFFINS

1 cup quick-cooking oats, uncooked
1 cup buttermilk
1 cup firmly packed light brown sugar
1 egg, slightly beaten
1¾ cups all-purpose flour
1 teaspoon baking powder
1 teaspoon baking soda
1 teaspoon salt
½ teaspoon ground cinnamon
¼ teaspoon ground cloves
¼ teaspoon ground mace
½ cup vegetable oil
½ teaspoon grated lemon rind
½ cup raisins

Combine oats and buttermilk in a large bowl; let stand 1 hour. Add brown sugar and egg; mix well.

Combine next 7 ingredients. Stir into oat mixture. Stir in oil, grated lemon rind, and raisins.

Spoon into greased muffin pans, filling one-half full. Bake at 400° for 20 minutes. Yield: about 1½ dozen.

*Note:* Wrap any leftovers in foil and freeze. To reheat, thaw to room temperature and bake in unopened foil at 350° for 15 minutes or until hot.
*Viva McCammon, Kansas City, Missouri.*

## DELUXE BUTTERMILK BISCUITS

1 package dry yeast
2 tablespoons warm water (105° to 115°)
5 cups all-purpose flour
¼ cup sugar
1 tablespoon baking powder
1 teaspoon baking soda
1 teaspoon salt
1 cup shortening
2 cups buttermilk
Melted butter or margarine

Dissolve yeast in warm water, and set aside.

Combine dry ingredients; cut in shortening with pastry blender until mixture resembles coarse meal. Add yeast mixture and buttermilk to dry ingredients, and mix well.

Turn dough out on a floured surface, and knead lightly 4 or 5 times. Roll dough to ½-inch thickness; cut with a 2-inch biscuit cutter. Place on greased baking sheets. Brush tops with melted butter. Bake at 400° for 12 to 15 minutes. Yield: 3½ dozen.

*Note:* Wrap any leftovers in foil and freeze. To reheat, thaw to room temperature and bake in unopened foil at 350° for 15 minutes or until hot, opening foil the last 5 minutes.

*Irene Hamric,*
*Birmingham, Alabama.*

## WHOLE WHEAT-WHITE BREAD

2 packages dry yeast
¼ cup sugar
4 cups warm water (105° to 115°)
5 cups whole wheat flour
5 cups all-purpose flour
½ cup sugar
1 tablespoon plus 1 teaspoon salt
1 cup instant nonfat dry milk powder
1 cup vegetable oil
1 tablespoon molasses
2 eggs, slightly beaten

Dissolve yeast and sugar in warm water; set aside.

Combine flour, sugar, salt, and dry milk in a very large bowl. Add yeast mixture, stirring well. Stir in oil, molasses, and eggs to make a soft dough. (Dough will be slightly sticky.)

Turn the soft dough out on a heavily floured surface, and knead until smooth and elastic (about 8 to 10 minutes).

Place dough in a well-greased bowl, turning to grease top. Cover and let rise in a warm place (85°), free from drafts, 1 hour or until doubled in bulk.

Punch dough down; cover and let rise again in a warm place, free from drafts, 1 hour or until doubled in bulk.

Punch dough down, and divide and shape into 4 loaves; place in greased 9- x 5- x 3-inch loafpans. Cover and let rise in a warm place, free from drafts, for 45 minutes or until doubled in bulk. Bake at 400° for 20 minutes; reduce heat to 325°, and bake for 15 minutes or until loaves sound hollow when tapped. Yield: 4 loaves.

*Note:* Wrap any leftovers in foil and freeze. To reheat, thaw to room temperature and bake in unopened foil at 350° for 30 minutes or until hot.

*Mrs. Timothy A. Pack,*
*Montevallo, Alabama.*

## SUPREME POTATO ROLLS

1 cup milk
½ cup water
1 package dry yeast
1 cup cooked, mashed potatoes
2 eggs
⅔ cup shortening
½ cup sugar
2 teaspoons salt
6 to 6½ cups all-purpose flour, divided
Melted butter or margarine (optional)

Combine milk and water in a heavy saucepan; cook over medium heat, stirring constantly, until very hot. (Do not boil.) Cool to lukewarm (105° to 115°). Stir in yeast; let stand 5 minutes.

Combine potatoes, eggs, shortening, sugar, and salt in a large mixing bowl; beat at medium speed of an electric mixer until smooth. Add yeast mixture. Gradually add 2 cups flour, beating until smooth; add enough remaining flour to form a stiff dough, beating well.

Turn dough out on a lightly floured surface, and knead until smooth and elastic (about 10 minutes). Place in a well-greased bowl, turning to grease top. Cover and let rise in a warm place (85°), free from drafts, 1 hour or until doubled in bulk.

Punch dough down. Roll to ½-inch thickness on a lightly floured surface; cut with a 2½-inch biscuit cutter. Place about ½ inch apart on greased baking sheets. Cover and let rise in a warm place, free from drafts, 30 minutes or until doubled in bulk. Bake at 400° for 10 to 12 minutes or until golden; brush tops with melted butter, if desired. Yield: 3 dozen.

*Note:* Wrap any leftovers in foil and freeze. To reheat, thaw to room temperature and bake in unopened foil at 350° for 15 minutes or until hot, opening foil the last 5 minutes.

*Mrs. James R. Lineberger,*
*Gastonia, North Carolina.*

# Lunch Ideas Quick To Please

"They'd eat it every day if I let them." Alice Pahl of Raleigh says that's how her five children feel about Pizza on French Bread. After trying it, we tend to agree with them. Alice fixes this treat often when the children are home for lunch during the summer because it's so simple to prepare.

If you're looking for other quick lunch ideas for your family, these recipes are for you. We've put together this assortment of recipes to get you in and out of the kitchen fast. Some are simple enough for older children to prepare themselves.

## SIMPLE SLOPPY JOES

1 pound ground beef
1 medium onion, chopped
½ cup catsup
3 tablespoons vinegar
2 tablespoons water
1 tablespoon brown sugar
1 tablespoon dry mustard
1 tablespoon Worcestershire sauce
¼ teaspoon salt
Hamburger buns

Cook meat and onion in a large skillet until meat is browned; drain. Stir in next 7 ingredients, and heat thoroughly. Serve on warm buns. Yield: 4 servings.

*Louise Pittenger,*
*Winchester, Tennessee.*

## SKILLET BEEF AND MACARONI

1 pound ground beef
¼ cup chopped onion
2 (8-ounce) cans tomato sauce
1 (12-ounce) can whole kernel corn, drained
1 cup cooked macaroni
2 teaspoons chili powder
½ teaspoon seasoned salt
½ cup (2 ounces) shredded Cheddar cheese

Cook ground beef and onion in a skillet until browned; drain well. Stir in next 5 ingredients. Simmer, stirring occasionally, 5 to 10 minutes or until thoroughly heated. Stir in Cheddar cheese. Yield: 4 to 6 servings.

*Marie Lazelle,*
*Grove, Oklahoma.*

## MEXICALI HOT DOGS

Vegetable cooking spray
8 frankfurters
1 (8-ounce) can tomato sauce
1 cup water
¾ cup chopped onion
½ cup chopped green pepper
1 tablespoon brown sugar
2 tablespoons prepared mustard
2 teaspoons chopped hot pepper
1 teaspoon chili powder
½ teaspoon salt
8 hot dog buns

Spray a large skillet with vegetable cooking spray. Pierce frankfurters with a fork in several places, and cook in skillet until lightly browned.

Combine next 9 ingredients in a large saucepan; bring to a boil. Add frankfurters; reduce heat, and simmer 10 minutes or until sauce is thickened. Serve on warm buns. Yield: 8 servings.
*Mabel Baldwin Couch,*
*Chelsea, Oklahoma.*

## TUNA-MACARONI TREAT

1 (7¼-ounce) package macaroni and cheese dinner
1 (7-ounce) can tuna, drained and flaked
1 (10¾-ounce) can cream of celery soup, undiluted
½ cup milk
1 tablespoon chopped onion

Prepare macaroni and cheese dinner according to package directions, decreasing butter to 2 tablespoons, if desired. Combine remaining ingredients in a large bowl, and mix well; stir in macaroni and cheese. Spoon tuna mixture into a lightly greased 1½-quart baking dish. Bake at 350° for 18 to 20 minutes or until lightly browned. Yield: 4 to 6 servings.
*Marilyn J. Gambill,*
*Goodlettsville, Tennessee.*

## PIZZA ON FRENCH BREAD

2 (5-ounce) loaves unsliced French bread
1 (6-ounce) can tomato paste
1 teaspoon dried whole oregano
1 medium onion, thinly sliced and separated into rings
1 (3½-ounce) package sliced pepperoni
2 cups (8 ounces) shredded mozzarella cheese

Slice each loaf in half horizontally; spread tomato paste over cut surface of each half, and sprinkle with oregano. Top each half with onion and pepperoni, and sprinkle with cheese. Bake at 400° for 6 minutes. Yield: 4 to 6 servings.
*Alice G. Pahl,*
*Raleigh, North Carolina.*

# Peppers Perk Up A Meal

Regardless of how green peppers come to the table—sliced, chopped, stuffed, or preserved—they bring along lots of color and flavor. A stuffing of rice and ham turns them into a tasty, attractive entrée. For an unusual side dish, fill the shells with a medley of vegetables. You can even preserve green peppers in a colorful jelly to serve as an appetizer along with cream cheese and crackers.

## STUFFED PEPPERS WITH RICE AND HAM

6 large green peppers
1 small onion, chopped
¾ cup chopped celery
2 tablespoons butter or margarine
2 medium tomatoes, chopped
2 cups cooked rice
1½ cups chopped cooked ham
½ cup chopped almonds, toasted
½ teaspoon salt
¼ teaspoon pepper
½ cup buttered breadcrumbs

Cut off tops of green peppers, and set aside; discard seeds. Cook peppers 5 minutes in boiling salted water; drain and set aside.

Chop tops of peppers; combine with onion and celery. Sauté vegetables in butter in a large skillet until tender; add next 6 ingredients. Cook 15 minutes or until most of liquid is absorbed.

Stuff vegetable mixture into peppers, and top with buttered breadcrumbs. Place in baking dish, and pour in 1 inch of water. Bake peppers at 350° for 10 minutes. Yield: 6 servings.
*Rublelene Singleton,*
*Scotts Hill, Tennessee.*

*Tip: Cooking vegetables with the least amount of water possible will preserve vitamins and maintain flavor.*

## STUFFED PEPPER MEDLEY

10 large green peppers
3 cups cooked corn, drained
1½ cups cooked lima beans, drained
1 cup cooked black-eyed peas, drained
¾ pound bacon, cooked and crumbled
2 cups chopped fresh tomatoes
2 cups soft breadcrumbs
½ teaspoon salt
¼ teaspoon pepper

Cut off tops of green peppers, and remove seeds. Cook peppers 5 minutes in boiling salted water; drain and set aside.

Combine remaining ingredients, stirring well. Stuff peppers with vegetable mixture, and place in a 13- x 9- x 2-inch baking dish. Bake at 350° for 10 minutes or until thoroughly heated. Yield: 10 servings.
*Janice G. Overman,*
*Lynchburg, Virginia.*

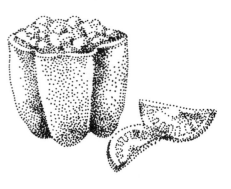

## ORIENTAL CHICKEN

¼ cup firmly packed brown sugar
2 tablespoons cornstarch
½ teaspoon salt
¼ cup vinegar
1 tablespoon soy sauce
1 (15¼-ounce) can pineapple chunks, undrained
1 large green pepper, cut into strips
1 small onion, thinly sliced and separated into rings
2 whole chicken breasts, skinned and boned
¼ cup butter or margarine, melted
Hot cooked rice

Combine first 3 ingredients, and stir until well blended; gradually add vinegar and soy sauce, stirring until cornstarch mixture is dissolved. Stir in pineapple, green pepper, and onion; set aside.

Cut chicken into thin strips; cook in butter in a large skillet until lightly browned. Add pineapple mixture, stirring until smooth. Cover and simmer 15 minutes. Serve over rice. Yield: 4 servings.
*Debra Leckie,*
*Shreveport, Louisiana.*

## CREAMY VEGETABLE DIP

2 eggs, beaten
2 tablespoons vinegar
1 to 2 tablespoons sugar
1 tablespoon butter or margarine
1 (8-ounce) package cream cheese,
    softened
⅔ cup chopped green pepper
⅓ cup grated onion
2 tablespoons chopped pimiento
¼ teaspoon hot sauce
⅛ teaspoon salt

Combine eggs, vinegar, and sugar in top of a double boiler; mix well. Cook over boiling water, stirring constantly, until smooth and thickened. Add butter and cream cheese; beat at medium speed of electric mixer until smooth. Stir in remaining ingredients.

Chill well, and serve with assorted raw vegetables. Yield: about 2 cups.
*Lexie Freeman,*
*Fort Worth, Texas.*

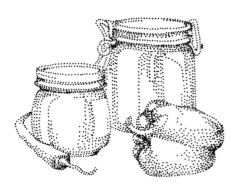

## UNUSUAL GREEN PEPPER JELLY

6 large green peppers
1½ cups vinegar, divided
1 teaspoon crushed red pepper
6 cups sugar
½ teaspoon salt
2 (3-ounce) packages liquid fruit pectin

Seed peppers, and chop coarsely. Place half of chopped peppers and ¾ cup vinegar in container of electric blender; process on high speed until smooth. Repeat with remaining chopped peppers and vinegar.

Combine pureed peppers, red pepper, sugar, and salt in a large Dutch oven; bring to a boil, and add pectin. Cook, stirring often, for 30 minutes or until mixture sheets from a metal spoon.

Quickly pour jelly into sterilized jars, leaving ½-inch headspace. Cover at once with a ⅛-inch layer of paraffin. Cover with metal lids, and screw metal bands tight. Yield: about 6 half pints.
*Kathleen Branson,*
*Thomasville, North Carolina.*

# Salads For Summer Outings

Looking for an unusual salad to brighten a summer menu? Consider a cool salad that not only adds color and texture to a meal but is nutritious too.

You'll find our Frozen Banana Salad very cool and pretty—just perfect for your next outdoor gathering. If you want to make the salad the meal, we suggest Confetti Macaroni Salad.

## APRICOT FRUIT SALAD

1 (20-ounce) can crushed pineapple
1 (6-ounce) package apricot-flavored
    gelatin
2 cups boiling water
2 cups cold water
2 bananas, chopped
1 cup miniature marshmallows
1 cup sugar
¼ cup all-purpose flour
¼ cup butter or margarine
2 eggs, slightly beaten
2 (3-ounce) packages cream cheese,
    softened
1 (1¼-ounce) package whipped topping
    mix

Drain pineapple, reserving juice. Combine gelatin and boiling water; stir until dissolved. Add cold water, bananas, marshmallows, and pineapple; mix well. Pour into a 13½- x 8¾- x 1¾-inch dish; chill until firm.

Add enough water to reserved pineapple juice to make 1 cup. Combine pineapple liquid, sugar, flour, butter, and eggs in a saucepan; cook over medium heat, stirring constantly, until thick. Add cream cheese; continue stirring until cheese is melted. Allow to cool; spoon over gelatin layer.

Prepare whipped topping mix according to package directions; spread over cooked layer. Chill; cut into squares to serve. Yield: 15 to 18 servings.
*Maxine Devore,*
*Knob Lick, Kentucky.*

## SUNSHINE CARROT SALAD

2 cups grated carrots
1 (11-ounce) can mandarin oranges,
    drained
1 cup pineapple chunks, drained
1 cup flaked coconut
½ cup raisins
1 (8-ounce) carton commercial sour cream
Lettuce leaves

Combine first 5 ingredients; stir well. Chill 2 to 3 hours. Stir in sour cream; serve salad on lettuce leaves. Yield: 6 to 8 servings.
*Gail Thompson,*
*Montgomery, Alabama.*

## FROZEN BANANA SALAD

4 bananas, mashed
1 (8½-ounce) can crushed pineapple,
    undrained
1 tablespoon lemon juice
1 (6-ounce) jar maraschino cherries,
    drained and cut into quarters
½ cup chopped pecans
¾ cup sugar
1 teaspoon salt
2 (8-ounce) cartons commercial sour
    cream
Lettuce leaves

Combine all ingredients except lettuce; stir well, and pour into a 9-inch square pan. Freeze until firm; cut into squares, and serve on lettuce. Yield: 9 servings.
*Mrs. Warren D. Davis,*
*Yulee, Florida.*

## CONFETTI MACARONI SALAD

1 (8-ounce) package or 2 cups elbow
    macaroni
1 (12-ounce) can luncheon meat, diced
1½ cups diced Cheddar cheese
½ cup chopped green pepper
⅓ cup chopped onion
½ cup mayonnaise
2 tablespoons milk
2 tablespoons vinegar
½ teaspoon salt
Lettuce leaves

Cook macaroni according to package directions; drain well. Combine macaroni, luncheon meat, cheese, green pepper, and onion; stir well, and chill.

Combine mayonnaise, milk, vinegar, and salt; pour over macaroni salad, and toss well. Serve salad in a lettuce-lined bowl. Yield: 10 to 12 servings.
*Pauline Lester,*
*Saluda, South Carolina.*

*Tip: Use a stiff vegetable brush to scrub vegetables rather than peel them. Peeling is not necessary for many vegetables and causes a loss of vitamins found in and just under the skin.*

# Try Boysenberries This Summer

Summer isn't the same without some kind of juicy berry dessert like pie, fresh baked cobbler, or sweet berries and cream. We tried boysenberries in these traditional summer dishes and enjoyed the delicious blend of blackberry and raspberry flavors.

This hybrid fruit looks like a blackberry and should be selected and stored in the same way. Choose plump, firm, full-colored berries, and store them unwashed and covered in the refrigerator.

## BOYSENBERRY COBBLER

4 cups fresh boysenberries or
  blackberries, washed and drained
¼ cup sugar
2 cups all-purpose flour
3 tablespoons sugar
1 tablespoon baking powder
½ teaspoon salt
½ cup butter or margarine
½ cup milk
1½ cups boiling water
½ teaspoon ground cinnamon
1 teaspoon sugar
Sauce (recipe follows)

Sprinkle boysenberries with ¼ cup sugar; set aside.

Combine flour, 3 tablespoons sugar, baking powder, and salt in a mixing bowl; cut in butter with pastry blender until mixture resembles coarse meal. Add milk, mixing well. Roll two-thirds of the dough to ⅛-inch thickness on a lightly floured surface. Place in a lightly greased 12- x 8- x 2-inch baking dish.

Pour berries into pastry-lined dish. Roll out remaining dough, and add top crust. Pour boiling water over crust. Combine cinnamon and 1 teaspoon sugar; sprinkle over cobbler. Bake at 350° for 35 minutes. Spoon cobbler into serving dishes, and top with sauce. Yield: 10 to 12 servings.

*Sauce:*

1 tablespoon cornstarch
¼ cup water
3 tablespoons butter or margarine
1 cup sugar
1 cup crushed boysenberries

Mix cornstarch with water until smooth. Melt butter in a saucepan; add sugar, berries, and cornstarch mixture. Cook over medium heat, stirring occasionally, until mixture thickens. Yield: about 1½ cups.                    *Billie Taylor,*
*Afton, Virginia.*

## BERRY-PEACH COMPOTE

6 large peaches, peeled and sliced
1 tablespoon lemon juice
2 cups fresh boysenberries, blueberries, or
  raspberries, washed and drained
⅓ cup sugar
1 cup whipping cream, whipped
⅛ teaspoon ground ginger
⅛ teaspoon ground nutmeg

Combine peaches and lemon juice; mix well. Add boysenberries; sprinkle with sugar. Let stand until sugar dissolves. Mix well, and spoon into individual serving dishes. Top with whipped cream. Combine ginger and nutmeg; mix well, and sprinkle over whipped cream. Yield: 6 to 8 servings.
*Wilda B. Bell,*
*Chattanooga, Tennessee.*

## BOYSENBERRIES AND CREAM SUPREME

1 (8-ounce) package cream cheese,
  softened
¼ cup plus 2 tablespoons sugar
1½ cups commercial sour cream
4 cups fresh boysenberries, washed and
  drained

Beat cream cheese with electric mixer until light and fluffy. Gradually add sugar, mixing well. Stir in sour cream. Cover mixture, and chill thoroughly before serving.

Divide boysenberries among individual dishes; spoon cream cheese mixture over berries. Yield: 6 to 8 servings.
*Peggy Revels,*
*Woodruff, South Carolina.*

## BOYSENBERRY PIE

4 cups fresh boysenberries, washed and
  drained
1 cup sugar
Pastry for double-crust 9-inch pie
¼ cup sugar
2 tablespoons all-purpose flour

Combine boysenberries and 1 cup sugar; let stand 30 minutes.

Roll half of crust to ⅛-inch thickness, and fit into a 9-inch pieplate.

Combine ¼ cup sugar and flour; stir well. Add flour mixture to fruit, stirring well. Pour into pastry-lined pieplate.

Roll out remaining pastry to ⅛-inch thickness, and cut into ten 10- x ½-inch strips. Arrange strips in lattice design over pie, and trim edges; seal and flute.

Bake at 375° for 55 to 60 minutes or until crust is golden brown. Yield: one 9-inch pie.

*Note:* The pie may be covered with a complete top crust rather than lattice strips, if desired.                    *Bertha Fowler,*
*Woodruff, South Carolina.*

# Pick A Meal From The Garden

Summer is the time to combine the season's freshest produce in an all-vegetable dinner. Our suggestions include the bright red, green, and yellow vegetables of summer—all prepared simply and seasoned with a light touch.

Yellow squash is cooked whole, cut in half, and filled with a savory bacon and breadcrumb mixture. Lima beans are combined with scallions sautéed in butter. And what could taste better than garden-fresh tomatoes and onion slices marinated in oil and vinegar.

To complete your vegetable dinner, add a wedge of steaming cornbread made with—what else, but—fresh corn. Green chiles and Cheddar cheese are added for an extra snap.

## FRESH LIMA BEANS AND SCALLIONS

3 cups shelled fresh lima beans
5 small scallions or green onions, cut into
  ½-inch pieces
3 tablespoons butter or margarine
1 tablespoon all-purpose flour
½ teaspoon salt
¼ teaspoon white pepper
¼ teaspoon paprika

Cook beans in boiling salted water 20 minutes or until tender; drain, reserving ½ cup liquid.

Sauté scallions in butter until tender. Add flour, stirring until smooth. Cook 1 minute, stirring constantly. Gradually stir in reserved liquid; cook over medium heat, stirring constantly, until thickened. Stir in lima beans, salt, pepper, and paprika. Yield: 4 to 6 servings.
*Ruth Horomanski,*
*Satellite Beach, Florida.*

## SEASONED BAKED CORN ON THE COB

4 ears fresh corn
¼ cup plus 1 tablespoon butter or
  margarine, softened
½ teaspoon freeze-dried chives
¼ teaspoon salt
¼ teaspoon prepared mustard
⅛ teaspoon pepper

Remove husks and silks from corn just before cooking. Combine remaining ingredients, stirring well. Spread herb butter on corn, and place each ear on a piece of aluminum foil; wrap tightly.

Bake at 400° for 45 minutes, turning occasionally. Yield: 4 servings.

*Sara Flowers,*
*North Little Rock, Arkansas.*

## GREEN CHILE CORNBREAD

1 cup cornmeal
¼ cup all-purpose flour
1 tablespoon sugar
1 teaspoon salt
½ teaspoon baking soda
1 cup fresh corn cut from cob, drained
1 (8-ounce) carton commercial sour cream
1 (4-ounce) can chopped green chiles,
  drained
1 cup (4 ounces) shredded Cheddar cheese
2 eggs, beaten
2 tablespoons butter or margarine

Combine first 5 ingredients; mix well. Stir in remaining ingredients except butter. Heat butter in an 8½-inch cast-iron skillet until very hot. Pour batter into hot skillet; bake at 350° for 1 hour or until browned. Yield: 8 to 10 servings.

*Lois Rodriquez,*
*Henryetta, Oklahoma.*

## MARINATED TOMATO SLICES

4 tomatoes, sliced
1 onion, thinly sliced
1 cup vegetable oil
⅓ cup wine vinegar
⅛ teaspoon garlic powder
Salt and pepper
Lettuce leaves (optional)

Arrange tomato and onion slices in a shallow container. Combine oil, vinegar, and garlic powder; stir well, and pour over tomato and onion. Sprinkle with salt and pepper. Cover and marinate in refrigerator at least 10 minutes. Serve over lettuce leaves, if desired. Yield: about 8 servings.

*Patricia Boschen,*
*Ashland, Virginia.*

## SOUTHERN STEWED OKRA

1 cup sliced fresh okra
1 medium onion, chopped
1 green pepper, chopped
¼ cup vegetable oil
3 tomatoes, peeled and quartered
1 tablespoon sugar
1 teaspoon all-purpose flour
½ teaspoon salt
½ teaspoon pepper

Cook okra in boiling salted water 10 minutes; drain well, and set aside.

Sauté onion and green pepper in oil. Add tomatoes; cook over medium heat 5 minutes. Stir in okra, sugar, flour, salt, and pepper. Cook over low heat 5 to 8 minutes or until vegetables are tender. Yield: 4 servings.

*Mrs. M. L. Shannon,*
*Fairfield, Alabama.*

## GERMAN POTATO SALAD

3 slices bacon
1 medium onion, chopped
1 tablespoon all-purpose flour
½ cup water
¼ cup cider vinegar
1 tablespoon sugar
1 tablespoon prepared mustard
½ teaspoon salt
⅛ teaspoon pepper
5 cups sliced, cooked potatoes
2 hard-cooked eggs, chopped
¼ cup chopped celery
2 tablespoons chopped fresh parsley

Cook bacon in a large skillet until crisp; drain well, reserving drippings in skillet. Crumble bacon, and set aside. Sauté onion in bacon drippings until tender. Add flour, stirring until smooth. Gradually add water; cook over medium heat, stirring until thickened. Add next 5 ingredients; stir well, and bring to a boil. Stir in bacon and remaining ingredients. Serve immediately. Yield: 8 servings.

*Mrs. Paul Raper,*
*Burgaw, North Carolina.*

## CHEESY STUFFED SQUASH

6 medium-size yellow squash
½ pound bacon
1 small onion, chopped
¾ cup soft breadcrumbs
1 cup (4 ounces) shredded sharp Cheddar
  cheese
Paprika
Fresh parsley (optional)

Wash squash thoroughly; cook in boiling salted water to cover 8 to 10 minutes or until tender but still firm. Drain and cool slightly. Remove and discard stems. Cut each in half lengthwise; remove and reserve pulp, leaving a firm shell.

Cook bacon in a large skillet until crisp; drain well, reserving 2 tablespoons bacon drippings in skillet. Crumble bacon, and set aside. Sauté onion in bacon drippings until tender; stir in bacon, breadcrumbs, and squash pulp.

Place squash shells in a 13- x 9- x 2-inch baking dish. Spoon squash mixture into shells; top with cheese. Broil 6 inches from heat about 5 minutes or just until cheese is melted. Sprinkle with paprika. Garnish with parsley, if desired. Yield: 6 servings.

*Mrs. H. D. Baxter,*
*Charleston, West Virginia.*

# A Fish Fry With All The Trimmings

The excitement of catching a fish is exceeded only by the anticipation of eating it. And the catch always seems to taste better when shared with friends at a fish fry. The focal point of the meal is the crisp fish fried to a delicate golden brown. We give you a choice of either Fried Catfish or Golden Fried Fish, which uses fish fillets. But it wouldn't be a fish fry without tartar sauce, hush puppies and coleslaw.

**Golden Fried Fish**
**or**
**Fried Catfish**
**Tartar Sauce**
**Coleslaw**
**Golden Hush Puppies**
**Brown Sugar Pound Cake**

## GOLDEN FRIED FISH

1 cup all-purpose flour
½ teaspoon salt
1 tablespoon vegetable oil
⅔ cup cold water
1 egg white
1 to 1¼ pounds fish fillets, cut into
  serving-size portions
Vegetable oil

Combine flour, salt, oil, and water; blend well. Beat egg white (at room temperature) until soft peaks form; fold into flour mixture.

Dip both sides of fish into batter. Fry fish until golden brown on both sides in ½ inch of oil heated to 370°. Drain on paper towels. Yield: about 4 servings.

*Note:* Drop any remaining batter by spoonfuls into hot oil; fry until golden brown. Serve with Golden Fried Fish.

*Mrs. Jack Hampton,*
*Elizabethton, Tennessee.*

## FRIED CATFISH

⅔ cup yellow cornmeal
¼ cup all-purpose flour
2 teaspoons salt
½ teaspoon paprika
4 small catfish, cleaned and dressed
½ cup vegetable oil

Combine cornmeal, flour, salt, and paprika. Dry fish thoroughly; coat both sides of fish with cornmeal mixture.

Fry fish in oil heated to 370° about 4 minutes on each side or until golden brown. Drain well on paper towels. Yield: 4 servings.

*Note:* Fish fillets may be substituted.
*Mildred Clute,*
*Marquez, Texas.*

## TARTAR SAUCE

1 cup mayonnaise
1½ tablespoons minced or grated sweet pickle
1½ tablespoons minced fresh parsley
1½ tablespoons capers
1½ tablespoons minced or grated onion

Combine all ingredients, mixing well. Chill several hours before serving. Yield: 1¼ cups.

## COLESLAW

4 cups shredded cabbage
1 cup finely grated carrot
¼ cup mayonnaise or salad dressing
2 teaspoons lemon juice
2 tablespoons sugar
1 tablespoon evaporated milk
Green pepper rings

Combine first 6 ingredients; mix well. Cover and chill thoroughly. Garnish with green pepper rings. Yield: 4 to 5 servings.

*Note:* Red cabbage may be substituted for 1 cup of green.
*Carolyn Beyer,*
*Fredericksburg, Texas.*

## GOLDEN HUSH PUPPIES

2 cups self-rising cornmeal
1 small onion, finely chopped
¾ cup milk
1 egg, slightly beaten
Vegetable oil or shortening

Combine cornmeal and onion; add milk and egg, stirring well.

Carefully drop batter by tablespoonfuls into deep hot oil (370°); cook only a few at a time, turning once. Fry until hush puppies are golden brown (3 to 5 minutes). Drain well on paper towels. Yield: about 2 dozen.

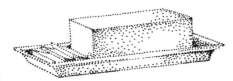

## BROWN SUGAR POUND CAKE

1 cup butter or margarine, softened
½ cup shortening
1 (16-ounce) package brown sugar
½ cup sugar
5 large eggs
½ teaspoon baking powder
3 cups all-purpose flour
1 cup milk
2 tablespoons vanilla extract
1 cup chopped pecans
Cream cheese frosting (recipe follows)

Cream butter and shortening in a large mixing bowl; gradually add sugar, beating until light and fluffy. Add eggs, one at a time, beating well after each addition.

Combine baking powder and flour; add to creamed mixture alternately with milk, beginning and ending with flour, and beating well after each addition. Stir in vanilla and pecans.

Pour batter into a greased and floured 10-inch tube pan. Bake at 350° for 1 hour and 10 minutes or until a wooden pick inserted in center comes out clean. Cool in pan 10 minutes; invert on wire rack to cool completely. Frost with cream cheese frosting. Yield: one 10-inch cake.

*Cream Cheese Frosting:*

½ cup butter or margarine, softened
1 (8-ounce) package cream cheese, softened
2 teaspoons vanilla extract
1 (16-ounce) package powdered sugar

Combine all ingredients, mixing until smooth. Yield: enough for one 10-inch tube cake.

*Mrs. William Frank Chambers, Sr.,*
*Clyde, North Carolina.*

# Serve A Stuffed Entrée For A Change

The next time you plan meat loaf for dinner, roll the meat loaf mixture around slices of ham and shredded cheese and have Cheesy Meat Roll instead. The flavor is Italian, owed to the oregano and garlic that season the meat and the slices of mozzarella cheese arranged on top.

Pork chops also invite a filling, and our Fruit-Stuffed Pork Chops are a delicious variation. Have the butcher cut a pocket in thick pork chops so you can fill them with a stuffing of breadcrumbs and prunes. Before baking, add pineapple juice to keep the chops moist and juicy.

## STUFFED STEAK ROLLS

2 (1-pound) top round steaks, ½ inch thick
3 slices bacon
⅓ cup finely chopped onion
¼ cup finely chopped celery
2 cups soft breadcrumbs
2 tablespoons chopped fresh parsley
1 egg, beaten
½ cup all-purpose flour
1 teaspoon poultry seasoning
¼ teaspoon salt
¼ teaspoon rubbed sage
¼ teaspoon pepper
¼ cup vegetable oil
1 (10½-ounce) can beef broth, undiluted
1 bay leaf

Trim excess fat from steaks; pound to ⅛-inch thickness, and cut each into 6 pieces. Set aside.

Fry bacon in a large skillet until crisp; drain well, reserving 2 tablespoons drippings in skillet. Crumble the bacon, and set aside.

Add onion and celery to skillet; sauté until tender. Combine bacon, sautéed vegetables, breadcrumbs, parsley, and egg; mix well. Place 1 heaping tablespoonful stuffing on each piece of steak. Roll up each piece, jellyroll fashion; secure with wooden picks.

Combine next 5 ingredients, stirring well. Dredge each steak roll in the flour mixture, and brown in hot oil in a large skillet.

Transfer steak rolls to a 2-quart casserole. Add broth and bay leaf. Cover and bake at 375° for 1 hour. Remove bay leaf before serving. Yield: 6 servings.

*Sue Virgil,*
*San Antonio, Texas.*

## CHEESY MEAT ROLL

2 pounds ground beef
¾ cup soft breadcrumbs
½ cup tomato juice
2 eggs, beaten
2 tablespoons chopped fresh parsley
½ teaspoon dried whole oregano
¼ teaspoon salt
¼ teaspoon pepper
1 small clove garlic, minced
8 thin slices ham
1½ cups (6 ounces) shredded mozzarella
   cheese
3 slices mozzarella cheese

Combine first 9 ingredients, mixing well; shape into a 12- x 10-inch rectangle on a sheet of waxed paper. Arrange ham slices over meat, leaving a 1-inch margin around edges. Top with shredded mozzarella cheese. Beginning at short end, roll meat jellyroll fashion, lifting waxed paper to help in rolling. Press edges and ends together to seal.

Place roll, seam side down, in a lightly greased 13- x 9- x 2-inch baking pan. Bake at 350° for 1 hour and 15 minutes; remove from oven. Cut each cheese slice into 2 triangles, and arrange on top of roll so they slightly overlap. Return to oven 2 minutes or until cheese melts. Let roll stand 5 minutes before serving. Yield: 8 servings.

*Mrs. Robert James,*
*Marion, Ohio.*

## CORNISH HENS WITH WILD RICE STUFFING

¼ cup minced celery
¼ cup minced shallots or onion
2 tablespoons minced green pepper
2 tablespoons butter or margarine
1⅓ cups chicken broth
2 tablespoons minced fresh parsley
1 teaspoon herb seasoning
⅔ cup wild rice, uncooked
2 (1- to 1¼-pound) Cornish hens
Salt and pepper
¼ cup butter or margarine
½ cup red currant jelly
¼ cup brandy

Sauté celery, shallots, and green pepper in 2 tablespoons butter in a medium saucepan. Stir in next 3 ingredients; bring to a boil, and add wild rice. Cover and reduce heat to medium low; cook about 25 minutes.

Remove giblets from hens, and reserve for another use. Rinse hens with cold water, and pat dry; sprinkle cavities with salt and pepper. Stuff hens lightly with rice mixture. Close cavities, and secure with wooden picks; truss.

Place hens, breast side up, in a shallow baking pan.

Melt ¼ cup butter in a saucepan; brush hens with butter, reserving any remaining butter in saucepan. Bake hens at 375° for 30 minutes.

Combine jelly and brandy in saucepan with remaining butter; cook over low heat, stirring often, until jelly melts. Brush hens with jelly mixture. Bake 30 to 40 additional minutes, depending on size of hens, basting every 10 minutes with jelly mixture. Yield: 2 servings.

*Carol Jerome,*
*Brevard, North Carolina.*

## FRUIT-STUFFED PORK CHOPS

2 cups soft breadcrumbs
1 cup chopped prunes
2 tablespoons shortening, melted
1 teaspoon lemon juice
½ teaspoon salt
6 (1¼-inch-thick) pork chops, cut with
   pockets
Salt
½ cup seasoned, dry breadcrumbs
1 cup pineapple juice

Combine first 5 ingredients, mixing well; stuff into pockets of chops, and secure openings with wooden picks. Sprinkle chops with salt, and dredge in seasoned dry breadcrumbs.

Place chops in a lightly greased 13- x 9- x 2-inch baking dish; pour ½ cup pineapple juice over chops, and bake at 350° for 30 minutes. Add remaining pineapple juice, and bake an additional 30 minutes. Yield: 6 servings.

*Mrs. C. D. Marshall,*
*Culpeper, Virginia.*

## BAKED SNAPPER WITH TARRAGON STUFFING

½ cup chopped celery
½ cup chopped onion
⅓ cup butter or margarine
½ teaspoon salt
½ teaspoon dried whole tarragon
⅛ teaspoon pepper
3 cups soft breadcrumbs
3 tablespoons milk
6 (8-ounce) red snapper fillets
2 tablespoons butter or margarine, melted

Sauté celery and onion in ⅓ cup butter in a medium skillet until tender. Add salt, tarragon, and pepper; mix well. Stir in breadcrumbs and milk.

Place 3 fillets in a greased 13- x 9- x 2-inch baking dish. Spoon breadcrumb mixture over fillets; top with remaining fillets, and brush with 2 tablespoons melted butter. Bake at 400° about 35 minutes or until fish flakes easily when tested with a fork. Yield: 6 to 8 servings.

*Sandra Souther,*
*Gainesville, Georgia.*

# Finger Foods For The Party

Everything you might need for that tea or reception you're planning is right here: delicious finger foods that are refreshing but not too filling.

Cooling Party Fruit Punch, a blend of pineapple, lemon, and orange flavors, makes a tingly golden drink. For garnish, add maraschino cherries and floating fruit slices or an ice ring made from the punch. With it, offer your guests sweet and spicy Glazed Pecans, Cherry Pecan Cookies, and Cheese Straws.

## GLAZED PECANS

1 cup sugar
½ cup water
1 teaspoon ground cinnamon
¼ teaspoon ground allspice
2 cups pecan halves
1 teaspoon vanilla extract

Combine first 4 ingredients in a large saucepan. Cook over medium heat 5 minutes, stirring constantly. Add pecans, and continue cooking 5 minutes. Remove from heat; stir in vanilla. Place pecans individually on waxed paper. Cool completely. Yield: 2 cups.

*Martha M. Dooley,*
*Chattanooga, Tennessee.*

## CHERRY PECAN COOKIES

1 cup butter or margarine, softened
1 cup sifted powdered sugar
1 egg
2½ cups all-purpose flour
¼ teaspoon cream of tartar
1 cup candied cherries, halved
½ cup finely chopped pecans

Cream butter; gradually add sugar, beating until light and fluffy. Add egg and beat well. Combine flour and cream of tartar; add to creamed mixture, and mix well. Stir in cherries and pecans.

Shape dough into two 10- x 2-inch rolls. Wrap in aluminum foil, and freeze until firm.

Cut into ¼-inch slices; place on ungreased cookie sheets. Bake at 375° for 10 to 12 minutes. Yield: 6½ dozen.
*Mrs. Clay Turner,*
*De Funiak Springs, Florida.*

## CHEESE STRAWS

1½ cups all-purpose flour
1 teaspoon baking powder
1 teaspoon salt
⅛ teaspoon sugar
1 teaspoon red pepper
⅓ cup butter or margarine
1 cup (4 ounces) shredded sharp Cheddar
    cheese
¼ cup cold water

Combine first 5 ingredients, mixing well; set aside.

Melt butter and let cool. Pour over cheese, and toss gently. Add to dry ingredients, and cut in until mixture resembles coarse meal. Sprinkle water evenly over flour mixture; stir with a fork until all ingredients are moistened. Shape into a ball.

Roll dough to ⅛-inch thickness on a lightly floured surface, and cut into 3- x ½-inch strips.

Place strips on ungreased cookie sheets. Bake at 325° for 10 to 12 minutes or until crisp. Place on wire racks to cool. Yield: about 6 dozen.
*Aileen Wright,*
*Nashville, Tennessee.*

## PARTY FRUIT PUNCH

2 (46-ounce) cans pineapple juice
2 (12-ounce) cans frozen orange juice
    concentrate, thawed and undiluted
1 (6-ounce) package lemon-flavored
    gelatin
4 quarts ginger ale, chilled
Fruit slices (optional)
Maraschino cherries (optional)

Combine first 3 ingredients, stirring well; chill.

To serve, combine chilled mixture and ginger ale in a punch bowl. Garnish with fruit slices and maraschino cherries, if desired. Yield: about 2 gallons.
*Ruby Vineyard,*
*Rutledge, Tennessee.*

# Discover The Sweet Side Of Carrots

Carrots are one of the most economical, nutritious, and readily available vegetables on the produce shelf. Young, tender carrots can almost be considered a convenience food because they store well and need only a scrubbing before being enjoyed as a between-meal snack.

But there are numerous ways to enjoy carrots. One suggestion is Sweet-and-Sour Carrots, perfect as a side dish. Or combine carrots with pineapple in a refreshing congealed salad. For the sweet side of carrots, use them as an ingredient in cookies and cake.

## SWEET-AND-SOUR CARROTS

1 pound carrots, scraped and diagonally
    sliced
1 medium-size green pepper, chopped
⅓ cup sugar
1 teaspoon cornstarch
½ teaspoon salt
1 (8-ounce) can pineapple chunks,
    undrained
2 teaspoons vinegar
2 teaspoons soy sauce

Cook carrots, covered, in a small amount of boiling salted water until tender. Add green pepper; cook 3 minutes. Drain and set aside. Combine sugar, cornstarch, and salt in a medium saucepan. Drain pineapple, and reserve juice. Add water to reserved pineapple juice to make ⅓ cup liquid; stir into sugar mixture. Stir in vinegar and soy sauce; cook over low heat until bubbly, stirring constantly. Stir in vegetables and pineapple; cook until well heated. Yield: 6 to 8 servings. *Mattye Holland,*
*Mineral Wells, Texas.*

## CARROT SALAD

1 (3-ounce) package orange-flavored
    gelatin
1½ cups boiling water
1 (8-ounce) can crushed pineapple,
    undrained
2 cups grated carrots
½ cup flaked coconut
¼ cup chopped pecans

Dissolve gelatin in boiling water; drain pineapple, and add juice to gelatin mixture. Chill until consistency of

unbeaten egg white. Stir in pineapple, carrots, coconut, and pecans. Pour into a lightly greased 1-quart mold or individual molds; chill until firm. Yield: 6 servings.
*Carolyn Beyer,*
*Fredericksburg, Texas.*

## CARROT CAKE

3 eggs
2 cups sugar
1¼ cups vegetable oil
3 cups all-purpose flour
2 teaspoons baking soda
1 teaspoon salt
2 teaspoons ground cinnamon
1½ cups grated carrots
1 cup chopped pecans
1 (20-ounce) can crushed pineapple, well
    drained
2 teaspoons vanilla extract

Combine eggs, sugar, and oil in a large mixing bowl; beat well. Combine flour, soda, salt, and cinnamon; add to sugar mixture, and beat well. Stir in carrots, pecans, pineapple, and vanilla. Pour into a greased and floured 10-inch tube pan. Bake at 350° for 1 hour and 15 minutes or until a wooden pick inserted in center comes out clean. Cool in pan 10 to 15 minutes; remove from pan, and let cool completely. Yield: one 10-inch cake. *Phyllis England,*
*Deer Lodge, Tennessee.*

## CARROT COOKIES

½ cup shortening
½ cup butter or margarine, softened
¾ cup sugar
2 eggs
1¼ cups cooked, mashed carrots
2 cups all-purpose flour
2 teaspoons baking powder
¼ teaspoon salt
1 cup flaked coconut
½ cup chopped pecans

Combine shortening, butter, and sugar in a large mixing bowl; beat until fluffy. Add eggs and carrots, mixing well.

Combine flour, baking powder, and salt; add to creamed mixture, and stir well. Stir in coconut and pecans.

Drop dough by teaspoonfuls onto greased cookie sheets. Bake at 400° for 10 minutes or until firm. Cool on wire racks. Yield: about 7 dozen.
*Cindy Tippett,*
*Shreveport, Louisiana.*

# From Our Kitchen To Yours

When fresh vegetables are plentiful, you might like to try some of our test kitchens staff's favorite methods for preparing them.

## The Basics of Cooking Vegetables

When we test any vegetable recipe, regardless of the cooking method used, we always keep these basic cooking principles in mind:

—To retain as many of the nutrients as possible, avoid cutting vegetables into tiny pieces. Leave them whole or cut into large chunks.

—Use as little water as possible in cooking. (Reserve the vegetable water, and use when making soups or stews to increase the nutritional value.) And avoid overcooking, since that drives out nutrients. When the vegetables are bright in color and crisp-tender, they are ready to eat.

**Steaming**—Among the many ways to cook vegetables, steaming is one of our favorites. This method not only retains the nutrients, it also retains much of the vegetables' natural color. To steam vegetables, use a pot with a tightly fitting lid and a steamer rack. Add about 1 inch of water to the pot, making sure the water does not touch the bottom of the rack. Remember, it's the steam from the water that cooks the vegetables, not the water.

Add the vegetables to the rack, and place it over the water. Cover and let the water boil over medium-high heat. The vegetables are done when crisp-tender. Depending on the vegetable used, you may need to add more water to complete cooking. (*Note:* Try layering sliced carrots, squash, and fresh mushrooms on the steamer rack, and steam them for about 10 minutes.)

**Stir-frying**—We get lots of recipes from our readers calling for this method. Cooking at a high temperature for a short period of time is the key to stir-frying. This ensures minimum nutritional loss while preserving natural color and flavor of vegetables.

Cut tender vegetables such as zucchini into large slices, or leave the smaller ones whole as with fresh mushrooms. Cut less tender vegetables such as carrots and celery diagonally into smaller slices to expose the largest possible area to the heat.

Heat a small amount of oil in a large skillet or wok; add vegetables, and stir constantly until they are crisp-tender.

Use a combination of vegetables such as squash, zucchini, onions, and tomatoes, or stir-fry only one vegetable, and add your favorite seasonings.

**Sautéing**—This method is a close relative of stir-frying but doesn't require the high temperatures needed to stir-fry. To sauté, cook vegetables in a small amount of oil in a skillet, just until crisp-tender.

One of our staff's favorite treats is an end-of-the-week vegetable medley sauté. If we have extra vegetables such as broccoli, squash, or carrots left over from a week of testing and photography, we'll add them to the skillet and sauté. It's an excellent way to use extras.

**Microwaving**—The microwave oven is rapidly becoming standard equipment in Southern kitchens, and some of the best foods to come out of them are vegetables. Microwaved vegetables retain essential nutrients and their natural flavor because they can be cooked with little or no water. Vegetables with a high water content such as fresh corn on the cob cook in their own juices. Here are some tips we follow when microwaving vegetables:

—Cover the vegetables tightly unless otherwise stated in the recipe.

—Stir vegetables halfway into the cooking time to distribute the heat.

—Arrange small or more tender portions of the vegetables toward the center of the dish. For example, when cooking broccoli, place the flowerets toward the center of the dish, while extending the tougher stem ends toward the outer edge of the dish.

—Rotate the dish during cooking to promote even cooking.

—Pierce vegetables cooked in their skins such as potatoes and acorn squash to release excess steam.

—To prevent dark spots from forming on vegetables, don't sprinkle salt directly on the vegetables before microwaving them. Add salt to taste after cooking or add it to the water just before you put in the vegetables.

—Vegetables will continue to cook after they are removed from the oven. Allow a standing time of three to five minutes to continue cooking.

If you're not familiar with microwaving vegetables, use these tips along with the manufacturer's instructions.

## More Kitchen Tips

**Garnishing guide:** Dress up an entrée, beverage, or dessert with fresh fruit. Try slicing a large strawberry about three or four times from the tip end to, but not through, the stem. Carefully spread the slices into a fan shape. Add a touch of fresh mint for a beautiful garnish. Also, cut a long narrow strip of rind from oranges, lemons, or limes with a zester, cutting in a circular fashion around the fruit. Tie the strip into a bow, and trim the ends. Use it to top your favorite citrus salad, beverage, or dessert.

**Timesaver:** If you're faced with peeling a bushel of tomatoes for canning or making relish, try this quick method. Dip the tomatoes into boiling water for 1 minute; plunge into cold water. The skin will slip off easily.

**Freezer keeper:** Keep foods such as strawberries, pork chops, diced green pepper, and bacon from sticking together in the freezer by placing in a single layer on a baking sheet and freezing until firm. Remove from the baking sheet, store in freezer bags or containers, and use as needed.

# Scrumptious Fruit Cobblers In A Hurry

"Cobble up" means to put together quickly, and that's just what you do with these quickie fruit cobblers. They make good use of either canned or fresh fruits and can be mixed up in a jiffy. Even so, that down-home flavor is still a part of each dish.

### APRICOT COBBLE UP

1 cup biscuit mix
1 tablespoon brown sugar
¼ teaspoon ground nutmeg
1 tablespoon butter or margarine, softened
⅓ cup milk
1 (17-ounce) can apricot halves, undrained
Whipping cream

Combine first 3 ingredients; stir in butter until evenly distributed. Add milk, and mix well. Spread batter in a greased 8-inch square baking pan.

Drain apricots, reserving syrup. Arrange apricot halves, cut side down, on top of batter; pour syrup over top. Bake at 400° for 30 to 35 minutes. Serve warm with cream. Yield: 4 to 6 servings.
*Bernadette Dirkman,*
*Green Bay, Wisconsin.*

## BLACKBERRY COBBLER

5 cups fresh blackberries
¾ cup sugar
1 tablespoon cornstarch
⅛ teaspoon salt
2 tablespoons butter or margarine
Pastry (recipe follows)
1 tablespoon milk
1 tablespoon sugar
Vanilla ice cream

Wash berries thoroughly, and drain well; place in a 9-inch square baking dish. Combine ¾ cup sugar, cornstarch, and salt; sprinkle mixture over berries. Dot with butter.

Roll pastry out on a lightly floured surface into a 9-inch square; place over berries, sealing edges to sides of dish. Cut slits in crust. Brush crust with milk, and sprinkle with 1 tablespoon sugar. Bake at 425° for 30 minutes or until crust is golden brown. Serve with vanilla ice cream. Yield: 6 servings.

*Pastry:*

1 cup all-purpose flour
½ teaspoon salt
⅓ cup shortening
2 tablespoons cold water

Combine flour and salt. Cut in shortening until mixture resembles coarse crumbs; sprinkle with water, and stir with a fork until mixture forms a ball. Yield: enough for one 9-inch cobbler.
*Florence L. Costello,*
*Chattanooga, Tennessee.*

## CHERRY COBBLER

1 cup all-purpose flour
½ cup sugar
2 teaspoons baking powder
Pinch of salt
2 tablespoons butter or margarine, melted
½ cup milk
1 (16-ounce) can tart red pitted cherries, undrained
1 cup sugar
½ cup hot water
Few drops of red food coloring (optional)

Combine flour, ½ cup sugar, baking powder, and salt; add butter and milk, mixing well. Pour batter into a greased 9-inch square baking pan.

Combine remaining ingredients, and pour over batter evenly. Bake at 400° for 30 minutes. Cool before serving. Yield: 6 servings. *Vicki Dutton,*
*Brownwood, Texas.*

## FRESH PEACH COBBLER

¼ cup plus 2 tablespoons butter or margarine
2 cups sugar, divided
¾ cup all-purpose flour
2 teaspoons baking powder
Dash of salt
¾ cup milk
2 cups sliced peaches

Melt butter in a 2-quart baking dish. Combine 1 cup sugar, flour, baking powder, and salt; add milk, and stir until mixed. Pour batter over butter in baking dish, but do not stir.

Combine peaches and remaining 1 cup sugar; spoon over the batter. Do not stir. Bake at 350° for 1 hour. Yield: 6 to 8 servings. *Mrs. Horace Edwards,*
*McCormick, South Carolina.*

# Bake An Old-Fashioned Molasses Favorite

Many old-fashioned home-baked favorites were flavored with a dab from the molasses jar. Although it may not be the staple it once was, molasses is still popular in today's baking. Here it's featured in cookies, bread, and baked beans.

## MOLASSES BAKED BEANS

½ pound ground beef
2 (16-ounce) cans pork and beans
1 (15¾-ounce) can barbecued beans
1 medium onion, chopped
½ cup chopped green pepper
½ cup firmly packed brown sugar
¼ cup molasses
¼ cup catsup
2 tablespoons prepared mustard
1 tablespoon Worcestershire sauce
1 clove garlic, crushed
1 teaspoon seasoned salt
½ teaspoon lemon-pepper seasoning
4 or 5 slices bacon

Cook ground beef until browned; drain well.

Combine all ingredients except bacon, and mix well; pour into a 13- x 9- x 2-inch baking dish. Top with bacon. Bake at 350° for 2 hours. Yield: 8 servings. *Mrs. Steve Toney,*
*Helena, Arkansas.*

## OAT-MOLASSES BREAD

2 packages dry yeast
½ cup warm water (105° to 115°)
1⅓ cups warm milk
1 cup hot water
¼ cup shortening
⅓ cup molasses
1 tablespoon plus 1 teaspoon salt
7 to 7¾ cups all-purpose flour, divided
2½ cups regular oats, uncooked
2 tablespoons butter or margarine, melted
1 tablespoon milk

Combine yeast and ½ cup warm water in a small bowl; let stand 5 minutes. Combine 1⅓ cups milk, 1 cup hot water, and shortening in a large bowl; stir until shortening melts. Stir in molasses, salt, and yeast mixture.

Gradually add 2 cups flour, beating well. Add oats and enough remaining flour to form a stiff dough.

Turn dough out onto a floured surface, and knead until smooth and elastic (about 10 minutes). Divide dough in half, and place each half in a well-greased bowl. Brush tops with butter. Cover with plastic wrap. Let rise in a warm place (85°), free from drafts, 1 hour or until doubled in bulk. Punch dough down, and let rest 10 minutes.

Shape each half into a loaf, and place each loaf into a greased 9- x 5- x 3-inch loafpan. Brush tops lightly with milk.

Cover; let rise in a warm place (85°), free from drafts, 45 minutes or until doubled in bulk. Bake loaves at 350° for 40 to 45 minutes. Yield: 2 loaves.
*Tissie M. Brown,*
*Livingston, Tennessee.*

## BUTTER PECAN COOKIES

2 cups all-purpose flour
½ teaspoon salt
1 cup butter, softened
2 tablespoons sugar
¼ cup light molasses
2 cups finely chopped pecans
Powdered sugar

Combine flour and salt; set aside.

Cream butter and sugar in a large mixing bowl until light and fluffy. Add molasses; mix until well blended. Gradually add flour mixture to butter mixture; mix well. Stir pecans into dough.

Roll dough into 1-inch balls; place about 2 inches apart on ungreased cookie sheets. Bake at 350° for 15 to 18 minutes. Dust or roll warm cookies in powdered sugar. Yield: about 5 dozen.
*Varniece R. Warren,*
*Hermitage, Arkansas.*

## MOLASSES SUGAR COOKIES

¾ cup shortening
1 cup sugar
¼ cup molasses
1 egg, beaten
2¼ cups all-purpose flour
2 teaspoons baking soda
½ teaspoon salt
½ teaspoon ground cloves
1 teaspoon ground ginger
1 teaspoon ground cinnamon
Sugar

Melt shortening and cool. Add 1 cup sugar, molasses, and egg; mix well. Combine flour, soda, salt, and spices; add to sugar mixture, mixing until blended.

Shape dough into 1-inch balls; roll in sugar. Place 2 inches apart on greased cookie sheets; bake at 375° for 8 minutes or until done. Yield: about 4 dozen.
*Mrs. Edgar Patterson,
Carrollton, Georgia.*

# Good Spreads, Good Sandwiches

This summer keep your refrigerator well stocked with a variety of sandwich spreads. Not only do they provide tasty meals for those on the go, but they're also great for picnics and impromptu get-togethers.

Salad Dressing Spread has the delicate flavor of cream cheese and Italian seasonings, while Zesty Cheese Spread is a scrumptious variation of pimiento cheese.

## CUCUMBER AND CREAM CHEESE SPREAD

2 (8-ounce) packages cream cheese, softened
2 teaspoons lemon juice
¼ teaspoon prepared horseradish
¼ teaspoon salt
⅛ teaspoon hot sauce
2 teaspoons minced onion
½ medium cucumber, peeled and finely chopped

Beat cream cheese until smooth. Add next 4 ingredients, and mix well. Stir in onion and cucumber. Spoon mixture into a covered container; chill at least 1 hour or until ready to use. Yield: 2 cups.

## CHUNKY SANDWICH SPREAD

1 (8-ounce) package cream cheese, softened
½ cup chopped onion
½ cup chopped green pepper
3 tablespoons chopped pimiento, drained
3 tablespoons catsup
3 hard-cooked eggs, chopped
1 cup finely chopped pecans or walnuts
¼ teaspoon salt
¼ teaspoon pepper

Combine all ingredients, mixing well. Spoon mixture into a covered container; chill at least 1 hour or until ready to use. Yield: about 3 cups.
*Gwyn Prows Groseclose,
Longwood, Florida.*

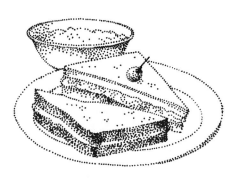

## ZESTY CHEESE SPREAD

2½ cups (10 ounces) shredded sharp Cheddar cheese
⅔ cup mayonnaise
2½ teaspoons lemon juice
1 teaspoon minced onion
2 tablespoons prepared mustard
2 teaspoons chopped pimiento, drained
Dash of pepper

Combine all ingredients, mixing well. Spoon mixture into a covered container; chill at least 1 hour or until ready to use. Yield: about 2 cups.
*Melanie Densmore,
Marietta, Georgia.*

## SALAD DRESSING SPREAD

2 (8-ounce) packages cream cheese, softened
1 (0.7-ounce) package Italian salad dressing mix
½ cup mayonnaise
½ cup chopped fresh parsley
1 (4-ounce) jar chopped pimiento, drained

Combine all ingredients, mixing well. Spoon mixture into a covered container; chill at least 1 hour or until ready to use. Yield: about 2½ cups.
*Sally Pedigo,
Dallas, Texas.*

## Microwave Cookery

# Chilled Desserts Start In The Microwave

When you want the dessert to be ready and waiting well in advance of mealtime, no choice could be better than one that chills for several hours before serving.

And since many chilled desserts feature sauces and custard-type fillings, microwaving is a great way to make them. In addition to faster cooking, microwaving also eliminates the constant stirring that sauces and fillings normally require, as well as scorching or sticking.

Our recipes offer a variety of chilled desserts, from cheesecake and chocolate pudding to fresh strawberries arranged in a pie shell and glazed with a lemon-lime sauce. Since the wattage of microwave ovens varies, so will cooking times. A time range is given in each of our recipes to allow for the difference. To prevent overcooking, always check for doneness at the lower end of the range.

Almost any chilled dessert can be converted to microwave preparation. Since less liquid evaporates during microwaving than in conventional cooking, you may need to increase the thickening agent or decrease the liquid. Here are

*Microwave the cheesecake filling briefly before pouring it into the crust, where it will be microwaved again. This will result in more even cooking.*

*Every step in the preparation of Pear-Berry Cheesecake takes place in the microwave oven, from the graham cracker crust to the pear sauce that's drizzled over the fruit topping.*

## PEAR-BERRY CHEESECAKE

**2 tablespoons butter or margarine**
**2 eggs**
**½ cup sugar**
**1 (8-ounce) carton commercial sour cream**
**2 teaspoons vanilla extract**
**2 (8-ounce) packages cream cheese, softened**
**Microwaved graham cracker crust (recipe follows)**
**1 (8½-ounce) can pear halves in heavy syrup**
**⅔ cup strawberry halves**
**2 teaspoons cornstarch**
**2 teaspoons lemon juice**

Place butter in a 3-quart glass bowl; microwave at HIGH for 45 seconds or until melted. Add next 5 ingredients, and beat at medium speed of electric mixer until well blended. Cover with waxed paper, and microwave at HIGH for 5 to 6 minutes or until very hot; using a wire whisk, stir well every 2 minutes during cooking. (Mixture will become smooth as it cooks.) Pour over microwaved graham cracker crust.

Microwave at MEDIUM (50% power) for 6 to 9 minutes or until almost set in center, giving the dish one quarter-turn every 3 minutes. (Mixture firms up as it chills.) Cool thoroughly, and chill.

Drain pears, reserving ½ cup liquid (add water, if necessary, to measure ½ cup). Slice each pear half into 4 wedges. Arrange pear wedges and strawberry halves on chilled cheesecake as desired.

Combine reserved pear liquid, cornstarch, and lemon juice in a 2-cup glass measure; stir until cornstarch is dissolved. Microwave at HIGH for 1½ to 2 minutes or until thickened, stirring once. Cool slightly, and spoon over cheesecake. Chill thoroughly before serving. Yield: 8 servings.

*Microwaved Graham Cracker Crust:*

**1 cup graham cracker crumbs**
**2 tablespoons sugar**
**3 tablespoons butter or margarine, melted**

Combine all ingredients; mix well, and press into a buttered 9-inch round baking dish. Microwave at HIGH for 1½ minutes or until firm, rotating dish after 1 minute. Yield: one 9-inch pie shell.

some other pointers to ensure your success with chilled desserts begun in the microwave oven.

—Use HIGH power when microwaving most sauces or fillings; however, to ensure a smooth consistency for sauces that contain a lot of eggs or sugar, use a lower setting. In general, recipes with cream cheese or sour cream should also be microwaved at a lower setting; these ingredients have a high fat content, making them attract more energy and thus cook faster.

—A glass mixing bowl is perfect for making sauces and fillings in the microwave oven. Just be sure to use one large enough to prevent the mixture from boiling over. A sauce yielding 1 to 1½ cups should be cooked in a container with at least a 1-quart capacity.

—Microwaved sauces need to be stirred occasionally to mix the cooked portion on the outside with the uncooked portion in the center. Thorough stirring at 2-minute intervals is sufficient for the recipes included here.

—If your recipe calls for a pie shell, microwave it before filling; otherwise, the crust won't cook properly. For a regular pastry shell, use dried peas or beans to keep the sides and bottom from puffing during microwaving (do not use metal pastry weights). To keep the rim from puffing and losing its shape, gently prick it with a fork. Graham cracker crusts microwave well without taking these extra steps.

—Some fillings should be partially cooked in the microwave oven before being poured into the pie shell. This allows the filling to be stirred for at least part of the microwaving time, resulting in more even cooking.

—When microwaving a filled pie shell, give the dish one quarter-turn every 2 to 3 minutes during cooking. This also promotes even cooking of the filling.

—Most sauces and fillings will not be completely thickened after microwaving is complete; however, they'll thicken as they chill.

*Tip: Avoid using dishes with sloping sides when cooking casseroles in the microwave. Food on the edges receive the most energy and can overcook.*

## CHOCOLATE-ALMOND PUDDING

2 cups milk
¾ cup sugar
2 tablespoons cocoa
2 tablespoons cornstarch
¼ teaspoon salt
2 egg yolks
½ teaspoon vanilla extract
¼ teaspoon almond extract
½ cup whipping cream
2 tablespoons powdered sugar
¼ cup sliced almonds, toasted

Place milk in a 1½-quart glass bowl, and microwave at HIGH for 3 to 3½ minutes. Combine sugar, cocoa, cornstarch, and salt; mix well, and stir into hot milk.

Beat egg yolks until thick and lemon colored; gradually add about one-fourth of hot mixture to egg yolks, then stir into remaining hot mixture. Microwave at HIGH for 5 to 7 minutes or until thickened, stirring at 2-minute intervals. Stir in vanilla and almond extract. Spoon into serving dishes, and chill.

Before serving, combine whipping cream and powdered sugar; beat until soft peaks form. Spoon a dollop onto each serving of pudding, and garnish with almonds. Yield: 4 servings.

## GLAZED STRAWBERRY PIE

1 cup sugar
2½ tablespoons cornstarch
1 cup lemon-lime carbonated beverage
1 drop red food coloring
1 quart whole strawberries
Basic microwave pastry (recipe follows)
Whipped cream

Combine sugar and cornstarch in a 1-quart glass bowl; gradually stir in carbonated beverage. Microwave at HIGH for 5½ to 6½ minutes or until thickened and clear, stirring at 2-minute intervals. Stir in food coloring, and set aside.

Wash and cap strawberries, and arrange, stem end down, to cover bottom of pastry shell; spoon on glaze. Chill. Serve with whipped cream. Yield: one 9-inch pie.

*Basic Microwave Pastry:*

1 cup all-purpose flour
½ teaspoon salt
⅓ cup plus 1 tablespoon shortening
2 to 4 drops yellow food coloring
    (optional)
2 to 3 tablespoons cold water

Combine flour and salt; cut in shortening with pastry blender until mixture resembles coarse meal. Add food coloring to the water if extra color is desired (pastry will not brown in microwave oven). Sprinkle water evenly over flour mixture, and stir with a fork until all ingredients are moistened.

Shape dough into a ball, and place on a lightly floured surface; roll dough into a circle that is 2 inches larger than an inverted 9-inch pieplate. Fit the pastry loosely into pieplate, trim edges, and fold under to form a standing rim; flute.

Place a piece of heavy-duty plastic wrap over pastry, and cover with dried peas or beans. Gently prick rim of pastry (this will help maintain fluted shape). Microwave at HIGH for 5½ to 7 minutes or until pastry is opaque and bottom is dry. Yield: one 9-inch pastry shell.

## CHARLOTTE RUSSE

1 envelope unflavored gelatin
¼ cup milk
2 eggs
1 cup sugar
⅛ teaspoon salt
2 cups milk
¼ cup cream sherry
1 teaspoon vanilla extract
2 cups whipping cream, whipped
About 7 ladyfingers, split lengthwise
2 tablespoons slivered almonds, toasted

Soften gelatin in ¼ cup milk, and set mixture aside.

Combine eggs and sugar in a 2½-quart glass bowl; beat until thick and lemon colored. Stir in salt and 2 cups milk. Microwave at HIGH, uncovered, for 6 to 8 minutes or until slightly thickened; stir at 2-minute intervals during cooking. Stir in gelatin mixture; let cool.

Stir sherry and vanilla into custard; fold in whipped cream. Line sides of a 2-quart bowl with ladyfingers; pour in filling, and chill until set. Sprinkle with almonds. Yield: 8 to 10 servings.

*Tip: Use the water-displacement method for measuring shortening if the water that clings to the shortening will not affect the product. Do not use this method for measuring shortening for frying. To measure ¼ cup shortening using this method, put ¾ cup water in a measuring cup; add shortening until the water reaches the 1-cup level. Be sure that the shortening is completely covered with water. Drain off the water before using the shortening.*

# Make It Hearty And Mexican

Mexico's lively cuisine is more and more in favor on Southern tables. Besides being spicy, Mexican food is known for being hearty—as these recipes show.

Beefy Jalapeño Cornbread is filled with a tempting mixture of beef, onion, peppers, and cheese. Also included are two chicken casseroles that combine the traditional south-of-the-border ingredients for spicy and hearty results.

## BEEFY JALAPENO CORNBREAD

1 cup yellow cornmeal
1 cup milk
2 eggs
¾ teaspoon salt
½ teaspoon soda
½ cup bacon drippings
1 (17-ounce) can cream-style corn
1½ pounds ground beef
1 tablespoon yellow cornmeal
1 large onion, chopped
2 cups (8 ounces) shredded Cheddar
    cheese
4 jalapeño peppers, finely chopped

Combine 1 cup cornmeal, milk, eggs, salt, soda, bacon drippings, and corn in a bowl; set aside. Cook ground beef until lightly browned; drain well, and set aside.

Sprinkle 1 tablespoon cornmeal in a greased 10½-inch cast-iron skillet; pour half of batter into skillet. Sprinkle evenly with beef; top with onion and cheese. Sprinkle peppers over top. Pour remaining batter over top. Bake at 350° for 50 minutes or until golden brown. Yield: 6 to 8 servings.

*Mrs. C. L. Nabours,*
*Ranger, Texas.*

## CHEESY MEXICAN CHICKEN PIE

1 (1½-pound) broiler-fryer
1 (10-ounce) can enchilada sauce
1 (10¾-ounce) can cream of mushroom
    soup, undiluted
1 large onion, chopped
½ teaspoon garlic salt
Dash of pepper
1 (8½-ounce) package regular corn chips
1 cup (4 ounces) shredded Cheddar cheese

Place chicken in a Dutch oven with water to cover. Bring to a boil; cover and simmer 1 hour or until tender. Remove chicken, reserving 1 cup broth (remaining broth may be reserved for use in other recipes); cool. Remove chicken from bone, and cut into bite-size pieces.

Combine chicken, enchilada sauce, soup, onion, garlic salt, and pepper. Place half of corn chips in a greased 12- x 7- x 2-inch baking dish. Top with chicken mixture, then with remaining corn chips. Sprinkle with cheese; pour chicken broth over casserole. Bake at 350° for 30 minutes. Yield: 6 to 8 servings.

*Phyllis Blue,*
*Slaughters, Kentucky.*

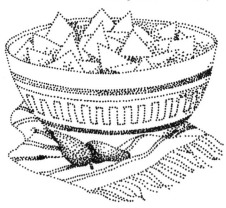

### MEXICAN CHICKEN CASSEROLE

1 (3½-pound) broiler-fryer
2 tablespoons butter or margarine
1 medium onion, chopped
1 green pepper, chopped
1 teaspoon garlic salt
1 (10¾-ounce) can cream of mushroom soup, undiluted
½ cup plus 2 tablespoons tomatoes and green chiles
1½ dozen frozen corn tortillas, thawed
2 cups (8 ounces) shredded Cheddar cheese

Place chicken in a large Dutch oven; add enough water to cover chicken. Bring to a boil; cover and simmer 1 hour or until tender. Remove chicken from Dutch oven, reserving ½ cup broth. Remove chicken from bone, and cut into bite-size pieces. Set aside.

Melt butter in a skillet; add onion, green pepper, and garlic salt. Sauté until tender. Combine onion mixture, soup, reserved chicken broth, and tomatoes and green chiles in a bowl; stir well.

Tear tortillas into bite-size pieces; place half of tortilla pieces in a greased 13- x 9- x 2-inch baking dish. Top with half of soup mixture, then add half of diced chicken. Sprinkle with half of cheese. Repeat layers. Bake at 350° for 30 minutes or until bubbly. Yield: 6 to 8 servings.

*Evalyn Mitchell,*
*Springlake, Texas.*

# Toss A Hearts Of Palm Salad

A Mexican friend introduced Mrs. Dean Piercy of Memphis to hearts of palm in a salad recipe. It's called Different Vegetable Salad—sliced hearts of palm and artichoke hearts make the difference. While Mrs. Piercy prefers the salad with Mexican food, she says it goes well with beef and barbecue pork.

A tropical vegetable with delicate flavor, hearts of palm are actually the young tender buds of a palm tree. In Florida they're available fresh, while in other parts of the country you'll find them in cans.

### DIFFERENT VEGETABLE SALAD

2 avocados, peeled and coarsely chopped
Lemon juice
1 (14-ounce) can hearts of palm, drained and sliced
1 (14-ounce) can artichoke hearts, drained and coarsely chopped
2 large tomatoes, coarsely chopped
2 cucumbers, thinly sliced
⅔ cup vegetable oil
¼ cup vinegar
2 tablespoons water
1 (0.6-ounce) package Italian salad dressing mix
Leafy lettuce (optional)

Sprinkle avocado with lemon juice, tossing to coat avocado. Combine avocado and next 4 ingredients; toss gently. Refrigerate until serving time.

Combine oil, vinegar, water, and salad dressing mix in a jar. Cover tightly, and shake vigorously. Chill. Toss salad with dressing just before serving. Serve on leafy lettuce, if desired. Yield: 8 servings.

*Mrs. Dean Piercy,*
*Memphis, Tennessee.*

# Blueberries, Ice Cream Too

Blueberries are ripe, and summer evenings are warm enough to churn ice cream outside—so it's only natural to think of plump blueberries and homemade ice cream for a cool, tempting summer combination.

Fresh Blueberry Crunch, a cobbler-like dessert baked with a crusty topping of rolled oats, brown sugar, and butter, conceals a juicy layer of fresh blueberries. Combine a hot serving of this fresh fruit dish with a cool mound of our Country Vanilla Ice Cream for a delectable blend of summertime flavors.

### COUNTRY VANILLA ICE CREAM

4 eggs
2¼ cups sugar
1 quart whipping cream
1 tablespoon plus 1½ teaspoons vanilla extract
½ teaspoon salt
5 cups milk

Beat eggs with electric mixer at medium speed until frothy. Gradually add sugar, beating until mixture becomes thick (about 5 minutes). Add remaining ingredients; mix well. Pour into freezer can of a 1-gallon hand-turned or electric freezer; freeze according to manufacturer's instructions. Let ripen at least 1 hour. Yield: about 1 gallon.

*Linda Wilson,*
*Little Rock, Arkansas.*

### BLUEBERRY ICE CREAM MUFFINS

1 cup vanilla ice cream, softened
1 cup self-rising flour
1 cup fresh blueberries

Combine ice cream and flour, stirring just until moistened. Fold in blueberries. Spoon batter into paper-lined miniature muffin pans, filling two-thirds full. Bake at 350° for 20 to 25 minutes. Yield: 1½ dozen muffins.

*Mrs. Rodger Giles,*
*Augusta, Georgia.*

### FRESH BLUEBERRY CRUNCH

4 cups fresh blueberries
1 cup firmly packed brown sugar
¾ cup all-purpose flour
¾ cup regular oats, uncooked
½ cup butter or margarine, melted

Place blueberries in a 2-quart baking dish, spreading evenly. Combine remaining ingredients, and sprinkle over blueberries. Bake at 350° for 45 minutes. Yield: 6 servings.

*Mrs. Paul Raper,*
*Burgaw, North Carolina.*

# Desserts To Cool And Tempt You

Each of these frozen desserts has a special added touch. One is a luscious and easy-to-make blend of vanilla ice cream, lime sherbet, and crème de menthe. Another boasts the refreshing flavor of cantaloupe in a sherbet made in your freezer. And when you're extra busy, try Creamy Peach Freeze. You'll be delighted that anything this good could be so simple!

### CREAMY PEACH FREEZE

1 (1¼-ounce) package whipped topping mix
1 (16-ounce) can sliced peaches, drained

Prepare whipped topping mix according to package directions. Combine whipped topping and peaches in container of electric blender; process until smooth. Spoon into 4 serving dishes, and freeze 2 to 3 hours or until firm. Remove from freezer 5 minutes before serving. Yield: 4 servings.

*Marie Raney,*
*Dogpatch, Arkansas.*

### LIME-MINT REFRESHER

1 (1¼-ounce) package whipped topping mix
½ cup cold milk
½ teaspoon vanilla extract
1 quart vanilla ice cream, softened
1 pint lime sherbet, softened
¼ cup crème de menthe

Combine whipped topping mix, milk, and vanilla; beat until smooth and stiff. Add remaining ingredients; stir well. Freeze. Yield: 10 to 12 servings.

*Mrs. C. B. Smith,*
*White Hall, Maryland.*

### FRUIT CREAM FREEZE

1 (3-ounce) package fruit-flavored gelatin
¼ cup sugar
Dash of salt
1 cup boiling water
1 pint vanilla ice cream, softened
½ cup whipping cream
¼ cup sugar
12 miniature marshmallows cut into quarters or 2 tablespoons chopped marshmallows
2 tablespoons chopped pecans
2 tablespoons flaked coconut

Combine gelatin, ¼ cup sugar, salt, and water; stir until gelatin dissolves. Add ice cream to gelatin; stir to blend.
Beat whipping cream until frothy; gradually add ¼ cup sugar, beating until stiff. Stir whipped cream into gelatin mixture. Freeze 25 minutes or until just firm but not solid; beat with electric mixer until fluffy. Stir in remaining ingredients. Freeze until firm. Yield: 8 servings.

*Carolyn Beyer,*
*Fredericksburg, Texas.*

### FROSTY CANTALOUPE SHERBET

1 envelope unflavored gelatin
½ cup milk
3 cups cantaloupe chunks
1 cup light corn syrup

Combine gelatin and milk in a saucepan; cook, stirring constantly, over low heat until gelatin dissolves. Combine gelatin mixture, cantaloupe, and corn syrup in the container of an electric blender; process on high speed 30 seconds. Pour into a 4-cup freezer container. Cover and freeze overnight.
Let stand at room temperature until slightly softened. Spoon into a large mixing bowl; beat on low speed of electric mixer until smooth (do not overbeat since mixture will melt). Pour into a 4-cup mold or freezer container; cover and freeze until firm. Yield: about 4 cups.
*Note:* Honeydew, watermelon, blueberries, strawberries, nectarines, or peaches may be used instead of cantaloupe. Add 1 tablespoon lemon juice when using peaches or nectarines.

# Tips On Buying Fresh Fruit And Vegetables

Farmers' markets across the South are overflowing with the very freshest of farm-fresh fruit and vegetables. To help ensure that you get the best of what's available, here are some tips on buying.

**Cantaloupe:** To test for ripeness, sniff the stem end for the characteristic aroma. Also look for pronounced netting and a skin color of yellow or tan; if the skin is green beneath the netting, the fruit is not ripe. Should the cantaloupe have a portion of stem still attached, give it a slight tug; if it pulls off, the cantaloupe is ripe.

**Corn:** Puncture a kernel with your thumbnail; if an opaque, milky liquid spurts out, the ear is at its peak of quality. A clear, watery liquid means the corn is immature; if thick and pasty, the ear is overripe and will taste starchy.

**Cucumbers:** Look for those 3 to 8 inches long and 3 inches or less in diameter; firmness also indicates good quality. A yellowish, puffy appearance is a sign of overmaturity. If in doubt about quality, ask the seller to cut one; large seeds and a tough skin indicate the cucumber is past its prime.

**Eggplant:** The smaller they are, the less "seedy" they will be; that's because the seeds will be immature. If the skin of the eggplant is glossy, the fruit is fresh; a dull sheen means the eggplant is either overripe or old.

**Greens:** With all types of greens—turnip greens, spinach, kale, collards, and mustard—the young leaves are the tenderest. Don't buy greens with wilted or yellowing leaves.

**Honeydew melons:** To check for ripeness, sniff for the characteristic aroma. Also, the blossom end of the melon should be slightly soft but not mushy.

**Limas or butterbeans:** The large white or speckled types are at their peak of flavor when the beans are fully formed in the pods. The best test is simply to shell several you think are full; then choose pods with a similar feel. Baby limas or baby butterbeans are immature limas or a small-seeded selection, so don't expect these pods to feel full.

**Okra:** Pods are best when 3 to 4 inches long; longer ones may be tough and stringy. If possible, ask the seller to cut a pod so you can check the seeds; they should be glossy white.

**Peaches:** A good-quality peach is firm but not hard, with no visible bruises or brown spots. For fresh use or freezing, choose peaches with a definite yellowish blush; for canning, purchase fruit that has a slightly greenish color.

**Peppers:** Size is no indication of quality. Look for peppers with smooth, slick skin that has not shriveled.

**Snap beans:** The younger bush beans are, the better. Those 3 to 6 inches long are best; larger ones may be tough and stringy. Pole beans are best when 4 to 6 inches long, and the seeds inside have not developed (indicated by flat pods rather than round ones).

**Southern peas:** Pod color is the key to choosing flavorful peas. Purple-podded selections are best when the ends and almost half of the pod have turned from green to purple. If the pod is completely purple, the peas are too dry for maximum flavor. Other types of Southern peas are best when the pods begin to show a color change. Green pods may be hard to shell, but the peas inside are at their peak of flavor. If the peas rattle inside the pods, they are much too dry to taste good. Peas that have been iced down should be carefully checked; if they feel mushy, don't buy them.

**Summer squash:** Size is the best sign of peak flavor. While large fruit is edible, it is generally seedy and less flavorful than smaller fruit. Yellow squash is best when 4 to 6 inches long and smooth skinned; zucchini, 6 to 8 inches long and shiny skinned; pattypan, 4 to 6 inches in diameter and a shiny-white skin color.

**Tomatoes:** Buy tomatoes that are brightly colored and firm. If soft, overcolored, or the skin is crinkly, they are overripe. Size is no indication of quality or flavor.

**Watermelon:** One of the best signs of ripeness is when the typically shiny surface becomes dull and the bottom of the melon turns from whitish to creamy yellow. The thump test (when a thump produces a muffled sound) may not be accurate because overripe melons make the same sound.

**Winter squash:** These squash are mature when you cannot pierce the skin with your thumbnail. Softening skin often means that the squash is old and past its peak.

# Fruit Salads On The Frosty Side

If a fruit salad seems to suit your menu, and a cool touch is in order, consider serving a frozen fruit salad. Choose the fruit and texture you prefer from our selection of recipes.

Frozen Waldorf Salad is much like its traditional refrigerated version—brimming with apples, celery, walnuts, and pineapple. For something different with peach halves, fill them with a banana concoction, freeze, then top with a whipped cream dressing.

We found that frozen salads are easier to slice when allowed to thaw a short period (even as much as 20 to 30 minutes in some cases) before serving. Any leftover salad should be refrozen as quickly as possible.

## FROZEN WALDORF SALAD

1 (8-ounce) can crushed pineapple
2 eggs, beaten
½ cup sugar
⅛ teaspoon salt
¼ cup lemon juice
½ cup chopped celery
2 medium apples, chopped
½ cup chopped walnuts
1 cup whipping cream, whipped

Drain pineapple, reserving juice. Add enough water to reserved pineapple juice to measure ½ cup, if necessary.

Combine juice mixture and next 4 ingredients in a medium saucepan; mix well. Cook over medium heat until thickened, stirring constantly; cool. Add pineapple, celery, apples, and walnuts; toss well. Fold in whipped cream.

Spoon mixture into an 8-inch square pan; cover and freeze until firm. To serve, let stand at room temperature 20 to 30 minutes; cut into squares. Yield: 9 servings.

*Elizabeth Moore,*
*Huntsville, Alabama.*

## PARTY FREEZE SALAD

1 (8-ounce) package cream cheese, softened
¼ cup honey
1 (10-ounce) package frozen sliced strawberries, partially thawed
2 medium bananas, sliced
2 cups miniature marshmallows
1 cup whipping cream, whipped

Beat cream cheese until smooth; add honey, and mix well. Add fruit and marshmallows, tossing gently to coat. Fold in whipped cream.

Spoon mixture into a 9-inch square pan; cover and freeze until firm. To serve, let stand at room temperature 20 to 30 minutes, and cut into squares. Yield: 9 servings. *Mrs. John Rucker,*
*Louisville, Kentucky.*

## FROSTED PEACH SALAD

1 (29-ounce) can peach halves, drained
1 large banana, mashed
¼ cup chopped pecans or walnuts
1 tablespoon powdered sugar
1 teaspoon lemon juice
Lettuce (optional)
Whipped Cream Salad Dressing

Place peach halves in a greased muffin pan. Combine next 4 ingredients, and mix well. Mound mixture in peach cavities, and freeze until firm.

To serve, remove peach halves from freezer; let stand at room temperature 20 to 30 minutes. Serve on lettuce, if desired, and top with Whipped Cream Salad Dressing. Yield: 6 to 8 servings.

*Whipped Cream Salad Dressing:*

½ cup whipping cream
2 tablespoons powdered sugar
2 teaspoons lemon juice

Beat whipping cream until foamy; gradually add powdered sugar, beating until soft peaks form. Fold in lemon juice. Yield: about 1 cup.

*Amelia M. Brown,*
*Pittsburgh, Pennsylvania.*

## FRUITY LEMON FREEZE

2 (3-ounce) packages cream cheese, softened
½ cup mayonnaise
2 teaspoons lemon juice
1 teaspoon lemon extract
1 (8-ounce) can crushed pineapple, drained
½ cup maraschino cherries, diced
½ cup chopped pecans
2 cups sliced banana
1 cup whipping cream
¼ cup sugar
Lettuce (optional)
Pineapple slices, halved (optional)
Maraschino cherries, halved (optional)
Lemon twists (optional)

Beat cream cheese until smooth; add next 3 ingredients, and mix well. Stir in pineapple, cherries, and pecans. Add bananas, tossing gently to coat.

Beat whipping cream until foamy; gradually add sugar, beating until soft peaks form. Fold into fruit mixture. Spoon mixture into a 9- x 5- x 3-inch loafpan; cover and freeze until firm.

To serve, unmold salad on lettuce, and garnish with pineapple slices, cherries, and lemon twists, if desired. Let stand at room temperature 20 to 30 minutes before serving. Yield: 10 servings.

*Teresa Poston,*
*Golden, Texas.*

# Add Some Cottage Cheese

If cottage cheese isn't regularly found in your refrigerator, you may not be aware of the versatility and nutrition it has to offer. High in protein and low in calories, cottage cheese adds texture and flavor to recipes ranging from cheese blintzes to a squash soufflé.

For a special breakfast or dessert, give Cheese Blintzes a try. Crêpes are folded around a creamy cottage cheese filling and topped with sour cream and strawberry preserves. A blend of Cheddar and cottage cheese adds to the rich yet delicate flavor of Cheesy Squash Soufflé.

Refrigerate cottage cheese in a tightly covered container, and use it within one week after purchase unless the date on the package indicates otherwise.

## CHEESE BLINTZES

2 (3-ounce) packages cream cheese, softened
1 (12-ounce) carton dry-curd cottage cheese
1 egg, beaten
2 tablespoons sugar
1 teaspoon grated lemon rind
Crêpes (recipe follows)
3 tablespoons butter or margarine, divided
Commercial sour cream
Strawberry preserves
Fresh strawberries (optional)

Combine cream cheese and cottage cheese; beat until smooth. Stir in next 3 ingredients; chill 15 to 20 minutes.

Spoon about 3 tablespoons cheese filling in center of each crêpe. Fold right and left sides over filling; then fold bottom and top over filling, forming a square.

Melt 2 tablespoons butter in a large skillet. Place half of blintzes in skillet, seam side down. Cook over medium heat until lightly browned, turning once; remove from skillet, and keep warm. Melt remaining tablespoon butter in skillet; repeat procedure with the remaining blintzes. Serve with sour cream and strawberry preserves. Garnish blintzes with fresh strawberries, if desired. Yield: 12 servings.

*Crêpes:*

1 cup all-purpose flour
½ teaspoon salt
1¼ cups milk
2 eggs, beaten
2 tablespoons butter or margarine, melted
Vegetable oil

Combine first 3 ingredients, beating until smooth. Add the eggs, and beat well; stir in butter. Refrigerate batter 1 hour. (This allows the flour particles to swell and soften so the crêpes will be light in texture.)

Brush the bottom of a 6- or 7-inch crêpe pan or heavy skillet with vegetable oil; place pan over medium heat until just hot, not smoking.

Pour 2 tablespoons batter into pan; quickly tilt pan in all directions so batter covers the pan with a thin film. Cook about 1 minute.

Lift edge of crêpe to test for doneness. Crêpe is ready for flipping when it can be shaken loose from pan. Flip crêpe, and cook about 30 seconds on other side (this side is rarely more than spotty brown and is the side on which the filling is placed).

Place crêpes on a towel, and allow to cool. Stack the crêpes between layers of waxed paper to prevent sticking. Yield: 12 crêpes. *Jane C. Webb,*
*Norris, Tennessee.*

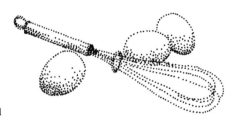

## CHEESY SQUASH SOUFFLE

1½ pounds yellow squash
1 tablespoon salt
1 tablespoon butter or margarine
½ cup finely chopped onion
4 eggs, beaten
¾ cup cream-style cottage cheese
½ cup (2 ounces) shredded Cheddar cheese
½ cup soft breadcrumbs
1 tablespoon butter or margarine, melted
1 teaspoon chopped fresh parsley
⅛ teaspoon pepper

Cut squash in half lengthwise; scoop out seeds. Coarsely grate squash; sprinkle with salt, and let stand 20 minutes. Place squash in a colander; rinse well, and drain. Press squash between paper towels until barely moist.

Melt 1 tablespoon butter in a large heavy skillet; sauté onion until tender. Remove from heat; add squash and remaining ingredients, mixing well. Pour into a lightly greased 1¾-quart baking dish; bake at 350° for 45 minutes or until golden. Yield: 6 servings.
*Betty R. Butts,*
*Kensington, Maryland.*

## EGGS MEXICANA

5 eggs, beaten
2 tablespoons butter or margarine, melted
¼ cup all-purpose flour
½ teaspoon baking powder
1 (8-ounce) carton cream-style cottage cheese
2 cups (8 ounces) shredded Monterey Jack cheese
1 (4-ounce) can chopped green chiles, drained

Combine first 4 ingredients in a medium mixing bowl; beat well. Stir in remaining ingredients, and pour into a well-greased 9-inch pieplate.

Bake at 400° for 10 minutes; reduce heat to 350°, and bake about 20 minutes or until set. Cut into wedges to serve. Yield: 6 servings. *Mrs. D. B. Stewart,*
*Littleton, Colorado.*

## COTTAGE-EGG SALAD SPREAD

6 hard-cooked eggs, chopped
1 (8-ounce) carton cream-style cottage cheese
1 teaspoon chopped chives
½ to 1 teaspoon dried whole dillweed
½ teaspoon dry mustard
¼ teaspoon salt
¼ teaspoon pepper

Combine all ingredients; mix well. Cover and chill. Serve as a sandwich spread. Yield: about 2 cups.
*Martha Edington,*
*Oak Ridge, Tennessee.*

## LEMON CHEESE PIE

2 eggs, separated
2 cups cream-style cottage cheese
¾ cup sugar
¼ teaspoon salt
¾ cup milk
1 (4¼-ounce) package egg custard mix
3 tablespoons butter or margarine, melted
1 teaspoon vanilla extract
¼ teaspoon lemon extract
1 unbaked 9-inch deep-dish pastry shell
Sliced strawberries (optional)

Beat egg yolks. Add cottage cheese, sugar, and salt; beat until smooth. Stir in next 5 ingredients.

Beat egg whites (at room temperature) until soft peaks form; fold into custard mixture. Pour mixture into pastry shell, and bake at 325° for 1 hour and 10 minutes or until filling is set. Chill. Top pie with sliced strawberries, if desired. Yield: one 9-inch pie.
*Lynne G. Wilkerson,*
*Livonia, Michigan.*

# July

In July, Southerners pull out jelly jars to pack away fresh summer flavors in jams, jellies, preserves, and marmalades. You'll find preserving tips in this chapter as well as recipes for old favorites like Apple Jelly, Blackberry Jam, and Old-Fashioned Peach Preserves. Orange-Pineapple Marmalade was something different for us—we loved the tangy citrus taste.

When the jelly making is finished, it's time to think about what to serve for supper. And once again, our *Summer Suppers* special section offers sizzling suggestions for cookouts, picnics, and other warm weather meals. We have some ideas for cooling off, too. How about serving a refreshing cold vegetable soup as an appetizer or chilling a dessert to top off the meal?

Ice cream parties are always popular summertime events. Churn a gallon of our Vanilla Ice Cream Spectacular and invite friends in to "build your own sundae." Our delicious toppings like Heavenly Chocolate Sauce, Fruity Dessert Topping, Sugared Pecans, and Whole Wheat Granola will start friendly competition to make the most impressive ice cream creation.

# Another Piece Of Fried Chicken, Please

What better picnic fare could you ask for than cold fried chicken with tossed salad and ice-cold watermelon. Whatever accompaniments your picnic includes, classic Southern fried chicken, with its crisp, savory crust and tender, juicy meat, is sure to be the center of attention.

And when it comes to making fried chicken, just ask a group of Southerners how they do it and you'll surely start an argument. Recipes vary within each state, neighborhood, and from family to family. Some keep it simple by just sprinkling the chicken with salt and pepper and then dredging it in flour. But others, like Jacquelyn Christopher of Asheville, North Carolina, prefer to shake the chicken in a bag of flour seasoned with salt, pepper, poultry seasoning, and a little paprika. One Alabama cook likes to soak chicken in a mixture of buttermilk and garlic before dredging it in flour.

Once the chicken is coated, how do you attain that crusty, golden exterior? Linda Whitt of Missouri City, Texas, says, "I brown my chicken quickly in a skillet and then bake it in the oven for the last 30 minutes." On the other hand, Maxie Young of Delray Beach, Florida, says, "I heat about an inch of oil until it's bubbly and fry the chicken to a nice brown color. You have to watch it carefully and turn it after about 15 minutes to prevent burning."

And then there is the question of whether to cover the chicken during frying. Some feel that the cover assures even cooking. Others believe an open skillet gives the chicken an extra-crispy crust that adheres better.

## TRADITIONAL FRIED CHICKEN

2 cups milk
2 eggs, beaten
2 tablespoons butter or margarine, melted
2 teaspoons paprika
1½ teaspoons salt
1 teaspoon pepper
1 (2½- to 3-pound) broiler-fryer, cut up and skinned
Additional pepper
All-purpose flour
Vegetable oil

Combine first 6 ingredients; mix well. Place chicken in a shallow pan, and pour milk mixture over top; refrigerate at least 15 minutes. Remove chicken from liquid. Sprinkle lightly with additional pepper, and dredge in flour. Let stand 5 minutes.

Heat 1 inch of oil in a large skillet to 325°; add chicken and fry 30 minutes or until golden brown, turning once. Drain on paper towels. Yield: 4 servings.
*Maxie Young,*
*Delray Beach, Florida.*

## GARLIC FRIED CHICKEN

1½ cups buttermilk
2 tablespoons lemon juice
2 cloves garlic, crushed
½ teaspoon salt
¼ teaspoon pepper
¼ teaspoon celery salt
1 (2½- to 3-pound) broiler-fryer, cut up and skinned
1 cup all-purpose flour
Vegetable oil

Combine first 6 ingredients; mix well. Place chicken in a shallow pan, and pour buttermilk mixture over top. Cover and refrigerate at least 3 hours or overnight.

Remove chicken from liquid. Dredge chicken in flour.

Heat 1 inch of oil in a large skillet to 325°; add chicken and fry 30 to 35 minutes, turning once. Drain chicken well on paper towels. Yield: 4 servings.
*Betty Nelson,*
*Dothan, Alabama.*

## SPICY COUNTRY-FRIED CHICKEN

1 cup all-purpose flour
2 teaspoons garlic salt
2 teaspoons pepper
1 teaspoon paprika
½ teaspoon poultry seasoning
½ cup milk
1 egg, beaten
1 (2½- to 3-pound) broiler-fryer, cut up and skinned
Vegetable oil

Combine first 5 ingredients in a plastic or paper bag; shake to mix, and set aside. Combine milk and egg; mix well.

Place 2 or 3 pieces of chicken in bag; shake well. Dip chicken in egg mixture; return to bag and shake again. Repeat procedure with remaining chicken.

Heat 1 inch of oil in a large skillet to 325°; add chicken and fry 30 to 35 minutes or until golden brown, turning once. Drain chicken on paper towels. Yield: 4 servings.
*Jacquelyn Christopher,*
*Asheville, North Carolina.*

## OVEN-FRIED PARMESAN CHICKEN

1 cup round buttery cracker crumbs
½ cup grated Parmesan cheese
2 tablespoons chopped fresh parsley
1 (2½- to 3-pound) broiler-fryer, cut up
½ cup butter or margarine, melted

Combine first 3 ingredients; mix well. Dip chicken in butter; dredge in cracker crumb mixture. Place chicken in a lightly greased 13- x 9- x 2-inch baking dish. Bake, uncovered, at 350° for 1 hour. Yield: 4 servings.
*Mrs. Ruby Vineyard,*
*Rutledge, Tennessee.*

## SESAME CHICKEN

1 egg, beaten
¼ cup milk
½ cup fine, dry breadcrumbs
¼ cup sesame seeds
¾ teaspoon salt
¼ teaspoon pepper
3 whole chicken breasts, split, skinned, and boned
½ cup all-purpose flour
Vegetable oil

Combine egg and milk; stir well. Combine breadcrumbs, sesame seeds, salt, and pepper, stirring well. Dredge chicken in flour; dip in egg mixture, and dredge in breadcrumb mixture.

Heat 1 inch of oil in a large skillet to 325°; add chicken, and fry 5 minutes on each side. Drain on paper towels. Yield: 6 servings.   *Mary Ann Lewis,*
*Houston, Texas.*

## SUPER FRIED CHICKEN

2 cups pancake mix
2 (0.7-ounce) packages Italian salad dressing mix, divided
⅓ cup club soda
1 egg, beaten
3 pounds chicken pieces, skinned
Vegetable oil

Combine pancake mix and 1 package salad dressing mix; mix well, and set aside. Combine club soda, egg, and remaining salad dressing mix; stir well. Dip chicken in club soda mixture; dredge in pancake mixture. Allow chicken to drain 5 minutes.

Heat 2 inches of oil in a large skillet to 400°; add chicken, and fry 3 to 5 minutes or until golden brown.

Place chicken on a lightly greased jellyroll pan; bake, uncovered, at 350° for 30 minutes. Yield: 4 servings.
*Linda Whitt,*
*Missouri City, Texas.*

# It's Jelly-Making Time

Along with enjoying the fresh fruit of summer straight from the tree or sweetened with sugar in a tasty cobbler, plan to extend that enjoyment by capturing their luscious flavors in a jam or jelly. Or try your hand at marmalade, preserves, or a jamlike conserve. There's at least one example of each in our collection of recipes, with fruit flavors ranging from strawberry and blueberry to peach and plum.

To help get you started off right when preserving fruit, here are some things you need to know.

## The Ingredients

Start with only top-quality fruit. When preparing the fruit, remove any damaged parts, along with the caps, stems, and blossom ends.

Some types of fruit contain enough natural pectin to make a gel; with others, you'll need to add commercial pectin. It comes in either liquid or powder form, but the two are not interchangeable; use what's called for in the recipe.

Follow the recipe exactly, measuring all ingredients accurately. Don't cut back on the sugar; it's necessary for proper gel formation with the pectin.

## Equipment and Containers

In making jams and jellies, it's essential to use a flat-bottom kettle large enough to allow the mixture to double or triple in size as it comes to a rolling boil. You'll also need a jelly or candy thermometer for recipes that suggest a cooking temperature for the mixture.

Use a jelly bag to strain juice from the fruit pulp when making jelly. The bag can be made of several thicknesses of cheesecloth or cotton flannel with the napped side turned inward. Place the jelly bag inside a colander or strainer while extracting the juice. Don't be tempted to squeeze the bag; you may cloud the jelly.

You'll need a funnel for pouring the prepared fruit mixture into jars. This helps to keep the jar rims clean.

Also have on hand a boiling-water bath canner to process any jellied fruit product that contains pieces of fruit, such as jams, marmalades, preserves, and conserves.

You may pack jelly in jelly glasses if paraffin will be used for sealing. But with jams and other preserves containing pieces of fruit, standard canning jars and lids must be used. Check the recipe for jar sizes so that processing time will be correct. Jars and glasses are reusable, provided they are in perfect condition. You may also reuse the metal bands, but always purchase new lids to ensure an adequate seal.

Before beginning any preparation of fruit, wash the jars, metal bands, and lids in hot soapy water, and rinse well in hot water. Cover with water in a large kettle, and boil for 10 minutes to sterilize; keep hot until ready for filling.

## Packing and Sealing

When **sealing with lids,** fill the hot jar to within ¼ inch of the top with hot fruit mixture. Wipe the jar rim clean, and place a metal lid on the jar with the sealing compound next to the glass. Screw the metal band firmly in place. Process jams or other products containing pieces of fruit in a boiling-water bath; jellies need not be processed.

After jars stand overnight, check each to see if a proper seal has been made (follow manufacturer's directions). If a seal was not made, store the product in the refrigerator; eat within a few weeks.

Glasses or jars of jelly may be **sealed with paraffin** instead of metal lids. Pour the hot fruit mixture into hot, sterilized jars, filling to within ½ inch of the top. Cover immediately with a ⅛-inch layer of hot paraffin (melted in the top of a double boiler). Prick air bubbles in the paraffin before it becomes firm, and cover the jars with lids.

After sealing, label each jar with the name of the jellied product and date; store in a cool, dark, dry place. Do not hold in storage longer than a year.

## APPLE JELLY

6 pounds apples, stemmed and coarsely
  chopped
6 cups water
3 cups sugar
2 tablespoons lemon juice

Combine apples and water in a large Dutch oven; bring to a boil. Cover, reduce heat, and simmer 20 to 25 minutes. Strain apples through a jelly bag or 4 layers of cheesecloth, reserving 4 cups juice. Discard pulp.

Combine 4 cups juice, sugar, and lemon juice in Dutch oven; bring to a rolling boil, stirring frequently. Boil until mixture reaches 220° on candy thermometer, stirring frequently. Remove Dutch oven from heat, and skim off foam with a metal spoon.

Quickly pour jelly into hot sterilized jars, leaving ½-inch headspace. Seal with a ⅛-inch layer of paraffin, and cover with lids. Yield: about 4 half pints.

## BLACKBERRY JELLY

4 to 6 quarts blackberries
7½ cups sugar
2 (3-ounce) packages liquid fruit pectin

Press enough blackberries through a sieve to extract 4 cups juice.

Combine 4 cups juice and sugar in a Dutch oven; bring to a rolling boil. Cook 1 minute, stirring frequently. Add fruit pectin, and bring to a boil; continue boiling 1 minute, stirring frequently. Remove from heat, and skim off foam with a metal spoon.

Quickly pour jelly into hot sterilized jars, leaving ½-inch headspace. Seal with a ⅛-inch layer of paraffin, and cover with lids. Yield: about 7 half pints.

## BLACKBERRY JAM

9 cups (about 4 pounds) crushed
  blackberries
6 cups sugar

Combine blackberries and sugar in a large Dutch oven; slowly bring to a boil, stirring occasionally until sugar dissolves. Boil 30 to 40 minutes, stirring frequently, until jam reaches desired consistency. Skim off foam with a metal spoon.

Quickly ladle jam into hot sterilized jars, leaving ¼-inch headspace; cover at once with metal lids, and screw bands tight. Process in boiling-water bath 15 minutes. Yield: 3 pints.

## BLUEBERRY CONSERVE

4 cups sugar
2 cups water
½ orange, thinly sliced
½ lemon, thinly sliced
1 quart blueberries

Combine sugar and water in a large Dutch oven; bring to a boil. Stir in orange and lemon slices; simmer, uncovered, 5 minutes. Add blueberries; cook over medium-high heat 40 minutes or until thick, stirring frequently.

Quickly ladle conserve into hot sterilized jars, leaving ¼-inch headspace; cover at once with metal lids, and screw bands tight. Process in boiling-water bath 15 minutes. Yield: 4 half pints.

## FIG PRESERVES

2 quarts (about 4½ pounds) figs
7 cups sugar
¼ cup lemon juice
6 cups water
2 lemons, thinly sliced

Cook figs 15 to 20 minutes in enough boiling water to cover; drain figs, and set aside.

Combine sugar, lemon juice, and 6 cups water in a large Dutch oven; cook over medium heat, stirring constantly, until sugar dissolves. Add figs; return to a boil and cook 10 minutes, stirring occasionally. Add lemon slices, and boil 15 minutes or until figs are tender and clear.

Carefully remove figs from syrup with a slotted spoon; boil syrup an additional 10 minutes or until desired thickness. Return figs to syrup; skim off foam with a metal spoon.

Quickly ladle preserves into hot sterilized jars, leaving ¼-inch headspace; cover at once with metal lids, and screw bands tight. Process in boiling-water bath 30 minutes. Yield: 5 half pints.

## PLUM JELLY

6 pounds plums, pitted and finely chopped
1½ cups water
1 (1¾-ounce) package powdered fruit pectin
7½ cups sugar

Combine plums and water in a large Dutch oven; cover and simmer 10 minutes, stirring occasionally. Remove from heat. Process plum mixture (undrained) in food mill; then strain through jelly bag or 4 layers of cheesecloth, reserving 5½ cups juice. Discard pulp.

Combine 5½ cups juice and pectin in Dutch oven, stirring well; bring to a rolling boil, stirring frequently. Add sugar, and return to a rolling boil; boil 1 minute, stirring frequently. Remove from heat, and skim off foam with a metal spoon.

Quickly ladle jelly into hot sterilized jars, leaving ½-inch headspace. Seal with a ⅛-inch layer of paraffin, and cover with lids. Yield: 4 pints.

## OLD-FASHIONED PEACH PRESERVES

2 quarts peeled, sliced peaches
6 cups sugar

Combine peaches and sugar in a large, shallow glass or plastic container. Cover and let stand in a cool place for 12 to 18 hours.

Pour peach mixture into a large Dutch oven; slowly bring to a boil, stirring frequently. Boil gently until peaches become transparent and syrup thickens (1½ to 2 hours), stirring frequently to prevent sticking. Skim off the foam with a metal spoon.

Quickly ladle preserves into hot sterilized jars, leaving ¼-inch headspace; cover at once with metal lids, and screw bands tight. Process in boiling-water bath 15 minutes. Yield: about 7 half pints.

## PEACH-ORANGE MARMALADE

2 quarts peeled, chopped peaches
¾ cup thinly sliced orange rind
1½ cups chopped orange sections
2 tablespoons lemon juice
5 cups sugar

Combine all ingredients in a large Dutch oven; slowly bring to a boil, stirring occasionally until sugar dissolves. Boil about 40 minutes or until thickened, stirring frequently to prevent sticking. Remove from heat, and skim off foam with a metal spoon.

Quickly pour marmalade into hot sterilized jars, leaving ¼-inch headspace; cover at once with metal lids, and screw bands tight. Process marmalade in boiling-water bath 15 minutes. Yield: 5 half pints.

## ORANGE-PINEAPPLE MARMALADE

6 oranges, thinly sliced
1 lemon, thinly sliced
4 cups water
3 medium-size fresh pineapples
About 8 cups sugar

Combine orange slices, lemon slices, and water in a large Dutch oven. Bring to a boil; cover, reduce heat, and simmer 1 hour. Let stand, covered, 12 to 18 hours in a cool place.

Remove leaves and stem end from pineapples. Peel pineapples, and trim out eyes; remove core. Chop pineapple, and measure 6 cups; reserve remaining pineapple for other uses.

Add 6 cups pineapple to orange mixture. Bring to a boil; boil rapidly, uncovered, about 20 minutes. Measure fruit mixture, including liquid; add 1 cup sugar per 1 cup fruit mixture. Stir well, and bring to a boil. Boil rapidly 25 to 30 minutes or until mixture registers 220° on candy thermometer; stir mixture frequently.

Quickly pour marmalade into hot sterilized jars, leaving ¼-inch headspace; cover at once with metal lids, and screw bands tight. Process marmalade in boiling-water bath 10 minutes. Yield: 9 half pints.

## STRAWBERRY PRESERVES DELUXE

1½ quarts strawberries
5 cups sugar
⅓ cup lemon juice

Wash and hull strawberries. Combine strawberries and sugar in a large Dutch oven; mix well, and let stand 3 to 4 hours.

Slowly bring strawberry mixture to a boil, stirring occasionally until sugar dissolves. Stir in lemon juice. Boil about 12 minutes or until berries are clear, stirring occasionally. Remove from heat, and skim off foam with a metal spoon.

Carefully remove fruit from syrup with a slotted spoon, and place in a shallow pan. Bring syrup to a boil; cook about 10 minutes or until syrup has thickened to desired consistency. Pour syrup over fruit. Let stand, uncovered, 12 to 24 hours in a cool place. Shake pan occasionally (do not stir) so the berries will absorb syrup and remain plump and whole. Skim off foam with a metal spoon.

Ladle preserves into hot sterilized jars, leaving ¼-inch headspace; cover at once with metal lids, and screw bands tight. Process in boiling-water bath 20 minutes. Yield: 4 half pints.

Right: *Surrounded with colorful fresh vegetables, a leafy, red cabbage serves as an unusual container for Spinach Dip in Cabbage (page 155). It's pretty enough to be a centerpiece.*

Page 154: *These fresh fruit desserts are all attractively served: Frozen Cantaloupe Cream (page 159) in tall parfaits, Strawberries With Brandied Orange Juice (page 160) in a clear glass basket, and Sherbet Ambrosia Cups (page 159) in natural orange shells.*

Far left: *For the ideal Southern picnic, team cold Spicy Country-Fried Chicken (page 148) with salad, watermelon, and a pretty summer day.*

Above: *Cold soups are an attractive addition to summer meals. From top: Curried Carrot Soup, Cold Strawberry Soup, Saucy Gazpacho, and Cucumber-Yogurt Soup (recipes on page 157).*

Left: *Lemon rind and juice perk up the flavor of Lemony New Potatoes (page 158).*

# summer Suppers.

## Gear Up For Summer Food And Fun

With the arrival of summer, the South begins blossoming with outdoor activities. Grills are readied for firing, baskets are filled with fresh vegetables from backyard gardens, and ice cream churns start turning. Most of all, it's a time for friends and family to gather for relaxing get-togethers.

Sometimes the occasion calls for a complete meal, or at other times it can simply revolve around tasty appetizers and a refreshing beverage. Regardless, food is generally the focus. That's why we've put together this special section of recipes and party ideas—to give you a fresh approach to all of your summertime entertaining.

We begin by heading to Anniston, Alabama, for a picnic—but this isn't your everyday picnic. It takes lots of planning to carry off the elaborate country-style spread organized by Margaret Wakefield, Jean Willett, Evie Connors, and Martha Cater. Each year, following the Museum Day Festival at the city's Museum of Natural History, these ladies invite friends to join them near a local lake to share an afternoon of old-fashioned fun.

Everyone settles back with an icy glass of Lemon Tea while last-minute touches are added to the meal. And what a spread it is. A leafy, red cabbage serves as a colorful container for Spinach Dip, surrounded with an assortment of fresh vegetables.

Equally colorful is Chilled Tomato Soup, which is poured from a glass pitcher into plastic cups so it will be easy to sip along with the meal. This picnic also has its own touch of the South, provided by a hearty Menfolks' Cornbread and black-eyed peas chilled in a tangy marinade.

But the focal point of the menu is Saucy Barbecued Beef tucked into Nannie's Biscuits. Before this picnic is over, most folks will have had at least two of these miniature sandwiches. Serving is made easier by assembling the beef and biscuits ahead of time and packing them in a basket.

You might not expect dessert with this lavish array of food, but three delectable choices are offered: Fruit Kabobs With Mint Marinade, Blond Nut Squares, and Lemon Tarts.

---

**Spinach Dip in Cabbage**
**Chilled Tomato Soup**
**Lemon Tea**
**Marinated Black-Eyed Peas**
**Menfolks' Cornbread**
**Saucy Barbecued Beef**
**Nannie's Biscuits**
**Blond Nut Squares**     **Lemon Tarts**
**Fruit Kabobs With Mint Marinade**

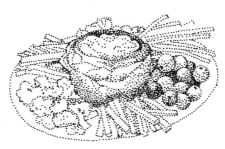

### SPINACH DIP IN CABBAGE

3 (10-ounce) packages frozen chopped
  spinach
1 cup chopped green onion
1 (16-ounce) carton commercial sour
  cream
2 cups mayonnaise
2 teaspoons herb-seasoned salt
1½ teaspoons dried whole oregano
1 teaspoon dried whole dillweed
Juice of 1 lemon
1 large red cabbage

Cook spinach according to package directions; drain well, and stir in next 7 ingredients. Chill.

Trim core end of cabbage to form a flat base. Cut a crosswise slice from the top, making it wide enough to remove about a fourth of the head; lift out enough inner leaves from the cabbage to form a shell about 1 inch thick. (Reserve slice and inner leaves of cabbage for use in other recipes.)

Spoon dip into cavity of cabbage, and serve with an assortment of fresh vegetables. Yield: about 6 cups.

### CHILLED TOMATO SOUP

9 cups tomato juice
¼ cup plus 2 tablespoons tomato paste
Grated rind of 1½ limes
¼ cup plus 2 tablespoons lime juice
6 small green onions, minced
1½ teaspoons sugar
1 teaspoon salt
1½ teaspoons curry powder
¾ teaspoon ground thyme
¼ teaspoon hot sauce
1 (16-ounce) carton commercial sour
  cream
Chopped fresh parsley

Combine first 10 ingredients in a large pitcher, stirring well; chill 4 to 6 hours.

Add sour cream to tomato mixture, beating with a wire whisk until blended. Garnish each serving with parsley. Yield: about 12 cups.
*Note:* Recipe may be doubled.

*Tip: Make certain your refrigerator or freezer is cold enough. Refrigerator temperature should be maintained at 34°F to 40°F and freezer temperature at 0°F or lower. To allow the cold air to circulate freely, foods should not be overcrowded.*

## LEMON TEA

6 quarts water
4 quart-size tea bags
1 cup sugar
2 (12-ounce) cans frozen lemonade
    concentrate, thawed and undiluted
Fresh mint leaves (optional)
Lemon slices (optional)

Bring water to a boil, and add tea bags. Remove from heat; cover and let stand 20 minutes. Add sugar and lemonade concentrate, stirring until dissolved. Add mint leaves, if desired. Serve over ice; garnish with lemon slices, if desired. Yield: about 7 quarts.

## MARINATED BLACK-EYED PEAS

3 (15-ounce) cans black-eyed peas, drained
1 cup vegetable oil
½ cup wine vinegar
¼ cup chopped onion
1 teaspoon garlic salt
⅛ teaspoon pepper
4 dashes of hot sauce
Onion rings
Green pepper rings

Combine first 7 ingredients in a large bowl, stirring well. Cover and marinate in refrigerator 3 days. To serve, garnish with onion rings and green pepper rings. Serve with slotted spoon. Yield: about 6 cups.

## MENFOLKS' CORNBREAD

2¼ cups yellow cornbread mix
3 tablespoons sugar
½ cup vegetable oil
3 eggs, beaten
1 (8½-ounce) can cream-style corn
1½ cups (6 ounces) shredded Longhorn
    cheese
1 large onion, grated
2 large canned jalapeño peppers, seeded
    and chopped

Combine all ingredients, mixing well. Heat a well-greased 13- x 9- x 2-inch baking pan in 400° oven for 3 minutes or until very hot.

Pour batter into hot pan, and bake at 450° for 20 minutes or until cornbread is golden brown. Cut bread into 2-inch squares to serve. Yield: about 2 dozen.

## SAUCY BARBECUED BEEF

1 (1½- to 2-pound) beef chuck roast
1 (8-ounce) can tomato sauce
1 (10½-ounce) can consommé,
    undiluted
1 large onion, chopped
1 cup catsup
¼ cup cider vinegar
¼ cup lemon juice
¼ cup chili sauce
¼ cup orange marmalade
2 tablespoons chopped fresh parsley
2 tablespoons frozen orange juice
    concentrate, thawed and undiluted
1 tablespoon Worcestershire sauce
2 teaspoons paprika
2 teaspoons chili powder
¼ teaspoon dried whole oregano
⅛ teaspoon garlic salt
Dash of hot sauce

Place roast in a Dutch oven; add water to cover, and bring to a boil. Cover, reduce heat, and simmer 1 hour. Remove cover, and cook an additional hour over low heat; drain. Remove and discard all fat and bone from roast; chop meat, and set aside.

Combine remaining ingredients in Dutch oven; bring to a boil, stirring sauce often. Add meat to sauce; reduce heat and simmer, uncovered, 1 to 1½ hours.

Serve barbecue with Nannie's Biscuits (recipe follows). Yield: about 5½ cups.

## NANNIE'S BISCUITS

⅔ cup shortening
1½ cups self-rising flour
⅔ cup buttermilk

Cut shortening into flour with a pastry blender until mixture resembles coarse meal. Add buttermilk, stirring with a fork until dry ingredients are moistened. Turn dough out on a lightly floured surface, and lightly knead 4 or 5 times.

Roll dough to ½-inch thickness, and cut with a 1½-inch biscuit cutter. Place biscuits on a lightly greased baking sheet; bake at 425° for 12 minutes or until golden brown.

Serve biscuits with Saucy Barbecued Beef (above). Yield: 3½ dozen.

## BLOND NUT SQUARES

¼ cup plus 2 tablespoons butter or
    margarine, softened
1 cup firmly packed brown sugar
1 egg
1 teaspoon vanilla extract
1 cup all-purpose flour
¼ teaspoon baking soda
¼ teaspoon salt
½ cup chopped pecans
½ cup semisweet chocolate morsels

Cream butter; gradually add sugar, beating well. Add the egg and vanilla; beat well.

Combine flour, baking soda, and salt; gradually add to creamed mixture, mixing well. Stir in chopped pecans and chocolate morsels.

Spread batter in a lightly greased 12- x 7½- x 1½-inch baking pan. Bake at 350° for 20 to 25 minutes. Cool and cut into 1½-inch squares. Yield: about 3 dozen.

## LEMON TARTS

1 cup plus 2 tablespoons all-purpose flour
¼ teaspoon salt
½ cup margarine, softened
1 egg, beaten
¼ cup whipping cream, whipped
½ (21-ounce) can lemon pie filling
Toasted coconut

Combine flour and salt; cut in margarine with a pastry blender until mixture resembles coarse meal. Add egg, and stir until well blended. Refrigerate dough 2 hours.

Shape dough into 35 balls; put each into a greased 1¾-inch muffin pan, and shape into a shell. Bake at 450° for 5 minutes; reduce heat to 400°, and bake 8 minutes. Gently remove pastry shells from pans; set aside to cool.

Fold whipped cream into lemon pie filling, and spoon 1 heaping tablespoonful into each shell. Top with coconut. Yield: 35 small tarts.

*Tip: Make spice cupcakes from a white or yellow cake mix by adding ground nutmeg, cinnamon, and cloves.*

## FRUIT KABOBS WITH MINT MARINADE

1½ cups water
1 cup sugar
1 cup fresh mint leaves
Juice of 1 orange
Juice of 1 lemon or lime
5 cups watermelon balls
1 cantaloupe, scooped into balls
3 cups (about 1 pound) green grapes
2 cups fresh strawberries, capped
Whole pears (optional)

Combine water and sugar in a heavy saucepan; bring to a boil, stirring frequently. Stir in mint and fruit juice; set aside to cool.

Combine melon, grapes, and strawberries in a large, shallow container; add mint mixture. Cover and marinate in refrigerator 1 to 2 hours. Drain well.

Alternate fruit on 6-inch skewers; insert skewers into whole pears, if desired. Yield: about 3 dozen kabobs.

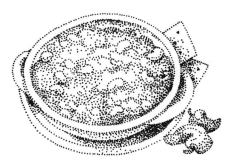

## Serve The Soup On Ice

What could taste better on a sultry summer day than a refreshing bowl of cold soup? Serve it as an enticing appetizer or add it to a lunchtime sandwich or salad. Choose from a range of colors and flavors that include light and creamy cucumber-yogurt, sweet strawberry, and spicy gazpacho.

To make cold soups even more appealing, serve them in stemmed glasses or crystal bowls nestled in crushed ice. Try adding an attractive garnish: a sprinkling of shredded cheese, fresh dillweed, celery leaves, or sliced fruit or vegetables.

## CURRIED CARROT SOUP

1 medium onion, chopped
2 tablespoons butter or margarine
4 carrots, scraped and coarsely chopped
4 cups chicken broth
1 (1- x 2-inch) strip lemon rind
2 teaspoons sugar
½ to 1 teaspoon curry powder
¼ teaspoon salt
¼ teaspoon pepper
3 tablespoons dry sherry
Toasted chopped almonds (optional)
Finely chopped green onion or chives (optional)
Thinly sliced carrot strips (optional)

Sauté onion in butter in a large skillet until tender. Add the next 7 ingredients. Reduce heat; cover and cook 20 minutes or until carrots are tender.

Pour half of mixture into container of electric blender; process until smooth. Pour into a bowl or pitcher; repeat with remaining mixture. Stir in sherry. Cover and chill. Garnish with almonds, green onion, and carrot strips, if desired. Yield: about 5 cups.

*Mrs. Howard B. Vaughn,*
*Nashville, Tennessee.*

## CUCUMBER-YOGURT SOUP

4 cups peeled, seeded, and chopped cucumber
2 cups water
2 (8-ounce) cartons plain yogurt
1 tablespoon honey
1 teaspoon salt
1 clove garlic, crushed
3 fresh mint leaves
¾ teaspoon minced fresh or ¼ teaspoon dried whole dillweed
Cucumber slices (optional)
Fresh dillweed (optional)

Combine first 8 ingredients in a large bowl. Pour about one-third of mixture into container of electric blender; process until smooth. Pour into a bowl or pitcher; repeat procedure with remaining mixture. Cover and chill several hours. Garnish with cucumber slices and fresh dillweed, if desired. Yield: about 5 cups.

*Michele Poynton,*
*Altamonte Springs, Florida.*

## SAUCY GAZPACHO

1 (16-ounce) can whole tomatoes, undrained
1 (46-ounce) can tomato juice
¼ cup vegetable or sesame seed oil
2 tablespoons red wine vinegar
1 clove garlic, minced
⅛ teaspoon pepper
1 small cucumber, peeled and finely chopped
1 medium tomato, chopped
1 medium carrot, scraped and shredded
1 stalk celery, finely chopped
1 small green pepper, finely chopped
Shredded Cheddar cheese (optional)
Celery leaves (optional)

Puree canned tomatoes in blender. Combine tomato puree and next 10 ingredients in a large bowl; stir well. Cover and chill at least 3 hours. Garnish with cheese and celery leaves, if desired. Yield: about 9 cups.

*Cookie McGee,*
*Raleigh, North Carolina.*

## COLD STRAWBERRY SOUP

2 cups unsweetened pineapple juice
⅓ cup sifted powdered sugar
2 cups fresh strawberries, washed and hulled
½ cup Burgundy or other dry red wine
½ cup commercial sour cream
Whipped cream (optional)
Fresh strawberries, sliced (optional)
Fresh mint leaves (optional)

Combine pineapple juice, powdered sugar, and strawberries in container of electric blender; process until smooth. Add Burgundy and sour cream; process an additional 2 minutes. Cover and chill several hours. Garnish with whipped cream, sliced strawberries, and mint leaves, if desired. Yield: about 4 cups.

*Marilyn Miller,*
*Birmingham, Alabama.*

*Tip: Before trying a new recipe, read through it at least once before beginning; check carefully to see if all ingredients are on hand.*

## Side Dishes From The Garden

Vegetable side dishes are never easier than in summer when an abundance of garden-fresh produce is available. Enhance your warm-weather meals with a serving of Creamed Fresh Corn cut straight from the cob. The juicy kernels are seasoned with butter, whipping cream, ground pepper, and a sprinkling of sugar.

Bacon-Flavored Squash is a savory casserole featuring Swiss and Cheddar cheese, sour cream, and crunchy bacon pieces. If you prefer a dish with a little more spice, try Zippy Zucchini Skillet. This corn and zucchini combination seasoned with green chiles, jalapeño peppers, garlic powder, and onion will liven up any menu.

### CREAMED FRESH CORN

4 ears fresh corn
1 teaspoon sugar
¼ cup butter or margarine
½ teaspoon freshly ground pepper
⅓ to ½ cup whipping cream
½ teaspoon salt

Cut corn from cob, scraping cob to remove the pulp. Combine corn and sugar; chill 1 hour.

Melt butter in a saucepan over medium heat. Add corn; cook 1 minute. Stir in pepper. Gradually add whipping cream, stirring constantly. Cook, uncovered, over medium heat 10 to 12 minutes or until liquid is absorbed, stirring corn frequently. Stir in salt. Yield: 4 servings.
*James T. Buck,*
*Richmond, Virginia.*

### LEMONY NEW POTATOES

2 pounds new potatoes
2 tablespoons lemon juice
2 tablespoons butter or margarine, melted
2 tablespoons chopped fresh parsley
1¾ teaspoons grated lemon rind

Wash potatoes; peel a thin strip around center. Cook potatoes, covered, in boiling salted water 10 minutes. Add lemon juice, and cook an additional 5 to 10 minutes or until tender; drain.

Combine butter, parsley, and rind; spoon over hot potatoes, and stir gently until coated. Yield: 6 to 8 servings.
*Ginger Barker,*
*Mesquite, Texas.*

### BACON-FLAVORED SQUASH

4 slices bacon
4 large yellow squash, sliced
2 green onions, chopped
1 egg, beaten
½ cup commercial sour cream
½ cup (2 ounces) shredded Swiss cheese
¾ cup (3 ounces) shredded Cheddar cheese

Cook bacon in a large skillet until crisp; drain on paper towels. Crumble and set aside, reserving drippings.

Sauté squash and onion in drippings 8 to 10 minutes.

Combine egg and sour cream; add to squash mixture. Stir in half the bacon. Spoon half the squash mixture into a greased shallow 2-quart casserole. Sprinkle Swiss cheese over top; spoon remaining squash mixture over cheese. Sprinkle Cheddar cheese over surface; top with remaining bacon.

Bake at 350° for 20 minutes or until bubbly. Yield: 6 servings.
*Betty L. Norman,*
*Anniston, Alabama.*

### ZIPPY ZUCCHINI SKILLET

2 tablespoons vegetable oil
4 medium zucchini, thinly sliced
1 medium onion, chopped
1 (16-ounce) can whole kernel corn, drained
1 (4-ounce) can chopped green chiles
2 teaspoons seeded chopped jalapeño peppers (optional)
¼ teaspoon salt
⅛ teaspoon garlic powder
½ cup (2 ounces) shredded Cheddar cheese

Heat oil in a large skillet; sauté zucchini and onion 10 minutes or until tender. Stir in remaining ingredients except cheese; cook, stirring occasionally, until thoroughly heated. Remove from heat; stir in cheese. Yield: 6 servings.
*June Crowder,*
*Dallas, Texas.*

### ZUCCHINI AND TOMATO BAKE

4 medium zucchini, sliced
½ teaspoon soy sauce
¼ teaspoon salt
¼ teaspoon garlic salt
¼ teaspoon pepper
2 medium tomatoes, cut into wedges
1 medium onion, sliced
1½ cups (6 ounces) shredded Cheddar cheese
3 tablespoons butter or margarine

Place zucchini in a 2½-quart casserole. Sprinkle with half each of soy sauce, salt, garlic salt, and pepper.

Layer tomatoes and onion over zucchini; sprinkle with remaining seasonings. Top with cheese, and dot with butter. Cover; bake at 350° for 40 minutes. Yield: 8 to 10 servings.
*Linda Bishop,*
*Omaha, Nebraska.*

## Chilled Desserts To Strike Your Fancy

Chilled fresh fruit—crunchy nuts—a dollop of whipped topping. That's just a hint of the good things in these refreshing chilled desserts. They're great to eat and guaranteed to make those hot summer days seem at least a few degrees cooler.

Take Frozen Cantaloupe Cream, for instance. It's a puree of the fresh fruit blended with orange juice for flavor and whipped cream for smoothness; then it's frozen to a thick and creamy consistency. For Sherbet Ambrosia Cups, orange shells are filled with orange sherbet, then topped with fruit, coconut, and almonds. Serve them straight from the freezer.

Summer's not summer without a parfait, and you'll love the layers of coffee ice cream, crunchy almonds, crushed English toffee, and chocolate syrup in Coffee Crunch Parfaits. The originator, Mrs. Pat Williams of Liberty, North Carolina, likes to keep them on hand in the freezer during the long hot summer. Just add a dollop of whipped topping and a cherry and serve.

## FROZEN CANTALOUPE CREAM

½ cup water
½ cup sugar
½ cup fresh orange juice
1 small cantaloupe
½ cup whipping cream, whipped
Additional whipped cream
Grated orange rind

Combine water, sugar, and orange juice in a small saucepan; bring to a boil, stirring well. Boil 5 minutes, stirring occasionally; set aside to cool.

Peel cantaloupe, and cut into ½-inch cubes. Place in container of electric blender, and process until smooth. Pour into a bowl, and stir in cooled juice mixture; fold in whipped cream.

Pour cantaloupe mixture into a 10- x 6- x 2-inch pan. Freeze 1½ hours or until slushy; remove from freezer, and process in blender until smooth. Repeat procedure. Return to freezer, and freeze 2 to 3 hours or until firm. Spoon into dessert dishes, and garnish with additional whipped cream and orange rind. Yield: 6 to 8 servings.
*Evelyn Short,*
*Knoxville, Tennessee.*

## COFFEE CRUNCH PARFAITS

1 quart coffee ice cream, slightly softened
1 (2¼-ounce) package slivered almonds, chopped and toasted
2 (⅞-ounce) English toffee candy bars, crushed
½ cup chocolate syrup
1 (4-ounce) carton frozen whipped topping, thawed
8 maraschino cherries with stems

Spoon ¼ cup ice cream into each of eight 4-ounce chilled parfait glasses; freeze 30 minutes. Layer ½ tablespoon each of almonds, crushed candy, and chocolate syrup. Repeat layers of ice cream, almonds, candy, and chocolate. Cover and freeze until firm.

Top each parfait with whipped topping and a cherry. Yield: 8 parfaits.
*Mrs. Pat Williams,*
*Liberty, North Carolina.*

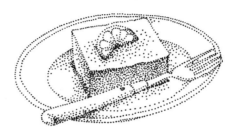

## LEMONY CREAM CHEESE SQUARES

1 cup graham cracker crumbs
3 tablespoons sugar
¼ cup butter or margarine, melted
1 (8-ounce) package cream cheese, softened
½ cup sugar
⅛ teaspoon salt
½ cup milk
1 teaspoon lemon juice
1 teaspoon vanilla extract
1 (4-ounce) carton frozen whipped topping, thawed
Lemon slices (optional)
Fresh mint leaves (optional)

Combine crumbs, 3 tablespoons sugar, and butter; mix well. Press mixture on bottom and sides of a lightly greased 8-inch square baking pan; bake at 375° for 6 to 8 minutes.

Beat cream cheese in a large mixing bowl until soft and creamy. Gradually add ½ cup sugar, beating until fluffy. Add salt, milk, lemon juice, and vanilla; beat at medium speed of electric mixer 1 minute.

Gently fold in whipped topping; spoon filling into prepared crust. Chill at least 6 hours. Cut into squares, and garnish with a lemon slice and mint, if desired. Yield: 9 servings. *Marie Davis,*
*Morganton, North Carolina.*

## LIME SHERBET

1 (3-ounce) package lime-flavored gelatin
1½ cups sugar
1 cup boiling water
1 tablespoon plus ½ teaspoon grated lime rind
⅓ cup lime juice
1 quart milk

Combine first 5 ingredients; stir well, and let cool. Add milk, mixing well. Pour into a 9-inch square pan, and place in freezer about 1 hour or until mixture is firm but not frozen.

Spoon into a mixing bowl, and beat well with electric mixer. Pour back into pan, and freeze several hours or overnight. Yield: 8 servings.
*Mrs. Harry B. Dawson,*
*Jacksonville, Florida.*

## SHERBET AMBROSIA CUPS

3 large seedless oranges
1 pint orange sherbet, slightly softened
½ cup strawberries, sliced
⅓ cup shredded coconut
¼ cup sliced almonds, toasted

Cut oranges in half crosswise; carefully remove sections, and set aside. Clip membranes inside orange shells, and carefully remove. Place orange shells in freezer until thoroughly chilled. Using a chilled spoon, spread sherbet evenly on bottom and sides of orange shells, leaving centers hollow. Freeze about 4 hours or until sherbet is firm.

Combine orange sections, strawberries, and coconut, mixing well. Spoon about ⅓ cup mixture into each frozen sherbet cup; freeze 30 additional minutes. Remove cups from freezer; top each with almonds. Serve immediately. Yield: 6 servings.
*Mrs. Randall L. Wilson,*
*Louisville, Kentucky.*

*Tip: Use the store's comparative pricing information for good buys. The unit-price data allows you to compare the cost of similar products of different sizes by weight, measure, or count.*

## STRAWBERRY SHERBET

1 envelope unflavored gelatin
¼ cup cold water
¼ cup boiling water
1 quart strawberries, washed and hulled
1 cup milk
⅔ cup honey
1 tablespoon lemon juice
2 egg whites

Soften gelatin in cold water; stir in boiling water.

Place strawberries and milk in container of an electric blender; process until smooth. Pour into a large bowl; stir in gelatin mixture, honey, and lemon juice.

Beat egg whites (at room temperature) until stiff but not dry; fold into strawberry mixture.

Pour mixture into freezer can of a 1-gallon hand-turned or electric freezer. Freeze according to manufacturer's instructions. Let ripen at least 1 hour before serving. Yield: 1½ quarts.

*Mrs. E. T. Williams,*
*Baton Rouge, Louisiana.*

## STRAWBERRIES WITH BRANDIED ORANGE JUICE

2 quarts fresh strawberries, washed and hulled
14 sugar cubes
3 oranges
½ cup brandy
Whipped cream
Fresh mint leaves

Place strawberries in a large bowl, reserving several for garnish; set aside.

Rub sugar cubes over rind of oranges until soaked with oil. Crush cubes with wooden spoon in a small bowl. Add juice of oranges and brandy; stir until sugar is dissolved. Pour over strawberries. Cover and chill 2 to 3 hours, stirring occasionally. Garnish with whipped cream, reserved strawberries, and mint leaves. Yield: 8 servings.

*Ruth E. Cunliffe,*
*Lake Placid, Florida.*

# Sip Summertime's Coolest

Whether you're lounging by the pool or enjoying a late afternoon on the deck, sipping on a cool beverage will make this relaxing time even better. Choose from our frosty beverages, guaranteed to keep your summer cool.

Dr. C. G. Herrington of Memphis shares his original Daiquirita recipe. He created this new drink while trying to make margueritas for his guests. Finding his bar short on tequila, he turned to invention and substituted rum. Dr. Herrington writes, "In desperation, I topped up the drinks with rum, took a deep breath, and stepped onto the patio announcing that we were about to try a new drink recipe: the Daiquirita."

Another delightful cooler is Fuzz Buzz, made with limeade, vodka, and peaches.

## DAIQUIRITAS

Lime wedge
Salt
1 (6-ounce) can frozen limeade concentrate, undiluted
¾ cup cold water
¾ cup light rum
⅓ cup tequila
Lime slices (optional)

Rub rim of 6 cocktail glasses with wedge of lime. Place salt in saucer; spin rim of each glass in salt. Set prepared glasses aside.

Combine limeade concentrate, water, rum, and tequila in container of electric blender; process well. Pour over ice in prepared glasses; garnish with a slice of lime, if desired. Yield: 6 servings.

*Dr. C. G. Herrington, Jr.,*
*Memphis, Tennessee.*

## FUZZ BUZZ

1 (6-ounce) can frozen limeade concentrate, undiluted
¾ cup vodka
2 medium peaches, unpeeled and sliced
Cracked ice

Combine first 3 ingredients in container of electric blender; process until smooth. Gradually add ice, processing until mixture reaches desired consistency. Yield: about 4½ cups.

*Fay S. Anderson,*
*Arcadia, California.*

## ORANGE-LIME PUNCH

2 (12-ounce) cans frozen orange juice concentrate, thawed and undiluted
3 (6-ounce) cans frozen limeade concentrate, thawed and undiluted
2 (6-ounce) cans frozen lemonade concentrate, thawed and undiluted
1 (8-ounce) bottle lime juice
1 quart water
2 cups sifted powdered sugar
1 quart light rum
1 pint fresh strawberries
1 (33.8-ounce) bottle club soda, chilled
Assorted fresh fruit slices (optional)

Combine first 7 ingredients, mixing well; chill. Stir in strawberries and club soda before serving. Serve over ice. Garnish with fresh fruit slices, if desired. Yield: about 4½ quarts.

*Ginger Barker,*
*Mesquite, Texas.*

## CITRUS COOLER

2½ cups sugar
2½ cups water
1 (46-ounce) can pineapple juice
1 (46-ounce) can orange juice
1½ cups lemon juice
1½ quarts ginger ale
Pineapple wedges (optional)

Combine sugar and water in a medium saucepan; bring to a boil, stirring until sugar dissolves. Pour sugar mixture into a 4½-quart freezer container. Stir in fruit juice; freeze until firm. Remove from freezer several hours before serving (mixture should be slushy). Stir in ginger ale. Garnish with pineapple wedges, if desired. Yield: 5½ quarts.

*Billye Johnson,*
*Beckville, Texas.*

## SUMMER SHAKE

1 (8-ounce) carton strawberry-flavored
   yogurt
¾ cup orange juice
2 eggs
1 tablespoon honey
3 to 4 ice cubes
Strawberries (optional)

Combine first 4 ingredients in container of electric blender; process on high speed until frothy. Add ice cubes, blending until crushed. Garnish with strawberries, if desired. Serve immediately. Yield: about 3 cups.
*Mrs. C. D. Marshall,*
*Culpeper, Virginia.*

# Appetizers Keep It Easygoing

Start your party with our creamy vegetable dip and a colorful platter of fresh vegetables—it's the perfect appetizer for informal entertaining. But then, so are our Spicy Nuts, Party Bread Spread, and pecan-coated Cheese Ball.

The Spicy Nuts are just that—spicy. They're coated with chili powder, red pepper, and garlic salt, then baked. Also on the spicy side is our Chili Dip; served warm with taco chips, it's a nice change from cold appetizers.

## APRICOT-CREAM CHEESE SPREAD

1 (3-ounce) package cream cheese,
   softened
1 cup drained canned apricots, chopped
¼ cup chopped walnuts or pecans
1 tablespoon honey

Beat cream cheese at medium speed of electric mixer until smooth and fluffy; stir in remaining ingredients. Serve on white or whole wheat bread. Yield: 1 cup.    *Mrs. Bruce Fowler,*
*Woodruff, South Carolina.*

## PARTY BREAD SPREAD

1 cup finely chopped pecans
2 hard-cooked eggs, finely chopped
1 small onion, minced
½ cup mayonnaise
1 (3-ounce) jar pimiento-stuffed olives,
   drained and finely chopped
Additional pimiento-stuffed olives, sliced
   (optional)

Combine first 5 ingredients; stir well. Serve spread on party rye bread or crackers. Garnish with olive slices, if desired. Yield: about 2 cups.
*Susan Ray,*
*Abbeville, South Carolina.*

## CHEESE BALL

2½ cups (10 ounces) shredded sharp
   Cheddar cheese
1 (8-ounce) jar process cheese spread
1 (8-ounce) package cream cheese,
   softened
1 tablespoon mayonnaise
1 tablespoon Worcestershire sauce
1 teaspoon frozen chopped chives, thawed
⅛ teaspoon garlic powder
⅛ teaspoon onion powder
½ cup chopped pecans

Combine all ingredients except pecans; beat on medium speed of electric mixer until smooth. Chill 2 hours. Shape into a ball, and roll in pecans. Serve with crackers. Yield: 1 cheese ball.    *Mrs. Bob Nester,*
*Charleston, West Virginia.*

## SPICY NUTS

¼ cup vegetable oil
¾ teaspoon chili powder
½ teaspoon red pepper
½ teaspoon garlic salt
1 teaspoon Worcestershire sauce
1 (7-ounce) jar dry roasted cashews
1 (8-ounce) jar dry roasted peanuts

Combine first 5 ingredients in a large bowl, mixing well; add cashews and peanuts, stirring to coat. Spread evenly in a 13- x 9- x 2-inch baking pan. Bake at 300° for 20 minutes, stirring once after 10 minutes. Yield: about 3 cups.
*Kathryn M. Elmore,*
*Demopolis, Alabama.*

## CHILI DIP

2 (15-ounce) cans chili without beans
1 (14½-ounce) can tamales, mashed
1 pound process cheese spread, cut into
   1-inch cubes
1 tablespoon Worcestershire sauce
¼ teaspoon hot sauce

Combine all ingredients in top of double boiler. Cook over low heat, stirring frequently until cheese melts. Serve warm with taco chips. Yield: about 1½ quarts.    *Eloise Haynes,*
*Greenville, Mississippi.*

## VEGETABLE DIP

1 cup mayonnaise
1 tablespoon lemon juice
½ teaspoon salt
½ teaspoon paprika
2 tablespoons instant minced onion
½ tablespoon frozen chopped chives,
   thawed
½ teaspoon curry powder
½ teaspoon Worcestershire sauce
1 (8-ounce) carton commercial sour cream
Chopped green onions (optional)

Combine all ingredients except green onions, mixing well. Chill. Garnish with green onions, if desired. Serve with fresh vegetables. Yield: about 2 cups.
*Mrs. J. F. Robertson,*
*Montgomery, Alabama.*

*Tip: To freshen air throughout the house, boil 1 tablespoon of whole cloves in a pan of water for a few minutes.*

# summer Suppers

## Get Fired Up For A Cookout

Whether the sun is shining or is quietly setting, the time is always right for cooking outdoors. Not only is entertaining easier, but it's also more leisurely as there's time to enjoy the company of your guests while the meat is on the grill.

Chicken is always a favorite, and we think you'll enjoy our tangy Lemonade Chicken; it tastes like it was marinated for hours, yet requires no advance preparation. Barbecue lovers won't be disappointed with Honey-Glazed Spareribs, which are basted with a spicy tomato and honey sauce.

If you like to smoke meats, be sure to try Dale Lloyd's Smoked Country-Style Backbones. Lemon juice, pineapple juice, and Chablis are added to the water pan to flavor the meat and keep it from drying out.

To keep grilled meats juicy, turn them with either a spatula or a pair of long-handled tongs; a fork will pierce the meat and cause some of the juices to drip out.

### MARINATED SIRLOIN KABOBS

¼ cup lemon-lime carbonated beverage
¼ cup dry sherry
¼ cup soy sauce
3 tablespoons sugar
3 tablespoons vinegar
½ teaspoon garlic powder
¼ teaspoon salt
¼ teaspoon pepper
2 pounds (1½-inch-thick) boneless sirloin steak, cut into 1-inch chunks
½ pound fresh medium mushroom caps
1 pint cherry tomatoes
2 onions, cut into eighths
2 green peppers, cut into 1-inch pieces
1 small fresh pineapple, cut into 1-inch pieces

Combine first 8 ingredients, mixing well; pour into a large shallow dish. Add meat; cover and marinate at least 2 hours in the refrigerator, turning meat occasionally.

Remove meat from marinade, reserving marinade. Alternate meat, vegetables, and pineapple on skewers. Grill over medium-hot coals 10 to 15 minutes or until desired degree of doneness, basting frequently with marinade. Yield: 4 to 5 servings. *Bernie Benigno, Gulfport, Mississippi.*

### MARINATED FLANK STEAK

2 (1¼-pound) flank steaks
½ cup soy sauce
¼ cup Pickapeppa sauce
¼ cup Worcestershire sauce
3 tablespoons vegetable oil
3 tablespoons Burgundy or other dry red wine
3 tablespoons red wine vinegar
2½ tablespoons brown sugar
2 cloves garlic, minced

Prick both sides of steak with fork, and place in a large shallow pan.

Combine remaining ingredients; pour over steak. Cover; marinate 24 hours in refrigerator, turning occasionally.

Remove steak from marinade. Grill over hot coals 4 to 5 minutes on each side, or until desired degree of doneness. To serve, slice steak across grain in thin slices. Yield: 6 to 8 servings. *Jane Campbell, Greenville, Mississippi.*

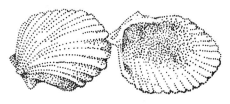

### SEA SCALLOP KABOBS

1 small onion, grated
1½ tablespoons lime juice
½ teaspoon sugar
¼ teaspoon salt
Pinch of pepper
1 pound fresh scallops
¼ cup butter or margarine, melted

Combine first 5 ingredients in a small shallow dish. Add scallops, tossing gently to coat. Cover and marinate at least 2 hours in the refrigerator, stirring often.

Place scallops on skewers. Grill 5 minutes on each side over medium-hot coals, brushing frequently with butter. Yield: 4 servings. *Cynthia Aaron, Tallahassee, Florida.*

### SMOKED COUNTRY-STYLE BACKBONES

1½ cups catsup
⅔ cup vinegar
½ cup firmly packed brown sugar
¼ cup butter or margarine
1 teaspoon celery seeds
2 teaspoons Worcestershire sauce
1 teaspoon liquid smoke
½ teaspoon dry mustard
¼ teaspoon paprika
Dash of hot sauce
Juice of 1 lemon
1 (46-ounce) can unsweetened pineapple juice
2 cups Chablis or other dry white wine
½ cup lemon juice
6 pounds country-style backbones

Combine first 11 ingredients in a medium saucepan. Bring mixture to a boil; reduce heat, and simmer 15 minutes. Set aside.

Combine pineapple juice, Chablis, and lemon juice; set aside.

Prepare charcoal fire in smoker, and let burn 10 to 15 minutes. Place water pan in smoker, and fill with pineapple juice mixture. Add enough hot water to fill pan, if necessary.

Place lower food rack on appropriate shelf in smoker. Arrange half of the backbones on food rack, and baste with barbecue sauce mixture. Place upper food rack on shelf; arrange remaining backbones on food rack, and baste with sauce.

Cover with smoker lid; cook about 3½ hours. Remove lid; turn meat, and baste with sauce. If water pan is dry, add hot water, pineapple juice, or wine, filling pan one-third to one-half full. Cover meat immediately, and continue cooking 2 to 3 hours or until desired degree of doneness. Yield: 6 servings. *Dale Lloyd, Birmingham, Alabama.*

## HONEY-GLAZED SPARERIBS

1 (8-ounce) can tomato sauce
½ cup honey
2 tablespoons minced onion
2 tablespoons red wine vinegar
1 teaspoon celery seeds
1 teaspoon Worcestershire sauce
½ teaspoon salt
¼ teaspoon pepper
1 clove garlic, minced
½ cup dry sherry
4 pounds spareribs

Combine first 9 ingredients in a heavy saucepan; simmer, stirring occasionally, about 20 minutes. Stir in sherry.

Cut ribs into serving-size pieces; place on grill over slow coals. Grill about 30 minutes, turning frequently. Brush with sauce, and cook an additional 2 hours, basting and turning frequently. Baste ribs with remaining sauce before serving. Yield: 4 servings.
*Mrs. W. A. Reid, Jr.,*
*Tuscumbia, Alabama.*

## LEMONADE CHICKEN

1 (6-ounce) can frozen lemonade
  concentrate, thawed and undiluted
½ cup soy sauce
1 teaspoon seasoned salt
½ teaspoon celery salt
⅛ teaspoon garlic powder
2 (2½- to 3-pound) broiler-fryers, cut up
Lemon slices (optional)

Combine first 5 ingredients; stir well. Place chicken on grill over medium-hot coals. Grill about 15 to 20 minutes, turning frequently. Brush with sauce, and grill an additional 30 to 35 minutes or until desired degree of doneness, basting and turning frequently. Garnish with lemon slices, if desired. Yield: 8 servings.
*Carolyn Epting,*
*Leesville, South Carolina.*

*Tip: Look for meat cuts that have the most lean for the money. When you buy less expensive cuts of meat, make sure you are not paying for large amounts of gristle, fat, and bone.*

## GRILLED STUFFED FRANKS

1 (8-ounce) can tomato sauce
1 tablespoon sugar
2 tablespoons spicy brown mustard
½ teaspoon garlic powder
8 frankfurters
6 small green onions, chopped
8 slices bacon
8 hot dog buns

Combine tomato sauce, sugar, mustard, and garlic powder; stir well. Slice frankfurters lengthwise to make a pocket. Brush inside each pocket with sauce; sprinkle with onion. Wrap each frankfurter with bacon, securing with a wooden pick.

Cook frankfurters over hot coals 10 to 15 minutes or until bacon is crisp, turning often and basting with remaining sauce. Serve in hot dog buns. Yield: 8 servings.
*Susan Settlemyre,*
*Raleigh, North Carolina.*

# Bring Garden Freshness To The Salad

When our Southern gardens and grocery bins are overflowing with fresh fruit and vegetables, it's time to turn our attention to salads. Consider making a big colorful tossed salad the center of your next luncheon, or mix up a quick marinated salad to accompany the weekend cookout. Serve a fruit salad along with a buffet, or make it the light, refreshing end to a picnic menu.

We especially recommend Marinated Salsa Tomatoes, a tomato salad with a difference; green chile salsa and garlic give garden-fresh tomatoes a spicy and adventuresome twist.

## MAKE-AHEAD ORIENTAL SALAD

1 (17-ounce) can English peas, drained
1 (14-ounce) can bean sprouts, drained
1 (12-ounce) can white shoe peg corn,
  drained
1 (8-ounce) can sliced water chestnuts,
  drained
1 (4½-ounce) jar sliced mushrooms,
  drained
1 (4-ounce) jar chopped pimiento, drained
1 large green pepper, thinly sliced
1 large onion, thinly sliced
1 cup sliced celery
1 cup sugar
1 cup vegetable oil
½ cup vinegar
½ cup water
2 tablespoons red wine vinegar
1 tablespoon soy sauce
1 teaspoon dry mustard
½ teaspoon salt
½ teaspoon paprika
¼ teaspoon pepper
1 clove garlic, crushed

Combine vegetables in a large bowl, and toss lightly. Combine remaining ingredients; stir well. Pour marinade over vegetables, stirring gently. Cover and chill overnight. Drain vegetables, or serve salad with a slotted spoon. Yield: 12 to 15 servings.
*June H. Johnson,*
*Mocksville, North Carolina.*

## MARINATED VEGETABLE SALAD

4 cups chopped tomatoes
1 cup chopped celery
1 cup chopped onion
½ cup chopped green pepper
¾ cup vinegar
½ cup vegetable oil
¼ cup sugar
2 tablespoons poppy seeds
1 tablespoon salt

Combine tomatoes, celery, onion, and green pepper in a large bowl; toss lightly.

Combine remaining ingredients in a jar. Cover tightly, and shake vigorously; pour marinade over vegetables. Cover and chill at least 3 hours. Yield: 6 to 8 servings.
*Mrs. Otis Shipman,*
*Bells, Tennessee.*

## MARINATED SALSA TOMATOES

1½ cups vegetable oil
1 cup vinegar
¼ cup sugar
½ teaspoon dried whole oregano
¼ teaspoon salt
⅛ teaspoon pepper
⅛ teaspoon celery seeds
3 to 4 small tomatoes, finely chopped
6 green onions, finely chopped
1 (7-ounce) can green chile salsa
1 clove garlic, minced
6 medium tomatoes, quartered
Lettuce leaves
1 (2-ounce) can anchovy fillets (optional)

Combine first 7 ingredients in a jar; cover tightly, and shake vigorously. Pour over chopped tomatoes and green onion; stir in salsa and garlic. Add tomato quarters, tossing gently; cover and marinate in refrigerator at least 2 hours.

Using a slotted spoon, remove vegetables from marinade; arrange the salad on a lettuce-lined platter. Garnish with anchovy fillets, if desired. Yield: 6 to 8 servings.

*Note:* Reserve marinade for other uses, if desired.

*Mrs. Roger Nelson Horn,*
*Houston, Texas.*

*Served with its own fruity dressing, Summer Fruit Salad is layered with a variety of mouth-watering fruit.*

## MARINATED ZUCCHINI SALAD

⅓ cup vinegar
¼ cup sugar
2½ tablespoons vegetable oil
1 tablespoon wine vinegar
½ teaspoon salt
¼ teaspoon pepper
5 small zucchini, thinly sliced
½ cup diced celery
½ cup diced onion
½ cup chopped green pepper

Combine first 6 ingredients; stir well. Add vegetables; toss to coat. Cover and marinate in refrigerator several hours or overnight. Yield: 6 to 8 servings.

*Gwyn Prows Groseclose,*
*Longwood, Florida.*

*Tip: Sand and dirt can be removed from fresh vegetables by soaking in warm salted water 5 minutes.*

## SUMMER FRUIT SALAD

Ascorbic-citric powder
2 large apples, unpeeled and sliced
2 fresh nectarines, unpeeled and cut into wedges
2 fresh peaches, peeled and cut into wedges
1 (11-ounce) can mandarin oranges
1 (16-ounce) can pear halves, sliced
1 (6-ounce) jar maraschino cherries
¼ cup sugar
1½ teaspoons cornstarch
½ cantaloupe
1 cup seedless green grapes
Fresh mint

Prepare ascorbic-citric solution according to manufacturer's directions. Toss apples, nectarines, and peaches separately in prepared solution; drain fruit, and set aside.

Drain canned fruit and combine juices; stir well and set aside 1 cup of the fruit juice mixture. Combine sugar and cornstarch in a saucepan; stir in reserved fruit juice mixture. Cook over medium heat, stirring constantly, until mixture is thickened and bubbly.

Scoop out melon balls, or peel melon and cut into cubes. Layer apples, mandarin oranges, grapes, cantaloupe, pears, nectarines, and peaches in a 3-quart serving bowl; garnish with mint and a few maraschino cherries (reserve remaining cherries for other use). Serve with fruit juice dressing. Yield: 10 to 12 servings.

*Katy Lou Horton,*
*Odessa, Texas.*

## AVOCADO-MELON SALAD

1 small cantaloupe, peeled, seeded, and cut into 4 wedges
1 avocado, peeled and cut into 8 wedges
Lettuce cups
Sour Cream Dressing

Arrange cantaloupe and avocado on lettuce-lined serving platter. Top with Sour Cream Dressing. Yield: about 4 servings.

*Sour Cream Dressing:*
¼ cup commercial sour cream
2 tablespoons apricot preserves
1 tablespoon mayonnaise or salad dressing

Combine all ingredients; stir well. Yield: about ½ cup. *Marge Killmon, Annandale, Virginia.*

### FRESH FRUIT SALAD

2 large apples, thinly sliced
2 medium peaches, peeled and sliced
2 medium pears, thinly sliced
2 cups seedless green grapes, halved
3 tablespoons honey
¾ to 1 cup mayonnaise
½ cup chopped pecans

Combine fruit and honey; set aside 3 to 4 minutes. Add mayonnaise and pecans; stir well. Cover and chill several hours or overnight. Yield: about 8 servings. *Mrs. William S. Bell, Chattanooga, Tennessee.*

## Cooking Light

## Entertaining Can Be Light

When planning your next summer supper, you don't have to interrupt your diet in order to enjoy a memorable meal with your guests. Start with a light appetizer beverage; then move on to a main course of marinated chicken kabobs on a bed of rice with a blue cheese-dressed spinach salad on the side. Peach Parfaits make a spectacular finale that everyone is sure to love.

How can such a delicious menu fit your low-calorie diet plan? For starters,

Bettina Hambrick's Fresh Vegetable Cocktail is a simple mixture of unsweetened pineapple juice combined with slices of carrot, cucumber, and celery— all pureed in the blender and served in attractive stemmed glasses.

As your guests catch the aroma of Sesame Chicken Kabobs on the grill, they'll be eager for mealtime to begin. The marinade for the chicken is soy sauce, reduced-calorie salad dressing, and other seasonings; this blend is lower in calories than the usual oil-based marinades and sweet barbecue sauces.

Chicken broth and sautéed onion add lots of flavor to Seasoned Onion Rice. We substitute cooking spray for oil to sauté the onion.

As with many other light menus, we've included a fresh vegetable salad that's high in fiber but low in calories. Our creamy Blue Cheese Dressing is made with low-fat cottage cheese and only a small amount of blue cheese. Blue cheese is relatively high in fat, but since its flavor is so strong, a little goes a long way.

Peach Parfait makes a delightful dessert for dieters and nondieters alike. Unsweetened fresh peaches are congealed in peach nectar and served in tall parfait glasses. Garnish each serving with a tablespoon of whipped topping (14 extra calories) if you like; but if you're watching your cholesterol intake, top with peach slices.

**Fresh Vegetable Cocktail**
**Sesame Chicken Kabobs**
**Seasoned Onion Rice**
**Spinach-Blue Cheese Salad**
**Peach Parfait**

### FRESH VEGETABLE COCKTAIL

3 cups unsweetened pineapple juice, chilled
1 medium carrot, sliced
1½ stalks celery, sliced
⅓ cucumber, peeled and sliced
2 slices lemon
Fresh mint (optional)

Combine all ingredients except mint in container of an electric blender. Process until smooth; chill. Garnish with fresh mint, if desired. Yield: 6 servings (about 70 calories per ⅔-cup serving). *Bettina Hambrick, Muskogee, Oklahoma.*

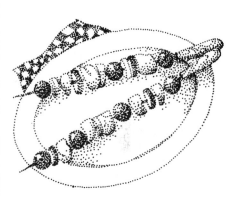

### SESAME CHICKEN KABOBS

2 whole chicken breasts, skinned and boned
¼ cup soy sauce
¼ cup Russian reduced-calorie salad dressing
1 tablespoon sesame seeds
2 tablespoons lemon juice
¼ teaspoon ground ginger
¼ teaspoon garlic powder
1 large green pepper, cut into 1-inch pieces
2 medium onions, cut into eighths
3 small zucchini, cut into ¾-inch pieces
1 pint cherry tomatoes
Vegetable cooking spray

Cut chicken breasts into 1-inch pieces; place chicken in a shallow container, and set aside.

Combine next 6 ingredients in a jar; cover tightly, and shake vigorously. Pour over chicken; cover and marinate in the refrigerator at least 2 hours.

Remove chicken from marinade, reserving marinade. Alternate chicken and vegetables on skewers. Coat grill with cooking spray. Grill kabobs about 6 inches from medium-hot coals for 15 to 20 minutes or until chicken is done, turning and basting often with marinade. Yield: 6 servings (about 156 calories per serving).

## SEASONED ONION RICE

**Vegetable cooking spray**
**1 medium onion, finely chopped**
**1 cup uncooked regular rice**
**1 (10¾-ounce) can chicken broth,**
**    undiluted**
**¾ cup water**
**1 tablespoon Worcestershire sauce**
**1 beef-flavored bouillon cube**
**¼ teaspoon pepper**

Coat a medium saucepan with cooking spray; add onion, and sauté 5 minutes. Add remaining ingredients, and bring to a boil. Coat a 1½-quart casserole with cooking spray; add rice mixture. Cover and bake at 350° for 1 hour. Yield: 6 servings (about 136 calories per serving).

## SPINACH-BLUE CHEESE SALAD

**1¼ pounds fresh spinach, torn**
**1 hard-cooked egg, chopped**
**5 water chestnuts, sliced**
**1 (2-ounce) jar sliced pimiento, drained**
**¼ pound fresh mushrooms, sliced**
**Blue Cheese Dressing**

Combine spinach, egg, chestnuts, pimiento, and mushrooms in a large bowl; toss. Serve with Blue Cheese Dressing. Yield: 6 servings (about 42 calories per serving, plus 19 calories per tablespoon of dressing).

*Blue Cheese Dressing:*
**½ cup low-fat cottage cheese**
**2 tablespoons crumbled blue cheese**
**¼ cup plus 2 tablespoons buttermilk**
**¼ teaspoon pepper**

Combine all ingredients in container of an electric blender; process until smooth. Chill thoroughly. Yield: ⅔ cup.

*Tip: The next time a recipe calls for 1 cup buttermilk, try this handy substitute: Put 1 tablespoon vinegar or lemon juice in a measuring cup, add enough whole milk to make 1 cup, and let stand 5 minutes to thicken slightly.*

## PEACH PARFAIT

**1 envelope plus 1 teaspoon unflavored**
**    gelatin**
**½ cup cold water**
**¼ cup sugar**
**1 (12-ounce) can peach nectar**
**2 tablespoons water**
**1 tablespoon lemon juice**
**4 medium peaches, peeled and cut into**
**    ¾-inch cubes**
**¼ cup plus 2 tablespoons frozen whipped**
**    topping, thawed (optional)**
**Additional peach slices (optional)**

Dissolve gelatin in ½ cup cold water; bring to a boil, stirring constantly. Remove from heat; stir in sugar and peach nectar. Chill until consistency of unbeaten egg white.

Combine 2 tablespoons water and lemon juice in a medium bowl; add 4 peaches, tossing gently to coat. Drain peaches, and combine with thickened nectar mixture; spoon evenly into 6 parfait glasses. Chill until firm.

To serve, top each parfait with 1 tablespoon whipped topping and an additional peach slice, if desired. Yield: 6 parfaits (about 98 calories per serving plus 14 calories per tablespoon whipped topping).

# Ice Cream Invites A Variety Of Toppings

Everyone knows that homemade ice cream is best, whether it's cranked by hand or turned in an electric freezer. That delicious rich cream that comes up with the dasher is always worth the extra effort homemade demands.

To share the enjoyment with friends, plan a make-your-own sundae party; all you need is a good basic vanilla ice cream and lots of toppings so your guests can have fun making their own creations.

We suggest you start with our Vanilla Ice Cream Spectacular; or, if you prefer, mix some crushed fresh fruit into the basic ingredients before freezing. You can serve the ice cream in individual scoops from an attractive bowl by making it well in advance of your party. Scoop out the frozen cream onto cookie sheets and store them, covered, in the coldest part of your freezer until party time. The balls of ice cream will be frozen hard and will stay frozen longer than when served directly from the freezer.

Let your guests choose from a variety of toppings. Besides a chocolate sauce—the number one favorite—we suggest Date-Nut Sundae Sauce, Honeyscotch Sundae Sauce, and Fruity Dessert Topping for a change of pace. Include some crunchy toppings, too, like Sugared Pecans and Whole Wheat Granola.

For the final touch, set out a tray of Butter-Nut Strips for guests to munch on while they indulge in their homemade sundaes. These tasty little butter cookies are topped with chopped almonds that are toasted as the cookie strips bake.

## VANILLA ICE CREAM SPECTACULAR

**2¼ cups sugar**
**¼ plus 2 tablespoons all-purpose flour**
**½ teaspoon salt**
**5 cups milk, scalded**
**5 eggs, beaten**
**1 quart whipping cream**
**1½ tablespoons vanilla extract**

Combine sugar, flour, and salt in a 3-quart saucepan; gradually stir in milk. Cook over medium heat 15 minutes or until thickened, stirring constantly.

Stir one-fourth of hot mixture into beaten eggs; add to remaining hot mixture, stirring constantly. Cook 1 minute; remove from heat and cool. Chill 2 hours.

Combine whipping cream and vanilla in a large bowl; add chilled custard, stirring with a wire whisk to combine. Pour mixture into freezer can of a 1-gallon hand-turned or electric freezer. Freeze according to manufacturer's instructions. Let ripen 1½ to 2 hours before serving. Yield: 1 gallon.

*Dorothy L. Anderson,*
*Manor, Texas.*

### HEAVENLY CHOCOLATE SAUCE

½ cup butter or margarine
4 (1-ounce) squares unsweetened chocolate
3 cups sugar
1 (13-ounce) can evaporated milk
½ teaspoon salt

Melt butter and chocolate in top of a double boiler; stir in remaining ingredients. Cook over medium heat, stirring until sugar is dissolved and sauce is smooth. Serve warm over ice cream. Yield: about 4 cups.    *Janis Moyer,*
*Farmersville, Texas.*

### DATE-NUT SUNDAE SAUCE

½ cup chopped dates
½ cup dark corn syrup
¼ cup firmly packed brown sugar
¼ cup water
¼ teaspoon salt
½ teaspoon vanilla extract
¼ cup chopped pecans

Combine first 5 ingredients in a small saucepan. Bring to a boil over medium heat, stirring constantly; continue to cook, stirring constantly, until mixture thickens (about 2 minutes). Remove from heat; stir in vanilla and pecans. Let cool. Serve over vanilla ice cream. Yield: 1 cup.    *Florence L. Costello,*
*Chattanooga, Tennessee.*

### HONEYSCOTCH SUNDAE SAUCE

1 (5.33-ounce) can evaporated milk, divided
¾ cup honey
½ cup sugar
¼ cup butter or margarine
¼ teaspoon salt

Combine ⅓ cup evaporated milk and remaining ingredients; mix well. Cook over medium heat, stirring occasionally, until mixture reaches soft ball stage (234°). Stir in remaining milk. Cook, stirring constantly, about 3 minutes, or until smooth. Serve sauce over ice cream. Yield: 1⅔ cups.

*Mrs. W. J. Scherffius,*
*Mountain Home, Arkansas.*

### FRUITY DESSERT TOPPING

1½ cups apple juice
¼ cup honey
4 peaches, peeled and sliced
2 bananas, peeled and sliced
1 cup pitted dark sweet cherries, halved

Combine apple juice and honey in a medium saucepan; stir well. Bring to a boil; reduce heat and cook, stirring occasionally, until mixture is reduced by about one-third. Stir in fruit; simmer 5 minutes or until fruit is thoroughly heated. Serve over vanilla ice cream. Yield: about 4 cups.

*Mrs. John F. Davis III,*
*Dallas, Texas.*

### BUTTER-NUT STRIPS

¾ cup butter or margarine, softened
¼ cup sugar
1 teaspoon almond extract
2 cups all-purpose flour
1 egg white, beaten
1 tablespoon sugar
⅓ cup chopped blanched almonds

Cream butter; gradually add ¼ cup sugar, beating until light and fluffy. Add extract and flour; beat until smooth. Shape into a ball; chill.

Roll dough to ¼-inch thickness on a lightly floured surface. Cut into 2½- x ½-inch strips; place on ungreased cookie sheets. Brush tops lightly with egg white. Combine 1 tablespoon sugar and almonds; sprinkle over egg white. Bake at 350° for 15 minutes or until lightly browned. Yield: about 4 dozen.

*Mrs. Donald C. Vanhoy,*
*Salisbury, North Carolina.*

### SUGARED PECANS

2 egg whites
1 cup sugar
1 pound (about 4 cups) pecans, coarsely chopped
½ cup butter or margarine, melted

Beat egg whites (at room temperature) until foamy. Gradually add sugar, 1 tablespoon at a time, beating until stiff peaks form. Fold in pecans.

Pour butter into a 15- x 10- x 1-inch jellyroll pan. Spread pecan mixture over butter. Bake at 325° for 30 minutes, stirring every 10 minutes. Cool and store in an airtight container. Yield: 4 cups.

*Laurie McReynolds,*
*Norman, Oklahoma.*

### WHOLE WHEAT GRANOLA

4 cups regular oats, uncooked
3 cups whole wheat flour
2 cups wheat germ
1 cup all-purpose flour
1 tablespoon ground cinnamon
1½ teaspoons salt
1 cup vegetable oil
1 cup honey
½ cup water
1 cup flaked coconut
½ cup sliced almonds
1 cup raisins

Combine first 6 ingredients in a large bowl; mix well. Combine vegetable oil, honey, and water; pour over oats mixture, and mix well.

Spread mixture evenly in two 15- x 10- x 1-inch jellyroll pans. Bake at 250° for 1 hour; remove from oven, and stir in coconut and almonds. Bake an additional 30 minutes; cool. Stir in raisins; store in airtight containers. Yield: 13 cups.

*Note:* Granola may be served as a cereal with milk.    *Regyna Day,*
*Westminster, Colorado.*

*Tip: Plastic bags that have been used to wrap dry foods, vegetables, and fruit can often be washed and reused.*

# From The Garden To The Casserole

During the summer when vegetables are plentiful and especially flavorful, there's no better time to combine them in a variety of baked casseroles. Whether your garden bears green beans, eggplant, cabbage, or squash, these recipes should start you on a season full of vegetable enjoyment.

Light and airy are two ways to describe Cheesy Zucchini Casserole—a combination of stiffly beaten egg whites, bacon, mushrooms, and zucchini. Savory Cabbage Casserole alternates layers of shredded cabbage and tomatoes with rice. And Elegant Eggplant Casserole is another winning combination—eggplant, onion, bacon, and potatoes are bound with creamy chicken mushroom soup.

## SAVORY CABBAGE CASSEROLE

4 cups shredded cabbage
1 (28-ounce) can tomatoes, undrained and chopped
1 teaspoon salt
¼ cup chopped onion
1 tablespoon butter or margarine
3 cups cooked regular rice
½ cup cracker crumbs
½ cup (2 ounces) shredded Cheddar cheese
2 tablespoons butter or margarine, melted

Combine first 5 ingredients in a large saucepan; bring to a boil. Reduce heat, and simmer 5 minutes. Place half of rice in a greased 2-quart casserole; top with half of cabbage mixture. Repeat layers. Combine remaining ingredients, stirring well; sprinkle over casserole. Bake at 375° for 45 minutes. Yield: 8 servings.

*Pat Andrus,*
*Scott, Louisiana.*

## ELEGANT EGGPLANT CASSEROLE

1 medium eggplant
2 slices bacon, diced
1 medium onion, chopped
1 medium potato, grated
1 (10¾-ounce) can creamy chicken mushroom soup, undiluted
½ cup round buttery cracker crumbs

Peel eggplant, and cut into 1-inch cubes; cook in a small amount of boiling water for 10 minutes or until tender. Drain well.

Fry bacon in a large skillet until crisp. Stir in onion and potato; cook until onion is tender. Add eggplant and soup, stirring well. Spoon into a lightly greased 1½-quart baking dish. Sprinkle with cracker crumbs. Bake at 350° for 30 minutes. Yield: 6 servings.

*Nell Kruger,*
*San Antonio, Texas.*

## GARDEN CASSEROLE

2 cups fresh green beans
1 tablespoon butter or margarine, melted
3 medium carrots, scraped and sliced into thin strips
1 large green pepper, cut into 1-inch pieces
1 large onion, thinly sliced
2 cups sliced celery
1½ teaspoons salt
½ teaspoon pepper
1 tablespoon sugar
2 tablespoons cornstarch
1 (16-ounce) can whole tomatoes, undrained and chopped
3 tablespoons butter or margarine

Remove strings from beans; cut beans into 1-inch pieces. Wash thoroughly, and drain.

Pour 1 tablespoon melted butter into a 3-quart baking dish; tilt to coat surface. Layer beans, carrots, green pepper, onion, and celery in baking dish.

Combine salt, pepper, sugar, and cornstarch; mix well, and sprinkle over vegetables. Top with chopped tomatoes, and dot with 3 tablespoons butter. Bake at 350° for 1 hour or until vegetables are tender. Yield: 10 servings.

*Anita Cox,*
*Fort Worth, Texas.*

## CHEESY ZUCCHINI CASSEROLE

2 pounds medium zucchini, thinly sliced
1 (4-ounce) can sliced mushrooms, undrained
1 tablespoon butter or margarine, melted
2 eggs, separated
1 (8-ounce) carton commercial sour cream
2 tablespoons all-purpose flour
½ teaspoon salt
1½ cups (6 ounces) shredded Cheddar cheese
6 slices bacon, cooked and crumbled
¼ cup fine, dry breadcrumbs
1 tablespoon butter or margarine, melted
Bacon curls (optional)
Fresh parsley sprigs (optional)
Sliced zucchini (optional)

Combine zucchini, mushrooms, and 1 tablespoon butter in a large skillet; cook over medium heat until zucchini is tender, stirring occasionally.

Beat egg yolks; add sour cream, flour, and salt, stirring until blended. Beat egg whites (at room temperature) until stiff; fold into sour cream mixture.

Layer half the squash mixture, sour cream mixture, cheese, and bacon in a 12- x 8- x 2-inch baking dish. Repeat the layers.

Combine breadcrumbs and 1 tablespoon butter; sprinkle over casserole. Bake at 350° for 25 minutes. Garnish with bacon curls (rolled-up slices of cooked bacon), parsley, and sliced zucchini, if desired. Yield: 8 servings.

*Leilah Williams,*
*Eustace, Texas.*

# Put Variety Into Burgers

Getting tired of your usual hamburgers? Try adding some extra flavor or maybe a surprise in the middle.

The addition of Burgundy and half-and-half gives Company Hamburger Steak a sophisticated appeal. Crowned with a zesty sauce, Barbecued Burgers prove that bran cereal with raisins is a surprisingly delicious way to stretch ground beef while adding some fiber to the diet.

In the supermarket, select ground beef that has a reddish pink color and feels cold to the touch. Use refrigerated ground beef within two days; frozen ground beef will keep up to two or three months without loss of quality.

Turn each patty just once during cooking; turning more than that tends to make the beef less juicy.

## BARBECUED BURGERS

1 pound ground beef
½ cup bran cereal with raisins
½ cup milk
1 egg, beaten
Dash of pepper
2 tablespoons butter or margarine
½ cup chopped onion
1 cup catsup
¼ cup water
¼ cup vinegar
2 tablespoons brown sugar
1 tablespoon prepared mustard

Combine first 5 ingredients; stir well. Shape into 6 patties about ¾ inch thick. Melt butter in a large skillet; cook patties until brown on each side. Remove burgers, and keep warm.

Sauté onion in pan drippings until tender. Add remaining ingredients, stirring until smooth.

Place burgers in the sauce; cover skillet, and simmer 5 to 10 minutes. Yield: 6 servings.          *Mrs. James E. Farrar,*
*Hamilton, Ontario.*

## COMPANY HAMBURGER STEAKS

1 pound lean ground beef
½ cup half-and-half
2 tablespoons Burgundy or other
  dry red wine
2 slices bread, crusts removed and
  crumbled
1 egg, beaten
¾ teaspoon salt
½ teaspoon pepper
2 tablespoons butter or margarine
1 (3½-ounce) can sliced mushrooms,
  undrained
1 (10¼-ounce) can beef gravy

Combine first 7 ingredients; mix well, and shape into 4 patties. Melt butter in a large skillet; cook patties until brown on each side.

Add mushrooms; cook 3 to 4 minutes. Add gravy, and bring to a boil; cover skillet, and simmer 15 to 20 minutes. Yield: 4 servings.          *Rhonda Cox,*
*Shawnee, Oklahoma.*

## SURPRISE BURGERS

¾ pound ground beef
½ cup soft breadcrumbs
2 teaspoons prepared mustard
1 clove garlic, crushed
¼ teaspoon salt
Dash of pepper
2 tablespoons milk
1 (10-ounce) package Swiss cheese, cut
  lengthwise into 4 slices
4 French rolls, split lengthwise and
  toasted
Leaf lettuce (optional)
Red peppers, sliced and seeded (optional)

Combine first 7 ingredients; mix well, and divide into 4 equal portions. Mold one portion of meat mixture around each cheese slice.

Place burgers in a 13- x 9- x 2-inch baking pan. Bake at 400° for 10 to 15 minutes or until cheese begins to melt. Place burgers in French rolls; garnish with lettuce and red peppers, if desired. Yield: 4 servings.          *Sandra Bowlin,*
*Morristown, Tennessee.*

## PINEAPPLE BURGERS

1 pound ground beef
1 (8-ounce) can sliced pineapple, drained
½ cup firmly packed brown sugar
1 cup catsup
¼ cup prepared mustard

Shape ground beef into 8 thin patties. Place a pineapple slice on 4 patties; top with remaining patties, and seal edges.

Place patties in a skillet over medium heat; cook about 15 minutes or until desired degree of doneness.

Combine sugar, catsup, and mustard in a small saucepan; simmer 5 minutes, and pour over patties. Yield: 4 servings.
*Cheryl J. Smith,*
*Bethune, South Carolina.*

# Try These Fresh Lemon Treats

Grated lemon rind or freshly squeezed juice gives these lemon dishes that famous tart and tangy taste. For example, our Lemon-Sour Cream Pie boasts a strong lemon flavor in a rich, butter-yellow filling capped with golden meringue. You'll find a more subtle fruit flavor in Lemon Soufflé, a pastel-colored dessert with a creamy texture that melts in your mouth.

When you use fresh lemons for cooking, remember that one medium lemon will yield 2 to 4 tablespoons of juice and 1 tablespoon of grated rind. You'll extract more juice if you use room temperature lemons and roll them firmly on the counter with the palm of your hand before juicing. It's best to grate the peel while the lemon is whole; freeze grated rind for later use if you don't need it right away.

## LEMON TEA CAKE

½ cup butter or margarine, softened
1 cup sugar
2 eggs
1⅔ cups all-purpose flour
1 teaspoon baking powder
½ teaspoon salt
½ cup milk
½ cup chopped walnuts
Grated rind of 1 lemon
Glaze (recipe follows)

Combine butter and sugar, creaming until light and fluffy. Add the eggs, one at a time, beating well after each addition. Combine flour, baking powder, and salt; add to creamed mixture alternately with milk, mixing well after each addition. Stir in walnuts and lemon rind.

Pour batter into a greased and floured 9- x 5- x 3-inch loafpan. Bake at 350° for 55 minutes or until a wooden pick inserted in center comes out clean. Pour glaze over bread. Cool 10 to 15 minutes before removing from pan. Yield: 1 loaf.

*Glaze:*

½ cup sifted powdered sugar
Juice of 1 lemon

Combine sugar and lemon juice, mixing well. Yield: about ½ cup.
*Betty Jane Morrison,*
*Lakewood, Colorado.*

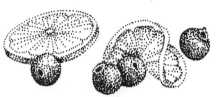

## LEMON-SOUR CREAM PIE

1 (8-ounce) carton commercial sour cream
4 eggs, separated
1 (4¾-ounce) package vanilla pudding mix
1⅓ cups milk
1 (6-ounce) can frozen lemonade
  concentrate, thawed and undiluted
⅓ cup sugar
2 tablespoons cornstarch
2 tablespoons water
¼ cup fresh lemon juice
1 baked 9-inch deep-dish pastry shell
½ teaspoon cream of tartar
½ cup sugar

Combine sour cream and egg yolks in a medium saucepan, mixing well. Stir in pudding mix, milk, lemonade concentrate, and ⅓ cup sugar.

Combine cornstarch and 2 tablespoons water, mixing well; add to lemon mixture. Cook mixture over medium heat, stirring constantly, until thickened. Remove from heat, and stir in lemon juice. Pour filling into baked pastry shell.

Combine egg whites (at room temperature) and cream of tartar; beat until foamy. Gradually add ½ cup sugar, 1 tablespoon at a time, beating until stiff peaks form. Spread meringue over lemon filling, sealing to edge of pastry. Bake at 350° for 12 to 15 minutes or until golden brown. Cool pie to room temperature. Yield: one 9-inch pie.
*Cille Caddell,*
*Charlotte, North Carolina.*

## LEMON SOUFFLE

3 eggs, separated
1 envelope unflavored gelatin
½ cup sugar
¼ teaspoon salt
1 cup water
Grated rind of 1 lemon
Juice of 1 lemon
⅓ cup sugar
1 cup whipping cream, whipped

Cut a piece of aluminum foil or waxed paper long enough to fit around a 1-quart soufflé dish, allowing a 1-inch overlap; fold lengthwise into thirds. Lightly oil one side of foil; wrap around outside of dish, oiled side against dish, allowing it to extend 3 inches above rim to form a collar. Secure foil with freezer tape.

Beat egg yolks; combine yolks and next 4 ingredients in a saucepan, stirring well. Cook over medium heat, stirring constantly, until mixture begins to bubble. Remove from heat; stir in lemon rind and juice. Cool.

Beat egg whites (at room temperature) until foamy; gradually add ⅓ cup sugar, beating until stiff peaks form. Fold egg whites and whipped cream into the yolk mixture.

Spoon into prepared dish, and chill until firm. Remove collar from dish. Yield: 6 servings.     *Adell Whitfield,*
*El Dorado, Arkansas.*

## LEMON CREAM DRESSING

½ cup mayonnaise
½ teaspoon prepared mustard
Grated rind of 1 lemon
Juice of 1 lemon
½ cup whipping cream, whipped

Combine mayonnaise and mustard, mixing well; stir in lemon rind and lemon juice. Fold in whipped cream. Serve over fresh fruit. Yield: 1½ cups.
*Ruth E. Cunliffe,*
*Lake Placid, Florida.*

# Fresh Peaches Sweeten The Summer

Southern summers bring ripe, juicy peaches to roadside stands, fresh-air markets, and the kitchen table. This golden fruit sweetens pies, cobblers,

and, of course, homemade ice cream. You'll find recipes here for these all-time favorites as well as some new ideas like our Bavarian Peach Cream—a delicate congealed dessert with a light, fluffy texture and a sweet peaches-and-cream flavor.

The best peach dishes start with top-quality fruit. Look for peaches with a creamy to gold undercolor; a green tint indicates that the fruit was picked too early and will never ripen. When cooking, it will help to remember that 4 medium peaches equal 2 cups of slices.

## PEACH BREAD

½ cup butter or margarine, softened
1 cup sugar
3 eggs
2¾ cups all-purpose flour
1½ teaspoons baking powder
½ teaspoon baking soda
1 teaspoon salt
1½ teaspoons ground cinnamon
2 cups sliced fresh peaches
3 tablespoons frozen orange juice
   concentrate, thawed and undiluted
1 teaspoon vanilla extract

Cream butter; gradually add sugar, beating well. Add eggs, one at a time, beating well after each addition.

Combine next 5 ingredients; add to creamed mixture alternately with the peaches, beginning and ending with flour mixture. Stir in orange juice concentrate and vanilla.

Pour batter into a greased and floured 9- x 5- x 3- inch loafpan. Bake at 350° for 1 hour or until wooden pick inserted in center comes out clean. Cool in pan 10 minutes; remove from pan, and cool completely. Yield: 1 loaf.
*Kathryn McCoy,*
*Bishop, Texas.*

## OVEN-BAKED PEACHES WITH GINGER

¾ cup firmly packed brown sugar, divided
2 tablespoons butter or margarine
6 large peaches, peeled and sliced
2 to 3 tablespoons crystallized ginger
½ cup light rum
1 tablespoon butter or margarine

Sprinkle half of sugar in a 12- x 8- x 2-inch baking dish; dot with 2 tablespoons butter. Place peaches on top of sugar and butter; sprinkle with ginger. Pour rum over peaches; sprinkle with remaining sugar. Dot with 1 tablespoon butter. Bake at 350° for 20 minutes. Yield: 6 servings.
*Mrs. J. Gordon Dixon,*
*Griffin, Georgia.*

## OLD-FASHIONED PEACH COBBLER

4 cups sliced fresh peaches
1 cup sugar
½ cup butter or margarine
1½ cups all-purpose flour
¾ teaspoon salt
½ cup shortening
¼ cup plus 1 tablespoon cold water

Combine first 3 ingredients in a medium saucepan; bring to a boil, and cook over low heat until peaches are tender and mixture thickens. Pour peach mixture into a lightly buttered 10- x 6- x 2-inch baking dish. Set aside.

Combine flour and salt; cut in shortening with a pastry blender until mixture resembles coarse meal. Sprinkle water evenly over flour mixture, and stir with a fork until all ingredients are moistened. Shape pastry into a ball.

Roll out pastry to ⅛-inch thickness on a lightly floured board; cut into 1-inch strips, and arrange half of the strips in lattice design over peaches. Bake at 350° for 35 minutes. Remove from oven, and gently press baked pastry into peach mixture. Repeat lattice design over peaches with remaining pastry strips. Return to oven, and bake an additional 40 minutes. Yield: 6 servings.     *Marie Davis,*
*Morganton, North Carolina.*

## FRESH PEACH PIE

5 cups sliced fresh peaches
1 unbaked 9-inch pastry shell
⅓ cup butter or margarine, melted
1 cup sugar
⅓ cup all-purpose flour
1 egg

Place peaches in pastry shell. Combine remaining ingredients, and pour over peaches. Bake at 350° for 1 hour and 10 minutes. Yield: one 9-inch pie.
*Karen Mangin,*
*Baton Rouge, Louisiana.*

## BAVARIAN PEACH CREAM

1 (3-ounce) package peach-flavored gelatin
1 cup whipping cream, whipped
2 cups chopped fresh peaches

Prepare gelatin according to package directions; chill until the consistency of unbeaten egg white.

Beat gelatin at high speed of electric mixer until foamy, about 2 to 3 minutes. Fold in whipped cream and peaches. Pour into a lightly oiled 6-cup mold. Cover and chill overnight. Unmold before serving. Yield: 6 to 8 servings. *Mrs. John N. Atkins, Jr., Nashville, Tennessee.*

## PEACH ICE CREAM

6 cups mashed peaches
1 cup sugar
5 eggs
2 cups sugar
¼ teaspoon salt
1 teaspoon vanilla extract
½ cup milk
1 cup whipping cream, whipped
1 cup half-and-half
About 1 quart milk

Combine peaches and 1 cup sugar; stir well, and set aside.

Beat eggs with electric mixer at medium speed until frothy. Gradually add 2 cups sugar, beating until thick. Add salt, vanilla, and ½ cup milk; beat until sugar is dissolved. Stir in whipped cream, half-and-half, and peaches.

Pour mixture into freezer can of 1-gallon hand-turned or electric freezer. Add enough milk to fill can two-thirds full. Freeze according to manufacturer's instructions. Let ripen at least 1 hour. Yield: about 1 gallon. *Rhonda Cox, Tallahassee, Florida.*

# From Our Kitchen To Yours

Our test kitchens staff has prepared many freezers of ice cream over the years, and we'd like to share some tips to make sure your special ice cream freezes just right every time.

## About Making Ice Cream

Whether using a cooked custard or a no-cook base for your ice cream, start with the best ingredients. Buy the freshest milk, cream, and eggs possible. Pure flavorings, not imitations, will give your ice cream a richer flavor. Use fully ripened fruit because underripe fruit freezes too hard. Always chop or mash fruit such as peaches or strawberries into small pieces. Be sure to sweeten the fruit before adding to the cream mixture because the sugar will keep the fruit from freezing too hard. If a recipe calls for whipped cream, whip only until soft peaks form, not until it's stiff. If possible, chill the cream mixture 4 hours or overnight. This allows the flavors to blend and helps make the ice cream smoother.

When freezing ice cream, follow manufacturer's instructions for your freezer. If your instructions are missing, follow these general guidelines.

■ Position the empty ice cream container in the freezer. Pour in the ice cream mixture, and add the dasher. Most freezers should be filled no more than two-thirds full. (Leaving this space allows for expansion of the ice cream as the rotating dasher incorporates air into the mixture.) Before adding the ice and salt, let the motor run, or turn the crank for 1 minute.

■ For a 1-gallon freezer, you'll need about 20 pounds of crushed ice and 3 to 4 cups rock salt. Don't skimp on the ice and salt; they're essential for the proper freezing of the ice cream. The ice cream freezes because its heat is absorbed by the ice and salt. Ice alone is not cold enough to freeze the ice cream.

Always use the amount of salt recommended for your freezer. If too little salt is used, the brine will not get cold enough to thoroughly freeze the ice cream. If too much salt is used, the ice cream will freeze too quickly, causing large ice crystals to form. Rock salt is usually preferred over table salt because table salt dissolves rapidly. (Some freezer manufacturers do recommend using table salt.)

When adding ice and salt, make four fairly thick layers of ice and four thin layers of salt, beginning with ice and ending with salt. You'll have some ice and salt left over to add as the ice melts and when ripening the ice cream.

■ When freezing the ice cream, always stay within earshot of your electric freezer. When the motor slows down or stops running, the ice cream is churned and the freezer should be unplugged immediately. (The motor can burn out if allowed to run too long after churning is complete.) Churning is usually complete in 25 to 35 minutes.

■ After freezing, let the ice cream ripen to harden and blend the flavors. Drain off the brine; then carefully wipe the can cover to remove any traces of salt before taking off the cover. Lift the dasher, scraping ice cream back into the can. Cover the can with foil or plastic wrap. Rinse the cover, and carefully place on the container. Pack the remaining ice and salt around and above the can. Insulate the freezer with several layers of newspapers or a heavy towel. Let stand in a cool place 1 to 2 hours; then it's ready to serve.

# Chicken Salad With A Flair

After one bite, our foods staff voted this chicken salad one of the tastiest they've ever sampled. There's nothing unusual about it, but they acclaimed it for just the right blend of ingredients. Serve it on lettuce leaves, and garnish with grapes and cantaloupe balls.

## CHICKEN SALAD WITH FRUIT

4 cups chopped cooked chicken
2 cups thinly sliced celery
1 to 2 tablespoons minced onion
¾ cup mayonnaise
¼ cup whipping cream
1 tablespoon lemon juice
½ teaspoon salt
White pepper to taste
Lettuce leaves
¼ to ½ cup slivered almonds, toasted
2 to 3 cups cantaloupe balls
Seedless green grapes

Combine chicken and celery. Combine next 6 ingredients, stirring well; add to chicken mixture, and toss well. Chill.

Serve salad on lettuce leaves. Sprinkle with toasted almonds, and garnish with melon balls and grapes. Yield: 8 to 10 servings. *Mrs. Kenneth Olson, Dunnellon, Florida.*

*Tip: Onions offer outstanding nutritive value. They are a good source of calcium and vitamins A and C. They contain iron, riboflavin, thiamine, and niacin, have a high percentage of water, and supply essential bulk. They are low in calories and have only a trace of fat.*

# Microwave Cookery

## Take The Mystery Out Of Browning Dishes

Microwave browning dishes will help take you one step closer to obtaining conventional results from your microwave oven. Browning dishes function much like conventional skillets or grills, except that they allow you to brown, grill, or sear foods such as Grilled Cheese Sandwiches or Easy French Toast in the microwave oven.

Browning dishes are available in two styles—a skillet and a grill. The skillet comes in several different sizes and has a cover. The grill has a slightly sloping surface with a recessed well around the rim of the dish to catch fats and drippings as they drain from food. The grill is designed to make it especially easy to turn foods over as they cook.

Each browning dish has a special coating on the underside of the dish. This coating absorbs microwaves when the dish is preheated; as a result, the cooking surface becomes very hot. When food is placed on the hot surface, it browns at the contact point—as it would on a conventional hot skillet or grill.

If you are experimenting with this new microwave accessory, here are some helpful hints:

—The first step in microwave browning is to preheat the browning dish in the microwave; this activates the special coating. Preheating times vary according to several factors: the size and shape of the browning dish, the wattage of the microwave oven, the type of food being cooked, and the personal preference of the cook. Try the minimum preheat time initially. If you prefer browner food products, you can increase the preheat time. However, never exceed the manufacturer's recommended preheating times—usually 5 minutes for small skillets and 8 minutes for larger skillets or grills.

—Always use hot pads when handling heated browning dishes. The coated part of the dish becomes hot enough to burn or scorch countertops and tables.

—Use browning dishes only in microwave ovens that have a glass-ceramic shelf or bottom. The dishes become so hot they could easily melt or crack a plastic shelf.

—Do not cover the browning skillet or grill with paper or plastic products while microwaving. Paper could burn and plastic will melt.

—Should you have to microwave more than one batch of food, the browning dish will need to be preheated between each batch; however, the second preheating usually takes about half as long as the first. Refer to manufacturer's directions.

—If you find foods are not browning evenly, try rotating the dish occasionally during cooking. There are hot spots in nearly every microwave oven, and rotating allows for even browning.

—Most browning dishes may be washed in the dishwasher or by hand. Avoid harsh cleaning pads such as steel wool; plastic scouring pads work better.

### HAMBURGER PATTIES

1 pound lean ground beef
2 teaspoons dried parsley flakes
¼ teaspoon salt
¼ teaspoon onion salt
⅛ teaspoon pepper
1 tablespoon catsup
1 teaspoon butter or margarine

Combine first 6 ingredients, mixing well; shape into 4 patties. Set aside.

Place a browning grill in microwave oven; preheat at HIGH for 6 minutes. Add butter to hot grill, tilting to coat the surface.

Place patties on grill; microwave at HIGH for 3 minutes. Turn patties over; microwave at HIGH for 1½ to 2½ minutes or until browned. Yield: 4 servings.

### VEGETABLE STIR-FRY

1 tablespoon soy sauce
½ teaspoon sugar
1 (6-ounce) package frozen Chinese pea pods, thawed and drained
1 cup sliced fresh mushrooms
½ cup fresh bean sprouts
¼ cup sliced water chestnuts
2 tablespoons butter or margarine

Combine soy sauce and sugar, stirring well; set aside. Combine next 4 ingredients, tossing gently; set aside.

Place a 10-inch browning skillet in microwave oven; preheat, uncovered, at HIGH for 3 minutes. Add butter to hot skillet, tilting to coat surface. Place vegetable mixture in skillet; cover with skillet top. Microwave at HIGH for 2 minutes. Remove skillet cover, and add soy sauce mixture; stir well. Cover and microwave at HIGH 1½ to 2½ minutes. Yield: 4 servings.

### QUICK BROWNED POTATOES

2 small potatoes
1½ tablespoons butter or margarine
1½ teaspoons grated Parmesan cheese
⅛ teaspoon salt
⅛ teaspoon garlic powder
⅛ teaspoon paprika
⅛ teaspoon pepper

Scrub potatoes, and cut into ¼-inch crosswise slices; place on paper towels to drain.

Place a 10-inch browning skillet in microwave oven; preheat, uncovered, at HIGH for 8 minutes. Add butter to hot skillet, tilting to coat surface. Place potatoes in skillet. Microwave at HIGH for 5 to 6 minutes. Turn potatoes over; microwave 2 to 3 minutes or until tender. Drain potatoes on paper towels.

Combine remaining ingredients, stirring well; sprinkle over potatoes. Yield: 2 servings.

### GRILLED CHEESE SANDWICHES

Butter or margarine
4 slices bread
4 slices process American cheese

Butter one side of each slice of bread. Place 2 slices of cheese between 2 bread slices, with buttered sides out.

Place a 10-inch browning grill in microwave oven; preheat at HIGH for 4 to 5 minutes.

Place sandwiches on grill; microwave at MEDIUM HIGH (70% power) for 30 seconds. Flatten sandwiches slightly with a spatula. Turn sandwiches over, and microwave for 25 seconds or until cheese melts. Yield: 2 servings.

### EASY FRENCH TOAST

2 eggs, slightly beaten
¼ cup milk
1 teaspoon sugar
⅛ teaspoon salt
¼ teaspoon vanilla extract
½ teaspoon butter or margarine
4 slices bread

Combine first 5 ingredients in a large bowl; beat well. Set aside.

Place a browning grill in microwave oven; preheat at HIGH for 4 to 5 minutes. Add butter to hot grill, tilting to coat surface.

Dip bread slices in egg mixture, coating both sides. Place slices on grill; microwave at HIGH for 1 minute. Turn slices over; microwave at HIGH for 1 minute. Yield: 2 servings.

# Spectacular Make-Ahead Dessert Soufflés

If you've ever made what you hoped would be a light, airy dessert soufflé only to have it fall before reaching the table, you're going to love chilled versions like Frozen Vanilla Soufflé and Brandy Alexander Soufflé. They're virtually fall-proof, thanks to the eggs and whipped cream (and gelatin in some cases) that hold them firm when removed from the refrigerator or freezer.

When preparing them, there's one thing that's essential: If a cooked custard is used in the recipe, it must be cooled before whipped cream or beaten egg whites are folded in; otherwise, the soufflé won't hold its shape.

## BRANDY ALEXANDER SOUFFLE

2 envelopes unflavored gelatin
2 cups water
4 eggs, separated
¾ cup sugar
1 (8-ounce) package cream cheese, softened
3 tablespoons crème de cacao
3 tablespoons brandy
¼ cup sugar
1 cup whipping cream, whipped

Cut a piece of aluminum foil or waxed paper long enough to fit around a 1½-quart soufflé dish, allowing a 1-inch overlap; fold lengthwise into thirds. Lightly oil one side of foil; wrap around outside of dish, oiled side against dish, allowing it to extend 3 inches above rim to form a collar. Secure the foil with freezer tape.

Combine gelatin and 1 cup water in top of a double boiler; bring water in bottom of double boiler to a boil. Cook, stirring constantly, until gelatin dissolves; stir in remaining water.

Beat egg yolks until thick and lemon colored; gradually add ¾ cup sugar, beating well. Stir into gelatin mixture. Cook over low heat 10 to 12 minutes or until thickened, stirring constantly.

Beat cream cheese until smooth; gradually add yolk mixture, beating well. Stir in crème de cacao and brandy; chill until slightly thickened.

Beat egg whites (at room temperature) until foamy; gradually add ¼ cup sugar, beating until stiff peaks form. Gently fold whipped cream and beaten egg whites into cream cheese mixture.

Spoon into a 1½-quart soufflé dish, and chill until firm. Remove collar from dish. Yield: 8 to 10 servings.

*Mrs. Travis M. Bedsole, Jr.,*
*Mobile, Alabama.*

## FROZEN VANILLA SOUFFLE

4 egg yolks
1 cup sugar
1 cup milk
1 cup half-and-half
1½ teaspoons vanilla extract
⅛ teaspoon salt
2 cups whipping cream, whipped
Additional whipped cream (optional)
Chocolate shavings

Cut a piece of aluminum foil or waxed paper long enough to fit around a 1-quart soufflé dish, allowing a 1-inch overlap; fold lengthwise into thirds. Lightly oil one side of foil; wrap around outside of dish, oiled side against dish, allowing it to extend 3 inches above rim to form a collar. Secure the foil with freezer tape.

Beat egg yolks in top of a double boiler until thick and lemon colored; gradually add sugar, beating well. Add milk, half-and-half, vanilla, and salt; beat well. Bring water in bottom of double boiler to a boil. Reduce heat to low; cook, stirring constantly, until mixture thickens and coats a metal spoon. Let cool.

Gently fold whipped cream into custard, and spoon into prepared soufflé dish; freeze until firm. Remove collar from dish. Garnish soufflé with additional whipped cream and chocolate shavings, if desired. Yield: 8 servings.

*Mrs. Charles P. McGenty,*
*Cape Girardeau, Missouri.*

## KAHLUA SOUFFLE

2 envelopes unflavored gelatin
½ cup milk
2 eggs, separated
⅔ cup sugar
1 cup strong coffee
½ cup Kahlúa or other coffee-flavored liqueur
¼ teaspoon salt
2 tablespoons sugar
2 cups whipping cream, whipped
½ cup almond brickle chips

Cut a piece of aluminum foil or waxed paper long enough to fit around a 1-quart soufflé dish, allowing a 1-inch overlap; fold lengthwise into thirds. Lightly oil one side of foil; wrap around outside of dish, oiled side against dish, allowing it to extend 3 inches above rim to form a collar. Secure the foil with freezer tape.

Combine gelatin and milk; stir until gelatin dissolves. Let stand 5 minutes.

Beat egg yolks until thick and lemon colored; gradually add ⅔ cup sugar, beating well. Add coffee, and beat until smooth. Pour coffee mixture into top of a double boiler, and bring water to a boil. Cook, stirring constantly, until mixture thickens and coats a metal spoon. Stir in gelatin mixture, Kahlúa, and salt. Chill until consistency of unbeaten egg white; beat well.

Beat egg whites (at room temperature) until foamy; gradually add 2 tablespoons sugar, beating until stiff peaks form. Gently fold whipped cream and beaten egg whites into coffee mixture.

Spoon into prepared soufflé dish, and chill until firm. Remove collar from dish, and sprinkle with brickle chips. Yield: 8 servings.

*Mrs. Roger Nelson Horn,*
*Houston, Texas.*

# Homemade Breads With A Plus

Poppy seeds and sour cream, tomato sauce, caraway seeds, and cheese—these are some of the best ways we know to boost the flavor of homemade breads.

Serve some of these breads at your next outdoor cookout or with a special meal. Freeze any leftovers for one of those too-busy-to-cook days.

## ONE-STEP BISCUITS

1 (8-ounce) carton commercial sour cream
1 egg
2 cups pancake mix
Poppy seeds

Combine sour cream and egg in a large mixing bowl; beat until well blended. Add pancake mix; stir until dry ingredients are moistened.

Drop by tablespoonfuls onto greased cookie sheet. Sprinkle with poppy seeds. Bake at 375° for 10 to 15 minutes or until golden. Yield: 1 dozen.

*Claudia Graves,*
*Columbus, Mississippi.*

## CARAWAY PUFFS

2 packages yeast
½ cup warm water (105° to 115°)
2 cups small-curd cottage cheese
¼ cup sugar
2 tablespoons caraway seeds
2 teaspoons salt
½ teaspoon baking soda
2 eggs, slightly beaten
4⅔ cups all-purpose flour
Melted butter or margarine

Combine yeast and warm water in a large mixing bowl; stir and set aside. Heat cottage cheese over low heat until lukewarm. Stir cottage cheese, sugar, caraway seeds, salt, soda, and eggs into yeast mixture. Gradually add flour, stirring until dough leaves the sides of the mixing bowl.

Cover and let rise in a warm place (85°), free from drafts, 1 hour or until doubled in bulk. Stir dough down; spoon into 24 large well-greased muffin pans. Cover and let rise in a warm place (85°), free from drafts, 45 minutes or until doubled in bulk. Bake at 350° for 25 minutes or until golden brown. Brush tops with butter. Yield: 2 dozen.
*Sophia Landrith,*
*Junction City, Kansas.*

## CHEESE BREAD

1 egg
3¾ cups biscuit mix
1½ cups milk
¾ cup (3 ounces) shredded sharp Cheddar cheese

Beat egg at low speed of electric mixer. Add biscuit mix, milk, and cheese; beat 1½ minutes at medium speed until well mixed. Spoon batter into a greased 9- x 5- x 3-inch loafpan. Bake at 350° for 50 to 60 minutes. Yield: 1 loaf.
*Vicki Dutton,*
*Brownwood, Texas.*

## TOASTED CORNBREAD

1 (6-ounce) package cornbread mix
1 egg, beaten
¾ cup tomato sauce
2 tablespoons instant onion flakes
Melted butter or margarine
Grated Parmesan cheese

Combine first 4 ingredients; stir just until cornbread mix is moistened. Spoon into a greased 8-inch cast-iron skillet or 8-inch cakepan. Bake at 425° for 20 minutes; let cool.

Remove from pan, and slice cornbread horizontally into 2 layers; cut each layer into 6 wedges. Place cut sides up on a cookie sheet; broil until golden brown. Brush tops with butter; sprinkle with cheese. Yield: 6 servings.
*Sara A. McCullough,*
*Louisville, Mississippi.*

## Are There Kids In Your Kitchen?

Many of today's best cooks began practicing their culinary skills while still in their early teens or before. If you have young chefs at your house, let them try their hands at this menu.

Before they begin, remind your children to read the entire recipe thoroughly before beginning work; this will speed up the cooking process and eliminate mistakes. Assemble all food and equipment first; then do any necessary chopping or slicing. Remember that many steps in a recipe can be completed well ahead of time to avoid a last-minute scramble.

---

**Grapefruit-Orange Refresher**
**Super Chicken Salad**
**Sesame Italian Green Beans**
**Herbed French Bread**
**Frozen Strawberry Delight**

---

## GRAPEFRUIT-ORANGE REFRESHER

1½ cups grapefruit juice
1½ cups orange juice
¼ cup lime juice
¼ cup plus 1 tablespoon sugar

Combine all ingredients, mixing well. Serve over ice. Yield: about 3½ cups.
*Joyce Maurer,*
*Christmas, Florida.*

## SUPER CHICKEN SALAD

3½ cups chopped cooked chicken
½ cup chopped celery
½ cup mayonnaise
¼ cup commercial French dressing
3 hard-cooked eggs, chopped
¼ teaspoon Worcestershire sauce
½ teaspoon salt
⅛ teaspoon pepper
½ cup chopped pecans
Lettuce leaves (optional)

Combine first 8 ingredients; mix well. Chill 2 hours. Stir in pecans just before serving. Serve on lettuce leaves, if desired. Yield: 6 servings.
*Barbara E. Bach,*
*Clearwater, Florida.*

## SESAME ITALIAN GREEN BEANS

2 (9-ounce) packages frozen Italian green beans
2 tablespoons butter or margarine, melted
1 tablespoon sesame seeds, toasted

Cook green beans according to package directions; drain. Add butter and sesame seeds; toss well. Yield: 4 to 6 servings.
*Ruth Moffitt,*
*Smyrna, Delaware.*

## HERBED FRENCH BREAD

1 (14-ounce) loaf unsliced French bread
½ cup butter or margarine, softened
½ teaspoon garlic powder
½ teaspoon celery seeds
1 tablespoon chopped green onion tops
Dash of dried whole dillweed
1 tablespoon grated Parmesan cheese
½ teaspoon dried parsley flakes

Slice French bread into ½-inch slices, not quite cutting through bottom crust. Combine remaining ingredients, mixing well; spread butter mixture between bread slices. Wrap loaf in aluminum foil; bake at 350° for 20 minutes. Yield: 1 loaf.
*Mrs. J. Craig Honaman,*
*Tallahassee, Florida.*

## FROZEN STRAWBERRY DELIGHT

1 (10-ounce) package frozen strawberries, thawed
1 (8-ounce) carton commercial sour cream
½ cup sugar
1 tablespoon vanilla extract

Combine all ingredients in container of an electric blender; process until smooth. Pour into an 8- x 4- x 3-inch loafpan, and freeze. Spoon into individual serving dishes. Yield: 4 to 6 servings.
*Mrs. Harry A. Smith,*
*Corbin, Kentucky.*

# August

**W**hen some cooks shy away from kitchen heat in August, you can cook and stay cool with our microwave cookie recipes. Nutty Oatmeal-Chocolate Chip Cookies, Peanut Butter Slice-and-Bakes, and Doubly-Good Chocolate Cookies all can be baked in minutes and are certain to disappear just as quickly. For the best tastes and textures, be sure to note our tips for baking cookies in the microwave oven.

If you prefer to do your summer cooking on the grill, skewer some kabobs and serve tender vegetables and chunks of beef, pork, lamb, or chicken livers on a stick. Rumaki Kabobs became our favorite, bacon-wrapped chicken livers and water chestnuts are skewered alternately with green pepper, onion, and carrots. The kabobs are basted with a sweet-and-sour sauce while the coals permeate them with a smoky, grilled-outdoors flavor.

But if sandwiches are more your style in hot weather, you'll like our recipes in this chapter for showy open-facers like Cheesy Chicken Sandwiches, Easy Pizza Burgers, and Beany Hot Dogs.

# Jellyrolls Swirl With Flavor

It's hard to imagine something so simple could be so impressive, but that's the sweet truth about jellyrolls.

Preparing this tasty dessert begins with baking the batter in a jellyroll pan; it bakes in less than half the time of a regular cake because it's such a thin layer. Then just roll the large rectangular cake into a log, and let it cool a few minutes. Unroll, spread with your favorite jelly, and roll it up again.

Although the traditional jellyroll is spread only with jelly and is dressed with nothing more than a sprinkling of powdered sugar, we couldn't resist some tasty variations—like piping whipped cream down the spine of Easy Jellyroll and nesting strawberries in the center.

When you have a little more time to spend, our Spiced Jellyroll and Heavenly Strawberry Roll are worth the extra effort. They start with the same sponge cake-type base but are spread with luscious homemade fillings instead of commercial jelly.

When making a jellyroll, you might want to trim off the crisp lengthwise edges with a sharp knife immediately after taking the cake from the oven. Trimming makes the jellyroll neater at the ends of the log, and the scraps are great for munching. Then quickly roll the hot layer to prevent it from crisping and cracking after you add the filling.

## EASY JELLYROLL

4 eggs
¾ teaspoon baking powder
¼ teaspoon salt
¾ cup sugar
¾ cup all-purpose flour
1 teaspoon lemon extract
Powdered sugar
1 cup strawberry jelly
Whipped cream (optional)
Whole fresh strawberries (optional)

Grease a 15- x 10- x 1-inch jellyroll pan, and line with waxed paper; grease and flour waxed paper. Set aside.

Combine eggs, baking powder, and salt; beat at high speed of an electric mixer until foamy. Gradually add ¾ cup sugar, beating until mixture is thick and lemon colored. Fold in flour and lemon extract. Spread batter evenly in prepared pan. Bake at 400° for 10 to 12 minutes.

Sift powdered sugar in a 15- x 10-inch rectangle on a linen towel. When cake is done, immediately loosen from sides of pan and turn out on sugar. Peel off waxed paper. Starting at narrow end, roll up cake and towel together; cool on a wire rack, seam side down, about 10 minutes.

Unroll cake; remove towel. Spread cake with jelly, and reroll. Place on serving plate, seam side down; let cool completely. Garnish roll with whipped cream and strawberries, if desired. Yield: 8 to 10 servings. *Sue Smith, Chelsea, Alabama.*

## SPICED JELLYROLL

3 eggs
1 egg yolk
½ cup sugar
½ teaspoon vanilla extract
½ cup all-purpose flour
1 teaspoon ground cinnamon
¼ teaspoon ground cardamom
¼ teaspoon ground nutmeg
2 tablespoons butter or margarine, melted and cooled
Powdered sugar
1 (8-ounce) carton frozen whipped topping, thawed
4 (1⅛-ounce) English toffee-flavored candy bars, crushed
1½ tablespoons amaretto or other almond-flavored liqueur
2 tablespoons flaked coconut, toasted

Grease a 15- x 10- x 1-inch jellyroll pan, and line with waxed paper; grease and flour waxed paper. Set aside.

Combine first 4 ingredients in a medium bowl; beat at high speed of an electric mixer 5 to 6 minutes or until thick and tripled in volume. Combine flour and spices, mixing well; fold into egg mixture until no streaks of flour remain. Fold in butter, blending well. Spread batter evenly in prepared pan. Bake at 350° for 11 to 13 minutes.

Sift powdered sugar in a 15- x 10-inch rectangle on a linen towel. When cake is done, immediately loosen from sides of pan, and turn out on sugar. Peel off waxed paper. Starting at narrow end, roll up cake and towel together; let cool completely on a wire rack, seam side down.

Combine whipped topping, crushed candy, and amaretto. Unroll cake; remove towel. Spread cake with two-thirds of whipped topping mixture, and reroll. Place on serving plate, seam side down. Spoon remaining whipped topping mixture down center of cake. Sprinkle coconut over topping. Chill 2 hours or until serving time. Yield: 8 to 10 servings.

## HEAVENLY STRAWBERRY ROLL

3 eggs
1 cup sugar
1 cup self-rising flour
⅓ cup water
1 teaspoon vanilla extract
Powdered sugar
⅔ cup sugar
2 tablespoons cornstarch
2 tablespoons strawberry-flavored gelatin
⅔ cup water
2 cups fresh strawberries, sliced
1 (3-ounce) package cream cheese, softened
1¼ cups sifted powdered sugar

Grease a 15- x 10- x 1-inch jellyroll pan, and line with waxed paper; grease and flour waxed paper. Set aside.

Beat eggs at high speed of an electric mixer until foamy. Gradually add 1 cup sugar, beating until mixture is thick and lemon colored. Fold flour, ⅓ cup water, and vanilla into egg mixture. Spread batter evenly in prepared pan. Bake at 375° for 10 to 12 minutes.

Sift powdered sugar in a 15- x 10-inch rectangle on a linen towel. When cake is done, immediately loosen from sides of pan and turn out on sugar. Peel off waxed paper. Starting at narrow end, roll up cake and towel together; let cool completely on a wire rack.

Combine next 4 ingredients in a medium saucepan; cook over medium heat, stirring constantly until mixture is thick, about 5 minutes. Cool completely, and stir in strawberries.

Beat cream cheese until fluffy; gradually add 1¼ cups powdered sugar, beating until smooth.

Unroll cake; remove towel. Spread cake with cream cheese mixture, then strawberry mixture; reroll. Place on serving plate, seam side down. Chill until serving time. Yield: 8 to 10 servings. *Pauline Russellburg, Mayfield, Kentucky.*

*Tip: Hull strawberries after washing so that they won't absorb too much water and become mushy.*

## Cooking Light

# Spoon On The Sauce–It's Light!

Who would think a dieter could indulge in Remoulade Sauce, Tangy Light Marinade, or Fresh Strawberry Sauce and enjoy it with a clear conscience? Lots of calories from fat or oil are usually hidden in main-dish sauces and marinades, and most dessert sauces get extra calories from a liberal sweetening with sugar. However, our special light sauces and marinades let you liven up your diet meals but still keep calories at a minimum.

Try a spicy Marinara Sauce for starters. Ruth Cunliffe of Lake Placid, Florida, serves this Italian-flavored sauce over spaghetti, rice, or noodles. For a total of about 125 calories, one-third cup of this sauce over a half-cup serving of pasta makes a filling accompaniment to fish or poultry.

Another way to dress up meals is with a light, but elegant, Remoulade Sauce. Joy Clinton of Brownsville, Tennessee, makes her version with reduced-calorie mayonnaise, chopped egg, and herbs. Spooned over broiled fish or other seafood, it gives her low-calorie diet a flavor lift.

You've probably heard that grilled meats are quite often recommended for dieters—excess fat drips away while the meat cooks over hot coals. For extra flavor, try marinating the meat overnight in Tangy Light Marinade; unlike other marinades, this one's made without oil. We particularly recommend it for flank steak, as the pineapple juice it contains acts as a tenderizer for this very lean cut of meat.

Your light dessert can be special when topped with a low-calorie sauce. Try Creamy Light Coconut Sauce over slices of fresh fruit or a scoop of ice milk. Even waffles and pancakes can be delicious and light when Peach-Blueberry Pancake Sauce or Fresh Strawberry Sauce replaces the usual butter and sweet syrup.

### SPICY APPLE DESSERT SAUCE

2 cups unsweetened apple juice
½ teaspoon ground cinnamon
2 tablespoons cornstarch
¼ cup plus 2 tablespoons water

Combine apple juice and cinnamon in a saucepan. Bring to a boil; then reduce heat to low. Dissolve cornstarch in water; gradually add to apple juice mixture, stirring constantly. Cook until smooth and thickened, stirring constantly. Chill.

Serve sauce over ice milk or plain low-fat yogurt. Yield: 2 cups (about 10 calories per tablespoon of sauce).

*Note:* Also good served warm over pancakes or waffles.

*Mrs. Paul A. Raper,*
*Burgaw, North Carolina.*

### CREAMY LIGHT COCONUT SAUCE

2 eggs, beaten
2 tablespoons sugar
1⅓ cups skim milk
1 teaspoon vanilla extract
¼ cup plus 2 tablespoons flaked coconut, toasted

Combine eggs and sugar in a small, heavy saucepan; mix well. Gradually stir in milk with a wire whisk. Cook over low heat, stirring constantly, 15 to 20 minutes or until thickened. Remove from heat, and stir in vanilla. Cover and chill.

To serve, stir in ¼ cup coconut; garnish with remaining coconut. Serve with fresh fruit or over ice milk. Yield: 1¾ cups (about 19 calories per tablespoon of sauce).

### PEACH-BLUEBERRY PANCAKE SAUCE

1 cup sliced fresh peaches
1 cup fresh blueberries
2 tablespoons sugar
½ cup unsweetened apple juice
Dash of ground nutmeg

Combine ½ cup peaches, ½ cup blueberries, and remaining ingredients in a small saucepan. Bring to a boil; then reduce heat and simmer, uncovered, 15 minutes. Add remaining fruit, stirring well. Serve warm over pancakes or waffles. Yield: 1½ cups (about 13 calories per tablespoon of sauce).

*Note:* Also good served chilled over ice milk or vanilla low-fat yogurt.

*Tip: For a great dessert, pour cream sherry over a chilled grapefruit.*

### FRESH STRAWBERRY SAUCE

2 cups fresh strawberries, sliced
2 tablespoons sugar
1½ teaspoons cornstarch
¼ teaspoon almond extract

Combine strawberries and sugar; cover and refrigerate several hours or overnight. Drain the strawberries, reserving juice; set aside.

Add enough water to strawberry juice to make ½ cup. Combine juice and cornstarch in a saucepan, stirring until cornstarch is dissolved. Cook over medium heat, stirring constantly, until smooth and thickened. Stir in strawberries and almond extract. Chill.

Serve sauce over slices of angel food cake. Yield: 1¼ cups (about 11 calories per tablespoon of sauce).

*Note:* Also good over pancakes, waffles, or ice milk.

### RAISIN-PINEAPPLE SAUCE

¾ cup unsweetened pineapple juice
½ cup raisins
1 tablespoon vinegar
Dash of Worcestershire sauce
⅛ teaspoon ground cloves
2 teaspoons cornstarch
2 tablespoons water

Combine first 5 ingredients, and bring to a boil; cook until raisins are plump. Dissolve cornstarch in water, and gradually add to hot mixture; cook until clear, stirring constantly. Serve hot over ham slices. Yield: ⅔ cup (about 33 calories per tablespoon of sauce).

### SPECIAL BARBECUE SAUCE

½ cup water
¼ cup vinegar
2 tablespoons lemon juice
1 tablespoon prepared mustard
½ teaspoon salt
½ teaspoon pepper
¼ teaspoon red pepper
1 medium onion, chopped
½ cup catsup
2 tablespoons Worcestershire sauce
1½ teaspoons liquid smoke

Combine first 8 ingredients in a large saucepan, mixing well. Bring to a boil; then reduce heat to medium. Cook, uncovered, 20 minutes, stirring occasionally; stir in the remaining ingredients. Use to baste chicken or other meats. Yield: about 1½ cups (about 10 calories per tablespoon of sauce).

## MARINARA SAUCE

1 (46-ounce) can tomato juice
½ pound fresh mushrooms, sliced
2 medium-size green peppers, chopped
1 sweet red pepper, chopped
2 teaspoons minced onion
½ teaspoon dried whole basil
½ teaspoon dried whole oregano
Dash of garlic powder

Combine all ingredients in a large Dutch oven; simmer, uncovered, 45 minutes. Serve over cooked spaghetti, rice, or noodles. Yield: 5 cups (about 4 calories per tablespoon of sauce).
*Ruth E. Cunliffe,*
*Lake Placid, Florida.*

## EASY BARBECUE SAUCE

1 medium onion, chopped
1 tablespoon margarine
1¼ cups tomato sauce
1 tablespoon vinegar
1 small bay leaf
¼ teaspoon salt
¼ teaspoon dry mustard
¼ teaspoon curry powder
¼ teaspoon hot sauce
⅛ teaspoon pepper

Sauté onion in margarine until tender; stir in remaining ingredients, and simmer 15 minutes. Use to baste chicken when baking or grilling. Yield: 1⅓ cups (about 11 calories per tablespoon of sauce).
*Sheri Beaver,*
*Hixson, Tennessee.*

## TANGY LIGHT MARINADE

1 cup unsweetened pineapple juice
⅓ cup soy sauce
1 teaspoon ground ginger
1 small clove garlic, crushed
⅓ cup Italian reduced-calorie salad dressing

Combine all ingredients, stirring well; use to marinate flank steak or pork chops before grilling. Baste meat with remaining marinade during grilling. Yield: 1⅔ cups (about 9 calories per tablespoon of marinade).

## LIGHT MUSTARD SAUCE

¼ cup sugar
2 tablespoons dry mustard
½ teaspoon salt
2 egg yolks, beaten
1 (13-ounce) can evaporated skim milk
½ cup vinegar

Combine first 4 ingredients in top of a double boiler; gradually add evaporated milk, and stir until smooth. Bring water to a boil; then reduce heat to low. Cook mixture until smooth and thickened, stirring constantly.

Stir in vinegar; cook until creamy and slightly thickened. Serve hot over ham slices. Yield: 2 cups (about 20 calories per tablespoon of sauce).

## REMOULADE SAUCE

1 cup reduced-calorie mayonnaise
1 hard-cooked egg, chopped
2 tablespoons minced fresh parsley
1 tablespoon red wine vinegar
2 teaspoons capers
½ to 1 teaspoon dry mustard
1 teaspoon dried whole tarragon
1 teaspoon minced garlic
1 teaspoon chopped chives
1 teaspoon anchovy paste
Dash of onion powder

Combine all ingredients, stirring well. Chill several hours. Serve sauce over broiled fish or other seafood. Yield: 1⅓ cups (about 35 calories per tablespoon of sauce).
*Joy Clinton,*
*Brownsville, Tennessee.*

# Roll Up A Fruit Pastry

Those who love fruit will find our fruit rolls delightful. Each starts with a special pastry, which is spread with sweetened fruit, rolled up like a jellyroll, and popped into the oven. The result is a delicious and flaky confection that's perfect for breakfast or dessert.

## BLACKBERRY ROLL

1½ cups all-purpose flour
1 tablespoon sugar
1 teaspoon salt
1 teaspoon grated orange rind
½ cup shortening
3 tablespoons orange juice
2 tablespoons butter or margarine, melted
4 cups fresh blackberries
1 cup sugar
¾ teaspoon sugar
1 cup boiling water
Vanilla ice cream or whipped cream

Combine first 4 ingredients; stir well. Cut in shortening with pastry blender until mixture resembles coarse meal. Sprinkle orange juice evenly over surface; stir with a fork until all dry ingredients are moistened. Shape into a ball; chill.

On a floured surface, roll dough into a 14- x 10-inch rectangle about ⅛-inch thick. Brush pastry with butter.

Combine blackberries and 1 cup sugar; stir well. Spoon 3 cups blackberry mixture onto dough. Starting with the short side, roll up jellyroll fashion.

Place roll, seam side down, in a greased 12- x 8- x 2-inch baking dish. Cut several small slits across top of pastry; sprinkle with ¾ teaspoon sugar. Spoon remaining blackberry mixture evenly around roll.

Bake at 450° for 10 minutes; pour boiling water around the roll. Reduce heat to 350°, and bake 35 minutes or until golden brown. To serve, slice roll and top with ice cream or whipped cream. Yield: about 8 servings.
*Betty Elliott,*
*Roanoke, Virginia.*

## APPLE ROLL

¾ cup butter, softened
1 (8-ounce) package cream cheese, softened
1 egg, separated
2 cups all-purpose flour
6 medium apples, peeled, cored, and thinly sliced
½ cup sugar
1 teaspoon ground cinnamon

Combine butter, cream cheese, and egg yolk; beat until smooth. Add flour, mixing well. Shape dough into 3 balls; chill.

Combine remaining ingredients except egg white in a medium saucepan. Cover and cook over low heat until apples are tender, stirring occasionally. Cool.

On a floured surface, roll one portion of dough into a 10- x 13-inch rectangle about ⅛-inch thick; spread one-third of apple mixture over dough. Starting with short side, roll up jellyroll fashion, and turn edges under. Repeat with remaining dough and apple mixture.

Place rolls, seam side down, on a greased 12- x 8- x 2-inch baking dish. Lightly beat egg white and brush on top of rolls. Bake at 375° for 40 minutes or until brown. Yield: 12 to 15 servings.
*Louise Kinsel,*
*Aberdeen, Maryland.*

*Honeydew Fruit Cups, topped with a creamy coconut-flavored sauce, make a refreshing addition to warm-weather meals.*

## Have A Bite Of Juicy Melon

Cool, succulent, light, and delicate in taste, melons are the perfect antidote to a hot day. They're wonderful sliced and served ice cold. But when the occasion calls for something elegant, spoon melon balls into dessert glasses or fold them into congealed salads.

### CANTALOUPE CREAM DELIGHT

1 small cantaloupe, cubed
½ cup sugar
¾ teaspoon vanilla extract
½ cup commercial sour cream
Fresh fruit

Combine cantaloupe and sugar in a medium saucepan; cook 10 minutes over low heat. Stir in vanilla; chill completely. Stir in sour cream; serve over fresh fruit. Yield: 1¼ cups.
*Cornelia Stewart,*
*Smithfield, North Carolina.*

### HONEYDEW FRUIT CUPS

6 cups honeydew balls
2 (15¼-ounce) cans pineapple chunks, drained
Lettuce leaves
1 (8-ounce) carton plain yogurt
¼ cup dry piña colada cocktail mix

Combine honeydew and pineapple; spoon into lettuce-lined sherbet or champagne glasses. Combine yogurt and cocktail mix; serve over fruit. Yield: 4 to 6 servings.
*Milly Butler,*
*Savannah, Georgia.*

### SOUTHERN PLANTATION CANTALOUPE

2 medium cantaloupes, halved and seeded
2 cups pineapple juice, divided
1 (3-ounce) package orange-flavored gelatin
Lettuce leaves
Mayonnaise

Carefully scoop out fruit from cantaloupe halves, reserving a ½-inch-thick shell. Cut the fruit into small cubes, and set aside.

Bring 1 cup pineapple juice to a boil; add gelatin, stirring until dissolved. Add remaining 1 cup pineapple juice, and stir well. Chill until consistency of unbeaten egg white.

Fold in cubed cantaloupe, and pour into reserved melon halves. Chill until firm. Cut cantaloupe halves in half, and arrange on lettuce. Garnish each with a dollop of mayonnaise. Yield: 8 servings.
*Dora Lee Thompson,*
*Chester, Maryland.*

## Spinach Straight From The Can

Canned spinach? Believe it or not, it provides plenty of vitamin A and good ideas for these easy-to-cook recipes.

For flavorful fettuccini, toss canned spinach with hot buttered noodles, cream, and cheese. And add an easy appetizer to your next party menu by serving Savory Spinach Spread with crackers, or round out a meal with Spinach-Stuffed Peppers.

You'll find canned spinach convenient because it doesn't have to be cooked or thawed—just make sure all the liquid is drained off before combining spinach with other ingredients.

### SPINACH FETTUCCINI

1 (14-ounce) can spinach
1 (8-ounce) package medium egg noodles
2 tablespoons chopped onion
1 clove garlic, crushed
1 tablespoon butter or margarine
¼ cup butter or margarine
½ cup whipping cream
1 cup grated Parmesan cheese
Coarsely ground black pepper

Drain spinach in a colander; place on paper towels, and press until spinach is barely moist.

Cook noodles according to package directions; drain well. Sauté onion and garlic in 1 tablespoon butter until tender; stir in spinach. Cover and simmer 3 minutes.

Add ¼ cup butter to warm noodles, tossing gently until butter melts. Add spinach mixture, whipping cream, and cheese; toss gently. Sprinkle with pepper. Yield: 8 servings. *Cindy Fields,*
*Courtland, Virginia.*

## GOURMET BAKED SPINACH

3 tablespoons butter or margarine
2 tablespoons minced onion
3 tablespoons all-purpose flour
2 cups milk
2 (14-ounce) cans spinach
3 hard-cooked eggs, finely chopped
1 teaspoon salt
¼ teaspoon pepper
½ cup crushed corn flakes
½ cup (2 ounces) shredded process
   American cheese
Paprika

Melt butter in a heavy saucepan; sauté onion until tender. Add flour, stirring until smooth. Cook 1 minute, stirring constantly. Gradually add milk; cook over medium heat, stirring constantly, until thickened and bubbly.

Drain spinach in a colander; place on paper towels, and press until barely moist. Stir spinach, eggs, salt, and pepper into sauce; spread in a lightly greased 8-inch square baking dish. Combine crushed corn flakes and cheese; mix well, and sprinkle over spinach mixture. Sprinkle lightly with paprika; bake at 375° for 20 minutes. Yield: 6 servings. *Mrs. H. G. Drawdy, Spindale, North Carolina.*

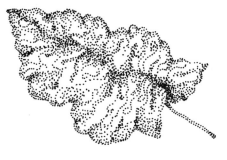

## SPINACH-STUFFED PEPPERS

3 medium-size green peppers
1 (14-ounce) can spinach
½ cup grated Parmesan cheese
2 (3-ounce) packages cream cheese,
   softened
¼ cup soft breadcrumbs
1 egg, beaten
¼ teaspoon salt
⅛ teaspoon pepper
1½ teaspoons olive oil

Trim stems from peppers. Cut peppers in half, and remove seeds. Cover the peppers with boiling water, and cook 3 minutes; drain.

Drain spinach in a colander; place on paper towels, and press until spinach is barely moist.

Set aside 2 tablespoons Parmesan cheese. Combine the spinach, remaining Parmesan cheese, cream cheese, breadcrumbs, egg, salt, and pepper; mix well. Fill peppers with spinach mixture, and place in a shallow baking dish. Sprinkle tops with 2 tablespoons reserved Parmesan cheese, and drizzle with olive oil. Bake peppers at 350° for 35 minutes. Yield: 6 servings. *Mary Patterson, Westwood, Massachusetts.*

## SAVORY SPINACH SPREAD

1 (14-ounce) can spinach
1 (3-ounce) package cream cheese,
   softened
½ cup commercial sour cream
3 slices bacon, cooked and crumbled
1 tablespoon minced green onion
Salt to taste
2 teaspoons prepared horseradish

Drain spinach in a colander; place on paper towels, and press until spinach is barely moist.

Combine spinach and cream cheese; mix well. Stir in remaining ingredients. Spoon into a lightly greased 2-cup baking dish. Bake at 350° for 25 to 30 minutes. Spread on crackers or party rye bread. Yield: 2 cups. *Joy W. Collins, Birmingham, Alabama.*

# Tomatoes Are A Taste Of Summer

Summer is the season when fresh tomatoes are in their full glory, blazing with color and brimming with juice. Sliced for sandwiches, cut into wedges for salads, or cooked down into a sauce, fresh tomatoes are one of the most exciting (and favored) tastes.

Marie Harris of Sevierville, Tennessee, fills tomato shells with a colorful mixture of spinach, celery, carrot, and green pepper and serves them warm. She describes her Buffet Tomatoes as both "pretty and delicious."

Roanoke, Virginia's, Nancy Duncan layers sliced tomatoes in a casserole with bacon and mushrooms. Floyd Stover likes to top fried tomatoes with a creamy, slightly sweet gravy.

If fully ripe, fresh tomatoes can be refrigerated after purchase. However, underripe tomatoes should be kept at room temperature to assist ripening. And while you're enjoying your tomato treats, remember they're packed with plenty of vitamins A and C.

## FRIED RIPE TOMATOES WITH GRAVY

4 medium tomatoes
½ cup all-purpose flour
¼ cup plus 2 tablespoons vegetable oil
1 cup whipping cream
2 tablespoons brown sugar
½ teaspoon salt
⅛ teaspoon pepper

Cut tomatoes into ⅓-inch slices, and dredge in flour. Set aside 1 tablespoon remaining flour.

Heat oil in a large skillet over medium heat, and add tomatoes; cook until golden brown, turning once. Arrange tomatoes on a serving platter; keep warm.

Add reserved tablespoon of flour to pan drippings, stirring until smooth. Cook 1 minute, stirring constantly. Gradually add whipping cream; cook over medium heat, stirring constantly, until thickened. Stir in brown sugar, salt, and pepper. Spoon over tomatoes. Serve immediately. Yield: 8 servings.
*Floyd C. Stover, Bakersfield, Missouri.*

## BUFFET TOMATOES

6 large firm tomatoes
½ teaspoon salt
1 (10-ounce) package frozen chopped
   spinach
1 large onion, chopped
3 stalks celery, chopped
2 carrots, chopped
⅓ cup chopped green pepper
2 tablespoons chopped fresh parsley
2 tablespoons butter or margarine
¾ cup seasoned, dry breadcrumbs
⅓ cup milk
1 egg, beaten
1 tablespoon grated Parmesan cheese

Remove stems from tomatoes, and cut a ¼-inch slice from top of each. Scoop out pulp, leaving shells intact (reserve pulp for other uses). Sprinkle inside of shells with salt; invert to drain.

Cook spinach according to package directions; drain spinach, and press until barely moist.

Sauté onion, celery, carrots, green pepper, and parsley in butter until vegetables are tender. Combine sautéed vegetables, spinach, breadcrumbs, milk, and egg, mixing well.

Spoon vegetable mixture into tomato shells, and place in a lightly greased 8-inch square baking dish. Sprinkle cheese over tomatoes. Bake at 400° for 15 minutes or until thoroughly heated. Yield: 6 servings. *Marie W. Harris, Sevierville, Tennessee.*

## TOMATOES PROVENCAL

4 slices bacon, diced
1 clove garlic, minced
1 medium onion, thinly sliced
¼ pound fresh mushrooms, sliced
1 tablespoon all-purpose flour
½ teaspoon seasoned salt
10 tomatoes
¼ cup plus 2 tablespoons grated Parmesan
    cheese
1 tablespoon butter or margarine

Fry bacon in a medium skillet until crisp; remove bacon, reserving pan drippings in skillet. Set bacon aside to drain. Sauté garlic, onion, and mushrooms in skillet until tender. Stir in bacon, flour, and seasoned salt.

Cut tomatoes into ½-inch slices. Place half of slices in a lightly greased 10- x 6- x 2-inch baking dish. Spoon half of bacon mixture over tomatoes; sprinkle with 3 tablespoons Parmesan cheese. Repeat layers and dot with butter. Bake at 350° for 25 minutes. Yield: 6 to 8 servings. *Nancy M. Duncan, Roanoke, Virginia.*

# These Frozen Desserts Begin With Ice Cream

Butter pecan, pralines and cream, chocolate-marshmallow-almond, and coffee. No, they're not the flavors of the month at the neighborhood ice cream shoppe, they're the irresistible beginnings of our fabulous ice cream desserts. Our foods staff savored every bite when taste testing these treats.

Two ice cream flavors, pralines and cream and butter pecan, are layered with chocolate fudge topping and toasted pecans for Absolutely Divine Ice Cream Pie. Each luscious slice is drizzled with a warm fudge topping and pecans just before serving.

Cool off a hot day with frosty Amaretto Freeze. Vanilla ice cream laced with amaretto and brown sugar is blended, then frozen in individual serving dishes. For a final touch, garnish each serving with whipped cream and stemmed maraschino cherries.

And don't miss our Heavenly Ice Cream Pie. A pecan pastry holds layers of chocolate-marshmallow-almond and vanilla ice cream and a rich, thick meringue. Homemade hot fudge sauce tops each slice of this frozen delight.

## ABSOLUTELY DIVINE ICE CREAM PIE

1¼ cups graham cracker crumbs
3 tablespoons sugar
⅓ cup butter or margarine, melted
1 quart butter pecan ice cream, softened
1 (16-ounce) can chocolate fudge topping
1 to 1½ cups chopped pecans, toasted
1 quart pralines and cream ice cream,
    softened

Combine graham cracker crumbs, sugar, and butter; mix well. Firmly press mixture into bottom of a 9-inch springform pan. Bake at 350° for 8 minutes. Cool completely.

Spread butter pecan ice cream evenly over crust; cover and freeze. Spread half of fudge topping over ice cream; sprinkle with ½ cup pecans. Cover pie and freeze.

Spread pralines and cream ice cream evenly over pie; cover and freeze until ice cream is firm.

Spoon remaining fudge topping into a heavy saucepan; cook over low heat just until thoroughly heated. To serve, drizzle warm fudge topping over each slice of pie, and sprinkle with remaining pecans. Yield: one 9-inch pie.

## HEAVENLY ICE CREAM PIE

¾ cup plus 1½ tablespoons all-purpose
    flour
½ teaspoon salt
⅓ cup shortening
2½ tablespoons all-purpose flour
2 tablespoons water
3 tablespoons chopped pecans
1 pint chocolate-marshmallow-almond ice
    cream, softened
1 pint vanilla ice cream, softened
4 egg whites
¼ teaspoon cream of tartar
½ cup sugar
½ teaspoon vanilla extract
Hot fudge sauce (recipe follows)

Combine first 2 ingredients; cut in shortening with pastry blender until mixture resembles coarse meal. Combine 2½ tablespoons flour and water, stirring to make a paste. Stir paste into flour mixture to make a dough.

Shape dough into a ball; chill. Roll dough to ⅛-inch thickness on a lightly floured surface. Fit pastry in a 9-inch pieplate, and flute edges of pastry as desired. Sprinkle pecans over pastry; press lightly into dough. Bake at 400° for 10 minutes; cool.

Spread the chocolate-marshmallow-almond ice cream evenly over pastry; cover pie and freeze. Spread vanilla ice cream over chocolate layer; cover and freeze until ice cream is firm.

Beat egg whites (at room temperature) and cream of tartar until foamy. Gradually add sugar, 1 tablespoon at a time, beating until stiff peaks form. Stir in vanilla. Spread meringue over ice cream, sealing to edge of pastry. Broil 1 minute or until golden brown. Freeze.

Let stand at room temperature 5 minutes before serving. Drizzle each slice with hot fudge sauce. Yield: one 9-inch pie.

*Hot Fudge Sauce:*

2 (1-ounce) squares unsweetened chocolate
¼ cup plus 2 tablespoons water
½ cup sugar
Dash of salt
¼ cup plus 2 tablespoons butter or
    margarine
½ teaspoon vanilla extract

Combine chocolate and water in a small saucepan over low heat; cook until chocolate melts. Add sugar and salt; simmer 5 minutes. Stir in butter and vanilla. Yield: about 1¼ cups.

*Elnora Denney, Columbiana, Alabama.*

## CARAMEL ICE CREAM PIE

1 cup all-purpose flour
½ cup butter or margarine, melted
½ cup chopped pecans
¼ cup firmly packed brown sugar
1 (12-ounce) jar caramel topping
1 quart vanilla ice cream, softened

Combine first 4 ingredients; mix well. Spread on a baking sheet, pressing with fingers to ¼-inch thickness. Bake at 400° for 12 minutes. Immediately transfer to a large mixing bowl, and stir until the mixture is crumbled.

Press crumbs into a buttered 9-inch pieplate, reserving ¼ cup crumbs. (Crumb crust firms as it freezes.) Pour ¾ cup caramel topping into crust; freeze. Spread ice cream evenly over crust; cover and freeze.

Sprinkle 2 tablespoons of the reserved crumbs over ice cream. Drizzle remaining caramel topping over pie; sprinkle with remaining crumbs. Freeze until firm.

Let frozen pie stand at room temperature 5 minutes before slicing. Yield: one 9-inch pie. *Mrs. Ken Vincent, Monroe, Louisiana.*

## AMARETTO FREEZE

⅓ cup amaretto
1 tablespoon brown sugar
1 quart vanilla ice cream
Whipped cream (optional)
Maraschino cherries (optional)

Combine amaretto and brown sugar; stir until sugar dissolves.

Combine ice cream and amaretto mixture in container of electric blender; process until smooth. Pour into 6 individual freezer-proof serving dishes, and freeze.

Garnish with whipped cream and maraschino cherries just before serving, if desired. Yield: 6 servings.

*Patricia Pashby,*
*Memphis, Tennessee.*

## COFFEE ICE CREAM CRUNCH

½ cup butter or margarine, softened
¾ cup firmly packed brown sugar
2½ cups crisp rice cereal
1 cup flaked coconut
½ cup chopped pecans
½ gallon coffee ice cream, softened

Cream butter; gradually add brown sugar, beating until light and fluffy. Stir in next 3 ingredients. Spread half of crumb mixture in a greased 13- x 9- x 2-inch pan. Spread ice cream evenly over crumb mixture; top with remaining crumb mixture. Cover and freeze until firm.

Let stand at room temperature 5 minutes before slicing. Yield: 15 servings.

*Mrs. W. J. Scherffius,*
*Mountain Home, Arkansas.*

# Grill A Special Kabob

Janice Elder of Spartanburg, South Carolina, sent us a delicious and unusual kabob recipe that she recommends for cookouts. A longtime fan of rumaki, a Hawaiian appetizer, Janice created Rumaki Kabobs by skewering bacon-wrapped chicken livers and water chestnuts alongside onion, green pepper, and carrots. She bastes the kabobs with a mixture of brown sugar, soy sauce, and ginger during grilling to give the kabob a tasty Hawaiian flavor.

You'll want to try our other kabob recipes, too. Coat cubes of boneless pork with a peanut butter and soy sauce mixture for Spicy Pork Kabobs. Marinate cubes of sirloin in a soy sauce mixture before grilling it with tomatoes, mushrooms, green pepper, and onion. And if you like lamb, be sure to try marinated chunks of lamb threaded onto skewers with onion, pepper, and tomatoes.

## BEEF KABOBS DELUXE

½ cup vegetable oil
¼ cup soy sauce
¼ cup vinegar
½ teaspoon pepper
2 pounds sirloin tip roast, cut into 2-inch cubes
6 to 8 boiling onions
½ pound fresh mushrooms
1 cup cherry tomatoes
1 large green pepper, cut into 1-inch pieces

Combine oil, soy sauce, vinegar, and pepper in a large shallow container. Add meat; cover and marinate in refrigerator 4 hours or overnight.

Parboil onions 3 to 5 minutes; drain. Remove meat from marinade. Alternate meat and vegetables on skewers. Grill kabobs 5 minutes on each side over medium coals or until desired degree of doneness, basting with marinade. Yield: 6 to 8 servings.

*Kathy C. Squires,*
*Charlottesville, Virginia.*

## SPICY PORK KABOBS

3 medium onions, minced
1 clove garlic, minced
¼ cup creamy peanut butter
3 tablespoons soy sauce
1½ tablespoons lemon juice
1 tablespoon brown sugar
1½ teaspoons ground coriander
1½ teaspoons salt
1 teaspoon ground cumin
½ teaspoon red pepper
½ teaspoon freshly ground pepper
2 pounds lean boneless pork, cut into 1½-inch cubes

Combine all ingredients except pork; mix well. Add pork, and stir to coat; cover and refrigerate 3 to 4 hours. Place pork on skewers.

Grill kabobs 30 to 35 minutes over medium coals, turning frequently. Yield: 6 servings.

*Helen Rainwater,*
*Weslaco, Texas.*

## SHISH KABOBS

2 pounds boneless lamb
¼ cup Burgundy or other dry red wine
½ cup diced onion
½ cup olive oil
1 small clove garlic, minced
½ teaspoon salt
½ teaspoon dried whole oregano, crushed
⅛ teaspoon freshly ground pepper
Dash of red pepper
1 medium onion, cut into eighths
1 medium-size green pepper, cut into eighths
8 cherry tomatoes

Remove fell (tissuelike covering) from lamb, if necessary; cut meat into 1½-inch cubes, and set aside.

Combine next 8 ingredients in a large shallow container. Add lamb; cover and marinate in refrigerator at least 6 hours or overnight.

Remove meat from marinade. Alternate meat and vegetables on skewers. Grill kabobs 15 to 20 minutes over medium coals, turning and basting frequently with marinade. Yield: 6 to 8 servings.

*Sara McCullough,*
*Broaddus, Texas.*

## RUMAKI KABOBS

2 large carrots, cut into ½-inch pieces
12 chicken livers (about 1 pound)
½ cup soy sauce
8 water chestnuts
12 slices bacon, cut in half
2 medium onions, quartered
1 large green pepper, cut into 1-inch pieces
¼ cup firmly packed brown sugar
¼ teaspoon ground ginger
Hot cooked rice (optional)

Parboil carrots 1 minute; set aside.

Cut chicken livers in half. Dip each chicken liver half into soy sauce; reserve remaining soy sauce.

Cut water chestnuts into thirds. Place a piece of water chestnut and a piece of chicken liver on each piece of bacon. Roll up, and alternate chicken liver bundles and vegetables on skewers.

Combine reserved soy sauce, brown sugar, and ginger; stir until sugar dissolves. Grill kabobs 15 to 20 minutes over medium coals or until desired degree of doneness, turning and basting frequently with the soy sauce mixture. Serve over rice, if desired. Yield: 4 to 6 servings.

*Janice S. Elder,*
*Spartanburg, South Carolina.*

*Tip: A quick way to give barbecue fare a garlic flavor is to toss garlic cloves on the coals while the food grills.*

# Steam Vegetables To Perfection

Vegetable steaming equipment has become a big seller in housewares departments and kitchen specialty shops. That's because steaming preserves the color, texture, and nutritional value of vegetables, making them attractive as well as better for us. And steaming is so easy, even novice cooks will have good results on the first try.

Boiling causes water-soluble vitamins such as riboflavin, niacin, and vitamin C to leach out into the cooking water. Steaming, however, preserves these nutrients by minimizing the contact of the vegetable with the cooking water. Vegetables have more color and crunch when they are steamed; but beware, prolonged steaming makes them mushy and destroys their vibrant colors.

Varying in size and shape, steamers generally have a perforated basket or colander (sometimes both) that suspends the food over boiling water. A good steamer should have a snugly fitting lid to prevent steam from escaping and be deep and wide enough for the steam to circulate around the food.

Since steam distributes heat evenly, you don't need a steamer made of heavy-gauge metal. However, if you intend to use the steamer for other cooking purposes, a heavy-gauge metal would be a worthwhile investment. The most common steamers are aluminum, but stainless steel, copper, and Calphalon® models are also available.

For those who would rather not invest in a complete steamer, several steaming accessories are available. The most familiar is the expanding **"daisy" steam basket.** Adjustable to fit almost any size of saucepan, the basket can usually accommodate up to six servings of vegetables.

An **aluminum steaming tray** will get more value out of your wok. Placed in the wok and supported by its sides, the steaming tray has a wide diameter that's especially good for steaming long vegetables such as asparagus and broccoli. It works well with almost any vegetable as long as the wok lid remains closed.

If you've tried steaming artichokes, you're familiar with the difficulty of getting the artichoke to stand upright during cooking. The relatively new **artichoke steaming stand** makes this a problem of the past. Set in a saucepan or Dutch oven with a small amount of water, each stand holds one artichoke. Not only is the stand practical, but it's attractive enough to bring to the table.

# Crêpes For Dessert

Dessert crêpes complete a meal with simple elegance. Great for entertaining, these crêpes and fillings can be made in advance and are quickly assembled. They start with the same basic crêpe batter.

Embracing a creamy orange filling, Orange Dream Crêpes are topped with orange marmalade, sprinkled with almonds, and quickly broiled in the oven. Chocolate Chantilly Crêpes are laced with almonds and rum.

Before cooking, let the crêpe batter stand for one hour at room temperature, or in the refrigerator for longer periods. If necessary, cover and store it in the refrigerator overnight; just stir before using.

As the crêpes are cooked, stack them on a flat surface between sheets of waxed paper. Spoon the filling onto the side of the crêpe that's least attractive, so the prettiest side is showing.

Our dessert crêpes recipe yields plenty of extra crêpes for you to use later. Store leftover crêpes by placing the stack between two paper plates and wrapping it tightly. They'll keep two or three days in the refrigerator or up to four months in the freezer.

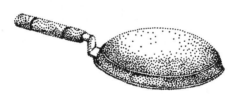

## BASIC DESSERT CREPES

1½ cups all-purpose flour
1 tablespoon sugar
¼ teaspoon salt
2 cups milk
1 teaspoon vanilla extract
3 eggs
2 tablespoons butter or margarine, melted
Vegetable oil

Combine first 5 ingredients, beating until smooth. Add eggs, and beat well; stir in butter. Refrigerate 1 hour. (This allows flour particles to swell and soften so the crêpes are light in texture.)

Brush the bottom of a 6-inch crêpe pan with oil; place over medium heat until just hot, not smoking.

Pour 2 tablespoons batter into pan; quickly tilt pan in all directions so that batter covers the pan in a thin film. Cook 1 minute.

Lift edge of crêpe to test for doneness. Crêpe is ready for flipping when it can be shaken loose from pan. Flip the crêpe, and cook about 30 seconds on other side. (This side is rarely more than spotty brown and is the side on which the filling is placed.)

Place crêpes on a towel to cool. Stack them between layers of waxed paper to prevent sticking. Yield: 2 dozen crêpes.

## ORANGE DREAM CREPES

1 (3-ounce) package cream cheese, softened
1 (8-ounce) carton commercial sour cream
1 cup orange marmalade, divided
2 teaspoons grated orange rind
¼ teaspoon grated lemon rind
12 dessert crepes
1½ teaspoons sliced almonds, toasted

Beat cream cheese until light and fluffy; stir in sour cream, ¼ cup orange marmalade, and rind.

Spread cream cheese mixture evenly over each crêpe; roll up, and place seam side down in a lightly greased 13- x 9- x 2-inch baking dish. Spread remaining marmalade over crêpes, and sprinkle with almonds. Broil 6 inches from heat until crêpe edges are light brown. Yield: 12 crêpes.

*Note:* When preparing Orange Dream Crêpes, substitute 1 teaspoon lemon extract for vanilla extract in the Basic Dessert Crêpes recipe, if desired.

*Diana Norvelle,
Ocala, Florida.*

## CHOCOLATE CHANTILLY CREPES

1 (4⅛-ounce) package chocolate instant pudding mix
1½ cups cold milk
¼ cup rum
1¼ cups whipping cream, whipped
¼ cup chopped almonds, toasted
16 dessert crepes
Sliced toasted almonds (optional)

Combine pudding mix and milk; beat at lowest speed of electric mixer until thickened, about 2 minutes. Stir in rum. Fold in 1½ cups whipped cream and chopped almonds. Chill.

Spoon 3 tablespoons of pudding mixture into center of each crêpe; roll up, and place seam side down on a serving plate. Garnish with remaining whipped cream and sliced almonds, if desired. Yield: 16 crêpes.

*Note:* When preparing Chocolate Chantilly Crêpes, substitute 1 teaspoon rum for vanilla extract in the Basic Dessert Crêpes recipe, if desired.

## PEACH CREPES

6 fresh peaches, peeled and sliced
½ cup sugar
1 tablespoon cornstarch
1 teaspoon ground cinnamon
Dash of ground nutmeg
2 teaspoons lemon juice
1 (8-ounce) carton commercial sour cream
2 tablespoons sugar
½ teaspoon vanilla extract
8 dessert crêpes
Fresh peach slices (optional)

Combine first 6 ingredients in a large saucepan; cook over low heat until peaches are tender, stirring mixture occasionally.

Combine sour cream, 2 tablespoons sugar, and vanilla; mix well, and set aside.

Spoon 3 tablespoons peach mixture into center of each crêpe; roll up, and place seam side down on a serving platter. Spoon sour cream mixture over crêpes. Garnish with fresh peaches, if desired. Yield: 8 crêpes.

# Churn Your Own Pralines And Cream

When you try Susan Temple's Pralines and Cream Ice Cream, you'll find it hard to believe it didn't come from the ice cream parlor. Toasted pecans are lightly coated with caramelized sugar to give it the characteristic flavor and crunch.

### PRALINES AND CREAM ICE CREAM

2 to 2½ cups chopped pecans
2 tablespoons butter or margarine
6 eggs
1 (14-ounce) can sweetened condensed milk
1 (13-ounce) can evaporated milk
1 tablespoon vanilla extract
1 pint whipping cream
2 cups sugar, divided
1 cup evaporated milk
About 2 cups milk

Sauté chopped pecans in butter, stirring constantly, about 5 minutes or until toasted. Set aside to cool.

Beat eggs in a large bowl at medium speed of electric mixer until frothy. Add next 4 ingredients; mix well.

Combine 1 cup sugar and 1 cup evaporated milk in a saucepan. Cook over low heat, stirring constantly, until the mixture begins to bubble; remove pan from heat.

Place remaining 1 cup sugar in a small saucepan; cook over medium heat, stirring constantly, until sugar dissolves and forms a smooth liquid. Stir in pecans. (Mixture may form lumps.)

Stir pecan mixture into sugar and milk mixture; break apart pecan lumps. Stir into egg mixture.

Pour into freezer can of a 1-gallon hand-turned or electric freezer. Add enough milk to fill can three-fourths full. Freeze according to manufacturer's instructions. Let ice cream ripen at least 1 hour. Yield: about 1 gallon.

*Susan Temple,*
*Longview, Texas.*

# Microwave Cookery

# Cookies, Made For The Microwave

If folks at your house love cookies, consider making them in your microwave oven. You bake only 6 at a time, but a batch of 2 to 3 dozen can be done in little more than the time required to preheat the conventional oven.

Some cookie recipes cannot be adapted to microwave cookery, and the texture and color of others may vary from conventionally baked cookies. You can get good results, however, by using proper microwave-cooking techniques and an adapted recipe.

Most microwaved cookies are soft and chewy, rather than crisp. To keep cookies from spreading thin and being too tender, use a stiffer dough than that of a conventional recipe.

Avoid recipes with a high proportion of shortening or butter. The high fat content attracts microwave energy and can cause overbaking in spots. Since cookies won't brown in a microwave oven, use recipes with ingredients that contain natural color, such as chocolate, brown sugar, or dark spices. Or dust the cookies with powdered sugar to give them an attractive finish.

Each recipe included here gives a time range for baking the cookies. To prevent overbaking, always check for doneness at the lower end of the range.

## Shaped or Drop Cookies

To bake shaped or drop cookies, arrange 6 at a time in a ring on a waxed paper-lined, microwave-safe plate, spacing them 2 inches apart. Use MEDIUM (50% power) for most cookies. Turn the plate of cookies occasionally during baking to ensure even doneness.

Cookies are done when they are fairly firm to the touch and almost dry on top. (A few wet spots will dry while the cookies cool.) Do not overcook, or cookies will appear done on top but be burned in the center.

Slide waxed paper with cookies onto counter. Let cool 2 minutes, remove cookies from paper, and place on a wire rack to finish cooling. Cookies will stick if cooled completely before being removed from the paper.

## Bar Cookies

Since corners of bar cookies cook faster than the center, you'll need to shield the corners with aluminum foil to reduce energy received and slow the cooking process. But before doing this, check your manufacturer's directions; some older models of microwave ovens can be damaged by the use of foil. If your oven doesn't allow shielding, bake cookies in a round dish.

To shield bar cookies, cut triangles of foil and place over the top corners of the dish, keeping foil smooth and close to the dish. Be sure the foil is at least 1 inch from the walls of the oven. If foil is not smooth or touches oven walls, it may cause an arc (spark of electricity). If an arc does occur, flatten the foil and continue microwaving.

For most bar cookies, shields should be left in place during the entire microwave cycle. However, you'll need to remove the shields earlier if the cycle is almost complete and the corners are not cooking as rapidly as the center.

## BLACKBERRY JAM BARS

¼ cup plus 3 tablespoons butter or
  margarine, softened
½ cup firmly packed brown sugar
1 cup all-purpose flour
¼ teaspoon salt
¼ teaspoon baking soda
1 cup quick-cooking oats, uncooked
¾ cup blackberry jam

Cream butter; gradually add sugar, beating well. Combine flour, salt, and soda; add to creamed mixture, mixing well. Stir in oats.

Press half of mixture into an ungreased 8-inch square baking dish. Shield corners of dish with triangles of foil, keeping foil smooth and close to dish. Microwave at MEDIUM (50% power) for 6 to 7 minutes or until firm, rotating the dish one quarter-turn at 2-minute intervals. Top with jam, spreading to within ¼ inch of edge. Press remaining crumb mixture on top.

Microwave, with edges shielded, at MEDIUM for 11 to 13 minutes or until firm, rotating dish one quarter-turn at 2-minute intervals. (Do not overcook; mixture will firm up as it cools.) Cool and cut into bars. Yield: about 2 dozen.

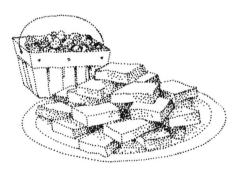

## DOUBLY-GOOD CHOCOLATE COOKIES

½ cup semisweet chocolate morsels,
  divided
1¼ cups all-purpose flour
½ teaspoon baking powder
¼ teaspoon salt
½ cup sugar
¼ cup shortening
1 egg
½ teaspoon vanilla extract
1½ teaspoons milk
½ cup chopped pecans

Place ¼ cup chocolate morsels in a small glass bowl; microwave at HIGH for 1½ minutes, and stir well. Let cool.

Combine flour, baking powder, and salt; set aside.

Combine sugar and shortening in a large bowl, creaming well. Add cooled chocolate, egg, vanilla, and milk; beat well. Add dry ingredients, and mix well. Stir in remaining chocolate morsels and chopped pecans.

Microwave 6 cookies at a time, dropping heaping teaspoonfuls of dough in a ring onto a waxed paper-lined glass pizza plate. Microwave at MEDIUM (50% power) for 2 to 3 minutes or until cookies are dry on the surface, rotating dish one half-turn at 1-minute intervals. Slide waxed paper with cookies onto counter, and let cool 2 minutes. Remove cookies to wire racks to complete cooling. Repeat procedure with remaining dough. Yield: about 2½ dozen.

## NUTTY OATMEAL-CHOCOLATE CHIP COOKIES

1 cup all-purpose flour
½ teaspoon baking soda
¼ teaspoon baking powder
¼ teaspoon salt
1 cup firmly packed brown sugar
½ cup shortening
1 egg
½ teaspoon vanilla extract
1 cup quick-cooking oats, uncooked
½ cup semisweet chocolate morsels
½ cup finely chopped pecans

Combine flour, soda, baking powder, and salt; set aside.

Combine sugar and shortening, creaming well; beat in egg and vanilla. Add flour mixture, and mix well. Stir in oats, chocolate morsels, and pecans.

Microwave 6 cookies at a time, dropping heaping teaspoonfuls of dough in a ring onto a waxed paper-lined glass pizza plate. Microwave at MEDIUM (50% power) for 2 to 3 minutes or until cookies are dry on the surface, rotating dish one half-turn at 1-minute intervals. Slide waxed paper with cookies onto counter, and let cool 2 minutes. Remove cookies to wire racks to complete cooling. Repeat procedure with remaining dough. Yield: about 3 dozen.

## PEANUT BUTTER SLICE-AND-BAKES

1¾ cups all-purpose flour
½ cup sugar
½ teaspoon baking soda
¼ teaspoon salt
½ cup shortening
¾ cup creamy peanut butter, divided
¼ cup light corn syrup
1 tablespoon milk

Combine flour, sugar, soda, and salt; cut in shortening and ½ cup peanut butter with pastry blender until mixture resembles coarse meal. Stir in corn syrup and milk.

Shape dough into a long roll, 2 inches in diameter; wrap in waxed paper, and chill 2 to 3 hours or until firm.

Unwrap roll, and cut into ¼-inch slices. Place 6 cookies on a waxed paper-lined glass pizza plate, arranging them in a ring. Microwave at MEDIUM (50% power) for 2 to 4 minutes or until cookies are dry on the surface, rotating dish one quarter-turn at 1-minute intervals. Slide waxed paper with cookies onto counter, and let cool 2 minutes. Remove cookies to wire rack to complete cooling. Repeat procedure with remaining dough.

Spread half of cookies with about ½ teaspoon peanut butter each. Top with the remaining cookie slices. Yield: about 2 dozen.

## WEDDING COOKIES

1 cup plus 2 tablespoons all-purpose flour
⅛ teaspoon ground cinnamon
½ cup butter or margarine, softened
½ cup finely chopped pecans
¼ cup sifted powdered sugar
½ teaspoon vanilla extract
Powdered sugar

Combine flour and cinnamon in a large bowl. Add butter, pecans, ¼ cup powdered sugar, and vanilla; stir until well blended (mixture will be stiff). Shape dough into 1-inch balls.

Place 6 cookies on a waxed paper-lined glass pizza plate, arranging them in a ring. Microwave at MEDIUM (50% power) for 3 to 4 minutes or until firm, rotating dish one quarter-turn at 1-minute intervals. Slide waxed paper with cookies onto counter, and let cool 2 minutes. Roll cookies in additional powdered sugar, and cool completely on wire racks. Repeat procedure with remaining dough. Yield: about 2½ dozen.

*Tip: Need a quick microwave frosting for cakes and cupcakes? Place about 16 mint chocolate patties over a layer cake, or top cupcakes with one patty. The layer cake patties will melt in 2 minutes at HIGH in a microwave and one patty on a cupcake will take 10 to 15 seconds at HIGH in a microwave.*

# Avoid Leftovers With Entrées For Two

If you're cooking for two, you'll find these small-scale entrées will suit your needs perfectly—and with lots of flavor.

For Beefed-Up Peppers, green pepper shells are filled with a spicy mixture of ground beef, corn, Cheddar cheese, and chili sauce; then the peppers are topped with crushed tortilla chips before baking. Also served in a tasty container, Tropical Chicken Boats for Two offers a combination of cubed chicken, pineapple chunks, celery, sour cream, and toasted almonds mounded into avocado halves and served on a bed of lettuce. Eggplant Parmigiana is a good selection for a savory meatless main dish for two.

## BEEFED-UP PEPPERS

2 large green peppers
½ pound ground beef
2 tablespoons chopped onion
½ cup whole kernel corn
¼ cup (1 ounce) shredded Cheddar cheese
¼ cup chili sauce
½ teaspoon chili powder
½ teaspoon Worcestershire sauce
¼ teaspoon salt
2 tablespoons crushed tortilla chips

Cut off tops of green peppers, and remove seeds. Remove stem portion from tops, and discard; chop remainder of tops, and set aside.

Cook pepper shells 5 minutes in boiling salted water; drain and set aside.

Cook ground beef, onion, and chopped pepper until beef is browned; drain well. Stir in next 6 ingredients.

Fill peppers with beef mixture; place in a 1-quart shallow baking dish. Top with tortilla chips. Bake at 350° for 40 minutes. Yield: 2 servings. *Pat Smith, Baton Rouge, Louisiana.*

## HERB CHICKEN BAKE

¼ cup dry breadcrumbs
1 tablespoon grated Parmesan cheese
½ teaspoon dried whole basil
½ teaspoon dried whole oregano
¼ teaspoon garlic salt
1 whole chicken breast, split and skinned
¼ cup butter or margarine, melted
¼ cup dry white wine
¼ cup chopped green onion
¼ cup dried parsley flakes

Combine the first 5 ingredients, mixing well. Dip chicken in butter; then dredge in breadcrumb mixture. Place in an 8-inch square baking dish. Bake at 375° for 30 minutes.

Combine wine, onion, and parsley with remaining butter; stir well. Pour over chicken; continue baking 20 minutes or until done. Yield: 2 servings.
*Karen L. Foster, Austin, Texas.*

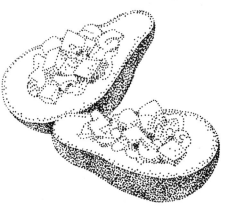

## TROPICAL CHICKEN BOATS FOR TWO

1 (8-ounce) can pineapple chunks
1 cup chopped cooked chicken
½ cup sliced almonds, toasted
½ cup chopped celery
¼ cup commercial sour cream
½ teaspoon honey
1 large ripe avocado, peeled and halved
Lettuce leaves

Drain the pineapple, reserving ¼ cup juice. Combine pineapple, chicken, almonds, and celery; mix well. Add sour cream, reserved pineapple juice, and honey; stir well. Fill avocado halves with chicken mixture. Arrange on lettuce leaves. Yield: 2 servings.
*Sandra Russell, Maitland, Florida.*

## DANISH PORK TENDERLOIN

¼ cup all-purpose flour
½ teaspoon salt
¼ teaspoon pepper
⅛ teaspoon rosemary leaves
¾ pound pork tenderloin, cut into ½-inch slices
2 tablespoons butter or margarine
1 tablespoon vegetable oil
1 medium onion, thinly sliced
½ cup Chablis or other dry white wine
4 fresh mushrooms, thinly sliced
2 tablespoons lemon juice
Hot cooked rice

Combine flour, salt, pepper, and rosemary; dredge pork in flour mixture.

Sauté pork in butter and oil in a large skillet 1 minute on each side or until brown. Remove pork. Add onion; cook 1 minute or until crisp-tender. Stir in wine; simmer 3 minutes. Stir in mushrooms. Add pork; cover and simmer 3 minutes on each side. Stir in lemon juice; simmer 2 minutes. Remove from heat; cover and let stand 10 minutes. Serve over rice. Yield: 2 servings.
*Lilly S. Bradley, Salem, Virginia.*

## EGGPLANT PARMIGIANA

3 tablespoons butter or margarine, melted
½ cup corn flake crumbs
¼ cup grated Parmesan cheese
½ teaspoon salt
Dash of pepper
1 small eggplant
1 egg, slightly beaten
1 (8-ounce) can tomato sauce
½ teaspoon dried whole oregano
½ teaspoon sugar
Dash of onion salt
2 (1-ounce) slices mozzarella cheese, cut in half diagonally

Pour melted butter into a 10- x 8- x 2-inch baking dish; set aside. Combine corn flake crumbs, Parmesan cheese, salt, and pepper; stir well, and set aside.

Peel eggplant, and cut into ¾-inch slices. Dip each slice in egg, and coat with crumb mixture; arrange in baking dish. Bake at 400° for 20 minutes; turn slices. Bake an additional 15 minutes.

Combine the tomato sauce, oregano, sugar, and onion salt in a small saucepan; bring to a boil, stirring occasionally. Pour sauce over eggplant, and top with mozzarella. Bake an additional 3 minutes or until the cheese is slightly melted. Yield: 2 servings.
*Ellen Meadows Shell, Powhatan, Virginia.*

Right: *Easy Jellyroll (page 176) wraps a filling of strawberry jam; a garnish of whipped cream and strawberries gives it an elegant look.*

Page 188: *The enjoyment of certain foods spans generations of good cooks. These traditional Southern dishes are the pick of the crop: Pecan Cake With Praline Glaze (page 196), assorted fresh vegetables, Cider-Baked Country Ham (page 195), Chow-Chow (page 196), Skillet Squash (page 195), Sunshine Sweet Potato Cups (page 195), and Baking Powder Biscuits (page 195).*

# From Our Kitchen To Yours

Fats and their liquid counterparts, oils, are often misunderstood. To some, the word fat means being overweight; to others, it's a messy cleanup after frying. But to a nutritionist, fat represents one of the three major dietary components of food—the other two being proteins and carbohydrates.

## Facts About Fats

■ Fats are the most concentrated source of food energy, yielding 9 calories per gram—over twice as many calories as are supplied by either carbohydrates or protein, both of which yield 4 calories per gram. Fats give foods distinctive flavors and aromas, leaving you with a feeling of satisfaction or "fullness" after eating.

They also contain the fat-soluble vitamins A, D, E, and K and are the sole source of linoleic acid, the essential fatty acid the body cannot manufacture for itself. Some fat is necessary in the diet to maintain good health. Consumption of moderate amounts of fat in addition to a balanced diet and regular exercise is generally acceptable for healthy people.

In cooking, fats have a number of roles to play. In pastry making, it's the melting of the fat that puffs the dough and makes a flaky crust. Fats are used in breads to add tenderness, moistness, and flavor. For frying, fats are a must. They can be heated to a much higher temperature than water so foods not only cook but brown, too.

■ Fats can be divided into two groups: fats and oils. Those that are solid at room temperature—such as butter, margarine, lard, shortening, and the fat of meat—are called fats. Corn, peanut, sesame seed, olive, and safflower oils are liquid at room temperature and are known as oils.

We've often had questions about the differences between shortening and vegetable oil. Basically, shortening is an oil that has hydrogen added under carefully controlled conditions. This process, hydrogenation, changes the oil from a liquid to a solid. We don't recommend substituting a fat for an oil or, in other words, shortening for vegetable oil. If our recipe calls for ¼ cup vegetable oil, we have used just that, not ¼ cup shortening.

■ Butter and margarine are two fats widely used in cooking and for flavoring foods. While butter and margarine are often used interchangeably, they are two different products. Butter has milk fat or cream as a base, while most margarines are made from vegetable oils, with some made from a combination of vegetable oils and animal fat.

Both butter and margarine are available in salted, unsalted, and whipped form. The whipped products have air incorporated to make them more spreadable. Don't substitute whipped for regular butter or margarine without making necessary adjustments. Usually 1½ cups whipped margarine equals 1 cup margarine.

Diet or imitation margarine is a soft margarine with about half the fat and more than three times the water of plain margarine. It is used primarily as a spread and isn't suitable for baking because of the high water content.

Butter and margarine have many uses in cooking, but they are not used for frying because of their low smoke points. (Smoke point is the temperature at which a fat or oil begins to smoke.)

■ Store fats and oils correctly to maintain freshness and increase their storage life. Keep oils tightly closed and stored at room temperature out of direct sunlight. (Light tends to deteriorate the oil; therefore, some oils are stored in tins so the light will be blocked out.) Many oils can be refrigerated after opening because they have been treated to prevent clouding and solidifying. Vegetable shortenings are stored at room temperature. Lard must be refrigerated. All forms of butter and margarine should be refrigerated as soon as possible after purchase. Keep unused portions in a covered container so they won't absorb odors of other food. Butter can be stored up to 30 days in the refrigerator and four months in the freezer.

## Some Other Tips

**Clarifying butter**—When your recipe calls for clarified butter, follow this easy method. Melt butter over low heat. The fat rises to the top and the milk solids sink to the bottom. Skim off the white froth that appears on the top. Then strain off the clear, yellow butter, keeping back the sediment of milk solids. This butter may be chilled until ready to use, then reheated.

**Butter curls**—Butter curls add a decorative touch to your table. You will need a butter curler and sticks of butter or margarine. Dip the butter curler in warm to hot water; then pull it firmly across the top of a slightly softened stick. The butter will curl up and over the curler. Place curls in ice water. When all curls have been made, remove from water and place on a serving dish.

Cover and refrigerate until ready to use.

**Butter balls**—To make butter balls for individual servings, dip a pair of butter paddles into scalding water, then into ice water. Using 1 tablespoon of slightly softened butter, roll into a ball between the paddles. Move the paddles in circles in opposite directions for easier shaping. When the butter has formed a textured ball, drop it into ice water. Dip paddles into ice water before forming each ball.

# Toss A Vermicelli Salad

Looking for a delicious but different salad to take on a picnic or to your family reunion? Try Vermicelli Vinaigrette Salad. It's an attractive combination of cooked pasta, artichoke hearts, tomatoes, mushrooms, and nuts, tossed with a vinaigrette dressing.

### VERMICELLI VINAIGRETTE SALAD

⅓ (12-ounce) package vermicelli
1 (6½-ounce) jar marinated artichoke hearts
2 large tomatoes, chopped
1 cup fresh mushrooms, sliced
½ cup chopped walnuts
2 tablespoons chopped fresh parsley
¼ cup vegetable oil
¼ cup red wine vinegar
1 large clove garlic, minced
¼ teaspoon salt
¼ teaspoon dried whole basil
⅛ teaspoon pepper
Lettuce leaves
Additional fresh parsley (optional)

Cook vermicelli according to package directions, omitting salt; drain and set aside. Drain artichoke hearts, reserving ¼ cup marinade; chop artichoke hearts. Combine vermicelli, artichoke hearts, tomatoes, mushrooms, walnuts, and parsley; mix well, and set aside.

Combine reserved marinade, oil, vinegar, garlic, salt, basil, and pepper in a jar. Cover tightly, and shake vigorously. Pour over vermicelli mixture; toss gently. Cover and chill thoroughly. Arrange salad on lettuce leaves before serving. Garnish with additional parsley, if desired. Yield: 6 servings.

*Earlene Ramay,*
*Englewood, Colorado.*

# Pack A Safe Picnic

When summer weather brings Southerners outdoors for picnics and cookouts, precautions should be taken to keep food from spoiling. Warm temperatures provide an excellent environment for the growth of harmful bacteria; and since contaminated foods don't necessarily change in odor, taste, or appearance, the danger could go undetected.

Protection against food poisoning begins with selection and preparation of the food; improper handling is more often the cause of bacterial contamination than is the food itself. Cautious selection of food in the supermarket, proper storage at home, and cleanliness during preparation are major factors in the prevention of food-borne illness. Here are a few specific pointers that should help keep your picnic safe.

■ First, plan the menu according to the distance you'll travel to the picnic site; for long distances, use less perishable food.

■ During preparation, place any cooked food (such as ham, chicken, and potatoes) in the refrigerator as soon as it stops steaming. Keep all dishes and the containers refrigerator-chilled until the last minute. Meat, poultry, and egg sandwiches should be refrigerated.

■ When preparing sandwiches or salads containing commercial mayonnaise, it's best to add the mayonnaise during the initial preparation stages. Contrary to popular belief, commercial mayonnaise actually helps protect food against bacterial growth because of the acid ingredients (vinegar and lemon juice) it contains. Commercial mayonnaise adds enough acidity to meat sandwiches and salads to retard bacterial growth and reduce spoilage. However, mayonnaise should not be considered a substitute for refrigeration and homemade mayonnaise may not contain enough acid ingredients to offer protection.

■ Pack picnic foods in insulated containers that will keep hot food hot and cold food cold since bacteria thrive at temperatures between 45° and 115°. Be sure to use ice, dry ice, or reusable cold packs to keep food chilled.

■ It's easy for food to reach warm temperatures in the hot sun, so keep picnic containers away from direct sun and pack food to be used first on top to avoid excessive opening of the container. Don't save leftovers since food may sit for a while during and after the picnic, and spoilage can occur without any obvious changes in the food.

# Spruce Up The Menu With Showy Sandwiches

Too pretty to hide beneath slices of bread, these open-face sandwiches give you a mouth-watering preview of tasty toppings. Smothered with tomato slices and melted cheese, Desiree Burington's Tuna Cheesies consist of creamy tuna salad on English muffins—perfect for a light luncheon.

Wieners get a new twist with Susie Dent's chili-spiced Beany Hot Dogs. Slice the wieners and team them with kidney beans, tomato sauce, and Cheddar cheese for a hearty mixture to spoon over hot dog buns. Sprinkle with crumbled bacon for garnish and added crunch.

## EASY PIZZA BURGERS

½ pound ground beef
2 tablespoons grated Parmesan cheese
2 tablespoons chopped onion
2 tablespoons chopped ripe olives
¼ teaspoon salt
½ teaspoon ground oregano
¼ cup plus 2 tablespoons catsup
2 slices mozzarella cheese, cut into ½-inch strips
2 hamburger buns, split and toasted
2 cherry tomatoes, halved

Cook beef until browned, stirring occasionally. Drain off pan drippings. Add next 6 ingredients; cook over low heat about 2 minutes, stirring constantly.

Place half the cheese strips on bun halves. Top each with meat mixture and remaining cheese. Broil until cheese melts. Garnish with cherry tomato halves. Yield: 2 to 4 servings.
*Hazel Jordan,*
*Euless, Texas.*

## BEANY HOT DOGS

4 slices bacon
1 medium-size green pepper, chopped
1 medium onion, chopped
6 wieners, thinly sliced
2 (15½-ounce) cans kidney beans, drained
1 (8-ounce) can tomato sauce
2 tablespoons chili powder
½ teaspoon salt
⅛ teaspoon pepper
2 cups (8 ounces) shredded sharp Cheddar cheese
8 hot dog buns

Cook bacon in a large skillet until crisp; remove bacon, reserving 2 tablespoons drippings in skillet. Crumble bacon, and set aside.

Sauté green pepper and onion in drippings until tender. Add wieners, beans, tomato sauce, and seasonings; cover and cook over medium heat 5 minutes. Remove from heat; add cheese, stirring until melted. Spoon mixture into hot dog buns. Sprinkle bacon pieces on top. Yield: 8 servings.
*Susie M. E. Dent,*
*Saltillo, Mississippi.*

## TURKEY OPEN-FACERS

1 (10-ounce) package frozen asparagus spears
¼ cup commercial French dressing
1 tablespoon chopped onion
⅛ teaspoon pepper
1 tablespoon butter or margarine, softened
2 teaspoons mayonnaise
2 slices bread, toasted
4 slices cooked turkey
2 slices Swiss cheese, cut diagonally

Cook asparagus according to package directions; drain and return to saucepan. Combine next 3 ingredients, stirring well; pour over asparagus. Cook over medium heat 3 to 4 minutes or until mixture comes to a boil; remove from heat.

Combine butter and mayonnaise, mixing well; spread on toast. Place 2 slices of turkey on each slice of toast. Arrange half of asparagus spears on top of turkey; top with cheese. Broil 1 to 2 minutes or until cheese melts. Yield: 2 servings.
*Emma Belle Armistead,*
*Thomasville, Alabama.*

## CHEESY CHICKEN SANDWICHES

6 slices cooked chicken
6 slices bread, toasted
1 cup plus 2 tablespoons milk
1 egg
½ teaspoon dry mustard
¼ teaspoon salt
½ teaspoon Worcestershire sauce
1½ tablespoons all-purpose flour
2 cups (8 ounces) shredded Cheddar cheese
Chopped fresh parsley

Arrange chicken on toast; set aside. Combine next 7 ingredients in container of electric blender; process until smooth. Transfer mixture to a heavy saucepan; cook over medium heat, stirring constantly, until thickened. Spoon over sandwiches, and sprinkle with parsley. Yield: 6 servings. *Carol Kempher,* ~~~~~ *, Florida.*

## TUNA CHEESIES

1 (6½-ounce) can tuna, drained and
   flaked
¼ cup finely chopped onion
¼ cup chopped celery
3 tablespoons mayonnaise
⅛ teaspoon pepper
4 English muffins, split and toasted
8 slices tomato
8 slices American cheese

Combine first 5 ingredients; mix well. Spoon tuna mixture onto English muffin halves; place on a baking sheet.

Top sandwiches with tomato slices and cheese. Broil until cheese melts. Yield: 8 sandwiches.

*Desiree Burington,*
*Valdosta, Georgia.*

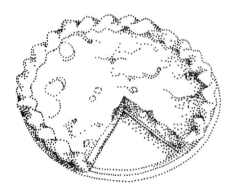

# These Pies Are Filled With Vegetables

If you're looking for something new to do with vegetables, why not bake them in a pie? Made with high-protein foods such as milk, eggs, or cheese, these vegetable pies rate high in nutrition and can be served as eye-catching main dishes for meatless meals.

Cauliflower-Carrot Pie has a rich and cheesy filling baked in a crust of herb-seasoned croutons. With onions in such abundance, bake them in a pie along with bacon and sour cream. It's so good you don't even have to be an onion-lover to enjoy it.

## CAULIFLOWER-CARROT PIE

3 cups herb-seasoned croutons, crushed
¼ cup butter or margarine, melted
1 medium head cauliflower
¼ cup butter or margarine
1 cup finely chopped onion
1 clove garlic, minced
½ cup thinly sliced carrots
¼ teaspoon salt
¼ teaspoon ground oregano
1 cup (4 ounces) shredded Cheddar
   cheese, divided
2 eggs
¼ cup milk

Combine first 2 ingredients; mix well. Press into a 9-inch pieplate; bake at 375° for 8 minutes. Set aside.

Remove outer leaves from cauliflower. Separate cauliflower into flowerets; wash thoroughly, and quarter flowerets.

Melt ¼ cup butter in a skillet; add cauliflower, onion, garlic, carrots, salt, and oregano. Cook over medium heat 10 minutes, stirring often.

Sprinkle ½ cup cheese over crust. Spoon cooked vegetables into shell, and top with remaining cheese. Combine eggs and milk; beat well, and pour over pie. Bake at 375° for 35 minutes. Yield: one 9-inch pie. *Mary Lou Welsh,*
*Hinsdale, Illinois.*

## QUICK AND CHEESY CORN PIE

2 cups biscuit mix
2 tablespoons butter or margarine, melted
½ cup cold water
½ cup milk
4 eggs
1 (17-ounce) can cream-style corn
¾ cup (6 ounces) shredded sharp Cheddar
   cheese
2 tablespoons minced onion
2 tablespoons minced green pepper
¼ teaspoon pepper

Combine first 3 ingredients; stir until a stiff batter forms. Spoon batter into a lightly greased 10-inch pieplate; spread to form a shell. Set aside.

Combine milk and eggs; beat well. Stir in remaining ingredients. Pour mixture into pastry shell. Bake at 375° for 50 to 55 minutes or until filling is set. Yield: one 10-inch pie.
*Mrs. J. L. Stringfield,*
*Cottageville, South Carolina.*

*Tip: Freeze very soft cheese 15 minutes to make shredding easier.*

## ONION PIE

Pastry for 9-inch pie
8 slices bacon
2 cups thinly sliced onion
3 eggs, slightly beaten
1 (8-ounce) carton commercial sour
   cream
⅛ teaspoon white pepper
1½ teaspoons minced chives
½ teaspoon caraway seeds

Line a 9-inch pieplate with pastry; trim excess pastry around edges and flute. Prick bottom and sides of pastry shell with a fork. Bake at 400° for 3 minutes; remove from oven, and gently prick with a fork. Bake 5 minutes longer. Let cool on a rack.

Cook bacon until crisp; drain, reserving 3 tablespoons drippings. Crumble bacon, and set aside. Sauté onion in bacon drippings until tender. Combine bacon, onion, and the next 4 ingredients in a bowl; stir well. Spoon mixture into pastry shell, and sprinkle with caraway seeds. Bake at 350° for 30 to 35 minutes or until set. Let stand 5 minutes before serving. Yield: one 9-inch pie.
*Trudy Dunn,*
*San Jose, California.*

## SPINACH PIE

Pastry for 9-inch pie
1 (10-ounce) package frozen chopped
   spinach
1 medium onion, chopped
2 tablespoons butter or margarine
1 cup cream-style cottage cheese
3 tablespoons grated Parmesan cheese,
   divided
⅛ teaspoon ground nutmeg

Line a 9-inch pieplate with pastry; trim excess pastry around edges and flute. Prick bottom and sides of pastry shell with a fork. Bake at 400° for 3 minutes; remove from oven, and gently prick with a fork. Bake 5 minutes longer. Let cool on rack.

Cook spinach according to package directions. Drain well, and squeeze spinach to remove excess liquid. Set aside.

Sauté onion in butter until tender. Add spinach, cottage cheese, 2 tablespoons Parmesan cheese, and nutmeg; stir well. Spoon mixture into pastry shell. Sprinkle with remaining Parmesan cheese. Bake at 350° for 25 to 30 minutes or until set. Yield: one 9-inch pie.
*Virginia Mathews,*
*Jacksonville, Florida.*

# Making Mayonnaise Is Easier Than You Think

For a delightfully fresh, rich-flavored mayonnaise seasoned to your own taste, why not make your own? If you've been reluctant to try making mayonnaise yourself, follow the instructions provided here and you'll find it isn't as hard as you may think.

Mayonnaise is simply an emulsion of egg yolk and vegetable oil with a flavoring of lemon juice, lime juice, or vinegar and a choice of seasonings. The emulsion is created by very rapid beating, especially at the beginning of the process.

Beating the egg yolks well before adding the oil is the key to making a mayonnaise that is less likely to separate or curdle. A deep, narrow bowl allows the ingredients to be well beaten, and using an electric mixer or blender is more effective than hand mixing.

When the emulsion becomes thick and the lemon juice or other acid ingredient is added, the mixture thins temporarily and thickens again after continued beating. Since homemade mayonnaise doesn't contain stabilizing ingredients present in most commercial types, excessive stirring should be avoided to prevent separation once all the oil is added.

If the emulsion should break down during mixing or storage, add the curdled mixture to a well-beaten egg yolk. The best method is to beat the yolk in a bowl and add the mayonnaise a spoonful at a time while using an electric mixer. Be sure to follow this procedure exactly, since adding the yolk to the mixture will not re-create the emulsion.

**Step 1**—*To make a good mayonnaise, beat the egg yolks well at the first stage of the process.*

**Step 2**—*Add oil 1 tablespoon at a time to help stabilize the emulsion.*

**Step 3**—*Gradually add lemon juice after the mixture becomes very thick.*

**Step 4**—*Fold in seasonings; to keep the emulsion from separating, be careful not to overstir. Store in covered plastic or glass container in the refrigerator.*

## HERBED MAYONNAISE

**2 egg yolks**
**2 tablespoons lemon juice**
**½ teaspoon salt**
**½ teaspoon dry mustard**
**Pinch of red pepper**
**2 cups vegetable oil**
**1½ teaspoons minced chives**
**1½ teaspoons chopped fresh parsley**

Combine first 5 ingredients in blender container; process on medium speed 5 seconds or until thick and lemon colored. Remove cover, and continue to process 55 seconds, adding oil in a thin, steady stream. Spoon mayonnaise into a small bowl; fold in herbs just until blended. Cover and refrigerate. Yield: 2 cups.

## TASTY MAYONNAISE

**2 egg yolks**
**2 cups vegetable oil**
**2 tablespoons lemon juice**
**½ teaspoon salt**
**¾ teaspoon dry mustard**
**¾ teaspoon paprika**
**3 drops hot sauce**

Beat egg yolks in a deep, narrow bowl at high speed of an electric mixer until thick and lemon colored. Add oil, 1 tablespoon at a time; beat until mixture begins to thicken. Gradually add lemon juice, beating until thickened. Add remaining ingredients, stirring well. Spoon mayonnaise into a glass or plastic container; cover and refrigerate. Do not store mayonnaise in a metal container. Yield: about 2 cups.

*Note:* If mayonnaise curdles in making, add curdled mixture, a teaspoonful at a time, to a well-beaten egg yolk.

# September

The air tingles with excitement as September kicks off the start of another football season and another reason for Southerners to entertain. Whether the party is before or after the game, we have the menu to suit the occasion. Our football brunch offers a main dish of Huevros Rancheros with Canadian-style bacon, fresh fruit, and coffee cake.

For months, our staff has been swamped with reader requests for the recipe for "Herman" sourdough starter. In this chapter, you'll find a recipe and step-by-step instructions for Herman as well as recipes for using the starter for Hot Rolls and Sourdough Biscuits.

And since tradition lives in the South's favorite recipes, we present some of the best-known recipes of the past. Remember Cider-Baked Country Ham, Chow-Chow, Cheddar Spoonbread, Baking Powder Biscuits, Lemon Chess Pie, and Pecan Cake With Praline Glaze? Like Southern hospitality, these recipes will never die.

# Enjoy The Mellow Goodness Of Fall Pears

Glistening green and gold or blushing with a tinge of red, fall pears capture the very essence of the season in their glowing colors and mellow goodness—a feast for both the eye and the palate. You will certainly want to enjoy some right off the tree or baked in an old-fashioned pie or cobbler, but we have several other irresistible ideas.

For starters, we present Poached Pears in Wine. This dessert is for those who like to end a meal on an elegant note, and preparation is surprisingly simple. Just peel each pear, leaving the stem intact; then poach in a light sauce flavored with rosé, cinnamon, and cloves.

Fall Salad With Ginger Dressing combines the flavors of pears and apples in a cool gelatin mold, with a dollop of spicy dressing adding the finishing touch. And one taste of Pear Preserves spread between warm biscuits or ladled over ice cream is sure to make you a winner, whether the judges are at the county fair or around your table.

If you're lucky enough to have a pear tree, you know it's best to pick pears before they are actually ripe. Select fruit that's mature in size but still firm and greenish. If left to ripen on the tree, the pears will develop a coarse texture.

It's easy to ripen firm pears—just place them in a paper or plastic bag for a few days at room temperature. You'll know they're ready to be enjoyed when the stem end becomes soft enough to yield to gentle pressure.

## POACHED PEARS IN WINE

8 medium pears
1 cup sugar
2 cups water
2 cups rosé
Grated rind of 1 lemon
1 teaspoon lemon juice
4 whole cloves
1 (2-inch) stick cinnamon
Additional grated lemon rind (optional)

Peel pears, removing core from bottom end but leaving stems intact. Slice about ¼ inch from bottom of each pear to make a flat base. Set pears aside.

Combine next 7 ingredients in a 5-quart Dutch oven; bring to a boil over medium heat, stirring until sugar dissolves. Place pears in Dutch oven in an upright position. Cover and simmer for 20 minutes (straighten pears if they tilt while cooking).

Using a slotted spoon, transfer pears to a 10- x 6- x 2-inch baking dish. Strain syrup, and pour over pears; cover and refrigerate until chilled.

Spoon pears and syrup into dessert dishes; sprinkle with lemon rind, if desired. Yield: 8 servings.

*Peggy Fowler Revels,*
*Woodruff, South Carolina.*

## FALL SALAD WITH GINGER DRESSING

1 (3-ounce) package apricot-flavored gelatin
2 cups boiling water
⅓ cup coarsely chopped dates
⅛ teaspoon salt
2 medium unpeeled pears, cored and diced (about 1 cup)
2 medium unpeeled apples, cored and diced (about 1 cup)
⅓ cup chopped walnuts
Lettuce leaves (optional)
Ginger Dressing

Dissolve gelatin in boiling water; stir in dates and salt. Chill until consistency of unbeaten egg white.

Fold in pears, apples, and walnuts. Pour into a lightly oiled 4-cup mold, and chill until firm. Unmold on lettuce leaves, if desired; serve with Ginger Dressing. Yield: 6 to 8 servings.

*Ginger Dressing:*

⅓ cup mayonnaise
⅓ cup commercial sour cream
2 tablespoons minced crystallized ginger

Combine all ingredients, stirring well. Chill. Yield: about ⅔ cup.

*Mrs. Charles R. Simms,*
*Palestine, Illinois.*

## BEST EVER PEAR COBBLER

6 medium pears, peeled, cored, and sliced (about 4 cups)
1 tablespoon lemon juice
3 tablespoons all-purpose flour
1 cup sugar
½ teaspoon ground cinnamon
½ teaspoon ground nutmeg
Dash of salt
1 tablespoon butter or margarine
Cheddar Cheese Pastry

Arrange pear slices evenly in a 10- x 6- x 2-inch baking dish; sprinkle with lemon juice. Combine flour, sugar, cinnamon, nutmeg, and salt; stir well, and sprinkle over pears. Dot with butter.

Roll pastry to ¼-inch thickness on a lightly floured surface; cut into 10- x ½-inch strips. Arrange in lattice fashion over pears; trim edges. Bake at 350° for 1 hour. Yield: 6 to 8 servings.

*Cheddar Cheese Pastry:*

1 cup all-purpose flour
½ teaspoon salt
⅓ cup shortening
¼ cup (1 ounce) shredded sharp Cheddar cheese
2 to 3 tablespoons cold water

Combine flour and salt; cut in shortening with a pastry blender until mixture resembles coarse meal. Stir in cheese. Sprinkle cold water evenly over surface, stirring with a fork until all dry ingredients are moistened. Shape dough into a ball. Yield: pastry for 1 cobbler.

## DOUBLE-CRUST PEAR PIE

Pastry for deep-dish, double-crust 9-inch pie
¼ cup firmly packed brown sugar
1 tablespoon all-purpose flour
½ teaspoon ground cinnamon
Dash of salt
12 medium pears, peeled, cored, and coarsely chopped (about 8 cups)
½ cup all-purpose flour
1 teaspoon lemon juice
¼ cup butter or margarine, melted
¾ cup firmly packed brown sugar

Roll half of pastry to ⅛-inch thickness on a lightly floured surface; fit into a deep-dish 9-inch pieplate.

Combine ¼ cup brown sugar, 1 tablespoon flour, cinnamon, and salt in a large bowl; stir well. Add pears, tossing lightly to coat; spoon into pastry shell.

Combine ½ cup flour, lemon juice, butter, and ¾ cup brown sugar; mix well, and sprinkle over pears. Roll out remaining pastry to ⅛-inch thickness, and place over filling. Trim edges; then seal and flute. Cut slits to allow steam to escape. Bake at 350° for 1 hour. Yield: one 9-inch pie. *Virgil Harmon, Raleigh, North Carolina.*

*Tip: Submerge a lemon or orange in hot water for 15 minutes before squeezing to yield more juice.*

## PEAR PRESERVES

10 large pears, peeled, cored, and
   chopped
4½ cups sugar
3 cups water
2 lemons, thinly sliced

Place pears in a 3-quart Dutch oven, and add water to cover. Bring to a boil; then reduce heat to medium. Cover and cook until pears are tender (about 15 minutes). Drain well.

Combine sugar and 3 cups water in a 6-quart Dutch oven; bring to a boil, and cook 10 minutes (mixture will be a thin, transparent syrup). Remove from heat, and let cool 15 minutes.

Stir in pears and lemon slices; bring mixture to a rapid boil. Boil rapidly until pears are transparent (about 45 minutes), stirring occasionally.

Pour pear mixture into a shallow 13- x 9- x 2-inch pan; skim off foam with a metal spoon. Let stand, uncovered, in a cool place for 12 hours; shake pan occasionally (do not stir) so pears will absorb the syrup. Skim off excess foam.

Using a slotted spoon, spoon the fruit into hot sterilized jars. Bring syrup to a boil; pour over fruit, leaving ¼-inch headspace. Cover at once with metal lids, and screw bands tight. Process in boiling-water bath 10 minutes. Yield: 7 half pints.

# Sample The Flavor Of Southern Tradition

Just as the South is known for good cooks, it's known for the foods those cooks have made famous. There's just no way to improve on traditional favorites like sweet potatoes, country ham, chess pie, and spoonbread.

A deep pride in cooking nurtures the continued interest in these special foods. Nothing else could explain basting a ham 15 times while it cooks, carving out orange shells and stuffing them with pineapple-flavored sweet potatoes, or lovingly mixing and baking a pecan-bourbon cake topped with a hot praline glaze.

When you sample these time-honored recipes, you enjoy the traditions that accompany each. It is delicacies like these that help to preserve the South's culinary fame.

■ Made famous by the people of Smithfield, Virginia, country hams are cured and smoked according to centuries-old traditions. Their distinctive flavor and texture make them a Southern classic.

## CIDER-BAKED COUNTRY HAM

1 (15-pound) country ham
About 1 (16-ounce) package light brown
   sugar
1 (46-ounce) bottle apple cider
Whole cloves
Spiced crabapples (optional)
Fresh parsley (optional)

Place ham in a very large container; cover with cold water, and soak overnight. Scrub ham thoroughly with a stiff brush. Drain. Place ham, skin side down, in a roaster; coat exposed portion generously with brown sugar. Pour cider into roaster; cover and bake at 350° for 4 hours, basting every 20 to 30 minutes.

Carefully remove ham from cider; remove skin. Place ham, fat side up, on a cutting board; score fat in a diamond design, and stud with cloves.

Drain off half of cider. Return ham to roaster, fat side up; coat top generously with brown sugar. Continue baking, uncovered, for 1 hour, basting frequently with remaining cider. Garnish with crabapples and parsley, if desired. Yield: about 30 servings.

*Note:* A larger or smaller ham may be used. Bake 20 minutes per pound; uncover during last hour of baking, after fat is scored and studded with cloves.

■ Whether baked whole, stirred into a casserole, or mashed for a pie, sweet potatoes were a staple in the Old South.

## SUNSHINE SWEET POTATO CUPS

8 large oranges
4 large sweet potatoes
⅓ cup butter or margarine, softened
1 (8-ounce) can crushed pineapple,
   drained
2 teaspoons grated orange rind
½ teaspoon salt
¼ cup flaked coconut, toasted

Cut a thin slice from bottom of each orange so it will sit flat. Cut a ¾-inch slice from top of each orange (reserve slices for grating orange rind). Gently remove pulp, leaving shells intact (reserve pulp for other uses). Set aside.

Cook sweet potatoes in boiling water 25 to 30 minutes or until tender. Let cool to touch; peel and mash.

Combine mashed potatoes, butter, pineapple, orange rind, and salt; mix well. Spoon mixture into orange cups. Bake at 325° for 10 minutes. Sprinkle each with 1½ teaspoons coconut. Yield: 8 servings. *Mrs. Robert L. Humphrey, Palestine, Texas.*

■ Often plucked fresh from the garden, summer squash is a mealtime favorite. With this recipe you'll taste the Southerner's skillful use of seasonings.

## SKILLET SQUASH

2 tablespoons olive oil
2 tablespoons butter or margarine
3 cups sliced zucchini
3 cups sliced yellow squash
1½ teaspoons chopped fresh parsley
1½ teaspoons chopped fresh chives
¼ teaspoon dried whole tarragon
¼ teaspoon dried whole basil
¼ teaspoon dried whole dillweed
1 clove garlic, minced
¼ teaspoon salt
¼ teaspoon pepper

Heat oil and butter in a large skillet; add remaining ingredients, and cook 10 to 15 minutes or until squash is crisp-tender. Yield: 6 servings.
*Mrs. James E. Krachey, Guymon, Oklahoma.*

■ Many Southern cooks still bake fresh biscuits for every meal of the day. This tasty baking powder version would keep that tradition thriving.

## BAKING POWDER BISCUITS

2 cups all-purpose flour
1 tablespoon plus 1 teaspoon baking
   powder
½ teaspoon salt
¼ cup plus 1 tablespoon shortening
¾ cup milk

Combine flour, baking powder, and salt; stir well. Cut in shortening until mixture resembles coarse meal. Sprinkle milk evenly over flour mixture, stirring until dry ingredients are moistened. Turn dough out onto a lightly floured surface; knead lightly 10 to 12 times.

Roll dough to ½-inch thickness; cut with a 2¾-inch biscuit cutter. Place biscuits on a lightly greased baking sheet. Bake at 450° for 12 minutes or until lightly browned. Yield: 1 dozen.
*Mrs. F. E. George, St. Augustine, Florida.*

■ A soufflélike bread made from corn-meal, spoonbread is named for the utensil used to serve it.

## CHEDDAR SPOONBREAD

2 cups milk
1 cup water
1 cup yellow cornmeal
2 tablespoons butter or margarine
1 teaspoon salt
3 eggs
1½ cups (6 ounces) shredded Cheddar
   cheese

Combine first 5 ingredients; cook over medium heat until thickened, stir-ring constantly. Remove from heat.

Beat eggs until thick and lemon col-ored. Gradually stir about one-fourth of hot mixture into eggs; add to remaining hot mixture, stirring constantly. Add cheese, stirring until melted. Pour into a lightly greased 1½-quart casserole.

Bake at 400° for 35 minutes or until a knife inserted in center comes out clean. Yield: 6 servings.

*Polly A. Hughes,*
*Tarpon Springs, Florida.*

■ The South's favorite desserts include pecans. They're mixed into this cake batter, and they make up the topping.

## PECAN CAKE WITH PRALINE GLAZE

1 cup raisins
½ cup bourbon
1 cup butter or margarine, softened
2¼ cups sugar
5 eggs
3¼ cups all-purpose flour
1 teaspoon baking powder
½ teaspoon baking soda
1½ teaspoons ground nutmeg
1 cup buttermilk
2 cups coarsely chopped pecans
Praline Glaze

Combine raisins and bourbon, stirring well. Cover and refrigerate at least 1 hour. Cream butter; gradually add sugar, beating well. Add eggs, one at a time, beating well after each addition.

Combine flour, baking powder, soda, and nutmeg; add to creamed mixture alternately with buttermilk, beginning and ending with flour mixture. Mix well after each addition. Fold in pecans and reserved raisin mixture.

Pour batter into a greased and floured 10-inch tube pan. Bake at 325° for 1 hour and 30 minutes or until

wooden pick inserted in center comes out clean. Cool in pan 10 minutes; re-move to wire rack, and drizzle Praline Glaze over cake. Cool completely. Yield: one 10-inch cake.

*Praline Glaze:*

½ cup firmly packed brown sugar
¼ cup sugar
¼ cup butter or margarine
¼ cup whipping cream
½ cup pecan halves

Combine first 4 ingredients in a heavy saucepan. Cook over low heat, stirring constantly, until mixture reaches soft ball stage (234°). Remove from heat, and stir in pecans. Drizzle over cake immediately. Yield: about 1 cup.

*Sue-Sue Hartstern,*
*Louisville, Kentucky.*

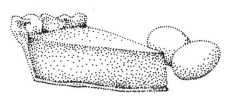

■ Chess pie starts with a blend of but-ter, sugar, and eggs, but then varies according to the other flavors Southern-ers add to it. This lemon version is definitely the most traditional.

## LEMON CHESS PIE

4 eggs, beaten
¼ cup milk
Grated rind of 1 lemon
¼ cup lemon juice
1½ cups sugar
1 tablespoon all-purpose flour
1 tablespoon cornmeal
¼ cup butter or margarine, melted
1 unbaked 9-inch pastry shell
Ground nutmeg

Combine first 4 ingredients; mix well. Combine dry ingredients; stir gently. Add dry ingredients to egg mixture, and mix until smooth. Stir in butter. Pour filling into pastry shell, and sprinkle nutmeg lightly over top. Bake at 350° for 45 to 50 minutes or until set. Let cool on a wire rack. Yield: one 9-inch pie.

*Annie E. Tubb,*
*Jacksonville, Florida.*

■ The last harvest of summer inspires cooks to stir up relishes to enjoy for a year. Chow-chow, flavored with mus-tard, is a savory example.

## CHOW-CHOW

2 quarts finely chopped cabbage
6 medium onions, chopped
6 green peppers, coarsely chopped
6 red peppers, coarsely chopped
1 quart peeled, chopped green tomatoes
¼ cup pickling salt
6 cups vinegar (5% acidity), divided
2 tablespoons prepared mustard
2½ cups sugar
2 tablespoons mustard seeds
1 tablespoon mixed pickling spices
1½ teaspoons ground turmeric
1 teaspoon ground ginger

Combine vegetables and salt; stir well. Cover and let stand 8 to 10 hours or overnight. Drain well.

Stir 2 tablespoons vinegar into mus-tard. Combine mustard, remaining vine-gar, and next 5 ingredients in a large kettle. Bring to a boil; reduce heat, and simmer 20 minutes. Add vegetables; simmer an additional 10 minutes.

Pack solidly into pint-size jars, leav-ing ¼-inch headspace. Cover at once with metal lids, and screw bands tight. Process in boiling-water bath 10 min-utes. Yield: 10 pints. *Cindy Murphy,*
*Cleveland, Tennessee.*

# Serve Brunch Before The Game

Wherever football fans hunger for ac-tion, food and entertaining are sure to be a part of the scene. If you live close enough to drive to the game, or if you're gathering friends in front of the television set, you'll find our football brunch menu a delicious way to kick off the day's events.

**Magnolias    Bacon Dip**
**Huevos Rancheros**
**Glazed Canadian-Style Bacon**
**Fresh Fruit Compote**
**Daisy Braid Coffee Cake**
**Coffee**

## MAGNOLIAS

4 cups orange juice
1 (25.4-ounce) bottle champagne
½ cup Grand Marnier
Orange slices
Maraschino cherries

Combine first 3 ingredients, and serve over ice. Garnish with orange slices and maraschino cherries. Yield: 7½ cups.
*David Holtzinger,*
*Yakima, Washington.*

## BACON DIP

1 (3-ounce) package cream cheese,
    softened
¼ cup commercial sour cream
2 teaspoons catsup
1 teaspoon prepared mustard
⅛ teaspoon ground ginger
8 slices bacon, cooked and crumbled

Combine first 5 ingredients; beat at medium speed of an electric mixer until smooth. Stir in bacon; serve with assorted crackers. Yield: about 1 cup.
*Becki Lanhardt,*
*Mechanicsville, Maryland.*

## HUEVOS RANCHEROS

1 cup chopped onion
1 cup chopped green pepper
2 cloves garlic, minced
3 tablespoons olive oil
1 tablespoon all-purpose flour
2 (16-ounce) cans tomatoes, drained and
    chopped
½ teaspoon dried whole oregano
½ teaspoon ground cumin
½ teaspoon chili powder
¼ teaspoon salt
⅛ teaspoon pepper
¼ cup white wine
6 eggs
½ cup (2 ounces) shredded sharp Cheddar
    cheese
¼ cup sliced ripe olives

Sauté onion, green pepper, and garlic in oil. Stir in flour, and cook 1 minute. Add next 7 ingredients; cook over medium heat 5 minutes. Pour sauce into a 12- x 8- x 2-inch baking dish. Make 6 indentations in sauce, and break an egg into each. Sprinkle with cheese and olives. Bake at 350° for 15 minutes or until eggs are set. Serve immediately. Yield: 6 servings.  *Mrs. W. M. Curls,*
*Anniston, Alabama.*

*Tip: To conserve energy, use pans with flat bottoms to absorb heat and use covers that fit tightly. Food will continue to cook 3 to 5 minutes after you turn off the electrical unit.*

## GLAZED CANADIAN-STYLE BACON

1½ pounds Canadian bacon
¼ cup firmly packed brown sugar
1½ teaspoons all-purpose flour
¼ teaspoon dry mustard
Dash of ground cloves
1 tablespoon water

Remove outer casing from bacon, if necessary. Place bacon in a lightly greased 9-inch square baking pan; bake, uncovered, at 350° for 1 hour.
Combine sugar, flour, mustard, and cloves; mix well. Stir in water. Brush half of mixture over bacon; bake at 350° for 10 minutes. Brush with remaining glaze; bake an additional 5 minutes. Yield: 6 servings. *Mary Brooke Casad,*
*Grand Prairie, Texas.*

## FRESH FRUIT COMPOTE

2 large seedless oranges, peeled and
    sectioned
1 pear, cut into ½-inch cubes
1 large apple, cut into ½-inch cubes
2 cups cubed fresh pineapple
1 banana, sliced
¼ cup Grand Marnier or other
    orange-flavored liqueur
3 tablespoons lemon juice
2 tablespoons sugar

Combine fruit in a large bowl, tossing lightly. Combine remaining ingredients, stirring until sugar is dissolved; pour over fruit, and mix well. Cover and chill at least 1 hour. Yield: 6 to 8 servings.
*Mrs. W. A. Ellis,*
*Talbott, Tennessee.*

## DAISY BRAID COFFEE CAKE

2½ to 3 cups all-purpose flour, divided
1 package dry yeast
¼ cup sugar
¾ teaspoon salt
¼ cup butter or margarine, softened
¾ cup warm water (105° to 115°)
1 egg
1 cup sifted powdered sugar
⅓ cup milk

Combine 1 cup flour, yeast, sugar, and salt in a large mixing bowl; stir well. Add butter and warm water; beat at medium speed of electric mixer 2 minutes. Stir in egg and 1 cup flour; beat at high speed of electric mixer 1 minute. Gradually add enough of remaining flour to make a soft dough (dough should remain soft and slightly sticky).

Turn dough out onto a heavily floured surface; knead 5 minutes or until dough is smooth and elastic. Cover and let rest 10 minutes.
Shape dough into a ball; place in a well-greased bowl, turning to grease top. Cover and let rise in a warm place (85°), free from drafts, 1 to 2 hours or until doubled in bulk.
Punch dough down; turn out onto a floured surface, and roll out to an 18- x 16-inch rectangle. Cut 3 lengthwise strips of equal width. Braid strips from center to ends, leaving ends loose. Place braided dough in a greased 9-inch cake-pan; braid loose ends together. Bake at 375° for 30 to 35 minutes or until golden brown and braids sound hollow when tapped with finger. Transfer to wire rack to cool.
Combine powdered sugar and milk, mixing until smooth; drizzle glaze over bread while warm. Yield: one 9-inch coffee cake.
*Note:* Recipe may be doubled to make 2 coffee cakes. Divide dough in half; let rise, then store reserved portion in the refrigerator up to 72 hours.
*Lucille Robinson,*
*Atlanta, Georgia.*

# From Our Kitchen To Yours

Selecting the right type of flour to use when making breads, pastries, cakes, or cookies can spell the difference between success and failure. Many of our readers have asked about the differences in kinds of flour and how they affect the baked product. The following are some answers.

## All About Flour

Flour is milled from all kinds of grains—wheat, corn, rye, barley, and oats—and each produces one or more kinds of flour. The differences lie in the grain used and how it's processed.
Before they are processed, all grains are alike in one respect. All are made up of kernels composed of three parts: bran, germ, and endosperm.
The *bran* (protective outer covering of kernel) adds fiber and texture to the flour. The *germ* (portion that would sprout if planted) contains fat and a large amount of thiamine. When milling certain flours, the germ is removed because its fat content limits how long the

flour can be stored. The *endosperm* (largest part of kernel) contains starch and provides the major source of protein in flour.

Flours milled from the entire kernel are the whole-grain type, such as whole wheat and rye. Other flours are made only from the endosperm; these include all-purpose, cake, and self-rising.

**The most popular grain is wheat:** Wheat flours are divided into two basic groups, whole grain and white. *Whole-grain wheat flours* include whole wheat, graham, and cracked wheat. Among the *white flours* are bread, unbleached, all-purpose, and cake; these are often enriched with iron and the B-vitamins to replace nutrients lost when the germ was removed.

Wheat flours also vary in protein content. Protein is important when it comes to how a flour performs during baking. When mixed with a liquid, protein forms a substance called gluten, which gives elasticity to batters and doughs, as well as provides the structure or framework for whatever you're baking. In addition, gluten affects the tenderness and volume of baked products.

The white flours have more protein (more gluten) than the whole-grain types. In the white flours, the hard-wheat types have more protein than the soft-wheat type.

For yeast bread, hard-wheat flour is best, resulting in a firmer crust and greater volume. Choose a soft-wheat type for biscuits, cakes, and pastries because the low protein content makes for a more tender product.

**What white flour to buy:** *Bread flour* is a hard-wheat flour milled especially for bread making. It can be difficult to find, but all-purpose flour can be substituted for it.

*All-purpose flour* is a combination of hard- and soft-wheat flour and commonly used for all types of baked products. If an all-purpose flour is labeled "higher protein," it's better suited for yeast breads. The all-purpose flours with a lower protein content give better results when used for cakes, quick breads, and sweet rolls. *Unbleached flour* is an all-purpose flour that has no bleaching agents added during processing and is often used interchangeably with all-purpose.

*Self-rising flour* is also an all-purpose flour to which leavening and salt have been added; it is not suitable for yeast breads. It is best not to substitute self-rising for all-purpose flour; however, all-purpose can be substituted for self-rising by making the following adjustments: For 1 cup self-rising flour, use 1 cup all-purpose flour plus 1 teaspoon baking powder and ½ teaspoon salt.

*Cake flour* is a soft-wheat type and has a much lower protein content than all-purpose. Products made with cake flour have a tender, delicate texture. Substitute all-purpose flour for cake flour by using 2 tablespoons less per cup.

*Instant blending flour* is used in making sauces and gravies but should never be used as a substitute in baked goods.

**When making bread:** If you've ever been unhappy with yeast breads you've baked using only whole-grain wheat flour, gluten was probably the culprit. Whole wheat flour has less gluten than white flour, so breads baked with only whole wheat are usually more dense and compact. Most recipes will add white flour to whole wheat to ensure both good volume and appearance.

Rye flours are usually combined with wheat flour because rye gluten lacks elasticity. Most of the other nonwheat flours—corn, barley, rice, soybean—should be combined with wheat or rye flour because they form no gluten.

**About sifting:** Since flour is sifted during milling, there's no need to sift before measuring. When we measure all-purpose or whole-grain flour, we stir the flour lightly; then spoon it into a standard measuring cup (we don't pack it in). Level with the straight edge of a spatula. Don't try to shake the cup level, as this packs the flour. The only flour we sift before measuring is cake flour.

**Storage:** Always place flour in an airtight container; then store in a cool dry place away from heat. Incorrectly stored flour can absorb a great deal of moisture, affecting the way it "handles" and causing problems with your recipes. Refrigerate or freeze whole-grain flour if it isn't used frequently. Because this type contains the oil-rich germ, it can become rancid if stored improperly.

## More Kitchen Tips

**Freezer keeper:** Keep spices and seasonings fresh longer by storing them in the freezer. We label the lids of all the containers; then arrange them in alphabetical order on shelves on the freezer door.

**About eggs:** To prevent curdling when adding eggs to a hot mixture, temper the eggs by beating in a small amount of hot mixture; then add to the remaining hot mixture.

**Quick cleanup:** Before cooking on your broiler pan, lightly spray both pan and rack with vegetable cooking spray. After broiling, cleanup is easy.

## cooking Light

# Dieting With Pasta And Rice

There's no reason to give up rice, spaghetti, and macaroni just because you're dieting. Although some diet books tell you these carbohydrate foods should be avoided, one ounce of cooked rice or pasta is actually lower in calories than the same amount of steak. What you have to give up are the rich sauces and butter—the culprits that shoot the calorie count straight up.

If you like pasta Italian style, try Spinach Manicotti—a combination of spinach, cottage cheese, and Parmesan cheese stuffed into manicotti shells and topped with a seasoned tomato sauce before baking. Garden Pasta also makes a satisfying entrée, with its sauce of fresh vegetables spooned over vermicelli and topped with shredded cheese. Add a green salad to complete the meal.

The flavor and look of pasta dishes can easily be varied. Just choose whole wheat or spinach pasta, and feel free to try the different sizes and shapes; each has about 100 calories per half-cup portion if cooked just to the *al dente* stage (barely tender). When cooked a few more minutes (until tender), the pasta absorbs more water, decreasing the calorie count to 80 per half-cup serving.

Rice is equally diverse when it comes to calorie-conscious cooking. Kathryn Bibelhauser of Louisville combines it with zucchini, onion, corn, and tomatoes for her Colorful Rice Casserole. By substituting brown rice for white in this dish, you'll get more protein and fiber, plus a chewy texture and delicious nutty flavor.

The outer coating of rice is stripped off to make polished white rice, losing valuable nutrients in the process. Although some nutrients are added back to polished rice, the best choice of white rice is parboiled (or converted) rice. It's hulled under special conditions, keeping the nutrient composition close to that of brown. While the calorie count of white rice is 80 per half-cup portion, the same amount of brown rice is 90 calories.

Wild rice is another option. Although not a true rice (it comes from a wild water grass), the texture and flavor are similar to brown rice. Wild rice is lower in calories than either white or brown; it measures in at about 70 calories for each half-cup serving.

## BAKED MACARONI AND CHEESE

1 cup uncooked elbow macaroni
2 eggs, beaten
1 cup skim milk
1 cup low-fat cottage cheese
¼ cup (1 ounce) shredded extra-sharp
  Cheddar cheese
½ teaspoon salt
¼ teaspoon freshly ground pepper
Vegetable cooking spray
1 tablespoon fine, dry breadcrumbs

Cook macaroni according to package directions, omitting salt; drain. Combine with next 6 ingredients, mixing well. Spoon macaroni mixture into a 1-quart baking dish coated with cooking spray; sprinkle with breadcrumbs.

Bake at 350° for 1 hour. Yield: 6 servings (about 158 calories per ⅔-cup serving).          *Jan Hughes,*
*Batesville, Arkansas.*

## SPINACH MANICOTTI

10 manicotti shells
2 (6-ounce) cans tomato paste
3 cups water
½ cup finely chopped onion
2 cloves garlic, crushed
½ teaspoon dried whole basil
½ teaspoon dried whole oregano
¼ teaspoon salt
¼ teaspoon pepper
2 (10-ounce) packages frozen chopped
  spinach
1 (16-ounce) carton low-fat cottage
  cheese
⅓ cup grated Parmesan cheese
¼ teaspoon ground nutmeg
Pepper to taste
Vegetable cooking spray
Chopped fresh parsley

Cook manicotti shells according to package directions, omitting salt; drain and set aside.

Combine next 8 ingredients; cover and cook over low heat for 1 hour.

Cook spinach according to package directions, omitting salt. Drain; place on paper towels, and squeeze until barely moist. Combine spinach, cottage cheese, Parmesan cheese, nutmeg, and pepper. Stuff manicotti shells with spinach mixture, and arrange in a 13- x 9- x 2-inch baking dish coated with cooking spray.

Pour tomato sauce over manicotti. Bake at 350° for 45 minutes. Garnish with parsley. Yield: 5 servings (about 300 calories per serving).     *Pat Helms,*
*Miami, Florida.*

## GARDEN PASTA

Vegetable cooking spray
1 cup chopped green onion
½ cup chopped fresh parsley
2 cloves garlic, crushed
2 cups finely shredded cabbage
2 cups peeled, chopped tomato
½ cup sliced radishes
½ cup chopped carrot
½ cup chicken broth
¼ cup tomato paste
1 teaspoon dried whole basil
Freshly ground pepper to taste
1 large tomato, cut into wedges
4 ounces uncooked vermicelli
1 cup (4 ounces) shredded Cheddar cheese

Coat a 10-inch skillet with cooking spray; place over medium heat until hot. Add onion, parsley, and garlic; sauté until tender. Add next 8 ingredients; cover and simmer 10 minutes. Stir in tomato wedges; cook just until well heated.

Cook vermicelli according to package directions, omitting salt; drain. Serve vegetable sauce over hot vermicelli. Top each serving with ¼ cup shredded cheese. Yield: 4 servings (about 292 calories per serving).     *Clarine Spetzler,*
*Salem, Virginia.*

## MAIN-DISH PASTA SALAD

1 cup uncooked corkscrew macaroni
2 small carrots, sliced
2 small green onions, chopped
1 (2-ounce) jar diced pimiento,
  drained
1 cup drained canned kidney beans
¾ cup sliced celery
¼ cup cooked English peas
2 tablespoons chopped parsley
¼ cup Italian reduced-calorie salad
  dressing
2 tablespoons reduced-calorie mayonnaise
⅛ teaspoon dried whole marjoram
⅛ teaspoon pepper
Lettuce leaves
2 medium tomatoes, sliced
2 hard-cooked eggs, cut into wedges
Parsley sprigs

Cook macaroni according to package directions, omitting salt. Drain. Combine with next 11 ingredients, tossing well; chill at least 1 hour.

Spoon into a lettuce-lined dish; arrange tomato slices and egg wedges around edges. Garnish with parsley. Yield: 4 servings (about 267 calories per serving).

## WILD RICE CASSEROLE

Vegetable cooking spray
1 (6-ounce) package long-grain and
  wild rice mix
6 green onions, chopped
8 medium mushrooms, sliced
2 cups chicken broth
1 (8-ounce) can sliced water chestnuts,
  drained

Spray a medium skillet with cooking spray; place over medium heat until hot. Add rice; cook until lightly browned, stirring occasionally. Stir in remaining ingredients, and spoon mixture into a 1¾-quart casserole.

Cover and bake at 350° for 1 hour or until rice is done. Yield: 6 servings (about 134 calories per serving).
*Lynne Weeks,*
*Midland, Georgia.*

## COLORFUL RICE CASSEROLE

Vegetable cooking spray
1½ pounds zucchini, thinly sliced
¾ cup chopped green onion
1 (17-ounce) can corn, drained
1 (16-ounce) can tomatoes, undrained
  and chopped
3 cups cooked regular rice or
  brown rice
½ teaspoon salt
¼ teaspoon pepper
¼ cup chopped fresh parsley
¼ teaspoon dried whole oregano

Coat an electric skillet with cooking spray; heat at 350° until hot. Add zucchini and onion; sauté about 5 minutes or until crisp-tender. Stir in remaining ingredients; cover, reduce heat, and simmer 15 minutes. Yield: 12 servings (about 84 calories per ½-cup serving).
*Kathryn Bibelhauser,*
*Louisville, Kentucky.*

*Tip: Cooked rice freezes well. It can be stored in the refrigerator up to one week, or in the freezer as long as 3 months.*

## ORANGE RICE

Vegetable cooking spray
1 cup uncooked regular rice
¾ cup chopped celery
1 tablespoon chopped onion
2 teaspoons grated orange rind
2 cups unsweetened orange juice
½ teaspoon salt

Coat a large skillet with cooking spray, and place over medium heat until hot. Add rice, celery, and onion; cook, stirring occasionally, until rice is lightly browned. Add remaining ingredients, and bring to a boil. Pour mixture into a 1½-quart casserole.

Cover and bake at 350° for 25 to 30 minutes or until done. Yield: 7 servings (about 130 calories per ½-cup serving).
*Diana Curtis,*
*Albuquerque, New Mexico.*

# Bake Sourdough Bread With Herman

Chances are, you're already familiar with Herman, the sourdough starter that's being passed around the South like gossip. The fermented batter is added to dough to give it the characteristic sourdough tang. As the starter ages, its flavor mellows, imparting progressively more sourdough flavor each time it's used. In the spirit of Southern hospitality, a cup of Herman starter is proudly given to favored friends, along with sourdough recipes and special instructions for care. The recipients, in turn, nurture their starters and soon present sample starters to other friends. If you don't already have a Herman starter, use our recipe to make your own.

Some instructions accompanying sourdough starters specify strict schedules for feeding and baking. However, we found you can use Herman Sourdough Starter anytime within 2 to 14 days from its previous use. Each time a cup is removed, replenish or "feed" it to maintain the volume and nourish the yeast. If cared for properly, your starter should last indefinitely.

Use your starter to bake all-time favorites such as Sourdough Biscuits and Sourdough Hot Rolls. Equally delicious, their textures differ widely: the biscuits are light and tender while the rolls have the characteristic hard crust. Sourdough Bread is another sure bet; one recipe will yield two tasty loaves.

*Enjoy the different textures of Sourdough Bread and Sourdough Biscuits, both made from Herman Sourdough Starter.*

## HERMAN SOURDOUGH STARTER

1 package dry yeast
½ cup warm water (105° to 115°)
2 cups all-purpose flour
1 teaspoon salt
3 tablespoons sugar
2 cups warm water (105° to 115°)
Herman Food (recipe follows)

Dissolve yeast in ½ cup warm water; let stand 5 minutes. Combine next 3 ingredients in a medium-size nonmetal bowl; mix well. Gradually stir in 2 cups warm water. Add yeast mixture, and mix well. Cover loosely with plastic wrap or cheesecloth and let stand in a warm place (80° to 85°) for 72 hours, stirring 2 to 3 times daily. Place fermented mixture in refrigerator, and stir daily; use within 11 days.

To use, remove sourdough starter from refrigerator and let stand at room temperature at least 1 hour. Stir well, and measure amount of starter needed for recipe. Replenish remaining starter with Herman Food, and return to refrigerator; use within 2 to 14 days, stirring daily.

Repeat the procedure for using and replenishing Herman Sourdough Starter. Yield: about 2 cups.

*Herman Food:*

½ cup sugar
1 cup all-purpose flour
1 cup milk

Stir all ingredients into remaining sourdough starter, and refrigerate.

*Note:* Herman Sourdough Starter may be frozen. Before using, let thaw at room temperature until mixture is bubbly (about 5 hours).
*Mrs. Ben F. Harper,*
*Chattanooga, Tennessee.*

*Tip: Sifting flour, with the exception of cake flour, is no longer necessary. Simply stir the flour, gently spoon it onto a dry measure, and level the top. Powdered sugar, however, should usually be sifted to remove the lumps.*

Combine the ingredients for Herman Sourdough Starter in a nonmetal bowl and cover loosely with cheesecloth. Once fermented, the starter should be stored in the refrigerator.

To use the starter in a recipe, let it stand at room temperature about 1 hour. Stir well, and measure the amount of starter needed in your recipe.

Be sure to replenish the remaining sourdough starter with Herman Food (sugar, flour, and milk). Properly "fed" and stored, your starter should last indefinitely.

## SOURDOUGH BISCUITS

2½ cups all-purpose flour
¾ teaspoon salt
½ teaspoon baking soda
1 teaspoon baking powder
¼ cup plus 2 tablespoons butter or margarine, softened
½ cup buttermilk
1 cup Herman Sourdough Starter (at room temperature)
1 tablespoon butter or margarine, melted

Combine first 4 ingredients in a nonmetal bowl; mix well. Cut in ¼ cup plus 2 tablespoons butter until mixture resembles coarse meal. Add buttermilk and sourdough starter; stir until moistened. Turn dough out onto a floured surface; knead lightly 10 to 12 times.

Roll dough to ½-inch thickness; cut with a 2¾-inch biscuit cutter. Place biscuits on a lightly greased baking sheet, and brush tops with 1 tablespoon melted butter. Cover and let rise in a warm place (85°), free from drafts, 30 minutes or until doubled in bulk. Bake at 425° for 15 to 17 minutes or until golden brown. Yield: about 1 dozen.

## SOURDOUGH BREAD

1 cup milk, scalded
¼ cup shortening
2 tablespoons sugar
2 packages dry yeast
¼ cup warm water (105° to 115°)
1 cup Herman Sourdough Starter (at room temperature)
1 egg, beaten
1 tablespoon salt
5 to 6 cups all-purpose flour

Combine scalded milk, shortening, and sugar; stir until sugar is dissolved. Cool to lukewarm (105° to 115°).

Dissolve yeast in ¼ cup water in a large nonmetal bowl; let stand 5 minutes. Add milk mixture, sourdough starter, egg, salt, and 3 cups flour; beat with an electric mixer until smooth. Stir in enough of remaining flour to make a soft dough.

Turn dough out onto a floured surface; knead until smooth and elastic (about 8 to 10 minutes). Place in a well-greased bowl, turning to grease top. Cover and let rise in a warm place (85°), free from drafts, 1 to 1½ hours or until doubled in bulk.

Punch dough down; divide in half, and place on a floured surface. Roll each half into an 8- x 6-inch rectangle. Starting at widest end, roll up jellyroll fashion. Fold under ends and place, seam side down, in 2 well-greased 9- x 5- x 3-inch loafpans. Cover and let rise in a warm place, free from drafts, 1 hour or until doubled in bulk. Bake at 350° for 40 minutes or until loaves sound hollow when tapped. Yield: 2 loaves.
*Aileen Wright,*
*Nashville, Tennessee.*

## SOURDOUGH HOT ROLLS

2 cups all-purpose flour
¼ teaspoon baking soda
2 teaspoons baking powder
¼ teaspoon salt
1 cup Herman Sourdough Starter (at room temperature)
¼ cup vegetable oil

Combine dry ingredients in a nonmetal bowl; mix well. Stir in sourdough starter and oil. Turn dough out onto a floured surface; knead until smooth and elastic (about 8 to 10 minutes).

Shape dough into 2-inch balls. Cover and let rise in a warm place (85°), free from drafts, 30 minutes or until doubled in bulk. Bake at 425° for 15 to 17 minutes. Yield: 1¼ dozen. *Marcia Owen,*
*Atlanta, Georgia.*

# Oven Potatoes Round Out The Menu

The next time you plan to include potatoes on your menu, try one of these delicious oven potato dishes. Our Saucy Potatoes for Company features cubed potatoes and bits of pimiento baked in a creamy cheese sauce.

## CREAMY POTATO BAKE

3 cups mashed potatoes
1 (8-ounce) carton commercial sour cream
5 to 6 slices bacon, cooked and crumbled
3 small green onions, chopped
1 cup (4 ounces) shredded Cheddar cheese

Spread potatoes evenly in a lightly greased 10- x 6- x 2-inch baking dish. Top with sour cream; sprinkle with bacon and green onion. Top with cheese. Bake potatoes at 300° for 30 minutes. Serve hot. Yield: 6 servings.
*Linda K. Tasker,*
*Greenville, Mississippi.*

## EASY OVEN-BAKED POTATOES

6 medium potatoes, unpeeled
6 medium onions
½ cup butter or margarine, melted
1 clove garlic, crushed
¾ teaspoon salt
¼ teaspoon pepper
¼ teaspoon celery seeds
¼ teaspoon paprika

Cut potatoes and onions into ¼-inch slices. Alternate slices, slightly overlapping, in a single layer in a 13- x 9- x 2-inch baking dish.

Combine next 5 ingredients; drizzle over potato and onion slices. Cover and bake at 400° for 40 minutes.

Sprinkle with paprika and bake, uncovered, for 20 additional minutes. Yield: 8 servings. *Gene Warner, Florence, South Carolina.*

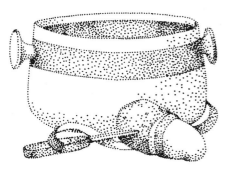

## SAUCY POTATOES FOR COMPANY

3 large potatoes, peeled and cubed
1 medium onion, chopped
3 tablespoons chopped green pepper
¼ cup butter or margarine
2½ tablespoons all-purpose flour
2 cups milk
⅓ cup shredded Cheddar cheese
½ teaspoon salt
¼ teaspoon pepper
3 tablespoons chopped pimiento

Cook potatoes in boiling water to cover 15 to 20 minutes or until tender. Drain and set aside.

Sauté onion and green pepper in butter until tender; add flour, stirring until well blended. Cook 1 minute, stirring constantly. Gradually add milk; cook over medium heat, stirring constantly, until thickened and bubbly. Add cheese, salt, and pepper; stir until cheese melts.

Stir in potatoes and pimiento. Spoon mixture into a lightly greased 1½-quart casserole. Bake, uncovered, at 350° for 30 minutes or until bubbly. Yield: about 6 servings. *Nelda Hase, Gainesville, Georgia.*

# Expert Tips On Muscadines

When it comes to cooking muscadines, Mrs. Cason J. Callaway, Sr., of Hamilton, Georgia, is an expert. Having grown the grapes for years, she has also developed several outstanding ways to highlight their distinctive flavor.

Mrs. Callaway suggests you pick muscadines that have turned a dark, almost black color and are soft to the touch.

## MUSCADINE PIE

Pastry for double-crust 9-inch pie
About 3½ pounds ripe muscadines
1 tablespoon fresh lemon juice
¼ cup all-purpose flour
1 to 1½ cups sugar
2 tablespoons butter or margarine

Roll half of pastry to ⅛-inch thickness onto a lightly floured surface; fit into a 9-inch pieplate. Set aside.

Wash and mash muscadines. Separate hulls from pulp; set hulls aside. Strain pulp, reserving juice; discard seeds. Combine juice and hulls in a heavy saucepan; cover and cook over low heat 20 to 25 minutes or until hulls are tender. Cool.

Combine hull mixture, lemon juice, flour, and sugar; mix well. Pour into pastry shell; dot with butter.

Roll out remaining pastry to ⅛-inch thickness; cut into ¾-inch-wide strips, and arrange lattice fashion over filling. Trim edges; seal and flute. Bake at 400° for 10 minutes; reduce heat to 375°, and bake 25 to 30 additional minutes. Yield: one 9-inch pie.

*Mrs. Cason J. Callaway, Sr., Hamilton, Georgia.*

## MUSCADINE ICE

About 14 pounds muscadines
1½ cups water
1½ cups sugar
2 teaspoons lemon juice

Wash and mash muscadines. Strain, reserving juice (will yield about 4 cups juice); set juice aside.

Place hulls and pulp in an 8-quart Dutch oven; add water, stirring well. Bring to a boil; boil 20 minutes, stirring occasionally. Remove from heat; cool.

Process hulls and pulp with food mill to remove remaining juice; strain juice

through 2 layers of cheesecloth (will yield about 2½ cups juice). Reserve juice, and discard processed hulls and pulp.

Combine all muscadine juice, sugar, and lemon juice in a large bowl; stir well. Pour mixture into freezer can of a 1-gallon hand-turned or electric freezer. Freeze according to manufacturer's instructions. Let ripen at least 1 hour. Yield: about 1 gallon.

*Mrs. Cason J. Callaway, Sr., Hamilton, Georgia.*

# Microwave Cookery

# Microwave Casseroles For Now And Later

Dinner for your family won't take hours of work if you use your microwave to prepare these freeze-ahead casseroles. Each recipe makes enough for two casseroles—one to enjoy now, and one to freeze and serve later.

Microwave the first casserole immediately, following usual procedures. The casserole to be frozen should be covered tightly with aluminum foil and stored no longer than three months.

To ensure quality of the frozen casserole, pay attention to the defrosting process. Many microwave ovens have a defrost setting, but the corresponding power level may vary from oven to oven. In our recipes, we recommend defrosting only on MEDIUM LOW (30% power) or MEDIUM (50% power). As the microwave oven cycles on and off at such low power levels, the heat will have time to equalize throughout the dish. This prevents the casserole from starting to cook or from drying out around the edges while defrosting. When defrosting is complete, follow the regular procedures to complete the microwaving.

Sometimes frozen casseroles require quite a bit of time to defrost and microwave. However, our test kitchens staff believes that most busy cooks would appreciate the convenience of having a casserole already assembled. While the frozen casserole defrosts and microwaves, you can prepare a salad and simple dessert to complete the meal.

## LAYERED BEEF CASSEROLE

2 pounds ground beef
2 medium onions, chopped
2 cloves garlic, minced
2 teaspoons olive oil
½ cup chili sauce
1 teaspoon onion powder
2 (10¾-ounce) cans vegetable beef soup,
    undiluted
¼ cup plus 2 tablespoons all-purpose flour
2 (10-ounce) packages frozen English peas,
    thawed
1 cup (4 ounces) shredded Cheddar cheese
4 large potatoes, cooked and mashed
2 tablespoons milk
2 eggs, slightly beaten
2 teaspoons dried parsley flakes
¼ teaspoon paprika

Crumble ground beef into a 2½-quart casserole; stir in onion, garlic, and oil. Cover and microwave at HIGH for 10 to 12 minutes or until meat is done, stirring twice. Drain well. Stir in chili sauce and onion powder. Microwave at HIGH for 45 seconds to 1 minute or until thoroughly heated.

Combine soup and flour, stirring well; blend into meat mixture, and microwave at HIGH for 3 to 4 minutes.

Spoon half of meat mixture into a 2-quart casserole; spread one package of peas evenly over top. Combine cheese, potatoes, milk, eggs, parsley, and paprika; stir well. Spread half of potato mixture over top of peas. Cover casserole with foil and freeze.

Spoon remaining meat mixture into another 2-quart casserole; top with remaining peas and remaining potato mixture. Microwave at HIGH for 5 minutes. Reduce power and microwave at MEDIUM (50% power) for 10 to 12 minutes or until thoroughly heated, rotating dish after half the time.

To serve frozen casserole, remove from freezer and discard foil wrapper. Cover and microwave at MEDIUM LOW (30% power) for 32 to 45 minutes, rotating dish after half the time. Microwave at HIGH for 5 minutes. Reduce power, and microwave at MEDIUM for 10 to 12 minutes, rotating dish after half the time. Yield: two 2-quart casseroles.

*Tip: Remove stems from fresh parsley, chives, basil, sage, and other herbs; rinse and pat dry. Spread ½ to 1 cup of the rinsed herbs between two sheets of paper towel. Microwave at HIGH for 2 to 2½ minutes. Store in airtight containers.*

## SAUSAGE JAMBALAYA CASSEROLE

1 cup uncooked regular rice
2 cups hot water
1 pound ground beef
1 pound smoked sausage, cut into ½-inch
    slices
1 medium-size green pepper, chopped
½ cup chopped green onion
3 cloves garlic, minced
1 (28-ounce) can tomatoes, undrained and
    chopped
½ teaspoon salt
¼ teaspoon pepper

Combine rice and water in a 2-quart casserole, stirring well. Cover and microwave at HIGH for 5 minutes. Stir well. Cover and microwave at MEDIUM (50% power) for 11 to 15 additional minutes; stir well, and set aside.

Crumble ground beef into a 2½-quart casserole; stir in sausage, green pepper, onion, and garlic. Cover and microwave at HIGH for 10 to 11 minutes or until meat is done, stirring twice. Drain well. Stir in rice and remaining ingredients.

Spoon half of mixture into a 2-quart casserole; cover with foil and freeze. Spoon remaining mixture into another 2-quart casserole. Cover and microwave at MEDIUM HIGH (70% power) for 8 to 10 minutes or until heated.

To serve frozen casserole, remove from freezer and discard foil wrapper. Cover and microwave at MEDIUM LOW (30% power) for 25 to 30 minutes, rotating and stirring after half the time. Microwave at MEDIUM HIGH for 8 to 10 minutes or until thoroughly heated. Yield: two 2-quart casseroles.

## CHICKEN DIVAN CASSEROLE

1 (3- to 3½-pound) broiler-fryer, cut up
    and skinned
1½ cups water
Pinch of dried whole rosemary
Salt and pepper to taste
2 tablespoons butter or margarine
3 tablespoons all-purpose flour
¾ cup milk
1 egg yolk
½ teaspoon grated lemon rind
Juice of ½ lemon
⅓ cup mayonnaise
3 tablespoons grated Parmesan cheese
2 (10-ounce) packages frozen broccoli
    spears, thawed

Arrange chicken in a 12- x 8- x 2-inch baking dish, placing meatier portions to outside of dish; pour water over chicken. Sprinkle with rosemary, salt,

and pepper. Cover with heavy-duty plastic wrap; microwave at HIGH for 6 to 8 minutes. Turn chicken and rearrange so the uncooked portions are to outside of dish. Cover; microwave at HIGH for 5 to 7 minutes.

Remove chicken from dish, and set aside; reserve ¾ cup chicken broth. Bone and chop chicken; set aside.

Place butter in a 4-cup glass measure. Microwave at HIGH for 35 to 45 seconds or until butter melts. Blend in flour; stir well. Gradually add milk and chicken broth, stirring well. Microwave at HIGH for 1½ minutes; stir well. Microwave at HIGH for 3 to 5 minutes; stir at 1-minute intervals until thickened.

Blend in egg yolk, lemon rind, and lemon juice; add mayonnaise and cheese, stirring well. Layer one-fourth each of broccoli, chicken, and sauce in a 1-quart casserole. Repeat layers; cover with foil and freeze. Repeat layers with remaining ingredients in another 1-quart casserole. Cover; microwave at HIGH for 9 to 10 minutes.

To serve frozen casserole, remove from freezer and discard foil wrapper. Cover and microwave at MEDIUM LOW (30% power) for 20 to 26 minutes, rotating after half the time. Microwave at HIGH for 7 to 9 minutes. Yield: two 1-quart casseroles.

## EASY TUNA CASSEROLE

2 (10¾-ounce) cans cream of celery soup,
    undiluted
1 cup milk
1 teaspoon paprika
1 (13-ounce) can tuna, drained and flaked
7 cups medium egg noodles, cooked and
    drained
2 cups thinly sliced celery
1 cup slivered almonds, toasted
½ cup chopped onion
1 (2-ounce) jar diced pimiento, undrained
½ teaspoon pepper

Combine all ingredients, stirring well. Spoon half of mixture into a 2-quart casserole; cover with foil and freeze. Spoon remaining mixture into another 2-quart casserole. Cover; microwave at HIGH for 8 to 10 minutes, stirring once.

To serve frozen casserole, remove from freezer and discard foil wrapper. Cover and microwave at MEDIUM (50% power) for 20 to 28 minutes, rotating dish after half the time. Microwave at HIGH for 6 to 11 minutes or until thoroughly heated, stirring once. Yield: two 2-quart casseroles.

# Vegetables To Brighten Any Meal

Yellow, green, red, or orange—just a few of the colors found in these tasty vegetable dishes. Not only will they brighten your table, but their nutritional value, flavor, and texture will enhance any meal.

If your time in the kitchen is limited, Buttered Peas and Mushrooms or Easy Cauliflower Casserole may be just the ticket to a quick and delicious dinner. Each requires minimal preparation and is ready for the table in minutes. Our Coconut-Stuffed Sweet Potatoes may take a little longer, but the zesty orange flavor makes every minute worthwhile.

## BEETS WITH PINEAPPLE

10 small beets
1 tablespoon vinegar
1 teaspoon salt
1 (8-ounce) can pineapple tidbits
2 tablespoons brown sugar
1 tablespoon cornstarch
1 tablespoon butter or margarine
1 tablespoon lemon juice

Leave root and 1 inch of stem on beets; scrub with a brush. Place beets in a saucepan, and add water to cover. Stir in vinegar and salt; bring to a boil. Cover, reduce heat, and simmer 30 to 35 minutes or until tender; drain. Pour cold water over beets, and drain. Let cool. Trim off beet stems and roots, and rub off skins. Cut beets into ¼-inch slices, and set aside.

Drain pineapple, reserving juice. Combine juice, sugar, and cornstarch in a heavy saucepan; cover and cook over medium heat, stirring constantly, until thickened and bubbly. Remove from heat. Add butter and lemon juice, stirring until butter melts. Add beets and pineapple; stir gently to coat. Cook over medium heat, stirring constantly, 5 minutes or until thoroughly heated. Yield: 4 servings. *Cecilia Breithaupt, Boerne, Texas.*

*Tip: Leftover vegetables go nicely in a salad. Or make a chef's salad with leftover meats, cheese, and cold cuts cut in strips and tossed with leftover vegetables, greens, and salad dressing.*

## EASY CAULIFLOWER CASSEROLE

1 medium head cauliflower
½ cup mayonnaise
½ cup (2 ounces) shredded sharp Cheddar cheese
½ teaspoon dry mustard
¼ teaspoon salt
⅛ teaspoon red pepper

Wash cauliflower, and break into flowerets. Cook, covered, in a small amount of boiling salted water 10 minutes or until crisp-tender; drain. Place cauliflower in a 1-quart casserole.

Combine remaining ingredients, stirring well. Spoon mayonnaise mixture evenly over cauliflower. Bake, uncovered, at 400° for 8 to 10 minutes or until bubbly. Yield: 4 servings.
*Mrs. Roger Williams, Arden, North Carolina.*

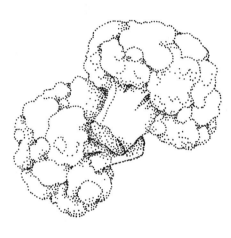

## CAULIFLOWER AU GRATIN

1 small cauliflower
2 cups milk
2 tablespoons quick-cooking tapioca
¾ teaspoon salt
⅛ teaspoon paprika
1 cup (4 ounces) shredded process American cheese
1 cup soft breadcrumbs
2 tablespoons butter or margarine, melted

Wash cauliflower, and break into flowerets. Cook, covered, in a small amount of boiling salted water 10 minutes or until crisp-tender; drain. Place cauliflower in a 1½-quart casserole.

Combine milk and tapioca in a heavy saucepan; cook over medium heat, stirring constantly, until thickened. Stir in salt and paprika. Add cheese, and stir until melted; spoon over cauliflower. Combine breadcrumbs and butter, stirring well; spoon over sauce. Bake at 350° for 20 minutes. Yield: 4 to 6 servings. *Mrs. Robert Collins, Fairfax, Missouri.*

## BUTTERED PEAS AND MUSHROOMS

2 tablespoons butter or margarine
¼ pound fresh mushrooms, sliced
¼ teaspoon salt
⅛ teaspoon pepper
1 (10-ounce) package frozen English peas
½ cup finely chopped green onion
1 green onion with top (optional)

Melt butter in a large skillet. Add mushrooms, and sauté 30 seconds; stir in salt and pepper. Add peas and chopped green onion; cook, stirring constantly, 2 to 3 minutes or until thoroughly heated. Garnish with green onion, if desired. Yield: 4 servings.
*Mrs. H. G. Drawdy, Spindale, North Carolina.*

## FRESH SQUASH CASSEROLE

2 tablespoons vegetable oil
1 pound yellow squash, cut into ¼-inch slices
½ cup mayonnaise
¼ cup diced pimiento
1 egg, beaten
½ cup chopped onion
½ cup (2 ounces) shredded Cheddar cheese
2 tablespoons butter or margarine, melted
½ cup potato chips, crushed

Heat oil in a large skillet over medium heat. Add squash, and sauté 5 minutes or until crisp-tender. Remove from heat, and set aside.

Combine next 6 ingredients, mixing well; stir into squash. Pour mixture into a lightly greased 1½-quart casserole; top with potato chips. Bake at 350° for 30 minutes. Yield: 4 servings.
*Felice Mayard, Abbeville, Louisiana.*

## COCONUT-STUFFED SWEET POTATOES

4 medium-size sweet potatoes
Vegetable oil
½ cup sugar
½ cup evaporated milk
⅓ cup orange juice
Pinch of salt
1 tablespoon grated orange rind
1 cup flaked coconut, divided

Scrub potatoes thoroughly, and rub skins with oil; bake at 375° for 1 hour or until tender. Let cool to touch. Slice skin away from top of each potato. Carefully scoop out pulp, leaving shells intact.

Combine potato pulp, sugar, milk, orange juice, and salt; beat with electric mixer until smooth. Stir in orange rind and ½ cup coconut.

Spoon potato mixture into shells; sprinkle with remaining coconut. Bake at 350° for 20 minutes or until thoroughly heated. Yield: 4 servings.

*Rosie Staley,*
*Randleman, North Carolina.*

# Rolls Baked With Sugar And Spice

A whiff of warm, spicy sweet rolls brings memories of favorite times and flavors. Mrs. Larry Edlefson remembers arriving home from school to the aroma of her mother's Spiral Cinnamon Rolls just pulled from the oven.

"I enjoy making them for my children now," she says. We think you'll enjoy these sweet yeast rolls, too—they're spiced with cinnamon and drizzled with a sugar glaze.

For something delightfully different, try Orange Butter Rolls, crescent-shaped yeast rolls enriched with sour cream and spread with a coconut and orange rind filling. They're coated with a mixture of orange juice, butter, sour cream, and sugar, then sprinkled with toasted coconut.

### SPIRAL CINNAMON ROLLS

¼ cup milk, scalded
¼ cup sugar
½ teaspoon salt
3 tablespoons butter or margarine
1 package dry yeast
¼ cup warm water (105° to 115°)
2¼ cups all-purpose flour, divided
1 egg
2 tablespoons butter or margarine, softened
¼ cup firmly packed brown sugar
½ teaspoon ground cinnamon
1 tablespoon butter or margarine, melted
1 cup sifted powdered sugar
2 tablespoons milk

Combine first 4 ingredients, stirring until butter melts. Cool to lukewarm (105° to 115°).

Dissolve yeast in warm water in a large mixing bowl. Stir in milk mixture,

1½ cups flour, and egg; beat at medium speed of electric mixer until smooth. Stir in the ¾ cup remaining flour to make a stiff dough.

Turn dough out onto a lightly floured surface; knead until smooth and elastic (about 8 minutes). Place dough in a greased bowl, turning to grease top. Cover and let rise in a warm place (85°), free from drafts, for 1 hour (dough will not double in bulk).

Turn dough out onto a lightly floured surface; roll into a 12- x 8-inch rectangle, and spread with 2 tablespoons butter. Combine brown sugar and cinnamon; sprinkle mixture over rectangle. Roll up jellyroll fashion, beginning at long side; moisten edges with water to seal. Cut rolls into 1-inch slices; place slices cut side down in greased muffin pans. Brush tops with 1 tablespoon melted butter. Using a fork, gently lift center of rolls to form a peak.

Cover and let rise in a warm place, free from drafts, about 40 minutes (rolls will not double in bulk). Bake at 350° for 20 minutes. Combine powdered sugar and 2 tablespoons milk, beating well. Drizzle over warm rolls. Yield: 1 dozen.

*Mrs. Larry Edlefson,*
*Houma, Louisiana.*

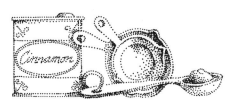

### RAISIN CINNAMON PULL-APARTS

1 package dry yeast
½ cup warm water (105° to 115°)
3 tablespoons sugar
½ teaspoon salt
2 tablespoons butter or margarine, softened
1 egg
About 2½ cups all-purpose flour, divided
2 tablespoons butter or margarine, melted
⅓ cup sugar
1 teaspoon ground cinnamon
⅓ cup raisins
1 cup sifted powdered sugar
2 tablespoons water

Dissolve yeast in warm water. Add next 4 ingredients and 1 cup flour; beat well. Gradually stir in enough remaining flour to make a soft dough. Turn out onto a lightly floured surface; knead 5 minutes. Roll dough into an 18- x 9-inch rectangle.

Brush dough with melted butter; sprinkle with ⅓ cup sugar, cinnamon,

and raisins. Roll dough up jellyroll fashion, beginning at long side; moisten edges with water to seal. Cut roll into 1½-inch slices; place slices cut side down in a greased 8-inch round cakepan. Cover; let rise in a warm place (85°), free from drafts, for 1 hour or until doubled in bulk.

Bake at 375° for 30 to 35 minutes. Combine powdered sugar and 2 tablespoons water, mixing well. Drizzle glaze over warm rolls. Yield: 1 dozen.

*Judy Cunningham,*
*Roanoke, Virginia.*

### BLUEBERRY PINWHEELS

2 cups biscuit mix
2 tablespoons sugar
1½ tablespoons grated orange rind
½ cup milk
¼ cup butter or margarine, melted
⅓ cup firmly packed brown sugar
½ teaspoon ground cinnamon
⅓ cup chopped pecans
¼ cup frozen blueberries, thawed and drained
1 cup sifted powdered sugar
2 tablespoons milk

Combine biscuit mix, 2 tablespoons sugar, and orange rind in a mixing bowl; mix well. Stir ½ cup milk into flour mixture to make a moderately stiff dough.

Turn dough out onto a floured surface, kneading lightly until dough is smooth. Roll out to a 15- x 9-inch rectangle (about ¼ inch thick); brush melted butter over dough, leaving a narrow margin on all sides.

Combine brown sugar, cinnamon, and pecans; sprinkle over dough. Sprinkle blueberries evenly over dough. Roll up jellyroll fashion, beginning at long side; moisten edges with water to seal. Cut roll into 15 (1-inch) slices; place slices cut side down in a greased 9-inch round cakepan.

Bake at 425° for 25 minutes or until rolls are lightly browned. Combine powdered sugar and 2 tablespoons milk, mixing well; drizzle over warm rolls. Yield: about 1¼ dozen.

*Frances Schoaps,*
*Houston, Texas.*

*Tip: To know when yeast is doubled in bulk, press dough flat in a bowl, mark level on outside of bowl, and mark a measure on outside of bowl that is double the first.*

## ORANGE BUTTER ROLLS

1 package dry yeast
¼ cup warm water (105° to 115°)
¼ cup plus 2 tablespoons butter or margarine, melted
½ cup commercial sour cream
¼ cup sugar
2 eggs
1 teaspoon salt
About 3¼ cups all-purpose flour
¾ cup sugar
1 cup flaked coconut, toasted and divided
2 tablespoons grated orange rind
2 tablespoons butter or margarine, melted
Orange glaze (recipe follows)

Dissolve yeast in warm water in a large mixing bowl. Add next 5 ingredients, mixing well. Gradually stir in enough flour to make a soft dough; mix well. Place in a well-greased bowl, turning to grease top. Cover and let rise in a warm place (85°), free from drafts, for 1½ to 2 hours or until doubled in bulk.

Combine ¾ cup sugar, ¾ cup coconut, and orange rind; set aside.

Punch dough down. Turn dough out onto a floured surface, and knead until smooth and elastic (about 7 minutes). Divide dough in half. Roll each half into a circle about 12 inches in diameter; brush each circle with 1 tablespoon butter. Sprinkle each with half the coconut mixture; cut into 12 wedges. Roll each wedge tightly, beginning at wide end.

Place rolls on greased baking sheets, point side down. Curve into crescent shape. Cover and let rise in a warm place, for 45 minutes or until doubled in bulk. Bake at 350° for 25 to 30 minutes or until lightly browned. Drizzle glaze over warm rolls. Sprinkle with remaining ¼ cup coconut. Yield: 2 dozen.

*Orange Glaze:*

¾ cup sugar
½ cup commercial sour cream
¼ cup butter or margarine
2 tablespoons orange juice

Combine all ingredients in a saucepan. Cook over low heat, stirring frequently, until thoroughly heated. (Do not boil.) Yield: about ½ cup.

*Betty Rabe,*
*Plano, Texas.*

*Tip: Plan your menus for the week, but stay flexible enough to substitute good buys when you spot them. By planning ahead, you can use leftovers in another day's meal.*

# There's Fruit In The Bread

For breakfast or an anytime snack, we suggest a fruit-laced quick bread. Blueberry Coffee Cake is especially easy to prepare. Just spread blueberry pie filling between two layers of batter, sprinkle on a crunchy topping, and it's ready to bake.

Mrs. Charles Lister of Danville, Kentucky, combines fresh apples, chopped pecans, and several spices for her Fresh Apple Loaf. She bakes the loaves in coffee cans to give them an unusual shape.

### FRESH APPLE LOAF

4 cups peeled, chopped apples
1 cup chopped pecans
2 cups sugar
3 cups all-purpose flour
2 teaspoons baking soda
¼ teaspoon salt
¼ teaspoon ground nutmeg
¼ teaspoon ground cloves
¾ teaspoon ground cinnamon
1 cup butter or margarine, melted
2 teaspoons vanilla extract
2 eggs, slightly beaten

Combine apples, pecans, and sugar; mix well. Let stand 1 hour, stirring often; do not drain.

Combine flour, soda, salt, and spices in a large bowl; add apple mixture, stirring well. Stir in butter, vanilla, and eggs.

Spoon the batter into 2 greased and floured 1-pound coffee cans. Tie a 2-inch band of foil around top of cans. Bake at 325° for 1 hour and 15 minutes or until a wooden pick inserted in center comes out clean. Let cool in cans 10 minutes; remove from cans to complete cooling. Yield: 2 loaves.

*Mrs. Charles Lister,*
*Danville, Kentucky.*

### BLUEBERRY COFFEE CAKE

1 cup butter or margarine, softened
1 cup sugar
2 eggs
1 (8-ounce) carton commercial sour cream
1 teaspoon vanilla extract
2 cups all-purpose flour
1 teaspoon baking powder
1 teaspoon baking soda
1 (21-ounce) can blueberry pie filling
Topping (recipe follows)

Cream butter; gradually add sugar, beating until light and fluffy. Add eggs, one at a time, beating well after each addition; stir in sour cream and vanilla.

Combine dry ingredients; gradually add to creamed mixture, beating well after each addition.

Spread half of batter in a greased 13- x 9- x 2-inch pan; spread with pie filling, top with remaining batter, and sprinkle with topping. Bake at 375° for 45 minutes. Cut cake into squares to serve. Yield: 15 servings.

*Topping:*

¼ cup all-purpose flour
¼ cup sugar
½ cup chopped pecans
3 tablespoons butter or margarine

Combine flour, sugar, and pecans; cut in butter until mixture resembles coarse meal. Yield: about 1 cup.

*Mrs. E. W. Hanley,*
*Macon, Georgia.*

# Whip The Meringue Problem

Tired of a weeping meringue? Mrs. Roy E. Gunnells of Dearing, Georgia, sent us her recipe for a cooked meringue that doesn't shrink or collect water droplets, even after refrigeration. And the chocolate filling that goes with it nets a high rating from us, too.

As with any meringue, be careful not to overbeat the egg whites. Cool the pie at room temperature, away from drafts, before serving.

### CHOCOLATE MERINGUE PIE

1¼ cups sugar
½ cup cocoa
⅓ cup cornstarch
¼ teaspoon salt
3 cups milk
3 egg yolks
3 tablespoons margarine
1½ teaspoons vanilla extract
1 baked 9-inch pastry shell
Easy Cooked Meringue

Combine sugar, cocoa, cornstarch, and salt in a heavy saucepan. Mix well to remove lumps. Gradually add milk, stirring until blended. Cook over medium heat, stirring constantly, until mixture thickens and comes to a boil; boil 1 minute, stirring constantly. Remove mixture from heat.

Beat egg yolks until thick and lemon colored. Gradually stir about one-fourth of hot mixture into yolks; add to remaining hot mixture, stirring constantly. Cook over medium heat 2 minutes, stirring constantly. Remove from heat; stir in margarine and vanilla. Immediately pour into pastry shell. Spread meringue over filling, sealing to edge of pastry. Bake at 425° for 5 to 7 minutes or until lightly browned. Cool before serving. Yield: one 9-inch pie.

*Easy Cooked Meringue:*

½ cup water
¼ cup plus 2 tablespoons sugar
1 tablespoon cornstarch
3 egg whites
Dash of salt

Combine water, sugar, and cornstarch in a small saucepan, stirring well; cook over medium heat, stirring constantly, until transparent and thickened. Beat egg whites (at room temperature) and salt until foamy. Continue beating while gradually pouring cooked mixture into egg whites. Beat 3 minutes or until stiff (but not dry) peaks form. Do not overbeat. Yield: enough for one 9-inch pie.

# Favorite Salads From The Sea

Seafood's so light and refreshing that many of our readers like to use it for a salad. It might take only a bed of lettuce for color, a little dressing to bind ingredients, and some onion and celery for flavor and crunch—and, of course, lots of seafood.

For an elegant offering, we suggest Lobster and Orange Salad. Toss chunks of lobster with fresh orange sections, and drizzle with a dressing that features whipped cream for body and horseradish for spunk.

The best part is that these salads can generally be made well ahead of serving time. In fact, most of these recipes recommend chilling before serving to allow flavors to blend.

## CRABMEAT LUNCHEON SALAD

2 (6-ounce) packages frozen crabmeat, thawed and drained
1 (10-ounce) package frozen English peas, thawed
1 cup chopped celery
1 small onion, minced
¾ cup mayonnaise
1 tablespoon lemon juice
⅛ teaspoon curry powder
1 teaspoon soy sauce
⅛ teaspoon garlic salt
1 (3-ounce) can chow mein noodles
½ cup slivered almonds, toasted

Combine first 4 ingredients; toss well. Combine next 5 ingredients; mix well. Pour dressing over crab mixture, and toss lightly; chill. To serve, stir in noodles; sprinkle with almonds. Yield: 8 servings. *Mrs. Harold Wagner, Hendersonville, North Carolina.*

## LOBSTER AND ORANGE SALAD

¼ teaspoon salt
1 (5-ounce) can lobster, drained and flaked or 1 cup coarsely chopped cooked lobster
3 large oranges, peeled and sectioned
½ cup whipping cream, whipped
¼ teaspoon grated orange rind
¼ cup orange juice
2 tablespoons mayonnaise
½ teaspoon prepared horseradish
Lettuce leaves
Ground nutmeg

Sprinkle salt over lobster; add orange sections, and toss gently. Chill 1 hour. Combine next 5 ingredients; mix well. Chill 1 hour. Spoon lobster mixture on lettuce leaves. Top with whipped cream dressing; sprinkle with nutmeg. Yield: about 4 servings. *Barbara E. Bach, Clearwater, Florida.*

## AVOCADO STUFFED WITH SHRIMP SALAD

5 cups water
1½ pounds unpeeled medium shrimp, uncooked
¼ cup lime or lemon juice, divided
½ cup chopped celery
½ cup chopped cucumber
½ cup mayonnaise
2 teaspoons dried whole dillweed
½ teaspoon salt
¼ teaspoon coarsely ground black pepper
3 large ripe avocados
Lettuce leaves

Bring water to a boil; add shrimp, and reduce heat. Simmer 3 to 5 minutes. Drain well, and rinse with cold water; chill. Peel and devein shrimp.

Sprinkle shrimp with 2 tablespoons lime juice; stir in celery, cucumber, mayonnaise, dillweed, salt, and pepper. Chill at least 1 hour.

Cut avocados in half lengthwise; remove seed, and peel. Gently rub the avocado halves with remaining 2 tablespoons lime juice. Place avocados on lettuce, and fill centers with shrimp mixture. Yield: 6 servings. *Claire Bastable, Chevy Chase, Maryland.*

## SHRIMP AND RICE SALAD

3 cups cooked rice, chilled
1 (6-ounce) or 1 (10-ounce) package frozen cooked shrimp, thawed
1½ cups diced celery
2 green onions, chopped
1 (8-ounce) can sliced water chestnuts, drained
1 (10-ounce) package frozen English peas, thawed
½ cup mayonnaise
2 teaspoons soy sauce
Lettuce leaves

Combine all ingredients except lettuce leaves, mixing well; chill 2 hours. Serve on lettuce leaves. Yield: 6 servings. *Jacquelyn Christopher, Asheville, North Carolina.*

## SUMMERTIME SALMON SALAD

1 (15½-ounce) can salmon
2 cups shredded cabbage
¼ cup diced celery
¼ cup sliced ripe olives
½ cup mayonnaise
6 large tomatoes
Lettuce leaves

Drain salmon, and flake with a fork. Add cabbage, celery, and olives; mix gently, and fold in mayonnaise. Cover and chill 2 hours.

With stem end up, cut each tomato into 6 wedges, cutting to, but not through, base of tomato. Spread wedges slightly apart; sprinkle inside of wedges with salt. Cover and chill 1½ hours.

Place each tomato on lettuce leaves; spoon salmon mixture into wedges. Yield: 6 servings. *Kathryn Knight, Sarasota, Florida.*

## CREAMY TUNA SALAD

2 envelopes unflavored gelatin
½ cup cold water
1 (10¾-ounce) can tomato soup, undiluted
2 (3-ounce) packages cream cheese, softened
1 (6½-ounce) can tuna, drained and flaked
1 cup mayonnaise or salad dressing
1 cup chopped celery
¼ cup chopped green pepper
¼ cup finely chopped onion
Lettuce leaves

Soften gelatin in cold water. Combine soup and cream cheese in saucepan over medium heat; cook until cream cheese dissolves. Remove from heat. Add gelatin mixture, stirring well; cool.

Combine remaining ingredients except lettuce, mixing well; stir in soup mixture. Pour into a lightly oiled 9- x 5- x 3-inch loafpan; chill until firm. Unmold on lettuce leaves. Yield: 8 servings.
*Wanda Bishop,*
*Little Rock, Arkansas.*

## FAVORITE TUNA SALAD

2 (6½-ounce) cans tuna, drained and flaked
4 hard-cooked eggs, chopped
¼ cup chopped pecans
3 tablespoons chopped sweet pickle
1 medium-size Delicious apple, unpeeled, cored, and coarsely chopped
½ cup mayonnaise
Lettuce leaves (optional)

Combine first 5 ingredients; mix well. Add mayonnaise, and stir gently. Serve salad on lettuce leaves, if desired. Yield: 6 servings.
*Betty Young,*
*Lexington, Kentucky.*

# Fresh Vegetables For Two

The abundance of fresh produce in the marketplace seems to invite family-size preparations. But if you're cooking for two, there's no reason you can't enjoy the best of the season's produce in casseroles and stir-fries geared for smaller servings.

Our Scalloped Corn for Two is a small-size version of a Southern favorite. It's made with fresh corn cut from the cob and baked with a cracker crumb topping. One large eggplant makes two generous servings when the halves are baked with a filling of mushrooms, tomatoes, green pepper, onion, and mozzarella. And watch a zucchini, an onion, and 10 large mushrooms turn into a delicious Oriental-style stir-fry.

## SCALLOPED CORN FOR TWO

½ cup fresh corn cut from cob
¼ teaspoon salt
Dash of pepper
1 egg, beaten
½ cup milk
1 tablespoon butter or margarine
¼ cup round buttery cracker crumbs
1 tablespoon butter or margarine, melted

Combine first 5 ingredients, mixing well. Pour into a lightly greased 2-cup baking dish; dot with 1 tablespoon butter. Combine cracker crumbs and melted butter, stirring well; sprinkle over corn mixture. Bake at 375° for 40 minutes. Yield: 2 servings.
*Mrs. J. T. Ballard,*
*Wichita Falls, Texas.*

## CHEESY STUFFED EGGPLANT

1 large eggplant
1 medium onion, chopped
1 medium-size green pepper, chopped
1 clove garlic, minced
1 tablespoon vegetable oil
1 large tomato, peeled and chopped
⅓ cup tomato juice
1 (3-ounce) can sliced mushrooms, drained
1 (8-ounce) package mozzarella cheese, diced
1 teaspoon dried whole oregano
Salt and pepper to taste
2 tablespoons grated Parmesan cheese

Wash eggplant, and cut in half lengthwise. Remove pulp, leaving a ¼-inch shell. Chop pulp, and set aside.

Sauté onion, pepper, and garlic in oil 5 minutes. Add eggplant, tomato, tomato juice, and mushrooms; cook over medium heat 15 to 20 minutes, stirring occasionally. Remove from heat. Stir in mozzarella, oregano, salt, and pepper.

Place eggplant shells in a 10- x 6- x 2-inch baking dish. Spoon mixture into shells; sprinkle with Parmesan. Bake at 350° for 15 to 20 minutes or until cheese melts. Yield: 2 servings. *Lynn Duncan,*
*Chapin, South Carolina.*

## FRIED PEPPER STRIPS

1 egg, beaten
1 (3-ounce) package cream cheese, softened
2 tablespoons self-rising flour
1 large green pepper, cut into ½-inch strips
Vegetable oil
Salt and pepper (optional)

Combine first 3 ingredients, mixing well. Dip green pepper strips in cream cheese mixture, turning to coat. Fry in hot oil (375°) until golden brown. Drain on paper towels. Sprinkle with salt and pepper, if desired. Yield: 2 servings.
*Mrs. Chris Horne,*
*North Macon, Georgia.*

## VEGETABLE STIR-FRY

2½ tablespoons vegetable oil
10 large mushrooms, sliced
1 medium onion, sliced
1 medium zucchini, sliced
1 tablespoon soy sauce
¼ teaspoon sugar
Salt and pepper to taste

Heat oil in a wok or heavy skillet. Add vegetables; stir-fry 5 minutes or until vegetables are crisp-tender. Add remaining ingredients; mix lightly. Yield: 2 servings. *Pamela Deutsch,*
*Dallas, Texas.*

## ZUCCHINI AND TOMATO AU GRATIN

¼ pound zucchini
1 tablespoon chopped onion
1 tablespoon vegetable oil
½ cup peeled, chopped fresh tomato
¼ teaspoon salt
Dash of pepper
¼ cup (1 ounce) shredded Cheddar cheese

Wash zucchini, and trim ends; cut into ¼-inch slices. Sauté onion in oil until tender. Add zucchini; cook 5 minutes, stirring constantly. Add tomato, salt, and pepper; cover and cook an additional 5 minutes. Spoon squash mixture into a 2-cup casserole; sprinkle with cheese. Bake at 375° for 5 minutes or until cheese melts. Yield: 2 servings.
*Eloise Juba,*
*Baltimore, Maryland.*

# Bake A Batch Of Bar Cookies

Chocolate, butterscotch, raspberry jam, and pecans flavor these easy-to-handle bar cookies. Since they're not sticky, you'll find them ideal for packing as carry-along snacks or in sack lunches.

Raspberry Bars feature a raspberry jam filling sandwiched by an oatmeal crust. We loved the raspberry flavor, but you can substitute your own favorite fruit jam or preserves.

Mary Helen Hackney says her Pecan Bars are a tasty alternative to pecan pie. To make them, she covers a crust consisting of butter, brown sugar, and flour with a mixture of corn syrup, eggs, butter, and pecans. The nuts rise during baking to make a crunchy topping for the chewy filling underneath.

### BUTTERSCOTCH BARS

4 eggs
1 (16-ounce) package brown sugar
2 cups biscuit mix
2 cups chopped pecans or walnuts
1 (6-ounce) package butterscotch morsels
1 teaspoon vanilla extract

Beat eggs with electric mixer at medium speed until frothy. Gradually add sugar, beating until thick. Add remaining ingredients, stirring well.

Spread batter in a greased and floured 13- x 9- x 2-inch pan. Bake at 325° for 45 minutes. Cool and cut into bars. Yield: about 4 dozen.
*Mary Linda Brooks,*
*Hayes, Virginia.*

### CHOCOLATE CINNAMON BARS

2 cups all-purpose flour
1 teaspoon baking powder
1 cup sugar
1 tablespoon ground cinnamon
½ cup butter or margarine, softened
½ cup shortening
1 egg, slightly beaten
1 egg, separated
⅓ cup sugar
1 teaspoon ground cinnamon
1 (6-ounce) package semisweet chocolate morsels
½ cup chopped pecans

Combine first 4 ingredients in a large bowl. Add butter, shortening, egg, and

egg yolk, mixing well. Press evenly into a lightly greased 15- x 10- x 1-inch jellyroll pan. Beat egg white slightly, and brush over mixture.

Combine remaining ingredients; sprinkle over bottom layer. Bake at 350° for 25 minutes. Cool and cut into bars. Yield: about 3 dozen.
*Adrian Palmer,*
*Chattanooga, Tennessee.*

### PECAN BARS

1⅓ cups all-purpose flour
2 tablespoons brown sugar
½ cup butter or margarine, softened
½ cup firmly packed brown sugar
2 eggs
½ cup dark corn syrup
2 tablespoons butter or margarine, melted
⅛ teaspoon salt
¾ cup chopped pecans

Combine flour and 2 tablespoons brown sugar. Cut in ½ cup butter with pastry blender until mixture resembles coarse meal. Press mixture evenly into a greased 9-inch square pan. Bake at 350° for 15 to 17 minutes.

Combine next 5 ingredients, beating well. Stir in pecans. Pour filling over prepared crust. Bake at 350° for 25 minutes or until firm. Let cool, and cut into bars. Yield: 2 dozen.
*Mary Helen Hackney,*
*Charlotte, North Carolina.*

### RASPBERRY BARS

¾ cup butter or margarine
1 cup firmly packed brown sugar
1½ cups all-purpose flour
1 teaspoon salt
½ teaspoon baking soda
1½ cups quick-cooking oats, uncooked
1 (10-ounce) jar red raspberry jam

Cream butter; gradually add sugar, beating until light and fluffy. Combine flour, salt, soda, and oats; add to creamed mixture.

Press half of crumb mixture into a greased 13- x 9- x 2-inch pan. Spread raspberry jam over crumb mixture. Sprinkle remaining half of crumb mixture over the jam. Bake at 400° for 20 minutes. Cool and cut into bars. Yield: about 4 dozen.
*Note:* Other fruit jams or preserves may be substituted for the raspberry jam, if desired.     *Mrs. W. Paul Jones,*
*Hopkinsville, Kentucky.*

# Great Pies Begin With The Crust

Although the filling of a delicious pie often gets the most attention, the crust will not go unnoticed. Our three flavorful pie shells are sure to get plenty of attention on their own.

Two very different alternatives to a traditional piecrust are rich Chocolate-Coconut Pie Shell and Crisp Cereal Piecrust. Fill them with ice cream or any other favorite pie filling.

### MAKE-AHEAD PASTRY

4 cups all-purpose flour
2 teaspoons salt
1 tablespoon sugar
1¾ cups shortening
1 egg, beaten
1 tablespoon white vinegar
½ cup cold water

Combine dry ingredients; cut in shortening until mixture resembles coarse meal. Combine egg, vinegar, and water in a small bowl; stir into flour mixture. Divide dough into 4 equal parts; shape each into a ball, and wrap tightly. Chill.

Roll each portion to ⅛-inch thickness on a lightly floured surface. Place in a 9-inch pieplate; trim off excess pastry along edges. Fold edges under and flute. To bake, prick bottom and sides with a fork; bake at 450° for 10 to 12 minutes or until golden brown. Do not prick shell if it will be filled before baking. Yield: four 9-inch pastry shells.

*Note:* Dough may be stored up to one week in refrigerator or stored in freezer for longer periods.     *Susan Erickson,*
*Pocahontas, Arkansas.*

### CRISP CEREAL PIECRUST

2 cups quick-cooking oats, uncooked
¼ teaspoon salt
½ cup sifted powdered sugar
½ teaspoon ground cinnamon
¼ cup plus 2 tablespoons butter or margarine, melted
Vegetable cooking spray

Combine first 4 ingredients in a mixing bowl; stir in butter, and mix well.

Spray a 9-inch pieplate with vegetable cooking spray; press piecrust mixture on bottom and sides of pieplate. Bake at 350° for 20 minutes; cool. Yield: one 9-inch piecrust.     *Greta Pinkston,*
*Harrison, Arkansas.*

## CHOCOLATE-COCONUT PIE SHELL

2 tablespoons butter or margarine
2 (1-ounce) squares unsweetened chocolate
⅔ cup sifted powdered sugar
2 tablespoons hot water
1½ cups flaked coconut
Vegetable cooking spray

Combine butter and chocolate in top of double boiler; bring water to a boil. Reduce heat to low; stir until the chocolate is melted.

Combine powdered sugar and hot water; add to chocolate mixture, stirring well. Stir in coconut.

Spray a 9-inch pieplate with vegetable cooking spray; firmly press piecrust mixture onto bottom and sides of pieplate. Cover and chill until firm. Yield: one 9-inch pie shell.

*Note:* Crust may be filled with softened ice cream and frozen until serving time. To serve, drizzle chocolate syrup over each slice.
*Lib Cunningham,*
*Atlanta, Georgia.*

# Snackin'-Good Quick Breads

Lynne Weeks of Midland, Georgia, likes to keep nutritious snacks on hand for her children. She often puts slices of Carrot-Pineapple Bread in their lunchboxes for snacktime, and usually they want more of the spicy bread with milk when they come home.

In fact, all of our quick breads make a great lunchbox snack. Even the muffins are as good at room temperature as they are fresh from the oven. And since these breads aren't very sweet, you'll feel good about them for between-meal eating.

## CARROT-PINEAPPLE BREAD

1½ cups all-purpose flour
1 cup sugar
1 teaspoon baking powder
1 teaspoon baking soda
1 teaspoon ground cinnamon
¼ teaspoon salt
2 eggs, beaten
1 cup scraped, shredded carrots
⅔ cup vegetable oil
½ cup crushed pineapple, undrained
1 teaspoon vanilla extract

Combine first 6 ingredients in a large mixing bowl; stir in remaining ingredients. Beat at medium speed of electric mixer 2 minutes. Pour into a greased and floured 9- x 5- x 3-inch loafpan; bake at 350° for 50 to 55 minutes or until a wooden pick inserted in center comes out clean. Yield: 1 loaf.
*Lynne T. Weeks,*
*Midland, Georgia.*

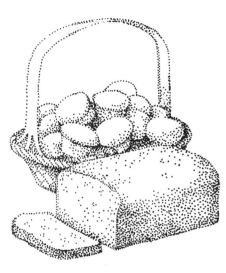

## ORANGE-CREAM CHEESE BREAD

1 (8-ounce) package cream cheese, softened
½ cup shortening
1⅔ cups sugar
2 eggs
2¼ cups all-purpose flour
1 tablespoon baking powder
1 teaspoon salt
1 cup milk
½ cup chopped walnuts
2 tablespoons grated orange rind
¼ cup orange juice

Combine cream cheese and shortening, creaming well. Gradually add sugar, beating until light and fluffy. Add eggs, beating well after each addition.

Combine flour, baking powder, and salt; add to creamed mixture alternately with milk, beginning and ending with flour mixture. Mix well after each addition. Stir in walnuts and orange rind.

Pour batter into 2 greased and floured 8½- x 4½- x 3-inch loafpans. Bake at 375° for 55 minutes or until a wooden pick inserted in center comes out clean. Let cool in pan 10 minutes; sprinkle orange juice over loaves. Remove to wire rack to finish cooling. Yield: 2 loaves.
*Patricia Boschen,*
*Ashland, Virginia.*

## COCONUT-MOLASSES MUFFINS

½ cup shortening
¼ cup sugar
1 egg
½ cup molasses
2 cups all-purpose flour
1 tablespoon baking powder
½ teaspoon salt
½ teaspoon ground ginger
⅔ cup milk
1 cup flaked coconut

Cream shortening; add sugar, beating until light and fluffy. Add egg and molasses, beating well.

Combine flour, baking powder, salt, and ginger; stir into creamed mixture alternately with milk, beginning and ending with flour mixture. Gently fold in the coconut.

Spoon into well-greased muffin pans, filling two-thirds full. Bake at 375° for 25 minutes. Serve warm or at room temperature. Yield: about 1½ dozen.
*Betty R. Butts,*
*Kensington, Maryland.*

## OATMEAL MUFFINS

2 cups all-purpose flour
2 cups quick-cooking oats, uncooked
1 cup firmly packed brown sugar
2 teaspoons baking powder
1 teaspoon salt
1 teaspoon baking soda
2 teaspoons ground cinnamon
2 eggs
2 cups buttermilk
⅔ cup shortening, melted

Combine first 7 ingredients in a large bowl; make a well in center of mixture, and set aside.

Combine eggs, buttermilk, and shortening, mixing well; add to dry ingredients, stirring just until moistened. Spoon into greased muffin pans, filling two-thirds full. Bake at 400° for 18 to 20 minutes. Serve warm or at room temperature. Yield: 1½ dozen.
*D. Harris Wise,*
*Fort Worth, Texas.*

*Tip: Disposable pans for heating vegetables, breads, or other foods on the grill are easily made from heavy-duty aluminum foil: Tear off a length of foil and turn up edges to make 1½- to 2-inch sides; pinch corners to prevent leaking.*

# Color The Meal With Greens

Turnip greens, collards, and spinach—all so dear to a Southerner's heart—get special attention in these three recipes. Simply prepared yet full of flavor, Seasoned Collard Greens are cooked with onion, salt pork, and a little vinegar. Mrs. William F. Smith enhances turnip greens by dropping cornmeal dumplings into the pot of simmering greens. And for a spinach salad the way you'll like it, toss it with a hot bacon dressing.

## SEASONED COLLARD GREENS

1 bunch (about 5 pounds) collard greens
½ pound salt pork
2 quarts water
1 medium onion, chopped
1 teaspoon seasoned salt
1 teaspoon sugar
1 teaspoon vinegar

Check leaves of collards carefully; remove pulpy stems and discolored spots on leaves. Wash leaves thoroughly; drain well and chop. Set aside.

Rinse salt pork thoroughly; pat dry, and cut into ½-inch-thick slices. Cook the salt pork in an 8-quart Dutch oven until golden brown. Slowly add water, and bring to a boil. Reduce heat and simmer, uncovered, 15 to 30 minutes. Add collards and remaining ingredients; bring to a boil. Cover, reduce heat, and simmer 30 to 45 minutes or until collards are tender, stirring occasionally. Add more water if necessary. Yield: 10 servings.          *Alice G. Pahl,*
*Raleigh, North Carolina.*

## SPINACH SALAD WITH HOT BACON DRESSING

1 pound fresh spinach, torn
4 slices bacon, diced
¼ cup sliced green onion
½ cup sliced fresh mushrooms 2 teaspoons brown sugar
⅛ teaspoon salt 1
½ tablespoons vinegar
⅛ teaspoon dry mustard Dash of paprika

Place spinach in a large salad bowl, and set aside.

Cook bacon in a medium skillet until crisp. Add onion and mushrooms; sauté until tender. Stir in next 5 ingredients; cook until thoroughly heated, stirring constantly. Pour hot mixture over spinach, and toss lightly. Serve immediately. Yield: 6 servings.          *Mary Boydston,*
*El Dorado Springs, Missouri.*

## TURNIP GREENS WITH CORNMEAL DUMPLINGS

About 1 pound ham hocks
2 quarts water
1 bunch (3 to 4 pounds) turnip greens with roots
Dash of pepper
1 cup cornmeal
1 teaspoon sugar
½ teaspoon salt
1½ cups boiling water
1 egg, beaten
About ½ cup all-purpose flour

Wash ham hocks, and place in an 8-quart Dutch oven; add 2 quarts water, and bring to a boil. Reduce heat, and simmer for 40 minutes or until the meat is tender.

Check leaves of turnips carefully; remove pulpy stems and discolored spots on leaves. Wash turnip greens and roots thoroughly; drain well. Chop turnip leaves; peel turnip roots, and cut in half.

Add greens, roots, and pepper to Dutch oven; bring to a boil. Cover, reduce heat, and simmer about 50 minutes or until greens and roots are tender.

Combine cornmeal, sugar, and salt; mix well. Stir in boiling water. Add egg, and mix well. Drop cornmeal mixture by tablespoonfuls onto a floured board, and roll in flour. Place dumplings over hot turnip greens, and cook over medium heat 15 minutes. Yield: 8 to 10 servings.          *Mrs. William F. Smith,*
*Lampasas, Texas.*

# You Won't Peel Potatoes For These Dishes

Packaged potatoes don't have to be plain. A few extra touches can turn these convenience products into fancy fare.

Mary Vaughn uses basil and paprika to spice up frozen potatoes in her recipe for Herb French Fries. Simply follow package directions for the potatoes, then toss with the seasonings while the French fries are hot.

Canned shoestring potatoes are a primary ingredient for Shoestring Potato Tuna Bake. This tasty casserole blends the potatoes with tuna, mushroom soup, celery, and pimiento.

## SHOESTRING POTATO TUNA BAKE

4 (1½-ounce) cans shoestring potatoes
1 (10¾-ounce) can cream of mushroom soup, undiluted
1 (6½-ounce) can tuna, drained and flaked
¾ cup evaporated milk
½ cup diced celery
¼ cup diced pimiento

Combine all ingredients except 1 can of shoestring potatoes; stir well. Spoon mixture into a lightly greased 1-quart casserole; top with remaining potatoes. Bake at 350° for 25 to 30 minutes. Yield: 4 servings.          *Janis Moyer,*
*Farmersville, Texas.*

## HERB FRENCH FRIES

1 (16-ounce) package frozen French fries
Vegetable oil
1½ teaspoons dried whole basil, crushed
½ teaspoon salt
¼ teaspoon paprika

Fry potatoes in vegetable oil according to package directions; drain well.

Add seasonings to potatoes, and toss well to coat. Serve immediately. Yield: 4 to 6 servings.          *Mary Vaughn,*
*Dallas, Texas.*

## CHEESY POTATOES

1 small onion, chopped
¼ cup butter or margarine
1 (8-ounce) jar process cheese spread
1 (8-ounce) carton commercial sour cream
1 (32-ounce) package frozen fried potato rounds, thawed

Sauté onion in butter until tender. Add next 2 ingredients; mix well. Set aside.

Place potatoes in a 12- x 8- x 2-inch baking dish. Pour cheese mixture over potatoes. Cover and bake at 350° for 30 minutes. Uncover casserole; bake 5 additional minutes. Yield: 8 servings.
*Mrs. Randy Throneberry,*
*Shelbyville, Tennessee.*

# Don't Frost The Cake, Spoon On A Sauce

We can't improve on pound cake or angel food cake still warm from the oven, but we do have a few tricks for dressing it up. Just spoon on Party Mint Sauce or Butterscotch-Pecan Sauce to keep the last slices as inviting as the first.

These and our other sauces yield enough for several servings, so just chill and reheat as needed. Keep some on hand even if there's no time to bake—these toppings make tasty treats out of commercial cake and ice cream, too.

## QUICK HOT FUDGE SAUCE

1 cup sugar
⅓ cup cocoa
2 tablespoons all-purpose flour
¼ teaspoon salt
1 tablespoon butter or margarine
1 cup boiling water
1 teaspoon vanilla extract

Combine first 5 ingredients in a saucepan; blend well. Gradually add water; cook over medium heat, stirring constantly, until smooth and thickened. Bring mixture to a boil; boil 2 minutes. Stir in vanilla. Serve hot over cake. Store in refrigerator; reheat as needed. Yield: 1¼ cups.    *Mrs. Paul Raper, Burgaw, North Carolina.*

## PARTY MINT SAUCE

1 (3⅛-ounce) package vanilla pudding mix
1½ cups milk
8 chocolate-covered mint patties, coarsely chopped
1 (1.25-ounce) envelope whipped topping mix
Grated chocolate (optional)
Fresh mint sprigs (optional)

Combine pudding mix, milk, and chopped mint patties in a saucepan. Cook, stirring constantly, over low heat until thickened and bubbly and mint patties melt. Remove from heat; cover with plastic wrap to prevent film from forming. Let cool completely.

Prepare whipped topping mix according to package directions; fold into chocolate mixture. Cover and chill. Serve over cake; garnish with grated chocolate and fresh mint sprigs, if desired. Yield: 2½ cups.

*Peggy Ann Hays, Rockmart, Georgia.*

## APRICOT SAUCE

1 cup dried apricots
2 cups warm water
¼ cup sugar
Pinch of salt
⅛ teaspoon almond extract

Soak apricots in warm water 1 hour; cover and cook over low heat for 15 to 20 minutes or until tender. Remove from heat.

Pour apricots and liquid into container of an electric blender; process until smooth. Stir in remaining ingredients, and mix well. Serve over cake. Yield: 1½ cups.    *Sarah Watson, Knoxville, Tennessee.*

## QUICK FRUIT SAUCE

1 (16-ounce) can chunky mixed fruit
¼ cup sugar
2 tablespoons cornstarch
½ teaspoon grated orange rind
Juice of 1 orange
2 tablespoons lemon juice
1 (3-inch) stick cinnamon
8 whole cloves

Drain mixed fruit, reserving liquid; set fruit aside.

Combine reserved liquid and remaining ingredients in a saucepan; cook over low heat, stirring constantly, until thickened and bubbly. Remove from heat; discard cinnamon stick and cloves. Stir in fruit; serve warm over cake. Yield: 2½ cups.    *Mrs. Robert Collins, Fairfax, Missouri.*

## BUTTERSCOTCH-PECAN SAUCE

½ cup light corn syrup
⅓ cup firmly packed brown sugar
3 tablespoons butter or margarine
⅛ teaspoon salt
2 tablespoons evaporated milk
½ cup chopped pecans
⅓ cup light rum

Combine first 4 ingredients in a heavy saucepan; bring to a boil, stirring constantly. Cook until mixture reaches soft ball stage (234°). Let cool 5 minutes.

Stir in evaporated milk, chopped pecans, and rum. Chill. Serve over cake. Yield: 1⅓ cups.

*Mrs. R. D. Walker, Garland, Texas.*

# Accent Chicken With Eggplant

Chicken and eggplant may seem an unlikely pair, but Chicken-Eggplant Parmigiana teams them in prize-winning fashion. Fried boneless chicken breasts are crowned with sliced eggplant and smothered in spaghetti sauce. Topped with Parmesan and mozzarella, it's baked and ready to serve in minutes.

## CHICKEN-EGGPLANT PARMIGIANA

2 whole chicken breasts, split, boned, and skinned
¾ cup fine, dry breadcrumbs
1 teaspoon salt
⅛ teaspoon pepper
1 egg, beaten
⅓ cup vegetable oil, divided
1 small eggplant, peeled and cut into 4 (½-inch-thick) slices
1 cup prepared meatless spaghetti sauce
2 tablespoons grated Parmesan cheese
1 cup (4 ounces) shredded mozzarella cheese

Place each chicken breast half on waxed paper; flatten to ¼-inch thickness using a meat mallet or rolling pin.

Combine breadcrumbs, salt, and pepper. Dip chicken in egg, and coat with breadcrumbs. Place chicken on a baking sheet; cover and chill 10 minutes.

Heat 2 tablespoons oil in a large skillet. Add chicken; sauté over medium-low heat 5 minutes on each side or until golden brown. Remove chicken, and place in a 12- x 8- x 2-inch baking dish.

Sauté eggplant in remaining oil over medium heat until golden brown on both sides; drain on paper towels.

Place 1 slice eggplant on each chicken breast half. Spoon spaghetti sauce over eggplant; sprinkle with Parmesan cheese, and top with mozzarella. Bake at 375° for 20 minutes or until cheese melts and sauce is bubbly. Yield: 4 servings.    *Connie Parvis, Milford, Delaware.*

*Tip: Use a blender or food processor to make crumbs from crackers or stale bread. If you don't have stale bread on hand, dry fresh bread in a microwave or toaster oven.*

# October

October brings brilliantly colored leaves, nippy breezes, and a rich fall harvest of pumpkins. The prettiest pumpkins may turn into jack-o'-lanterns, but most folks agree that the best are found in pies, cookies, chiffons, or baked and covered with a maple syrup glaze. Look for these recipes on the pages to follow.

And while leaves are changing colors, Southern sportsmen are donning hunting gear and heading for the woods to bag their first game meal of the season. Several of our editors traveled from North Carolina to Texas to see how these men cook and entertain with their game specialties. We share their tips and recipes for fried quail, barbecued rabbit, venison, and more.

Once again, our *Mexican Food Fest* special section offers more south-of-the-border favorites from our readers. This year you'll find recipes for authentic main dishes, and rich Mexican desserts.

# Sportsmen Put Dinner On The Table

The leaves are gold and the early morning air is crisp. Clusters of men dressed in camouflage hats and jackets pile into pickup trucks and campers to celebrate an age-old ritual. It's hunting season again.

Later in the day, the guns are cleaned and put away, the game is dressed, and the hunters change into warm, dry clothes. But the best part is still to come, when friends sit down to an autumn feast of wild game.

## Meet Me at Charlie's Place

"When you see a dog on a point, your heart stops beating," says Fred Curlin, who has seen many dogs on point. Fred loves to hunt—quail, deer, and dove are his favorites—and, according to his son, Pat Curlin, "he also loves to eat."

During hunting season, word of another of Fred's game suppers spreads fast in Statesboro, Georgia. By evening, 40 or 50 men have gathered at "Charlie's place" for a feast of fried quail, barbecued venison, and pit-cooked boar. Along with the game, there will be hot, buttered grits, coleslaw, baked beans, rolls, and a cake.

At smaller parties, Fred prepares Quail Magnificent, which is always a favorite with his guests. For this dish, he simmers whole quail, celery, carrots, onion, mushrooms, and spices in broth until the birds are juicy and tender. Quail meat is all white and tends to be dry, but cooking with moist heat preserves the natural juices and delicate flavor of the birds.

Fred hosts most of his game suppers at a cozy creekside house owned by his friend, Charlie Hendrix, also of Statesboro. Occasionally, Charlie pitches in and prepares his smoked, barbecued venison or boar, which he cooks all day. Meanwhile, Fred maintains his post at an outdoor cast-iron deep fryer preparing fried quail.

"I like to hunt, and I like to entertain," says Fred, "so the game suppers are an ideal way to combine these interests." It's also a refreshing outlet from the long hours he spends over a drafting board as an architect.

Fred and his friends make their quail-hunting expeditions as informal as the game suppers. "Normally, we have lunch together and hunt in the afternoon," he says. "We let the dogs run about a hundred yards ahead; it's always real peaceful and a good chance to visit."

By dusk, Fred and his friends have flushed several coveys and bagged enough quail to feed a hungry crowd. It's important to keep the birds cool and to dress them as soon as possible, says Fred. "Some like to dress them in the field if they only want the breast of the bird, but we like to take them back to dress them since we enjoy cooking the whole bird."

When dressing the birds, says Fred, it's easier to skin them than to dry-pluck them. "After removing the heads, we cut the feet off at the knees, which leaves a nice little drumstick. Then we take the birds by the back and pull, and skin and feathers will all come off at once."

Most of Fred's game suppers involve men only. "Sometimes we have couples over," he says, "but we have a lot of parties just for men. There's a group of us that really loves to eat."

To Fred, these game suppers mean more than just good eating. Remembering when he shot his first quail at the age of 12, Fred says, "It was a delightful sense of accomplishment that I had something to put on the table just like my dad, who had been putting food on the table for years. It made me feel good, big, older, more mature, just like the big guys—and I was ready to go again."

Below are two of Fred's favorite quail recipes.

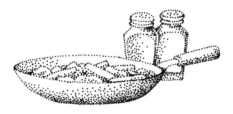

## QUAIL MAGNIFICENT

6 quail, cleaned
½ teaspoon salt
½ teaspoon pepper
⅓ cup all-purpose flour
Vegetable oil
2½ cups chicken broth
¼ teaspoon ground cinnamon
½ teaspoon poultry seasoning
1 tablespoon plus 1 teaspoon molasses
1 clove garlic, pressed
1 teaspoon lemon juice
4 medium carrots, cut into 2-inch pieces
2 stalks celery, cut into 2-inch pieces
¼ pound fresh mushrooms
2 green onions
½ cup dry sherry

Sprinkle quail with salt and pepper; dredge in flour. Brown quail on both sides in hot oil in a large, heavy skillet. Remove quail, and drain off oil; return quail to skillet.

Combine next 6 ingredients, mixing well; pour over quail. Reduce heat; cover and cook 30 minutes. Add remaining ingredients; cover and cook 30 additional minutes. Yield: 3 servings.

## FRIED QUAIL WITH ONION GRAVY

30 quail, cleaned
Salt
Pepper
All-purpose flour
8 slices bacon
2 cups peanut oil
¼ cup all-purpose flour
1 cup water
⅔ cup minced onion
Dash of garlic salt

Sprinkle quail with salt and pepper to taste; dredge in flour, and set aside.

Fry bacon in a large skillet. Remove bacon; reserve for other uses. Add peanut oil to drippings in skillet; heat over medium heat. Add quail; cook 10 to 12 minutes on each side or until done. Remove quail from pan; drain on paper towels. Reserve ¼ cup drippings in pan.

Add flour to drippings, stirring until smooth. Cook 1 minute, stirring constantly. Gradually add water, stirring well. Add onion and cook over medium heat, stirring constantly, until thickened and bubbly. Stir in ½ teaspoon salt, ⅛ teaspoon pepper, and garlic salt. Yield: 15 servings.

## 6 a.m. at Oakland Plantation

It's still dark in rural southeastern North Carolina when the toll of a heavy iron bell awakens the hunters. The aroma of sizzling sausage drifts through the morning air, calling them to a big country breakfast of piping-hot coffee, grits, and platters laden with sausage, eggs, and buttered toast.

While the dew is still on the ground, the dogs are released from their pens. Red-capped hunters pile into cars and trucks and ride to their stands on the hunting preserve nearby.

If Joe Neisler, Jr., of Kings Mountain, North Carolina, could have his way, deer season would never end. Each fall, he and his wife, Marlene, pack their bags and head for Oakland, the 200-year-old plantation home they now use as a hunting lodge.

Inviting family, friends, and business associates, Joe traditionally hosts 10 hunts each season. Five of the hunts are exclusively for men; the others include women, too. "We have about four couples hunts," he says. "The kids also like to hunt, so we'll have a 'cousins hunt' and invite our unmarried nieces and nephews."

A game rack and walk-in cooler on the Oakland grounds are in constant use throughout hunting season. When a deer is shot, it's loaded on the truck and carried back to the house, where it's photographed, weighed, and dressed. The skinned carcass is hung in the cooler to age a full week. "It doesn't work to hang the deer longer than a week," says Joe. "There's not enough fat, and it dries out." Once aged, the meat is butchered, placed in plastic bags, and wrapped in freezer paper for freezing.

When it comes to cooking venison, Joe is second to none. "The way I cook the hindquarter is unusual," he says. "Believe it or not, I can prepare it so it actually tastes like tenderloin."

His secret lies in removing the fascia, or white membrane separating the muscles. "It's tough and chewy, and it gives venison that wild or gamey flavor," says Joe. "You have to remove all of the white membrane to make the meat tender."

Joe's Grilled Venison Steaks are basted with a special marinade and then grilled until medium-rare. "Venison is a dry meat," he says. "You have to be careful not to overcook it, or it'll be dry and rubbery."

Venison Kabobs are another specialty. Joe skewers chunks of venison loin along with onion, green pepper, mushrooms, and tomato slices. "While I'm cutting the meat, I simmer the green pepper and mushrooms in butter to make them more tender," he says. He cooks the kabobs on the grill and bastes with butter to keep them juicy.

### VENISON KABOBS

2 large green peppers, quartered
1 pound fresh mushroom caps
½ cup butter or margarine
2 pounds venison loin, cut into 1-inch cubes
2 to 3 large tomatoes, sliced
2 to 3 medium onions, sliced
Garlic salt to taste
Pepper to taste

Sauté green pepper and mushrooms in butter until crisp-tender; drain, reserving the butter.

Alternate meat and vegetables on skewers. Sprinkle with garlic salt and pepper. Grill kabobs about 6 inches over medium-hot coals 10 to 12 minutes or until done, basting with the reserved butter. Yield: 6 to 8 servings.

### GRILLED VENISON STEAKS

1 (12- to 14-pound) venison hindquarter
1 (16-ounce) bottle commercial Italian dressing
1 (2.75-ounce) package dry onion soup mix
¾ cup butter or margarine, melted
2 teaspoons pepper

Separate each muscle of the hindquarter, and cut away from bone. Slice each muscle across the grain into 1-inch-thick slices (reserve remaining meat for use in another recipe). Remove and discard the white membrane surrounding each steak.

Combine salad dressing and soup mix in a large shallow dish, stirring well; add steaks. Cover and marinate steaks in refrigerator for 1 hour, turning once.

Combine butter and pepper, stirring well; set aside. Remove steaks from marinade. Grill about 5 inches from hot coals 8 to 10 minutes on each side or until done, basting occasionally with butter mixture. Yield: 10 to 12 servings.

### COUNTRY-STYLE VENISON STEAKS

1 (12- to 14-pound) venison hindquarter
1½ cups all-purpose flour
1½ teaspoons salt
¾ teaspoon pepper
¼ cup vegetable oil
¾ teaspoon rubbed sage, divided
¾ teaspoon dried whole thyme, divided
3 medium onions, sliced and divided
4½ cups water

Separate each muscle of the hindquarter, and cut away from bone. Slice each muscle across the grain into 1-inch-thick slices (reserve remaining meat for use in another recipe). Remove and discard the white membrane surrounding each steak; set steaks aside.

Combine flour, salt, and pepper; stir well. Dredge venison in flour mixture and reserve remaining flour mixture. Brown meat on both sides in hot oil in a large Dutch oven. Remove meat from Dutch oven, and discard drippings.

Layer one-third of steaks in Dutch oven; sprinkle with ¼ teaspoon sage and ¼ teaspoon thyme. Top with one-third of onion slices. Repeat layers twice, using remaining steaks, spices, and onion.

Gradually add water to reserved flour mixture, stirring until smooth; pour over steaks. Cover and simmer 1 to 1½ hours or until tender. Yield: 10 to 12 servings.

## At a Campsite in Texas

As he leans over the smoky grill and brushes quarters of rabbit with his pungent barbecue sauce, Claude Steele, of Duncanville, Texas, describes how he combines two favorite outdoor activities—hunting and camping. "We load up the camper with my rifles and cooking supplies and head for the woods. Sometimes we're gone for days."

Claude usually hunts with five regular hunting companions in the woods and fields near Brady, Texas. They go after rabbit, venison, quail, dove, Russian boar, and antelope.

While Claude hunts mainly for the sport of it, he also enjoys campside cooking. With the help of a barbecue grill and a portable oven and stove, he can cook "just about anything." Among his specialties are Hickory Barbecued Rabbit, Venison Chili, and a venison soup, thick with potatoes, carrots, and celery.

"Preparation of game starts right in the field with the kill," says Claude. There should be a clean kill so the animal dies immediately and the internal organs are not ruptured.

The animal is cooled as soon as possible. "It should be a maximum of 40 degrees—no warmer—in order to hang the game outside," says Claude. "Otherwise, the meat must be taken to a locker plant within a few hours."

Claude usually quarters the animal and makes arrangements for it to be frozen. "First I pack it in paper and then in plastic wrap to prevent freezer burn."

The cooking method selected for the meat is determined by the age and tenderness of the animal. Rabbit is young and delicately flavored, so it's good broiled or fried. "If you cook it over a grill, be sure to use real slow coals. If you don't, the meat will dry out because it doesn't contain much fat," Claude points out. Older, less tender game is better braised, stewed, or simmered.

Game that has been killed and dressed properly shouldn't have a tainted or wild flavor. "If you're ever in doubt of how the animal was handled, you can always marinate it to help reduce any strong flavor," says Claude. He suggests using milk or wine for a marinade.

## HICKORY BARBECUED RABBIT

1½ cups catsup
1 (12-ounce) can beer
1 (8-ounce) jar salsa jalapeño
1 cup tomatoes and green chiles
1 cup red wine
½ cup butter or margarine
½ cup vinegar
¼ cup plus 3 tablespoons Worcestershire sauce
1 medium onion, chopped
1 lemon, thinly sliced
⅓ cup prepared mustard
¼ cup pepper
3 tablespoons chili powder
2 tablespoons garlic salt
1 tablespoon celery salt
1 tablespoon hot sauce
½ teaspoon salt
1 canned jalapeño pepper, seeded, rinsed, and chopped
2 rabbits, skinned and quartered

Combine all ingredients except rabbit in a large Dutch oven; stir well. Bring to a boil; reduce heat and simmer 10 minutes, stirring occasionally. Set aside to cool.

Place rabbit in a large shallow container; pour sauce over top. Let stand 3 to 4 hours.

Place 5 or 6 soaked hickory chips on slow coals. Remove rabbit from sauce, and place cavity side down on grill. Grill about 30 minutes, brushing occasionally with sauce; turn. Cook an additional 30 minutes or until done, brushing occasionally with the sauce. Yield: 8 servings.

*Tip: When using skewers, select long sturdy ones that reach completely across the grill. Place food on skewers, leaving space between each piece to allow for heat penetration and thorough basting. Unless some vegetables are parboiled, they may require a longer cooking time than meat cubes.*

## VENISON SOUP

1 pound venison, cut into bite-size pieces
1 (46-ounce) can vegetable cocktail juice
1 (28-ounce) can whole tomatoes, undrained and chopped
2 medium-size red onions, chopped
1 tablespoon Worcestershire sauce
⅛ teaspoon hot sauce
4 large potatoes, peeled and cubed
3 medium carrots, sliced
4 small yellow squash, sliced
3 to 4 stalks celery, thinly sliced
2 medium-size green peppers, cut into 1-inch pieces

Combine first 6 ingredients in an 8-quart Dutch oven; bring to a boil. Reduce to medium heat; cover and cook 30 minutes, stirring occasionally. Stir in potatoes and carrots; cover and cook for 20 minutes.

Add remaining vegetables to soup; cook, uncovered, 10 additional minutes or until vegetables are crisp-tender. Yield: 4 quarts.

## VENISON CHILI

2 pounds venison, cut into ½-inch cubes
1 pound ground beef
2 large red onions, chopped
2 (15½-ounce) cans kidney beans, undrained
3 (8-ounce) cans tomato sauce
1 (6-ounce) can tomato paste
1 cup water
3 to 4 tablespoons chili powder

Combine venison, ground beef, and onion in a Dutch oven; cook until meat is browned, stirring to crumble beef. Drain off pan drippings. Stir in remaining ingredients; cover and simmer 1½ hours or until venison is tender, adding more water as needed. Yield: about 7 cups.

# Taste Fall In Pumpkin Sweets

There's more to a pumpkin than a potential Halloween jack-o'-lantern. Inside each plump, brightly colored shell lies the beginning of such tempting sweet treats as Pumpkin Pie Supreme, Baked Pumpkin, and Frosted Pumpkin-Walnut Cookies.

Egg whites, beaten until fluffy, are folded into the pumpkin filling to make Pumpkin Pie Supreme unusually light and creamy. Baked Pumpkin makes a delicious side dish for any meal; the moist, mashed pumpkin is topped with a delicious brown sugar and maple syrup glaze.

When selecting pumpkins for cooking, remember that the biggest may not necessarily be the best; smaller pumpkins contain less water, resulting in less waste.

To prepare a fresh pumpkin for cooking, start by slicing it in half crosswise. Place the halves, cut side down, on a jellyroll pan. Bake at 325° for 45 minutes or until fork tender. When it's cool, the pumpkin can be peeled and the pulp mashed. You'll find that a 5-pound pumpkin will yield about 4½ to 5 cups of cooked, mashed pulp.

While pumpkins are harvested during the fall months, they can be stored for enjoyment in the winter. A pumpkin will keep about one month at room temperature or for two or three months if refrigerated.

## PUMPKIN CHIFFON

1¾ cups graham cracker crumbs
¼ cup sugar
½ cup butter or margarine, melted
1 (8-ounce) package cream cheese, softened
2 eggs, beaten
¾ cup sugar
2 (3¾-ounce) packages vanilla instant pudding mix
¾ cup milk
2 cups cooked, mashed pumpkin
Dash of ground cinnamon
1 (8-ounce) carton frozen whipped topping, thawed and divided
½ cup chopped pecans

Combine first 3 ingredients; press into a 13- x 9- x 2-inch baking dish. Set aside.

Combine cream cheese, eggs, and ¾ cup sugar; beat until fluffy. Spread over crust. Bake at 350° for 20 minutes; set aside to cool.

Combine pudding mix and milk; beat 2 minutes at medium speed of electric mixer. Add pumpkin and cinnamon; mix well. Stir in 1 cup whipped topping.

Spread pudding mixture over cream cheese layer. Spread remaining whipped topping over pudding layer. Sprinkle top with pecans. Store in refrigerator. Yield: about 15 servings.

*Jacqueline Dorn,*
*Leesville, South Carolina.*

## BAKED PUMPKIN

3 cups cooked, mashed pumpkin
2 eggs, beaten
½ cup pecans, chopped
2 tablespoons sugar
2 tablespoons butter or margarine, melted
½ teaspoon salt
¼ teaspoon ground mace
Dash of pepper
½ cup pecan halves
½ cup firmly packed brown sugar
¼ cup maple or maple-flavored syrup

Combine first 8 ingredients, stirring well. Pour pumpkin mixture into a lightly greased 1½-quart casserole. Arrange pecan halves on top of casserole.

Combine brown sugar and syrup in a small saucepan; cook, stirring constantly, over medium heat until mixture reaches a boil. Cool slightly. Spoon glaze evenly over casserole. Bake, uncovered, at 350° for 40 minutes. Yield: 6 servings.
*Carla C. Hunter,*
*Fort Valley, Georgia.*

## PUMPKIN PIE SUPREME

2 eggs, separated
½ cup firmly packed dark brown sugar
1¼ cups cooked, mashed pumpkin
¾ cup evaporated milk
½ teaspoon salt
½ teaspoon ground cinnamon
½ teaspoon ground nutmeg
¼ teaspoon ground ginger
1 envelope unflavored gelatin
¼ cup cold water
½ cup sugar
½ teaspoon vanilla extract
1 baked 9-inch pastry shell
1 cup whipping cream
2 tablespoons powdered sugar
Additional ground cinnamon (optional)

Beat egg yolks until thick and lemon colored. Gradually add brown sugar, beating until thick. Add pumpkin, milk, salt, ½ teaspoon cinnamon, nutmeg, and ginger, stirring well.

Pour pumpkin mixture into top of double boiler; bring water to a boil. Cook over water until mixture is thickened. Soften gelatin in cold water; add to pumpkin, stirring well. Set mixture aside to cool.

Beat egg whites (at room temperature) until foamy. Gradually add ½ cup sugar, 1 tablespoon at a time, beating until stiff peaks form. Beat in vanilla. Fold egg whites into pumpkin mixture. Pour filling into pastry shell. Chill.

Beat whipping cream until foamy; gradually add powdered sugar, beating

until soft peaks form. Spread whipped cream over filling. Garnish with cinnamon, if desired. Yield: one 9-inch pie.
*Jean Clayton,*
*Birmingham, Alabama.*

## PUMPKIN FLAN

1¼ cups sugar, divided
¼ teaspoon salt
1 teaspoon ground cinnamon
1 cup cooked, mashed pumpkin
1½ cups evaporated milk
5 eggs, beaten
⅓ cup water
1½ teaspoons vanilla extract
½ cup whipping cream
1 tablespoon sugar
¼ teaspoon grated orange rind

Sprinkle ½ cup sugar evenly in a 9-inch cast-iron skillet; place over medium heat. Caramelize sugar by stirring often until sugar melts and is light golden brown; pour immediately into a 9-inch cakepan, tipping pan quickly until the sugar is evenly spread.

Combine ¾ cup sugar, salt, and cinnamon; stir well. Add pumpkin, milk, eggs, water, and vanilla; stir until smooth. Pour over caramelized sugar; place cakepan in a larger shallow pan. Pour about 1 inch of hot water in larger pan. Bake at 350° for 1 hour or until a knife inserted near center comes out clean. Remove pan from water; chill several hours or overnight. Loosen edges with a spatula. Place serving plate upside down on top of cakepan; quickly invert flan onto serving plate.

Combine whipping cream, 1 tablespoon sugar, and orange rind; beat until stiff peaks form. Serve with flan. Yield: one 9-inch flan.
*Charlotte Ann Pierce,*
*Greensburg, Kentucky.*

## FROSTED PUMPKIN-WALNUT COOKIES

½ cup butter or margarine, softened
1½ cups firmly packed brown sugar
2 eggs
1 cup cooked, mashed pumpkin
½ teaspoon lemon extract
½ teaspoon vanilla extract
2½ cups all-purpose flour
1 tablespoon baking powder
1 teaspoon salt
2 teaspoons pumpkin pie spice
1 cup chopped walnuts
Maple Frosting

Cream butter; gradually add brown sugar, beating well. Add eggs, one at a

time, beating well after each addition. Stir in pumpkin and flavorings.

Combine flour, baking powder, salt, and pumpkin pie spice; stir well. Gradually add to creamed mixture, mixing well. Stir in walnuts.

Drop dough by teaspoonfuls onto greased cookie sheets, 2 inches apart. Bake at 375° for 12 minutes. Cool cookies on wire racks. Frost with Maple Frosting. Yield: about 7½ dozen.

*Maple Frosting:*

¼ cup butter or margarine, softened
2¼ cups sifted powdered sugar
2 tablespoons milk
¾ teaspoon maple extract

Cream butter; gradually add 1 cup powdered sugar, beating well with electric mixer. Add remaining sugar alternately with milk, beating until smooth enough to spread. Add maple extract, and beat well. Yield: enough for 7½ dozen cookies.
*Mrs. Billie Taylor,*
*Afton, Virginia.*

## PUMPKIN NUT BARS

1 cup all-purpose flour
1 cup firmly packed brown sugar
½ teaspoon baking powder
½ teaspoon baking soda
1½ teaspoons pumpkin pie spice
⅔ cup cooked, mashed pumpkin
½ cup shortening
2 eggs, beaten
1 cup chopped pecans
Powdered sugar

Combine first 5 ingredients in a large mixing bowl; add next 3 ingredients. Beat on medium speed of electric mixer 1 minute or until smooth. Stir in pecans. Pour into a greased and floured 13- x 9- x 2-inch baking pan; bake at 350° for 25 to 30 minutes or until a wooden pick inserted in center comes out clean. Cool; sprinkle with powdered sugar. Cut into bars to serve. Yield: about 2½ dozen.
*Carol Forcum,*
*Marion, Illinois.*

# Chicken Livers With A New Look

Mrs. Loren Martin of Knoxville says that most people are surprised when she tells them about Chicken Livers in Orange Sauce. Who'd think of combining the two? Mrs. Martin cooks livers with ham, onion, and several herbs before adding an orange juice sauce—it's a wonderful flavor combination.

Another way to enjoy this iron-rich meat is in Janet Scherffius' Chicken Livers Risotto. Janet stirs sautéed livers into seasoned cooked mushrooms and rice and then sprinkles Parmesan cheese on top. This dish is a favorite meal at her house—even for her son, who always shied away from livers before.

## CHICKEN LIVERS IN ORANGE SAUCE

1 pound chicken livers, cut in half
All-purpose flour
¼ cup butter or margarine
1 cup diced cooked ham
½ cup chopped onion
½ teaspoon salt
¼ teaspoon dried whole thyme
¼ teaspoon dried whole basil
¼ teaspoon dried whole tarragon
1¼ cups orange juice
1 tablespoon cornstarch
¼ teaspoon hot sauce
1 (3½-ounce) can sliced mushrooms, drained
Hot cooked noodles or rice

Dredge chicken livers in flour; brown in butter. Add ham, onion, salt, and herbs; cook about 5 minutes over medium heat or until livers are done.

Combine orange juice, cornstarch, and hot sauce; stir until smooth. Add mixture to livers and cook, stirring constantly, until sauce is smooth and thickened. Stir in mushrooms. Serve over noodles. Yield: 4 servings.
*Mrs. Loren D. Martin,*
*Knoxville, Tennessee.*

## CHICKEN LIVERS AND POTATOES

2 slices bacon, cut into 1-inch pieces
1 pound chicken livers
1 (10½-ounce) can condensed onion soup, undiluted
1 tablespoon vegetable oil
1 (16-ounce) package frozen hash brown potatoes

Fry bacon in a large, heavy skillet over low heat until crisp; remove bacon, reserving drippings in skillet. Set bacon aside to drain.

Sauté chicken livers in reserved drippings 5 minutes or until browned. Spoon livers into a shallow 1½-quart casserole, reserving drippings in skillet. Sprinkle bacon over livers, and pour onion soup over top.

Stir oil into reserved bacon drippings; add potatoes and cook until browned, turning once. Spoon potatoes over liver mixture. Bake at 375° for 30 minutes. Yield: 4 servings.
*Lilly B. Smith,*
*Richmond, Virginia.*

## CHICKEN LIVERS RISOTTO

1 pound chicken livers
2 tablespoons vegetable oil
2 tablespoons chopped onion
8 mushrooms, sliced
1 tablespoon tomato paste
1 cup uncooked regular rice
2½ cups chicken broth
1 tablespoon butter or margarine
3 tablespoons grated Parmesan cheese

Sauté chicken livers in oil 5 minutes or until browned. Remove livers and set aside, reserving drippings in skillet. Sauté onion in drippings until tender; add mushrooms, and cook 2 minutes. Stir in tomato paste and rice; cook 5 minutes over low heat.

Add broth to rice mixture and cook, covered, 20 minutes or until liquid is absorbed. Stir livers and butter into rice, cooking just until livers are thoroughly heated. Sprinkle with Parmesan cheese. Yield: 4 to 6 servings.
*Janet Scherffius,*
*Mountain Home, Arkansas.*

## CHICKEN LIVERS AND RICE DISH

1 pound chicken livers
1 pound mushrooms
3 tablespoons butter or margarine
1 cup uncooked regular rice
3 tablespoons butter or margarine
1 (10½-ounce) can beef broth, undiluted
1 (10¾-ounce) can cream of mushroom soup, undiluted
¼ cup dry sherry

Sauté chicken livers and mushrooms in 3 tablespoons butter in a large skillet 5 to 8 minutes or until livers are browned. Remove livers and mushrooms from skillet; set aside. Reserve the pan drippings in a small bowl.

Sauté rice in remaining butter until golden. Add beef broth, mushroom soup, sherry, and reserved drippings to rice; stir well. Cover and simmer 20 minutes or until liquid is absorbed. Stir livers and mushrooms into rice; cook until livers are thoroughly heated. Yield: 6 servings.
*Glyna Meredith Gallrein,*
*Anchorage, Kentucky.*

# Sweeten Bread With Persimmons

Just bite into an unripe persimmon and you'll immediately know it lacks the sweet, pleasing flavor so characteristic of the ripe fruit. A persimmon isn't ripe until it starts to shrivel; wait until after the first frost to pick persimmons, but they're usually ready to eat when they start falling off the tree. Persimmons are a delicate fruit and should be refrigerated as soon as they are ripe.

## PERSIMMON DATE-NUT BREAD

¼ cup plus 2 tablespoons butter or margarine, softened
1 cup sugar
2 eggs
1 teaspoon baking soda
1 cup persimmon pulp
2 cups all-purpose flour
1 teaspoon baking powder
½ teaspoon salt
½ teaspoon ground cinnamon
½ teaspoon ground nutmeg
½ teaspoon ground cloves
1 cup chopped pecans
1 cup chopped dates

Cream butter; gradually add sugar, beating well. Add eggs, one at a time, beating well after each addition.

Combine soda and persimmon pulp; let stand until soda is dissolved. Add to creamed mixture, blending well. Combine next 6 ingredients, stirring well; gradually add to batter. Beat well. Stir in pecans and dates. Pour into a lightly greased 9- x 5- x 3-inch loafpan. Bake at 350° for 1 hour and 20 minutes or until a wooden pick inserted in the center comes out clean. Cool in pan for 10 minutes; remove from pan, and cool on wire rack. Yield: 1 loaf.
*Mary Belle Purvis,*
*Greeneville, Tennessee.*

# MEXICAN FOOD FEST™

## Enjoy Mexican Entrées North Of The Border

From the sunny beaches of the Yucatán to the northern reaches of Sonora, the cuisine of Mexico is as rich with history as it is ingredients. A blend of Spanish, French, Italian, and native influences, it evolved over several centuries, as the staple corn diet of the Aztecs expanded to include rice, garlic, onions, and other European foods now basic to Mexican cooking. Mexico enhanced these basics with native foods and established a cuisine like no other.

Begin your Mexican dining adventure with Ceviche. Highly popular in Acapulco, it's a spicy blend of scallops, tomatoes, garlic, and oregano. Without heat, a lime juice marinade "cooks" the scallops and adds a zesty flavor. Chiles Rellenos, Pollo Con Calabacita, and Chilaquiles are some of our other offerings you'll want to try.

### BEEF SALTILLO
#### (Beef With Tomatillos)

2½ pounds boneless round steak, cut into 8 pieces
2 tablespoons vegetable oil
½ pound chorizo or other spicy sausage, sliced
1 medium onion, sliced
1 clove garlic, minced
1 (8½-ounce) can tomatillos or small green tomatoes, undrained
2 (4-ounce) cans chopped green chiles, undrained
¼ cup chopped fresh cilantro or 1 teaspoon dried cilantro
½ teaspoon salt
¼ teaspoon pepper
12 small new potatoes, peeled and halved

Brown steak on both sides in hot oil in a large skillet. Remove from skillet, and set aside. Add sausage, onion, and garlic to skillet; cook until tender. Return steak to skillet; add next 5 ingredients. Cover, reduce heat, and simmer 1 hour or until steak is tender. Add potatoes; cover and simmer 20 to 30 minutes or until potatoes are tender. Yield: 8 servings. *Kathleen D. Stone, Houston, Texas.*

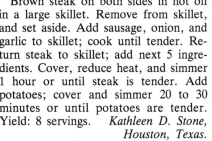

### COSTILLAS RELLENOS
#### (Stuffed Pork Chops)

2 tablespoons minced onion
¼ cup butter or margarine
1 cup fine, dry breadcrumbs
½ teaspoon salt
½ teaspoon chili powder
3 to 4 tablespoons milk
6 (1-inch-thick) pork chops, cut with pockets
Chili Butter
Lemon twists (optional)
Fresh parsley sprigs (optional)

Sauté onion in ¼ cup butter in a small saucepan over low heat until tender. Stir in next 3 ingredients. Add milk; stir until mixture is moistened.

Stuff pockets of pork chops with breadcrumb mixture, and secure with wooden picks. Place chops on broiler rack; broil 4 inches from heat, 10 minutes on each side. Baste with Chili Butter, and continue to broil an additional 5 minutes on each side. Garnish with lemon twists and parsley, if desired. Yield: 6 servings.

*Chili Butter:*

¼ cup butter or margarine, melted
2 tablespoons lemon juice
1 tablespoon minced fresh parsley
1 small clove garlic, minced
1 teaspoon chili powder
½ teaspoon salt

Combine all ingredients; stir well. Yield: about ⅓ cup. *Mrs. Fred Best, Naples, Texas.*

### POLLO CON CALABACITA
#### (Mexican Chicken With Zucchini)

1 (2½- to 3-pound) broiler-fryer, cut up
Vegetable oil
1 large zucchini or 1 small calabaza, cubed
1 tablespoon chopped onion
1 tablespoon chopped green pepper
1 clove garlic, minced
3 tablespoons all-purpose flour
1 teaspoon salt
1 teaspoon pepper
½ teaspoon ground cumin
3 cups water

Brown chicken in hot oil in a large skillet. Combine next 8 ingredients; toss gently. Spoon vegetable mixture over chicken, and add water. Bring mixture to a boil. Reduce heat; simmer, uncovered, 40 to 45 minutes or until chicken is tender and sauce is slightly thickened, stirring often. Yield: 4 servings.
*Rachel Perez, Brownfield, Texas.*

*Tip: Always try to match pan size with the burner. A pan that is smaller in diameter than its accompanying burner will allow heat to escape.*

# MEXICAN FOOD FEST

## CEVICHE
### (Marinated Raw Fish)

1 pound scallops
1½ cups lime juice or lemon juice
1 clove garlic, crushed
2 large tomatoes, chopped
1 to 2 jalapeño peppers, minced
3 tablespoons olive oil
½ teaspoon salt
½ teaspoon dried whole oregano
¼ teaspoon freshly ground pepper
4 to 5 medium avocados, halved, peeled,
　　and seeded
Lettuce leaves
Lemon half (optional)
Lemon and lime wedges (optional)
Fresh parsley sprigs (optional)

Place scallops in a glass or earthenware bowl (do not use metal). Add lime juice and garlic; stir gently. Cover and refrigerate 6 hours or overnight. Drain scallops, and place them in a large bowl.

Combine next 6 ingredients; stir into scallops. Cover and refrigerate 2 hours. Spoon scallop mixture into avocado halves; place avocado halves on lettuce leaves. Garnish with lemon half, lemon and lime wedges, and parsley, if desired. Yield: 4 to 5 servings.

## CHILAQUILES

2 medium onions, chopped
1 clove garlic, minced
2 tablespoons vegetable oil
2 (28-ounce) cans whole tomatoes,
　　undrained
2 (4-ounce) cans whole green chiles,
　　drained and cut into strips
½ teaspoon ground cumin
¼ teaspoon salt
¼ teaspoon pepper
1 (8-ounce) package corn tortillas
Vegetable oil
4 cups (16 ounces) shredded Monterey
　　Jack cheese
1 (8-ounce) carton commercial sour cream
　　(optional)

Sauté onion and garlic in hot oil in a Dutch oven until tender. Stir in next 5 ingredients; cover and simmer 20 minutes. Remove from heat.

Cut tortillas into fourths; fry in ¼ inch hot oil about 5 seconds on each side or until softened. Drain well on paper towels.

Layer half each of tortillas, tomato mixture, and cheese in a lightly greased 13- x 9- x 2-inch baking dish; repeat layers. Bake at 350° for 20 to 25 minutes. Serve with sour cream, if desired. Yield: 8 to 10 servings.
*Mrs. A. C. Crysler,*
*El Paso, Texas.*

## CHILES RELLENOS
### (Stuffed Chiles)

3 (4-ounce) cans whole green chiles,
　　drained
1 (8-ounce) package Monterey Jack
　　cheese, cut lengthwise into 9 strips
½ cup all-purpose flour
⅛ teaspoon salt
⅛ teaspoon pepper
3 eggs, separated
3 tablespoons all-purpose flour
Vegetable oil
1 jalapeño pepper, sliced and seeded
　　(optional)
Green Chile Sauce

Slit each chile lengthwise, and remove seeds; stuff each with a strip of cheese. Combine ½ cup flour, salt, and pepper; dredge each stuffed chile in flour mixture. Set aside.

Beat egg whites (at room temperature) in a large mixing bowl until stiff peaks form. Beat egg yolks until thick and lemon colored; gently fold yolks and 3 tablespoons flour into beaten egg whites.

Dip each floured chile in egg batter, and fry in deep hot oil (400°) for 2 to 3 minutes or until golden brown, turning once. Drain well on paper towels. Garnish with pepper slices, if desired. Serve with Green Chile Sauce. Yield: about 4 servings.

*Green Chile Sauce:*

½ pound ground beef
1 teaspoon chopped onion
1 small clove garlic, minced
2 cups water
¼ teaspoon Worcestershire sauce
2 (4-ounce) cans chopped green chiles,
　　undrained
⅛ teaspoon salt
⅛ teaspoon pepper
1½ tablespoons cornstarch

Combine beef, onion, and garlic in a large skillet, stirring to crumble beef. Cook until beef is browned and onion is tender. Drain off drippings. Stir in 2 cups water, Worcestershire sauce, chopped green chiles, salt, and pepper; cook over medium heat 10 minutes, stirring occasionally.

Add 3 tablespoons of hot mixture to cornstarch, stirring to make a paste; gradually add to sauce in skillet. Stir constantly until mixture thickens. Yield: 2½ cups sauce.
*C. C. Kibbe,*
*Diana, Texas.*

Right: *Seafood Paella (page 245) is a gourmet's delight. Chicken, shrimp, and soft-shelled clams are nestled in a savory bed of rice and surrounded with a ring of English peas and pimiento.*

Page 222: *A specialty of Acapulco, Mexico, Ceviche (page 220) is a zesty dish of scallops marinated in lime juice and garlic, then tossed with tomatoes and jalapeño peppers and served in avocado halves.*

# MEXICAN FOOD FEST

## End The Fiesta With One Of These Desserts

Desserts may not immediately come to mind when Mexican food is mentioned, but they are a truly heavenly part of the country's cuisine.

### MEXICAN FIESTA CONFECTION

1 (11-ounce) package piecrust sticks, crumbled
½ cup cocoa
¼ cup sugar
¼ cup plus 2 tablespoons hot water
3 ounces sweet baking chocolate
2 tablespoons butter or margarine
1 egg
1 cup sifted powdered sugar
1 teaspoon ground cinnamon
¼ teaspoon salt
1 teaspoon vanilla extract
1 cup whipping cream
Additional whipped cream
Chocolate curls

Combine first 3 ingredients; mix well. Sprinkle water evenly over cocoa mixture; work with a pastry blender, or process in food processor until all ingredients are moistened. Divide pastry into fourths. Press each portion onto the bottom of an inverted 8-inch square pan or 9-inch round pan to within ¼ inch of edge. Bake at 425° for 4 minutes. (Do not overbake. Layers will be soft until cooled.) Lift layers carefully, and transfer to wire racks to cool.

Combine baking chocolate and butter in top of a double boiler; bring water to a boil. Reduce heat to low; cook until chocolate melts. Beat egg well. Gradually stir about one-fourth of hot chocolate mixture into egg; add to remaining hot mixture, stirring constantly. Add powdered sugar, cinnamon, and salt; beat 1 minute at high speed of electric mixer. Remove from heat.

Fill bottom of double boiler with ice and water; set top in place. Beat chocolate mixture 1 minute or until slightly cool. Add vanilla, beating well. Slowly add whipping cream, beating until soft peaks form, about 5 minutes.

Spread chocolate mixture between pastry layers and over top. Chill overnight. Garnish dessert with whipped cream and chocolate curls. Yield: 8 to 10 servings. *Mrs. P. H. Czarowitz, Temple, Texas.*

### PUMPKIN EMPANADAS

1 (16-ounce) can pumpkin
¾ cup sugar
1 teaspoon ground allspice
4 cups all-purpose flour
½ cup sugar
1 tablespoon plus 1 teaspoon baking powder
1 teaspoon salt
1⅓ cups shortening
1 cup milk
Milk
1 egg white, beaten
¼ cup sugar
½ teaspoon ground cinnamon

Combine pumpkin, ¾ cup sugar, and allspice; stir well, and set aside.

Combine flour, ½ cup sugar, baking powder, and salt; cut in shortening with pastry blender until mixture resembles coarse meal. Sprinkle 1 cup milk evenly over surface; stir with a fork until all dry ingredients are moistened. Shape into a ball; chill. Roll out to ⅛-inch thickness; cut into 4-inch circles.

Place about 1 tablespoon pumpkin mixture in center of each circle. Moisten edges with additional milk; fold in half, and press edges together with a fork. Brush empanadas with egg white; place on ungreased baking sheets, and bake at 450° for 8 to 10 minutes or until golden. Combine ¼ cup sugar and cinnamon; sprinkle over empanadas while still warm. Yield: about 1½ dozen.
*Mrs. Mack C. Ivy, Alta Loma, Texas.*

### FRUIT IN TEQUILA

1 cup whipping cream
2 tablespoons powdered sugar
3 tablespoons butter or margarine
2 tablespoons sugar
2 fresh peaches, sliced or 1 (16-ounce) can sliced peaches, drained
2 fresh mangoes, cut into chunks or 2 (8-ounce) cans mangoes, drained and cut into chunks
2 cups fresh pineapple chunks or 1 (13¼-ounce) can pineapple chunks, drained
⅓ cup tequila
2 tablespoons Triple Sec or other orange-flavored liqueur
3 kiwi fruit, peeled and sliced crosswise
1 cup fresh strawberries, sliced in half lengthwise
3 tablespoons sliced almonds, toasted

Beat whipping cream until foamy; gradually add powdered sugar, beating until soft peaks form. Chill.

Melt butter in a large skillet; stir in sugar. Add peaches, mangoes, and pineapple; cook over medium heat for 2 minutes, spooning syrup over the fruit occasionally. Add tequila and Triple Sec, and continue to cook 1 minute. Add kiwi fruit and strawberries; toss gently.

Spoon fruit and syrup into individual serving dishes. Top each with a dollop of whipped cream, and sprinkle with almonds. Yield: 6 to 8 servings.

*Tip: If only drained fruit is called for in a recipe, use quarters and halves rather than the more costly whole fruit.*

# Main Dishes That Say Cheese

Cheese can liven up even the simplest ingredients, turning them into delicious and satisfying main dishes. Take Cheesy Lasagna, for example; cream cheese, cottage cheese, and mozzarella lend this pasta dish a creamy texture while providing lots of protein, calcium, and vitamin A. Chile Pepper Quiche is another tasty dish that combines Cheddar with Monterey Jack.

Once cut, ripened cheese should be wrapped tightly in plastic wrap or aluminum foil to keep it moist and fresh tasting. If surface molding occurs, simply cut off the molded area; the remaining cheese will be safe to eat. Soft, unripened varieties such as ricotta, cream cheese, and cottage cheese should be tightly covered and used soon after being purchased.

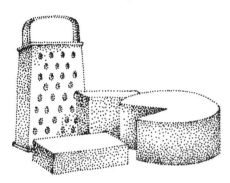

## CHEESY LASAGNA

1 pound ground beef
1 medium onion, chopped
1 medium-size green pepper, chopped
2 (8-ounce) cans tomato sauce
1 teaspoon Italian seasoning
½ teaspoon crushed fennel seeds
½ teaspoon garlic powder
½ teaspoon pepper
1½ teaspoons dried parsley flakes
1 (8-ounce) package lasagna noodles
1 (12-ounce) carton cottage cheese
1 (8-ounce) carton commercial sour cream
1 (3-ounce) package cream cheese, softened
4 cups (16 ounces) shredded mozzarella cheese

Combine beef, onion, and green pepper in a large skillet; cook until meat is browned, stirring to crumble meat. Drain off drippings. Add next 6 ingredients; simmer, uncovered, for 20 minutes, stirring occasionally.

Cook lasagna noodles according to package directions, omitting salt; drain.

Combine cottage cheese, sour cream, and cream cheese; mix well. Spread about ½ cup of meat sauce in a greased 13- x 9- x 2-inch baking dish. Layer half each of the noodles, cottage cheese mixture, meat sauce, and mozzarella cheese. Repeat layers. Bake at 350° for 30 minutes; let stand 10 minutes before serving. Yield: 6 to 8 servings.

*Joan B. Piercy,*
*Memphis, Tennessee.*

## CHEESY MEXICAN CASSEROLE

1½ pounds ground beef
2 medium onions, chopped
1 clove garlic, minced
1 (16-ounce) can whole tomatoes, undrained and chopped
1 (10-ounce) can tomatoes with green chiles, undrained
½ teaspoon salt
1 (4-ounce) can chopped green chiles, drained
1 dozen corn tortillas
Vegetable oil
4 cups (16 ounces) shredded Cheddar cheese
1 (8-ounce) carton commercial sour cream (optional)

Combine ground beef, onion, and garlic in a large skillet; cook until meat is browned, stirring to crumble meat. Drain off drippings. Add tomatoes and salt; reduce heat and simmer, uncovered, 25 to 30 minutes. Stir in chiles.

Fry tortillas, one at a time, in ¼ inch of hot oil; cook about 5 seconds on each side or just until softened. Drain tortillas well on paper towels. Cut each tortilla into quarters, and then set aside.

Layer half each of the tortillas, meat mixture, and cheese in a greased 13- x 9- x 2-inch baking dish; repeat layers. Bake at 350° for 10 to 15 minutes or until cheese melts. Serve with sour cream, if desired. Yield: 6 servings.

*Mrs. Karl Koenig,*
*Dallas, Texas.*

## BIRDS OF PARADISE

3 whole chicken breasts, skinned and boned
1 egg
1 tablespoon milk
¾ cup grated Parmesan cheese
¼ cup butter or margarine
¾ cup dry white wine

Cut chicken into 1½-inch pieces, and set aside.

Combine egg and milk in a bowl; mix well. Dip chicken pieces in egg mixture, and dredge in grated Parmesan cheese, coating well.

Melt butter in a nonstick electric skillet. Add chicken, and cook until lightly browned on each side. Sprinkle remaining cheese over chicken. Add wine; cover, reduce heat, and simmer 35 minutes. Remove cover, and simmer 10 additional minutes or until liquid is reduced. Yield: 6 servings.

*Teresa Sands,*
*Columbia, South Carolina.*

## CHILE PEPPER QUICHE

Pastry for 9-inch pie
1 cup (4 ounces) shredded Cheddar cheese
1½ cups (6 ounces) shredded Monterey Jack cheese, divided
1 (4-ounce) can chopped green chiles, drained
3 eggs
1 cup half-and-half

Line a 9-inch quiche dish or pieplate with pastry; trim excess pastry around edges. Prick bottom and sides of pastry with a fork. Bake at 400° for 3 minutes; remove from oven, and gently prick with a fork. Bake 5 minutes longer. Let cool on rack.

Layer Cheddar cheese, ¾ cup Monterey Jack cheese, chiles, and remaining Monterey Jack cheese in pastry shell.

Beat eggs until foamy; stir in half-and-half. Pour mixture into pastry shell; bake at 350° for 1 hour or until set. Yield: one 9-inch pie. *Carolyn Morris,*
*Baton Rouge, Louisiana.*

## DOUBLE CHEESE MACARONI

1 cup elbow macaroni
¼ cup butter or margarine
1½ cups cubed cooked ham
1½ cups milk
1 cup soft breadcrumbs
1 cup (4 ounces) shredded Cheddar cheese
½ cup (2 ounces) shredded Swiss cheese
3 eggs, beaten
1 tablespoon dried minced onion
1 tablespoon chopped fresh parsley
¼ teaspoon salt
¼ teaspoon pepper
Paprika

Cook macaroni in a large saucepan according to package directions; drain. Add butter; stir until melted. Stir in remaining ingredients except paprika. Pour into a lightly greased 2-quart shallow casserole; sprinkle paprika lightly over top. Bake at 350° for 40 minutes. Yield: 6 to 8 servings.

*Martha M. Dooley,*
*Chattanooga, Tennessee.*

## FRESH VEGETABLE CASSEROLE

3 stalks celery, cut into 2-inch pieces
2 small onions, quartered
1 cup water
8 small new potatoes, peeled
8 baby carrots, scraped
1 small head cauliflower, broken into flowerets
1 cup English peas
1 cup baby lima beans
¼ cup butter or margarine
¼ cup all-purpose flour
2 cups milk
1 teaspoon salt
2 cups (8 ounces) shredded Cheddar cheese
1 tablespoon grated Parmesan cheese
1 tablespoon chopped fresh parsley

Place celery and onion in 1 cup water; bring to a boil. Reduce heat and simmer, uncovered, 30 minutes. Strain liquid, reserving ¼ cup. Discard celery and onion.

Place next 5 ingredients in a Dutch oven. Cover with water, and bring to a boil. Cover, reduce heat, and simmer 10 minutes; drain. Arrange vegetables in a lightly greased 12- x 8- x 2-inch baking dish; set aside.

Melt butter in a heavy saucepan over low heat; add flour, stirring until smooth. Cook 1 minute, stirring constantly. Gradually add milk; cook over medium heat, stirring constantly, until thickened and bubbly. Stir in salt, Cheddar cheese, and reserved vegetable broth. Pour over vegetables; bake at 350° for 30 minutes. Sprinkle Parmesan cheese and parsley over top. Yield: 8 to 10 servings.
*DeLois Gates,*
*Blue Springs, Mississippi.*

*Tip: A special topping for cooked vegetables or casseroles can be made by crushing ½ cup herb-seasoned stuffing mix with 2 tablespoons melted butter or margarine; top dish with this mixture and sprinkle with 1 cup shredded cheese.*

# He Specializes In Smoked Pork

Whenever his busy schedule allows, Hal Tyler of Richmond pulls the smoker out of storage and fires up the coals. He starts by making a big pot of tangy barbecue sauce to add to the water pan during cooking. And when the Smoked Pork Shoulder is done, Hal reheats the sauce to spoon over slices of the meat on buns. His recipe makes plenty of sauce—even when Hal expects a large crowd for supper and smokes two roasts at a time.

Hal doesn't stop with just the meat; he takes care of the entire meal. Soon after starting the smoker, he slices lots of different vegetables for Vegetables Vinaigrette—a simple but delicious salad to go with the smoked pork. And like many barbecue lovers, Hal likes to spoon coleslaw atop the pork as a sandwich relish.

Following Hal's recipes are a selection of favored dishes from other men who have a flair for cooking.

## SMOKED PORK SHOULDER

2 cups catsup
2 cups vinegar
1 cup butter or margarine
1 (5-ounce) bottle Worcestershire sauce
1 tablespoon brown sugar
1 tablespoon dried onion flakes
1 tablespoon salt
1 tablespoon hot sauce
2 small cloves garlic, minced
⅛ teaspoon red pepper
⅛ teaspoon pepper
1 (6- to 8-pound) pork shoulder roast
Hamburger buns (optional)

Combine first 11 ingredients in a large saucepan, and bring to a boil; reduce heat, and simmer 10 minutes. Set aside.

Prepare charcoal fire in smoker, and let burn 10 to 15 minutes. Place water pan in smoker; fill with ¼ cup sauce and about 2 quarts water. Mix an additional ¼ cup sauce and 2 quarts water; set aside.

Trim skin from roast. Place roast on food rack, and baste generously on all sides with sauce.

Cover with smoker lid; cook 9 to 11 hours or until desired doneness, refilling water pan with prepared water-and-sauce mixture as needed. To serve,

thinly slice roast and heat remaining sauce. Serve on buns, if desired. Yield: 10 to 12 servings.

*Note:* Remaining sauce may be refrigerated and reheated for basting grilled chicken or other meats.

## OLD-FASHIONED COLESLAW

1⅓ cups evaporated milk
¼ cup sugar
¾ teaspoon salt
½ teaspoon pepper
¼ cup plus 2 tablespoons vinegar
6 cups finely shredded cabbage

Combine first 4 ingredients; mix well. Gradually add vinegar, stirring constantly; cover and chill at least 1 hour.

Pour dressing over cabbage; mix well. Cover and chill at least 1 hour. Serve with pork on buns or as a salad. Yield: 6 to 8 servings.

## VEGETABLES VINAIGRETTE

1 cup olive oil
⅓ cup white wine vinegar
2 cloves garlic, minced
2 teaspoons dried whole oregano
1 teaspoon salt
½ teaspoon pepper
½ teaspoon dry mustard
2 medium zucchini, sliced
2 medium-size yellow squash, sliced
2 medium cucumbers, sliced
4 medium tomatoes, sliced
2 large onions, sliced

Combine first 7 ingredients in a jar; shake well. Layer half of each vegetable in a large bowl in the order given; repeat layers with remaining vegetables. Pour marinade over vegetables, and refrigerate at least 2 hours before serving. Yield: 10 servings.

■ Allan A. Pollock of Hendersonville, North Carolina, enjoys making and eating this delightful dessert that looks like a pie and tastes like a cake.

## APPLE PIE CAKE

¼ cup butter or margarine, softened
1 cup sugar
2 eggs
1 cup all-purpose flour
1 teaspoon baking soda
¼ teaspoon salt
1 teaspoon ground cinnamon
½ teaspoon ground nutmeg
3 tablespoons orange juice
1 teaspoon vanilla extract
2½ cups peeled, finely chopped apples
½ cup raisins
Whipped cream (optional)

Cream butter; gradually add sugar, beating well. Add eggs; mix well.

Combine next 5 ingredients; add to creamed mixture alternately with orange juice, beginning and ending with the flour mixture. Stir in vanilla. Fold in apples and raisins.

Pour batter into a greased and floured 9-inch pieplate. Bake at 350° for 45 minutes or until a wooden pick inserted in center comes out clean. Cut cake into wedges; serve with whipped cream, if desired. Yield: one 9-inch pie.
*Allan A. Pollock,*
*Hendersonville, North Carolina.*

■ Many folks shy away from making doughnuts because they seem so complicated, but Ralph Monin of Elizabethtown, Kentucky, has shared one of the easiest and tastiest recipes we've seen.

## QUICK CAKE DOUGHNUTS

¼ cup butter or margarine, softened
1 cup sugar
1 egg
1 teaspoon baking soda
1 cup buttermilk
4 cups all-purpose flour
1 teaspoon baking powder
Vegetable oil
2 cups sifted powdered sugar
2 tablespoons milk

Cream butter; gradually add sugar, beating well. Add egg; beat well.

Dissolve soda in buttermilk. Combine flour and baking powder; add to creamed mixture alternately with buttermilk mixture, beginning and ending with the flour mixture.

Divide the dough in half. Working with one portion at a time, place dough on a floured surface; roll out to ¼-inch thickness. Cut dough with a floured doughnut cutter.

Heat 3 to 4 inches of oil to 375°; drop in 3 or 4 doughnuts at a time. Cook about 1 minute or until golden brown on one side; turn and cook other side about 1 minute. Drain on paper towels.

Combine powdered sugar and milk, beating well; drizzle over warm doughnuts. Yield: about 2½ dozen.

*Note:* Doughnuts may be sprinkled with a cinnamon-sugar mixture or powdered sugar instead of the powered-sugar glaze.
*Ralph Monin,*
*Elizabethtown, Kentucky.*

■ For a hearty gumbo, Joel Allard of San Marcos, Texas, simmers cubes of round steak with okra, tomato, green pepper, and onion.

## TEXAS RANCH-STYLE GUMBO

2½ pounds boneless round steak
¼ cup all-purpose flour
1 teaspoon dried whole thyme
½ teaspoon salt
¼ teaspoon pepper
3 tablespoons butter or margarine
3 tablespoons vegetable oil
¾ cup chopped green onion
1 large green pepper, chopped
1 (10-ounce) package frozen cut okra
3 large tomatoes, chopped
1 bay leaf
½ teaspoon hot sauce
2 cups chicken broth
6 cups hot cooked rice

Trim excess fat from steak; cut into 1-inch cubes.

Combine flour, thyme, salt, and pepper; dredge meat in flour mixture. Heat butter and oil in Dutch oven; add meat, and cook until browned on all sides. Remove meat, reserving drippings in Dutch oven. Add onion and green pepper to reserved drippings; sauté until tender. Stir in meat and remaining ingredients except rice. Cover and simmer 1½ hours. Remove bay leaf before serving. Serve over rice. Yield: 8 to 10 servings.
*Joe Allard,*
*San Marcos, Texas.*

*Tip: Shop alone and after you have eaten. Studies show that people tend to buy more when hungry or when accompanied by others.*

■ Before baking a venison roast, Jack Morrow of Porterdale, Georgia, marinates the meat overnight.

## VENISON ROAST

1 cup water
1 cup vinegar
2 teaspoons salt
⅛ teaspoon pepper
1 cup dry red wine, divided
2 cloves garlic
1 (3- to 5-pound) venison roast
10 to 12 slices bacon
2 tablespoons all-purpose flour
2 cups water

Combine 1 cup water, vinegar, salt, pepper, ¾ cup wine, and garlic; pour over roast, and marinate overnight in refrigerator.

Drain roast, and place in a shallow roasting pan. Cover top of roast with bacon slices. Place aluminum foil over pan, and fold under to seal edges. Bake at 550° for 7 minutes. Reduce heat to 350°; bake for 1½ hours, basting every 10 minutes with pan drippings.

Place flour in a skillet over medium heat; cook, stirring constantly, until lightly browned. Let cool. Combine ½ cup pan drippings, 2 cups water, and remaining ¼ cup wine; stir well. Slowly add drippings mixture to flour; cook over medium heat, stirring constantly, until smooth. Serve gravy with roast. Yield: 8 to 10 servings. *Jack Morrow,*
*Porterdale, Georgia.*

# Desserts That Melt In Your Mouth

These four chilled desserts will get a warm welcome at your next dinner party. They range from sinfully rich Brownie-Mint Dessert to easily prepared Frosty Fruit Medley.

## FROSTY FRUIT MEDLEY

1 (10-ounce) package frozen mixed fruit, thawed
2 bananas, sliced
¼ cup commercial sour cream
2 tablespoons brown sugar

Combine mixed fruit and bananas; mix gently. Cover and chill. To serve, spoon fruit mixture into individual serving dishes. Top each with sour cream, and sprinkle with brown sugar. Yield: 4 servings. *Mrs. H. C. Quesenberry, Dugspur, Virginia.*

## BERRIES ON SNOW

2 cups graham cracker crumbs
½ cup butter or margarine, softened
3 tablespoons powdered sugar
1 (2.5-ounce) package whipped topping mix
1 cup sugar
1 cup cold milk
1 teaspoon vanilla extract
1 (8-ounce) package cream cheese, softened
1 (3-ounce) package cream cheese, softened
1 (21-ounce) can blueberry or cherry pie filling

Combine graham cracker crumbs, butter, and powdered sugar; mix well. Press into bottom and ½ inch up sides of a 13- x 9- x 2-inch baking pan. Bake at 350° for 5 minutes. Cool.

Combine whipped topping mix, sugar, milk, and vanilla in a large mixing bowl. Beat until soft peaks form (about 2 minutes). Gradually add cream cheese, beating until smooth and well blended. Spread over crust; chill 30 minutes.

Spread pie filling evenly over cream cheese layer, and chill several hours or overnight. Store in refrigerator. Yield: about 15 servings. *Eva Crockett Carter, Rose Hill, Virginia.*

## LEMON DELIGHT

½ cup butter or margarine
1 cup all-purpose flour
¾ cup chopped pecans or walnuts, divided
1 (8-ounce) package cream cheese, softened
1 cup sifted powdered sugar
3 cups frozen whipped topping, thawed and divided
2 (3¾-ounce) packages lemon instant pudding and pie filling
3 cups milk

Cut butter into flour until mixture resembles coarse meal; stir ½ cup pecans into flour mixture. Press pecan mixture into a 13- x 9- x 2-inch baking pan. Bake at 350° for 15 minutes.

Combine cream cheese and powdered sugar; beat until fluffy. Fold 1 cup

whipped topping into cream cheese mixture. Spread over crust; chill.

Combine pudding mix and milk; beat 2 minutes at low speed of electric mixer. Spread pudding over cream cheese layer. Spread remaining whipped topping over pudding layer. Sprinkle with remaining pecans. Chill thoroughly. Store in refrigerator. Yield: about 15 servings. *Mrs. Guy Williams, Greenville, South Carolina.*

## BROWNIE-MINT DESSERT

3 egg whites
¾ cup sugar
¾ cup chocolate wafer crumbs
½ cup chopped walnuts or pecans
½ teaspoon vanilla extract
1 cup whipping cream
2 tablespoons powdered sugar
¼ cup crushed soft peppermint stick candy
Chocolate curls (optional)
Grated chocolate (optional)

Beat egg whites (at room temperature) until foamy. Gradually add sugar, 1 tablespoonful at a time, beating until mixture is glossy. Fold in crumbs, walnuts, and vanilla. Spread mixture into a buttered 8-inch square dish. Bake at 325° for 30 minutes. Cool completely.

Beat whipping cream until foamy; gradually add powdered sugar, beating until soft peaks form. Fold in peppermint; spread over prepared layer. Garnish with chocolate curls and grated chocolate, if desired. Cover and chill at least 3 hours. Cut into squares to serve. Store in refrigerator. Yield: 9 servings.
*Mrs. Lake A. Anderson, Old Fort, North Carolina.*

# Here's Why Southerners Love Sweet Potatoes

Like most Southerners, Sally Pedigo of Dallas loves sweet potatoes. But instead of preparing them the usual way, candied or in a casserole, she cuts them in half and fills them with apples and cinnamon. Sally says her Sweet Potatoes Stuffed With Apples tastes great with baked ham.

Stuffed is just one way to enjoy sweet potatoes. Try them baked with apricots or mashed and baked into a cake. And one of the best things about this delicious vegetable is the storehouse of vitamin A, vitamin C, and other nutrients hidden underneath the skin.

## SWEET POTATO LOG ROLL

3 eggs
1 cup sugar
¾ cup cooked, mashed sweet potatoes
1 teaspoon lemon juice
¾ cup all-purpose flour
1 teaspoon baking powder
2 teaspoons ground cinnamon
½ teaspoon ground cloves
¼ teaspoon ground ginger
¼ teaspoon salt
1 cup chopped pecans
Powdered sugar
Filling (recipe follows)

Grease and flour bottom and sides of a 15- x 10- x 1-inch jellyroll pan; line bottom of pan with waxed paper.

Beat eggs at high speed of electric mixer until thick and lemon colored (about 5 minutes); gradually add sugar, beating 5 additional minutes. Continue beating, and gradually add sweet potatoes and lemon juice.

Combine next 6 ingredients, and stir into sweet potato mixture. Pour batter into prepared pan, spreading evenly. Sprinkle with pecans. Bake at 375° for 12 to 15 minutes or until a wooden pick inserted in center comes out clean.

Sift powdered sugar in a 15- x 10-inch rectangle on a linen towel. When cake is done, immediately loosen from sides of pan, and turn out on sugar. Peel off waxed paper. Starting at narrow end, roll up cake and towel together; cool on a wire rack, seam side down.

Unroll cake, and remove towel. Spread cake with filling and reroll. Chill. Yield: 8 to 10 servings.

*Filling:*

¼ cup butter or margarine, softened
½ (8-ounce) package cream cheese, softened
1 cup sifted powdered sugar
½ teaspoon vanilla extract
¼ teaspoon butter flavoring
Pinch of salt

Combine butter and cream cheese, beating until light and fluffy. Add powdered sugar, flavorings, and salt; beat until smooth. Yield: enough filling for one log roll. *Nancy J. Mareau, Church Point, Louisiana.*

## APRICOT SWEET POTATOES

1 (6-ounce) package dried apricots
2 cups hot water
6 medium-size sweet potatoes
1 cup firmly packed brown sugar
3 tablespoons butter or margarine, melted
1 teaspoon grated orange rind
2 teaspoons orange juice
1 cup pecan halves

Combine apricots and hot water in a saucepan; let stand 1 hour. Cover and cook over low heat 15 to 20 minutes or until tender. Remove from heat; drain, reserving ¼ cup liquid.

Cook sweet potatoes in boiling water 20 to 25 minutes or until tender. Let cool to touch; peel and cut into ½-inch slices.

Layer half the sweet potatoes, apricots, and brown sugar in a lightly greased 13- x 9- x 2-inch baking dish; repeat layers.

Combine reserved apricot liquid and next 3 ingredients, mixing well; pour over layers in casserole. Cover and bake at 375° for 40 minutes. Top with pecans; bake 5 additional minutes. Yield: about 10 servings.
*Ann M. Klein,*
*Savannah, Georgia.*

## SWEET POTATOES STUFFED WITH APPLES

4 medium-size sweet potatoes
3 cups peeled, sliced apples
¼ cup butter or margarine
½ cup sugar
1 teaspoon ground cinnamon

Scrub sweet potatoes thoroughly; bake at 425° for 1 hour or until done.

Allow potatoes to cool to touch. Cut in half lengthwise; carefully scoop out sweet potato pulp, leaving ¼ inch of shells intact. Mash pulp.

Sauté apples in butter until tender. Combine sweet potato pulp, apples, sugar, and cinnamon; stir well. Stuff shells with potato mixture. Place in a 13- x 9- x 2-inch baking dish; bake at 425° for 25 minutes or until well heated. Yield: 8 servings.
*Sally Pedigo,*
*Dallas, Texas.*

*Tip: Wash most vegetables; trim any wilted parts or excess leaves before storing in crisper compartment of refrigerator. Keep potatoes and onions in a cool, dark place with plenty of air circulation to prevent sprouting.*

## Cooking Light

# Season Light With Herbs And Spices

Preparing low-calorie, salt-free meals is routine for Amy Shuman of Frostburg, Maryland. She knows that it's smart to cut back on the sugar, salt, and fat in her family's diet. You might think that food cooked without salt and the usual fattening seasonings tastes bland, but Amy has learned to liven up her meals with low-calorie, low-sodium herbs and spices. Chili Surprise is one of her favorites—it's a nutritious, meatless chili seasoned with chili powder and several herbs that are salt free.

Herbs and spices can open up a new world of flavors for your light cooking. Start with basic seasonings and become familiar with their strength and flavor. Basil, bay, curry, dill, ginger, marjoram, mint, mustard, oregano, rosemary, sage, thyme, and turmeric are strong herbs. Use these alone as accent flavors in food, or combine them carefully with milder seasonings. Delicately flavored herbs, such as parsley, chervil, and chives, can easily be used with stronger flavors.

Use finely chopped fresh herbs when possible, and when you do, use three times more than you would of the more potent dried form. Dried whole herbs are usually the next best choice since they maintain their strength longer than the commercially ground form. When possible, crush or grind the dried herbs to release flavor; grate your own nutmeg and peppercorns with a nutmeg grater or pepper mill.

You can purchase vanilla, a popular flavoring for sweets, in the whole bean form as well as in the less expensive extract with alcohol and water. When used in low-calorie desserts, vanilla extract helps make up for the decreased amount of sugar. Try adding a few drops of extract to a cup of unsweetened hot tea to bring out the flavor.

While the major role of herbs and spices is to enhance food's natural flavor, many also add visual interest. Chop parsley or chives for an attractive addition to rice; or sprinkle on orange-colored turmeric for an interesting change of pace. Toss strips of bright-red pimiento with vegetable salads or cooked pasta to liven up a family meal.

Poppy seeds and sesame seeds can also dress up diet food while adding a nutlike taste. Use poppy seeds to season cooked noodles. Sesame seeds, also known as benne seeds to Southerners, are good in stir-fries and vegetables. But don't use either of the seeds liberally if you're counting calories—both have about 15 calories per teaspoon.

If you're cutting back on salt, be sure to look for hidden sources of sodium on the spice rack. Some seasoning blends such as onion salt, garlic salt, celery salt, and lemon-pepper seasoning contain large amounts of sodium, as do MSG (monosodium glutamate), meat tenderizers, bouillon cubes and granules, and prepared horseradish.

Discover how other dieters have used herbs and spices in these recipes, which are low in both calories and sodium. See how several seasonings are combined in Chili Surprise and White Wine Stew, and how cinnamon is used effectively in Spiced Fruit Delight. Use your food processor to blend freshly grated horseradish with tart apples for Apple-Horseradish Sauce; add a sprinkle of fennel seeds, and you've got a delicious sauce for your pork or poultry entrées.

## WHITE WINE STEW

2¼ pounds lean boneless round steak, trimmed and cut into 1-inch cubes
Vegetable cooking spray
2 large onions, diced
1 large green pepper, cut into 1-inch pieces
1 pound carrots, scraped and cut into 1-inch pieces
3 stalks celery, cut into 1-inch pieces
2 cups light Chablis
2 cups water
1 teaspoon dried whole rosemary
1 teaspoon dried whole basil
1 teaspoon dried whole thyme
Freshly ground pepper to taste
2 tablespoons cornstarch
¼ cup cold water
Minced fresh parsley (optional)

Sauté cubed round steak in a Dutch oven sprayed with cooking spray. Add onion and pepper; cook, stirring often, until vegetables are tender. Add next 8 ingredients; bring to a boil. Cover and simmer stew 1 hour and 15 minutes.

Combine cornstarch and ¼ cup cold water, mixing well; stir into stew. Cook over medium-high heat, stirring constantly, until thickened and bubbly. Garnish with parsley, if desired. Yield: 8 servings (about 295 calories and 213 milligrams sodium per 1-cup serving).
*Eleanor N. McDowell,*
*West Chester, Pennsylvania.*

## HERB-BAKED CHICKEN

1 teaspoon dried whole rosemary, crushed
¼ teaspoon pepper
1 (3-pound) broiler-fryer, cut up and skinned
½ cup unsweetened pineapple juice
¼ teaspoon ground ginger
5 shallots, minced
Paprika

Rub rosemary and pepper into the chicken; arrange, meaty side up, in a 9-inch baking dish. Combine pineapple juice and ginger; pour over chicken. Sprinkle with shallots and paprika.

Cover and bake at 350° for 30 minutes; remove cover, and bake 25 to 30 minutes or until done. Yield: 4 servings (about 217 calories and 87 milligrams sodium per serving). *Doris Garton, Shenandoah, Virginia.*

■ Chili powder normally contains salt; but a salt-free version is available in some specialty stores.

## CHILI SURPRISE

1 cup dried kidney beans
1 cup dried pinto beans
½ cup dried black beans
5 stalks celery and leaves, chopped
1 large carrot, shredded
3 large tomatoes, peeled and cubed
1 large green pepper, chopped
1 medium onion, chopped
½ cup raisins
2 cloves garlic, minced
2 bay leaves
2 tablespoons chili powder
¼ cup plus 2 tablespoons fresh minced parsley
1 teaspoon dried whole dillweed
1 teaspoon dried whole basil
1 teaspoon dried whole oregano
1 teaspoon ground cumin
1 teaspoon ground allspice
¼ teaspoon freshly ground pepper
¼ teaspoon hot sauce
½ cup unsalted dry roasted cashews
¼ cup unsalted sunflower kernels
Beans sprouts (optional)

Sort and wash beans; place in a large Dutch oven. Cover with water 2 inches above beans; let soak overnight. Drain beans; cover with water. Cover and bring to a boil; reduce heat, and simmer for 1 hour.

Add the next 17 ingredients; simmer 30 minutes or until beans are tender and chili is thickened. (Add more water if necessary.) Remove and discard bay leaves. Stir in cashews and sunflower kernels. Serve topped with beans sprouts, if desired. Yield: 10 servings (about 259 calories and 137 milligrams sodium per 1-cup serving).
*Amy Shuman, Frostburg, Maryland.*

## CHIVE-POTATO BAKE

3 medium-size baking potatoes, thinly sliced
1 tablespoon minced chives
2 to 3 tablespoons minced fresh parsley
½ teaspoon freshly ground pepper
¼ teaspoon paprika

Layer one-third of potatoes in a 13- x 9- x 2-inch pan; sprinkle with one-third of chives, parsley, pepper, and paprika. Repeat layers until remaining ingredients are used.

Cover with foil, and bake at 400° for 45 minutes or until done. Yield: 6 servings (about 46 calories and 6 milligrams sodium per serving).

## DILLED CUCUMBER SALAD

2 medium cucumbers, thinly sliced
1 medium onion, sliced
⅓ cup vinegar
½ teaspoon dried whole dillweed
⅛ teaspoon pepper

Combine cucumbers and onion in a shallow dish. Combine remaining ingredients, and pour over cucumbers. Cover and refrigerate at least 1 hour. Yield: 4 servings (about 25 calories and 11 milligrams sodium per serving).

## SPICED FRUIT DELIGHT

4 cups unsweetened apple juice
2 to 3 (3-inch) sticks cinnamon
2 tablespoons lemon juice
2 apples, cored and cut into thin wedges
2 peaches, peeled and cut into thin wedges
2 pears, cored and cut into thin wedges
¼ pound cherries, pitted
2 cups fresh strawberries, hulled

Combine apple juice and cinnamon in a saucepan; bring to a boil. Boil 10 minutes. Cool. Add lemon juice and all fruit except strawberries. Chill. Stir in strawberries just before serving. Yield: 8 servings (about 103 calories and 3 milligrams sodium per serving).

## APPLE-HORSERADISH SAUCE

¼ small onion, cubed
½ stalk celery, cut into 1-inch pieces
1½ pounds tart apples, pared, cored, and cubed
2 tablespoons unsweetened orange juice
1 tablespoon freshly grated horseradish
¼ teaspoon fennel seeds, crushed

Position knife blade in food processor bowl; add onion and celery. Process until vegetables are finely chopped. Add apple, orange juice, and horseradish to bowl; process at high speed until mixture is almost smooth (scrape bowl during chopping if necessary). Stir in fennel seeds. Refrigerate several hours. Serve sauce with poultry or pork. Yield: 2 cups (about 12 calories and 4 milligrams sodium per tablespoon).

# Our Eggplant Will Surprise You

Most people serve eggplant as part of a meal, but Mrs. William T. Hunter of Princeton, Kentucky, offers her fried Jackstraw Eggplant as a snack. "My family eats it like potato chips," she confides, "and we prefer eggplant because it's a nourishing snack."

In Forest, Mississippi, Grace Russell is equally inventive with this versatile vegetable. She places ham and cheese between two slices of eggplant; then she coats and bakes the stacks into tender sandwiches that are eaten with a fork.

## EGGPLANT A LA MEXICANO

4 small onions, coarsely chopped
2 green peppers, coarsely chopped
3 tablespoons bacon drippings
1 medium eggplant, cubed
4 medium tomatoes, cubed
1 teaspoon salt
2 teaspoons chili powder
2 tablespoons all-purpose flour

Sauté onion and green pepper in bacon drippings in a large skillet. Add next 4 ingredients; cover and cook over medium heat 10 to 12 minutes. Stir in flour and cook, uncovered, for 2 minutes. Yield: 8 to 10 servings.
*Mrs. Lee Underwood, Spring Branch, Texas.*

## EGGPLANT PARMESAN

1 large eggplant
Salt
2 eggs, beaten
1½ cups cracker crumbs
Vegetable oil
Quick Italian Sauce
2 cups (8 ounces) shredded mozzarella
    cheese
¼ cup plus 2 tablespoons grated Parmesan
    cheese
Hot cooked vermicelli (optional)

Peel eggplant, and cut into ¼-inch slices. Sprinkle each slice with salt, and place in a bowl. Let stand 30 minutes; drain well. Dip each slice in egg, and coat with cracker crumbs. Fry in hot oil until golden brown. Drain on paper towels.

Place half the eggplant in a lightly greased 12- x 8- x 2-inch baking dish; spread half the Quick Italian Sauce over slices. Top with half the mozzarella cheese and half the Parmesan cheese; repeat layers. Bake at 350° for 20 to 25 minutes or until mixture is thoroughly heated. Serve over vermicelli, if desired. Yield: 6 servings.

*Quick Italian Sauce:*

½ cup chopped onion
1 clove garlic, minced
1 tablespoon vegetable oil
1 (12-ounce) can tomato paste
1 (7¾-ounce) can tomato soup, undiluted
1¼ cups water
1½ teaspoons dried whole oregano
½ teaspoon ground basil

Sauté onion and garlic in hot oil until tender. Stir in remaining ingredients. Bring to a boil; reduce heat and simmer 15 minutes, stirring occasionally. Yield: about 4 cups.    *Brett Van Dorsten,*
*Arcadia, California.*


## EGGPLANT AND NOODLE CASSEROLE

1 medium eggplant, peeled and sliced ½
    inch thick
3 tablespoons butter or margarine, melted
1 (5-ounce) package wide egg noodles,
    cooked
1 (8-ounce) carton commercial sour cream
1 (15-ounce) jar spaghetti sauce
2 cups (8 ounces) shredded mozzarella
    cheese

Brush each side of eggplant slices with butter; broil 4 inches from heat 3 to 4 minutes on each side.
Combine noodles and sour cream; spoon into a greased 13- x 9- x 2-inch baking dish. Arrange eggplant slices on noodles; cover with spaghetti sauce. Bake at 350° for 25 minutes or until bubbly. Sprinkle with cheese, and bake 5 minutes longer. Yield: 6 to 8 servings.
*Robbin Dorrier,*
*Charlotte, North Carolina.*


## STUFFED EGGPLANT CREOLE

2 small eggplant
4 slices bacon, cut into small pieces
¼ cup chopped onion
¼ cup chopped green pepper
½ cup sliced fresh mushrooms
2 cups peeled, chopped tomato
¼ teaspoon salt
⅛ teaspoon pepper
1 cup (4 ounces) shredded mozzarella
    cheese

Wash eggplant, and cut in half lengthwise. Remove pulp, leaving a ¼-inch shell; set shells aside. Chop the pulp, and set aside.
Combine bacon, onion, green pepper, and mushrooms in a large skillet; sauté until bacon is cooked. Add eggplant pulp, tomato, salt, and pepper; bring to a boil. Reduce heat, and simmer 10 minutes, stirring occasionally.
Place eggplant shells in a 10- x 6- x 2-inch baking dish. Spoon hot mixture into shells; add water to ½-inch depth. Bake at 350° for 25 minutes. Sprinkle cheese on top; bake an additional 5 minutes. Yield: 4 servings.
*Norma Edsill,*
*Aplington, Iowa.*


## JACKSTRAW EGGPLANT

1 medium eggplant
1 cup all-purpose flour
1 cup ice water
1 egg, beaten
2 tablespoons vegetable oil
½ teaspoon sugar
½ teaspoon salt
All-purpose flour
Vegetable oil
Grated Parmesan cheese

Peel eggplant, and cut into finger-size strips. Combine 1 cup flour, water, egg, 2 tablespoons vegetable oil, sugar, and salt; mix well. Dredge strips in additional flour; then dip in batter.
Fry strips in hot oil (375°) until golden brown; drain on paper towels. Sprinkle with Parmesan cheese. Serve hot. Yield: 4 to 6 servings.
*Mrs. William T. Hunter,*
*Princeton, Kentucky.*


## BAKED EGGPLANT SANDWICHES

1 large eggplant, peeled and cut into 12
    slices
1 teaspoon salt
1 cup fine, dry breadcrumbs
¼ cup grated Romano cheese
¼ cup chopped fresh parsley
¼ cup extra thick spaghetti sauce
6 slices thin cooked ham
6 slices Swiss cheese
2 eggs, beaten

Sprinkle eggplant slices with salt; set aside 1 hour. Rinse and gently pat dry.
Combine the breadcrumbs, Romano cheese, and parsley; stir well. Spread spaghetti sauce evenly on one side of each eggplant slice. On 6 eggplant slices, arrange a slice of ham and Swiss cheese over spaghetti sauce, folding ham and cheese as needed to fit. Cover with remaining eggplant slices, sauce side down.
Dip each sandwich into the beaten egg, and coat on all sides with breadcrumb mixture. Place in a lightly greased 13- x 9- x 2-inch baking pan. Cover and bake at 350° for 45 minutes. Yield: 6 sandwiches.    *Grace Russell,*
*Forest, Mississippi.*


# Try These Dressed-Up Breakfast Dishes

Bacon and eggs, ham and eggs, waffles—just what you'd expect for breakfast. But the surprise comes when you look over these recipes.

Eggs and bacon get a different twist with our Breakfast Eye-Openers. The eggs are baked in a cheese sauce, placed on toasted English muffins, then sprinkled with crumbled bacon.

Instead of serving scrambled eggs and a slice of ham, chop up the ham, mix it with seasonings, and stuff the mixture into hard-cooked egg halves for Savory Ham and Eggs. After stuffing, the eggs are baked in a light cream sauce and topped with Cheddar cheese.

Waffles get new flair with Southern Chicken-Pecan Waffles from Marijke Lee of Springfield, Virginia. She mixes cooked chicken in a sauce seasoned with wine and lemon juice and studded with mushrooms and pecans, then serves it all over hot waffles. "It's my favorite brunch recipe," she says.

## SOUTHERN CHICKEN-PECAN WAFFLES

¼ cup butter or margarine
1 tablespoon chicken-flavored bouillon granules
⅓ cup all-purpose flour
2 cups milk
½ cup white wine
1 tablespoon lemon juice
¼ teaspoon poultry seasoning
2 cups chopped cooked chicken
½ cup diced celery
2 tablespoons chopped pimiento
1 (6-ounce) can sliced mushrooms, drained
½ cup chopped pecans, divided
6 waffles

Melt butter in a heavy saucepan over low heat; add bouillon granules, and stir until blended. Add flour; cook 1 minute, stirring constantly. Gradually add milk to flour mixture; cook over medium heat, stirring constantly, until smooth. Reduce heat; stir in wine and lemon juice. Cook, stirring constantly, until thickened.

Stir in next 6 ingredients, reserving 2 tablespoons pecans. Cook, stirring constantly, until thoroughly heated.

Serve sauce over waffles; top with reserved pecans. Yield: 6 servings.
*Marijke A. Lee,*
*Springfield, Virginia.*

## SAVORY HAM AND EGGS

8 hard-cooked eggs
¼ cup butter or margarine, melted
½ teaspoon Worcestershire sauce
¼ teaspoon prepared mustard
1 tablespoon grated onion
⅓ cup chopped cooked ham
¼ teaspoon chopped fresh parsley
1 chicken-flavored bouillon cube
1 cup boiling water
3 tablespoons butter or margarine
¼ cup all-purpose flour
¾ cup half-and-half
¼ teaspoon paprika
⅛ teaspoon pepper
1 cup (4 ounces) shredded Cheddar cheese

Slice eggs in half lengthwise, and carefully remove yolks. Mash yolks, and add next 6 ingredients; mix well. Stuff whites with mixture; arrange eggs in a 12- x 8- x 2-inch baking dish. Set aside.

Dissolve bouillon cube in boiling water; set aside. Melt 3 tablespoons butter in a heavy saucepan over low heat; add flour, stirring until smooth. Cook 1 minute, stirring constantly. Gradually add bouillon and half-and-half; cook over medium heat, stirring

constantly, until thickened and bubbly. Stir in seasonings.

Pour sauce over eggs; sprinkle cheese on top. Cover with foil, and bake at 325° for 25 minutes. Yield: 6 to 8 servings.
*Edith M. VeuCasovic,*
*Bexar, Arkansas.*

## BREAKFAST EYE-OPENERS

3 slices bacon
1 cup coarsely chopped onion
1 (10¾-ounce) can cream of chicken soup, undiluted
⅓ cup milk
½ teaspoon prepared mustard
½ cup (2 ounces) shredded sharp Cheddar cheese
4 eggs
2 English muffins, split, toasted, and buttered

Cook bacon in a large skillet until crisp; remove bacon, reserving 2 tablespoons drippings in skillet. Crumble bacon and set aside.

Sauté onion in reserved drippings until tender. Add next 3 ingredients, stirring constantly until thoroughly heated. Add cheese, and stir until cheese melts.

Spoon two-thirds of sauce into an 8-inch square baking dish. Make 4 indentations in sauce; break an egg into each. Spoon remaining sauce around eggs; sprinkle with reserved bacon. Bake at 350° for 20 to 25 minutes or until eggs are set.

Top muffin halves with sauce and eggs. Serve immediately. Yield: 2 to 4 servings.
*Wynn Montgomery,*
*Atlanta, Georgia.*

# Soups And Stews Warm Autumn

Whether it's flavored with meat or vegetables, a steaming bowl of soup or stew seems especially right on a brisk autumn day. We've put together a collection of soup and stew recipes that we think are especially tempting.

Cream of Artichoke Soup is an excellent choice for an appetizer. Its rich yet delicate flavor whets the appetite for the meal to come. Our tasty and satisfying Lentil-Rice Stew makes a nutritious meatless main dish; only a salad and bread are needed to complete the meal.

## MEXICAN STEW

3 pounds lean boneless beef, cut into 1-inch cubes
½ cup chopped onion
3 tablespoons bacon drippings
1 (28-ounce) can whole tomatoes, undrained and chopped
1 (4-ounce) can whole green chiles, drained
½ cup beef broth
½ cup chicken broth
2 teaspoons garlic salt
2 teaspoons pepper
1 teaspoon ground cumin
3 to 4 potatoes, sliced

Brown beef and onion in bacon drippings in a Dutch oven. Add next 7 ingredients, and bring to a boil. Cover and reduce heat; simmer 1 hour. Add potatoes; cover and simmer 30 minutes or until potatoes are tender. Yield: about 3½ quarts. *Mrs. Ronny Bumpus,*
*Lampasas, Texas.*

## SMOKED SAUSAGE STEW

1 (17-ounce) can tiny English peas
1¼ pounds smoked sausage, cut into ½-inch slices
1 (16-ounce) can onion soup, undiluted
1 (16-ounce) can whole tomatoes, undrained
2 cups peeled, cubed potatoes
½ teaspoon Worcestershire sauce
¼ cup all-purpose flour

Drain peas, reserving ½ cup liquid; set both aside.

Cook sausage until browned in a Dutch oven; drain. Add next 4 ingredients and peas. Bring mixture to a boil; reduce heat and simmer, uncovered, 20 minutes or until potatoes are tender.

Stir reserved pea liquid into flour; gradually add to sausage mixture. Cook over medium heat, stirring constantly, until thickened and bubbly. Yield: about 2½ quarts. *Marie Elrod,*
*Warner Robins, Georgia.*

## LENTIL-RICE STEW

¾ cup chopped onion
¾ cup chopped celery
2 tablespoons butter or margarine
6 cups water
¾ cup dried lentils, washed and sorted
2 (16-ounce) cans whole tomatoes,
    undrained and chopped
¾ cup uncooked brown rice
1½ teaspoons garlic salt
½ teaspoon dried whole basil
½ teaspoon dried whole oregano
¼ teaspoon pepper
½ cup shredded carrots

Sauté onion and celery in butter in a Dutch oven until tender; add water and lentils. Bring mixture to a boil; cover, reduce heat, and simmer 20 minutes.

Stir in next 6 ingredients. Cover and simmer 1 hour or until rice is done. Add carrots; cook an additional 5 minutes. Yield: about 2 quarts.

*Jill Heatwole,*
*Dayton, Virginia.*

## CREAM OF ARTICHOKE SOUP

1 medium carrot, finely chopped
1 stalk celery, finely chopped
½ cup chopped green onion
2 tablespoons butter or margarine
4 cups chicken broth
1 bay leaf
Pinch of dried whole thyme
1 (8½-ounce) can artichoke hearts,
    drained and sliced
2 egg yolks
1 cup whipping cream

Sauté carrot, celery, and onion in butter in a heavy saucepan until onion is tender. Add broth, bay leaf, and thyme; cook over low heat 15 minutes, stirring often. Add artichoke hearts; cook an additional 10 minutes, stirring often.

Beat egg yolks until thick and lemon colored. Gradually stir about one-fourth of hot mixture into yolks; add to remaining hot mixture, stirring constantly. Add the whipping cream, and cook over low heat, stirring constantly, until thoroughly heated. Remove bay leaf and serve immediately. Yield: about 5 cups. *Mrs. Bernie Benigno,*
*Gulfport, Mississippi.*

*Tip: If soup or stew is too heavily salted, drop in a peeled, raw potato and cook for a few minutes. Remove the potato and taste the difference.*

# Salads For Chilly Days

Enjoy salads in the fall as much as in the summer. Make them substantial with hearty ingredients like meat, beans, and potatoes.

Hawaiian Ham-Sweet Potato Salad pairs two fall favorites in an unusual fashion: Ham and sweet potatoes are tossed with pineapple, onion, and green pepper. A generous topping of toasted almonds adds flavor and crunch.

A great make-ahead dish, Macaroni-Salmon Salad includes Cheddar cheese and pimiento-stuffed olives and is tossed with a spicy garlic dressing.

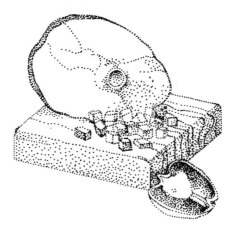

## HAWAIIAN HAM-SWEET POTATO SALAD

4 medium-size sweet potatoes
1 (15¼-ounce) can pineapple chunks
2 cups diced cooked ham
1 small onion, minced
1 medium-size green pepper, chopped
½ cup mayonnaise
1 teaspoon curry powder
¼ teaspoon paprika
Lettuce leaves
½ cup slivered almonds, toasted

Cook sweet potatoes in boiling water 20 to 25 minutes or until tender; drain. Let cool to touch; peel and cut into ¼-inch slices. Set aside.

Drain pineapple, reserving 2 tablespoons juice. Combine pineapple, ham, onion, and green pepper.

Combine mayonnaise, reserved pineapple juice, curry powder, and paprika; mix well.

Line a large salad bowl with lettuce leaves. Arrange sweet potato slices over lettuce. Place ham mixture over potatoes; top with mayonnaise mixture. Sprinkle with almonds; cover and chill. Yield: 6 servings. *Lisa Varner,*
*Fairborn, Ohio.*

## MEAL-IN-ONE SALAD

3 medium potatoes
1 medium head lettuce, torn
1 (17-ounce) can English peas, drained
3 medium tomatoes, coarsely chopped
1 (6½-ounce) can tuna, drained and
    flaked
2 avocados, peeled, seeded, and chopped
½ cup chopped green onion
3 hard-cooked eggs, sliced
Paprika
¾ cup vegetable oil
½ cup pickle relish
¼ cup vinegar
1 clove garlic, minced
½ teaspoon salt
½ teaspoon sugar
Dash of pepper

Cook potatoes in boiling salted water about 30 minutes or until tender; drain. Let cool to touch; peel and cut potatoes into bite-size pieces.

Combine the potatoes and next 6 ingredients in a large salad bowl; toss gently. Arrange hard-cooked eggs on top, and sprinkle lightly with paprika. Set salad aside.

Combine remaining ingredients in a small bowl; mix well. Serve with salad. Yield: 8 to 10 servings.

*Evelyn Weisman,*
*Kingsville, Texas.*

## MACARONI-SALMON SALAD

1 (8-ounce) package elbow macaroni
1 (15½-ounce) can pink salmon, drained
    and flaked
1 cup (4 ounces) shredded Cheddar
    cheese
⅓ cup chopped green pepper
¼ cup finely chopped onion
¼ cup sliced pimiento-stuffed olives
2 tablespoons chopped fresh parsley
¾ cup vegetable oil
¼ cup vinegar
1 teaspoon garlic salt
1 teaspoon sugar
1 teaspoon dry mustard
1 teaspoon paprika
⅛ teaspoon pepper

Cook macaroni according to package directions; drain. Rinse with cold water, and drain.

Combine macaroni and next 6 ingredients in a large salad bowl; toss gently. Combine remaining ingredients in a jar; screw lid tight and shake until mixed well. Pour over macaroni mixture; toss gently. Cover and chill 1 to 2 hours. Yield: 6 servings. *Irene A. Murry,*
*Herculaneum, Missouri.*

## HEARTY RICE SALAD

¼ pound smoked sausage, cut into ¼-inch
    slices
2 cups cooked regular rice, cooled
1 medium-size green pepper, chopped
⅔ cup chopped purple onion
1 (15½-ounce) can kidney beans, rinsed
    and drained
⅓ cup vinegar
¼ cup vegetable oil
¼ teaspoon garlic salt
½ teaspoon pepper
Leaf lettuce (optional)
Purple onion rings (optional)

Cook sausage in a skillet until browned; drain well on paper towels. Combine sausage and next 8 ingredients in a large bowl, mixing well; cover and chill. Serve on leaf lettuce, and garnish with onion rings, if desired. Yield: 6 servings.

*Monisa Wright,*
*Shawmut, Alabama.*

# Meatballs With Lots Of Flavor

If you're looking for a new way to serve ground beef, try meatballs for a change. These recipes offer a delicious array of flavor combinations.

Oven Barbecued Meatballs boast a favorite Southern flavor; they're baked in a barbecue sauce seasoned with celery seeds, then mounded on a bed of hot noodles. And cheese lovers will favor Golden Nugget Meatballs—each is filled with melted Cheddar cheese.

Our Sweet-and-Sour Meatballs simmer in a tangy pineapple sauce with carrot, onion, green pepper, and pineapple. Enjoy this hearty entrée served over a bed of rice.

## OVEN BARBECUED MEATBALLS

1½ pounds ground beef
1 cup soft breadcrumbs
½ cup chopped onion
⅓ cup milk
1 egg, beaten
1 teaspoon salt
½ teaspoon Worcestershire sauce
⅛ teaspoon pepper
2 tablespoons all-purpose flour
1 teaspoon paprika
1 tablespoon vegetable oil
Oven Barbecue Sauce
Hot cooked noodles

Combine first 8 ingredients, mixing well. Shape mixture into 1½-inch meatballs. Combine flour and paprika; dredge meatballs in flour mixture. Brown in oil over medium heat in a large skillet. Remove meatballs from skillet, and drain on paper towels.

Place meatballs in a lightly greased shallow 2-quart casserole. Pour Oven Barbecue Sauce over meatballs. Cover and bake at 350° for 45 minutes. Serve over noodles. Yield: 6 to 8 servings.

*Oven Barbecue Sauce:*

¾ cup catsup
¾ cup water
¼ cup chopped onion
3 tablespoons vinegar
1 tablespoon Worcestershire sauce
1 tablespoon sugar
½ teaspoon celery seeds

Combine all ingredients, stirring well; bring to a boil. Yield: about 2 cups.

*Mrs. Joe D. Wilson,*
*Radford, Virginia.*

## SWEET-AND-SOUR MEATBALLS

1 (8-ounce) can pineapple chunks
¾ pound lean ground beef
3 tablespoons minced green onion
1 egg, beaten
¼ teaspoon salt
¼ teaspoon ground ginger
2 tablespoons soy sauce
2 tablespoons vegetable oil
1 small green pepper, cut into thin strips
1 cup cooked sliced carrots
¼ cup sliced water chestnuts
1½ tablespoons vinegar
2 tablespoons soy sauce
1 tablespoon cornstarch
1½ tablespoons sugar
Hot cooked rice

Drain pineapple, reserving juice. Set both aside.

Combine next 6 ingredients, mixing well. Shape mixture into 1½-inch meatballs; brown in oil over medium heat in a large skillet. Remove meatballs from skillet, and drain on paper towels.

Add green pepper to pan drippings; sauté 2 minutes. Add pineapple, carrots, and water chestnuts; sauté 3 minutes. Remove mixture from skillet, and set aside with meatballs.

Combine reserved pineapple juice, vinegar, and 2 tablespoons soy sauce in a measuring cup. Add enough water to make 1 cup liquid. Dissolve cornstarch and sugar in a small amount of vinegar mixture; stir into remaining liquid. Add cornstarch mixture to skillet; cook over medium heat, stirring constantly, until sauce is smooth and thickened. Add meatballs and vegetables to sauce; simmer 5 minutes or until well heated. Serve over rice. Yield: 3 to 4 servings.

*Mrs. Lawrence Starkey, Jr.,*
*Charles City, Virginia.*

## MEATBALLS CREOLE

1 pound ground beef
½ cup regular oats, uncooked
½ cup tomato sauce
½ teaspoon garlic salt
¼ teaspoon salt
¼ cup all-purpose flour
2 tablespoons vegetable oil
¾ cup water
½ cup tomato sauce
½ cup chili sauce
2 small onions, chopped
Hot cooked rice

Combine first 5 ingredients, mixing well. Shape mixture into 1¼-inch meatballs; dredge in flour. Brown in oil over medium heat in a large skillet; drain off drippings. Combine remaining ingredients except rice; mix well, and pour over meatballs. Simmer 20 minutes, stirring occasionally. Serve over hot cooked rice. Yield: 4 servings.

*Mrs. N. C. O. Houston,*
*Tuscaloosa, Alabama.*

## GOLDEN NUGGET MEATBALLS

1½ pounds ground beef
1½ cups soft breadcrumbs
⅓ cup chopped green pepper
⅓ cup catsup
2 eggs, beaten
½ teaspoon garlic salt
¼ teaspoon dry mustard
⅛ teaspoon pepper
4 ounces sharp Cheddar cheese, cut into
    16 cubes
¼ cup all-purpose flour
3 tablespoons bacon drippings
2 (8-ounce) cans tomato sauce

Combine first 8 ingredients, mixing well. Shape mixture around each cheese cube, molding to make 16 meatballs; dredge in flour. Brown in bacon drippings over medium heat in a large skillet; pour off drippings, draining well.

Pour tomato sauce over meatballs in skillet; cover and simmer 20 minutes. Remove cover, and simmer 5 minutes or until sauce thickens. Yield: 6 servings.

*Norma Cowden,*
*Shawnee, Oklahoma.*

## Team These Flavors From The Sea

Diana McConnell of Arlington, Texas, has a great idea for fish fillets—she spreads sole or flounder with a mixture of shrimp, onion, garlic, and breadcrumbs. The fillets are simply rolled up and baked. Served with Blender Hollandaise Sauce, her Shrimp-Stuffed Rollups are a delightful way to enjoy a taste of the sea.

### SHRIMP-STUFFED ROLLUPS

2 cups water
14 to 16 fresh or frozen medium shrimp
1 small onion, minced
1 clove garlic, crushed
¼ cup plus 2 tablespoons butter or margarine, melted and divided
¼ cup soft breadcrumbs
1 tablespoon chopped fresh parsley
½ teaspoon salt
⅛ teaspoon pepper
6 to 8 sole or flounder fillets (about 1½ pounds)
Blender Hollandaise Sauce

Bring water to a boil; add shrimp, and return to a boil. Reduce heat and simmer, uncovered, 3 to 5 minutes. Drain well, and rinse shrimp in cold water; peel and devein. Chop 8 shrimp; set aside. Reserve remaining shrimp for garnish.

Sauté onion and garlic in 2 tablespoons butter until onion is tender. Add chopped shrimp, breadcrumbs, parsley, salt, and pepper; mix well, and remove from heat. Divide shrimp mixture evenly to spread over fillets. Roll up each fillet, and secure with a wooden pick.

Pour half of remaining butter into a 10- x 6- x 2-inch baking dish. Arrange fillets in baking dish; brush with remaining butter. Bake at 350° for 25 to 30 minutes or until fish flakes easily when tested with a fork. Remove fillets to serving dish. Top with Blender Hollandaise Sauce, and garnish with remaining shrimp. Yield: 6 servings.

*Blender Hollandaise Sauce:*

3 egg yolks
2 tablespoons lemon juice
Dash of salt
Dash of red pepper
½ cup butter or margarine, melted

Combine first 4 ingredients in container of an electric blender; set on high speed, and process until mixture is thick and lemon colored.

Turn blender to low speed; add butter to yolk mixture in a slow, steady stream. Turn blender to high speed, and process until thick. Yield: about ¾ cup.
*Diana McConnell,*
*Arlington, Texas.*

## From Our Kitchen To Yours

With holiday baking just around the corner, this is a good time to brush up on your piecrust-making skills.

### Making Perfect Piecrust

**Equipment:** Start with standard measuring cups and spoons so you'll be sure the ingredients are in the correct proportions. Too much flour will mean a tough crust; too much water, and it will be soggy and sticky; too much shortening makes the crust greasy and crumbly.

Cutting the shortening into the dry ingredients is a snap with a pastry blender, or you can use two knives. Some cooks prefer combining shortening and dry ingredients with their fingers; however, body heat can cause the shortening to get too soft, and the dough will need to be chilled to firm up the shortening.

For rolling out the piecrust, use any surface the dough won't stick to once you add a little flour. A stockinette covering on the rolling pin will help reduce the flour needed to prevent sticking.

To ensure good browning, use non-shiny pieplates, such as ovenproof glass, dull metal, or enamel. Shiny metal pans reflect heat, keeping the pastry from baking properly. And always use the size pieplate specified in the recipe. Standard sizes are 8, 9, and 10 inches in diameter, with a depth of 1¼ inches.

**Mixing:** The most critical preliminary step is to chill the shortening. Your goal is to work the chilled shortening into the dry ingredients so quickly that it doesn't have time to soften. It's the melting of the shortening during baking that pushes up the flour to create layers and layers of flaky pastry.

Combine the flour and salt in a mixing bowl, and cut in the chilled shortening until the mixture resembles coarse meal. Then sprinkle ice water, 1 tablespoonful at a time, over the flour mixture; stir with a fork only enough to moisten the dry ingredients. Don't overwork the dough; the more you handle it, the more gluten will develop, toughening the pastry.

Form the dough into a ball, cover with plastic wrap, and chill at least an hour (or overnight). Chilling makes the dough easier to handle, minimizes shrinkage during baking, and promotes tenderness.

**Rolling:** Lightly dust the rolling surface with flour, and place the chilled dough on it; flatten the dough with the side of your hand. Carefully roll the dough from the center out to the edges; do not roll back and forth across the dough, as this will stretch it. Roll to ⅛-inch thickness and 2 inches larger in diameter than the pieplate. Fold the dough in half; place the folded edge in the center of the pieplate, and unfold. Be careful not to pull at the dough, as this will also stretch it.

**Finishing:** Trim the edges of the dough, leaving about ½-inch overhang (kitchen shears or scissors are easier to use than a knife). Fold the overhanging dough under, pressing firmly against pieplate edge to seal; flute as desired.

When your recipe calls for a baked pastry shell, liberally prick the bottom and sides of the dough with a fork before baking; otherwise, the pastry will puff up and lose its shape. Instead of pricking, you can line the shell with aluminum foil and fill it with dried beans or pastry weights. Remove the beans or weights before crust is done to allow even baking.

Do not prick a piecrust to be filled before baking; just fill, and bake as directed. To keep the crust from getting soggy from juicy fillings, try brushing it with a slightly beaten egg white before filling.

**Variations:** For a *double-crust pie,* line the pieplate with half of pastry, following the procedure for a single crust; then add the filling. Trim off the overhanging edges. Roll remaining pastry about 1 inch larger than the pieplate; either prick it with a fork, or fold it in half and make decorative slits (when unfolded, the halves will be identical). These openings are necessary to allow steam to escape during baking. Moisten the edge of the bottom pastry with water; fit the top over the filling. Trim edge of top pastry so there's a ½-inch overhang, and fold the overhang under edge of bottom pastry, pressing firmly to seal; then flute and bake.

For a quick *lattice-topped pie,* roll and fit bottom pastry as you would for a double crust, but leave a 1-inch overhang around edge. Roll out remaining pastry, and cut into ½-inch strips (use a pastry wheel for a pretty finish). Moisten the edge of the bottom pastry with water; then lay half of strips across the filling, spacing them about ¾ inch apart; press ends of strips to bottom pastry. Repeat with remaining strips, arranging them in the opposite direction. (For a more decorative look, you may want to weave the strips or twist them.) Trim ends of strips even with 1-inch overhang; turn overhang over ends of strips, pressing firmly; flute as desired.

Both a double-crust and lattice-topped pie can be given a shiny surface by brushing the pastry with milk before baking; for a glazed look, use a beaten egg white mixed with a little water.

## Try These Shredded Carrot Favorites

Like every cook, Carol Keith has a favorite recipe for carrot salad. She tosses shredded carrots with canned pineapple, mandarin oranges, raisins, and coconut. But unlike most carrot salads, Carrot-Fruit Toss calls for sour cream as the flavorful dressing.

Another shredded carrot specialty is Claire Bastable's Easy Carrot Snack Cake, full of carrots, chopped pecans, and raisins. Cut the spicy, moist cake into squares for a delicious afternoon snack.

### EASY CARROT SNACK CAKE

1¼ cups all-purpose flour
1 cup sugar
1½ teaspoons baking powder
1 teaspoon salt
2 teaspoons ground cinnamon
¼ cup vegetable oil
2 eggs
2 teaspoons vanilla extract
1 cup shredded carrots
1 cup chopped pecans
½ cup raisins
Powdered sugar (optional)

Combine first 8 ingredients in a large mixing bowl; beat 1 minute at low speed of an electric mixer. Beat 2 minutes at medium speed of an electric mixer. Stir carrots, pecans, and raisins into batter.

Spoon batter into a lightly greased 8-inch square baking pan. Bake at 325°

for 40 minutes or until a wooden pick inserted in center comes out clean. Sprinkle cake with powdered sugar, if desired. Yield: 9 servings.

*Claire Bastable,*
*Chevy Chase, Maryland.*

### CARROT-FRUIT TOSS

2 cups shredded carrot
1 (15¼-ounce) can pineapple chunks, drained
1 (11-ounce) can mandarin oranges, drained
1 cup flaked coconut
½ cup raisins
1 (8-ounce) carton commercial sour cream
Lettuce leaves

Combine first 5 ingredients in a medium bowl; stir well. Cover and chill 2 to 3 hours. Gently stir sour cream into carrot mixture; serve on lettuce leaves. Yield: 8 servings. *Carol T. Keith,*
*Roanoke, Virginia.*

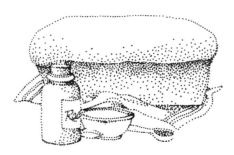

## Flavor Breads With Herbs And Spices

Ever tasted a well-seasoned bread that makes you ask, "What *is* that flavor?" If so, you've likely detected an herb or spice that has been used correctly—the seasoning whispers, but not loud enough for you to identify it. We think you'll find that's the case with these delectable herb and spice breads.

Our Cardamom White Bread rises high and light and bakes into a snow-white loaf wrapped with a golden crust. Mae Harkey tells us it's a family favorite, as is the hint of cardamom. "I've been putting cardamom in my breads for over 25 years," she says. "I like the flavor it adds." So did we.

For a spicy cakelike loaf, Parmesan Herb Bread is really easy to make; it starts with a biscuit mix and includes oregano, wine, and a sprinkling of Parmesan cheese. It's the perfect accompaniment to an Italian meal.

### ITALIAN-STYLE FLAT BREAD

1 (13¾-ounce) package hot roll mix
¾ cup warm water (115° to 125°)
1 egg
½ teaspoon dried whole rosemary
2 tablespoons olive oil
¼ teaspoon salt (optional)
⅛ teaspoon red pepper

Dissolve contents of yeast packet (included in roll mix) in water. Combine yeast mixture, egg, flour packet, and rosemary; stir well to form a soft dough. Place in a greased bowl. Cover and let rise in a warm place (85°), free from drafts, 45 minutes or until doubled in bulk.

Punch dough down, and turn out onto a lightly floured surface. Knead until smooth and elastic, about 1 to 2 minutes. Shape dough into a round, flat loaf; place on a greased cookie sheet. Cover and let rise in a warm place (85°), free from drafts, for about 45 minutes. Score top of loaf.

Combine remaining ingredients, and brush lightly over surface of loaf. Bake at 350° for 40 minutes or until bread sounds hollow when tapped. Cut into wedges to serve. Yield: 1 loaf.

*Susan Bellows,*
*Birmingham, Alabama.*

### PARMESAN HERB BREAD

1½ cups biscuit mix
1 tablespoon sugar
1 tablespoon instant minced onion
1 egg, beaten
¼ cup milk
¼ cup white wine or apple juice
½ teaspoon dried whole oregano
¼ cup grated Parmesan cheese

Combine first 7 ingredients; stir well. Spread dough into a greased 8-inch round cakepan. Sprinkle cheese over dough. Bake at 400° for 20 minutes or until wooden pick inserted in center comes out clean. Cut into wedges to serve. Yield: 6 to 8 servings.

*Kathryn Bibelhauser,*
*Louisville, Kentucky.*

*Tip: Store spices in a cool place and away from any direct source of heat as the heat will destroy their flavor. Red spices (chili powder, paprika, and red pepper) will maintain flavor and retain color longer if refrigerated.*

## CARDAMOM WHITE BREAD

2 cups milk, scalded
3 tablespoons sugar
1 tablespoon salt
1 teaspoon ground cardamom
¼ cup plus 1 tablespoon margarine
3 tablespoons sugar
2 packages dry yeast
2 cups warm water (105° to 115°)
10 cups bread flour, divided
1½ tablespoons margarine, melted

Combine first 5 ingredients; stir until margarine melts. Cool to lukewarm (105° to 115°).

Dissolve 3 tablespoons sugar and yeast in warm water in a large bowl; stir well. Add 2 cups bread flour, mixing well (mixture will be very thin). Cover and let rise in a warm place (85°), free from drafts, about 20 minutes. Stir in milk mixture and remaining 8 cups bread flour; beat at medium speed of electric mixer until smooth.

Turn dough out onto a lightly floured surface; knead until smooth and elastic (about 8 to 10 minutes). Place dough in a greased bowl, turning to grease top. Cover and let rise in a warm place (85°), free from drafts, 1 hour and 15 minutes or until doubled in bulk. Punch dough down, and turn out onto a lightly floured surface. Let dough rest for 10 minutes.

Divide dough in thirds, and shape each into a loaf. Place the loaves in 3 greased 9- x 5- x 3-inch loafpans. Cover and let rise in a warm place (85°), free from drafts, 1 hour or until doubled in bulk. Brush each loaf with melted margarine. Bake at 400° for 30 minutes or until golden brown.

Remove loaves from pans, and cool on wire racks. Yield: 3 loaves.
*Mae Harkey,*
*Mount Pleasant, North Carolina.*

# Main Dishes From The Wok

Just a few minutes is all it takes to stir up a delicious main course right in the wok. These dishes cook so rapidly that they retain a maximum of color, flavor, and nutrients.

Since there's no time to prepare ingredients once the stir-frying process begins, be sure to chop, measure, and assemble all meats and vegetables before heating the wok. Meat should be cut into small pieces or thin slices so it can be browned quickly but remain juicy.

When you add vegetables to the wok, cook them only until they're crisp-tender. Cut fibrous vegetables, such as broccoli or celery, diagonally to expose the largest possible area to the heat. Add the more delicate vegetables, such as tomatoes or mushrooms, to prevent overcooking.

## CHINESE PEPPER STEAK

1 pound boneless round steak
3 tablespoons soy sauce
1 tablespoon minced green onion
1 tablespoon sherry
2 teaspoons cornstarch
1 teaspoon sugar
1 teaspoon ground ginger
¼ cup peanut oil
2 large green peppers, cut into 1-inch squares
Hot cooked rice
Soy sauce (optional)

Partially freeze steak; slice across grain into 2- x ¼-inch strips, and set aside. Combine next 6 ingredients in a shallow container, mixing well; add steak. Cover and refrigerate 1 to 4 hours.

Pour oil around top of preheated wok, coating sides; allow to heat at medium high (325°) for 1 minute. Add steak mixture; stir-fry 2 to 3 minutes or until browned. Reduce heat to low (225°). Stir in green pepper; cook 5 minutes, stirring constantly, until crisp-tender. Serve over rice with additional soy sauce, if desired. Yield: 4 servings.
*Fannie Miller,*
*Chesapeake, Virginia.*

## SAUSAGE STIR-FRY

1 pound bulk pork sausage
1 medium onion, chopped
1 (8-ounce) can tomato sauce
1 (10-ounce) package frozen Japanese-style vegetables in sauce
1 (8-ounce) package medium egg noodles, cooked
2 tablespoons extra spicy catsup
2 medium tomatoes, peeled and chopped
½ cup (2 ounces) shredded sharp Cheddar cheese

Combine sausage and onion in wok; heat to medium high (350°). Cook sausage 4 or 5 minutes or until browned, stirring to crumble; drain well.

Add tomato sauce and vegetables to sausage mixture; stir-fry 4 to 5 minutes or until vegetables are crisp-tender. Stir in noodles and catsup. Add tomatoes and cheese; stir-fry over low heat (225°) until cheese melts. Yield: 8 to 10 servings.
*Linda Moon,*
*Atlanta, Georgia.*

## ORIENTAL CHICKEN WITH PEANUTS

1 chicken-flavored bouillon cube
1 cup boiling water
3 whole chicken breasts, skinned and boned
3 tablespoons peanut oil or vegetable oil
1 tablespoon cornstarch
2 tablespoons soy sauce
¼ cup dry roasted peanuts
Hot cooked rice

Dissolve bouillon cube in water; set aside. Cut chicken breasts into 1-inch pieces; set aside.

Pour oil around top of preheated wok, coating sides; allow to heat at medium high (325°) for 2 minutes. Add chicken; stir-fry 1 or 2 minutes or until lightly browned. Add bouillon; reduce heat to low (225°), and simmer 5 minutes, stirring occasionally. Combine cornstarch and soy sauce, mixing well. Increase heat to medium high; stir in cornstarch mixture. Cook, stirring constantly, until thickened. Stir in peanuts; serve over hot cooked rice. Yield: 4 servings.
*Suzie Berg,*
*Charlotte, North Carolina.*

## CHICKEN WITH PLUM SAUCE

2 whole chicken breasts, skinned and boned
3 tablespoons dry white wine
1 tablespoon catsup
2 tablespoons Chinese plum sauce (recipe follows)
½ teaspoon sugar
½ teaspoon salt
3 tablespoons peanut oil or vegetable oil
¼ cup chicken broth
1 tablespoon Chinese plum sauce (recipe follows)
1 teaspoon cornstarch
1 tablespoon water
Hot cooked rice

Cut chicken breasts into 1-inch pieces. Combine next 5 ingredients in a shallow container, mixing well; add chicken, and mix well. Cover and refrigerate at least 30 minutes.

Pour oil around top of preheated wok, coating sides; allow to heat at medium high (325°) for 2 minutes. Add chicken; stir-fry 1 or 2 minutes or until lightly browned. Add chicken broth and 1 tablespoon plum sauce. Reduce heat to low (225°); simmer 2 to 3 minutes.

Combine cornstarch and water; mix well. Pour over chicken; cook, stirring constantly, until thickened. Serve over hot cooked rice. Yield: 2 to 4 servings.

*Chinese Plum Sauce:*

½ cup plum jam
¼ cup chutney
1½ teaspoons vinegar
⅛ teaspoon hot sauce

Combine all ingredients in a small saucepan; cook until thoroughly heated. Store in refrigerator. Yield: ¾ cup.

*Note:* Commercial Chinese plum sauce may be substituted, if desired.

*Kay Castleman Cooper,*
*Burke, Virginia.*

## CHICKEN AND VEGETABLE STIR-FRY

1 chicken-flavored bouillon cube
1 cup boiling water
1 tablespoon cornstarch
¼ cup water
2 whole chicken breasts, skinned and boned
2 tablespoons peanut oil or vegetable oil
1 cup chopped onion
1 cup diagonally sliced celery
3 cups diagonally sliced fresh broccoli flowerets
½ teaspoon salt
¼ teaspoon ground ginger
1 tablespoon vegetable oil
Hot cooked rice

Dissolve bouillon cube in 1 cup boiling water. Combine cornstarch and ¼ cup water, stirring well; stir into bouillon mixture, and set aside. Cut chicken breasts into 1-inch pieces; set aside.

Pour 2 tablespoons oil around top of preheated wok, coating sides; allow to heat at medium high (325°) for 2 minutes. Add vegetables, salt, and ginger; stir-fry 4 minutes or until vegetables are crisp-tender. Remove vegetables from wok, and set aside.

Pour 1 tablespoon oil around top of wok; allow to heat at medium high for 2 minutes. Add chicken, and stir-fry 1 or 2 minutes or until lightly browned. Return vegetables to wok. Pour bouillon mixture over chicken and vegetables,

stirring well. Reduce heat to low (225°); simmer 2 to 3 minutes or until thickened. Serve over rice. Yield: 4 servings.

*Janet Kasper,*
*Fort Worth, Texas.*

Microwave
Cookery

# Cooking Apples In The Microwave

Can you imagine whole apples that bake in 6 minutes instead of 45? With the aid of your microwave oven, you can enjoy apples this way and in other delicious preparations, all ready in minutes. Our test kitchens have developed this range of apple recipes for your microwave—from desserts like Brandied Apples and Cream to an entrée of Baked Ham and Apples.

Any type of cooking apple that's firm and free of blemishes will work well for microwave cooking. Large apples are attractive, but small ones tend to have better flavor and texture.

To encourage even cooking, stir the apples or turn the dish as specified during the cooking time. When sliced apples are called for, slice the same thickness to promote even doneness.

Whole apples continue to cook after the microwave cycle is complete, so let them stand as long as the recipe directs before checking for doneness. Don't attempt to microwave until they are done, or they'll be overcooked after standing.

## BRANDIED APPLES AND CREAM

4 large cooking apples
¼ cup lemon juice
2 tablespoons butter or margarine
3 tablespoons brandy
⅓ cup firmly packed brown sugar
1½ teaspoons grated lemon rind
½ teaspoon ground cinnamon
3 tablespoons brandy
Lemon Cream

Peel and core apples; cut into ½-inch-thick wedges. Sprinkle with lemon juice, and toss gently.

Place butter in an 8-inch square baking dish. Microwave at HIGH for 40

seconds or until butter melts. Drain apples, and stir into butter. Combine 3 tablespoons brandy, brown sugar, lemon rind, and cinnamon; mix well, and spoon over apples. Microwave at HIGH for 4 to 5 minutes or until apples are tender, stirring once.

Place 3 tablespoons brandy in a 1-cup glass measure. Microwave at HIGH for 25 to 30 seconds or until hot. Ignite brandy, and pour over apples. When flames die down, spoon the brandied apples into individual serving dishes, and top with Lemon Cream. Yield: 4 to 6 servings.

*Lemon Cream:*

½ cup whipping cream
¾ teaspoon lemon juice
¼ teaspoon vanilla extract

Combine all ingredients, mixing well. Chill. Yield: about ½ cup.

## BAKED HAM AND APPLES

3 cups diced cooked ham
3 cooking apples, unpeeled and cut into wedges
½ cup firmly packed brown sugar
2 tablespoons all-purpose flour
2 tablespoons lemon juice
1 to 2 tablespoons prepared mustard
1 teaspoon grated orange rind
1 tablespoon chopped fresh parsley

Combine first 7 ingredients, mixing well. Spoon mixture into a 2-quart casserole, and cover with heavy-duty plastic wrap. Microwave at HIGH for 7 to 9 minutes or until apples are tender, stirring mixture after 4 minutes. Sprinkle parsley over top. Yield: 6 servings.

## CINNAMON APPLE RINGS

3 tablespoons butter or margarine
2 tablespoons lemon juice
2 tablespoons honey
¼ teaspoon ground cinnamon
4 medium cooking apples, unpeeled, cored, and cut into ½-inch rings

Place butter in a 12- x 8- x 2-inch baking dish. Microwave at HIGH for 50 seconds or until butter melts. Stir in lemon juice, honey, and cinnamon.

Place apple slices in butter mixture, turning to coat both sides. Cover with heavy-duty plastic wrap. Microwave at HIGH for 5 to 6 minutes or until apples are tender, giving dish a half-turn after 2 minutes. Let stand 2 minutes before serving. Yield: 6 to 8 servings.

## EASY BAKED APPLES

4 large cooking apples
¼ cup firmly packed brown sugar
1 teaspoon ground cinnamon
1 teaspoon ground nutmeg
2 tablespoons butter or margarine
⅓ cup water

Core apples, and slice a thin circle of peel from top of each. Place apples in a 9-inch pieplate.

Combine sugar, cinnamon, and nutmeg; spoon sugar mixture into cavities of apples. Top each with ½ tablespoon butter. Pour water into pieplate; cover with heavy-duty plastic wrap.

Microwave at HIGH for 6 to 8 minutes or until apples are crisp-tender, giving dish a half-turn after 3 minutes. Let stand 5 minutes before serving. Yield: 4 servings.

## APPLE-NUT CRUNCH

5 cups peeled sliced cooking apples
1 cup firmly packed brown sugar, divided
1 tablespoon lemon juice
¼ cup all-purpose flour
⅓ cup butter or margarine, softened
½ cup regular oats, uncooked
½ cup chopped pecans

Combine apples, ½ cup brown sugar, and lemon juice; toss lightly. Place mixture in an 8-inch square baking dish.

Combine remaining ½ cup brown sugar and flour; cut in butter with a pastry blender until well blended. Stir in oats and pecans. Spoon mixture evenly over the apples.

Microwave at HIGH for 9 to 12 minutes or until apples are tender, giving dish a quarter-turn at 3-minute intervals. Yield: 6 servings.

# Start Dinner With Escargots

Snails, commonly referred to by their French name, escargots, are considered a delicacy of the first order. Baked in their own shells along with a highly seasoned combination of butter, garlic, and parsley, snails are usually served as a savory light appetizer.

The final cooking may be done in a special snail pan (available in most gourmet shops) designed to keep the

*Baked on a bed of rock salt, Escargots Provençal are seasoned with a garlic-and-parsley butter and served in their shells.*

shells from rolling around. Or, if you prefer, simply fill a baking pan with rock salt, and nestle the shells in the salt to keep them still while cooking.

## ESCARGOTS PROVENCAL

1 (7½-ounce) can snails, drained and rinsed
½ cup Chablis or other dry white wine
½ cup beef broth
⅛ teaspoon salt
⅛ teaspoon pepper
Dash of ground nutmeg
18 snail shells, rinsed and drained
½ cup butter or margarine, softened
1 cup coarsely chopped fresh parsley
4 cloves garlic, minced
Rock salt (optional)
Parsley sprigs (optional)

Combine first 6 ingredients, stirring well. Cover and chill at least 3 hours. Drain; insert each marinated snail into a shell. Set aside.

Combine butter, coarsely chopped parsley, and garlic in container of electric blender; blend well. Pack about 2

teaspoons of butter mixture into each shell.

Place filled shells in snail pan, or pour enough rock salt into an 8-inch square baking dish to cover bottom (salt helps shells sit upright); arrange filled shells, open end up, on salt. Bake at 400° for 15 minutes. Garnish with parsley sprigs, if desired; serve immediately. Yield: 6 appetizer servings.     *Maryse H. Rose,*
*Mary Esther, Florida.*

# Feature Vegetables In The Salad

Add some excitement to your salads by combining a variety of crunchy, colorful vegetables. Crispy Green Bean Salad, for example, combines green beans, cooked until crisp but tender, with cubed potatoes; the vegetables are lightly coated with an oil-and-vinegar dressing and served cold.

Chopped tomatoes, cucumber, green pepper, and carrots add color and crunch to Congealed Fresh Vegetable Salad. Mixed Vegetable Salad is a rainbow combination of fresh broccoli and cauliflower flowerets, carrots, and purple onion tossed with commercial Italian dressing.

## ARTICHOKE-TOMATO SALAD

1 (8½-ounce) can artichoke hearts, drained and quartered
4 hard-cooked eggs, chopped
⅓ cup mayonnaise or salad dressing
2 tablespoons chopped dill pickle
1 tablespoon chopped pimiento
¼ teaspoon salt
¼ teaspoon pepper
2 to 3 large tomatoes, sliced
Lettuce leaves
2 tablespoons capers (optional)

Combine first 7 ingredients; stir well. Arrange tomato slices on a lettuce-lined plate. Spoon artichoke heart mixture in center of tomato slices. Garnish with capers, if desired. Yield: 6 servings.
*Aline S. Fuller,*
*Springdale, Arkansas.*

## PICKLED GREEN BEAN SALAD

2 pounds fresh green beans
1¾ cups vinegar (5% acidity)
1½ cups water
¾ cup sugar
1 tablespoon plus 1 teaspoon salt
1 tablespoon mustard seeds
1 tablespoon whole black peppercorns
1 (3-inch) stick cinnamon
2 cloves garlic, halved
3 medium onions, thinly sliced

Wash beans; trim ends, and remove strings. Cut beans into 1½-inch pieces. Cook beans, covered, in a small amount of boiling water 5 minutes; drain well.

Combine vinegar, water, sugar, and salt in a Dutch oven. Tie mustard seeds, peppercorns, cinnamon, and garlic in cheesecloth. Add spice bag to vinegar mixture; bring to a boil.

Stir beans and onion into vinegar mixture; simmer 10 minutes. Remove spice bag. Pack beans, onion, and liquid into hot sterilized jars, leaving ½-inch headspace. Cover at once with metal lids, and screw bands tight. Process in boiling-water bath 10 minutes. Yield: 4 pints.
*Sara A. McCullough,*
*Broaddus, Texas.*

## CRISPY GREEN BEAN SALAD

½ pound new potatoes, peeled and cubed
1 pound fresh green beans
3 tablespoons olive oil
1 tablespoon white wine vinegar
½ teaspoon salt
⅛ teaspoon garlic powder
⅛ teaspoon pepper
Lettuce leaves (optional)
Lemon twist (optional)

Cook potatoes in enough boiling water to cover for 15 to 20 minutes; drain well, and set aside.

Wash beans; trim ends, and remove strings. Cut beans into 1½-inch lengths. Cover beans with water, and bring to a boil. Reduce heat, cover, and simmer 8 minutes until crisp-tender. Drain well.

Combine potatoes and beans, tossing lightly. Combine next 5 ingredients, stirring well; pour over vegetables, tossing gently to coat. Cover and chill at least 4 hours. Serve over lettuce leaves and garnish with a lemon twist, if desired. Yield: 4 to 6 servings.
*Mrs. Floyd C. Stover,*
*Bakersfield, Missouri.*

## GARDEN SALAD BOWL

½ cup vegetable oil
⅓ cup red wine vinegar
1 tablespoon water
1 (.75-ounce) package Italian salad dressing mix
1 (1-pound) bunch fresh broccoli
8 medium fresh mushrooms, sliced
2 medium zucchini, thinly sliced
1 (4-ounce) jar diced pimiento, drained
1 to 2 tablespoons minced onion

Combine oil, vinegar, water, and salad dressing mix in a jar. Cover tightly, and shake vigorously; set aside.

Trim off large leaves of broccoli. Wash broccoli, and break off flowerets; reserve stalks for another use.

Combine broccoli flowerets and remaining vegetables in a large bowl. Pour dressing over vegetables; toss gently. Cover and refrigerate several hours. Yield: 6 to 8 servings.
*Mrs. H. G. Drawdy,*
*Spindale, North Carolina.*

## MIXED VEGETABLE SALAD

1 (1-pound) bunch fresh broccoli
1 small head cauliflower, broken into flowerets
2 medium carrots, scraped and thinly sliced
1 medium-size purple onion, thinly sliced
1 medium-size green pepper, cut into 1-inch pieces
1 (15-ounce) can garbanzo beans, drained
1 cup sliced ripe olives
1 (8-ounce) bottle commercial Italian dressing

Trim off large leaves of broccoli. Wash broccoli, and break off flowerets; cut into bite-size pieces. Reserve stalks for another use. Combine broccoli, cauliflower flowerets, and remaining ingredients in a large bowl; toss gently. Cover and chill at least 1 hour. Yield: 8 servings.
*Cynthia R. Newberry,*
*Gainesville, Florida.*

## GERMAN POTATO SALAD

4 medium potatoes
8 slices bacon
¼ cup sugar
2 tablespoons all-purpose flour
⅓ cup water
⅓ cup vinegar
1 small green pepper, chopped
1 small onion, chopped
¼ cup chopped celery
1 tablespoon chopped pimiento

Scrub potatoes; cook in boiling water 30 minutes or until tender. Drain and cool slightly. Peel potatoes; cut into ½-inch cubes.

Cook bacon in a large skillet until crisp; remove bacon, reserving ¼ cup drippings in skillet. Crumble bacon, and set aside. Add sugar, flour, water, and vinegar to pan drippings, stirring well. Cook mixture over medium heat until slightly thickened.

Combine potatoes, bacon, green pepper, onion, celery, and pimiento in a large bowl; top with vinegar mixture, tossing gently. Yield: 6 servings.
*Mrs. Lowell R. Wilkins,*
*Rome, Georgia.*

*Tip: To save the unused portion of a jar of pimientos or olives, cover with a little vinegar and water; cover tightly and refrigerate.*

## CONGEALED FRESH VEGETABLE SALAD

1 (6-ounce) package lemon-flavored gelatin
1½ cups boiling water
1 teaspoon salt
¼ teaspoon white pepper
2 tablespoons vinegar
Dash of Worcestershire sauce
2 cups cold water
2 cups diced tomato
1½ cups diced cucumber
1½ cups diced green pepper
1 cup diced carrot
¾ cup diced green onion
½ teaspoon celery seeds
Lettuce leaves (optional)
Lemon slices (optional)

Dissolve gelatin in boiling water; add salt, pepper, vinegar, and Worcestershire sauce. Stir in cold water. Chill until the consistency of unbeaten egg white. Fold in vegetables and celery seeds; spoon into a 7-cup mold. Refrigerate until firm. Unmold on lettuce leaves and garnish with lemon, if desired. Yield: 12 to 14 servings.

*Mildred Jacobs,*
*Eads, Colorado.*

# Crêpes For An Easy Brunch

Brunch can be easy if you make your entrée ahead of time. That's what you can do with Cheesy Sausage Crêpes. Fill a batch of crêpes with cooked sausage, cheese, and mushrooms; refrigerate it overnight, or freeze the dish if your brunch is two or more days away.

## CHEESY SAUSAGE CREPES

1 pound bulk pork sausage
¼ cup chopped onion
½ cup (2 ounces) shredded sharp Cheddar cheese
1 (3-ounce) package cream cheese, softened
¼ teaspoon ground thyme
1 (4½-ounce) jar sliced mushrooms, drained
¼ teaspoon garlic salt
Crêpes (recipe follows)
½ cup commercial sour cream
¼ cup butter or margarine, softened

Cook sausage and onion in a heavy skillet until sausage is browned, stirring

to crumble meat; drain. Stir in next 5 ingredients.

Fill each crêpe with about 2 tablespoons sausage mixture. Roll up, and place seam side down in two greased 12- x 8- x 2-inch baking dishes. Cover and bake at 350° for 25 minutes. Combine sour cream and butter, mixing well; spoon over crêpes. Bake, uncovered, 5 minutes. Yield: 8 servings.

*Crêpes:*

3 eggs
1 cup all-purpose flour
1 cup milk
1 tablespoon vegetable oil
Additional vegetable oil

Combine first 4 ingredients in container of electric blender; process 1 minute. Scrape down sides of blender container with rubber spatula; process an additional 15 seconds. Refrigerate 1 hour. (This allows flour particles to swell and soften so crêpes are light in texture.)

Brush the bottom of a 6-inch crêpe pan with oil; place pan over medium heat until oil is just hot, not smoking.

Pour 2 tablespoons batter into pan; quickly tilt pan in all directions so batter covers the pan in a thin film. Cook about 1 minute.

Lift edge of crêpe to test for doneness. Crêpe is ready for flipping when it can be shaken loose from pan. Flip crêpe, and cook about 30 seconds on other side. (This side is rarely more than spotty brown.) Place on a towel to cool. Stack crêpes between layers of waxed paper to prevent sticking. Yield: 16 crêpes.

*Note:* Crêpes may be frozen, if desired. Thaw to room temperature, and bake as directed.

*Mrs. Leslie Villeneuve,*
*Neptune Beach, Florida.*

# Fry Your Own Egg Rolls

If you've never made egg rolls, now's the time to start. Shrimp and Pork Egg Rolls are loaded with crunch and fried to crispy perfection, and—best of all—they're easy to make. That's because you make them with commercial egg roll wrappers. And although Chinese cooks say it's best to chop the vegetables by hand, you may want to try chopping them in the food processor.

## SHRIMP AND PORK EGG ROLLS

1½ teaspoons cornstarch
1 tablespoon soy sauce
½ pound lean boneless pork, cut into ¼-inch cubes
1 (6-ounce) package frozen cooked shrimp, thawed and drained
1 teaspoon dry sherry
3 tablespoons peanut or vegetable oil, divided
3 cups shredded cabbage
2½ cups fresh bean sprouts, chopped
½ pound fresh mushrooms, thinly sliced
½ cup finely chopped celery
1 (8-ounce) can bamboo shoots, drained and finely chopped
½ teaspoon salt
¼ teaspoon pepper
1 egg, beaten
1½ teaspoons water
2 (1-pound) packages egg roll wrappers
Peanut oil
Commercial sweet-and-sour sauce (optional)
Commercial mustard sauce (optional)

Combine cornstarch and soy sauce in a small bowl; mix well. Stir in pork, and let stand 20 minutes. Combine shrimp and sherry in another small bowl; stir well. Let stand 20 minutes.

Heat 2 tablespoons oil in a preheated wok, coating sides; allow to heat at medium high (325°) for 2 minutes. Add pork and shrimp mixtures; stir-fry 2 minutes or until pork is lightly browned. Remove from wok and drain.

Heat 1 tablespoon oil in wok. Add cabbage, bean sprouts, mushrooms, and celery; stir-fry 2 minutes or until vegetables are crisp-tender. Add bamboo shoots, pork, and shrimp; sprinkle with salt and pepper. Cook 1 minute; stir constantly. Remove mixture from wok; chill.

Combine egg and water in a custard cup; mix well and set aside.

Mound ⅓ cup of chilled filling in center of each egg roll wrapper. Fold top corner of wrapper over filling; then fold left and right corners over filling. Lightly brush exposed corner of wrapper with egg mixture. Tightly roll the filled end of the wrapper toward the exposed corner; gently press to seal.

Heat 1½ inches peanut oil to 375° in wok. Place 2 egg rolls in hot oil and fry for 35 to 45 seconds on each side, or until golden brown; drain on paper towels. Repeat with remaining egg rolls. Serve with sweet-and-sour sauce and mustard sauce, if desired. Yield: about 20 egg rolls.

*Note:* Remaining egg roll wrappers may be frozen and reserved for later use.

*Cherry Tyree,*
*Pelham, Alabama.*

# November

Holiday parties begin in November and Southerners look for food with a festive flair. We present our fifth annual *Holiday Dinners* special section in this chapter, where you'll find creative, new ideas to add sparkle to your holiday entertaining. This year our special section includes a formal dinner on Avery Island, Louisiana, which features Roast Ducklings With Blackberry Sauce and a luscious lemon dessert. We continue with recipes for gourmet entrées, dazzling desserts, a "Cooking Light" holiday feast for dieters, and some special coffee mixes you can keep on hand.

Many of our readers will smile when they see familiar recipes like Hummingbird Cake, Chicken Breasts Lombardy, Texas Cornbread Dressing, and Kahlúa Velvet Frosty on the next few pages—these recipes are just a few of the all-time favorites we compiled as a holiday gift to you. Among them are our most requested recipes, as well as those most remembered by our foods staff after testing literally thousands of dishes over the past few years. And, of course, we tasted each and every one again just to make sure they were still as wonderful as we recalled them to be the first time!

# These Recipes Deserve An Encore

Over the years, there have been a number of *Southern Living* recipes that have stood out as all-time favorites. We know because you've told us. Southern Gumbo, for example, was published eleven years ago, and we still get requests for the recipe. A steady stream of letters since September 1977 was your response to Perfect Chocolate Cake. And you also agreed with our choice of Hummingbird Cake for our February 1978 issue, making it our most requested recipe to date.

We also have our own favorite recipes, and these were compared with those you've written about to arrive at this slate of all-time favorites. Our home economists tested each recipe again, making a few adjustments when possible to incorporate your suggestions, such as reducing sugar, salt, and oil.

■ When Joe Broussard of Lafayette, Louisiana, sent us his favorite chicken recipe, he had no idea what a hit it would make with our foods staff. We've not only served it often at dinner parties in our own homes and at company-sponsored functions, but we've also recommended it to many readers requesting an entrée for a special occasion. It originally appeared in our November 1978 issue.

## CHICKEN BREASTS LOMBARDY

6 whole chicken breasts, boned, skinned, and quartered
½ cup all-purpose flour
1 cup butter or margarine, divided
Salt and pepper
1½ cups sliced mushrooms
¾ cup Marsala wine
½ cup chicken stock
½ cup (2 ounces) shredded Fontina or mozzarella cheese
½ cup grated Parmesan cheese

Place each piece of chicken between 2 sheets of waxed paper, and flatten to ⅛-inch thickness using a meat mallet or rolling pin.

Dredge chicken lightly with flour. Place 4 pieces at a time in 2 tablespoons melted butter in a large skillet; cook over low heat 3 to 4 minutes on each side or until golden brown. Place chicken in a greased 13- x 9- x 2-inch baking dish, overlapping edges; sprinkle with salt and pepper to taste. Repeat procedure with remaining chicken, adding 2 tablespoons butter to skillet each time. Reserve drippings in skillet.

Sauté mushrooms in ¼ cup butter until tender; drain. Sprinkle evenly over chicken.

Stir wine and chicken stock into drippings in skillet. Simmer 10 minutes, stirring occasionally. Stir in ½ teaspoon salt and ⅛ teaspoon pepper. Spoon about one-third of sauce evenly over chicken; reserve remaining sauce.

Combine cheese, and sprinkle over chicken. Bake at 450° for 10 to 12 minutes. Place under broiler 1 to 2 minutes or until lightly browned. Serve with reserved sauce. Yield: 8 servings.

*Note:* Turkey breast may be substituted for chicken. Instead of Marsala wine, ¾ cup dry white wine may be used.
*Joe Broussard,*
*Lafayette, Louisiana.*

■ Lois O. Ward of Louisville, Mississippi, won first place in the 1977 National Farm-Raised Catfish Cooking Contest with this recipe, and she graciously shared it with our readers in November 1977. We think it's the way Southern catfish was meant to be served.

## CRISP FRIED CATFISH

6 medium catfish, cleaned and dressed
1 teaspoon salt
¼ teaspoon pepper
1 (2-ounce) bottle hot sauce
2 cups self-rising cornmeal
Vegetable oil
Fresh parsley sprigs (optional)
Fluted lemon halves (optional)

Sprinkle catfish with salt and pepper. Marinate in hot sauce for 1 to 2 hours in the refrigerator.

Place cornmeal in a paper bag; drop in catfish, one at a time, and shake until completely coated. Fry in deep hot oil over high heat until fish float to the top and are golden brown; drain well. Serve hot. Garnish with parsley and lemon halves, if desired. Yield: 6 servings.
*Lois O. Ward,*
*Louisville, Mississippi.*

■ Southern Gumbo originally appeared in our February 1971 issue, submitted by Dr. William White of Seguin, Texas. Even now, we still receive frequent requests for reprints of the recipe.

## SOUTHERN GUMBO

1 cup vegetable oil
1 cup all-purpose flour
8 stalks celery, chopped
3 large onions, chopped
1 green pepper, chopped
2 cloves garlic, minced
About ½ cup chopped fresh parsley (optional)
1 pound okra, sliced
2 tablespoons shortening
2 quarts chicken stock
2 quarts water
½ cup Worcestershire sauce
Hot sauce to taste
½ cup catsup
1 large tomato, chopped
1 tablespoon salt
4 slices bacon or 1 large ham slice, chopped
1 or 2 bay leaves
¼ teaspoon dried whole thyme
¼ teaspoon dried whole rosemary
Red pepper flakes to taste (optional)
2 cups chopped, cooked chicken
1 to 2 pounds fresh crabmeat
4 pounds shrimp, peeled and deveined
1 pint oysters, undrained (optional)
1 teaspoon molasses or brown sugar
Hot cooked rice

Combine oil and flour in a large Dutch oven; cook over medium heat, stirring constantly, 10 to 15 minutes or until roux is the color of a copper penny. Stir in celery, onion, green pepper, and garlic; add parsley, if desired. Cook 45 minutes to 1 hour, stirring mixture occasionally.

Fry okra in 2 tablespoons hot shortening until browned. Add to gumbo, and stir well over low heat for a few minutes. (At this stage, the mixture may be cooled, packaged, and frozen or refrigerated for later use.)

Add next 12 ingredients; simmer 2½ to 3 hours, stirring occasionally.

About 30 minutes before serving, add chicken, crabmeat, and shrimp; simmer 30 minutes. Add oysters, if desired, during last 10 minutes of simmering period. Stir in molasses. Serve over rice. Yield: about 7½ quarts.
*Dr. William White,*
*Seguin, Texas.*

*Tip: Use a bulb baster to remove fat from broth, stew, or soup.*

■ Many readers remember their favorite quiche recipe only as "the one with the mayonnaise." We remember the recipe well. Appearing in our May 1977 issue as a specialty of Margaret Beasley of Timpson, Texas, it's definitely been our most requested quiche.

## CRAB QUICHE

**Pastry for 9-inch quiche pan or pieplate**
**½ cup mayonnaise**
**2 tablespoons all-purpose flour**
**2 eggs, beaten**
**½ cup milk**
**1 (6-ounce) package frozen crabmeat, thawed and drained**
**2 cups (8 ounces) shredded Swiss cheese**
**⅓ cup chopped green onion**
**Fresh parsley sprigs (optional)**
**Tomato rose (optional)**

Line a 9-inch quiche pan with pastry, and trim off excess around edge of pan. Place a piece of buttered aluminum foil, buttered side down, over pastry; gently press into pastry shell. This will keep the sides of the shell from collapsing. Cover foil with a layer of dried peas or beans. Bake at 400° for 10 minutes; remove foil and peas. Prick shell, and bake 3 to 5 additional minutes or until lightly browned. Cool.

Combine mayonnaise, flour, eggs, and milk; mix thoroughly. Stir in crabmeat, cheese, and onion. Spoon into quiche shell, and bake at 350° for 30 minutes or until firm in center. Garnish with parsley and tomato rose, if desired. Yield: one 9-inch quiche.

*Margaret Beasley,*
*Timpson, Texas.*

■ When it comes to dressing for the holiday turkey, our test kitchens staff thinks this version is the ultimate. It graced our pages in December 1975, submitted by Mrs. Raymond F. Buck of College Station, Texas.

## TEXAS CORNBREAD DRESSING

**10 (2-inch) cornbread muffins, crumbled**
**6 slices white bread, crumbled**
**5 cups chicken or turkey broth**
**2 medium onions, chopped**
**4 stalks celery, chopped**
**3 tablespoons butter or margarine**
**½ pound mild bulk pork sausage**
**2 eggs, beaten**
**Salt and pepper to taste**

Soak cornbread and white bread in chicken broth in a large bowl about 10 minutes; stir until liquid is absorbed.

Sauté onion and celery in butter until vegetables are tender; add sausage, and cook over low heat until sausage is browned. Drain. Add sausage mixture to bread mixture, along with eggs, salt, and pepper; mix well.

Stuff turkey lightly with dressing, or spoon dressing into a greased 13- x 9- x 2-inch baking dish. Bake at 350° for 45 minutes or until lightly browned. Yield: 8 to 10 servings.

*Note:* One 8½-ounce package corn muffin mix may be substituted for homemade muffins, if desired. Prepare mix according to package directions.

*Mrs. Raymond F. Buck,*
*College Station, Texas.*

■ This Monkey Bread recipe from Judy G. Neal of Abilene, Texas, was the granddaddy of our pull-apart breads. Published five years ago, it sparked many readers to experiment and send in recipes with tasty variations; but this original version remains one of our most requested.

## MONKEY BREAD

**1 cup milk**
**½ cup butter or margarine**
**¼ cup sugar**
**1 teaspoon salt**
**1 package dry yeast**
**3½ cups all-purpose flour**
**½ cup butter or margarine, melted**

Combine milk, ½ cup butter, sugar, and salt in a saucepan; heat until butter melts. Cool to 105° to 115°; add yeast, stirring until dissolved. Place flour in a large bowl; add milk mixture, and stir until well blended.

Cover and let rise in a warm place (85°), free from drafts, about 1 hour and 20 minutes or until doubled in bulk. Roll into 1½-inch balls; dip each in melted butter.

Layer balls of dough in a 10-inch one-piece tube pan or Bundt pan. Cover and let rise about 45 minutes or until doubled in bulk. Bake at 375° for 35 minutes. Cool in pan 5 minutes; invert onto serving plate. Yield: one 10-inch loaf.

*Judy G. Neal,*
*Abilene, Texas.*

*Tip: Keep staples such as sugar, flour, and spices in tightly covered containers at room temperature. Staples that are frequently replenished should be rotated so that the oldest is always used first.*

■ "Please send another copy of Cream Cheese Braids. My original is so battered from use that I can hardly read it." That's one reader's plea for this recipe that appeared in our December 1977 issue, compliments of Phyllis Cannon of Stanley, North Carolina.

## CREAM CHEESE BRAIDS

**1 (8-ounce) carton commercial sour cream, scalded**
**½ cup sugar**
**½ cup butter or margarine, melted**
**1 teaspoon salt**
**2 packages dry yeast**
**½ cup warm water (105° to 115°)**
**2 eggs, beaten**
**4 cups all-purpose flour**
**Filling (recipe follows)**
**Glaze (recipe follows)**

Combine scalded sour cream, sugar, butter, and salt; mix well, and let cool to lukewarm. Dissolve yeast in warm water in a large mixing bowl; stir in sour cream mixture and eggs. Gradually stir in flour (dough will be soft). Cover tightly, and chill overnight.

Divide dough into 4 equal portions. Turn each portion out onto a heavily floured surface, and knead 4 or 5 times. Roll each into a 12- x 8-inch rectangle. Spread one-fourth of filling over each rectangle, leaving a ½-inch margin around edges. Carefully roll up jellyroll fashion, beginning at long side. Firmly pinch edge and ends to seal. Carefully place rolls, seam side down, on greased baking sheets.

Make 6 equally spaced x-shaped cuts across top of each loaf. Cover and let rise in a warm place (85°), free from drafts, for 1 hour or until doubled in bulk. Bake at 375° for 15 to 20 minutes. Spread loaves with glaze while warm. Yield: four 12-inch loaves.

*Filling:*

**2 (8-ounce) packages cream cheese, softened**
**¾ cup sugar**
**1 egg, beaten**
**⅛ teaspoon salt**
**2 teaspoons vanilla extract**

Combine all ingredients. Process in food processor or electric mixer until well blended. Yield: about 2 cups.

*Glaze:*

**2 cups sifted powdered sugar**
**¼ cup milk**
**2 teaspoons vanilla extract**

Combine all ingredients, mixing well. Yield: about 1 cup. *Phyllis Cannon, Stanley, North Carolina.*

■ We're not sure what hummingbirds have to do with this cake, but it certainly caught our readers' attention in the February 1978 issue. In fact, we'd rate it as our all-time most requested recipe. Sent to us by Mrs. L. H. Wiggins of Greensboro, North Carolina, it's known to have won a blue ribbon at several county fairs.

### HUMMINGBIRD CAKE

3 cups all-purpose flour
2 cups sugar
1 teaspoon baking soda
1 teaspoon salt
1 teaspoon ground cinnamon
3 eggs, beaten
1 cup vegetable oil
1½ teaspoons vanilla extract
1 (8-ounce) can crushed pineapple,
  undrained
1 cup chopped pecans
2 cups chopped bananas
Cream Cheese Frosting
½ cup chopped pecans

Combine first 5 ingredients in a large mixing bowl; add eggs and oil, stirring until dry ingredients are moistened. Do not beat. Stir in vanilla, pineapple, 1 cup pecans, and bananas.

Spoon batter into 3 greased and floured 9-inch round cakepans. Bake at 350° for 25 to 30 minutes or until a wooden pick inserted in center comes out clean. Cool in pans 10 minutes; remove from pans, and cool completely.

Spread frosting between layers and on top and sides of cake; then sprinkle ½ cup chopped pecans on top. Yield: one 3-layer cake.

*Cream Cheese Frosting:*

1 (8-ounce) package cream cheese,
  softened
½ cup butter or margarine, softened
1 (16-ounce) package powdered sugar,
  sifted
1 teaspoon vanilla extract

Combine cream cheese and butter, beating until smooth. Add powdered sugar and vanilla; beat until light and fluffy. Yield: enough frosting for one 3-layer cake. *Mrs. L. H. Wiggins, Greensboro, North Carolina.*

■ The name of this recipe describes this cake to a tee. Submitted by Dondee Gage Steves of San Antonio for our September 1977 issue, it's kept a steady stream of letters coming ever since. One reader even declares she's given away as many copies of the recipe as we have.

### PERFECT CHOCOLATE CAKE

1 cup cocoa
2 cups boiling water
1 cup butter or margarine, softened
2½ cups sugar
4 eggs
1½ teaspoons vanilla extract
2¾ cups all-purpose flour
2 teaspoons baking soda
½ teaspoon baking powder
½ teaspoon salt
Filling (recipe follows)
Frosting (recipe follows)
Pecan halves (optional)

Combine cocoa and boiling water, stirring until smooth; set aside to cool.

Combine butter, sugar, eggs, and vanilla; beat at high speed of electric mixer 5 minutes until light and fluffy. Combine dry ingredients; add to sugar mixture alternately with cocoa mixture, beating at low speed of electric mixer, and beginning and ending with flour mixture. Do not overbeat.

Pour batter into 3 greased and floured 9-inch round cakepans. Bake at 350° for 25 to 30 minutes or until a wooden pick inserted in center comes out clean. Cool in pans 10 minutes; remove from pans, and cool the layers completely.

Spread filling between layers, and spread frosting over top and sides of cake. Garnish with pecans, if desired. Serve at once, or refrigerate until ready to serve. Yield: one 3-layer cake.

*Filling:*

1 cup whipping cream
1 teaspoon vanilla extract
¼ cup sifted powdered sugar

Beat whipping cream and vanilla until foamy; gradually add powdered sugar, beating until peaks hold their shape. Chill. Yield: about 2 cups.

*Frosting:*

1 (6-ounce) package semisweet chocolate
  morsels
About ½ cup half-and-half
¾ cup butter or margarine
2½ cups sifted powdered sugar

Combine chocolate morsels, ½ cup half-and-half, and butter in a saucepan; cook over medium heat, stirring until chocolate melts. Remove from heat; add powdered sugar, mixing well.

Set saucepan in ice, and beat until frosting holds its shape and loses its gloss. Add a few more drops of half-and-half if needed to make spreading consistency. Yield: about 3 cups.
*Dondee Gage Steves,
San Antonio, Texas.*

■ Many of you have written to tell us that you keep a supply of our December 1978 Hot Buttered Rum mix in the freezer all winter. Ginger Burch of Waldorf, Maryland, was responsible for the recipe, and we weren't surprised at its popularity.

### HOT BUTTERED RUM

1 pound butter, softened
1 (16-ounce) package light brown sugar
1 (16-ounce) package powdered sugar,
  sifted
2 teaspoons ground cinnamon
2 teaspoons ground nutmeg
1 quart vanilla ice cream, softened
Light rum
Whipped cream
Cinnamon sticks

Combine butter, sugar, and spices; beat until light and fluffy. Add ice cream, and stir until well blended. Spoon mixture into a 2-quart freezer-proof container; freeze.

To serve, thaw slightly. Place 3 tablespoons butter mixture and 1 jigger of rum in a large mug; fill with boiling water, stirring well. (Any unused butter mixture can be refrozen.) Top with whipped cream, and serve with cinnamon stick. Yield: about 25 cups.
*Ginger Burch,
Waldorf, Maryland.*

■ The brainchild of one of our own staff members, Kahlúa Velvet Frosty made such a name for itself around our offices that we shared the recipe in our December 1977 issue. Letters tell us it made a hit with you, too.

### KAHLUA VELVET FROSTY

1 cup Kahlúa or other coffee-flavored
  liqueur
1 pint vanilla ice cream
1 cup half-and-half
⅛ teaspoon almond extract
Ice cubes

Combine first 4 ingredients in container of electric blender; add enough ice cubes to bring the mixture to the 6-cup level. Process until frothy. Yield: 6 cups.

*Tip: For even blending, fill the blender container only three-fourths full for liquids and one-fourth full for solids.*

# Pilafs And Paellas Are Distinctive Rice Dishes

Rice is at its most elegant when served in pilafs and paellas. Perfect for dinner parties and family meals alike, these dishes adorn rice with flavor, color, and even a touch of history.

Pilaf, a classic Turkish dish, is a long-time Southern favorite. Rice is sautéed in butter and simmered with a choice of meat, poultry, fish, or vegetables. Depending on its ingredients, pilaf may be served as either an entrée or side dish.

For our Chicken Pilaf, perfect as an entrée, boneless chicken pieces are breaded, browned in butter, and simmered with rice, carrot, and onion. A helping is so filling and nutritious, it's almost a one-dish meal.

Near-Eastern Pilaf is excellent as a meatless main dish or may be served alongside an entrée. You'll love its crunchy topping of peanuts, almonds, raisins, and fried onion rings.

A variation of pilaf, paella originated in Spain, taking its name from the flat, two-handled baking pan in which it was prepared. Traditional paella is a flavorful blend of saffron-flavored rice, chicken, seafood, tomatoes, and other vegetables.

We highly recommend Adrian Palmer's Seafood Paella. Filled with chicken, shrimp, and soft-shelled clams, it's expensive to make, but the beauty and exciting flavor are worth every penny. Be sure to try Chicken-Pork-Shrimp Paella, too. It includes chicken, pork, shrimp, and Italian sausage—an exquisite blend of flavors.

## GARDEN PAELLA

1 cup chopped onion
1 green pepper, chopped
1 red pepper, chopped
¼ cup vegetable or peanut oil
1½ cups uncooked regular rice
3½ cups chicken broth
¾ pound broccoli, cut into 1-inch pieces
2 ripe tomatoes, chopped
1 tablespoon tomato paste
¼ teaspoon salt
¼ to ½ teaspoon pepper
½ teaspoon dried whole saffron, crushed or ¼ teaspoon ground saffron
Dash of Worcestershire sauce
2 small zucchini, cut into 1-inch pieces
1 (10-ounce) package frozen English peas
12 fresh or frozen asparagus spears, cut into 1-inch pieces

Sauté onion, green pepper, and red pepper in oil in a heavy, ovenproof Dutch oven until tender. Stir in next 9 ingredients, and bring to a boil. Remove from heat; cover and bake at 350° for 15 minutes.

Stir remaining vegetables into rice mixture. Cover and bake 30 minutes or until liquid is absorbed and vegetables are crisp-tender. Yield: 10 to 12 servings.
*Cynthia Kannenberg, Brown Deer, Wisconsin.*

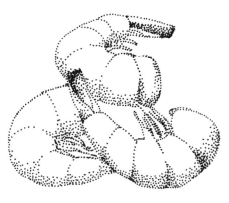

## CHICKEN-PORK-SHRIMP PAELLA

1 pound Italian link sausage
½ cup olive or vegetable oil
2 (2-pound) broiler-fryers, cut up
1 pound boneless pork, cut into 1-inch cubes
2 cups chopped onion
2 cloves garlic, crushed
2 cups uncooked regular rice
1 teaspoon salt
1 teaspoon dried whole oregano
½ teaspoon dried whole saffron, crushed or ¼ teaspoon ground saffron
¼ teaspoon pepper
2 medium tomatoes, peeled and chopped
3 (10¾-ounce) cans chicken broth, undiluted
1 bay leaf
1½ pounds large shrimp, peeled and deveined
1 (10-ounce) package frozen English peas
Pimiento strips (optional)
Lemon wedges (optional)

Cut sausage links in half crosswise; cook in a large skillet until browned. Drain sausage, and place in a lightly greased 4½-quart shallow baking dish.

Heat oil in skillet; add chicken, and brown on both sides. Remove chicken from skillet, and place in baking dish. Add pork to oil and cook until browned, stirring frequently; remove from skillet, and place in baking dish.

Add onion and garlic to skillet; sauté until tender. Add rice, salt, oregano, saffron, and pepper; cook over medium heat 10 minutes, stirring occasionally. Add tomatoes, chicken broth, and bay leaf; bring to a boil. Spoon over meat in baking dish; cover and bake at 350° for 1 hour.

Place shrimp and peas over rice mixture; cover and continue to bake 20 minutes or until shrimp are pink. Remove bay leaf before serving. Garnish with pimiento and lemon wedges, if desired. Yield: 10 to 12 servings.
*Carolyn Brantley, Greenville, Mississippi.*

## SEAFOOD PAELLA

3 pounds chicken breasts, thighs, and legs
¼ cup olive oil
2 large onions, chopped
2 cloves garlic, minced
1 (28-ounce) can whole tomatoes, undrained and chopped
½ teaspoon salt
1 cup uncooked regular rice
½ teaspoon dried whole oregano
½ teaspoon salt
½ teaspoon dried whole saffron or ¼ teaspoon ground saffron
¼ cup boiling water
2¼ pounds medium shrimp, peeled and deveined
1 (15-ounce) can soft-shelled or steamer clams in shells, drained
1 (10-ounce) package frozen English peas
1 (4-ounce) jar whole pimiento, drained and cut into strips

Brown chicken in hot oil in a large Dutch oven; remove chicken, and set aside. Add onion and garlic; sauté until tender. Add tomatoes and ½ teaspoon salt; return chicken to Dutch oven. Cover and simmer 30 minutes. Stir in rice, oregano, and ½ teaspoon salt. Dissolve saffron in boiling water; pour over chicken. Cover and simmer 25 minutes. Add shrimp and clams; cover and cook 10 minutes or until shrimp are pink. Spoon into center of a large serving dish.

Cook peas according to package directions; drain and stir in pimiento. Spoon peas around paella. Serve immediately. Yield: 6 servings.
*Adrian Palmer, Chattanooga, Tennessee.*

*Tip: When you are out of canned tomatoes for a recipe—do not panic! Try substituting 1 (6-ounce) can tomato paste plus 1 cup water. The substitution will make very little difference in most recipes.*

## PAELLA VALENCIANA

2 tablespoons vegetable oil
2 tablespoons olive oil
2½ pounds chicken breasts, thighs, and
   legs, skinned
2 cups uncooked regular rice
7 cups water
¼ pound chorizo or bulk sausage, cooked
   and drained
2 (6½-ounce) cans minced clams,
   undrained
2 cloves garlic, minced
1 (1.25-ounce) package taco seasoning mix
1 tablespoon seasoned salt
1 pound large shrimp, peeled and
   deveined
1 (10-ounce) package frozen English peas
1 cup pitted ripe olives

Heat oil in an 8-quart Dutch oven. Add chicken, and brown on both sides. Remove chicken from Dutch oven, and drain off drippings.

Add rice to Dutch oven; cook over low heat until lightly browned, stirring frequently. Add next 6 ingredients, and stir well. Arrange chicken pieces over the rice mixture. Bring mixture to a boil. Reduce heat; cover and simmer 1 hour, stirring occasionally.

Stir shrimp and peas into rice mixture, and cook 10 additional minutes. Add olives, and cook just until thoroughly heated. Yield: 8 servings.
*Mrs. David Williams,*
*Baton Rouge, Louisiana.*

## SHRIMP PILAF

4 slices bacon
½ cup finely chopped celery
2 tablespoons chopped green pepper
1 tablespoon all-purpose flour
1 teaspoon salt
¼ teaspoon pepper
1 pound medium shrimp, peeled and
   deveined
¼ cup plus 1 tablespoon Worcestershire
   sauce
1 tablespoon butter or margarine
1 cup uncooked regular rice
2⅔ cups water

Cook bacon in a large skillet until crisp; remove bacon, reserving 2 tablespoons drippings in skillet. Crumble bacon, and set aside.

Sauté celery and green pepper in bacon drippings until tender. Combine flour, salt, and pepper; dredge shrimp in flour mixture, and add to skillet. Stir in Worcestershire sauce. Cover and cook over low heat 30 minutes, stirring occasionally.

Melt butter in a medium saucepan. Add rice, and cook over low heat until lightly browned, stirring constantly. Add water, and bring to a boil. Reduce heat and simmer, covered, 20 minutes or until tender.

Stir rice into shrimp mixture, and place in a serving dish. Sprinkle with crumbled bacon. Yield: 4 servings.
*Mrs. Steve Lundquist,*
*Corpus Christi, Texas.*

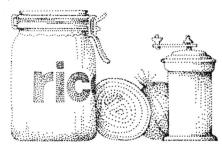

## FRUITED PORK PILAF

1 large onion, chopped
1 large green pepper, chopped
2 tablespoons vegetable oil
1 cup uncooked regular rice
2 cups cooked, cubed pork
1 (10½-ounce) can beef broth, diluted
1 (8-ounce) can pineapple tidbits, drained
1 tablespoon soy sauce
½ teaspoon ground allspice
¼ teaspoon pepper

Sauté onion and green pepper in oil in a large skillet until tender. Add rice and pork; cook over low heat until rice is lightly browned, stirring frequently. Add remaining ingredients, and bring to a boil. Cover and cook over medium heat 20 minutes or until rice is tender. Yield: 4 to 6 servings. *Carolyn Epting, Leesville, South Carolina.*

## CHICKEN PILAF

½ cup all-purpose flour
1 teaspoon paprika
½ teaspoon salt
Dash of pepper
4 whole chicken breasts, skinned, boned,
   and quartered
3 tablespoons butter or margarine
2 cups boiling water
2 chicken-flavored bouillon cubes
4 medium carrots, diced
1 medium onion, chopped
1 cup uncooked regular rice
½ teaspoon dried whole thyme

Combine first 4 ingredients; dredge chicken in flour mixture. Melt butter in a large, heavy ovenproof skillet; add chicken, and brown on both sides. Remove chicken from skillet, and set aside. Reserve drippings in skillet.

Combine boiling water and bouillon cubes, stirring until bouillon dissolves.

Sauté carrots and onion in reserved drippings until tender. Add rice; cook over low heat until lightly browned. Add bouillon mixture and thyme, stirring well. Arrange chicken pieces over rice mixture. Cover and bake at 350° for 1 hour. Yield: 8 servings.
*Randall De Trinis,*
*Brevard, North Carolina.*

## NEAR-EASTERN PILAF

⅓ cup chopped onion
¼ cup butter or margarine
1 cup uncooked regular rice
¼ cup raisins, divided
2 cups water
2 chicken-flavored bouillon cubes
⅛ teaspoon salt
Dash of pepper
Pinch of ground thyme
Pinch of ground oregano
¼ cup coarsely chopped salted peanuts
1 tablespoon vegetable oil
¼ cup plus 1 tablespoon coarsely chopped
   almonds, toasted and divided
½ cup canned fried onion rings

Sauté onion in butter in a medium skillet until tender. Add rice; cook over low heat until lightly browned, stirring frequently. Pour into a lightly greased 1½-quart baking dish; sprinkle with 3 tablespoons raisins.

Combine water and bouillon cubes in a small saucepan; bring to a boil. Stir in salt, pepper, thyme, and oregano; pour mixture over rice. Cover and bake at 350° about 20 minutes or until rice is tender.

Sauté peanuts in oil; stir 2 tablespoons peanuts and ¼ cup almonds into rice. Garnish with onion rings and remaining raisins, peanuts, and almonds. Yield: 4 to 6 servings.
*Mrs. Jeff Caldwell,*
*West Monroe, Louisiana.*

*Tip: To determine the size or capacity of a utensil, fill a liquid measure with water, and pour into utensil. Repeat until utensil is full, noting amount of water used. To determine a utensil's dimensions, measure from the inside edges.*

# Welcome Guests With Appetizers

Southern homes fill with laughter and the aromas of baking bread, roasting turkey, and simmering cider. Another year ends with a season of celebration; and where there's celebrating in the South, there's lots of good food.

This special section brings the best of holiday entertaining to you with a wealth of recipes and party ideas. On the following pages our readers share their favorites for appetizers, gourmet entrées, fruits, vegetables, and more.

Get holiday parties off to the right start with a tempting display of appetizers. Offer your guests a variety of items, both hot and cold.

Spinach Tarts look pretty, in addition to tasting good. A garnish of pimiento adds a nice splash of red to the spinach-filled cream cheese patty shells.

## SWEET-AND-SOUR MEATBALLS

1 pound hot bulk pork sausage
1 pound mild bulk pork sausage
1¼ cups catsup
¼ cup water
¼ cup firmly packed brown sugar
1 tablespoon soy sauce
1 tablespoon lemon juice
1 (15¼-ounce) can pineapple chunks, drained

Combine first 2 ingredients, mixing well; shape into 1-inch meatballs. Cook in a large skillet over medium heat until browned. Drain off drippings.

Combine remaining ingredients except pineapple; mix well, and pour over meatballs. Simmer 10 minutes, stirring occasionally. Add pineapple, and simmer an additional 10 minutes, stirring often. Yield: about 3½ dozen.
*Joyce Petrochko,*
*St. Albans, West Virginia.*

## BARBECUED OYSTERS

1 egg
2 tablespoons milk
1 (12-ounce) can fresh Select oysters, drained
½ cup all-purpose flour
1 cup cracker crumbs
½ cup chopped onion
1 tablespoon butter or margarine
½ cup apple juice
1 cup catsup
1 tablespoon brown sugar
1 tablespoon Worcestershire sauce
2 tablespoons vinegar
2 tablespoons prepared mustard
1 to 2 teaspoons liquid smoke
Vegetable oil

Combine egg and milk in a small bowl; mix well. Dredge each oyster in flour; dip in egg mixture, and coat with cracker crumbs. Set aside.

Sauté onion in butter in a large skillet until tender. Add next 7 ingredients, and mix well. Bring mixture to a boil; reduce heat and simmer, uncovered, 10 minutes, stirring frequently.

Heat 1 inch of oil to 350°. Fry oysters in oil until golden brown; drain on paper towels. Place oysters in sauce and simmer, uncovered, 5 minutes, turning once. Serve immediately. Yield: about 6 appetizer servings.
*Dick Edwards,*
*La Grange, Texas.*

## SMOKY SALMON CHEESE BALL

1 (7¾-ounce) can pink salmon
1 (8-ounce) package cream cheese, softened
1¼ cups (5 ounces) shredded mild Cheddar cheese
2 tablespoons minced onion
1 tablespoon dried parsley flakes
1 tablespoon lemon juice
1 to 2 teaspoons liquid smoke
¾ teaspoon celery salt
½ teaspoon garlic powder
½ cup finely chopped pecans

Drain salmon; remove skin and bones. Flake salmon with a fork; stir in remaining ingredients, except pecans. Chill until slightly firm. Shape mixture into a ball, and roll in pecans. Chill several hours or overnight. Yield: 1 cheese ball.
*Karen B. Brown,*
*Vienna, Georgia.*

## CHEESY SURPRISE LOG

¼ cup mayonnaise
1 hard-cooked egg, chopped
3 tablespoons chopped green pepper
2 tablespoons chopped onion
2 tablespoons diced pimiento
1 canned jalapeño pepper, seeded and chopped
1 tablespoon sugar
½ teaspoon salt
1 (16-ounce) can chopped sauerkraut, drained
4 cups (16 ounces) shredded Cheddar cheese
2 (3-ounce) packages cream cheese, softened
1 to 2 tablespoons milk
Chopped green pepper (optional)
Diced pimiento (optional)

Combine first 8 ingredients in a large mixing bowl; mix well. Stir in sauerkraut and Cheddar cheese. Shape into a log, and place on a serving tray.

Combine cream cheese and milk; beat well. Spread mixture over log. Chill 4 hours or overnight. Garnish with chopped green pepper and pimiento, if desired. Serve with crackers. Yield: 1 cheese log.
*Millie Ebel,*
*Louisville, Kentucky.*

*Tip: Refrigerate cheese in its original wrap until opened. After opening, rewrap tightly in plastic wrap, plastic bags, or aluminum foil, or place in airtight containers.*

## BLUE CHEESE-OLIVE BALL

1 (8-ounce) package cream cheese,
  softened
3 tablespoons butter or margarine,
  softened
1 tablespoon brandy
1 (4-ounce) package blue cheese, crumbled
1 tablespoon fresh or frozen chopped
  chives
½ cup finely chopped ripe olives
1 cup chopped pecans
Ripe olives (optional)
Fresh parsley sprigs (optional)

Combine first 3 ingredients; beat at
medium speed of an electric mixer until
smooth. Add blue cheese, and beat
well. Stir in chives and chopped olives.
(Mixture will be soft.)

Shape mixture into a ball, and roll in
pecans. Refrigerate several hours or
overnight. Garnish with ripe olives and
parsley, if desired. Serve with crackers.
Yield: 1 cheese ball. *Agnes H. Fisher,*
*Sylva, North Carolina.*

## COLD HAM SPREAD

1 tablespoon plus 1 teaspoon unflavored
  gelatin
¼ cup Chablis or other dry white wine
2 tablespoons butter or margarine
1 tablespoon all-purpose flour
1 cup half-and-half
2½ cups ground cooked ham
¼ cup mayonnaise
2 teaspoons Dijon mustard
½ cup whipping cream, whipped
Fresh parsley sprigs (optional)
Parsley Sauce

Soften gelatin in wine, and set aside.
Melt butter in a heavy saucepan over
low heat; add flour, stirring until
smooth. Cook 1 minute, stirring constantly. Gradually add half-and-half;
cook over medium heat, stirring constantly, until thickened and bubbly. Remove from heat; add softened gelatin,
and stir well. Cool.

Combine ham, mayonnaise, and mustard; add to cooled gelatin mixture, stirring well. Chill until slightly thickened.
Fold whipped cream into chilled mixture and spoon into a 1-quart mold
lightly oiled with mayonnaise. Refrigerate until set.

Unmold on serving plate; garnish
with parsley sprigs, if desired. Serve
with crackers and Parsley Sauce. Yield:
14 to 16 appetizer servings.

*Parsley Sauce:*

1 (8-ounce) carton commercial sour cream
½ cup mayonnaise
¾ cup chopped fresh parsley
¼ cup finely chopped fresh spinach
2 drops onion juice
⅛ teaspoon white pepper
⅛ teaspoon salt

Combine all ingredients, and mix
until smooth. Yield: 1¾ cups.
*Mrs. Werner A. Senff,*
*Longboat Key, Florida.*

## JALAPENO-CHEESE SPREAD

2½ cups (10 ounces) shredded Cheddar
  cheese
8 pimiento-stuffed olives, finely chopped
2 or 3 canned jalapeño peppers, seeded
  and finely chopped
2 teaspoons canned jalapeño pepper liquid
1 (2-ounce) jar diced pimiento, drained
2 tablespoons finely chopped dill pickle
3 to 4 tablespoons mayonnaise or salad
  dressing

Combine all ingredients; mix well.
Cover and refrigerate. Serve with crack-
ers or corn chips. Yield: 2 cups.
*Mrs. Harry Zimmer,*
*El Paso, Texas.*

## HOT CHILE DIP

2 or 3 dried red chile peppers, seeded
1 small onion, quartered
1 clove garlic
1 (16-ounce) can whole tomatoes,
  undrained
1 tablespoon sugar
1 teaspoon salt
¼ teaspoon ground oregano
⅛ teaspoon ground cumin

Place peppers, onion, and garlic in
container of electric blender; process 30
seconds. Add remaining ingredients,
and blend well. Serve with corn chips or
tortilla chips. Yield: 2¼ cups.

## STARBURST VEGETABLE DIP

¼ cup peeled, finely chopped cucumber
Salt
1 (8-ounce) carton commercial sour cream
1 (0.75-ounce) package Italian salad
  dressing mix
3 tablespoons finely chopped green pepper
3 tablespoons diced pimiento
Cucumber slice (optional)
Radish rose (optional)

Sprinkle cucumber with salt, and let
stand 20 minutes. Place cucumber in a
colander; rinse well and drain. Press cucumber between paper towels until
barely moist; set aside.

Combine sour cream and salad dressing mix in a bowl; mix well. Stir in
cucumber, green pepper, and pimiento.
Garnish with a cucumber slice and radish rose, if desired. Serve with assorted
fresh vegetables. Yield: about 1½ cups.
*Ginger Barker,*
*Mesquite, Texas.*

## PARMESAN PARTY ROUNDS

¾ cup mayonnaise
¾ cup grated Parmesan cheese
1 tablespoon milk
⅓ cup finely chopped green onion
2 (8-ounce) loaves sliced party rye bread

Combine first 3 ingredients; mix well.
Stir in green onion. Spread a thin layer
of mixture on each slice of bread; place
on a baking sheet. (Reserve remaining
bread for use in another recipe.) Broil
about 4 inches from heat until bread is
lightly toasted. Serve immediately.
Yield: about 5½ dozen.
*Eleanor Nelson,*
*Ludington, Michigan.*

## CHEESY PECAN BITES

2 cups all-purpose flour
1 teaspoon salt
2 cups (8 ounces) shredded sharp Cheddar
  cheese
1 cup butter or margarine, softened
About 1¼ cups pecan halves

Combine flour and salt in a mixing
bowl; add cheese, and mix well. Cut in
butter until mixture resembles coarse

meal. Mix with hands until dough is smooth; shape into a ball.

Roll dough to ¼-inch thickness on a lightly floured surface; cut into rounds with a 2-inch cookie cutter. Place on a lightly greased baking sheet. Place a pecan half in the center of each round. Fold 2 opposite edges of dough to center of pecan, overlapping edges slightly; press gently to seal. Bake at 425° for 10 minutes. Yield: about 6 dozen.

*Debbie Wilson,*
*College Station, Texas.*

### SUGARED PEANUTS

1 cup sugar
½ cup water
¼ teaspoon maple flavoring
2½ cups raw shelled peanuts

Combine all ingredients in a medium saucepan. Cook over medium heat, stirring frequently, 10 to 15 minutes or until peanuts are coated with syrup. Spread peanuts on a well-greased baking sheet. Bake at 300° for 15 minutes.

Remove from oven, and stir well; return nuts to oven, and bake 15 additional minutes. Yield: about 3 cups.

*Florence Miner,*
*Nevada, Iowa.*

### SPINACH TARTS

1 (10-ounce) package frozen chopped
    spinach, thawed and drained
1 egg, beaten
¼ teaspoon salt
⅛ teaspoon pepper
2 tablespoons chopped onion
1 cup crumbled feta or grated Romano
    cheese
¼ cup butter or margarine, melted
Cream Cheese Patty Shells
2 tablespoons grated Romano cheese
Diced pimiento (optional)

Place spinach on paper towels, and squeeze until barely moist. Combine spinach and next 6 ingredients; mix well. Fill each patty shell with 1 heaping teaspoonful of spinach mixture; sprinkle with Romano cheese. Bake at 350° for 30 to 35 minutes. Garnish tarts with pimiento, if desired. Yield: 2½ dozen appetizer servings.

*Cream Cheese Patty Shells:*
1 (3-ounce) package cream cheese,
    softened
½ cup butter or margarine, softened
1½ cups all-purpose flour

Combine softened cream cheese and butter; cream until smooth. Add flour, and mix well.

Shape dough into thirty 1-inch balls. Place in ungreased 1¾-inch muffin pans, and shape each ball into a shell. Yield: 2½ dozen.

*Deborah Styers,*
*Reidsville, North Carolina.*

### MUSHROOMS STUFFED WITH CRAB

24 large fresh mushrooms (about 1 pound)
½ cup milk
1 tablespoon butter
½ cup cracker crumbs
1 teaspoon dry mustard
1 teaspoon minced onion
¼ teaspoon salt
½ teaspoon prepared horseradish
Dash of pepper
1 (6½-ounce) can crabmeat, drained and
    flaked
2 tablespoons butter, melted

Clean mushrooms with damp paper towels. Remove mushroom stems, and reserve for use in another recipe. Set mushroom caps aside.

Combine milk and 1 tablespoon butter in a small saucepan. Cook over low heat until butter melts, stirring frequently. Remove from heat, and stir in next 7 ingredients.

Spoon crabmeat mixture into mushroom caps. Place in a lightly greased 13- x 9- x 2-inch baking dish, and brush tops with melted butter. Bake at 350° for 18 to 20 minutes. Yield: 2 dozen.

*Frances Ewing,*
*De Soto, Texas.*

*Tip: Every time the door is opened to the oven, the temperature drops 25 to 30 degrees. Use the oven window—the energy is not wasted as when the door is open.*

## Share Brandied Fruit

Whether received as gifts or nurtured from scratch, brandied fruit starters are making their way into thousands of Southern kitchens.

Our Brandied Fruit Starter can be served atop pound cake or ice cream and used to bake our Friendship Cake.

The starter should last indefinitely if handled properly. Use clean equipment, and keep it covered.

### BRANDIED FRUIT STARTER

1 (15¼-ounce) can pineapple chunks,
    drained
1 (16-ounce) can sliced peaches, drained
1 (17-ounce) can apricot halves, drained
1 (10-ounce) jar maraschino cherries,
    drained
1¼ cups sugar
1¼ cups brandy

Combine all ingredients in a clean, nonmetal bowl; stir gently. Cover and let stand at room temperature 3 weeks, stirring fruit twice a week. Serve fruit over ice cream or pound cake, reserving at least 1 cup starter at all times.

To replenish starter, add 1 cup sugar and one of the first 4 ingredients every 1 to 3 weeks, alternating fruit each time; stir gently. Cover and let stand at room temperature 3 days before using. Yield: 6 cups.

*Note: Apricot or peach brandy may be substituted for plain brandy, if desired.*

*Liz Dixon,*
*Knoxville, Tennessee.*

## FRIENDSHIP CAKE

1 cup butter or margarine, melted
1¾ cups sugar
3 cups all-purpose flour
1 teaspoon baking soda
1 teaspoon ground cinnamon
½ teaspoon salt
¼ teaspoon ground cloves
¼ teaspoon ground nutmeg
2 eggs
2 cups drained brandied fruit
1 cup chopped pecans
¼ cup brandied fruit juice
Powdered sugar (optional)

Combine butter and sugar in a large bowl; beat well. Combine next 6 ingredients; add to butter mixture, beating well. Add eggs; beat well.

Coarsely chop brandied fruit, and stir into batter. Add pecans and juice; mix well. Pour batter into a well-greased and floured 10-inch Bundt pan. Bake at 350° for 1 hour. Cool in pan 10 minutes; remove from pan, and cool completely on a wire rack. Sprinkle with powdered sugar, if desired. Yield: one 10-inch cake. *Janice S. Vaughn, Nashville, Tennessee.*

# Here's To A Delicious Holiday Season

For our formal dinner menu, we travel to lush Avery Island, Louisiana, and Sundown, the cottage retreat of Matt and Ginja Moseley of New Orleans. Holidays and weekends usually find Matt and Ginja on the island hosting parties and get-togethers.

Guests at Sundown know they are in for a treat; both Matt and Ginja are accomplished cooks and delight in creating their own recipes. "We often stumble onto new recipes," says Matt. "When we go out somewhere to eat, if we really like a certain dish, we come home and try to duplicate it."

One such dish is part of the holiday menu featured here. "The Crabmeat

Ravigote is our favorite dish at Galatoire's," says Ginja.

"Basically, it's a cream sauce combined with a Hollandaise sauce," explains Matt. "We're not exactly sure how they do it, but I think our recipe is pretty darn close."

Ginja also extracts ideas from cookbooks and magazines. "We enjoyed developing the Ducklings With Blackberry Sauce," she says. "I read about it, checked several similar recipes, then created this one."

Matt and Ginja begin their holiday feast by offering Spicy Curried Nuts and drinks in the living room. Crabmeat Ravigote is served at the dining table as the appetizer, followed by Ginja's refreshing Cranberry Sorbet. Oyster Bread Dressing, Saucy Minted Carrots, Zucchini Boats With Spinach, and Homemade Potato Rolls complement the main course of Ducklings With Blackberry Sauce.

The meal's crowning touch comes with dessert—Lemon Soufflé lavished with whipped cream and strawberries.

**Spicy Curried Nuts**
**Crabmeat Ravigote**
**Cranberry Sorbet**
**Ducklings With Blackberry Sauce**
**Oyster Bread Dressing**
**Saucy Minted Carrots**
**Zucchini Boats With Spinach**
**Homemade Potato Rolls**
**Lemon Soufflé**
**Wine      Coffee**

## SPICY CURRIED NUTS

½ teaspoon grated whole nutmeg
1 tablespoon plus 1 teaspoon curry powder
2 teaspoons ground ginger
2 teaspoons ground allspice
2 teaspoons ground cinnamon
¾ cup sugar
4 egg whites
10 to 12 drops hot sauce
4 cups pecan halves

Combine first 6 ingredients in a paper bag; shake to mix, and set aside. Lightly beat egg whites (at room temperature) and hot sauce until combined. Add pecans, a few at a time, stirring well to coat. Place pecans in bag; shake well.

Spread pecans in a single layer on a lightly greased 15- x 10- x 1-inch jellyroll pan. Bake at 200° for 2½ hours. Yield: 4 cups.

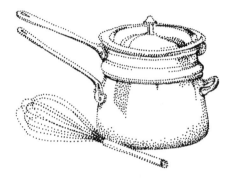

## CRABMEAT RAVIGOTE

1 frozen patty shell, thawed
6 egg yolks
1 cup butter
Juice of 1 lemon
Dash of hot sauce
¼ teaspoon salt
2 tablespoons butter
3 tablespoons all-purpose flour
1¾ cups milk
½ teaspoon salt
¼ teaspoon white pepper
1 pound fresh lump crabmeat
3 tablespoons chopped green onion
3 tablespoons finely chopped fresh parsley
Fresh parsley sprigs
Chopped pimiento

Roll patty shell out to ⅛-inch thickness on a lightly floured surface. Cut into 16 leaf shapes. Place on a lightly greased baking sheet, and bake at 350° for 5 to 8 minutes or until lightly browned. Set pastry leaves aside.

Combine egg yolks and 1 cup butter with a wire whisk in top of double boiler. Bring water to a boil (water in bottom of double boiler should not touch top pan). Reduce heat to low; cook, stirring constantly, until butter melts. Remove pan from water, and stir rapidly 2 minutes. Stir in lemon juice, 1

teaspoonful at a time; add hot sauce and salt. Place over boiling water; cook, stirring constantly, 2 to 3 minutes or until thickened and bubbly. Immediately remove from heat.

Melt 2 tablespoons butter in a heavy saucepan; add flour and cook 1 minute, stirring constantly. Gradually add milk; cook over medium heat, stirring constantly, until thickened. Stir in ½ teaspoon salt and white pepper.

Add cream sauce to mixture in double boiler. Gently fold in crabmeat, green onion, and chopped parsley. Spoon into individual serving dishes, and garnish with pastry leaves, parsley sprigs, and pimiento. Yield: 8 servings.

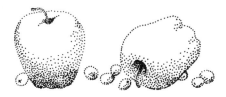

## CRANBERRY SORBET

**8 Granny Smith or other variety green apples**
**Lemon juice**
**4 cups fresh cranberries, finely ground**
**¾ cup orange juice**
**1 cup water**
**1 cup sugar**
**2 tablespoons lemon juice**

Cut a 1½-inch slice in a scallop pattern from top of each apple; reserve apple tops. Hollow each apple to within 1 inch from bottom, leaving a ½-inch shell. Sprinkle inside of apples with lemon juice. Freeze apples overnight.

Combine fresh cranberries and orange juice, mixing well. Set mixture aside.

Combine 1 cup water and sugar in a large heavy saucepan; bring to a boil. Reduce heat; cover and simmer 5 minutes. Stir in cranberry mixture and 2 tablespoons lemon juice; simmer, uncovered, an additional 5 minutes, stirring occasionally. Skim off foam, and cool.

Pour cranberry mixture into freezer can of a 2-quart freezer. Freeze according to manufacturer's instructions. Mound sorbet into frozen apple shells; place apple tops on side of mound. Store in freezer until serving time. Yield: 8 servings.

## DUCKLINGS WITH BLACKBERRY SAUCE

**2 (5- to 5½-pound) dressed ducklings**
**2 medium onions, quartered**
**2 medium apples, quartered**
**1 teaspoon salt**
**¼ teaspoon pepper**
**1 quart water**
**2 cups chopped onion**
**1 cup chopped celery**
**1 cup chopped carrots**
**2 (16-ounce) cans blackberries, undrained**
**¼ cup Cointreau**
**¼ cup blackberry jam**
**1 tablespoon plus 1 teaspoon all-purpose flour**
**1 tablespoon plus 1 teaspoon butter, softened**

Remove giblets and neck from ducklings; set aside. Prick fatty areas of ducklings (not breast) with a fork at intervals. Stuff each cavity with quartered onion and apple. Close cavity of ducklings with skewers. Sprinkle with salt and pepper. Fold neck skin under and place ducklings, breast side up, on a rack in a large roasting pan. Bake, uncovered, at 350° for 2 hours or until drumsticks and thighs move easily. Discard onions and apples. Set ducklings aside; keep warm.

Combine reserved giblets and neck, 1 quart water, chopped onion, celery, and carrots in a medium saucepan. Bring to a boil, stirring well. Reduce heat; cover and simmer 20 to 25 minutes. Drain mixture, reserving 2 cups duck stock. Discard giblets, neck, and vegetables.

Drain blackberries, reserving 2 cups blackberry juice; set blackberries aside.

Combine scrapings from roasting pan, reserved blackberry juice, Cointreau, and reserved duck stock in a medium saucepan. Bring to a boil, and boil 15 minutes or until liquid is reduced by half. Make a paste by combining jam, flour, and butter; gradually add to liquid in pan, stirring well. Cook over medium heat, stirring constantly, until thickened. Stir in blackberries.

Cut ducklings into quarters; place under broiler to crisp skin. Transfer to serving platter. Serve with blackberry sauce. Yield: 8 servings.

## OYSTER BREAD DRESSING

**1 (1-pound) loaf French bread**
**¼ pound chicken gizzards**
**3 cups water**
**1 cup finely chopped onion**
**¼ cup finely chopped celery**
**¼ cup finely chopped green pepper**
**1 bunch green onions, finely chopped**
**1 bunch fresh parsley, finely chopped**
**2 cloves garlic, crushed**
**¼ cup butter or margarine**
**½ pound ground lean beef**
**¼ pound ground pork**
**¼ pound chicken livers, finely chopped**
**1 teaspoon instant-blending flour**
**½ teaspoon salt**
**¼ teaspoon black pepper**
**¼ teaspoon ground red pepper**
**2 dashes of hot sauce**
**2½ pints oysters, undrained**

Cut bread in half lengthwise and place cut side up on a baking sheet; bake at 350° for 15 to 20 minutes or until lightly browned. Cool. Tear bread into about 1-inch pieces. Place in a large bowl, and set aside.

Place gizzards and 3 cups water in a saucepan; cover and cook over medium heat 45 minutes or until tender. Remove gizzards, reserving 1½ cups broth. Finely chop gizzards; set aside.

Sauté vegetables, parsley, and garlic in butter in a large skillet. Add gizzards, ground beef, pork, and livers; cook over medium-high heat until meat is no longer pink, stirring to crumble meat. Add reserved chicken broth; reduce heat to low, and simmer 30 minutes or until broth has been reduced to about ½ cup. Stir in flour and seasonings; simmer 10 minutes.

Spoon mixture over bread. Cut oysters in half; add oysters and oyster liquid to bread mixture. Stir until well combined. Spoon mixture into a well-greased 3-quart casserole. Bake at 350° for 20 minutes or until thoroughly heated. Yield: 8 servings.

*Tip: Stains or discolorations inside aluminum utensils can be removed by boiling a solution of 2 to 3 tablespoons cream of tartar, lemon juice, or vinegar to each quart of water in the utensil for 5 to 10 minutes.*

## SAUCY MINTED CARROTS

4 cups water
2 teaspoons sugar
1 teaspoon salt
2 pounds baby carrots
½ cup butter
¼ cup plus 2 tablespoons firmly packed
    brown sugar
1 tablespoon cornstarch
¼ cup fresh mint leaves, finely chopped

Combine water, sugar, and salt in a large saucepan; add carrots, stirring well. Bring to a boil; reduce heat, and cook 12 to 15 minutes or until tender. Drain carrots, reserving 1 cup liquid. Set carrots aside, and keep warm.

Melt butter in a heavy saucepan over low heat; add brown sugar and cornstarch, stirring until smooth. Cook 1 minute, stirring constantly. Gradually add 1 cup liquid reserved from carrots; cook over medium heat, stirring constantly, until thickened and bubbly. Stir in mint. Pour sauce over carrots, stirring gently to coat. Yield: 8 servings.

## ZUCCHINI BOATS WITH SPINACH

1 (10-ounce) package frozen chopped
    spinach
4 medium zucchini
3 tablespoons finely chopped onion
3 tablespoons butter or margarine
3 tablespoons all-purpose flour
1 cup half-and-half
½ cup milk
½ cup (2 ounces) shredded Swiss or
    Gruyère cheese
1 teaspoon salt
¼ teaspoon white pepper
5 drops hot sauce
1 tablespoon grated Parmesan cheese

Cook spinach according to package directions; drain and press dry. Set aside.

Cook zucchini in boiling salted water to cover 5 minutes. Drain and cool slightly; trim off stems. Cut zucchini in half lengthwise; remove and reserve pulp, leaving ¼-inch-thick shells. Drain shells, and set aside. Chop pulp; drain well, and set aside.

Sauté onion in butter in a saucepan. Reduce heat to low; add flour, and stir until smooth. Cook 1 minute, stirring constantly. Gradually add half-and-half and milk; cook over medium heat, stirring constantly, until thickened and bubbly. Add spinach, zucchini pulp, Swiss cheese, salt, pepper, and hot sauce.

Place zucchini shells in a 12- x 8- x 2-inch baking dish. Spoon spinach mixture into shells; sprinkle with Parmesan cheese. Bake, uncovered, at 350° for 15 minutes or until thoroughly heated. Yield: 8 servings.

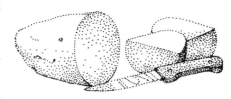

## HOMEMADE POTATO ROLLS

2 medium potatoes, peeled and quartered
½ cup milk
1 package dry yeast
½ cup sugar
⅔ cup vegetable oil
1 egg
1½ teaspoons salt
About 5½ cups all-purpose flour

Cook potatoes in boiling water to cover 15 to 20 minutes or until tender. Drain, reserving ½ cup potato water; set potatoes aside.

Combine potato water and milk; heat to 105° to 115°. Stir in yeast and sugar; let stand 5 minutes.

Mash potatoes to measure ¾ cup. Combine potatoes, oil, egg, salt, and yeast mixture in a large mixing bowl. Beat on medium speed of electric mixer until blended. Gradually beat in enough flour to form a moderately stiff dough.

Place dough in a well-greased bowl, turning to grease top. Cover and let rise in a warm place (85°), free from drafts, 1½ hours or until doubled in bulk.

Punch dough down; turn onto a lightly floured surface; knead about 5 minutes or until smooth and elastic.

Lightly grease muffin pans. Shape dough into 1-inch balls; place 3 balls in each muffin cup. Cover and let rise in a warm place (85°), free from drafts, 1 hour or until doubled in bulk. Bake at 400° for 12 to 15 minutes or until golden brown. Yield: 2 dozen.

## LEMON SOUFFLE

2 dozen ladyfingers
1 envelope unflavored gelatin
¼ cup cold water
8 eggs, separated
1 cup sugar
Pinch of salt
3 tablespoons grated lemon rind
½ cup lemon juice
1 cup sugar
Whipped cream
Lemon slices
Fresh strawberries

Line the bottom and sides of a 9-inch springform pan with ladyfingers. Set aside.

Soften gelatin in water; let mixture stand 5 minutes.

Combine egg yolks, 1 cup sugar, and salt in top of a double boiler; beat well. Bring water to a boil in bottom of double boiler. Reduce heat to low; cook, stirring constantly, until sugar dissolves. Add lemon rind and juice; cook, stirring constantly, until mixture thickens and coats a metal spoon. Add gelatin; stir until combined. Cool.

Beat egg whites (at room temperature) until foamy; gradually add 1 cup sugar, 1 tablespoon at a time, beating until soft peaks form. Fold egg whites into custard mixture; pour into springform pan. Chill until firm (4 to 5 hours). Unmold on a serving platter; garnish with piped whipped cream, lemon slices, and strawberries. Yield: 16 servings.

# Jazz Up The Bread With Nuts

Pecans and walnuts go into this festive array of holiday breads. Peggy Amos of Martinsville, Virginia, keeps plenty of pecans in the pantry for special holiday baking. Chopped pecans taste great in her cherry- and chocolate-flavored Merry Muffins. Their unusual two-tone appearance always draws compliments from Peggy's guests.

Flavored with pumpkin pie spice and white wine, and frosted with a powdered sugar glaze, Wine-Date Nut Bread is another favorite for the holidays. Make it with walnuts or pecans—whichever you have on hand.

## WINE-DATE NUT BREAD

6 cups all-purpose flour
2 cups firmly packed dark brown sugar
2 tablespoons baking powder
1 tablespoon plus 1 teaspoon pumpkin pie spice
1 teaspoon salt
1 (16-ounce) package chopped dates
2 cups chopped pecans or walnuts
4 eggs, beaten
2⅔ cups Chablis or other dry white wine
1 cup butter or margarine, melted
1 cup sifted powdered sugar
2½ tablespoons Chablis or other dry white wine
1 teaspoon pumpkin pie spice

Combine first 5 ingredients in a large mixing bowl, stirring well; add dates and pecans, stirring to coat.

Combine eggs, 2⅔ cups wine, and butter; add to dry ingredients, stirring just until blended. Pour batter into 2 greased 9- x 5- x 3-inch loafpans. Bake at 350° for 1 hour and 25 minutes or until bread tests done. Cool in pans 10 minutes. Remove to cooling rack.

Combine remaining ingredients, mixing well. Drizzle over warm loaves. Cool bread completely before slicing. Yield: 2 loaves.

*Mrs. J. Russell Buchanan,*
*Monroe, Louisiana.*

## MERRY MUFFINS

2 cups all-purpose flour
⅔ cup chopped pecans
½ cup sugar
1 tablespoon baking powder
½ teaspoon salt
¾ cup milk
⅓ cup vegetable oil
1 egg, beaten
¼ cup chopped maraschino cherries
¼ cup chocolate-flavored drink mix
Powdered sugar (optional)

Combine first 5 ingredients in a large bowl, stirring well; make a well in the center of mixture. Combine milk, oil, and egg; add to dry ingredients, stirring just until moistened.

Divide batter in half; stir cherries into one portion. Stir chocolate drink mix into remaining portion. Spoon about 1 tablespoon cherry batter into one side of each greased muffin tin. Spoon about 1 tablespoon chocolate batter into other side, filling two-thirds full. Bake at 400° for 15 to 20 minutes. Sprinkle with powdered sugar, if desired. Yield: 14 muffins.

*Peggy H. Amos,*
*Martinsville, Virginia.*

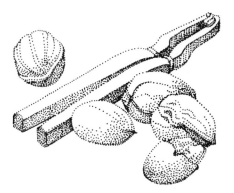

## FRUIT-NUT TWISTS

1½ cups all-purpose flour
3 tablespoons sugar
1 tablespoon baking powder
¼ teaspoon salt
⅓ cup shortening
½ cup plus 1 tablespoon milk
1 cup chopped mixed candied fruit
½ cup chopped walnuts

Combine first 4 ingredients in a mixing bowl; cut in shortening with a pastry blender until mixture resembles coarse meal. Sprinkle milk evenly over surface of flour mixture; stir with a fork until all ingredients are moistened. Stir in fruit and walnuts.

Roll dough to ½-inch thickness on a lightly floured surface. Cut into 4- x ½-inch strips. Twist strips into S shapes; place on lightly greased baking sheets. Bake at 450° for 6 to 8 minutes or until lightly browned. Yield: about 3½ dozen.

*Amelia M. Brown,*
*Pittsburgh, Pennsylvania.*

# European Coffees—Instantly

Here's a delightful holiday idea from Janice S. Elder of Spartanburg, South Carolina. By adding either cocoa, orange rind, or cinnamon to dry milk and instant coffee, she makes four European instant coffee mixes. To serve the coffee, she measures the mixes into cups or mugs and adds boiling water. They are delicious to sip and thoughtful, inexpensive gifts.

## CAFE CAPPUCCINO

½ cup instant coffee granules
¾ cup sugar
½ teaspoon dried orange peel, crushed
1 cup instant nonfat dry milk powder
Boiling water
Orange slices (optional)

Combine first 4 ingredients, and mix well. Store mix in an airtight container.

For each serving, place 2½ to 3 tablespoons mix in a cup. Add 1 cup boiling water; stir well. Serve with orange slices, if desired. Yield: about 10 servings.

## SWISS-STYLE MOCHA

½ cup instant coffee granules
½ cup sugar
2 tablespoons cocoa
1 cup instant nonfat dry milk powder
Boiling water

Combine first 4 ingredients, and mix well. Store mix in an airtight container.

For each serving, place 1 tablespoon plus 1 teaspoon mix in a cup. Add 1 cup boiling water, and stir well. Yield: about 24 servings.

*Tip: Nonfat dry milk costs about half as much as fluid whole milk. Keep a supply of reconstituted dry milk in the refrigerator and use it for cooking. Serve it very cold for drinking—or combine it half-and-half with whole milk if you prefer the taste.*

## ITALIAN MOCHA ESPRESSO

1 cup instant coffee granules
1 cup sugar
4½ cups instant nonfat dry milk powder
½ cup cocoa
Boiling water
Whipped cream (optional)
Grated chocolate (optional)

Combine first 4 ingredients, and mix well. Store mix in an airtight container.

For each serving, place ¼ cup plus 2 tablespoons mix in a cup. Add 1 cup boiling water; stir well. Garnish with whipped cream and grated chocolate, if desired. Yield: about 18 servings.

## CAFE VIENNESE

1 cup instant coffee granules
1 cup sugar
⅔ cup instant nonfat dry milk powder
½ teaspoon ground cinnamon
Boiling water
Cinnamon sticks (optional)

Combine first 4 ingredients, and mix well. Store mix in an airtight container.

For each serving, place 2½ to 3 tablespoons mix in a cup. Add 1 cup boiling water, and stir well. Serve each cup with a cinnamon stick, if desired. Yield: about 14 servings.

# Fruit On The Side For Color, Flavor

No holiday feast is complete without lots of festive and colorful side dishes. This year, along with the vegetables that always grace the holiday table, include a side dish of sparkling fruit. Each of these simply prepared fruits brings sweetness and elegance to special meals.

Select from stately pears poached in red wine or sliced apples cooked in sweetened orange juice. You'll find that ham, turkey, or roast tastes better when accompanied by Spiced Cranberries or Scalloped Pineapple.

## GOLDEN APPLES

3 medium cooking apples, unpeeled and cut into ¼-inch slices
½ cup orange juice
¼ cup honey
2 tablespoons apricot preserves

Combine apples and orange juice in a skillet; place over high heat, and bring juice to a boil. Stir in honey and apricot preserves; cover, reduce heat, and simmer 5 minutes. Serve warm. Yield: 4 to 6 servings. *Mrs. James E. Krachey, Guymon, Oklahoma.*

## SPICED CRANBERRIES

4 cups sugar
1½ cups vinegar
⅔ cup water
1 tablespoon plus 1 teaspoon ground ginger
1 teaspoon ground cloves
8 cups fresh cranberries

Combine first 5 ingredients in a large Dutch oven; bring to a boil, stirring constantly. Add cranberries; reduce heat and simmer 25 minutes, stirring frequently.

Quickly ladle cranberry mixture into hot sterilized jars, leaving ½-inch headspace; cover at once with metal lids, and screw bands tight. Process in boiling-water bath 10 minutes. Yield: 7 cups. *Mrs. Earl L. Faulkenberry, Lancaster, South Carolina.*

## PEARS IN RED WINE

6 medium pears
2 cups red wine
1½ cups water
½ cup sugar
½ cup firmly packed brown sugar
3 lemon slices
3 orange slices
Orange rind strips (optional)

Peel pears, removing core from bottom and leaving stems intact. Slice about ¼ inch from base of each pear so they will sit flat.

Combine next 6 ingredients in a Dutch oven over medium heat; bring to a boil. Cover, reduce heat, and simmer 5 minutes. Place pears in Dutch oven in upright position; cover and continue to cook 40 minutes or until pears are tender. Remove from heat; allow to cool. Cover and refrigerate several hours.

To serve, spoon pears and syrup into serving dishes; garnish with a strip of orange rind, if desired. Yield: 6 servings. *Wilda B. Bell, Chattanooga, Tennessee.*

## SCALLOPED PINEAPPLE

½ cup butter or margarine, melted
4 cups fresh bread cubes
3 eggs
1 cup sugar
½ cup evaporated milk
1 (20-ounce) can crushed pineapple, undrained

Combine butter and bread cubes; mix well, and set aside.

Combine eggs, sugar, and milk; beat with electric mixer just until blended. Add bread cube mixture and pineapple, stirring well. Pour into a lightly greased 2-quart baking dish. Bake, uncovered, at 350° for 1 hour. Yield: 6 to 8 servings. *Milli Marriott, Herkimer, New York.*

Right: *Readers tell us that Hummingbird Cake (page 244), Perfect Chocolate Cake (page 244), and Cream Cheese Braids (page 243) are among their favorite ways to satisfy a sweet tooth.*

Page 258: *Take a holiday break with nut-filled Merry Muffins, Wine-Date Nut Bread, and Fruit-Nut Twists (recipes on page 253).*

Below: *Christmas Snow Salad (page 266),
studded with red and green maraschino
cherries, is sweet enough to be served for
dessert.*

Right: *Candied Carrots and Brussel Sprouts
in Lemon Sauce are both special enough for
a fancy holiday meal (recipes on page 269).*

Above: *Pears in Red Wine (page 254),
served in stemmed glasses, are an attractive
addition to holiday tables.*

Right: *Chocolate lovers will especially enjoy
Crème de Menthe Cheesecake (page 263).*

Far right: *Inside each of the Individual Beef
Wellingtons (page 259) you'll find a tender
filet mignon smothered with mushroom
sauce.*

# Choose A Memorable Entrée

A hint of the unusual in each of these extraordinary entrées makes each one a gourmet treat. Dinner guests will relish our individually wrapped beef Wellingtons or Lemon Roasted Cornish Hens, rubbed with fresh mint and served with a lemon-seasoned sauce.

Joanne Champagne's Pork St. Tammany was a recipe contest winner in New Orleans. Joanne mixes up a stuffing of wild rice, vegetables, pecans, and apricots, then spoons it between pork tenderloins for a prize-winning dish.

### INDIVIDUAL BEEF WELLINGTONS

6 (4- to 5-ounce) filets mignons
1 teaspoon salt
¼ teaspoon pepper
½ cup chopped onion
½ cup chopped carrots
½ cup chopped celery
⅓ cup vegetable oil
1 cup red wine
2 tablespoons brandy
½ teaspoon fines herbes
1 tablespoon butter
Mushroom filling (recipe follows)
Pastry (recipe follows)
2 egg yolks
2 teaspoons water
2 cups beef broth
1 tablespoon tomato paste
2 tablespoons cornstarch
¼ cup Madeira or other dry sweet wine
Sliced fresh mushrooms
Carrot curls
Celery fans
Fresh parsley sprigs

Sprinkle filets with salt and pepper, and place in a shallow dish. Sauté onion, carrots, and celery in oil until tender. Add wine, brandy, and herbs. Pour mixture over filets; cover and marinate in refrigerator overnight.

Drain steaks, reserving marinade. Sauté filets in 1 tablespoon butter in a skillet just until lightly browned on both sides. Place filets in pan; cover and freeze 10 minutes. Remove from freezer, and refrigerate 2 hours.

Prepare mushroom filling; chill at least 2 hours.

Prepare pastry; chill 2 hours. Roll into an 18-inch square on a lightly floured board or pastry cloth; cut into six 9- x 6-inch rectangles. Spread each pastry rectangle with ⅓ cup mushroom filling; top with a filet.

Combine egg yolks and 2 teaspoons water; brush edges of pastry with egg mixture to seal. Fold pastry over, and pinch together. (Trim excess pastry if necessary.) Place Wellingtons, seam side down, on a lightly greased baking sheet. Brush with egg mixture; repeat after 1 minute. Roll pastry trimmings; cut into decorative shapes and arrange on top of Wellingtons, if desired. Brush with remaining egg mixture. Bake at 400° for 25 minutes or until golden brown.

Combine reserved marinade, reserved mushroom juice, beef broth, and tomato paste in a saucepan; simmer 1 hour. Dissolve cornstarch in Madeira; stir into broth mixture and cook, stirring constantly, until thickened. Serve with Beef Wellingtons. Garnish with sliced mushrooms, carrot curls, celery fans, and parsley sprigs. Yield: 6 servings.

*Mushroom Filling:*

2 pounds fresh mushrooms, finely chopped
¼ cup minced green onion
2 tablespoons butter
½ cup Madeira or other dry sweet wine
Salt and pepper to taste

Place mushrooms in a clean towel or cheesecloth and squeeze until barely moist, reserving juice. Sauté mushrooms and onion in butter; cook over medium heat until all liquid is evaporated. Add Madeira; cook until evaporated. Add salt and pepper. Yield: 2⅓ cups.

*Pastry:*

3 cups all-purpose flour
1½ teaspoons salt
¾ cup plus 2 tablespoons chilled butter or margarine, cubed
¼ cup shortening, chilled
⅓ to ½ cup ice water

Combine flour and salt in a large bowl; cut in chilled butter and shortening with a pastry blender until mixture resembles coarse meal. Sprinkle ice water evenly over surface; stir with a fork until all dry ingredients are moistened. Shape dough into a ball. Yield: enough for 6 individual Wellingtons.

*Trudy Dunn,*
*San Jose, California.*

### BEEF BURGUNDY

1 pound boneless round steak
2½ tablespoons all-purpose flour
1 teaspoon salt
⅛ teaspoon pepper
1½ tablespoons bacon drippings
½ cup water
½ cup Burgundy
6 small onions
1 tablespoon catsup
1 beef-flavored bouillon cube
1 teaspoon chopped fresh parsley
¼ teaspoon ground thyme
1 small bay leaf
Dash of garlic powder
¼ pound fresh mushrooms, sliced in half
1½ tablespoons chopped fresh parsley
Hot buttered noodles

Trim excess fat from steak, and pound to ¼-inch thickness. Partially freeze steak; slice across grain into 2- x ⅛-inch strips.

Combine flour, salt, and pepper. Dredge steak in flour mixture; sauté in hot drippings until browned. Add next 9 ingredients to steak, and stir well. Cover skillet, and cook over low heat 45 minutes.

Stir in mushrooms; cover and cook 15 minutes. Remove bay leaf, and sprinkle with remaining parsley. Serve over hot buttered noodles. Yield: 4 servings.

*Mary Scott,*
*Albuquerque, New Mexico.*

## PORK ST. TAMMANY

1 (6-ounce) package long grain and wild
  rice mix
½ cup boiling water
½ cup chopped dried apricots
2 green onions, finely chopped
½ cup chopped fresh mushrooms
¼ cup chopped green pepper
2 tablespoons butter or margarine
3 tablespoons chopped pecans
1 tablespoon chopped fresh parsley
⅛ teaspoon salt
⅛ teaspoon pepper
Dash of red pepper
Dash of garlic powder
4 (1½-pound) boneless pork tenderloins
4 slices bacon
Canned apricot halves
Fresh parsley sprigs

Cook rice according to package directions. Set aside.

Pour boiling water over apricots; let stand 20 minutes to soften. Drain.

Sauté green onions, mushrooms, and green pepper in butter until tender. Add rice, apricots, pecans, parsley, and seasonings; stir until combined.

Cut a lengthwise slit on top of each tenderloin, being careful not to cut through the bottom and sides. Spoon half of stuffing into the opening of one tenderloin; place cut side of second tenderloin over stuffing. Tie tenderloins together securely with string, and place on a rack in a roasting pan. Top with two bacon slices. Repeat procedure with remaining tenderloins.

Place an aluminum foil tent over tenderloins; bake at 325° for 1½ to 2 hours or until meat thermometer registers 170°. Remove foil the last 30 to 40 minutes of baking. Remove from oven; let stand 5 minutes. Remove string; slice and garnish with apricot halves and parsley. Yield: 8 to 10 servings.
  *Joanne Champagne,*
  *Covington, Louisiana.*

*Tip: Grills or pans with a nonstick finish may become scratched or lose their finish with use. Spray the damaged surface with a nonstick vegetable spray to prevent food from sticking.*

## BAKED CHICKEN AND ARTICHOKE HEARTS

3 pounds chicken breasts, boned and
  skinned
1 teaspoon salt
½ teaspoon paprika
¼ teaspoon pepper
¼ cup plus 2 tablespoons butter or
  margarine, divided
1 (9-ounce) package frozen artichoke
  hearts, thawed
¼ pound fresh mushrooms, sliced
2 tablespoons all-purpose flour
⅔ cup chicken broth
3 tablespoons dry sherry

Sprinkle chicken with salt, paprika, and pepper. Melt ¼ cup butter in a large skillet. Brown chicken in butter over low heat; transfer to a greased shallow 2-quart casserole, reserving drippings in skillet. Arrange artichoke hearts in between chicken breasts; set aside.

Add remaining butter to reserved drippings; melt over low heat. Add mushrooms, and sauté 4 to 5 minutes. Stir flour into mushrooms; gradually add chicken broth and sherry, mixing well. Cook over medium heat, stirring constantly, until thickened and bubbly (about 5 minutes).

Pour sauce over chicken and artichokes. Cover and bake at 375° for 40 minutes. Yield: 6 to 8 servings.
  *Sherry Boger Phillips,*
  *Knoxville, Tennessee.*

## LEMON ROASTED CORNISH HENS

4 (1¼-pound) Cornish hens
1 lemon
3 tablespoons butter or margarine,
  softened
2 teaspoons chopped fresh mint
1 teaspoon salt
¼ teaspoon pepper
1 small onion, sliced
1 clove garlic, crushed
2 tablespoons vegetable oil
1 cup chicken broth
¼ cup lemon juice
1½ tablespoons cornstarch
2 teaspoons water
Chopped fresh mint
Watercress (optional)

Remove giblets from hens; reserve for another use. Rinse hens with cold water, and pat dry.

Grate enough lemon rind to equal 1 teaspoon; cut remaining rind into thin strips, and set aside. Combine grated lemon rind, butter, 2 teaspoons chopped mint, salt, and pepper; rub mixture over hens. Place hens breast side up in a shallow baking pan. Bake at 375° for 1 hour and 10 minutes, basting hens every 15 minutes with pan drippings.

Sauté reserved lemon rind strips, onion, and garlic in oil 5 minutes. Combine broth, lemon juice, cornstarch, and water in a small saucepan; stir well. Cook over medium heat, stirring constantly, until sauce is thickened. Stir in sautéed mixture, and serve sauce over hens. Sprinkle with chopped fresh mint, and garnish with watercress, if desired. Yield: 4 servings.
  *Tammy Smith,*
  *Talbott, Tennessee.*

## BAKED STUFFED SQUAB

1 (6-ounce) package long grain and wild
  rice mix
6 squabs
Salt and pepper
¾ teaspoon ground ginger
¼ cup sliced fresh mushrooms
¼ cup chopped fresh parsley
¼ cup chopped celery
¼ cup butter or margarine
1 tablespoon soy sauce
2 teaspoons Worcestershire sauce
½ cup white wine

Cook rice according to package directions; set aside.

Remove giblets from squabs; reserve for another use. Rinse squabs with cold water, and pat dry; rub with salt, pepper, and ginger.

Sauté the mushrooms, parsley, and celery in butter until tender. Stir in rice, and mix well.

Stuff squabs with rice mixture; sprinkle with soy sauce and Worcestershire sauce. Place squabs in a 4½-quart baking dish. Fill baking dish with ½ inch water. Cover and bake at 450° for 45 minutes. Remove cover; reduce heat to 350°. Add white wine, and bake an additional 30 minutes. Yield: 6 servings.

*Patty Barnett,*
*Sumter, South Carolina.*

## Desserts Sweeten The Season

Southerners treasure desserts, but never so much as during the holidays. Served with piping-hot coffee, a beautiful and delicious dessert is the perfect ending to any holiday meal.

To get everyone into a festive spirit, try Teresa Sands' Bûche de Noël Cake, a version of the traditional French Christmas dessert. Resembling a branched yule log, this confection nestles a creamy mocha filling and has a rich chocolate frosting.

Coconut cake is always in demand at this time of year, and Christmas Coconut Cake—all three layers of it—is an elegant choice. Coconut extract flavors both cake and frosting.

White Christmas Dessert is made in advance and chilled in a mold. Light and fruity, it's nice to serve after a large holiday meal. For Chocolate Torte Royale, a cinnamon meringue shell is filled with layers of chocolate and whipped cream.

### OLD-FASHIONED EGG CUSTARD PIE

¼ cup butter or margarine, softened
⅔ cup sugar
2 eggs
3 tablespoons all-purpose flour
¾ cup evaporated milk
¼ cup water
1 teaspoon vanilla extract
1 unbaked 9-inch pastry shell

Cream butter; gradually add sugar, beating well. Add eggs, one at a time, beating well after each addition. Add flour, and mix thoroughly. Stir in milk, ¼ cup water, and vanilla.

Pour custard mixture into pastry shell. Bake at 400° for 20 minutes. Reduce heat to 300°, and bake an additional 15 minutes. Cool. Refrigerate until thoroughly chilled. Yield: one 9-inch pie.

*June H. Johnson,*
*Mocksville, North Carolina.*

### BRANDY FRUITCAKE

1 (16-ounce) package candied yellow pineapple, chopped
1 (8-ounce) package candied red pineapple, chopped
1 (8-ounce) package candied green pineapple, chopped
1 (8-ounce) package candied red cherries, halved
1 (8-ounce) package candied green cherries, halved
1 (8-ounce) package candied citron, finely chopped
6 cups chopped pecans
4 cups all-purpose flour, divided
1½ cups butter or margarine, softened
2 cups sugar
10 eggs
1 teaspoon baking powder
1 teaspoon salt
½ cup brandy
1 teaspoon almond extract
1 teaspoon lemon extract
1 teaspoon vanilla extract
1 cup brandy, divided

Combine first 7 ingredients; dredge with 2 cups flour, stirring to coat well. Set mixture aside.

Cream butter in a large mixing bowl; gradually add sugar, beating until light and fluffy. Add eggs, one at a time, beating well after each addition.

Combine remaining 2 cups flour, baking powder, and salt; mix well. Add to creamed mixture alternately with ½ cup brandy, beginning and ending with flour mixture. Mix well after each addition. Stir in flavorings and fruit-nut mixture.

Spoon batter into 3 paper-lined and greased 9- x 5- x 3-inch loafpans. Place a large pan of boiling water on lower oven rack. Cover pans tightly with foil, and bake at 300° for 2 hours and 15 minutes. Remove foil, and bake an additional 30 minutes or until a wooden pick inserted in center comes out clean.

Sprinkle each loaf with ⅓ cup brandy; cool 10 minutes in pans. Remove loaves from pans; place on wire racks, and cool completely. Yield: 3 loaves.

*Adeline Bartling,*
*New Bern, North Carolina.*

### WHITE CHRISTMAS DESSERT

2 envelopes unflavored gelatin
2½ cups pineapple juice, divided
1 tablespoon grated lemon rind
2 tablespoons lemon juice
1 cup sugar
1 cup whipping cream
½ cup flaked coconut
Flaked coconut (optional)
Maraschino cherries (optional)
Pineapple slices (optional)

Sprinkle gelatin over 1 cup pineapple juice in top of double boiler; let stand 5 minutes. Place over boiling water and cook, stirring constantly, until gelatin dissolves. Remove from heat; stir in lemon rind, lemon juice, sugar, and remaining pineapple juice. Chill mixture until consistency of unbeaten egg white. Beat at high speed of electric mixer 10 seconds.

Beat whipping cream until soft peaks form; fold into gelatin mixture, and fold in coconut. Pour into a lightly oiled 7-cup mold, and chill until set.

Unmold on a serving plate; garnish with flaked coconut, maraschino cherries, and pineapple slices, if desired. Yield: 8 to 10 servings.

*Annette Van Ordstrand,*
*Paducah, Kentucky.*

*Tip: When squeezing fresh lemons or oranges for juice, first grate the rind by rubbing the washed fruit against surface of grater, taking care to remove only the outer colored portion of the rind. Wrap in plastic in teaspoon portions and freeze for future use.*

## SOUR CREAM APPLE SQUARES

2 cups all-purpose flour
2 cups firmly packed brown sugar
½ cup butter or margarine, softened
1 (8-ounce) carton commercial sour cream
1 egg, slightly beaten
1½ teaspoons baking soda
½ teaspoon salt
2 teaspoons ground cinnamon
1 teaspoon vanilla extract
1 cup chopped pecans
2 cups peeled, finely chopped apples

Combine flour and brown sugar in a medium bowl; cut in butter with a pastry blender until mixture resembles coarse meal. Firmly press 2¾ cups of mixture evenly into an ungreased 13- x 9- x 2-inch baking pan, reserving the remaining mixture in bowl.

Add next 6 ingredients to reserved mixture in bowl, and beat well. Fold in pecans and apples. Pour filling over crust in pan. Bake at 350° for 35 minutes or until filling is firm. Cool and cut into 2-inch squares. Yield: 2 dozen.

*Marji Moore,*
*Tallahassee, Florida.*

## CHRISTMAS COCONUT CAKE

1 cup butter, softened
2 cups sugar
7 eggs
2¾ cups all-purpose flour
1 teaspoon baking powder
1 teaspoon baking soda
Dash of salt
1 cup buttermilk
2 tablespoons vegetable oil
1 teaspoon vanilla extract
1 teaspoon coconut extract
Coconut Frosting
1 cup flaked coconut
Red and green candied cherries
   (optional)

Cream butter; gradually add sugar, and beat 10 to 15 minutes at medium speed of electric mixer. Add eggs, one at a time, beating well after each addition. Combine flour, baking powder, soda, and salt; add to creamed mixture alternately with buttermilk and oil, beginning and ending with flour mixture, mixing well after each addition. Stir in flavorings.

Pour batter into 3 greased and floured 9-inch round cakepans. Bake at 350° for 20 to 25 minutes or until a wooden pick inserted in center comes out clean. Cool cake in pans 10 minutes. Remove layers from pans; place on wire racks, and let cool completely.

Spread Coconut Frosting between layers and on top and sides of cake. Sprinkle top and sides with 1 cup coconut; garnish with candied cherries, if desired. Cover and chill before serving. Yield: one 3-layer cake.

*Coconut Frosting:*

1 cup milk
¼ cup all-purpose flour
½ cup butter, softened
½ cup shortening
1 cup sugar
1 teaspoon coconut extract
1 teaspoon vanilla extract
1 cup flaked coconut

Combine milk and flour in a medium saucepan; cook over medium heat, stirring constantly, until mixture thickens. Remove saucepan from heat, and let mixture cool completely.

Add butter, shortening, and sugar; beat well. Add flavorings and 1 cup coconut, stirring well. Yield: enough frosting for one 3-layer cake.

*Carolyn S. Swiger,*
*Front Royal, Virginia.*

## BUCHE DE NOEL CAKE

Vegetable oil
4 eggs, separated
¼ cup plus 2 tablespoons sugar
2 tablespoons water
1 teaspoon vanilla extract
¼ cup plus 2 tablespoons sugar
¾ cup all-purpose flour
1 teaspoon baking powder
¼ teaspoon salt
2 to 3 tablespoons powdered sugar
1 tablespoon rum extract
Mocha Filling
Chocolate Frosting
⅓ cup finely chopped pecans

Grease a 15- x 10- x 1-inch jellyroll pan with vegetable oil, and line with waxed paper. Grease waxed paper lightly with vegetable oil, and set pan aside.

Beat egg yolks until thick and lemon colored; gradually add ¼ cup plus 2 tablespoons sugar, beating well. Stir in water and vanilla.

Beat egg whites (at room temperature) in a large mixing bowl until foamy; gradually add ¼ cup plus 2 tablespoons sugar, 1 tablespoon at a time, beating until stiff peaks form. Fold in egg yolk mixture.

Combine flour, baking powder, and salt; mix well, and fold into egg mixture. Spread batter evenly in prepared pan. Bake at 375° for 15 minutes.

Sift powdered sugar in a 15- x 10-inch rectangle on a linen towel. When cake is done, immediately loosen from sides of pan, and turn out onto sugar. Peel off waxed paper. Starting at wide end, roll up warm cake and towel together; let cake cool completely on a wire rack, seam side down.

Unroll cake; remove towel. Sprinkle rum extract evenly over cake. Spread with Mocha Filling, and reroll.

Diagonally cut a 4-inch piece of cake from the roll. Place rolls on a serving plate, positioning cut edge of short piece against side of longer piece, to resemble a tree branch. Frost with Chocolate Frosting, and lightly score with fork tines to resemble bark. Press chopped pecans into frosting on each end. Yield: 10 to 12 servings.

*Mocha Filling:*

¼ cup sifted powdered sugar
1 tablespoon cocoa
1 teaspoon instant coffee granules
1 cup whipping cream

Combine powdered sugar, cocoa, and coffee granules; mix well.

Beat whipping cream until foamy; gradually add sugar mixture, beating until soft peaks form. Yield: enough filling for 1 yule log.

*Chocolate Frosting:*

2 (1-ounce) squares unsweetened chocolate
¼ cup butter
2½ cups sifted powdered sugar
¼ cup milk
½ teaspoon almond extract

Melt chocolate and butter over hot water in top of a double boiler. Remove from heat, and cool.

Add powdered sugar and milk to chocolate mixture; beat until smooth. Stir in almond extract. Yield: enough frosting for 1 yule log. *Teresa Sands, Columbia, South Carolina.*

## CHOCOLATE TORTE ROYALE

1 (6-ounce) package semisweet chocolate morsels
Cinnamon Meringue Shell
2 egg yolks
¼ cup water
1 cup whipping cream
¼ teaspoon ground cinnamon
¼ cup sugar
Additional whipped cream (optional)
Whole pecans (optional)

Melt chocolate morsels over hot water in top of a double boiler. Cool slightly, and spread 2 tablespoons over bottom of meringue shell (layer will be thin).

Beat egg yolks until thick and lemon colored. Add remaining chocolate and ¼ cup water, beating until thoroughly blended. Cover and chill.

Beat 1 cup whipping cream and cinnamon until foamy; gradually add sugar, beating until soft peaks form. Spread half of sweetened whipped cream in meringue shell. Fold remaining whipped cream into chocolate mixture, and carefully spread mixture over whipped cream layer. Chill several hours or overnight. Garnish with whipped cream and pecans, if desired. Yield: 8 servings.

*Cinnamon Meringue Shell:*

2 egg whites
½ teaspoon vinegar
¼ teaspoon salt
¼ teaspoon ground cinnamon
½ cup sugar

Combine egg whites (at room temperature), vinegar, salt, and cinnamon; beat until frothy. Gradually add sugar, 1 tablespoon at a time, beating until stiff peaks form. (Do not underbeat the mixture.)

Spoon meringue onto unglazed brown paper. (Do not use recycled paper.) Using back of spoon, shape meringue into a circle about 8 inches in diameter; shape the circle into a shell (sides should be about 1¾ inches high).

Bake at 275° for 1 hour. Turn oven off, and allow meringue to cool in oven 2 hours. Yield: one 8-inch meringue shell. *Sherry Boger Phillips, Knoxville, Tennessee.*

## CREME DE MENTHE CHEESECAKE

1½ cups graham cracker crumbs
1 teaspoon ground cinnamon
⅓ cup butter or margarine, melted
3 (1-ounce) squares semisweet chocolate
3 eggs
⅔ cup sugar
1 (8-ounce) package cream cheese, softened
1 cup whipping cream
3 tablespoons crème de menthe
¼ cup plus 1 tablespoon all-purpose flour
⅛ teaspoon baking soda
⅛ teaspoon salt
Additional whipped cream
Green food coloring (optional)
Chocolate curls

Combine first 3 ingredients, mixing well. Firmly press mixture into a 9-inch springform pan; chill.

Melt chocolate squares over hot water in top of a double boiler. Set aside.

Combine eggs and sugar; beat at medium speed of an electric mixer until thick and lemon colored.

Beat cream cheese until smooth; gradually add 1 cup whipping cream, and beat well. Stir in melted chocolate, mixing well. Add egg mixture and crème de menthe; stir until blended.

Combine flour, baking soda, and salt; stir well, and add to cream cheese mixture; mix well. Pour batter into graham cracker crust. Bake at 300° for 1 hour. Turn oven off, and allow cheesecake to cool in oven for 1 hour. Chill cake several hours.

Tint whipped cream with a couple of drops of green food coloring, if desired. Pipe whipped cream in a decorative design around base and on top of cake. Garnish with chocolate curls. Yield: 8 to 10 servings. *Lynn R. Koenig, Charleston, South Carolina.*

# Sip A Sparkling Holiday Punch

A steaming cup of Holiday Cider, spiced with red cinnamon candies, offers a warm welcome to friends gathering to celebrate the holidays. So does Hot Pineapple Punch, a golden mixture of pineapple juice and white wine. A cinnamon stick in each cup adds a festive touch.

Chilled punches are great for winter parties, too. Patricia Flint says her Cranberry Frappé is especially pretty to serve during the holidays; it's a creamy blend of cranberry juice cocktail, pineapple juice, strawberry ice cream, whipped cream, and ginger ale.

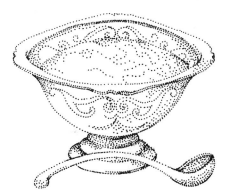

## CRANBERRY FRAPPE

1 quart cranberry juice cocktail, chilled
1 quart unsweetened pineapple juice, chilled
1½ cups sugar
1 to 2 teaspoons almond extract
½ gallon strawberry ice cream, softened
1 pint whipping cream
½ cup sugar
1 quart ginger ale, chilled

Combine first 5 ingredients in a large punch bowl, stirring well. Beat whipping cream until foamy; gradually add ½ cup sugar, beating until soft peaks form. Fold whipped cream mixture into ice cream mixture in punch bowl. Gently stir in ginger ale just before serving. Yield: about 5 quarts.

*Patricia Flint, Staunton, Virginia.*

## HOLIDAY CIDER

1 medium-size orange
1½ teaspoons whole cloves
1 gallon apple cider
¾ cup red cinnamon candies
2 (3-inch) sticks cinnamon

Slice orange into 6 wedges; stud wedges with cloves. Set aside.

Combine cider and candies in a Dutch oven over medium heat; cook until candies are dissolved and mixture is thoroughly heated. Pour cider mixture into a heat-proof punch bowl. Add clove-studded orange wedges and cinnamon sticks. Serve hot. Yield: 1 gallon.
*Terri Burke,*
*Belington, West Virginia.*

## FOAMY LIME PUNCH

2 (0.25-ounce) packages lemon-lime flavor
　unsweetened soft drink mix
2 quarts water
2 cups sugar
1 (46-ounce) can unsweetened pineapple
　juice
1 quart ginger ale, chilled
1 quart lime sherbet

Combine first 4 ingredients, mixing well; chill. To serve, combine chilled mixture and ginger ale in a punch bowl. Drop sherbet by scoops into punch. Yield: about 4 quarts. *Jayne Perala,*
*Salem, Virginia.*

## HOT PINEAPPLE PUNCH

1 (46-ounce) can unsweetened pineapple
　juice
½ cup sugar
¼ cup lime juice
¼ teaspoon ground nutmeg
3¼ cups dry white wine
Cinnamon sticks (optional)

Combine first 4 ingredients in a large Dutch oven, mixing well. Bring to a boil, stirring until sugar dissolves. Reduce heat, and stir in wine; simmer until mixture is thoroughly heated. Serve punch with cinnamon sticks, if desired. Yield: 2¼ quarts.
*Anne S. Reynolds,*
*Raleigh, North Carolina.*

# A Busy Day, A Casual Menu

With all the hustle and bustle of holiday shopping, it's nice to sit back and enjoy a relaxing meal at home. You'll find this menu, featuring quiche and soup, easy to prepare; in fact, most of the recipes can be assembled or completely prepared ahead.

For starters, there's Cauliflower and Caraway Soup, a creamy appetizer just right to warm up with. The soup is followed with Tasty Quiche, thick with bacon, mushrooms, and Swiss cheese. For the salad, citrus fruit and avocados are topped with Celery Seed Dressing. Stuffed tomatoes add a touch of color to the plate. Afterwards, continue the enjoyment with a slice of Cocoa Marbled Cake, flavored with a hint of rum.

**Cauliflower and Caraway Soup**
**Tasty Quiche　　Easy Stuffed Tomatoes**
**Citrus-Avocado Salad**
**Cocoa Marbled Cake**
**Coffee**

## CAULIFLOWER AND CARAWAY SOUP

2½ cups chicken broth
1 small head cauliflower, broken into
　flowerets
6 green onions, chopped
1 teaspoon salt
¼ teaspoon dried whole basil
¼ teaspoon dried whole thyme
2 cups evaporated milk
½ teaspoon caraway seeds
Shredded Cheddar cheese (optional)
Chopped fresh parsley (optional)

Combine first 6 ingredients in a heavy saucepan; simmer 10 to 15 minutes or until cauliflower is tender. Pour cauliflower mixture into container of electric blender; process until smooth. Return mixture to saucepan; add milk and cook, stirring often, until thoroughly heated. Sprinkle with caraway seeds. Garnish with cheese and parsley, if desired. Yield: about 5 cups. *Sue Fowler,*
*Maryville, Tennessee.*

## TASTY QUICHE

Pastry for 9-inch pie
4 slices bacon
1 medium onion, chopped
1 (3½-ounce) can sliced mushrooms,
　drained
1 cup (4 ounces) shredded Swiss cheese
4 eggs, beaten
2 cups half-and-half
¼ cup grated Parmesan cheese
½ teaspoon salt
½ teaspoon pepper
¼ teaspoon ground nutmeg
Carrot curls (optional)

Line a 9-inch quiche dish with pastry; trim excess pastry around edges. Prick bottom and sides of pastry with a fork. Bake at 400° for 3 minutes; remove from oven, and gently prick with a fork. Bake 5 minutes longer.

Cook bacon in a skillet until crisp; remove bacon, reserving 1 tablespoon drippings. Crumble bacon, and set aside. Sauté onion in bacon drippings until tender. Sprinkle bacon, onion, mushrooms, and Swiss cheese in pastry shell. Combine next 6 ingredients, mixing well. Pour into pastry shell. Bake at 350° for 45 minutes or until filling is set. Garnish with carrot curls, if desired. Yield: one 9-inch quiche. *Faye Price,*
*Tarboro, North Carolina.*

## EASY STUFFED TOMATOES

6 large tomatoes
2 tablespoons butter or margarine
½ cup chopped onion
1 cup chopped celery
¼ cup chopped green pepper
1 cup cooked regular rice
1 (2¼-ounce) can deviled ham
1 teaspoon Worcestershire sauce
1 teaspoon salt
⅛ teaspoon pepper
1 tablespoon butter or margarine, melted
½ cup soft breadcrumbs

Remove stems from tomatoes, and cut a ¼-inch slice from top of each. Scoop out pulp, leaving shells intact. Chop pulp and drain; set aside. Invert tomato shells on paper towels to drain; set aside.

Melt 2 tablespoons butter in a skillet; sauté onion, celery, and green pepper

*A menu that can be prepared ahead is always welcome during the busy holiday season. This one centers around Tasty Quiche.*

until vegetables are tender. Stir in tomato pulp and next 5 ingredients, mixing well.

Place tomatoes in a 12- x 8- x 2-inch baking dish; spoon rice mixture into shells, mounding slightly. Combine butter and breadcrumbs, mixing well; sprinkle over tops of tomatoes. Bake at 350° for 15 minutes or until tops are browned. Yield: 6 servings.

*Margaret Warren,*
*Crofton, Kentucky.*

### CITRUS-AVOCADO SALAD

**3 oranges**
**1 grapefruit**
**2 small avocados, peeled and sliced**
**Lettuce leaves**
**Celery Seed Dressing**

Peel and section oranges and grapefruit, reserving juice that drains from fruit. Sprinkle avocado slices with reserved fruit juice, and arrange on lettuce leaves. Top with sectioned fruit. Serve salad with Celery Seed Dressing. Yield: 6 servings.

*Celery Seed Dressing:*
**½ cup sugar**
**¾ cup vegetable oil**
**⅓ cup lemon juice**
**1 teaspoon paprika**
**1 teaspoon celery seeds**
**1 teaspoon dry mustard**
**½ teaspoon salt**

Combine all ingredients in a jar. Cover tightly, and shake vigorously. Yield: 1¼ cups. *Barbara Beacom,*
*Kernersville, North Carolina.*

### COCOA MARBLED CAKE

**3 tablespoons cocoa**
**2 tablespoons sugar**
**¼ cup water**
**½ cup plus 2 tablespoons butter or margarine, softened**
**1 cup sugar**
**4 eggs, separated**
**1½ cups self-rising flour**
**⅓ cup half-and-half**
**1 teaspoon rum**
**½ teaspoon vanilla extract**

Combine first 3 ingredients; stir until blended. Set aside.

Cream butter; gradually add 1 cup sugar, beating well. Add egg yolks, one at a time, beating well after each addition. Add flour, and mix well. Gradually add half-and-half, beating at low speed of an electric mixer. Stir in rum and vanilla.

Beat egg whites (at room temperature) until stiff peaks form; fold into batter. Pour two-thirds of batter into a greased and floured 10-inch Bundt pan. Stir cocoa mixture into remaining batter; pour over plain batter. Draw knife through batter to make a swirl design. Bake at 375° for 10 minutes; reduce to 350°, and bake 30 minutes or until a wooden pick inserted in center comes out clean. Cool in pan 10 minutes; remove from pan, and let cool completely. Yield: one 10-inch cake.

*Ella C. Stivers,*
*Abilene, Texas.*

*Tip: For just a squirt of lemon juice, poke a hole in one end and squeeze.*

# Salads For That Special Meal

Every holiday menu deserves a salad. Fruit and vegetables in a tossed or congealed salad offer a refreshing contrast to the main course and also add color and texture to the meal.

Orange-Cauliflower Salad is a simple, yet eye-catching, toss of fresh spinach, cauliflower, and mandarin oranges—topped with a sweet orange dressing.

Our congealed vegetable salads have a holiday look and taste. Beet Salad Mold is rich in color and filled with tangy diced beets. Vegetable Relish Salad conceals crispy cabbage, celery, and green pepper; top with mayonnaise for an attractive garnish.

We've also included congealed fruit salads— Christmas Snow Salad, Holiday Cranberry Salad, and Sparkling Fruit Salad—including maraschino cherries, cranberries, mandarin oranges, and pineapple molded in a variety of shapes and colors.

## CHRISTMAS SNOW SALAD

2 envelopes unflavored gelatin
½ cup cold water
1 (15¼-ounce) can crushed pineapple, undrained
1 (1.25-ounce) envelope whipped topping mix
⅓ cup mayonnaise
¼ cup sifted powdered sugar
1 (10-ounce) jar red maraschino cherries, drained and chopped
1 (6-ounce) jar green maraschino cherries, drained and chopped
½ cup chopped pecans or walnuts
Additional red and green maraschino cherries (optional)

Soften gelatin in ½ cup cold water; set aside. Drain pineapple, reserving juice; add enough water to juice to make 1 cup. Bring pineapple juice mixture to a boil; remove from heat, and

stir in softened gelatin. Chill mixture until consistency of unbeaten egg white.

Prepare whipped topping mix according to package directions, omitting vanilla; fold 1 cup topping into gelatin mixture (reserve remaining topping for other uses). Gently fold next 5 ingredients and pineapple into gelatin mixture; pour into a lightly oiled 4-cup mold. Chill until firm. Unmold on serving tray; garnish with additional cherries, if desired. Yield: 8 servings.

*Mrs. Paul Raper,*
*Burgaw, North Carolina.*

## HOLIDAY CRANBERRY SALAD

3 envelopes unflavored gelatin
½ cup cold water
1 (15¼-ounce) can crushed pineapple, undrained
2 cups sugar
4 cups fresh cranberries
½ cup seedless green grapes
1 cup finely chopped pecans

Soften gelatin in cold water; set aside. Drain pineapple, reserving juice; set pineapple aside. Add enough water to juice to make 3½ cups. Bring juice mixture and sugar to a boil; add cranberries, and cook 7 to 10 minutes or until berries pop. Stir in softened gelatin. Chill until consistency of unbeaten egg white. Stir in grapes, pecans, and pineapple; pour into a lightly oiled 8-cup mold. Chill until firm. Yield: about 12 servings.

*Jane Beverly,*
*Fayetteville, Tennessee.*

## MANDARIN ORANGE AND PINEAPPLE SALAD

1 (11-ounce) can mandarin oranges, drained
1 (20-ounce) can pineapple chunks, drained
2 cups large-curd cottage cheese
1 (8-ounce) carton frozen whipped topping, thawed
1 teaspoon vanilla extract
1 (6-ounce) package orange-flavored gelatin
¼ cup chopped pecans
¼ cup flaked coconut

Combine first 5 ingredients. Sprinkle gelatin over mixture, and stir well. Spoon mixture into a 13- x 9- x 2-inch dish. Combine pecans and coconut; sprinkle over salad. Chill 6 hours or overnight. Yield: 15 servings.

*Betty J. Moore,*
*Belton, Texas.*

## SPARKLING FRUIT SALAD

1 (11-ounce) can mandarin oranges, undrained
1 (8-ounce) can pineapple chunks, undrained
1 (3-ounce) package raspberry-flavored gelatin
1 cup boiling water
1 (16-ounce) can whole cranberry sauce
¼ cup chopped pecans

Drain oranges and pineapple, reserving juice; set fruit aside. Add enough water to juice to make ½ cup; set aside.

Dissolve gelatin in boiling water; stir in juice mixture. Chill until consistency of unbeaten egg white. Stir in cranberry sauce, pecans, oranges, and pineapple; pour into a lightly oiled 4-cup mold. Chill until firm. Yield: 8 servings.

*Kathryn M. Elmore,*
*Demopolis, Alabama.*

## ORANGE-CAULIFLOWER SALAD

2 (11-ounce) cans mandarin oranges, drained
2 cups cauliflower flowerets
¼ cup chopped green pepper
4 cups torn fresh spinach
Orange Blossom Dressing

Combine first 4 ingredients in a medium salad bowl, tossing gently. Serve with Orange Blossom Dressing. Yield: 6 servings.

*Orange Blossom Dressing:*

¾ cup evaporated milk
⅓ cup frozen orange juice concentrate, thawed and undiluted

Combine evaporated milk and orange juice concentrate, mixing well. Yield: about 1 cup.
*Mina De Kraker,*
*Holland, Michigan.*

## VEGETABLE RELISH SALAD

1 (3-ounce) package lime-flavored gelatin
¾ teaspoon salt
1 cup boiling water
¾ cup cold water
2 tablespoons vinegar
2 teaspoons grated onion
½ cup finely shredded cabbage
½ cup grated carrots
¼ cup finely chopped celery
3 tablespoons finely chopped green pepper
Lettuce leaves (optional)
Mayonnaise (optional)

Dissolve gelatin and salt in boiling water; stir in ¾ cup cold water, vinegar, and onion. Chill until consistency of unbeaten egg white.

Stir cabbage, carrots, celery, and green pepper into thickened gelatin mixture. Pour into a lightly oiled 3-cup mold; chill until firm. Unmold salad on lettuce leaves; garnish with a dollop of mayonnaise, if desired. Yield: 6 servings.
*Jodie McCoy,*
*Tulsa, Oklahoma.*

## MARINATED COMBO SALAD

1 (16-ounce) can cut green beans, drained
1 (15½-ounce) can wax beans, drained
1 (12-ounce) can whole kernel corn, drained
1 small head cauliflower, broken into flowerets
1 cup chopped celery
1 cup grated carrots
⅔ cup vegetable oil
½ cup lemon juice
2 to 3 tablespoons sugar
1½ teaspoons salt
1 teaspoon pepper
Lettuce leaves

Combine first 6 vegetables; set aside. Combine remaining ingredients except lettuce, mixing well. Pour over vegetables, and toss gently. Cover and chill at

least 2 hours or overnight, stirring occasionally. Drain salad, and serve on lettuce leaves. Yield: 10 servings.
*Lori Seets,*
*Lubbock, Texas.*

## BEET SALAD MOLD

1 (16-ounce) can diced beets, undrained
1 (3-ounce) package lemon-flavored gelatin
¼ cup sugar
¼ cup vinegar
1 tablespoon prepared horseradish

Drain beets, reserving liquid; set beets aside. Add enough water to beet liquid to make 1½ cups. Bring beet liquid to a boil; add gelatin and sugar, stirring until dissolved. Stir in vinegar and horseradish. Chill until consistency of unbeaten egg white. Stir in beets; pour into a lightly oiled 4-cup mold. Chill until firm. Yield: 6 servings.
*Helen J. Wright,*
*Leesville, South Carolina.*

# Feast On Leftover Turkey

When you select your holiday turkey, choose one large enough to have plenty of leftovers. Then you can continue the feasting by serving such tasty entrées as Turkey Parmesan, a hearty gumbo, and Oriental Turkey.

Turkey leftovers require careful storage. As soon as possible, separate the stuffing from the meat; then refrigerate both immediately. Use the stuffing and gravy within two days; the meat will

keep up to three days. If you need more broth, cover the turkey carcass with water and simmer for two to three hours with your favorite seasonings.

Or extend the storage life of your turkey leftovers by freezing them. Slice, chop, or cube the meat; then package it in meal-size portions. Place gravy and broth in plastic freezer containers, leaving ½-inch headspace. Tightly wrap cooked stuffing, and plan to use it within four weeks.

## TURKEY-AND-OYSTER PIE

Pastry for 10-inch double-crust pie
1 cup milk
1 (12-ounce) jar turkey gravy or 1 cup leftover turkey gravy
1 tablespoon butter or margarine, melted
3 tablespoons all-purpose flour
2 cups chopped cooked turkey
1 (12-ounce) can fresh Standard oysters, drained
1 tablespoon chopped fresh parsley
1 tablespoon finely chopped celery
½ teaspoon salt
¼ teaspoon pepper

Roll half of pastry to ⅛-inch thickness on a lightly floured board; fit into an 8-inch square baking dish. Set aside.

Combine milk and gravy in a large saucepan; cook over medium heat until mixture comes to a boil, stirring constantly. Reduce heat to low; simmer 10 minutes, stirring often.

Combine butter and flour, mixing well to form a smooth paste; stir into gravy mixture. Add turkey and oysters. Cook over medium heat until mixture comes to a boil, stirring constantly; remove from heat. Stir in parsley, celery, salt, and pepper; spoon mixture into pastry shell.

Roll out remaining pastry to ⅛-inch thickness; carefully place over pie, leaving a 1-inch overhang at edge of dish. Seal edges and flute; cut slits in top for steam to escape.

Bake at 350° for 40 to 50 minutes or until golden brown. Yield: one 8-inch pie.
*Gladys Johnston,*
*Elberton, Georgia.*

## TURKEY PARMESAN

½ cup chopped onion
½ cup chopped celery
½ cup sliced fresh mushrooms
2 cloves garlic, minced
½ cup butter or margarine
½ cup all-purpose flour
4 cups milk
4 cups cubed cooked turkey
⅔ cup grated Parmesan cheese
2 tablespoons chopped fresh parsley
2 tablespoons dry white wine
2 teaspoons Worcestershire sauce
½ teaspoon salt
½ teaspoon pepper
½ teaspoon poultry seasoning
5 drops hot sauce
Pinch of red pepper
Hot cooked noodles

Sauté onion, celery, mushrooms, and garlic in butter in a large heavy skillet until tender. Blend in flour, and cook 1 minute, stirring constantly. Gradually add milk; cook over medium heat, stirring constantly, until thickened and bubbly. Add next 10 ingredients; stir well, and cook until thoroughly heated. Serve over noodles. Yield: 8 servings.
*Joanne Champagne,*
*Covington, Louisiana.*

## ORIENTAL TURKEY

3 tablespoons vegetable oil
1 cup thinly sliced onion
1 cup thinly sliced celery
1 medium-size green pepper, cut into thin strips
1 (14-ounce) can Chinese mixed vegetables, undrained
1 (8-ounce) can sliced water chestnuts, undrained
1½ tablespoons cornstarch
3 cups cooked turkey strips
2 tablespoons soy sauce
1 teaspoon teriyaki sauce
Pepper to taste
Hot cooked rice

Sauté onion, celery, and green pepper in oil in a large skillet until tender.
Drain Chinese vegetables and water chestnuts, reserving liquid. Add enough water to reserved liquid to make 2 cups. Dissolve cornstarch in a small amount of liquid; add to remaining liquid, stirring well. Add liquid to sautéed vegetables; cook until smooth and thickened.
Add turkey, Chinese vegetables, water chestnuts, soy sauce, teriyaki sauce, and pepper to sautéed vegetables; stir well. Cook until thoroughly heated. Serve over rice. Yield: 8 servings.
*Mrs. W. Harold Groce,*
*Arden, North Carolina.*

## TURKEY DIVAN

2 (10-ounce) packages frozen broccoli spears
1 (10¾-ounce) can cream of celery soup, undiluted
¼ cup Chablis or other dry white wine
1 pound sliced cooked turkey
1 cup (4 ounces) shredded Cheddar cheese

Cook broccoli according to package directions, omitting salt; drain. Arrange in a lightly greased shallow 2-quart casserole. Combine soup and wine; pour half over broccoli. Arrange turkey slices over broccoli, and pour remaining soup mixture over top.
Cover and bake at 350° for 25 minutes. Sprinkle with cheese, and bake an additional 5 minutes or just until cheese melts. Yield: 6 servings.
*Romanza Johnson,*
*Bowling Green, Kentucky.*

## TURKEY GUMBO

5 slices bacon
1 small onion, chopped
2 tablespoons all-purpose flour
1 (16-ounce) can whole tomatoes, undrained
1 clove garlic, minced
½ teaspoon salt
½ teaspoon pepper
2 quarts water
2 bay leaves
2 cups chopped cooked turkey
1 cup turkey broth
1 (10-ounce) package frozen cut okra
Hot cooked rice
Gumbo filé

Fry bacon in a Dutch oven; drain, reserving 2 tablespoons drippings in Dutch oven. Crumble bacon, and set aside.
Add onion to drippings; sauté until tender. Stir in flour; cook over medium heat, stirring constantly, 4 to 5 minutes. Add reserved bacon and next 8 ingredients, stirring well. Bring mixture to a boil, and reduce heat; simmer, uncovered, for 1½ hours.
Stir in okra; cook an additional 30 minutes. Remove bay leaves. Serve gumbo over rice. Add a small amount of gumbo filé to each serving. Yield: 2 quarts.
*Mrs. Jack Broadway,*
*Richmond, Virginia.*

# Serve The Season's Dressiest Vegetables

A golden turkey may be the key attraction at your holiday dinner—but every Southerner knows that it takes a delicious selection of vegetable side dishes to make the menu special and complete. Since you'll want to include dishes that are both tasty and attractive, we suggest Corn-Stuffed Tomatoes or Candied Carrots for starters. The tomato shells are filled with corn, seasonings, and cheese. The carrots are sliced diagonally and cooked with a flavorful cranberry glaze.
Use side dishes as you would use a centerpiece—to add color and interest to your table. Choose either Asparagus Delight or Spinach and Egg Casserole to complement the yellow and red of Corn-Stuffed Tomatoes. And Brussels Sprouts in Lemon Sauce makes a perfect partner to Candied Carrots.

## ASPARAGUS DELIGHT

2 (15-ounce) cans asparagus spears,
  undrained
3 tablespoons butter or margarine
3 tablespoons all-purpose flour
1 cup milk
⅛ teaspoon salt
¼ teaspoon white pepper
6 hard-cooked eggs, sliced
2 (3-ounce) cans mushroom stems and
  pieces, drained
2 tablespoons fine, dry breadcrumbs

Drain asparagus, reserving 1 cup liquid; set aside.

Melt butter in a heavy saucepan over low heat; add flour, stirring until smooth. Cook 1 minute, stirring constantly. Gradually add 1 cup asparagus liquid and milk; cook over medium heat, stirring constantly, until thickened and bubbly. Stir in salt and pepper.

Spread ¼ cup sauce in a greased 10- x 6- x 2-inch baking dish. Layer half each of the asparagus, eggs, mushrooms, and sauce. Repeat layers; then sprinkle with breadcrumbs. Bake at 325° for 20 to 25 minutes or until bubbly. Yield: 8 servings. *Mary M. Hoppe,*
*Kitty Hawk, North Carolina.*

## BRUSSELS SPROUTS IN LEMON SAUCE

2 (10-ounce) packages frozen brussels
  sprouts
¼ cup butter or margarine
⅔ cup mayonnaise
2 tablespoons lemon juice
½ teaspoon celery salt
2 tablespoons grated Parmesan cheese
¼ cup sliced almonds, toasted

Cook brussels sprouts according to package directions, omitting salt; drain. Place brussels sprouts in a shallow 2-quart casserole, and keep warm.

Melt butter in a saucepan; add mayonnaise, lemon juice, and celery salt. Beat with a wire whisk until smooth; cook over medium heat until hot, stirring constantly (do not boil). Pour sauce over sprouts; sprinkle with cheese and almonds. Yield: 6 servings.
*Mrs. Richard Pearce,*
*Fayetteville, North Carolina.*

## BROCCOLI-CHEESE CASSEROLE

1 large bunch broccoli
1 (6-ounce) roll process cheese food with
  garlic
1 (10¾-ounce) can cream of mushroom
  soup, undiluted
1 tablespoon Worcestershire sauce
¼ teaspoon hot sauce
Pepper to taste
½ cup soft breadcrumbs
2 tablespoons butter or margarine, melted

Cook broccoli in small amount of boiling water 15 minutes or until crisp-tender; drain. Chop coarsely, and set aside.

Place cheese in the top of a double boiler; cook over boiling water, stirring constantly, until cheese melts. Add broccoli, mushroom soup, Worcestershire sauce, hot sauce, and pepper; mix thoroughly. Pour into a lightly greased 1½-quart casserole. Combine breadcrumbs and butter; mix well, and sprinkle over broccoli mixture. Bake at 350° for 35 to 40 minutes. Yield: 6 servings.
*Jeanne Higgins,*
*Baton Rouge, Louisiana.*

## SCALLOPED CABBAGE

1 medium cabbage, coarsely chopped
6 slices bacon
2 tablespoons chopped green pepper
1 cup (4 ounces) shredded Cheddar
  cheese, divided
2 tablespoons diced pimiento
White sauce (recipe follows)
½ cup soft breadcrumbs
1 tablespoon butter or margarine, melted

Cook cabbage, covered, in a small amount of boiling salted water for 10 minutes or until crisp-tender; drain well, and set aside.

Cook bacon in a heavy skillet until crisp; remove bacon, reserving 1 tablespoon drippings in skillet. Crumble bacon, and set aside. Sauté green pepper in drippings until tender.

Spoon half of cabbage into a lightly greased shallow 2½-quart casserole. Sprinkle with bacon, green pepper, ½ cup cheese, and pimiento. Spoon on remaining cabbage, and sprinkle with remaining cheese. Pour white sauce over

top. Combine breadcrumbs and butter; mix well, and sprinkle over casserole. Bake, uncovered, at 375° for 15 to 20 minutes. Yield: 8 servings.

*White Sauce:*

2 tablespoons butter or margarine
2 tablespoons all-purpose flour
1 cup milk
⅛ teaspoon salt
⅛ teaspoon pepper
Dash of paprika

Melt butter in a heavy saucepan over low heat; add flour, stirring until smooth. Cook 1 minute, stirring constantly. Gradually add milk; cook over medium heat, stirring constantly, until thickened and bubbly. Stir in salt, pepper, and paprika. Yield: 1 cup.
*René Harper,*
*Calvert City, Kentucky.*

## CANDIED CARROTS

4 cups diagonally sliced carrots
¼ cup butter or margarine
¼ cup jellied cranberry sauce
2 tablespoons brown sugar
Fresh parsley sprigs (optional)

Cook carrots in a small amount of boiling salted water 10 minutes; drain, and set aside.

Combine next 3 ingredients in a medium skillet; cook over low heat, stirring constantly, until cranberry sauce melts. Add carrots, and stir gently. Cook over medium heat, stirring constantly, until thoroughly heated. Garnish with parsley, if desired. Yield: 6 servings.
*Marie W. Harris,*
*Sevierville, Tennessee.*

*Tip: Burned food can be removed from an enamel saucepan by using the following procedure: Fill the pan with cold water containing 2 to 3 tablespoons salt, and let stand overnight. The next day, cover and bring water to a boil.*

## CAULIFLOWER WITH ALMOND SAUCE

½ teaspoon salt
1 large head cauliflower, broken into flowerets
¼ cup butter or margarine
¼ cup all-purpose flour
¼ teaspoon salt
⅛ teaspoon pepper
1 cup half-and-half
½ cup Chablis or other white wine
½ cup water
½ cup slivered almonds, toasted
½ cup (2 ounces) shredded Cheddar cheese

Bring 1 inch of water and ½ teaspoon salt to a boil in a large saucepan; add cauliflower flowerets. Cover and cook 8 to 10 minutes or until crisp-tender. Drain and place in a greased 2-quart casserole.

Melt butter in a medium saucepan over low heat. Add flour, ¼ teaspoon salt, and pepper; stir until smooth. Cook 1 minute, stirring constantly. Gradually add half-and-half, wine, and water; cook over medium heat, stirring constantly, until thickened and bubbly. Stir in almonds. Pour sauce over cauliflower, and bake at 375° for 15 minutes. Sprinkle with cheese, and bake an additional 5 minutes. Yield: 6 servings.

*Karen Davage,*
*Spring, Texas.*

## STUFFED MUSHROOMS FLORENTINE

24 large fresh mushrooms
1 (10-ounce) package frozen leaf spinach
1 clove garlic, minced
½ cup butter or margarine
1 small onion, finely chopped
2 (3-ounce) packages cream cheese, softened
½ cup fine, dry breadcrumbs
⅛ teaspoon pepper
¾ teaspoon dry mustard
¼ teaspoon ground nutmeg
2½ tablespoons grated Parmesan cheese

Clean mushrooms with damp paper towels. Remove mushroom stems and chop; set aside.

Cook spinach according to package directions, omitting salt. Drain well; place spinach in container of electric blender, and process until smooth. Set aside.

Sauté garlic in butter in a medium skillet over low heat 1 minute; remove from heat. Dip mushroom caps in butter and garlic mixture, coating well; place in a 13- x 9- x 2-inch baking dish.

Stir the chopped mushroom stems and onion into remaining butter and the garlic mixture; sauté until tender.

Combine spinach, cream cheese, breadcrumbs, and seasonings in a medium bowl; add mushroom mixture, stirring well. Spoon spinach mixture into mushroom caps, and sprinkle with Parmesan cheese. Bake at 375° for 15 minutes. Yield: 8 servings.

*Mrs. Tommy W. Ellison,*
*Matthews, North Carolina.*

## CORN-STUFFED TOMATOES

6 medium tomatoes
¼ cup chopped onion
1 tablespoon butter or margarine
1 (17-ounce) can whole kernel corn, drained
¼ cup (1 ounce) shredded Cheddar cheese
1 tablespoon dried whole basil
1 tablespoon chopped fresh parsley
½ teaspoon pepper
¼ teaspoon salt
Lemon roses (optional)
Fresh parsley sprigs (optional)

Cut a thin slice from bottom of each tomato so it will sit flat. Cut a ¾-inch slice from top of each tomato. Gently remove pulp, leaving shells intact. Chop tomato pulp, and set aside ¾ cup (reserve remaining pulp for other uses).

Sauté onion in butter in a medium skillet until tender. Add ¾ cup chopped tomato pulp and next 6 ingredients, stirring well. Spoon mixture into tomato shells, and place in a 10- x 6- x 2-inch baking dish. Bake at 350° for 15 minutes. Garnish with lemon roses and parsley, if desired. Yield: 6 servings.

*Rebecca Ashley,*
*Dalton, Georgia.*

## PARMESAN POTATOES

½ cup grated Parmesan cheese
¼ cup all-purpose flour
¼ teaspoon garlic salt
⅛ teaspoon pepper
5 medium potatoes, unpeeled and cut into ¼-inch slices
¼ cup plus 2 tablespoons butter or margarine

Combine first 4 ingredients, stirring well. Dredge potatoes in flour mixture.

Layer sliced potatoes in a lightly greased 2-quart casserole, dotting each layer with butter. Bake at 400° for 1 hour. Yield: 4 to 6 servings.

*Mary Harris,*
*Elkin, North Carolina.*

## SPINACH AND EGG CASSEROLE

1 pound fresh spinach
¼ cup butter or margarine
¼ cup all-purpose flour
1½ cups milk
½ teaspoon salt
⅛ teaspoon red pepper
1 cup soft breadcrumbs, divided
2 hard-cooked eggs, sliced
1 cup (4 ounces) shredded sharp Cheddar cheese
2 slices bacon, cut into 1-inch pieces
Fresh parsley sprigs (optional)

Remove stems from spinach; wash leaves thoroughly in lukewarm water. Place spinach in a Dutch oven (do not add water); cover and cook over high heat 3 to 5 minutes. Drain spinach well; chop and set aside.

Melt butter in a heavy saucepan over low heat; add flour, stirring until smooth. Cook 1 minute, stirring constantly. Gradually add milk; cook over medium heat, stirring constantly, until mixture is thickened and bubbly. Stir in salt and red pepper. Set sauce aside.

Sprinkle ½ cup of breadcrumbs in a greased 10- x 6- x 2-inch baking dish. Layer half each of spinach, egg slices, cheese, and sauce in baking dish. Repeat layers; sprinkle top with ½ cup breadcrumbs. Arrange bacon evenly over top. Bake at 350° for 40 minutes.

Garnish casserole with parsley, if desired. Yield: 6 servings.

*Note:* Two 10-ounce packages frozen chopped spinach may be substituted for fresh spinach. *Lynn Abbott, Southern Pines, North Carolina.*

## Cooking Light

# Fit For A Feast, But Light

For most Southerners the coming holidays mean lots of tempting, rich foods. How can you enjoy this festive season without gaining back all the pounds you've lost with "Cooking Light"? Start by preparing a calorie-trimmed holiday feast that looks and tastes sinfully good.

Lead off the menu with bowls of smooth Peppery Pea Soup. The thickness comes from pureed vegetables—not heavy cream. Garnish the soup, as well as the rest of the meal, elegantly. Visual appearance can help turn light recipes into delicacies suited for holiday dining.

Before opening the wine bottle for this special occasion, remember that alcohol calories add up quickly. But if wine is traditional with your holiday meals, you can save some calories with one of the new light versions. A 6-ounce glass of light Chablis contains about 90 calories, compared to 130 calories for a glass of regular wine.

Continue your feast with a delicious entrée of Herbed Cornish Hens. They're marinated and roasted in a mixture of herbs and light rosé. Basting during the last minutes of cooking makes the hens moist and golden brown.

What Southern holiday menu would be complete without sweet potatoes? Save calories by seasoning them with orange juice, cinnamon, and butter flavoring instead of the usual sugar and butter. By spooning fourth-cup portions of potato mixture into orange cups, you can keep the calorie count to only 79 each.

Offer Broccoli With Mock Hollandaise Sauce for another side dish and Zesty Marinated Vegetables for the salad. Both dishes use low-calorie, fresh vegetables to round out the menu at a minimal number of calories.

Top off your light feast with an impressive dessert of Petits Pots de Chocolat or Fresh Fruit Compote. Either choice keeps the meal's total calories surprisingly low—under 560. What a pleasant surprise for the holidays!

**Peppery Pea Soup**
**Herbed Cornish Hens**
**Sweet Potatoes in Orange Cups**
**Broccoli With Mock Hollandaise Sauce**
**Zesty Marinated Vegetables**
**Petits Pots de Chocolat**
**or**
**Fresh Fruit Compote**
**Coffee**

## PEPPERY PEA SOUP

1 quart water
4 chicken-flavored bouillon cubes
2 (16-ounce) packages frozen English peas
  and carrots
¼ cup minced onion
½ teaspoon celery seeds
½ teaspoon pepper
Green onion strips
Thin carrot strips

Bring water to a boil; add bouillon, stirring to dissolve. Add next 4 ingredients; cover, reduce heat, and simmer 8 to 10 minutes.

Pour soup mixture into container of an electric blender, and process until smooth. Garnish with green onion strips and thin carrot strips. Serve immediately. Yield: 7 cups (about 68 calories per ⅞-cup serving). *Ann Criswell, Shreveport, Louisiana.*

## HERBED CORNISH HENS

4 (1-pound 6-ounce) Cornish hens
1½ cups light rosé
½ teaspoon garlic powder
½ teaspoon onion powder
½ teaspoon celery seeds
½ teaspoon poultry seasoning
½ teaspoon paprika
½ teaspoon dried whole basil
½ teaspoon pepper
½ cup light rosé

Remove giblets from hens; reserve for other uses. Rinse hens with cold water, and pat dry. Split each hen lengthwise using an electric knife. Place the hens, cavity side up, on a rack in a shallow roasting pan.

Pour 1½ cups wine over hens in pan. Combine seasonings; sprinkle half of seasoning mixture over cavities of hens. Cover and marinate in refrigerator 2 hours.

Bake, uncovered, at 350° for 1 hour. Remove from oven, and turn hens breast side up. Pour ½ cup wine over hens; sprinkle with remaining seasoning mixture. Bake an additional 30 minutes, basting every 10 minutes with wine mixture in pan. Yield: 8 servings (about 157 calories per serving). *Jerry Williams, Henderson, North Carolina.*

*Tip: Use a timer when cooking. Set the timer so it will ring at various intervals, and check the progress of the dish. However, try to avoid opening the oven door unless necessary.*

## SWEET POTATOES IN ORANGE CUPS

4 small oranges
2 cups cooked, mashed sweet
  potatoes
1 teaspoon grated orange rind
¼ cup plus 2 tablespoons unsweetened
  orange juice
1 teaspoon butter flavoring
¾ teaspoon ground cinnamon
¼ teaspoon salt
Orange rind curls (optional)

Cut oranges in half crosswise. Clip membranes, and carefully remove pulp (do not puncture bottom). Reserve orange pulp for other uses.

Combine next 6 ingredients; stir well. Stuff each orange cup with ¼ cup potato mixture. Place orange cups in a 13- x 9- x 2-inch baking pan; cover and bake at 350° for 20 minutes. Top each with an orange rind curl, if desired. Yield: 8 servings (about 79 calories per serving).
*Becky Burnett,*
*Knoxville, Tennessee.*

## BROCCOLI WITH MOCK HOLLANDAISE SAUCE

2 (1-pound) bunches fresh broccoli
½ cup reduced-calorie mayonnaise
3 tablespoons water
1 tablespoon lemon juice
⅛ teaspoon white pepper
Pimiento strips (optional)

Trim off large leaves of broccoli, and remove tough ends of lower stalks. Wash broccoli thoroughly, and separate into spears. Arrange broccoli in steaming rack with stalks to center of rack. Place over boiling water; cover and steam 10 to 15 minutes or to desired degree of doneness. Arrange broccoli spears in serving dish.

Combine remaining ingredients except pimiento strips; heat thoroughly, stirring constantly (do not boil). Spoon sauce over broccoli; garnish with pimiento strips, if desired. Yield: 8 servings (about 63 calories per serving).

## ZESTY MARINATED VEGETABLES

4 medium carrots, scraped and diagonally
  sliced
1 small head cauliflower, broken into
  flowerets
2 small zucchini, sliced
¼ pound fresh mushrooms, sliced
1 cup water
⅓ cup vinegar
1 (0.6-ounce) package reduced-calorie
  Italian salad dressing mix
Leaf lettuce

Combine first 4 ingredients in a large shallow dish. Combine 1 cup water, vinegar, and dressing mix in a jar; cover tightly, and shake vigorously. Pour over vegetables, tossing lightly to coat. Cover and chill overnight. Serve on lettuce. Yield: 8 servings (about 33 calories per serving).
*Mary Boydston,*
*El Dorado Springs, Missouri.*

## PETITS POTS DE CHOCOLAT

1 envelope unflavored gelatin
1½ cups skim milk, divided
3 eggs, separated
¼ cup sugar
⅓ cup sifted cocoa
⅛ teaspoon salt
1 teaspoon vanilla extract
¼ cup sugar
½ cup frozen whipped topping, thawed
1 teaspoon chocolate shavings

Combine gelatin and ½ cup skim milk in a medium saucepan, stirring well; let stand 1 minute. Cook over medium heat, stirring constantly, about 1 minute or until gelatin is dissolved.

Combine remaining 1 cup skim milk and egg yolks, beating well. Add yolk mixture, ¼ cup sugar, cocoa, and salt to saucepan; stir well. Cook over medium heat, stirring constantly, about 5 minutes or until smooth and thickened. Remove from heat; stir in vanilla, and chill 20 minutes.

Beat egg whites (at room temperature) in a medium mixing bowl until foamy; gradually add ¼ cup sugar, 1 tablespoon at a time, beating until stiff

peaks form. Gradually add chilled chocolate mixture, folding gently.

Divide evenly into eight 4-ounce serving dishes. Chill at least 2 hours. Garnish each serving with 1 tablespoon whipped topping and ⅛ teaspoon chocolate shavings. Yield: 8 servings (about 117 calories per ⅜-cup serving).
*Mrs. William J. Morgan,*
*Roanoke, Virginia.*

## FRESH FRUIT COMPOTE

1 (15¼-ounce) can pineapple tidbits in
  unsweetened juice, undrained
3 tablespoons cornstarch
2 teaspoons sugar
½ teaspoon ground nutmeg
1 cup water
3 tablespoons lemon juice
2 medium-size oranges, peeled, seeded,
  and sectioned
2 medium apples, unpeeled and chopped
2 medium bananas, sliced
1 medium-size yellow apple, unpeeled and
  chopped
1 medium pear, unpeeled and chopped
1 cup seedless green grapes, halved
1 cup red grapes, halved and seeded

Drain pineapple, reserving juice; set aside.

Combine cornstarch, sugar, and nutmeg in a medium saucepan; gradually add 1 cup water, stirring until smooth. Cook over medium heat, stirring constantly, until mixture comes to a boil; boil 1 minute. Remove from heat, and stir in reserved pineapple juice and lemon juice; cool.

Combine reserved pineapple and remaining ingredients; pour dressing over top, tossing gently to coat. Cover and chill thoroughly. Yield: 8 servings (about 157 calories per 1½-cup serving) or 12 servings (about 105 calories per 1-cup serving).
*Pamela Copenhaver,*
*Springfield, Illinois.*

*Tip: Easily remove the white membrane when peeling an orange by soaking the unpeeled orange in boiling water for 5 minutes.*

# Enjoy These Apple Favorites

When it's apple-picking time, Southern kitchens are filled with the aroma of freshly baked apple pies and other favorites like baked apples, apple dumplings, and sugar-sprinkled apple fritters.

You'll want to try Annelies Covalt's Dutch Apple Pie; it's a little different from most recipes since it's baked in a springform pan and has an unusual crust of butter, sugar, and flour. For the filling, apple slices are coated with a lemon-flavored syrup and then mixed with golden raisins simmered in rum.

## IMPERIAL BAKED APPLES

6 large baking apples
¼ cup firmly packed brown sugar
1 tablespoon butter or margarine, melted
3 tablespoons chopped almonds, toasted
2 tablespoons apricot preserves
¾ cup orange juice
½ cup sugar
1 teaspoon quick-cooking tapioca

Core apples to within ½ inch from bottom; peel top third of each. Place apples in a shallow baking dish. Set aside.

Combine next 4 ingredients, mixing well. Stuff each apple with about 2 tablespoons of sugar mixture.

Combine remaining ingredients; pour over apples. Bake at 350° for 45 minutes or until tender. Baste occasionally with orange juice syrup in bottom of dish. Yield: 6 servings.

*Mrs. Kris Ragan,*
*Midlothian, Virginia.*

## APPLE DUMPLINGS

2 cups all-purpose flour
2 teaspoons baking powder
1 teaspoon salt
⅔ cup shortening
½ cup milk
3 cooking apples, peeled, cored, and sliced into wedges
½ teaspoon sugar
¼ teaspoon ground cinnamon
1½ cups sugar
¼ teaspoon ground cinnamon
¼ teaspoon ground nutmeg
1½ cups water
2 tablespoons butter

Combine first 3 ingredients; cut in shortening with pastry blender until mixture resembles coarse meal. Gradually add milk, stirring to make a soft dough. Roll dough out on a lightly floured surface to ¼-inch thickness and shape into an 18- x 12-inch rectangle; cut dough into six 6-inch squares.

Place 3 to 4 pieces of apple on each square. Moisten edges of each dumpling with water; bring corners to center, pinching edges to seal. Place dumplings in a lightly greased 12- x 8- x 2-inch baking dish. Combine ½ teaspoon sugar and ¼ teaspoon cinnamon; sprinkle evenly over top. Combine remaining ingredients in a medium saucepan; place over low heat, stirring until butter melts and sugar dissolves. Pour syrup over dumplings. Bake at 375° for 45 minutes, basting once with syrup. Yield: 6 servings.

*Ranaé Phelps,*
*Balch Springs, Texas.*

## DUTCH APPLE PIE

2 cups all-purpose flour
1 cup sugar
¾ cup cold butter
1 cup golden raisins
¼ cup light rum
¼ cup butter
½ cup sugar
1 tablespoon ground cinnamon
Juice and grated rind of 2 lemons
9 medium cooking apples, peeled, cored, and thinly sliced
3 tablespoons water
2 tablespoons sugar

Combine flour and 1 cup sugar; cut in ¾ cup cold butter with pastry blender until mixture resembles coarse meal. Knead crumb mixture until dough forms a ball. Measure ¼ cup dough; set aside. Press remaining dough in bottom and 1½ inches up the sides of an ungreased 9-inch springform pan. Set aside.

Press reserved ¼ cup dough into a 5- x 4-inch rectangle on a floured surface. Cut into 4- x ¼-inch strips; place strips on waxed paper, and freeze until ready to use.

Combine raisins and rum in a medium skillet; simmer 8 to 10 minutes or until raisins are soft. Stir in next 4 ingredients; continue to simmer 5 to 10 minutes or until mixture is slightly thickened.

Place apples and 3 tablespoons water in a Dutch oven; cover and cook over low heat about 5 minutes, or until apples are soft. Stir occasionally. Drain liquid from apples; pour sugar syrup over cooked apples, stirring to coat slices. Place apples in prepared crust. Arrange reserved dough strips to resemble wheel spokes on top of pie.

Set pie on a cookie sheet and bake at 350° for 40 minutes. Remove from oven; sprinkle 2 tablespoons sugar evenly over pie. Cool on a wire rack 20 minutes; remove to serving platter. Release rim, and continue cooling. Yield: one 9-inch pie. *Annelies H. Covalt,*
*Roswell, Georgia.*

## APPLE FRITTERS

1 egg, beaten
½ cup milk
2 teaspoons sugar
1 teaspoon ground cinnamon
1 cup self-rising flour
1 (8-ounce) carton commercial sour cream
¼ cup vegetable oil, divided
3 cooking apples, cored and thinly sliced
Powdered sugar

Combine first 5 ingredients, and mix well. Stir in the sour cream.

Heat 2 tablespoons vegetable oil in a large skillet. Dip apple slices in batter. Cook several slices at a time 3 to 4 minutes on each side or until golden brown. Drain fritters on paper towels. Add remaining vegetable oil to skillet as needed.

Dust fritters with powdered sugar, and serve hot. Yield: 4 to 6 servings.

*Audrey Bledsoe,*
*Smyrna, Georgia.*

*Tip: To prevent fruit or nuts from sinking to the bottom of bread or cake batter, shake them in a bag with a small amount of flour to dust lightly before adding to batter.*

# Enjoy Turnips As A Side Dish

Southerners love turnip greens so much it's easy to forget that the bulb beneath the tops can be just as tasty in its own right.

A good example is Gay Evaldi's Baked Turnip Casserole—she combines turnips, green pepper, chopped green onion, parsley, and crunchy bacon pieces in a hearty casserole. Charlotte Farmer of Richmond created her Gingered Turnips by adding soy sauce, onion, beef stock, and ginger to mashed turnips.

### GINGERED TURNIPS

2 pounds turnips, peeled and cubed
1 tablespoon minced onion
1¼ cups beef stock
½ teaspoon ground ginger
½ teaspoon sugar
2 teaspoons soy sauce
Chopped fresh parsley

Combine all ingredients except parsley in a Dutch oven over low heat. Cover and simmer 15 minutes or until turnips are tender. Remove from heat; drain. Beat turnip mixture on medium speed of electric blender until smooth. Sprinkle with parsley. Yield: 4 to 6 servings.           *Charlotte Farmer, Richmond, Virginia.*

### BAKED TURNIP CASSEROLE

12 turnips, peeled and cubed
½ pound bacon, chopped
2 onions, chopped
1 clove garlic, minced
1 medium-size green pepper, chopped
2 egg yolks, beaten
⅓ cup evaporated milk
3 slices bread, toasted and crumbled
¼ cup butter or margarine, melted
1 tablespoon chopped green onion with
   tops
2 teaspoons chopped fresh parsley
½ teaspoon salt
¼ teaspoon pepper

Place turnips in a large saucepan; cover with water, and bring to a boil. Cover and cook 30 minutes or until turnips are tender. Drain and mash; set aside.

Cook bacon in a large skillet until crisp; remove bacon, reserving 2 tablespoons drippings in skillet. Set bacon aside. Sauté onion, garlic, and green pepper in reserved drippings until tender. Stir in turnips and remaining ingredients except bacon. Spoon into a 3-quart casserole; top with reserved bacon. Bake at 350° for 30 minutes. Yield: 8 to 10 servings.     *Gay Evaldi, East Windsor, New Jersey.*

# Depend On Chicken

Some of the most nutritious, economical, and tasty main dishes start with chicken. An excellent source of protein, chicken is recommended by nutritionists because it's lower in fat than red meats.

If your schedule calls for easy recipes, try Betty Jane Morrison's Hawaiian Chicken. Pineapple juice, brown sugar, and vinegar penetrate the chicken with a sweet-and-sour flavor during baking.

Company Chicken Cordon Bleu takes a little longer to assemble, but the result is worth the extra effort. Clonelle Jones of Nashville often prepares this special entrée for guests and says she's had many requests for her recipe.

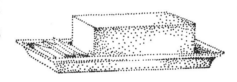

### COMPANY CHICKEN CORDON BLEU

2 whole chicken breasts, split, boned, and
   skinned
⅛ teaspoon salt
⅛ teaspoon white pepper
1 egg, beaten
½ cup milk
2 (1-ounce) slices cooked ham, cut in half
2 (1-ounce) slices Swiss cheese, cut in half
½ cup all-purpose flour
⅔ cup fine, dry breadcrumbs
¼ cup butter or margarine

Place each chicken breast half on a sheet of waxed paper; flatten to ¼-inch thickness, using a meat mallet or rolling pin. Sprinkle with salt and pepper.

Combine egg and milk; brush both sides of chicken pieces with milk mixture. Place a piece of ham and a piece of cheese in center of each chicken piece. Brush top of cheese slices with milk mixture; fold chicken in half, securing edges with wooden picks. Dredge chicken in flour; dip in remaining milk mixture, and coat well with breadcrumbs. Cover and chill 1 hour.

Melt butter in a heavy skillet; brown chicken on both sides. Remove to a lightly greased 9-inch square pan; bake, uncovered, at 350° for 40 to 45 minutes or until done. Yield: 4 servings.
          *Clonelle G. Jones, Nashville, Tennessee.*

### CHICKEN CONTINENTAL

1 (3- to 3½-pound) broiler-fryer, cut up
½ cup all-purpose flour
¼ cup butter or margarine
1 (10¾-ounce) can cream of chicken soup,
   undiluted
1⅓ cups water
1 medium onion, chopped
1 teaspoon celery flakes
1 teaspoon ground thyme
½ teaspoon salt
⅛ teaspoon pepper
1⅓ cups uncooked regular rice
1 (12-ounce) can whole kernel corn,
   undrained

Dredge chicken in flour. Melt butter in a large skillet. Add chicken, and cook over medium heat 15 to 20 minutes or until golden brown, turning occasionally. Drain on paper towels, and set aside; reserve drippings in skillet.

Add next 7 ingredients to drippings; cook over low heat until bubbly.

Combine rice, corn, and half of soup mixture, stirring well; spread evenly in a greased 13- x 9- x 2-inch baking dish. Arrange chicken over rice mixture, and top with remaining soup mixture. Cover and bake at 375° for 30 to 40 minutes or until done. Yield: 4 to 6 servings.
          *Mrs. James Collins, De Funiak Springs, Florida.*

### HAWAIIAN CHICKEN

¾ cup unsweetened pineapple juice
⅓ cup catsup
¼ cup firmly packed brown sugar
¼ cup butter or margarine
¼ cup vinegar
2 tablespoons cornstarch
1 teaspoon salt
1 teaspoon chili powder
1 teaspoon soy sauce
½ teaspoon Worcestershire sauce
1 (2½- to 3-pound) broiler-fryer, cut up
   and skinned

Combine first 10 ingredients in a small saucepan. Bring to a boil; cook 1 minute, stirring constantly.

Place chicken in a 13- x 9- x 2-inch baking dish; pour sauce over chicken. Cover and bake at 350° for 45 minutes. Uncover and bake an additional 30 minutes, basting occasionally. Yield: about 4 servings.

*Betty Jane Morrison,*
*Lakewood, Colorado.*

## LEMON FRIED CHICKEN

**4 whole chicken breasts, split and skinned**
**3 tablespoons lemon juice**
**1 cup crispy rice cereal, finely crushed**
**2 tablespoons grated lemon rind**
**1 tablespoon paprika**
**¼ teaspoon dried whole thyme**
**¼ teaspoon ground nutmeg**
**⅛ teaspoon pepper**
**Vegetable oil**

Sprinkle chicken with lemon juice; cover and refrigerate 15 minutes.

Combine cereal, lemon rind, paprika, thyme, nutmeg, and pepper; mix well. Dredge chicken in cereal mixture; let stand 5 minutes.

Heat 1 inch of oil in a large skillet to 350°; add chicken and fry 30 minutes or until golden brown, turning once. Drain on paper towels. Yield: 8 servings.

*Jay Jerome,*
*Charlottesville, Virginia.*

## CHICKEN MONTEREY

**4 whole chicken breasts, split, boned, and**
  **skinned**
**1 tablespoon all-purpose flour**
**½ teaspoon salt**
**¼ teaspoon pepper**
**¼ cup butter or margarine**
**½ cup chopped onion**
**8 large mushrooms, sliced**
**1 clove garlic, minced**
**2 tablespoons all-purpose flour**
**1 teaspoon celery salt**
**½ teaspoon white pepper**
**½ cup chicken broth**
**½ cup Chablis or other dry white wine**
**1 avocado, peeled, seeded, and mashed**
**1½ cups (6 ounces) shredded Monterey**
  **Jack cheese, divided**

Place each chicken breast half on a sheet of waxed paper; flatten to ¼-inch thickness, using a meat mallet or rolling pin. Sprinkle chicken with 1 tablespoon flour, salt, and pepper.

Lightly brown chicken in butter in a large skillet over low heat. Place chicken in a 13- x 9- x 2-inch baking dish, reserving pan drippings in skillet.

Add onion, mushrooms, and garlic to pan drippings; sauté until tender but not brown. Stir in next 5 ingredients; cook over low heat 5 minutes. Stir in avocado and ½ cup cheese. Spoon cheese mixture over chicken; top with remaining cheese. Cover and bake at 350° for 15 minutes. Yield: 8 servings.

*Martha T. Leoni,*
*New Bern, North Carolina.*

# Fancy Entrées Just For Two

It's easier to splurge on elegant dishes when there are just two of you. So when an occasion calls for something special, serve a memorable entrée such as LaJean Grannan's Cornish Hens With Brown Rice. LaJean says it is part of her holiday menu for two.

"My husband and I enjoyed this dish for our first Thanksgiving dinner alone," she says. "It's much easier than cooking a turkey and the trimmings, and we found it to be a real treat." You will too—the hens are basted with a red currant jelly and port wine sauce and served with a side dish of Brown Rice.

Another elegant dish for two, Steak Diane, offers juicy beef tenderloin sautéed with butter, shallots, and mustard. For our Veal Steak dish, veal cutlets are given a cheesy twist; Parmesan is added to the breadcrumb coating and sprinkled over the cutlets after sautéing.

## CORNISH HENS WITH BROWN RICE

**2 (1¼-pound) Cornish hens**
**½ teaspoon salt**
**¼ teaspoon pepper**
**1 tablespoon butter or margarine**
**¼ cup red currant jelly**
**1 tablespoon butter or margarine**
**½ teaspoon lemon juice**
**2 whole cloves**
**Dash of salt**
**Dash of pepper**
**¼ cup port wine**
**Brown Rice**

Remove giblets from hens; reserve for other uses. Rinse hens with cold water, and pat dry. Sprinkle cavity of hens with ½ teaspoon salt and ¼ teaspoon pepper. Place hens breast side up in a shallow baking pan. Rub hens with 1 tablespoon butter. Close cavities, and secure with wooden picks; truss.

Combine next 6 ingredients in a small saucepan; cook over low heat, stirring often, until jelly melts. Stir in wine, and pour mixture over hens.

Bake at 400° for 15 minutes. Reduce heat to 350°, and bake an additional 1 hour, basting occasionally with pan drippings. (If hens begin to overbrown, cover loosely with aluminum foil.) Serve with Brown Rice. Yield: 2 servings.

*Brown Rice:*

**1¾ cups chicken broth**
**½ cup uncooked brown rice**
**½ teaspoon salt**
**1½ cups coarsely chopped celery**
**½ cup sliced mushrooms**
**2 tablespoons butter or margarine**
**1 (8-ounce) can water chestnuts, drained**
  **and diced**
**½ teaspoon dried whole thyme**
**¼ teaspoon dried whole rosemary**
**⅛ teaspoon pepper**

Combine broth, rice, and salt in a heavy saucepan; bring to a boil. Cover, reduce heat, and simmer 45 to 50 minutes or until all liquid is absorbed.

Sauté celery and mushrooms in butter until crisp-tender; add water chestnuts and seasonings. Stir into rice. Yield: 2 servings.

*LaJean Grannan,*
*Poplar Grove, Arkansas.*

## STEAK DIANE

**4 (½-inch-thick) tenderloin steaks**
**⅛ teaspoon salt**
**⅛ teaspoon freshly ground pepper**
**2 tablespoons butter**
**½ teaspoon dry mustard**
**2 tablespoons minced shallots**
**2 tablespoons butter**
**1 tablespoon lemon juice**
**1½ teaspoons Worcestershire sauce**
**1 tablespoon minced fresh parsley**
**1 tablespoon minced fresh chives**

Pound steaks to ¼-inch thickness. Sprinkle both sides of steaks with salt and pepper. Combine 2 tablespoons butter, mustard, and shallots in a heavy skillet; cook over medium heat 1 minute, stirring frequently. Add steaks; cook 1 minute on each side or until desired degree of doneness. Remove steaks to serving plate, and keep warm.

Add 2 tablespoons butter, lemon juice, and Worcestershire sauce to pan drippings; cook over medium-high heat 2 minutes. Stir in parsley and chives. Pour butter sauce over steaks. Serve immediately. Yield: 2 servings.

*Carol Jerome,*
*Brevard, North Carolina.*

## DRESSED CRAB

2 slices bread
½ pound fresh crabmeat, drained and
    flaked
3 tablespoons dry sherry
2 teaspoons lemon juice
½ teaspoon salt
⅛ teaspoon white pepper
¼ cup whipping cream, whipped
½ cup soft breadcrumbs
2 tablespoons butter or margarine, melted
Fresh parsley sprigs

Remove crusts from bread slices; tear bread into coarse crumbs. Combine breadcrumbs, crabmeat, sherry, lemon juice, salt, and pepper; stir well.

Fold whipped cream into crabmeat mixture, and spoon into two greased ovenproof serving dishes. Combine ½ cup breadcrumbs and butter; sprinkle over crabmeat mixture. Bake at 375° for 15 minutes or until lightly browned. Garnish with parsley. Yield: 2 servings.
*Mrs. C. C. Kerns,*
*Exmore, Virginia.*

## SAILOR SHRIMP FOR TWO

1 clove garlic, minced
1 tablespoon olive oil
1 (16-ounce) can pear-shaped tomatoes,
    undrained and chopped
¼ cup tomato paste
¼ cup water
1 tablespoon minced fresh parsley
½ teaspoon salt
½ teaspoon garlic salt
½ teaspoon dried whole oregano
¼ teaspoon dried whole basil
Dash of pepper
3 cups water
1 pound unpeeled shrimp
Hot cooked rice
Grated Parmesan cheese (optional)
Lemon slices (optional)

Sauté garlic in oil in a heavy skillet. Stir in next 9 ingredients; simmer, uncovered, 15 to 20 minutes.

Bring 3 cups water to a boil. Add shrimp; return to a boil. Reduce heat, and simmer 3 to 5 minutes. Drain; rinse with cold water. Peel and devein shrimp.

Add shrimp to tomato mixture, cooking just until thoroughly heated. Serve shrimp over rice; sprinkle with Parmesan cheese and garnish with lemon, if desired. Yield: 2 servings.
*Patsy Hull,*
*Montgomery, Alabama.*

*Tip: Whenever a recipe calls for a re-heating process, the dish can be made in advance up to that point.*

## VEAL STEAK

½ pound (½-inch-thick) veal cutlets
1 tablespoon lemon juice
1 egg
1 tablespoon water
1 tablespoon vegetable oil
½ cup fine, dry breadcrumbs
¼ cup grated Parmesan cheese
¼ cup all-purpose flour
½ teaspoon salt
⅛ teaspoon pepper
¼ cup butter or margarine
Grated Parmesan cheese

Flatten cutlets to ¼-inch thickness, using a meat mallet or rolling pin; sprinkle with lemon juice, and set aside for 30 minutes.

Combine egg, water, and oil; beat well. Combine the breadcrumbs and ¼ cup cheese, stirring well. Combine flour, salt, and pepper; dredge cutlets in flour mixture. Dip cutlets in egg mixture; dredge in breadcrumb mixture, coating well.

Sauté cutlets in butter about 3 minutes on each side or until browned. Sprinkle with additional Parmesan cheese. Yield: 2 servings.
*Virginia M. Griffin,*
*Princeton, Kentucky.*

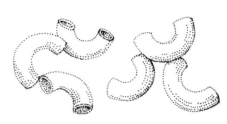

# Toss An Imaginative Pasta Salad

Pasta salads are more versatile than you may think; with a little imagination, countless variations are possible. For instance, Dorothy Burgess makes Barbecue Macaroni Salad by tossing elbow macaroni with barbecue sauce, chopped olives, and sweet pickles. Sandy Lamp combines spaghetti with ham, Cheddar, and lots of fresh vegetables for her hearty Spaghetti Salad. Patricia Boschen's Spiral Macaroni Salad is a pretty combination of spiral macaroni, cherry tomatoes, cheese, and green pepper.

Keep in mind that you cook pasta only until it's tender and yet slightly firm to the bite; overcooking makes it soft and mushy. Using a colander, drain the pasta immediately after it's cooked, and rinse it with cold water to cool it before adding other ingredients.

## BARBECUE MACARONI SALAD

1 (16-ounce) package elbow macaroni
1½ cups chopped sweet pickles
2 tablespoons sweet pickle juice
1½ cups chopped celery
1¼ cups commercial barbecue sauce
1 cup chopped ripe olives
1 cup mayonnaise
½ cup chopped onion
½ teaspoon chili powder

Cook macaroni according to package directions; drain. Rinse macaroni with cold water; drain.

Combine all ingredients, and toss gently. Chill at least 1 hour. Yield: 12 to 15 servings.
*Dorothy Burgess,*
*Huntsville, Texas.*

## SPIRAL MACARONI SALAD

1 (8-ounce) package spiral macaroni
1 cup cherry tomatoes, halved
1 cup (4 ounces) shredded Cheddar cheese
1 small cucumber, peeled and cut into
    chunks
2 tablespoons chopped green pepper
2 tablespoons chopped celery
2 tablespoons chopped green onion
1 tablespoon pickle relish
¼ cup mayonnaise
½ teaspoon prepared mustard
Pinch of dillseeds
Pinch of celery salt
Pinch of celery seeds

Cook macaroni according to package directions; drain. Rinse macaroni with cold water; drain.

Combine macaroni and next 7 ingredients; toss gently. Combine remaining ingredients, and mix well. Pour over salad; toss gently. Cover and chill at least 1 hour. Yield: 6 servings.
*Patricia Boschen,*
*Ashland, Virginia.*

## OVERNIGHT PASTA SALAD

1 cup (4 ounces) tiny shell macaroni,
    uncooked
2 cups shredded lettuce
2 hard-cooked eggs, sliced
2 (1-ounce) slices cooked ham, cut into
    thin strips
1 (10-ounce) package frozen English peas,
    thawed
½ cup (2 ounces) shredded Swiss cheese
½ cup mayonnaise
¼ cup commercial sour cream
1 tablespoon chopped green onion
1 teaspoon prepared mustard
1 teaspoon hot sauce
1 teaspoon paprika
Chopped fresh parsley

Cook macaroni according to package directions, using 1½ teaspoons salt; drain. Rinse macaroni with cold water; drain.

Layer lettuce, macaroni, egg slices, ham, peas, and cheese in a 1½-quart salad bowl. Combine next 5 ingredients, and mix well. Spread mixture evenly over top, sealing to edge of bowl. Sprinkle with paprika and parsley. Cover bowl tightly, and chill overnight. Yield: 6 to 8 servings.
*Carol T. Keith,*
*Roanoke, Virginia.*

## SPAGHETTI SALAD

1 (8-ounce) package spaghetti
½ cup shredded lettuce (optional)
1 small onion, chopped
3 slices cooked ham, chopped
½ cup (2 ounces) cubed Cheddar cheese
3 small sweet pickles, chopped
½ cup chopped green pepper
¼ cup chopped radishes
½ cup chopped celery
¼ cup chopped carrots
⅔ cup mayonnaise
1 tablespoon prepared mustard
1½ tablespoons lemon juice
1½ teaspoons salt
¼ teaspoon pepper
2 tablespoons sugar
Lettuce leaves (optional)

Cook spaghetti according to package directions; drain. Rinse spaghetti with cold water; drain and set aside.

Combine next 9 ingredients, mixing well; stir in spaghetti.

Combine mayonnaise, mustard, lemon juice, salt, pepper, and sugar; stir well. Pour over spaghetti mixture, and toss to coat. Serve over lettuce leaves, if desired. Yield: 6 servings.
*Sandy Lamp,*
*Waynesboro, Georgia.*

# A Bounty Of Winter Squash

Hidden within the hard, outer shells of acorn, butternut, and other kinds of winter squash is a sweet, delicious pulp that inspires a bounty of cold-weather dishes.

Acorn squash becomes a main attraction when it's halved, baked, and stuffed. Our Stuffed Acorn Squash boasts a filling of ground beef, sausage,

onion, celery, and cream of mushroom soup.

The pulp of either hubbard or butternut squash may be used to prepare Tasty Whipped Squash. Laced with nutmeg and golden raisins, the dish is lightly sweetened and topped with a delicate brown sugar and pecan glaze.

Select winter squash that are fully mature, with hard, tough rinds that can't be perforated with a thumbnail. Avoid those with cuts, punctures, and sunken spots, which are all signs of decay.

Winter squash should last several weeks if stored in a cool (50° to 60°), dry area that's well ventilated. Squash kept at room temperature should be used within one week.

## STUFFED ACORN SQUASH

3 large acorn squash
¾ pound ground beef
¼ pound bulk pork sausage
⅓ cup chopped onion
1 (10¾-ounce) can cream of mushroom soup, undiluted
½ cup chopped celery
1 cup soft breadcrumbs
2 tablespoons butter or margarine, melted

Cut squash in half lengthwise, and remove seeds. Place cut side down in shallow baking pans, and add 1 inch water. Bake, uncovered, at 400° for 30 minutes. Drain.

Cook ground beef, sausage, and onion in a large skillet over medium heat until meat is brown, stirring to crumble. Remove from heat, and drain off drippings. Stir in soup and celery. Spoon evenly into squash halves. Combine breadcrumbs and butter; sprinkle over squash. Bake, uncovered, at 400° for 20 minutes. Yield: 6 servings.
*Mrs. H. G. Drawdy,*
*Spindale, North Carolina.*

## TASTY WHIPPED SQUASH

5 pounds hubbard or butternut squash
2 tablespoons butter or margarine, softened
2 tablespoons brown sugar
⅓ cup golden raisins
½ teaspoon salt
¼ teaspoon ground nutmeg
⅛ teaspoon pepper
1 tablespoon butter or margarine
1 tablespoon brown sugar
1 tablespoon light corn syrup
2 tablespoons finely chopped pecans

Cut squash in half lengthwise, and remove seeds. Place cut side down in shallow baking pans; add ½ inch water. Cover and bake at 400° for 40 to 50 minutes or until tender. Drain. Scoop out pulp, and discard shell.

Combine squash pulp, 2 tablespoons butter, and 2 tablespoons brown sugar in a large bowl; beat with an electric mixer until smooth.

Spoon squash mixture into a large saucepan; cook over medium heat 5 minutes, stirring often. Stir in raisins, salt, nutmeg, and pepper; cook 10 minutes, stirring often. Spoon squash into a serving dish, and keep warm.

Combine remaining ingredients in a small saucepan; cook over medium heat until sugar dissolves, stirring constantly. Pour over squash. Yield: 6 to 8 servings.
*Alice McNamara,*
*Eucha, Oklahoma.*

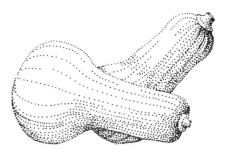

## SQUASH PUDDING

5 medium butternut squash
¼ cup butter or margarine, softened
2 eggs
1 tablespoon milk
1 teaspoon vanilla extract
½ teaspoon grated lemon rind
½ teaspoon ground nutmeg
½ teaspoon ground cinnamon
1 teaspoon ground mace
½ cup sugar
½ cup firmly packed brown sugar
½ cup chopped pecans, divided

Cut squash in half lengthwise, and remove seeds. Place cut side down in shallow baking pans; add ½ inch water. Cover and bake at 400° for 40 to 50 minutes or until tender. Drain. Scoop out pulp, and discard shell.

Combine squash pulp and next 10 ingredients in a large bowl; beat with an electric mixer until smooth. Stir in ¼ cup pecans. Spoon mixture into a greased 2-quart baking dish. Bake, uncovered, at 350° for 45 minutes. Sprinkle with remaining ¼ cup pecans; continue to bake pudding an additional 5 minutes. Yield: 6 to 8 servings.
*Cheryl Corriveau,*
*De Land, Florida.*

# Soup-And-Sandwich Meals Go Light

A steaming bowl of soup served with a hearty sandwich makes good eating when the weather turns cool—even if you're eating light.

This month's "Cooking Light" soups have been stripped of extras like butter, bacon drippings, fatty meats, and cream. We substituted skim milk for whole milk or cream in three of our soups and cut back on the margarine used for sautéing vegetables in Creole Seafood Gumbo.

We've all been told that dieters should avoid sandwiches because of the bread. But if a sandwich is high in calories, the culprit is probably the filling. You can choose breads that are lower in calories than others by taking note of nutritional information on the label. It's the mayonnaise, butter, margarine, fatty meats, and cold cuts that are the ingredients to avoid.

Spread the bread with reduced-calorie mayonnaise instead of regular mayonnaise, or use diet margarine instead of butter. Regular or spicy mustards are good choices (only 5 to 10 calories per teaspoonful). You might also try spreading the bread with Neufchâtel cheese, which has about one-third fewer calories than regular cream cheese.

Keep calories low in sandwich fillings by choosing lean cuts of beef, pork, lamb, and veal. Skinned chicken and turkey are two of the best low-calorie fillings because their fat content is naturally low. Stay away from luncheon meats; most are fatty, high in calories, and also contain excess sodium.

The best way to make your light sandwich seem like more is to add low-calorie vegetables such as lettuce, tomatoes, mushrooms, cucumbers, cabbage, and alfalfa or bean sprouts.

## PIMIENTO CHEESE SANDWICHES

1 (8-ounce) package Neufchâtel cheese, softened
2 cups (8 ounces) shredded Colby or Longhorn cheese
1 (4-ounce) jar diced pimiento, drained
3 tablespoons dill pickle juice
Dash of garlic powder
4 (6-inch) whole wheat pocket bread rounds
Leaf lettuce

Combine cheese, mixing well. Add next 3 ingredients, mixing well. Chill at least 1 hour.

Cut pocket bread rounds in half; line each half with lettuce, and fill with ¼ cup cheese mixture. Yield: 8 servings (about 211 calories per serving).
*Mitze Waddle,*
*Hewitt, Texas.*

## EASY SLOPPY JOES

2½ pounds lean ground chuck
2 cups chopped onion
1 (6-ounce) can tomato paste
½ cup catsup
¼ cup tomato juice
2 tablespoons Worcestershire sauce
2 tablespoons prepared mustard
2 tablespoons lemon juice
1 teaspoon salt
¼ teaspoon pepper
6 hamburger buns, split and toasted

Combine ground chuck and onion in a large skillet; cook until meat is browned and onion is tender. Pour mixture into a colander, and pat dry with a paper towel; wipe pan drippings from skillet with a paper towel.

Return meat mixture to skillet, and add next 8 ingredients; simmer 15 to 20 minutes, stirring frequently.

To serve, spoon ½ cup meat mixture over each bun half. Yield: 12 servings (about 265 calories per serving).
*Note:* Sloppy Joe mixture freezes well. To serve, thaw in refrigerator and heat.
*Ruth E. Cunliffe,*
*Lake Placid, Florida.*

## VEGETABLE SALAD ROLLS

½ cup chopped green pepper
½ cup chopped cucumber
½ cup chopped tomato
½ cup chopped celery
2 tablespoons chopped onion
2 tablespoons chopped fresh parsley
2 tablespoons chopped dill pickle
⅓ cup low-fat cottage cheese
¼ cup reduced-calorie mayonnaise
⅛ teaspoon garlic powder
8 (1.2-ounce) hard rolls
Leaf lettuce

Combine first 7 ingredients, tossing well; set aside.

Combine cottage cheese, mayonnaise, and garlic powder in container of electric blender; process until smooth. Add to vegetable mixture, tossing gently; chill until ready to serve.

To serve, cut a ¾-inch slice from top of each roll; scoop out center, leaving a ½-inch shell (reserve crumbs for other uses). Line inside of rolls with leaf lettuce, and top with vegetable mixture. Yield: 8 servings (about 80 calories per serving).

## CREOLE SEAFOOD GUMBO

Vegetable cooking spray
1 teaspoon margarine
1 cup chopped onion
1 clove garlic, minced
7 cups water
1 pound shrimp, peeled and deveined
1 (10-ounce) package frozen sliced okra
1 cup sliced celery
¾ cup chopped green pepper
½ cup uncooked regular rice
1 (16-ounce) can whole tomatoes, undrained and chopped
1 (8-ounce) bottle clam juice
3 tablespoons all-purpose flour
1 teaspoon Worcestershire sauce
¾ teaspoon salt
1 teaspoon gumbo filé or ½ teaspoon dried whole thyme
¼ teaspoon pepper
⅛ teaspoon hot sauce
1 pound fresh crabmeat
1 (4-ounce) jar diced pimiento, drained

Coat a 5-quart Dutch oven with cooking spray; add margarine, and place over medium heat until margarine melts. Add onion and garlic, and sauté until tender. Add next 6 ingredients, and bring to a boil. Reduce heat; simmer, uncovered, 30 to 35 minutes. Stir in tomatoes. Combine clam juice, flour, Worcestershire sauce, salt, gumbo filé, pepper, and hot sauce; add to gumbo mixture, stirring well. Cook over medium heat until mixture begins to thicken. Stir in crabmeat and pimiento. Yield: 17 cups (about 91 calories per 1-cup serving). *Mrs. W. J. Wallace,*
*Orlando, Florida.*

## POTATO SOUP

5 medium potatoes, peeled and cubed
1 medium onion, chopped
⅓ cup chopped celery
3 cups water
1 cup skim milk
1 teaspoon salt
1 teaspoon chicken-flavored bouillon granules
2 teaspoons chopped chives
⅛ teaspoon pepper
Additional chopped chives (optional)

Combine potatoes, onion, celery, and 3 cups water in a 3-quart Dutch oven.

Bring to a boil; cover, reduce heat, and simmer 20 minutes or until potatoes are tender. Drain, setting vegetables aside and reserving 1½ cups cooking liquid in Dutch oven.

Mash vegetable mixture with a potato masher or electric mixer; add to reserved cooking liquid, along with next 5 ingredients. Cook, stirring constantly, until soup is thoroughly heated. Garnish with chopped chives, if desired. Yield: 6 cups (about 116 calories per 1-cup serving).
*Lynda L. Medaugh,*
*Sassafras, Kentucky.*

## LIGHT CREAM-OF-CELERY SOUP

6 stalks celery, coarsely chopped
6 green onions, coarsely chopped
3 medium potatoes, coarsely chopped
1 quart skim milk
½ teaspoon salt
⅛ teaspoon pepper

Combine all ingredients in a large saucepan. Cook over low heat 30 minutes or until vegetables are tender, stirring occasionally (do not boil).

Pour half of milk mixture into container of electric blender, and process 30 seconds; strain mixture through a sieve into a saucepan. Repeat blending and straining process with remaining mixture. Cook over low heat until thoroughly heated. Serve hot or cold. Yield: 4 cups (about 188 calories per 1-cup serving).

## DELICIOUS CORN CHOWDER

2 cups water
2 cups diced potatoes
½ cup chopped onion
½ cup diced celery
½ teaspoon dried whole basil
1 large bay leaf
1 (16½-ounce) can cream-style corn
2 cups skim milk
1 cup drained canned tomatoes, chopped
½ teaspoon salt
⅛ teaspoon pepper
½ cup (2 ounces) shredded Cheddar cheese
Fresh parsley sprigs

Combine first 6 ingredients in a large Dutch oven, and bring to a boil. Reduce heat, and simmer about 10 minutes or until potatoes are tender. Discard bay leaf. Stir in corn, skim milk, tomatoes, salt, and pepper; heat thoroughly (do not boil).

Add cheese; cook over low heat, stirring constantly, until cheese is melted and mixture thickens. Garnish with fresh parsley sprigs. Yield: 8 cups (about 130 calories per 1-cup serving).

# Cupcakes To Rave About

You'll find everything from chocolate bits to fruit preserves in these delectable cupcakes. Apple-Nut Cupcakes are chock full of raisins, nuts, and apples and flavored with coffee and cinnamon. Black Bottom Cups bake into moist, two-toned cakes with a chocolate base and a cream cheese topping filled with semisweet chocolate morsels.

## APPLE-NUT CUPCAKES

½ cup shortening
1 cup sugar
1 egg
½ teaspoon baking soda
½ cup cold coffee
2 cups all-purpose flour
½ teaspoon salt
1 tablespoon ground cinnamon
1 cup chopped pecans or walnuts
1 cup raisins
1 cup peeled, finely chopped cooking apples

Cream shortening; gradually add sugar, beating well. Add egg; beat well.

Stir soda into coffee. Combine flour, salt, and cinnamon; add to creamed mixture, alternately with coffee, beginning and ending with flour mixture. Stir in pecans, raisins, and apples. Spoon into paper-lined muffin pans, filling two-thirds full. Bake at 350° for 18 to 20 minutes. Yield: 1½ dozen.
*Juliette Rabon,*
*Uriah, Alabama.*

## BLACK BOTTOM CUPS

1½ cups all-purpose flour
1 cup sugar
¼ cup cocoa
1 teaspoon baking soda
½ teaspoon salt
1 cup water
⅓ cup vegetable oil
1 tablespoon vinegar
1 teaspoon vanilla extract
1 (8-ounce) package cream cheese, softened
⅓ cup sugar
1 egg
⅛ teaspoon salt
1 (6-ounce) package semisweet chocolate morsels

Combine first 5 ingredients, mixing well. Stir in water, oil, vinegar, and vanilla. Spoon batter into paper-lined muffin pans, filling two-thirds full.

Combine cream cheese and ⅓ cup sugar, creaming until light and fluffy. Add egg and salt, beating well; stir in chocolate morsels. Spoon 1 heaping teaspoon cream cheese mixture into center of each cupcake. Bake at 350° for 30 to 35 minutes. Cool in pans 10 minutes; remove to wire rack to complete cooling. Yield: 2 dozen.
*Mrs. R. M. Lancaster,*
*Brentwood, Tennessee.*

## CREAM CHEESE PARTY CUPCAKES

3 (8-ounce) packages cream cheese, softened
1 cup sugar
5 eggs
1½ teaspoons vanilla extract
1 (8-ounce) carton commercial sour cream
¼ cup sugar
½ teaspoon vanilla extract
Strawberry preserves

Beat cream cheese in a large mixing bowl until soft and creamy. Gradually add 1 cup sugar, beating until light and fluffy. Add eggs, one at a time, beating well after each addition. Stir in 1½ teaspoons vanilla. Spoon batter into paper-lined miniature muffin pans, filling two-thirds full. Bake at 300° for 30 minutes.

Combine sour cream, ¼ cup sugar, and ½ teaspoon vanilla, stirring well. Spoon ¼ teaspoon of sour cream mixture on each cupcake; top with small amount of strawberry preserves in the center of sour cream mixture. Return cupcakes to oven; continue baking 5 minutes. Yield: about 6 dozen.
*Linda Denson,*
*Little Rock, Arkansas.*

## BROWNIE CUPCAKES

4 (1-ounce) squares semisweet chocolate
1 cup butter or margarine
1¾ cups sugar
1 cup all-purpose flour
4 eggs
1 teaspoon vanilla extract
¼ teaspoon butter flavoring
1½ cups chopped pecans

Combine chocolate and butter in a heavy saucepan; cook over low heat, stirring constantly, until melted. Cool mixture slightly.

Combine sugar, flour, eggs, and flavorings in a large mixing bowl. Add chocolate mixture, stirring until batter is smooth. Stir in pecans. Spoon batter into paper-lined muffin pans, filling two-thirds full. Bake at 325° for 35 minutes. Yield: about 2 dozen.

*Cindy Winburn,*
*Butler, Missouri.*

# From Our Kitchen To Yours

Don't think of garnishes as extras. Whether you use a garnish as simple as hard-cooked egg slices on top of a casserole or as elaborate as piped whipped cream over a chocolate mousse, these attractive details are essential when it comes to adding sparkle to meals. And that's especially important during the holiday season.

## Some Ideas for Garnishes

**Frosted cranberries**—Serve your holiday turkey surrounded with mounds of frosted cranberries. Just dip fresh cranberries into beaten egg white, and roll them in granulated sugar. Place the berries on a wire rack (mesh type), and let dry in a cool place. Don't refrigerate them because the moisture will make the sugar melt.

**Notched citrus cups**—Lemons, limes, oranges, and grapefruit make a colorful garnish for seafood and vegetables or for use as a decorative container for a multitude of foods.

To make notched cups, first cut a thin slice from each end of the fruit so the halves will sit level. Insert the blade of a small knife at a downward angle into the middle of the fruit; remove the blade. Insert knife again at an upward angle to make a zigzag pattern. Continue cutting in this fashion completely around the fruit. Separate the halves by twisting slightly and carefully pulling them apart. Accent the notches, if desired, by dipping the tips into paprika, cinnamon, or chopped parsley.

If the fruit will be used as a container for salads, vegetables, or desserts, simply scoop out the pulp (reserve for another use), and fill the shell.

**Fluted mushrooms**—Use raw, fluted mushrooms as a garnish for salads, casseroles, or for adding interest to the dinner plate. Lightly sautéed, mushrooms are especially attractive for garnishing steaks or roast beef.

Begin with fresh, medium to large, firm mushrooms. Rub the entire mushroom with lemon juice to prevent browning. Make several slits at even intervals around the mushroom cap, cutting from the center of the cap to the edge and using a curving motion with the knife. Make another set of slits parallel to the first slits, allowing about 1/16 inch between. Remove the thin strip of mushroom between the slits and discard.

**Lemon roses**—Use lemon roses to brighten up a serving bowl filled with broccoli or other vegetables, or to spruce up a luncheon or dinner plate.

Using a sharp knife, peel a ½-inch-wide strip of rind in a continuous spiral from top to bottom of the lemon. Then with flesh side inward, coil the strip tightly at first to form the center of the rose; gradually let it become looser to form the outer petals. (Tomato roses can be made using the same procedure.)

**Hard-cooked eggs**—This colorful, nutritious garnish can be used in several ways. Overlap thin slices in a circle to top a casserole, vegetable, or salad; then fill the center of the circle with sprigs of parsley. Or cut the egg into quarters, and arrange the wedges in pinwheel fashion.

Sieved egg yolk makes an appealing topping for asparagus, broccoli, or spinach because of the distinct color contrast. Press only the yolk through a sieve, and lightly sprinkle it over the vegetable. Finely chopped egg is another option for vegetables and salads.

**Piped garnishes**—Using a decorator bag, pipe stiffly beaten whipping cream on top or around the base of desserts. Add a finishing touch by sprinkling the mounds of cream with finely chopped nuts or chocolate shavings.

Pipe mayonnaise or softened cream cheese on aspics or other congealed salads. Stuff celery quickly by piping cream cheese or other fillings through a large decorator tip. Stuffed eggs look even better when the filling is piped in.

Mashed potatoes serve as both garnish and side dish when piped around meats, such as roast beef or lamb.

**Vegetable and fruit garnishes**—Red or green pepper rings, celery leaves, cherry tomatoes, parsley sprigs, fresh herbs, and onion rings are all good choices for garnishing a casserole. Use one, or group several. For a particularly eye-catching combination, place several celery leaves off-center on a casserole and top with a cherry tomato or two. Or interlock rings of red and green pepper to add a dash of color.

Use baked fruit, such as peach, apricot, or pear halves, to garnish a platter of meat. For added color and flavor, fill the center of the fruit halves with spiced cream cheese, nuts, or currant jelly. For a quick garnish, arrange clusters of red and green grapes and nuts in the shell around the meat.

# Vegetable Casseroles In 30 Minutes

When time is running short, you'll appreciate the convenience of these delicious vegetable casseroles. Made with canned or frozen vegetables, they take only 30 minutes to bake.

For a zesty side dish, try our Spinach-Parmesan Casserole. It features chopped spinach mixed with sour cream, onion, lemon juice, and Parmesan cheese. Equally tasty, Pea Casserole Supreme blends tiny English peas with crunchy water chestnuts and celery.

## ITALIAN BROCCOLI CASSEROLE

2 (10-ounce) packages frozen chopped broccoli
2 eggs, beaten
1 (11-ounce) can condensed Cheddar cheese soup, undiluted
½ teaspoon dried whole oregano
1 (8-ounce) can stewed tomatoes, drained
3 tablespoons grated Parmesan cheese

Cook broccoli according to package directions, omitting salt; drain well.

Combine next 3 ingredients; mix well. Stir in broccoli and tomatoes. Spoon mixture into a greased 10- x 6- x 2-inch baking dish; sprinkle with Parmesan cheese. Bake, uncovered, at 350° for 30 minutes. Yield: 8 servings.

*Barbara Schildgen,*
*Dothan, Alabama.*

## CHEESY ASPARAGUS CASSEROLE

2 tablespoons butter or margarine
1 tablespoon all-purpose flour
1 (10¾-ounce) can cream of mushroom soup, undiluted
2 cups (8 ounces) shredded Cheddar cheese
2 hard-cooked eggs, sliced
2 (15-ounce) cans asparagus spears, drained
½ cup soft breadcrumbs

Melt butter in a heavy saucepan over low heat; add flour, stirring until smooth. Add soup and Cheddar cheese; cook until cheese melts and mixture is smooth, stirring constantly.

Layer half each of egg slices, asparagus spears, and cheese sauce in a lightly greased 10- x 6- x 2-inch baking dish; repeat layers. Sprinkle with breadcrumbs. Bake at 325° for 30 minutes. Yield: 8 servings. *Margaret Smith, Lauderdale-by-the-Sea, Florida.*

## PEA CASSEROLE SUPREME

3 tablespoons butter or margarine
⅓ cup finely chopped green pepper
1 small onion, grated
2 cups finely chopped celery
2 (17-ounce) cans tiny English peas, drained
2 tablespoons diced pimiento
1 (8-ounce) can water chestnuts, drained and thinly sliced
1 (10¾-ounce) can cream of mushroom soup, undiluted
2 tablespoons milk
¾ cup soft breadcrumbs

Melt butter in a large saucepan. Add green pepper, onion, and celery; sauté until tender. Remove from heat. Add next 5 ingredients; mix well. Spoon mixture into a greased 10- x 6- x 2-inch baking dish; sprinkle with breadcrumbs. Bake, uncovered, at 350° for 30 minutes. Yield: 8 servings.
*Mrs. Windsor Pipes, Baton Rouge, Louisiana.*

## SPINACH-PARMESAN CASSEROLE

2 (10-ounce) packages frozen chopped spinach
1 tablespoon butter or margarine
½ cup chopped onion
1 (8-ounce) carton commercial sour cream
½ cup grated Parmesan cheese
2 tablespoons lemon juice
¼ teaspoon garlic salt
½ cup soft breadcrumbs

Cook spinach according to package directions; drain well, and set aside.

Melt butter in a large saucepan. Add onion, and sauté until tender; remove from heat. Add spinach and remaining ingredients except breadcrumbs; mix well. Spoon mixture into a greased 1-quart casserole; sprinkle with breadcrumbs. Bake, uncovered, at 350° for 30 minutes. Yield: 6 servings.
*Brett Van Dorsten, Arcadia, California.*

# Sprouts Add Crunch, Taste Green

More people are eating bean sprouts and alfalfa sprouts than ever before— and with good reason. These vegetables add lots of flavor and a crispy texture to salads and sandwiches.

When buying fresh sprouts, remember that they spoil after a day or two, losing their bright-white color and crispness. Sprouts that are brownish or coated with a slippery film have already begun to spoil. Store fresh sprouts in the refrigerator, and always wash them thoroughly before using.

## FRESH SPINACH-SPROUT SALAD

1½ pounds fresh spinach, torn into bite-size pieces
1 cup fresh alfalfa sprouts or bean sprouts, washed and drained
1 small onion, thinly sliced and separated into rings
1 (8-ounce) can sliced water chestnuts, drained
8 slices bacon, cooked and crumbled
2 hard-cooked eggs, sliced
Dressing (recipe follows)

Combine vegetables, bacon, and egg in a large bowl; toss well. Serve with dressing. Yield: 10 servings.

*Dressing:*

½ cup sugar
½ cup vegetable oil
½ cup red wine vinegar
⅓ cup catsup
Dash of salt

Combine all ingredients in a jar. Cover jar tightly, and shake vigorously. Yield: 1⅔ cups. *Virginia Cavender, Memphis, Tennessee.*

## RISING SUN OMELET

¾ cup fresh bean sprouts, washed and drained
1 tablespoon butter or margarine
4 eggs
2 tablespoons water
¼ teaspoon salt
¼ teaspoon pepper
1 tablespoon butter or margarine
⅓ cup sliced water chestnuts
Grated Parmesan cheese
Fresh parsley sprigs (optional)

Sauté bean sprouts in 1 tablespoon butter until tender; set aside.

Combine eggs, water, salt, and pepper; mix just until blended.

Heat 1 tablespoon butter in a 10-inch omelet pan or heavy skillet over medium heat until bubbly. Pour egg mixture into skillet. As mixture starts to cook, gently lift edges of omelet with a spatula, and tilt pan so uncooked portion flows underneath.

When egg mixture is set, spoon bean sprouts in center; top with water chestnuts. Fold 2 outer edges of omelet toward center to cover filling; slide onto a warm platter, and sprinkle with Parmesan cheese. Garnish with parsley, if desired. Yield: 2 servings.
*Mrs. George P. Robinson, High Point, North Carolina.*

## BEEF AND BEAN SPROUTS

½ pound boneless round steak
3 tablespoons vegetable oil
½ cup chopped green onion
½ teaspoon seasoned salt
½ teaspoon garlic powder
1 pound fresh bean sprouts, washed and drained
½ cup sliced fresh mushrooms
1 small green pepper, cut into ¼-inch strips
¼ cup water
3 to 4 tablespoons soy sauce
1 tablespoon vinegar
1 tablespoon cornstarch
Hot cooked rice

Partially freeze steak; slice across grain into 3- x ½-inch strips.

Heat oil in large skillet over medium heat; add green onion, and stir-fry 1 minute. Add steak, seasoned salt, and garlic powder; stir-fry 4 minutes. Add bean sprouts, mushrooms, and green pepper; stir-fry 3 minutes.

Combine next 4 ingredients, mixing well; add to bean sprout mixture. Cook, stirring constantly, for 3 minutes or until thickened. Serve over rice. Yield: about 4 servings. *Dianna Woody, Bunnell, Florida.*

## ALFALFA POCKET BREAD SANDWICHES

1 (3-ounce) package cream cheese, softened
1 tablespoon mayonnaise
4 (6-inch) pocket bread rounds
4 lettuce leaves
8 tomato slices
2 (5-ounce) cans chunk chicken, drained and flaked
1 (4½-ounce) package fresh alfalfa sprouts, washed and drained

Combine cream cheese and mayonnaise, mixing well.

Cut slit halfway around edge of each bread round; spread cream cheese mixture on inside of each. Evenly divide lettuce, tomato slices, chicken, and alfalfa sprouts among sandwiches. Yield: 4 servings.            *Sara A. McCullough,*
*Broaddus, Texas.*

## Microwave Cookery

# Microwave Menus Keep It Simple

Busy schedules call for menus that can be prepared in minutes. With this in mind, we're sharing two simple menus to prepare in your microwave oven.

Our first menu features Chunky Chili, just right on a cold night. Corn Muffins go perfectly with the chili and take only about 2 minutes to microwave. For dessert, there's Double Chocolate Pie. With this menu, begin your preparation with the pie, since it needs to be chilled before it's served.

Individual Taco Pies are the order of the day for our second menu, requiring less than 30 minutes for all the preparation and microwaving. These fiery little casseroles are topped with cheese, lettuce, tomato, and your own microwaved Taco Sauce. Afterwards, cool off your taste buds with our refreshing Orange-Tapioca Creme.

---

**Chunky Chili**
**Corn Muffins**
**Double Chocolate Pie**
**Coffee**

## CHUNKY CHILI

1 large onion, finely chopped
1 green pepper, finely chopped
1 pound lean beef for stewing, cut into ½-inch cubes
1 (16-ounce) can kidney beans, drained
1 (16-ounce) can tomatoes, undrained
1 (8-ounce) can tomato sauce
1 (4-ounce) can chopped green chiles, drained
2 tablespoons chili powder
¼ teaspoon garlic powder
¼ teaspoon ground cumin
½ teaspoon salt
¼ teaspoon pepper
Shredded Cheddar cheese (optional)

Combine onion and green pepper in a 5-quart casserole or bowl. Cover with casserole lid or heavy-duty plastic wrap. Microwave at HIGH for 6 to 7 minutes or until crisp-tender. Stir in remaining ingredients except cheese. Cover and microwave at HIGH for 10 minutes; stir well. Cover and microwave at MEDIUM (50% power) for 30 to 35 minutes. Sprinkle individual servings with cheese, if desired. Yield: 10 cups.

## CORN MUFFINS

½ cup all-purpose flour
½ cup yellow cornmeal
½ cup drained canned whole kernel corn
¼ cup chopped green pepper
1 tablespoon sugar
2 teaspoons baking powder
½ teaspoon salt
⅓ cup milk
1 egg, beaten
¼ cup vegetable oil

Combine all ingredients in a bowl; mix just until dry ingredients are moistened. Place paper liners in four 6-ounce custard cups; fill half full with batter. Arrange cups in a ring on a glass pizza plate. (May use microwave cupcake dish, alternating cups for even baking.) Microwave at HIGH 1½ to 2 minutes or until surface is almost dry, rotating plate after half the time. Let stand on a wire rack 2 minutes. Repeat procedure with remaining batter. Yield: 8 muffins.

---

## DOUBLE CHOCOLATE PIE

¼ cup plus 2 tablespoons butter or margarine
1½ cups chocolate wafer crumbs
6 (1-ounce) squares semisweet chocolate
3 tablespoons sugar
2 tablespoons milk
3 eggs, separated
2 tablespoons crème de cacao
Sweetened whipped cream
Chocolate curls

Place butter in a 9-inch glass pieplate. Microwave at HIGH for 1 minute or until butter melts; stir in wafer crumbs, mixing well. Press mixture evenly into pieplate. Microwave at HIGH for 2 to 2½ minutes, rotating dish one half-turn after 1 minute. Chill well.

Combine chocolate, sugar, and milk in a 2-cup glass measure. Microwave at MEDIUM (50% power) for 2½ to 3½ minutes or until chocolate begins to melt, stirring after 1½ minutes. Stir until chocolate melts completely.

Beat egg yolks, and stir in one-fourth of chocolate mixture; then add to remaining chocolate mixture. Stir in the crème de cacao.

Beat egg whites (at room temperature) until stiff peaks form; fold in chocolate mixture. Pour filling into crust, and chill until firm. Top with whipped cream and chocolate curls before serving. Yield: one 9-inch pie.

---

**Individual Taco Pies**
**Taco Sauce**
**Orange-Tapioca Creme**
**Iced Tea**

## INDIVIDUAL TACO PIES

½ cup chopped green pepper
½ cup chopped onion
1 pound lean ground beef
1 (1.25-ounce) package taco seasoning mix
½ cup chopped tomato
1 egg, beaten
½ cup finely crushed corn chips
1 (15½-ounce) can kidney beans, drained
4 (6-inch) corn tortillas
1 cup (4 ounces) shredded Cheddar cheese
Shredded lettuce
Chopped tomato

Combine green pepper and onion in a 1-quart casserole; cover with casserole lid or heavy-duty plastic wrap. Microwave at HIGH 1½ to 2½ minutes or until onion is tender. Combine with next 6 ingredients; stir well, and set aside.

Cut four evenly spaced 2-inch slashes in edge of each tortilla. Shape tortillas, overlapping cut edges, to fit four 12-ounce casserole dishes. Press a fourth of meat mixture into each of the tortilla-lined casseroles. Cover with waxed paper, and microwave at HIGH 8 to 10 minutes.

Top each casserole with ¼ cup cheese. Let stand 3 minutes or until cheese begins to melt. Top with lettuce and tomato; serve with Taco Sauce (recipe below). Yield: 4 servings.

### TACO SAUCE

¾ cup chopped onion
1 clove garlic, minced
½ cup chopped tomato, drained
2 tablespoons vegetable oil
2 tablespoons chopped jalapeño pepper
½ teaspoon dried whole oregano
½ teaspoon ground cumin
¼ teaspoon salt
1½ teaspoons cornstarch
½ cup water
1 (8-ounce) can tomato sauce
2 tablespoons vinegar

Combine onion and garlic in a 1-quart casserole or bowl; cover with casserole lid or heavy-duty plastic wrap. Microwave at HIGH for 1½ to 3 minutes. Add next 6 ingredients; cover and microwave at HIGH for 2 to 5 minutes.

Combine cornstarch and water; stir in tomato sauce and vinegar. Add to onion mixture, stirring well. Microwave, uncovered, at HIGH for 2 to 5 minutes or until thickened, stirring at 1-minute intervals. Yield: 2 cups.

*Note:* For a thicker sauce, use 1 tablespoon cornstarch.

### ORANGE-TAPIOCA CREME

1¾ cups milk
⅓ cup sugar
¼ cup quick-cooking tapioca
⅛ teaspoon salt
2 eggs, separated
2 tablespoons sugar
2 teaspoons grated orange rind
¼ cup orange juice

Combine milk, ⅓ cup sugar, tapioca, salt, and egg yolks in a 2-quart glass bowl; beat at low speed of electric mixer until well blended. Microwave at HIGH, uncovered, for 6 to 7½ minutes or until thickened, stirring at 2-minute intervals.

Beat egg whites (at room temperature) until frothy. Gradually add 2 tablespoons sugar, beating until stiff peaks form; fold in orange rind and juice. Fold egg white mixture into pudding mixture, and spoon into dessert dishes. Chill until set. Yield: 4 servings.

# There's Rum In The Beans

Mrs. Roger Williams of Arden, North Carolina, discovered a way to turn ordinary dried navy beans into a spirited main dish—by adding rum. Besides the rum, she flavors her Rum-Laced Bean Bake with chopped smoked ham, onion, salt pork, mustard, and garlic.

### RUM-LACED BEAN BAKE

1 pound dried navy beans
2 whole cloves
1 small onion
½ pound lean salt pork
1 small bay leaf
1½ teaspoons salt
2 medium onions, chopped
½ pound smoked ham, chopped
2 small cloves garlic, minced
1 tablespoon dry mustard
¼ cup light rum

Sort and wash beans; place in a large Dutch oven. Cover with water 2 inches above beans; let soak overnight. Drain beans well.

Insert cloves in small onion. Add onion, salt pork, bay leaf, and salt to beans. Cover beans with water 3 inches above beans. Cover and bring to a boil; reduce heat, and simmer 1 hour or until beans are tender. Drain, reserving liquid. Add enough water to bean liquid to make 2¼ cups; set aside. Discard onion, cloves, and bay leaf. Remove salt pork; dice and set aside.

Layer half of beans in a 2½-quart casserole. Combine salt pork with chopped onion, ham, and garlic; spoon over beans. Top with remaining beans.

Combine reserved bean liquid and dry mustard, stirring well; pour over beans. Bake at 350° for 1 hour. Pour rum over top, and bake an additional 45 minutes. Yield: 10 to 12 servings.

*Mrs. Roger Williams,*
*Arden, North Carolina.*

*Tip: Lower oven temperature 25° when using heat-proof glass dishes to ensure even baking.*

# Cranberry Flavors This Coffee Cake

Here's a coffee cake that's special enough to give to friends during this holiday season. In fact, Aileen Lorberg, of Cape Girardeau, Missouri, says her friends often ask for it as a birthday gift. "I just bake it, stick a candle on it, and take it to them," she says.

Aileen invented Cranberry-Orange Coffee Cake while experimenting with a coffee cake recipe she'd followed for years. Substituting cranberry-orange relish for whole-berry cranberry sauce, pecans for walnuts, and milk for water, she produced a coffee cake that has been a much requested favorite of family and friends ever since.

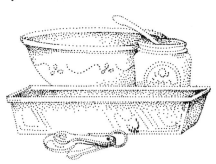

### CRANBERRY-ORANGE COFFEE CAKE

¼ cup firmly packed brown sugar
½ cup chopped pecans
¼ teaspoon ground cinnamon
2 cups biscuit mix
2 tablespoons sugar
⅔ cup milk
1 egg, beaten
½ (14-ounce) jar cranberry-orange relish
Powdered sugar glaze (recipe follows)

Combine brown sugar, pecans, and cinnamon; mix well, and set aside.

Combine biscuit mix, sugar, milk, and egg; beat 30 seconds at medium speed of electric mixer. Pour batter into a greased 9-inch square pan. Sprinkle batter with prepared pecan mixture, and spoon relish evenly over top.

Bake at 400° for 25 minutes or until wooden pick inserted in center comes out clean. Drizzle glaze over warm cake. Yield: one 9-inch coffee cake.

*Powdered Sugar Glaze:*

1 cup sifted powdered sugar
½ teaspoon vanilla extract
1 tablespoon milk

Combine all ingredients; mix well. Yield: about ½ cup. *Aileen Lorberg,*
*Cape Girardeau, Missouri.*

# Entrées For Your Chafing Dish

If you're planning a buffet for your next dinner party, use your chafing dish and serve one of these choice entrées. Not only will the food stay warm, but you'll have an attractive centerpiece.

Beef Marengo proved to be our favorite. It's made with chuck roast and simmered with Chablis, onion, mushrooms, and herbs. Served over noodles, it's an elegant dish with exquisite flavor.

## BEEF MARENGO

1 (4-pound) boneless chuck roast
½ cup vegetable oil
1 cup chopped onion
1 cup chopped celery
1 clove garlic, crushed
1 cup Chablis or other dry white wine, divided
2 (8-ounce) cans tomato sauce
2 bay leaves
1 teaspoon dried whole oregano
½ teaspoon dried whole rosemary
½ teaspoon salt
½ teaspoon pepper
1 tablespoon chopped fresh parsley
1 pound fresh mushrooms, sliced
2 tablespoons lemon juice
¼ cup butter or margarine
1 tablespoon all-purpose flour
2 tablespoons water
Chopped fresh parsley (optional)
Hot cooked noodles

Trim excess fat from roast; cut into 1-inch cubes.

Brown meat in hot oil in a large Dutch oven; remove meat. Add onion, celery, and garlic to pan drippings; sauté until tender. Add meat, ½ cup wine, and next 7 ingredients to vegetable mixture; bring to a boil. Cover, reduce heat, and simmer 1 hour or until meat is tender, stirring occasionally. Discard bay leaves.

Combine mushrooms and lemon juice, tossing gently. Melt butter in a large skillet; add mushrooms, and sauté until tender.

Combine flour and 2 tablespoons water; stir until smooth. Stir flour mixture, sautéed mushrooms, and remaining ½ cup wine into meat mixture. Cover and cook over medium heat 15 minutes. Transfer mixture to a chafing dish; sprinkle with chopped parsley, if desired. Serve over noodles. Yield: 8 to 10 servings. *Carolyn Brantley, Greenville, Mississippi.*

## TANGY ROUND STEAK

2 pounds boneless round steak
½ cup commercial spicy-sweet French dressing, divided
½ cup chopped onion
1½ cups water
1 (1.25-ounce) package sour cream sauce mix
1 teaspoon Worcestershire sauce
½ cup chopped celery
1 (3-ounce) can sliced mushrooms, drained
Hot cooked noodles

Trim excess fat from steak; cut steak into 2- x ¼-inch strips.

Heat ¼ cup dressing in a Dutch oven; add steak and onion. Cook until steak is browned and onion is tender, stirring often.

Stir in next 5 ingredients and remaining ¼ cup dressing; bring to a boil. Cover, reduce heat, and simmer 1 hour, stirring occasionally. Transfer mixture to a chafing dish. Serve over noodles. Yield: 6 servings. *Charlene Keebler, Savannah, Georgia.*

## CHAFING DISH CHICKEN

2 whole chicken breasts, split, boned, and skinned
¼ cup plus 2 tablespoons all-purpose flour
2 tablespoons grated Parmesan cheese
½ teaspoon salt
½ cup vegetable oil
1 cup chicken broth
¼ cup Chablis or other dry white wine
¼ cup chopped green pepper
1 clove garlic, minced
½ teaspoon salt
White pepper to taste
Hot cooked rice

Cut chicken into bite-size pieces. Combine flour, cheese, and ½ teaspoon salt in a bowl; mix well. Dredge chicken in flour mixture; set aside remaining flour mixture.

Heat oil in a large skillet to 325°; add chicken, and fry 8 to 10 minutes or until golden brown, turning once. Remove chicken; drain on paper towels. Drain off pan drippings, reserving 2 tablespoons in skillet. Add reserved flour mixture, stirring until smooth. Cook 1 minute, stirring constantly. Gradually add broth, stirring until smooth. Stir in next 5 ingredients; cook over medium heat until thickened, stirring constantly. Add chicken, and cook until thoroughly heated. Transfer mixture to a chafing dish. Serve over hot cooked rice. Yield: 4 servings. *Frances Bellows, Birmingham, Alabama.*

## CREAMED CHICKEN

1 (3- to 3½-pound) broiler-fryer
1 (10-ounce) package frozen English peas
3 tablespoons butter or margarine
3 tablespoons all-purpose flour
3 cups milk
¾ teaspoon salt
¾ teaspoon white pepper
1 (3-ounce) can sliced mushrooms, drained
1 (2-ounce) jar diced pimiento, drained
⅓ cup slivered almonds, toasted
Commercial patty shells, baked

Place chicken in a Dutch oven, and cover with water; bring to a boil. Cover, reduce heat, and simmer 1 hour or until tender. Remove chicken from broth; let cool. (Reserve broth for use in other recipes.) Bone chicken, and cut into bite-size pieces; set aside.

Cook peas according to package directions; drain and set aside.

Melt butter in a large saucepan over low heat; add flour, stirring until smooth. Cook 1 minute, stirring constantly. Gradually add milk; cook over medium heat, stirring constantly, until thickened and bubbly. Add next 5 ingredients; mix well. Stir in chicken and peas. Cook over low heat until thoroughly heated, stirring frequently. Transfer mixture to a chafing dish. Serve over patty shells. Yield: 6 servings. *Kathryn Ryan, Noblesville, Indiana.*

## SEAFOOD SUPREME

1 cup water
½ teaspoon salt
1 pound fresh small scallops
1 (10¾-ounce) can cream of shrimp soup, undiluted
⅔ cup milk
1 teaspoon paprika
1½ teaspoons Worcestershire sauce
Dash of red pepper
⅛ teaspoon white pepper
1½ pounds medium shrimp, peeled
Commercial patty shells, baked

Combine 1 cup water and salt in a medium saucepan, and bring to a boil; add scallops. Cover, reduce heat, and simmer 5 minutes; drain.

Combine next 6 ingredients in a large saucepan; cook over low heat, stirring until smooth and bubbly. Stir in scallops and shrimp; cook, uncovered, 3 to 5 minutes or until shrimp are pink, stirring occasionally. Transfer mixture to a chafing dish. Serve over patty shells. Yield: 6 servings. *Lilly B. Smith, Richmond, Virginia.*

# December

Since December is the month for feasting in the South, we compiled our readers' favorite recipes into two holiday menus to make your meal planning easier. You'll find a traditional seated dinner complete with turkey and all the trimmings and Cherry Bourbon Cake for the finale. Our buffet menu will make serving simpler if you're short on dining space; this meal features Beef Bourguignon and a chocolate Yule Log.

Then travel with us to Decatur, Alabama, where one Southern hostess celebrates the holidays with a sinfully delicious dessert party. On the upcoming pages she shares her recipes for cheesecakes, fruit tarts, candies, cakes, and even an ice cream bombe.

If you'd rather give your holiday treats away, then you'll enjoy putting together our gift box selections. We devised Christmas food packages especially for dieters, picnickers, chocolate lovers, and New Year's Eve partiers so you can tailor each gift to the receivers' individual tastes.

# Spread The Table With A Holiday Feast

When your holiday guests arrive, you want everything to be special—the gifts, the decorations, and, of course, the food. This year, we've assembled two impressive menus to help you plan your entertaining. The first is for a formal seated dinner, and the second is suitable for buffet service.

Our seated dinner is a spectacular feast for 8 to 10 people. Starting this traditional bill of fare is a rich-and-creamy Mushroom Soup topped with Parmesan cheese and toasted almonds. Following is a traditional stuffed roast turkey served with an array of winter vegetables. Besides Creamy Broccoli Supreme and Sweet Potato Soufflé, there's an unusual side dish that features a combination of crisp-tender carrots tossed with green grapes in an orange-wine sauce.

Add a touch of color and elegance to each of these dishes with an appropriate garnish. Wedges of lemon or lime, orange sections, tomato roses, frosted grapes, whole nuts, and sprigs of parsley are just some possibilities.

Dinner comes to a close with Cherry Bourbon Cake—a buttery cake filled with chopped cherries and walnuts—and refreshing Citrus Ambrosia.

Our buffet menu will serve 10 to 12 and centers around an entrée of Beef Bourguignon. Along with the beef, which is to be served over hot rice, there are side dishes of peas and cauliflower, spiced squash, and a colorful, molded Holiday Cranberry Salad.

Dessert is definitely the highlight of this meal. Choose between a delicately flavored rum pudding crowned with spoonfuls of bright-red raspberry sauce, and a beautifully decorated chocolate Yule Log filled with whipped cream. A steaming cup of Kahlúa-laced Mocha Deluxe Hot Drink complements both desserts, deliciously.

---

**Mushroom Soup**
**Roast Turkey With Rice Dressing**
**Sweet Potato Soufflé**
**Creamy Broccoli Supreme**
**Glazed Carrots With Grapes**
**Spiced Cranberries**
**Refrigerator Rolls**
**Cherry Bourbon Cake**
**Citrus Ambrosia**
**Wine          Coffee**

## MUSHROOM SOUP

4 medium onions, minced
2 cloves garlic, minced
¼ cup butter or margarine
2 pounds fresh mushrooms, coarsely chopped
2 cups whipping cream
2 cups beef broth
1 cup grated Parmesan cheese
1 cup sliced almonds, toasted
Chopped fresh parsley

Sauté onion and garlic in butter in a Dutch oven over medium heat until onion is tender. Add mushrooms; cook over low heat 10 minutes or until tender. Gradually add cream and broth; continue to cook until thoroughly heated. Do not boil. Sprinkle each serving with cheese, almonds, and parsley. Yield: 2½ quarts. *Mrs. R. E. Coffman, Natchez, Mississippi.*

## ROAST TURKEY WITH RICE DRESSING

1 (14- to 15-pound) turkey
2 teaspoons salt
2 teaspoons pepper
1 cup sliced celery
½ cup chopped onion
½ cup butter or margarine
2 cups herb-seasoned croutons
3 (10-ounce) packages frozen rice with green pepper and parsley, thawed
1 (8-ounce) can sliced water chestnuts, drained
1½ teaspoons poultry seasoning
About ¼ cup butter or margarine, melted
Red and green grapes
Orange wedges
Lime wedges
Apple wedges
Whole walnuts
Fresh parsley sprigs

Remove giblets and neck from turkey; reserve for giblet gravy, if desired. Rinse turkey thoroughly with cold water; pat dry. Combine salt and pepper; sprinkle over surface and in cavity of turkey.

Sauté celery and onion in ½ cup butter until tender. Combine sautéed vegetables, croutons, rice, water chestnuts, and poultry seasoning in a large mixing bowl; mix well.

Stuff dressing into cavity of turkey, and close cavity with skewers. Tie ends of legs to tail with string or tuck them under flap of skin around tail. Lift wingtips up and over back so they are tucked under bird securely.

Brush entire bird with about ¼ cup melted butter; place breast side up on a rack in roasting pan. Insert meat thermometer in breast or meaty part of thigh, making sure it does not touch bone. Bake at 325° until meat thermometer registers 185° (about 4½ to 5½ hours); baste turkey frequently with pan drippings. If turkey gets too brown, cover lightly with aluminum foil.

When turkey is two-thirds done, cut the cord or band of skin holding the drumstick ends to the tail; this will ensure that the inside of the thighs is cooked. Turkey is done when drumsticks are easy to move.

Transfer turkey to serving platter. Let stand 15 minutes before carving. Garnish with fruit, nuts, and parsley. Yield: 20 to 24 servings.

*Note:* If turkey and dressing are prepared in advance, refrigerate separately and stuff just prior to cooking. After serving, remove dressing from turkey cavity as soon as possible. Cool meat and dressing promptly, and refrigerate separately. *Tammy Smith, Talbott, Tennessee.*

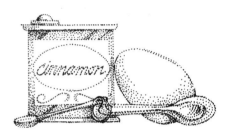

## SWEET POTATO SOUFFLE

1¾ cups whipping cream
1 cup firmly packed brown sugar
1 teaspoon salt
4 cups cooked, mashed sweet potatoes
6 eggs, separated
2 teaspoons ground cinnamon
2 teaspoons ground nutmeg
1 cup finely chopped pecans
¼ cup butter or margarine
¼ cup whipping cream
1 cup firmly packed brown sugar
1 cup flaked coconut
1 cup finely chopped pecans
⅓ cup self-rising flour
1 teaspoon rum extract
Mandarin orange slices
Pecan halves

Combine first 3 ingredients in a heavy saucepan; cook over medium heat, stirring constantly, thoroughly heated (do not boil). Pour over potatoes; beat at low speed of an electric mixer until smooth. Beat yolks; stir yolks, spices, and 1 cup pecans into potatoes. Beat egg whites (at room temperature) until stiff peaks form; fold into potato mixture. Pour into two greased 2-quart casseroles. Set aside.

Combine butter, ¼ cup whipping cream, 1 cup brown sugar, coconut, and 1 cup pecans in a heavy saucepan; cook over medium heat, stirring constantly, until bubbly. Stir in flour and rum extract; spoon half over each casserole. Bake at 350° for 30 minutes. Garnish with orange slices and pecans. Yield: 12 servings.
*Dr. G. Othell Hand,*
*Columbus, Georgia.*

## CREAMY BROCCOLI SUPREME

**4 (10-ounce) packages frozen broccoli**
**spears**
**2 tablespoons minced onion**
**2 tablespoons butter or margarine**
**2 (8-ounce) cartons commercial sour**
**cream**
**2 teaspoons sugar**
**½ teaspoon red wine vinegar**
**½ teaspoon paprika**
**⅓ cup chopped salted peanuts**
**Tomato roses (optional)**

Cook broccoli according to package directions; drain.

Sauté onion in butter in a heavy skillet until tender. Remove from heat; stir in sour cream, sugar, vinegar, and paprika. Arrange broccoli on serving dish. Spoon sauce over broccoli; sprinkle with peanuts. Garnish with tomato roses, if desired. Yield: 8 to 10 servings.
*Mrs. Lester Rolf,*
*Stillwater, Oklahoma.*

## GLAZED CARROTS WITH GRAPES

**2 pounds carrots, diagonally sliced**
**½ cup water**
**¼ cup plus 1 tablespoon cornstarch**
**2 cups orange juice**
**½ cup sugar**
**¼ cup dry white wine**
**1 pound seedless green grapes**

Cook carrots in a small amount of boiling water 12 to 15 minutes or until crisp-tender; drain and set aside.

Stir ½ cup water into cornstarch and set aside.

Combine orange juice, sugar, and wine in a saucepan; bring to a boil. Add cornstarch mixture and cook, stirring constantly, until smooth and thickened. Remove from heat and stir in carrots and grapes. Yield: 8 to 10 servings.
*Sherry Phillips,*
*Knoxville, Tennessee.*

## SPICED CRANBERRIES

**4 cups fresh cranberries**
**2 cups water**
**3 cups sugar**
**1 teaspoon ground cinnamon**
**½ teaspoon ground cloves**
**Pinch of ginger**

Wash cranberries and drain; set aside. Combine remaining ingredients in a large saucepan; bring to a boil. Add cranberries; cook 7 to 10 minutes or until cranberry skins pop. Reduce heat, and simmer 1 hour, stirring occasionally. Remove from heat, and let cool. Chill until ready to serve. Yield: 2 cups.
*Jane Cleary,*
*Burlington, North Carolina.*

## REFRIGERATOR ROLLS

**2 medium potatoes, peeled and**
**quartered**
**⅔ cup shortening**
**½ cup sugar**
**1 teaspoon salt**
**2 eggs, beaten**
**1 cup milk**
**1 package dry yeast**
**½ cup warm water (105° to 115°)**
**About 7 cups all-purpose flour**

Cook potatoes in boiling water to cover 15 to 20 minutes or until tender; drain. Mash potatoes to measure 1 cup; add shortening, sugar, salt, and eggs. Beat at medium speed of electric mixer until well blended.

Scald milk; cool to 105° to 115°. Dissolve yeast in warm water; add to milk, stirring well. Stir into potato mixture; gradually add enough flour to make a soft dough.

Turn dough out onto a floured surface, and knead until smooth and elastic (about 8 to 10 minutes). Place in a well-greased bowl, turning to grease top. Cover and let rise in a warm place (85°), free from drafts, 1 hour or until doubled in bulk.

Turn dough out onto a floured surface, and knead again. Return dough to bowl; cover and chill until needed. (Dough may be stored in refrigerator several days.)

Lightly grease muffin pans. Shape dough into 1-inch balls; place 3 balls in each muffin cup. Cover and let rise in a warm place (85°), free from drafts, 1 hour or until doubled in bulk. Bake at 400° for 15 to 20 minutes or until golden brown. Yield: about 3 dozen.
*Mildred Teal,*
*Manchester, Georgia.*

## CHERRY BOURBON CAKE

**2 cups butter, softened**
**2 cups sugar**
**8 eggs, separated**
**3 cups all-purpose flour**
**1 (6-ounce) jar maraschino cherries,**
**drained and chopped**
**½ cup chopped walnuts**
**½ teaspoon ground nutmeg**
**⅓ cup bourbon**
**½ cup sugar**

Cream butter; gradually add 2 cups sugar, beating until light and fluffy. Add egg yolks, one at a time, beating well after each addition.

Combine flour, cherries, walnuts, and nutmeg, mixing well; add to creamed mixture alternately with bourbon, beginning and ending with flour mixture.

Beat egg whites (at room temperature) until foamy. Gradually add ½ cup sugar, 1 tablespoon at a time, beating until stiff peaks form. Gently fold into batter.

Pour batter into a greased and floured 10-inch tube pan. Bake at 350° for 1 hour and 30 minutes or until a wooden pick inserted in center comes out clean. Cool in pan 10 to 15 minutes; remove from pan, and let cool completely. Yield: one 10-inch cake.
*Audrey Bledsoe,*
*Smyrna, Georgia.*

## CITRUS AMBROSIA

**9 large oranges, peeled, seeded,**
**and sectioned**
**1 (20-ounce) can pineapple chunks,**
**drained**
**1 (16-ounce) can fruit cocktail,**
**drained**
**2 medium apples, unpeeled and**
**coarsely chopped**
**2 cups sliced bananas**
**1 cup flaked coconut**
**1 cup chopped pecans**

Combine all ingredients, tossing well. Chill thoroughly. Yield: 10 servings.
*Lora Blocker,*
*Dade City, Florida.*

*Tip: For an interesting change, use fresh pineapple, cantaloupe, or other shells as containers for dips and spreads. Pineapple halves scooped out are beautiful for serving cheese dips or salads. Other fruit like melon shells are nice for salads or appetizers.*

Beef Bourguignon
Peas and Cauliflower
Golden Squash Puff
Holiday Cranberry Salad
French-Style Crescent Rolls
Rum Pudding With Raspberry Sauce
Yule Log
Mocha Deluxe Hot Drink
Wine

## BEEF BOURGUIGNON

1 (4- to 5-pound) boneless sirloin roast
1 cup Burgundy or other dry red wine
1 cup water
2 (10¾-ounce) cans cream of mushroom
  soup, undiluted
1 (2.75-ounce) package onion soup mix
2 pounds fresh mushrooms, sliced
1 cup chopped green pepper
1 pound pearl onions, peeled
½ teaspoon garlic powder
10 cherry tomatoes
Fresh parsley sprigs
Hot cooked rice

Cut beef into 1½-inch cubes; place in a 2½-quart casserole. Combine wine, 1 cup water, soup, and soup mix; stir well, and pour over beef. Stir in mushrooms; cover and bake at 325° for 2 hours.

Add green pepper, onion, and garlic powder; cover and bake an additional 30 minutes. Stir in cherry tomatoes. Garnish with parsley sprigs. Serve over rice. Yield: 10 to 12 servings.

*Jane Roden,*
*Athens, Georgia.*

## PEAS AND CAULIFLOWER

¼ cup plus 2 tablespoons vegetable oil
3 heads cauliflower, broken into flowerets
3 (10-ounce) packages frozen English peas
3 whole pimientos, sliced into ¼-inch
  strips
1 teaspoon salt
½ teaspoon pepper

Heat oil in a skillet over low heat; add cauliflower; cover and cook 10 minutes, stirring occasionally. Add peas; continue cooking 10 minutes or until vegetables are tender. Stir in pimiento, salt, and pepper. Yield: 10 to 12 servings.

*Dorothy Lewis,*
*Bealeton, Virginia.*

## GOLDEN SQUASH PUFF

6 cups cooked, mashed hubbard squash
½ cup milk
¼ cup plus 2 tablespoons all-purpose flour
¼ cup firmly packed brown sugar
4 eggs, beaten
¼ cup cooking sherry
1 teaspoon salt
1 teaspoon ground nutmeg
⅛ teaspoon pepper
1 cup chopped pecans
Whipped cream
Additional chopped pecans

Combine first 9 ingredients. Beat with electric mixer until light and fluffy. Pour into a buttered 12- x 8- x 2-inch baking dish; sprinkle 1 cup pecans on top. Bake at 350° for 30 to 35 minutes. Garnish with piped whipped cream and additional pecans. Yield: 10 to 12 servings.

*Mrs. Ralph Chase,*
*Hendersonville, North Carolina.*

## HOLIDAY CRANBERRY SALAD

3 (3-ounce) packages cherry-flavored
  gelatin
1 cup sugar
2 cups boiling water
1 (15¼-ounce) can crushed pineapple,
  undrained
2 tablespoons lemon juice
2 cups fresh cranberries, ground
2 small oranges, unpeeled, seeded, and
  ground
2 cups finely chopped celery
1 cup chopped walnuts
Lettuce leaves
Sugar-frosted cranberries
Orange twists

Dissolve gelatin and sugar in boiling water. Drain pineapple, reserving juice; set pineapple aside. Add water to pineapple juice to measure 1 cup. Stir in lemon juice. Stir juice mixture into gelatin mixture; chill until consistency of unbeaten egg white.

Add cranberries, oranges, celery, and walnuts to gelatin mixture; mix well. Pour into a lightly oiled 10-cup mold; chill until set. Unmold on lettuce leaves. Garnish with frosted cranberries and orange twists. Yield: 15 to 18 servings.

*Mrs. Gary W. Taylor,*
*Afton, Virginia.*

*Tip: Many gelatin molds do not have their size stamped on them. You can determine the capacity of a mold by measuring the number of cups of water it will hold.*

## FRENCH-STYLE CRESCENT ROLLS

5 cups all-purpose flour, divided
¼ cup sugar
2 packages dry yeast
2 teaspoons salt
1 cup water
¾ cup evaporated milk
¼ cup vegetable oil
1 egg
¾ cup butter or margarine, softened

Combine 1 cup flour, sugar, yeast, and salt in a large mixing bowl.

Combine 1 cup water, milk, and oil in a saucepan; heat to 120° to 130°. Add to flour mixture. Add egg; beat 5 minutes at medium speed of an electric mixer.

Cut butter into remaining 4 cups flour with a pastry blender until mixture resembles coarse meal. Stir flour mixture into yeast mixture; mix well. Place into a well-greased bowl, turning to grease top. Cover and refrigerate 2 hours.

Punch dough down, and turn out onto a floured surface; knead 4 to 5 times to remove air bubbles.

Divide dough into 4 portions. Roll each portion on a lightly floured surface into a circle 14 inches in diameter and ¼ inch thick; cut into 10 wedges. Roll each wedge tightly, beginning at wide end.

Place rolls on greased baking sheets, point side down. Curve into crescent shapes. Cover and let rise in a warm place (85°), free from drafts, 30 minutes or until doubled in bulk. Bake at 400° for 15 to 20 minutes or until lightly browned. Yield: about 3 dozen.

*Carol Forcum,*
*Marion, Illinois.*

## RUM PUDDING WITH RASPBERRY SAUCE

3 envelopes unflavored gelatin
½ cup cold water
1¾ cups boiling water
¾ cup light rum
4 egg yolks
¾ cup sugar
2 cups whipping cream
Raspberry Sauce

Soften gelatin in cold water; let stand 1 minute. Add boiling water, stirring until gelatin dissolves, scraping sides and bottom of bowl occasionally. Let cool. Stir in rum.

Beat egg yolks until thick and lemon colored. Add sugar; beat well, and stir in gelatin mixture. Chill until consistency of unbeaten egg white.

Beat whipping cream until soft peaks form (do not overbeat); fold into gelatin mixture. Spoon into a lightly oiled 6-cup mold, and chill until set. Unmold onto serving platter, and serve with Raspberry Sauce. Yield: 12 servings.

*Raspberry Sauce:*
2 (10-ounce) packages frozen raspberries, thawed
1 cup sugar
2 tablespoons cornstarch

Combine raspberries and sugar in a saucepan; bring to a boil, and boil 5 minutes. Put mixture through a food mill. Combine a small amount of raspberry sauce and cornstarch; stir into remaining raspberry sauce. Cook over low heat, stirring constantly, until smooth and thickened. Cool. Yield: about 2 cups.
*Shirley Kickliter,*
*Auburn, Alabama.*

## YULE LOG
¾ cup sifted cake flour
¼ cup cocoa
¼ teaspoon salt
5 eggs, separated
1 cup sugar
1 tablespoon lemon juice
2 to 3 tablespoons powdered sugar
1 cup whipping cream, whipped
Creamy Mocha Frosting
Candied cherries

Grease bottom and sides of a 15- x 10- x 1-inch jellyroll pan with vegetable oil; line with waxed paper, and grease lightly. Set aside.

Sift together flour, cocoa, and salt; beat egg yolks at high speed of an electric mixer 5 minutes or until thick. Gradually add sugar, beating well. Stir in lemon juice, and set aside.

Beat egg whites (at room temperature) until stiff but not dry. Gently fold yolk mixture into whites. Gradually fold flour mixture into egg mixture. Spread batter evenly in prepared pan. Bake at 350° for 15 minutes.

Sift powdered sugar in a 15- x 10-inch rectangle on a linen towel. When cake is done, immediately loosen from sides of pan, and turn out on sugar. Peel off waxed paper. Starting at narrow end, roll up cake and towel together; cool on a wire rack, seam side down.

Unroll cake; remove towel. Spread cake with whipped cream and reroll. Place on serving plate, seam side down; chill at least 1 hour.

Spread Creamy Mocha Frosting over cake roll. Garnish with candied cherries. Yield: 10 to 12 servings.

*Creamy Mocha Frosting:*
1 tablespoon instant coffee granules
⅓ cup boiling water
3 (1-ounce) squares unsweetened chocolate
¼ cup butter or margarine
Dash of salt
2½ cups sifted powdered sugar

Combine coffee granules and boiling water, stirring until dissolved; set aside.

Combine chocolate, butter, and salt in top of a double boiler. Cook over medium heat, stirring until smooth. Remove from heat; cool.

Stir in coffee mixture. Gradually add powdered sugar, beating at medium speed of electric mixer until smooth and creamy (about 1 minute). Use immediately. Yield: enough for one cake roll.
*Note:* Yule log will slice neatly if stored in refrigerator until serving time.
*Connie Stark,*
*Newburg, Missouri.*

## MOCHA DELUXE HOT DRINK
½ cup Swiss-style instant coffee beverage
12 cups boiling water
1½ cups Kahlúa or other coffee-flavored liqueur

Spoon powdered coffee beverage into a large saucepan. Add boiling water; mix well. Stir in liqueur. Serve immediately. Yield: 3 quarts.
*Dora S. Hancock,*
*Plano, Texas.*

Cooking Light

# Let Dieters Enjoy The Party

Most Southerners put out a lavish array of rich holiday foods for the season's parties. Unfortunately, many dieters abandon their good intentions during the festivities, indulging in rich eggnog, sweet candies and cookies, and calorie-laden chips and dips. Instead of weighing your party down with the usual high-calorie fare, treat your guests to our special "Cooking Light" party ideas.

Hot Spiced Cider and Banana Nog are both welcome changes from the usual high-calorie beverages. By omitting the sugar from a typical mulled cider and adding 2 cups of water, we've diluted the calories from 86 to about 49 per half-cup serving of Hot Spiced Cider.

For a cooler beverage, whirl up a blender full of Banana Nog. Frozen, naturally sweet bananas are blended with skim milk and rum extract, then dusted with ground nutmeg before serving. Be sure to use very ripe bananas; that way, you'll get more of the sweet fruit flavor without any extra calories.

Fill your party table with a variety of low-calorie treats, each attractively garnished and arranged. Give Fresh Fruit With Lemon Sauce a prominent spot, as it's especially colorful.

Low-Fat Chicken Spread is a delicious, light alternative to the popular, more fattening pâté. Calories are kept low by mixing finely chopped, lean chicken with Neufchâtel cheese and a reduced-calorie mayonnaise. Offer the spread with melba toast or crisp celery sticks (celery sticks will keep the calorie count lower).

In addition to being low in calories, Cranberry-Apple Ice contains practically no sodium. Let your salt-conscious guests know that Hot Spiced Cider, Fresh Fruit With Lemon Sauce, and Vegetables Vinaigrette are almost sodium free, while the only sodium in Banana Nog comes from the skim milk.

## CRAB-STUFFED CHERRY TOMATOES
36 cherry tomatoes
Salt
¼ cup low-fat cottage cheese
1½ teaspoons minced onion
1½ teaspoons lemon juice
½ teaspoon prepared horseradish
Dash of garlic salt
½ pound fresh crabmeat, drained and flaked
¼ cup minced celery
1 tablespoon finely chopped green pepper

Cut top off each tomato; scoop out pulp, reserving pulp for other uses. Sprinkle inside of tomato with salt, and invert on paper towels to drain.

Place cottage cheese in container of electric blender; process until smooth. Add next 4 ingredients, blending well. Stir in remaining ingredients. Spoon crabmeat mixture into tomatoes. Chill before serving. Yield: 36 appetizers (about 12 calories each).

## LOW-FAT CHICKEN SPREAD

1½ pounds chicken breasts, skinned
¼ (8-ounce) package Neufchâtel cheese, softened
1 tablespoon reduced-calorie mayonnaise
1 tablespoon grated onion
1 tablespoon sweet pickle juice
½ cup finely chopped celery
Dash of curry powder
¼ teaspoon salt
¼ teaspoon pepper
½ tablespoon chopped pimiento
Dash of hot sauce
Dash of garlic powder
Vegetable cooking spray
Leaf lettuce
Radishes (optional)

Cook chicken in unsalted water to cover until tender. Remove from broth, reserving 2 tablespoons broth; cool. Bone chicken, and chop fine. Set aside.

Combine Neufchâtel cheese and mayonnaise, beating until smooth; add next 9 ingredients, and mix well. Stir in chicken and reserved chicken broth. Lightly coat four ½-cup molds or one 2-cup mold with cooking spray; press in chicken mixture, and chill.

Unmold on lettuce-lined plate; garnish with radishes, if desired. Serve with melba toast or celery. Yield: 2 cups (about 22 calories per tablespoon).

*Note:* Chicken will be more moist if cooked and boned the day before using and placed in the broth to chill.

## VEGETABLES VINAIGRETTE

1 (1¼-pound) bunch broccoli
1 (1½-pound) head cauliflower, broken into flowerets
1 pound fresh brussels sprouts
¾ pound baby carrots, scraped
½ pound fresh mushrooms
1 pint cherry tomatoes
1 large cucumber, sliced
2 cups water
1 cup white wine vinegar
2 teaspoons sugar
1 teaspoon dry mustard
1 teaspoon paprika
1 teaspoon dried whole oregano
¼ teaspoon dried whole thyme
4 whole cloves garlic, crushed

Trim off leaves of broccoli; discard tough ends of lower stalks. Cut broccoli into bite-size pieces.

Steam broccoli, cauliflower, brussels sprouts, and carrots separately until crisp-tender; drain well, and chill. Place mushrooms, tomatoes, cucumber, and steamed vegetables in a large, shallow glass or plastic container.

Combine remaining ingredients in a jar; cover tightly, and shake vigorously. Pour over vegetables; cover and refrigerate overnight. Drain vegetables, and arrange on serving platter. Yield: 20 appetizer servings (about 45 calories per serving).

## FRESH FRUIT WITH LEMON SAUCE

2 Delicious apples, unpeeled and cut into wedges
2 tablespoons lemon juice
3 kiwi, peeled and sliced crosswise
3 medium oranges, peeled and sliced crosswise
1 medium pineapple, peeled and cubed
1 pound seedless green grapes
1 head romaine lettuce, shredded
¼ cup flaked coconut
Lemon Sauce

Toss apple wedges in lemon juice. Arrange apple wedges and other fruit on a bed of lettuce. Sprinkle with coconut, and serve with Lemon Sauce. Yield: 20 appetizer servings (about 61 calories per serving plus 20 calories per tablespoon sauce).

*Lemon Sauce:*

1 (1¾-ounce) package powdered fruit pectin
1 cup unsweetened pineapple juice
2 tablespoons honey
½ teaspoon grated lemon rind
1 tablespoon lemon juice

Combine all ingredients, mixing well. Cover and refrigerate 2 hours or until thoroughly chilled. Yield: 1¼ cups.

## CRANBERRY-APPLE ICE

2 pounds fresh cranberries
4 cups unsweetened apple juice, divided
¾ cup sugar
1 teaspoon grated orange rind

Wash cranberries; combine with 2 cups apple juice and sugar in a large saucepan. Cook 7 to 10 minutes or until cranberry skins pop; put through a food mill. Add remaining apple juice and orange rind to cranberry mixture. Chill.

Pour mixture into freezer can of a 1-gallon hand-turned or electric freezer. Freeze according to manufacturer's instructions. Yield: 2 quarts (about 91 calories per ½-cup serving).

*Note:* Ice may be stored in freezer compartment of refrigerator until serving time. Let stand at room temperature 10 to 15 minutes before serving.

## PEARS STUFFED WITH CHEESE

6 large ripe pears
1 (8-ounce) package Neufchâtel cheese, softened
½ cup low-fat cottage cheese
¼ cup crumbled blue cheese

Wash pears, and pat dry; cut out center of each pear with an apple corer. Combine remaining ingredients, mixing well. Fill pears with cheese mixture; cover and chill.

Just before serving, cut each pear into 8 wedges. Yield: 48 appetizers (about 30 calories each).

## BANANA NOG

6 medium-size ripe bananas, peeled and frozen
1 quart skim milk
1 teaspoon rum extract
Ground nutmeg

Combine 3 bananas, 2 cups milk, and ½ teaspoon rum extract in container of electric blender; process until mixture is smooth and thick. Repeat with remaining ingredients.

Sprinkle each serving with nutmeg, and serve immediately. Yield: 7½ cups (about 63 calories per ½-cup serving).

## HOT SPICED CIDER

1 medium orange, sliced
2 quarts unsweetened apple cider
2 cups water
1 teaspoon whole allspice
16 whole cloves
2 (2-inch) sticks cinnamon
Additional sticks cinnamon (optional)

Combine first 6 ingredients in a 3-quart saucepan, and bring to a boil; reduce heat, and simmer 15 minutes. Strain mixture, discarding spices; pour into cups. Serve with stick cinnamon, if desired. Yield: 10 cups (about 49 calories per ½-cup serving).

*Right:* Cauliflower, mandarin oranges, and spinach leaves are tossed together for Orange-Cauliflower Salad (page 266).

Far left: *Let guests help themselves to a buffet meal of Beef Bourguignon served over rice. Pecan-sprinkled Golden Squash Puff, Peas and Cauliflower, Holiday Cranberry Salad, and French-Style Crescent Rolls complete the menu (recipes on page 288).*

Blue Cheese-Olive Ball (page 248) is a *flavorful departure from the traditional cheese ball; it blends the distinctive flavor of blue cheese with cream cheese, olives, and pecans.*

Serve luscious holiday desserts like our *whipped cream-filled Yule Log (page 289) or Rum Pudding With Raspberry Sauce (page 288).*

Above: *With our holiday gift boxes, you can give an assortment of good things to eat. The Children's Gift Box features Fruit Balls, Peanut Butter Granola, and Candied Popcorn and Peanuts; the Chocolate Gift Box features Hot Fudge Sauce, Chocolate Snowball Cookies, Chocolate-Covered Pretzels, and Creamy Dark Fudge; and the Picnic Gift Box features Hot German Mustard, Chocolate Dream Bars, and Italian Bread (recipes begin on page 295).*

Right: *Containing Old-Fashioned Cranberry Relish, Curried Almonds, Gourmet Seasoning Salt, and Sesame-Cheese Cutouts, the Gourmet's Gift Box boasts a wealth of great tastes (recipes on page 296).*

Above left: *Welcome January with the New Year's Gift Box. It features Sugar and Spice Pecans, Parmesan Sticks, and Great Cereal Nibblers (recipes begin on page 297).*

# Boxes Of Gifts From The Kitchen

This year, why not say "Merry Christmas" with a personalized selection of gifts from your kitchen? Our six holiday gift boxes make it easy. One of the boxes is meant especially for children, while others are designed to delight dieters, chocolate lovers, gourmet cooks, and picnickers. Our New Year's Gift Box is a thoughtful present to the host and hostess of a New Year's party.

Pack the food in plastic or glass containers, baskets, or festively wrapped boxes. Sand pails, picnic baskets, hat boxes, and decorative tins are large enough to hold several items and also have practical uses after the food is gone. As a bonus, you can embellish each box with assorted utensils or knickknacks that suit the gift and its recipient.

Proper storage is important. Foods that require refrigeration should not be packed too far in advance or left out under the Christmas tree. To be sure each item receives proper care, it's a good idea to include a note with each gift detailing special instructions for storage.

■ The perfect gift for a chocoholic is our Chocolate Gift Box.

**Creamy Dark Fudge**
**Hot Fudge Sauce**
**Chocolate-Covered Pretzels**
**Chocolate Snowball Cookies**

## CREAMY DARK FUDGE

3 (6-ounce) packages semisweet chocolate morsels
1 (14-ounce) can sweetened condensed milk
1½ teaspoons vanilla extract
⅓ cup chopped pecans

Combine chocolate morsels and condensed milk in a heavy saucepan; cook over low heat until chocolate melts, stirring constantly. Remove from heat, and stir in vanilla.

Spread chocolate mixture in a lightly greased 8-inch square pan. Sprinkle with pecans. Chill 2 to 3 hours or until firm; cut into squares. Cover and store in refrigerator. Yield: 24 squares.
*Heather Riggins,*
*Nashville, Tennessee.*

## HOT FUDGE SAUCE

4 (1-ounce) squares unsweetened chocolate
2 tablespoons butter or margarine
¾ cup boiling water
2 cups sugar
3 tablespoons light corn syrup
2 teaspoons vanilla extract

Combine chocolate, butter, and water in a heavy saucepan; cook over low heat until chocolate melts, stirring constantly. Add sugar and corn syrup; mix well. Bring mixture to a boil; reduce heat, and simmer, uncovered, 7 minutes without stirring. Remove from heat, and stir in vanilla.

Serve sauce warm over ice cream. Store in refrigerator; reheat as needed. Yield: 2⅓ cups. *Mary Dishon,*
*Stanford, Kentucky.*

## CHOCOLATE-COVERED PRETZELS

1 (5.75-ounce) package milk chocolate morsels
2 tablespoons shortening
24 (3-inch) pretzels

Combine chocolate morsels and shortening in top of a double boiler; bring water to a boil. Reduce heat to low; cook until chocolate melts, stirring occasionally. Remove double boiler from heat, leaving chocolate mixture over hot water.

Dip each pretzel in chocolate; allow excess to drain. Place on waxed paper-lined cookie sheets; chill until firm. Arrange pretzels between layers of waxed paper in an airtight container; store in a cool place. Yield: 2 dozen.

## CHOCOLATE SNOWBALL COOKIES

¼ cup butter or margarine, softened
½ cup sugar
1 egg
1 (1-ounce) square unsweetened chocolate, melted
1 teaspoon vanilla extract
1½ cups all-purpose flour
½ teaspoon baking powder
¼ teaspoon salt
Snowy Glaze

Cream butter; gradually add sugar, beating until light and fluffy. Add next 3 ingredients, and beat well.

Combine flour, baking powder, and salt; gradually add to creamed mixture, beating just until smooth. Chill dough 1 to 2 hours.

Shape dough into 1-inch balls. Place on greased cookie sheets. Bake at 350° for 12 minutes. Cool on wire racks. Dip tops of cookies in Snowy Glaze. Store in an airtight container. Yield: about 3 dozen.

*Snowy Glaze:*

1 cup sifted powdered sugar
1 tablespoon plus 2 teaspoons milk
½ teaspoon vanilla extract

Combine all ingredients; beat until smooth. Yield: about ½ cup.
*Mrs. Ed Holby,*
*Birmingham, Alabama.*

■ Our Children's Gift Box is designed for children as well as the young at heart.

**Candied Popcorn and Peanuts**
**Peanut Butter Granola**
**Fruit Balls**

## CANDIED POPCORN AND PEANUTS

5 quarts freshly popped popcorn, unsalted
1 cup raw peanuts
1 cup butter or margarine
2 cups firmly packed light brown sugar
½ cup dark corn syrup
½ teaspoon baking soda
½ teaspoon salt
½ teaspoon vanilla extract

Combine popcorn and peanuts in a lightly greased roasting pan; mix well, and set aside.

Melt butter in a large saucepan; stir in sugar and corn syrup. Bring to a boil; boil 5 minutes, stirring occasionally. Remove from heat; stir in soda, salt, and vanilla.

Pour sugar mixture over popcorn mixture, stirring until evenly coated. Bake at 250° for 1 hour, stirring every 15 minutes. Cool, and store in an airtight container. Yield: about 5 quarts.
*Deanne Anthony,*
*Poteau, Oklahoma.*

*Tip: Tinted coconut makes a child's cake more festive. Fill a pint jar one-third to one-half full of coconut. Add a few drops of cake coloring to 1 to 2 tablespoons water, and add to coconut; cover jar, and shake well to distribute color.*

## PEANUT BUTTER GRANOLA

3 cups regular oats, uncooked
1 cup salted sunflower kernels
1 cup chopped pecans
½ cup wheat germ
½ cup sesame seeds
½ cup honey
¼ cup vegetable oil
½ cup peanut butter
¼ teaspoon vanilla extract
1 cup raisins

Combine first 5 ingredients in a large bowl; mix well, and set aside.

Combine honey and oil in a small saucepan; place over medium heat, stirring until mixture is thoroughly heated. Remove from heat; stir in peanut butter and vanilla, mixing well. Pour over oats mixture, and stir until evenly coated.

Spread mixture in a lightly greased 15- x 10- x 1-inch jellyroll pan. Bake at 250° for 50 minutes, stirring every 10 minutes; cool. Add raisins, and mix well. Store granola in an airtight container. Yield: about 8 cups.

*Janice Hilmer,*
*Melbourne, Florida.*

## FRUIT BALLS

1 cup pitted prunes
1 cup pitted dates
1 cup dark raisins
1 cup golden raisins
1 cup flaked coconut
¼ cup wheat germ
1 teaspoon grated orange rind
2 tablespoons orange juice
2 tablespoons honey
1½ cups finely chopped pecans,
    divided

Position knife blade in food processor bowl. Add prunes and dates; cover. Process 35 to 40 seconds or until finely chopped. Place in a large mixing bowl. Repeat chopping procedure with raisins and coconut; add raisin mixture to prune-date mixture, and stir well.

Stir in next 4 ingredients and ½ cup pecans; mix well. Shape into 1-inch balls, and roll each in remaining chopped pecans. Store in an airtight container, placing waxed paper between layers; refrigerate. Yield: 4 dozen.

*Kathryn M. Elmore,*
*Demopolis, Alabama.*

*Tip: For easy chopping of dried fruit, place fruit in freezer 2 hours before chopping. Cut with knife or kitchen shears dipped frequently in hot water to prevent sticking.*

■ The Dieter's Gift Box is a considerate gift for calorie watchers.

**Banana Jam**
**Spicy Applesauce**
**Seasoning Blend**
**Hot Mocha-Cocoa Mix**

## BANANA JAM

1 (6-ounce) can frozen apple juice
    concentrate, thawed and undiluted
2 tablespoons cornstarch
3 cups sliced ripe bananas
3 tablespoons lemon juice
2 whole cloves
1 (2-inch) stick cinnamon

Combine apple juice concentrate and cornstarch in a heavy saucepan; stir until smooth. Add remaining ingredients, stirring well. Cook over medium heat, stirring constantly, until thickened and bubbly. Cook an additional 3 to 5 minutes. Remove cloves and cinnamon stick; discard.

Quickly spoon banana mixture into hot sterilized jars, leaving ¼-inch headspace. Cover at once with metal lids, and screw bands tight. Cool. Store in refrigerator. Yield: 2 half-pints (about 23 calories and less than 1 milligram sodium per tablespoon). *Nettie Hackley, Cartersville, Georgia.*

## SPICY APPLESAUCE

10 large cooking apples (about 4 pounds)
1 cup apple juice
1½ teaspoons ground cinnamon
¼ teaspoon ground cloves
¼ teaspoon ground nutmeg

Peel, core, and quarter apples; combine with remaining ingredients in a large Dutch oven. Cook over medium-low heat 25 to 30 minutes or until apples are tender, stirring frequently. Mash apple mixture.

Quickly spoon applesauce into hot sterilized jars, leaving ¼-inch headspace. Cover at once with metal lids, and screw bands tight. Process in boiling-water bath 25 minutes. Yield: 3 pints (about 11 calories and less than 1 milligram sodium per tablespoon).

## SEASONING BLEND

1 tablespoon garlic powder
1 tablespoon dry mustard
1 tablespoon paprika
1½ teaspoons white pepper
1 teaspoon dried whole basil
½ teaspoon ground thyme

Combine all ingredients; mix well. Store in an airtight container. Sprinkle over meat or vegetables. Yield: about ¼ cup (less than 1 calorie and less than 1 milligram sodium per teaspoon).

*Sherry Bauersachs,*
*Henderson, Kentucky.*

## HOT MOCHA-COCOA MIX

3 cups instant nonfat dry milk powder
1 cup sugar
1 cup cocoa
½ cup instant coffee powder
1 teaspoon ground cinnamon
½ teaspoon ground nutmeg
⅛ to ¼ teaspoon ground cloves
Boiling water

Combine first 7 ingredients in a large bowl, and mix well. Store mix in an airtight container.

For each serving, place 2 tablespoons mix in a cup. Add 1 cup boiling water, and stir well. Yield: 44 servings (about 41 calories and 25 milligrams sodium per serving).

■ Our Gourmet's Gift Box will please the most discriminating of tastes.

**Sesame-Cheese Cutouts**
**Curried Almonds**
**Old-Fashioned Cranberry Relish**
**Gourmet Seasoning Salt**

## SESAME-CHEESE CUTOUTS

½ cup butter or margarine, softened
1 (3-ounce) package cream cheese,
    softened
1 cup all-purpose flour
½ teaspoon chili powder
¼ teaspoon salt
1 tablespoon sesame seeds

Combine butter and cream cheese in a medium mixing bowl; beat until light and fluffy.

Combine flour, chili powder, and salt; stir well. Gradually add flour mixture to creamed mixture, beating well. Shape dough into a ball; wrap in waxed paper, and freeze 45 minutes or until firm.

Roll dough to ⅛-inch thickness on a lightly floured surface; cut out rounds with a 2-inch cookie cutter. Place on lightly greased cookie sheets; sprinkle with sesame seeds. Bake at 400° for 12 minutes or until lightly browned. Cool. Store in airtight containers, placing waxed paper between layers. Yield: about 3 dozen. *Mary Belle Purvis, Greeneville, Tennessee.*

## CURRIED ALMONDS

3 cups blanched whole almonds
1 tablespoon butter or margarine, melted
2 teaspoons seasoned salt
¾ teaspoon curry powder

Place almonds in a shallow roasting pan; brush butter over nuts, and stir well. Roast almonds at 350° for 20 minutes or until golden brown.

Combine salt and curry powder; sprinkle over almonds, and stir until well coated. Bake an additional 10 minutes. Drain on paper towels; cool. Store in an airtight container. Yield: about 3 cups.
*D. R. Heun,*
*Louisville, Kentucky.*

## OLD-FASHIONED CRANBERRY RELISH

4 cups fresh cranberries, ground
4 oranges, unpeeled, seeded, and ground
4 apples, unpeeled, cored, and ground
3 lemons, peeled, seeded, and ground
4 cups sugar

Combine all ingredients in a large mixing bowl; mix well. Chill. Store in an airtight container in the refrigerator. Yield: 3 quarts.
*Dot McFarland,*
*Resaca, Georgia.*

## GOURMET SEASONING SALT

1 cup salt
2 teaspoons dry mustard
1½ teaspoons dried whole oregano
1 teaspoon ground marjoram
1 teaspoon dried whole thyme
1 teaspoon garlic powder
1 teaspoon curry powder
½ teaspoon onion powder
½ teaspoon celery seeds
¼ teaspoon dried whole dillweed (optional)

Combine all ingredients; mix well. Store in an airtight container. Yield: 1¼ cups.
*Inez Thornburg,*
*Long Beach, Mississippi.*

■ Our New Year's Gift box is the perfect present for a New Year's host.

**Parmesan Sticks**
**Great Cereal Nibblers**
**Sugar and Spice Pecans**
**Champagne**

## PARMESAN STICKS

1 (8-ounce) can crescent dinner rolls
½ cup grated Parmesan cheese

Separate dough into 4 rectangles, and set aside. Sprinkle 1 tablespoon cheese on waxed paper; place a rectangle of dough on cheese, and sprinkle top with 1 tablespoon cheese. Roll dough out to a 10- x 5-inch rectangle. Cut lengthwise into 6 strips, and cut each strip in half crosswise. Twist each strip, and place on a greased cookie sheet.

Repeat procedure with remaining dough and cheese. Bake at 375° for 6 to 8 minutes or until lightly browned; cool. Arrange cheese sticks between layers of waxed paper in an airtight container. Yield: 4 dozen.
*Mary Vaughn,*
*Dallas, Texas.*

## GREAT CEREAL NIBBLERS

6 cups puffed wheat or rice cereal
2 cups dry roasted, unsalted peanuts
¼ cup sesame seeds, toasted
½ cup firmly packed brown sugar
¼ cup honey
¼ cup butter or margarine

Combine first 3 ingredients in a large bowl; mix well, and set aside.

Combine remaining ingredients in a small saucepan; place over medium heat, stirring until sugar is dissolved. Pour over cereal mixture; stir until evenly coated. Spread mixture in a lightly greased 15- x 10- x 1-inch jellyroll pan.

Bake at 275° for 45 minutes or until golden brown, stirring every 15 minutes. Remove cereal mixture to waxed paper while still warm; cool. Store in an airtight container. Yield: about 8½ cups.
*Jodie McCoy,*
*Tulsa, Oklahoma.*

## SUGAR AND SPICE PECANS

¾ cup sugar
1 egg white
2½ tablespoons water
1 teaspoon ground cinnamon
½ teaspoon salt
¼ teaspoon ground allspice
¼ teaspoon ground cloves
¼ teaspoon ground nutmeg
8 cups pecan halves

Combine first 8 ingredients in a large bowl; mix well. Add pecans; stir until evenly coated.

Spread pecans in a greased 15- x 10- x 1-inch jellyroll pan. Bake at 275° for 50 to 55 minutes. Remove to waxed paper while still warm; cool. Store in an airtight container. Yield: 9 cups.
*Janie King,*
*San Antonio, Texas.*

■ Extend an invitation for a sunny day meal when giving our Picnic Gift Box.

**Italian Bread**
**Hot German Mustard**
**Commercial Sausage or Ham**
**Chocolate Dream Bars**
**Wine**

## ITALIAN BREAD

1¾ cups boiling water
1 tablespoon butter or margarine
1 tablespoon sugar
2 teaspoons salt
2 packages dry yeast
4½ to 5 cups all-purpose flour, divided
2 tablespoons cornmeal
Vegetable oil
1 egg white
1 tablespoon water

Combine boiling water and butter; stir until butter melts. Cool to lukewarm (105° to 115°).

Combine sugar, salt, yeast, and 2 cups flour in a large mixing bowl. Gradually add butter mixture, beating at low speed of an electric mixer until moistened. Increase to medium speed, and beat 2 minutes. Add ½ cup flour, and beat an additional 2 minutes. Gradually stir in enough remaining flour to make a soft dough (dough should remain soft and slightly sticky).

Turn dough out onto a heavily floured surface, and knead until smooth and elastic (about 8 to 10 minutes). Divide in half; cover and let rest 20 minutes.

Grease a cookie sheet, and sprinkle with cornmeal; set aside.

Place dough on a lightly floured surface. Roll each half into a 15- x 10-inch rectangle. Roll up jellyroll fashion, beginning at wide edge. Place dough seam side down on cookie sheet; turn under edges, and brush with oil. Cover loosely with plastic wrap, and chill at least 2 hours.

Remove loaves from refrigerator; uncover and let stand 10 minutes. Cut several diagonal slashes, ¾ inch deep, in top of each loaf. Bake at 400° for 20 minutes. Combine egg white and 1 tablespoon water, mixing well; brush over loaves. Bake an additional 5 minutes. Yield: 2 loaves.
*Teresa Poston,*
*Golden, Texas.*

*Tip: Use shiny cookie sheets and cakepans for baking rather than darkened ones. Dark pans absorb more heat and cause baked products to overbrown.*

## HOT GERMAN MUSTARD

¼ cup sugar
¼ cup dry mustard
2 tablespoons all-purpose flour
Dash of salt
3 tablespoons boiling water
⅓ cup vinegar
1 (16-ounce) jar prepared mustard

Combine first 4 ingredients in a mixing bowl; mix well. Add boiling water; stir to form a thick paste. Stir in vinegar and mustard; mix well. Store in an airtight container, and refrigerate. Yield: 2 cups.
*Mrs. James Hunt,*
*Dallas, Texas.*

## CHOCOLATE DREAM BARS

½ cup butter or margarine
¼ cup plus 1 tablespoon cocoa
¼ cup sugar
1 egg, slightly beaten
1 teaspoon vanilla extract
1 cup flaked coconut
½ cup chopped pecans
2 cups graham cracker crumbs
Custard filling (recipe follows)
1 (6-ounce) package semisweet chocolate morsels
1 tablespoon butter or margarine

Combine first 4 ingredients in top of double boiler; bring water to a boil. Reduce heat to low; cook until mixture thickens, stirring constantly. Remove from heat. Add vanilla, coconut, pecans, and cracker crumbs; mix well. Press mixture into a 9-inch square pan; chill 15 minutes.

Spread custard filling over chocolate mixture. Chill 30 minutes or until custard mixture becomes firm.

Combine remaining ingredients in a saucepan over low heat; stir until chocolate melts and mixture is smooth. Spread over custard filling. Cool and cut into bars. Cover and store in refrigerator. Yield: 2½ dozen.

*Custard Filling:*

¼ cup butter or margarine, softened
3 tablespoons milk
2 tablespoons vanilla instant pudding mix
2 cups sifted powdered sugar

Cream butter; add milk and pudding mix, beating until well blended. Add powdered sugar, and mix well. Yield: 1 cup.
*Mrs. Walter Wickstrom,*
*Pelham, Alabama.*

## Microwave Cookery

# Double Crusts For The Microwave

If you baked Grandmother's lattice-topped apple pie in the microwave oven, you'd have a soggy, white mess. But by following these tips for double-crust pies, you'll have brown, flaky pastry every time—microwave quick. You'll enjoy the tasty fillings, too.

You can't brown pastry in the microwave oven, but a few drops of yellow food coloring will give it a golden appearance. Spices will also add color, or you can substitute whole wheat flour for part of the all-purpose flour; these options enhance the flavor, too.

To ensure doneness, the pastry shell, filling, and top crust must be microwaved separately. Then the pie is assembled and again microwaved. The total cooking time, however, is still only a fraction of the time a double-crust pie would require in a conventional oven.

Here are other pointers for working with pastry:

■ When microwaving a bottom pastry shell, use dried peas or beans to keep the sides and bottom from puffing during microwaving (do not use metal pastry weights). To keep the rim from puffing and losing its shape, gently prick it with a fork.

■ The pastry should appear opaque and dry when done. If a few wet spots remain after microwaving to the top of the time range given in the recipe, remove the beans or peas and continue microwaving briefly (30 seconds is usually enough time).

## DOUBLE-CRUST PASTRY

1½ cups all-purpose flour
¾ teaspoon salt
½ cup plus 1 tablespoon shortening
4 drops yellow food coloring
4 to 6 tablespoons cold water

Combine flour and salt; cut in shortening with pastry blender until mixture resembles coarse meal. Add food coloring to the water if extra color is desired (pastry will not brown in microwave oven). Sprinkle water evenly over flour mixture, and stir with a fork until all ingredients are moistened.

Set aside about ⅓ of pastry for top crust. Shape remaining dough into a ball, and place on a lightly floured surface; roll dough into a circle that is 2 inches larger than an inverted 9-inch pieplate. Fit the pastry loosely into pieplate, trim edges, and fold under to form a standing rim; flute.

Place a piece of heavy-duty plastic wrap over pastry, and cover with dried peas or beans. Gently prick rim of pastry (this will help maintain fluted shape). Microwave at HIGH for 5½ to 7 minutes or until pastry is opaque and bottom is dry, turning after 3 minutes. Set aside.

Roll remaining pastry to ⅛-inch thickness on lightly floured surface. Cut into decorative shapes, or cut into strips and weave into a lattice to fit top of pie. Arrange cutouts in a ring on lightly greased waxed paper, or weave lattice directly on waxed paper. Place waxed paper on a flat microwave-safe plate. Microwave at HIGH for 2 to 3 minutes or until pastry is dry, giving dish one quarter-turn at 1-minute intervals. Peel pastry from paper, and place on pie filling. Yield: one 9-inch double-crust pastry shell.

*Spice Crust:*

Add 2 tablespoons sugar, ½ teaspoon ground cinnamon, and ¼ teaspoon ground nutmeg to flour and salt.

*Whole Wheat Crust:*

Substitute ¾ cup whole wheat flour for ¾ cup all-purpose flour.

## NUTTY CRANBERRY PIE

1 recipe Double-Crust Pastry
2 cups sugar
¾ cup water
4 cups fresh cranberries
4 egg yolks
2½ tablespoons all-purpose flour
Dash of salt
½ cup chopped pecans
2 tablespoons butter or margarine
½ teaspoon almond extract

Prepare and microwave bottom pastry shell and cutouts or lattice for top. Set aside.

Combine sugar, ¾ cup water, and cranberries in a 2½-quart glass bowl; stir well. Cover with waxed paper, and microwave at HIGH for 9 to 11 minutes or until cranberry skins pop, stirring once. Let cool.

Beat egg yolks; stir in flour and salt. Beat a small amount of the cranberry mixture into yolk mixture; stir yolk mixture into cranberry mixture. Cover and

*For a traditional double-crust pie, cut a 6½-inch round of pastry using a fluted pastry wheel. Slice into serving-size wedges and microwave; then arrange on top of pie.*

*Easy Cherry Pie slices easily when topped with pastry cutouts; just slice between the flowers.*

*Shape cutouts with cookie cutters to make a simple top crust. Arrange cutouts in a circle on waxed paper; microwave, and place on top of pie.*

mixture into yolk mixture; stir yolk mixture into cranberry mixture. Cover and microwave at HIGH for 4 to 6 minutes or until thickened, stirring at 1-minute intervals. Stir in pecans, butter, and almond extract.

Spoon filling evenly into pastry shell, and cover with pastry cutouts or lattice. Microwave at HIGH for 1½ to 2 minutes. Cool before slicing. Yield: one 9-inch pie.

### EASY CHERRY PIE

**1 recipe Double-Crust Pastry**
**1 cup sugar**
**3 tablespoons cornstarch**
**2 (16-ounce) cans red tart pitted cherries**
**3 to 4 drops red food coloring (optional)**
**¼ teaspoon almond extract**

Prepare and microwave bottom pastry shell and cutouts or lattice for top. Set aside.

Combine sugar and cornstarch in a 1½-quart glass bowl, stirring well to remove lumps.

Drain cherries, reserving ¾ cup juice. Stir juice into sugar mixture; add food coloring, if desired. Cover with waxed paper, and microwave at HIGH for 5 to 6 minutes or until thickened, stirring at 1-minute intervals. Stir in cherries and almond extract.

Spoon filling evenly into pastry shell and cover with pastry cutouts. Microwave at HIGH for 2 to 3 minutes. Cool before slicing. Yield: one 9-inch pie.

### OLD-FASHIONED APPLE PIE

**1 recipe Double-Crust Pastry**
**6 cups peeled, thinly sliced cooking apples**
**¾ cup honey**
**¼ cup all-purpose flour**
**½ teaspoon ground cinnamon**
**½ teaspoon ground nutmeg**
**Dash of salt**
**2 tablespoons butter or margarine**

Prepare and microwave bottom pastry shell and cutouts or lattice for top. Set aside.

Combine apples and honey in a 2½-quart glass bowl, tossing gently. Combine flour, spices, and salt, stirring well; spoon over apple mixture. Add butter, and toss gently. Cover with waxed paper, and microwave at HIGH for 10 to 12 minutes or until apples are tender, stirring apples at 4-minute intervals.

Spoon filling evenly into pastry shell, and cover with pastry cutouts or lattice. Microwave at HIGH for 1½ to 2 minutes. Cool before slicing. Yield: one 9-inch pie.

*For a lattice-topped pie, cut ⅛-inch strips of dough using fluted pastry wheel; weave strips, trimming as necessary to make a 7-inch round. Microwave lattice, and carefully transfer to pie.*

# A Harvest Of The Season's Freshest Vegetables

Market bins everywhere are brimming with broccoli, carrots, cauliflower, and vegetables of the winter harvest. Here, our readers share a wealth of ideas for giving these vegetables a special look, and just in time for the holidays.

Frances Jean Neely of Jackson, Mississippi, has discovered a great way to prepare fresh broccoli. She simmers it with oregano and serves the broccoli spears with a creamy cheese sauce. The result is her simple yet elegant Broccoli Italienne.

## BROCCOLI ITALIENNE

2 (1-pound) bunches fresh broccoli
2 cups water
½ teaspoon dried whole oregano
½ teaspoon salt
½ cup mayonnaise
¼ cup (1 ounce) shredded Cheddar
  cheese
1 tablespoon milk

Trim off large leaves of broccoli, and remove tough ends of lower stalks. Wash broccoli thoroughly, and separate into spears. Combine water, oregano, and salt in a Dutch oven; bring to a boil, and add broccoli. Cover, reduce heat, and simmer 10 minutes or until tender. Drain well, and place in a serving dish.

Combine remaining ingredients in a small saucepan; cook over low heat until cheese melts, stirring constantly. Spoon mixture over broccoli. Yield: 8 servings.
*Frances Jean Neely,*
*Jackson, Mississippi.*

## CARROTS AND BRUSSELS SPROUTS

¾ pound fresh brussels sprouts or 2
  (10-ounce) packages frozen brussels
  sprouts
1 (10¾-ounce) can chicken broth,
  undiluted
¾ pound baby carrots
2 tablespoons butter or margarine,
  melted
⅛ teaspoon ground ginger
¼ teaspoon seasoned salt

Place brussels sprouts and chicken broth in a saucepan; bring to a boil. Cover, reduce heat, and simmer 5 to 10 minutes or until tender; drain and set aside.

Add carrots to a small amount of boiling salted water in a large saucepan; cook 5 minutes or until tender. Drain off liquid. Pour butter over carrots; sprinkle with ginger. Cook over medium heat 5 minutes, stirring occasionally. Add brussels sprouts and seasoned salt; mix well. Cook 1 minute or until thoroughly heated. Yield: 6 to 8 servings.
*Rosie Thompson,*
*Beaumont, Texas.*

## LEMON CARROTS

8 carrots, cut into 1-inch slices
¾ cup water
¼ cup sugar
1½ tablespoons lemon juice
⅛ teaspoon salt
2 tablespoons butter or margarine
Fresh parsley sprigs (optional)

Combine first 5 ingredients in a saucepan. Cover and cook over medium heat 15 to 17 minutes or until carrots are tender. Add butter; stir until butter melts. Serve immediately. Garnish with parsley, if desired. Yield: 4 servings.
*Betty J. Moore,*
*Belton, Texas.*

## CHEESY CAULIFLOWER ITALIANO

2 small heads cauliflower (about 4 cups
  flowerets)
3 tablespoons all-purpose flour
½ teaspoon garlic powder
½ teaspoon pepper
1 small onion, thinly sliced
3 tablespoons butter or margarine
1 cup sliced ripe olives
2 cups (8 ounces) shredded mozzarella
  cheese
½ cup grated Parmesan cheese
2 tablespoons chopped parsley
¼ cup dry white wine
¾ cup milk
Paprika

Arrange flowerets in steaming rack. Place over boiling water; cover and steam 10 minutes or until crisp-tender. Remove from heat.

Combine flour, garlic powder, and pepper; set aside.

Arrange half of flowerets in a greased 8-inch square baking dish; top with half of onion slices. Sprinkle half of flour mixture over onion; dot with half of butter. Top with half each of olives, mozzarella, and Parmesan cheese. Sprinkle with parsley. Repeat layers with remaining cauliflower, onion, flour mixture, butter, olives, and cheese.

Combine wine and milk; stir well, and pour over casserole. Sprinkle with paprika. Bake, uncovered, at 350° for 40 minutes. Yield: 6 to 8 servings.
*Nancy M. Duncan,*
*Roanoke, Virginia.*

## SCALLOPED POTATOES

5 to 6 large potatoes, peeled and sliced
1½ cups chicken broth
½ teaspoon salt
¼ teaspoon pepper
1 cup (4 ounces) shredded Swiss cheese
3 tablespoons grated Parmesan cheese

Combine first 4 ingredients in a Dutch oven; bring to a boil. Cover, reduce heat, and simmer 5 minutes. Remove potatoes from broth, reserving broth.

Layer half each of potatoes and Swiss cheese in a lightly greased 2-quart casserole; repeat layers. Pour reserved broth over top; sprinkle with Parmesan cheese. Cover and bake at 350° for 55 minutes. Remove cover, and bake an additional 5 minutes or until potatoes are tender. Yield: 8 servings.
*Anita McLemore,*
*Knoxville, Tennessee.*

# Give A Flavorful Herb Jelly

Jars of bright red, yellow, or green herb jelly make special holiday gifts. Jellies made with rosemary or sage go well with poultry, while Mint Jelly makes a nice accompaniment to lamb. When you're giving Basil Jelly, suggest it be served with roast pork or beef. Bright-red Rose Geranium Jelly, with a sweet, mild herb flavor, is delicious on buttered toast for breakfast.

You can make your jelly with fresh herbs in the winter if you have an indoor herb garden; if you can't find fresh, substitute one-third as much of the dried form. In most of our recipes the herb is cooked with fruit juice and sugar and is removed before the jelly is poured into jars. But for Rose Geranium Jelly, place a single leaf of the herb in each jar of jelly to release its flavor during storage.

## BASIL JELLY

6 pounds apples, stemmed and chopped
6 cups water
3 cups sugar
2 tablespoons coarsely chopped fresh basil leaves
2 tablespoons lemon juice

Combine apples and 6 cups water in a large Dutch oven; bring to a boil. Cover, reduce heat, and simmer 20 to 25 minutes. Strain apples through a jelly bag or 4 layers of cheesecloth, reserving 4 cups juice. Discard pulp.

Combine 4 cups juice, sugar, basil, and lemon juice in Dutch oven; bring to a rolling boil, stirring frequently. Boil until mixture reaches 220° on candy thermometer, stirring frequently. Remove from heat, and skim off foam with a metal spoon.

Quickly pour jelly through a sieve into hot sterilized jars, leaving ¼-inch headspace; cover at once with metal lids, and screw bands tight. Process in boiling-water bath 5 minutes. Yield: 4 half-pints.

## MINT JELLY

6 pounds apples, stemmed and chopped
6 cups water
3 cups sugar
¾ cup fresh mint leaves, crushed
2 tablespoons lemon juice
2 drops green food coloring

Combine apples and 6 cups water in a large Dutch oven; bring to a boil. Cover, reduce heat, and simmer 20 to 25 minutes. Strain apples through a jelly bag or 4 layers of cheesecloth, reserving 4 cups juice. Discard pulp.

Combine 4 cups juice, sugar, mint, lemon juice, and food coloring in Dutch oven; bring to a rolling boil, stirring frequently. Boil until mixture reaches 220° on candy thermometer, stirring frequently. Remove from heat, and skim off foam with a metal spoon.

Quickly pour jelly through a sieve into hot sterilized jars, leaving ¼-inch headspace; cover at once with metal lids, and screw bands tight. Process in boiling-water bath 5 minutes. Yield: 4 half-pints.

## ROSE GERANIUM JELLY

4 cups apple juice
About 8 drops red food coloring
1 (1¾-ounce) package powdered fruit pectin
5½ cups sugar
7 fresh rose geranium leaves

Combine first 3 ingredients in a large Dutch oven. Quickly bring to a rolling boil, stirring frequently. Add sugar, and return to a rolling boil, stirring constantly. Boil 1 minute, stirring frequently. Remove from heat, and skim off foam with a metal spoon.

Place 1 rose geranium leaf in each hot sterilized jar. Quickly pour jelly into jars, leaving ¼-inch headspace; cover at once with metal lids, and screw bands tight. Process in boiling-water bath 5 minutes. Yield: 7 half-pints.

## ROSEMARY JELLY

1½ cups white grape juice
½ cup water
3½ cups sugar
3 tablespoons fresh rosemary leaves, crushed
About 8 drops red food coloring
About 8 drops yellow food coloring
1 (3-ounce) package liquid fruit pectin

Combine first 6 ingredients in a large Dutch oven. Quickly bring to a rolling boil, stirring constantly; cook 1 minute, stirring frequently. Add fruit pectin; cook, stirring constantly, until mixture returns to a rolling boil. Continue boiling 1 minute, stirring frequently. Remove from heat, and skim off foam with a metal spoon.

Quickly pour jelly through a sieve into hot sterilized jars, leaving ¼-inch headspace; cover at once with metal lids, and screw bands tight. Process in boiling-water bath 5 minutes. Yield: 4 half-pints.

## SAGE JELLY

1½ cups apple cider
½ cup water
3½ cups sugar
¼ cup coarsely chopped fresh sage leaves
About 6 drops yellow food coloring
1 (3-ounce) package liquid fruit pectin

Combine first 5 ingredients in a large Dutch oven. Quickly bring to a rolling boil, stirring constantly; cook 1 minute, stirring frequently. Add fruit pectin; cook, stirring constantly, until mixture returns to a rolling boil. Continue boiling 1 minute, stirring frequently. Remove from heat, and skim off foam with a metal spoon.

Quickly pour jelly through a sieve into hot sterilized jars, leaving ¼-inch headspace; cover at once with metal lids, and screw bands tight. Process in boiling-water bath 5 minutes. Yield: 4 half-pints.

## THYME JELLY

1½ cups white grape juice
½ cup water
3½ cups sugar
3 tablespoons fresh thyme leaves, crushed
About 8 drops red food coloring
1 (3-ounce) package liquid fruit pectin

Combine first 5 ingredients in a large Dutch oven. Quickly bring to a rolling boil, stirring constantly; cook 1 minute, stirring frequently. Add fruit pectin; cook, stirring constantly, until mixture returns to a rolling boil. Continue boiling 1 minute, stirring frequently. Remove from heat, and skim off foam with a metal spoon.

Quickly pour jelly through a sieve into hot sterilized jars, leaving ¼-inch headspace; cover at once with metal lids, and screw bands tight. Process in boiling-water bath 5 minutes. Yield: 4 half-pints.

# Be Creative With Winter Salads

Ever thought of stirring avocado into shredded cabbage for coleslaw? Guacamole Mexican Coleslaw tastes great with almost any Mexican entrée, and it's just one of our delicious variations on basic winter salads.

Make rice salad crunchy with sliced water chestnuts and celery, or add a surprise to potato salad with garbanzo beans and olives.

## POTATO-BEAN SALAD

4 cups diced cooked potatoes
1 (16-ounce) can garbanzo beans, drained
1 cup chopped celery
½ cup chopped salad olives
2 tablespoons dried parsley flakes
2 teaspoons onion salt
¼ teaspoon pepper
1 cup mayonnaise
4 hard-cooked eggs, sliced
Paprika (optional)

Combine first 7 ingredients in a large bowl; toss lightly. Add mayonnaise, stirring to coat vegetables. Gently stir in egg slices. Chill thoroughly. Sprinkle with paprika, if desired. Yield: 8 to 10 servings.
*Greydon Baker,*
*Venice, Florida.*

## CRUNCHY RICE SALAD

1 cup uncooked regular rice
1 (11-ounce) can mandarin oranges, drained
1 cup chopped green onion
1 cup diagonally sliced celery
1 (8-ounce) can sliced water chestnuts, drained
1 (3½-ounce) can sliced mushrooms, drained
¼ cup rice vinegar
¼ cup vegetable oil
¼ cup soy sauce
Lettuce leaves (optional)

Cook rice according to package directions, omitting salt. Cool.

Combine rice and next 5 ingredients, tossing lightly. Combine vinegar, oil, and soy sauce; pour over rice mixture, and toss lightly. Chill thoroughly. Serve on lettuce leaves, if desired. Yield: 10 to 12 servings. *Katherine Oliver, Tulsa, Oklahoma.*

## GUACAMOLE MEXICAN COLESLAW

3 ripe avocados, mashed
2 tablespoons lemon juice
6 cups shredded cabbage
1 cup finely chopped onion
1 cup finely chopped green pepper
½ cup mayonnaise or salad dressing
1 tablespoon sugar
1 tablespoon tarragon vinegar
½ teaspoon salt
¼ teaspoon garlic powder
¼ teaspoon pepper
Dash of hot sauce
Dash of Worcestershire sauce
¼ teaspoon paprika

Combine avocado and lemon juice in a large bowl, mixing well. Add cabbage, onion, and green pepper; mix well.

Combine remaining ingredients except paprika; stir into cabbage mixture. Sprinkle with paprika. Yield: 8 to 10 servings. *Eunice Ochoa, Schertz, Texas.*

## WILTED LETTUCE SALAD

2 cups torn leaf lettuce
2 cups torn iceberg lettuce
3 small green onions, chopped
5 slices bacon
2 tablespoons vinegar
1 teaspoon sugar

Combine lettuce and green onion in a salad bowl. Cook bacon in a large skillet until crisp; remove bacon, reserving drippings in skillet. Crumble bacon, and set aside.

Add vinegar and sugar to bacon drippings; bring to a boil, and pour over lettuce. Toss gently. Sprinkle with bacon before serving. Yield: 4 servings. *Judy A. Myers, Pensacola, Florida.*

## BEST CHERRY SALAD

1 (16½-ounce) can pitted, dark sweet cherries, undrained
1 (11-ounce) can mandarin oranges, undrained
1 (8-ounce) can crushed pineapple, undrained
1 (6-ounce) package cherry-flavored gelatin
1 cup boiling water
½ cup chopped pecans
Lettuce leaves (optional)

Drain fruit, reserving juice. Dissolve gelatin in boiling water; add fruit juice, stirring well. Chill until consistency of unbeaten egg white.

Fold fruit and pecans into gelatin. Pour into a lightly oiled 1½-quart mold, and chill until firm. Unmold on lettuce leaves, if desired. Yield: 10 to 12 servings. *Mrs. H. G. Drawdy, Spindale, North Carolina.*

# Serve Two, With Tradition

You can still enjoy a traditional holiday meal even if you're cooking just for two. Instead of turkey and dressing, serve Rice-Stuffed Cornish Hens; filled with rice, mushrooms, and crunchy almonds, this is a perfect entrée for two.

Our menu includes vegetable dishes of spinach, sweet potatoes, and cauliflower. Creamy Lemon Spinach is blended with cream cheese and flavored with lemon. For Apple-Glazed Sweet Potatoes, sliced, cooked potatoes are broiled under a topping of apple butter, cinnamon, and orange rind. Finish the meal with Delicious Apple Crisp. Add a scoop of vanilla ice cream for a perfect ending.

**Rice-Stuffed Cornish Hens**
**Creamy Lemon Spinach**
**Apple-Glazed Sweet Potatoes**
**Marinated Cauliflower Salad**
**Delicious Apple Crisp**
**White Wine**

## RICE-STUFFED CORNISH HENS

2 tablespoons slivered almonds
2 tablespoons finely chopped onion
⅓ cup uncooked regular rice
3 tablespoons butter or margarine
1 cup water
1 chicken-flavored bouillon cube
1 teaspoon lemon juice
½ teaspoon salt
1 (3-ounce) can mushroom stems and pieces, drained
2 (1- to 1½-pound) Cornish hens
Salt and pepper
¼ cup butter or margarine, melted
Red and green grapes (optional)

Sauté almonds, onion, and rice in 3 tablespoons butter in a medium saucepan over medium heat 5 minutes. Stir in 1 cup water, bouillon cube, lemon juice, and ½ teaspoon salt. Cover, reduce heat, and simmer 20 minutes or until liquid is absorbed. Stir in mushrooms.

Remove giblets from hens; reserve for another use. Rinse hens with cold water, and pat dry; sprinkle with salt and pepper. Stuff hens lightly with rice mixture. Close cavities, and secure with wooden picks; truss. Place hens breast side up in a shallow baking pan; brush with melted butter. Cover, and bake at 350° for 20 minutes. Remove cover; bake an additional 30 to 40 minutes, brushing occasionally with butter. Place hens on a serving platter, and garnish with grapes, if desired. Yield: 2 servings. *Charlotte R. Johnson, Orlando, Florida.*

## CREAMY LEMON SPINACH

1 (10-ounce) package frozen chopped spinach
1 (3-ounce) package cream cheese, softened
1 tablespoon butter or margarine, softened
1 teaspoon grated lemon rind
1 teaspoon lemon juice
2 tablespoons seasoned, dry breadcrumbs
1 tablespoon butter or margarine, melted
Lemon rind strips (optional)

Cook spinach according to package directions; drain well.

Combine next 4 ingredients; mix well. Stir in spinach. Spoon mixture into a lightly greased 2-cup casserole.

Combine breadcrumbs and melted butter; mix well, and spoon over spinach. Bake, uncovered, at 350° for 25 minutes. Garnish with lemon strips, if desired. Yield: 2 servings. *Sara Porter, Birmingham, Alabama.*

## APPLE-GLAZED SWEET POTATOES

2 small sweet potatoes
Salt to taste
½ teaspoon ground cinnamon
¼ cup plus 2 tablespoons apple butter
1 teaspoon grated orange rind
1 tablespoon butter or margarine, melted

Cook sweet potatoes in boiling water 20 to 25 minutes or until tender. Let cool to touch; peel and cut into ½-inch slices. Arrange slices in a lightly greased 8-inch square pan; sprinkle lightly with salt.

Combine remaining ingredients; mix well. Spread mixture over sweet potatoes. Broil 6 inches from heat until bubbly. Yield: 2 servings.

*Mrs. A. C. Schaller,*
*Florissant, Missouri.*

## MARINATED CAULIFLOWER SALAD

1 (10-ounce) package frozen cauliflower
¼ cup green pepper strips
¼ cup commercial Italian dressing
½ teaspoon lemon juice
Lettuce leaves (optional)

Cook cauliflower according to package directions; drain. Combine cauliflower and remaining ingredients except lettuce; stir well. Cover and chill 3 hours, stirring occasionally. Serve on lettuce leaves, if desired. Yield: 2 servings.

*Kathy Helwick,*
*Dallas, Texas.*

## DELICIOUS APPLE CRISP

2 medium-size cooking apples, peeled, cored, and chopped
1 teaspoon all-purpose flour, divided
⅓ cup bran flakes cereal, crushed
2 tablespoons all-purpose flour
¼ teaspoon ground cinnamon
⅛ teaspoon ground nutmeg
3 tablespoons brown sugar
2 tablespoons butter or margarine, softened
Vanilla ice cream (optional)

Divide apples evenly into two lightly greased 6-ounce ovenproof dessert cups. Sprinkle ½ teaspoon flour over each cup.

Combine crushed cereal, 2 tablespoons flour, cinnamon, nutmeg, and brown sugar; mix well. Cut butter into cereal mixture with pastry blender until mixture resembles coarse meal. Sprinkle over apples. Bake, uncovered, at 350°

for 25 minutes or until apples are tender and topping is golden brown. Serve warm with ice cream, if desired. Yield: 2 servings.

*F. L. Graham,*
*Lexington, Kentucky,*

# Stop By For Dessert

The scent of evergreens and the aroma of freshly baked pastries and cookies greet guests in the foyer of Bette and William Haney's lovely Decatur, Alabama, home. Then William steers everyone into the dining area where a rainbow of sweets forms a sparkling buffet.

Each year, the Haneys host a late-evening dessert party following the Morgan-Lawrence County Medical Society Christmas dinner-dance. Bette, along with friend Jackie Guice, has fun planning and preparing the menu, which may include up to 16 show-stopping desserts.

The Haneys' guests have a glorious time narrowing down their dessert selections. The buffet begins with Miniature Cheesecakes, Dainty Lemon Tarts, and five types of cookies. But that's not all—an Amaretto Torte, a Chocolate Cheesecake, two beautiful fruit tarts, and an Ice Cream Bombe are included in the sumptuous display.

Once their plates are filled, the guests choose a glass of champagne or a cup of coffee and head to the living room where Bette settles down to the piano and strikes up a lively Christmas tune.

Bette prepares most of her specialties in advance. "Some of these desserts can be partially completed ahead of time and then baked early on the day of the party. The Ice Cream Bombe is frozen and the cheesecakes and the Wine Jelly and Charlotte Russe are refrigerated until the last minute."

Finally, Bette and Jackie garnish each dessert with decorator frosting, chocolate leaves, or marzipan flowers.

## AMARETTO TORTE

1 (8-ounce) package dried apricots
1 cup warm water
3 tablespoons sugar
½ cup amaretto
½ cup butter or margarine, softened
1 egg yolk
1½ cups sifted powdered sugar
3 tablespoons amaretto
6 egg whites
¼ teaspoon cream of tartar
⅛ teaspoon salt
1½ cups sugar
1 teaspoon cider vinegar
1 teaspoon vanilla extract
1¾ cups ground pecans, divided
1 pint whipping cream, whipped and divided
Green and purple grapes (optional)
Fresh strawberries (optional)

Grease bottom and sides of two 8-inch round cakepans; line bottom of pans with waxed paper. Grease waxed paper.

Combine apricots and warm water in a large saucepan; soak 30 minutes. Stir in 3 tablespoons sugar. Bring mixture to a boil. Reduce heat; cover and simmer 20 to 25 minutes or until apricots are tender. Pour apricot mixture and ½ cup amaretto into container of electric blender; process until smooth. Set aside.

Combine butter, egg yolk, and powdered sugar; beat at medium-high speed of electric mixer 10 minutes. Add 3 tablespoons amaretto; beat well. Set aside.

Beat egg whites (at room temperature), cream of tartar, and salt until foamy. Gradually add 1½ cups sugar, 1 tablespoon at a time, beating until stiff peaks form. Add vinegar and vanilla, beating well. Fold in 1¼ cups pecans.

Spoon meringue into prepared pans, spreading evenly; sprinkle top of each with ¼ cup pecans. Bake at 350° for 40 minutes. Gently loosen layers around edges, and immediately turn out of pans onto wire racks; remove waxed paper, and cool completely. (Layers may crumble around edges and have a cracked appearance on top.)

Place one meringue layer, pecan side up, on serving platter; top with butter mixture, spreading to edges. Spread apricot mixture evenly over butter mixture; top with 2 cups whipped cream. Place remaining meringue layer, pecan side up, over whipped cream. Spread remaining whipped cream on sides of torte. Chill at least 3 hours before serving. Store in refrigerator. Garnish with grapes and strawberries, if desired. Yield: 8 to 10 servings.

## DAINTY LEMON TARTS

2 cups sugar
1½ teaspoons grated lemon rind
½ cup lemon juice
1 cup butter or margarine
4 eggs, beaten
Tart shells (recipe follows)
Decorator frosting or whipped cream
  (optional)
Blueberries (optional)

Combine first 4 ingredients in top of double boiler; bring water to a boil. Reduce heat to low, and cook until butter melts, stirring constantly.

Gradually stir about one-fourth of hot mixture into eggs; add to remaining hot mixture, stirring constantly. Cook in top of double boiler, stirring constantly, 20 minutes or until thickened. Chill 2 hours. Spoon about 1 teaspoon filling into each tart shell. Garnish each tart with decorator frosting or whipped cream and blueberries, if desired. Yield: about 8 dozen.

*Tart Shells:*

3 cups all-purpose flour
1½ teaspoons salt
1 cup shortening
5 to 6 tablespoons ice water

Combine flour and salt in a bowl; cut in shortening with a pastry blender until mixture resembles coarse meal. Sprinkle water evenly over surface; stir with a fork until all dry ingredients are moistened. Shape dough into a ball; chill.

Roll dough to ⅛-inch thickness on a lightly floured suface; cut into rounds with a 2-inch scalloped cutter. Fit each pastry into a 1¾-inch muffin pan; prick each with a fork. Bake at 400° for 10 to 12 minutes. Yield: about 8 dozen tarts.


## RAINBOW FRUIT TART

2 cups all-purpose flour
½ cup sugar
1¾ teaspoons grated lemon rind
½ teaspoon salt
¼ teaspoon ground cinnamon
¾ cup butter or margarine
3 egg yolks, slightly beaten
Luscious Pastry Cream
2 cups fresh strawberries
1 cup seedless green grapes
½ cup mandarin orange sections,
  drained
⅓ cup fresh or frozen blueberries,
  drained
Sweet Apricot Glaze

Combine first 5 ingredients; cut in butter with pastry blender until mixture resembles coarse meal. Add egg yolks, stirring well. Knead dough until smooth; shape into a ball. Roll dough between two sheets of waxed paper to ¼-inch thickness. Fit pastry to an 11-inch round tart pan (dough will be fragile; smooth with fingers to fit pan). Cover; chill 1 hour.

Place a piece of aluminum foil over pastry. Cover foil with a layer of dried peas or beans. Bake at 400° for 8 to 10 minutes; remove peas and foil. Prick shell, and bake 8 to 10 minutes or until lightly browned. Cool completely.

Spread Luscious Pastry Cream evenly over bottom of pastry. Arrange fruit over pastry cream in an attractive pattern. Spoon Sweet Apricot Glaze over fruit. Yield: 10 to 12 servings.

*Luscious Pastry Cream:*

5 egg yolks
1 cup sugar
⅔ cup all-purpose flour
2 cups scalded milk
3 tablespoons Grand Marnier or other
  orange-flavored liqueur
1 tablespoon butter or margarine

Beat egg yolks until frothy. Gradually add sugar, beating until thick. Add flour, beating well. Gradually add hot milk, beating constantly. Pour mixture into a large, heavy saucepan; cook over low heat, stirring constantly, until thickened and smooth. (Mixture may be lumpy while cooking; beat with a wire whisk to remove lumps, if necessary.)

Remove from heat, and stir in Grand Marnier and butter. Cover cream with plastic wrap; cool completely. Yield: about 3½ cups.

*Sweet Apricot Glaze:*

¼ cup apricot preserves
2 tablespoons red currant jelly
1 tablespoon sugar
1 tablespoon water
1 tablespoon Grand Marnier or other
  orange-flavored liqueur

Combine first 4 ingredients in a small saucepan. Cook over medium heat, stirring often, just until mixture reaches a boil. Press mixture through a sieve, reserving syrup. Discard preserves. Stir liqueur into syrup; cool completely. Yield: about ½ cup.

*Tip: Save lemon and orange rinds. Store in the freezer, and grate as needed for pies, cakes, breads, and cookies. Or the rinds can be candied for holiday uses.*


## PEAR TART

1½ cups all-purpose flour
½ teaspoon baking powder
½ teaspoon salt
¼ cup butter or margarine
¼ cup shortening
4 to 6 tablespoons milk
¾ cup blanched, slivered almonds
½ cup sugar
1 egg
1 tablespoon butter or margarine,
  melted
2 cups water
2 tablespoons lemon juice
8 to 10 fresh pears
¼ cup sugar
¼ cup butter or margarine
3 tablespoons slivered almonds,
  toasted
¼ cup plus 2 tablespoons apricot
  preserves
¼ cup water
2 tablespoons sugar
1 tablespoon Kirsch
Marzipan leaves and berries
  (optional)

Combine flour, baking powder, and salt in a bowl; cut in ¼ cup butter and shortening with pastry blender until mixture resembles coarse meal. Sprinkle milk evenly over surface; stir with a fork until all dry ingredients are moistened. Shape into a ball; chill at least 1 hour.

Roll dough to ⅛-inch thickness on a lightly floured surface. Fit pastry to an 11-inch round tart pan. Set aside.

Position knife blade in processor bowl. Add ¾ cup almonds; process 40 to 50 seconds or until finely ground. Add next 3 ingredients; process until well mixed. Spread evenly over bottom of pastry. Set aside.

Combine 2 cups water and lemon juice; mix well. Peel and core pears. Dip pears in lemon juice mixture; drain well. Cut pears in half vertically, and then cut into ½-inch-thick lengthwise slices. Arrange pears so slices are overlapping, curved side up, in rows on top of almond mixture. Sprinkle with ¼ cup sugar; dot with ¼ cup butter, and sprinkle with toasted almonds. Bake at 400° for 1 hour and 15 minutes.

Combine next 3 ingredients; cook over low heat, stirring constantly, until sugar dissolves. Press preserve mixture through a sieve, reserving syrup. Discard preserves. Stir Kirsch into syrup. Carefully brush syrup over tart. Remove tart from pan before serving. Garnish with marzipan leaves and berries, if desired. Yield: 16 servings.

*Note:* Marzipan garnishes may be purchased from bakeries or caterers.

## ICE CREAM BOMBE

1 pint French vanilla ice cream, slightly softened
1 tablespoon rum extract
¼ cup maraschino cherries, drained and chopped
½ pint French milk chocolate ice cream, slightly softened
1 tablespoon cocoa
½ (1-ounce) square unsweetened chocolate, melted
1 cup whipping cream
2 tablespoons sugar
½ pint raspberry sherbet, slightly softened
3 egg yolks
3 tablespoons sugar
2 teaspoons almond extract
¼ cup coconut macaroon crumbs
Decorator frosting (optional)
Marzipan flowers (optional)
Green and purple grapes (optional)

Lightly brush inside of a 5-cup mold or bowl with unflavored oil. Place in freezer until thoroughly chilled.

Combine vanilla ice cream and rum extract; mix until smooth. Using a chilled spoon, spread half of vanilla ice cream evenly on bottom and sides of mold, leaving center hollow. (It may be necessary to place ice cream in freezer until workable.) Freeze about 4 hours or until ice cream is firm. Stir maraschino cherries into remaining vanilla ice cream; return to freezer until firm.

Soften maraschino cherry ice cream mixture, if necessary; spread evenly over vanilla layer, leaving center hollow. Freeze about 4 hours or until firm.

Combine chocolate ice cream, cocoa, and melted chocolate in container of an electric blender; blend well. Beat whipping cream until foamy; gradually add 2 tablespoons sugar, beating until soft peaks form. Fold 1 cup whipped cream into chocolate mixture, and spread evenly over cherry layer, leaving center hollow. Freeze about 4 hours or until firm. Reserve remaining whipped cream.

Spread raspberry sherbet evenly over chocolate layer, leaving center hollow. Freeze about 4 hours or until firm.

Combine egg yolks, 3 tablespoons sugar, and almond extract in top of double boiler; bring water to a boil. Reduce heat to low and cook, stirring constantly, until thickened. Cool.

Fold remaining 1 cup whipped cream into egg yolk mixture. Stir in macaroon crumbs. Spoon into center of ice cream-lined mold. Cover tightly, and freeze overnight.

Using tip of knife, gently loosen edges of ice cream from mold. Invert mold onto a chilled serving plate. Wrap a warm towel around the mold for 30 seconds. Remove towel, and firmly hold plate and mold together. Shake gently, and slowly lift off mold. Garnish with decorator frosting, marzipan flowers, and grapes, if desired. Freeze until serving time. Yield: 8 servings.

## WINE JELLY AND CHARLOTTE RUSSE

2 envelopes unflavored gelatin
½ cup cold water
1⅔ cups boiling water
1 cup sugar
1 cup dry sherry
⅓ cup orange juice
3 tablespoons lemon juice
Red food coloring
1 envelope unflavored gelatin
¼ cup cold water
2 eggs
½ cup sugar
1 cup milk
1 teaspoon vanilla extract
2 cups whipping cream, whipped
Fresh strawberries (optional)

Soften 2 envelopes gelatin in ½ cup cold water. Add 1⅔ cups boiling water and 1 cup sugar; stir until gelatin and sugar are dissolved. Stir in sherry and fruit juice. Add food coloring to desired shade of red. Pour into a lightly oiled 2½-quart ring mold. Chill just until set (should be slightly firm, but sticky to the touch).

Soften 1 envelope gelatin in ¼ cup cold water. Set aside. Beat eggs in a heavy saucepan; add ½ cup sugar, beating well. Stir in milk; cook over low heat, stirring constantly, until thickened. Add softened gelatin, stirring until dissolved. Let cool, and stir in vanilla. Fold in whipped cream. Spoon mixture over wine layer. Chill until firm; unmold and garnish with strawberries, if desired. Yield: 12 servings.

## MINIATURE CHEESECAKES

½ cup graham cracker crumbs
2 tablespoons butter or margarine, melted
1 (8-ounce) package cream cheese, softened
¼ cup sugar
1 egg
½ teaspoon vanilla extract
1 (10-ounce) jar cherry preserves

Combine graham cracker crumbs and butter, mixing well. Line 1¾-inch muffin pans with miniature paper liners. Spoon 1 teaspoon graham cracker mixture into each liner; gently press into bottom.

Beat cream cheese with electric mixer until light and fluffy; gradually add sugar and mix well. Add egg and vanilla, beating well. Spoon mixture into liners. Bake at 350° for 10 minutes.

Place cherry preserves in a small saucepan; heat just until preserves melt. Spoon about 1 teaspoon preserves over each cheesecake. Chill thoroughly. Yield: 2 dozen.

## CHOCOLATE CHEESECAKE

1 cup chocolate wafer crumbs
¼ cup butter or margarine, melted
1 (12-ounce) package semisweet chocolate morsels
3 (8-ounce) packages cream cheese, softened
¾ cup sugar
3 eggs
½ cup amaretto
1 (8-ounce) carton commercial sour cream
2 tablespoons whipping cream
2 teaspoons vanilla extract
1 (4-ounce) carton frozen whipped topping, thawed
Chocolate leaves (optional)

Combine chocolate wafer crumbs and butter, mixing well; firmly press into bottom of a 9-inch springform pan.

Place chocolate morsels in top of double boiler; bring water to a boil. Reduce heat to low; cook until chocolate melts.

Beat cream cheese with electric mixer until light and fluffy; gradually add sugar, mixing well. Add eggs, one at a time, beating well after each addition. Stir in melted chocolate, and beat until blended. Stir in next 4 ingredients (mixture may appear slightly lumpy). Pour into prepared pan. Bake at 350° for 45 minutes (center may be soft but will firm when chilled). Let cool to room temperature on a wire rack; refrigerate overnight.

Remove sides of springform pan; top with whipped topping. Garnish with chocolate leaves, if desired. Yield: 10 to 12 servings.

## CHOCOLATE-ALMOND DESSERT

½ cup butter or margarine, softened
⅔ cup sugar
3 eggs
4 (1-ounce) squares semisweet chocolate, melted
1 cup whole almonds, very finely ground
Grated rind of 1 orange
¼ cup commercial corn flake crumbs
Chocolate-Honey Glaze
Toasted slivered almonds

Grease bottom and sides of one 8-inch round cakepan; line bottom of pan with waxed paper.

Cream butter; gradually add sugar, beating until light and fluffy. Add eggs, one at a time, beating well after each addition. Stir in chocolate, ground almonds, orange rind, and corn flake crumbs, mixing well.

Pour into prepared pan; bake at 350° for 35 minutes or until a wooden pick inserted in center comes out clean. Remove from oven, and cool in pan on a wire rack at least 30 minutes.

Gently turn out of pan onto serving plate; remove waxed paper, and cool. Spread Chocolate-Honey Glaze on top and sides. Arrange slivered almonds around edges. Yield: 10 servings.

*Chocolate-Honey Glaze:*

2 (1-ounce) squares unsweetened chocolate
2 (1-ounce) squares semisweet chocolate
¼ cup butter or margarine
2 teaspoons honey or light corn syrup

Combine all ingredients in top of a double boiler; bring water to a boil. Reduce heat to low; cook just until chocolate and butter melt, beating well. Yield: about ½ cup.

## ALMOND SPRITZ COOKIES

1 cup butter or margarine, softened
⅔ cup sugar
3 egg yolks
1 teaspoon vanilla extract
2½ cups all-purpose flour
⅛ teaspoon salt
1 egg white, slightly beaten
½ cup ground blanched almonds
1 (12-ounce) package semisweet chocolate morsels

Cream butter; gradually add sugar, beating until light and fluffy. Add egg yolks, one at a time, beating well after each addition. Stir in vanilla.

Combine flour and salt; add to creamed mixture, beating well.

Use a cookie press to shape dough into 2½-inch-long cookies, following manufacturer's instructions, or use the following procedure: Sift powdered sugar lightly over working surface. Shape 2 tablespoons dough by hand into a 2½-inch-long rope; repeat with remaining dough. Place cookies on a lightly greased cookie sheet.

Brush each cookie with egg white, and lightly sprinkle with almonds (reserve remaining almonds). Bake at 400° for 8 to 10 minutes or until lightly browned. (Cookies rolled by hand may require 2 to 3 minutes additional baking time.) Remove cookies to wire racks, and cool completely.

Place chocolate in top of double boiler; bring water to a boil. Reduce heat to low; cook just until chocolate melts. Remove from heat.

Dip ends of cookies in chocolate, covering about ½ inch on each end. Sprinkle ends with remaining almonds. Place cookies on wire racks until chocolate is firm. Yield: about 6 dozen.

## GRANDMOTHER'S SANDWICH COOKIES

1 cup butter or margarine, softened
⅔ cup sugar
2 eggs, separated
2½ cups all-purpose flour
¼ teaspoon salt
Powdered sugar
½ cup sugar
½ cup ground blanched almonds
About 1½ cups raspberry preserves or ½ cup semisweet chocolate morsels

Cream butter; gradually add ⅔ cup sugar, beating until light and fluffy. Add egg yolks, one at a time, beating well after each addition.

Combine flour and salt; add to creamed mixture, beating well. Shape dough into a ball; cover and chill at least 2 hours.

Work with half of dough at a time; store remainder in refrigerator. Sift powdered sugar lightly over working surface. Roll half of dough out to ⅛-inch thickness; cut into rounds with a 2½-inch cookie cutter. Roll remaining dough out to ⅛-inch thickness; cut with a 2½-inch doughnut cutter, reserving centers. (Dough may require chilling at this point for ease in handling.)

Combine ½ cup sugar and almonds; mix well. Beat egg whites (at room temperature) until frothy. Brush one side of all cookie cutouts with egg white, and coat with almond mixture; place coated side up on lightly greased cookie sheets. Bake at 375° for 8 to 10 minutes or until lightly browned. Cool on wire racks.

*For Raspberry Sandwich Cookies:* Dip almond side of 2½-inch solid cookies in powdered sugar. Spread other side of cookie with a thin layer of raspberry preserves. (Cookies are very delicate and must be handled carefully to prevent breaking.) Dip almond side of doughnut-shaped cookies in powdered sugar; place sugar side up on top of raspberry filling. Yield: about 1½ dozen cookies.

*For Chocolate Sandwich Cookies:* Place chocolate morsels in top of double boiler; bring water to a boil. Reduce heat to low; cook until chocolate melts.

Using half of reserved cookie centers, spread a thin layer of melted chocolate on side without almonds. Top with remaining cookie centers, almond side up. Drizzle tops of cookies with remaining chocolate. Yield: 8 cookies.

## BRAZIL SQUARES

1 cup butter or margarine, softened
1 cup firmly packed brown sugar
1 egg
2 cups all-purpose flour
½ teaspoon baking powder
½ teaspoon salt
1 teaspoon vanilla extract
1 (12-ounce) package semisweet chocolate morsels
1 cup toasted pecans, ground

Cream butter; gradually add brown sugar, beating until light and fluffy. Add egg, beating well. Combine flour, baking powder, and salt; gradually add to creamed mixture. Stir in vanilla. Spread dough evenly in a lightly greased 15- x 10- x 1-inch jellyroll pan. Bake at 350° for 20 to 22 minutes.

Sprinkle cookie crust with chocolate morsels; return to oven, and bake 1 minute or just until chocolate melts. Spread chocolate evenly over top, and sprinkle with pecans. Cut into squares while warm. Yield: about 6 dozen.

## SWEDISH COOKIES

1 cup butter or margarine, softened
½ cup sifted powdered sugar
1½ cups all-purpose flour
¼ cup cornstarch
¼ teaspoon salt
½ teaspoon almond extract
½ teaspoon vanilla extract
Decorator frosting (recipe follows)

Cream butter; gradually add sugar, beating until light and fluffy. Combine dry ingredients; gradually add to creamed mixture, mixing well. Stir in flavorings. Chill dough 1½ hours.

Shape dough into 1-inch balls; place on ungreased cookie sheets. Gently press cookies with fingers to flatten. Bake at 350° for 10 to 12 minutes. Top with flowers made from decorator frosting. Yield: 4 dozen.

*Decorator Frosting:*

⅔ cup shortening
¼ teaspoon salt
½ teaspoon almond or vanilla extract
⅓ cup water
1 (16-ounce) package powdered sugar, sifted
Paste food coloring (optional)

Combine shortening, salt, and extract in a medium mixing bowl; beat at medium speed of electric mixer until blended. Alternately add small amounts of water and powdered sugar, beating constantly at low speed, until blended. Beat 8 minutes at medium speed of electric mixer. Color portions of frosting with paste food coloring, if desired. Prepare decorating bags. Decorate as desired. Yield: about 2⅓ cups.

*Note:* Frosting may be stored at room temperature or in refrigerator for several days.

### COCONUT-BLACK WALNUT BONBONS

1 (8-ounce) package cream cheese, softened
7 cups sifted powdered sugar
1 teaspoon black walnut flavoring
About 1¼ cups black walnut pieces
1 (8-ounce) package flaked coconut

Beat cream cheese with electric mixer until light and fluffy; gradually add powdered sugar, beating well. Add flavoring and mix well. Shape cream cheese mixture around each walnut piece, forming 1-inch balls. Roll in coconut. Chill. Yield: about 5 dozen.

### VANILLA CRESCENTS

1 cup butter or margarine, softened
½ cup sugar
2 egg yolks
⅛ teaspoon salt
1 teaspoon vanilla extract
3 cups all-purpose flour
1 cup blanched, slivered almonds, finely ground
Powdered sugar

Cream butter; gradually add sugar, beating well. Add egg yolks, salt, and

vanilla; beat well. Stir in flour and almonds. Chill 1 hour.

Break off dough by heaping teaspoonfuls, and shape into 2-inch crescents. Place on lightly greased cookie sheets. Bake at 325° for 20 minutes. Remove immediately from cookie sheets, and coat with powdered sugar. Yield: about 5 dozen.

# Dressings With A Difference

There are as many recipes for dressing as there are Southern cooks, and here are three more versions you'll enjoy. Rosie Thompson, of Beaumont, Texas, says she doesn't need turkey or chicken to serve with her Cajun Dressing. "I've served it as a main dish many times," she says. In this spicy dish Rosie mixes hot and mild sausage with onion, green pepper, celery, chicken soup mix, and rice.

Our other recipes are equally savory. One is a combination of cornbread, sausage, vegetables, and pecans; the other calls for cream-style corn and is shaped into individual servings.

### ZESTY CORN DRESSING BALLS

1 (8-ounce) package herb-seasoned stuffing mix
½ cup chopped onion
½ cup chopped celery
¼ cup butter or margarine
1 (17-ounce) can cream-style corn
½ cup water
1 teaspoon poultry seasoning
⅛ teaspoon pepper
3 eggs, beaten
2 tablespoons butter or margarine, melted

Place stuffing mix in a large bowl; set aside.

Sauté onion and celery in ¼ cup butter in a large skillet until tender. Add next 4 ingredients, and bring to a boil; pour over stuffing mix, and mix well. Stir in eggs. Let cool 10 minutes.

Shape stuffing mixture into 8 balls, and place in a lightly greased 9-inch square pan. Pour melted butter evenly over dressing. Bake at 375° for 25 minutes. Yield: 8 servings.

*Eileen MaCutchan,*
*Largo, Florida.*

### CAJUN DRESSING

1 pound hot bulk pork sausage
1 pound mild bulk pork sausage
1 large onion, chopped
1 large green pepper, chopped
3 stalks celery, chopped
2 (0.375-ounce) envelopes instant chicken noodle soup mix
2 cups uncooked regular rice
6 cups water

Brown sausage in a Dutch oven, stirring to crumble; drain. Stir in remaining ingredients, mixing well.

Place mixture in a 4½-quart casserole. Cover and bake at 350° for 1 hour; uncover and bake an additional 15 to 20 minutes or until moisture is absorbed. Yield: 12 to 15 servings.

*Rosie Thompson,*
*Beaumont, Texas.*

### CORNBREAD-SAUSAGE DRESSING

6 cups cornbread crumbs
5 cups toasted soft breadcrumbs
6 chicken-flavored bouillon cubes
4 cups boiling water
1 cup finely chopped celery
1 cup finely chopped onion
1 cup finely chopped green pepper
¼ cup butter or margarine
½ pound bulk pork sausage
1 teaspoon poultry seasoning
½ teaspoon salt
¼ teaspoon pepper
4 eggs, beaten
1 cup finely chopped pecans

Combine cornbread crumbs and breadcrumbs in a large bowl.

Dissolve bouillon cubes in boiling water; pour over crumb mixture, and stir well.

Sauté celery, onion, and green pepper in butter until tender; add to crumb mixture, stirring well.

Brown sausage in a heavy skillet; drain. Stir sausage and remaining ingredients into cornbread mixture. Spoon into a lightly greased 13- x 9- x 2-inch baking dish; bake at 350° for 45 minutes. Yield: 8 to 10 servings.

*Mary Belle Purvis,*
*Greeneville, Tennessee.*

*Tip: An uncooked or cooked stuffed turkey or chicken should never be refrigerated. The stuffing should be thoroughly removed and refrigerated in a separate container.*

# Cider Bugs Charm Visitors

When friends and relatives drop in to visit during the holidays, wouldn't it be nice to send a small favor home with them? Our recipe for Beetle Cider Mix makes a dozen little creatures eager to be adopted. One cider beetle will spice up 1½ quarts apple cider.

Wrap each beetle tightly with plastic wrap, and tie with ribbon. Attach directions for use.

### BEETLE CIDER MIX

6 oranges
About 2¼ cups firmly packed brown sugar
12 (1½-inch) sticks cinnamon
12 small whole nutmeg
24 large whole allspice
96 whole cloves

Slice oranges in half crosswise; scoop out pulp, and reserve for other uses. Place orange halves cut side up on a wire rack on a baking sheet. Bake at 250° for 2 hours or until dry and hard. Let cool.

Pack brown sugar firmly into each orange half, mounding it slightly. Arrange spices in brown sugar to resemble a beetle, pressing slightly into sugar. Use cinnamon sticks for bodies, nutmegs for heads, allspices for eyes, and cloves for feet. Cover tightly with plastic wrap. Store in refrigerator. Yield: 12 cider beetles.

To use, unwrap beetle and drop into 1½ quarts apple cider; simmer 30 minutes. Add ¼ cup to ½ cup brandy, if desired; heat well. Remove orange rind and spices to serve. Store unused cider in refrigerator.

# Sweet Spreads Suited For Winter

Summer's not the only time to ladle hot sweetened fruit into sterilized jars, and then seal in the flavor. We've collected several recipes for marmalades, butters, and conserves that are suitable for winter because they use dried, canned, or seasonal fresh fruit.

The home economists in our test kitchens especially liked Dried Fruit Conserve and recommend it for holiday giving. It's made with dried apricots, peaches, and pears; raisins, a whole orange, and pecans add extra flavor.

### DRIED FRUIT CONSERVE

1½ cups (about ½ pound) chopped dried apricots
1⅓ cups (about ½ pound) chopped dried peaches
1⅓ cups (about ½ pound) chopped dried pears
1 medium-size orange, unpeeled, seeded, and chopped
3 cups water
2 cups sugar
½ cup raisins
1 tablespoon lemon juice
½ teaspoon ground cinnamon
⅛ teaspoon ground cloves
½ cup chopped pecans or walnuts

Combine first 5 ingredients in a large Dutch oven, stirring well. Cover and cook over medium heat 15 to 20 minutes or until fruit is tender. Stir in remaining ingredients except pecans; bring mixture to a boil. Boil rapidly 10 minutes, stirring frequently. Stir in pecans, cook an additional 5 minutes or until thick, stirring frequently.

Quickly pour conserve into hot sterilized jars, leaving ¼-inch headspace; cover at once with metal lids, and screw bands tight. Process in boiling-water bath 15 minutes. Yield: 6 half-pints.

### APPLE-CRANBERRY CONSERVE

5 apples, unpeeled, cored, and ground
3 cups fresh cranberries, ground
1 orange, unpeeled, seeded, and ground
1 lemon, unpeeled, seeded, and ground
1 (20-ounce) can crushed pineapple, undrained
1 (1¾-ounce) package powdered fruit pectin
5½ cups sugar
1 (2¼-ounce) package slivered almonds, toasted

Combine fruit in a large Dutch oven; stir well. Place over high heat and bring to a boil, stirring frequently. Stir in fruit pectin, and return mixture to a boil. Quickly stir in sugar; return to a boil and boil 1 minute, stirring constantly.

Remove from heat, and skim off foam with a metal spoon. Stir in almonds.

Quickly spoon conserve into hot sterilized jars, leaving ¼-inch headspace; cover at once with metal lids, and screw bands tight. Process in boiling-water bath 5 minutes. Yield: 11 half-pints.

### GRAPEFRUIT MARMALADE

⅔ cup thinly sliced grapefruit rind
3 cups water, divided
1⅓ cups chopped grapefruit sections
1 quart water
About 3¼ cups sugar

Combine grapefruit rind and 1 cup water in a large Dutch oven; bring to a boil. Boil, uncovered, 10 minutes; drain. Repeat procedure twice.

Combine rind, chopped grapefruit, and 1 quart water; cover and let stand in a cool place 12 to 18 hours.

Bring mixture to a boil; cover, reduce heat to medium, and boil 40 minutes or until rind is tender. Measure fruit mixture, including liquid; add 1 cup sugar per 1 cup fruit mixture. Stir well; bring mixture to a boil, and boil rapidly until mixture registers 218° on a candy thermometer, stirring frequently.

Pour marmalade into hot sterilized jars, leaving ¼-inch headspace; cover at once with metal lids, and screw bands tight. Process in boiling-water bath 10 minutes. (Mixture will thicken as it cools.) Yield: 3 half-pints.

### APRICOT BUTTER

2 cups firmly packed dried apricots
4 cups water
2 cups sugar

Combine apricots and 4 cups water in a Dutch oven; let stand 8 hours. Cook apricots, uncovered, 8 to 10 minutes or until very tender.

Press apricots through a coarse sieve, discarding pulp. Bring to a boil in Dutch oven; add sugar, and simmer 40 to 45 minutes, stirring frequently.

Quickly spoon apricot mixture into hot sterilized jars, leaving ¼-inch headspace; cover at once with metal lids, and screw bands tight. Process in boiling-water bath 10 minutes. Yield: 4 half-pints.

### PEACH BUTTER

1 (8-ounce) package dried peaches
2 cups water
1 cup sugar

Combine peaches and 2 cups water in a Dutch oven; let stand 5 hours. Cook peaches over low heat 30 minutes or until very tender. Remove from heat; mash peaches with a potato masher. Stir in sugar; cook over low heat 5 to 8 minutes or until thick, stirring butter frequently.

Quickly spoon butter into hot sterilized jars, leaving ¼-inch headspace; cover at once with metal lids, and screw bands tight. Process in boiling-water bath 10 minutes. Yield: 3 half-pints.

# Homemade Rolls Highlight Dinner

The only thing better than the aroma of freshly baked yeast rolls is biting into one and letting it melt in your mouth. If you take the time to prepare any of these dinner rolls, you'll discover that their sweet, yeast flavor and aroma make them worth the extra effort.

Yeast rolls can be baked in a variety of pretty shapes. Parker House Refrigerator Rolls are made by cutting the dough into circles and then folding each circle in half. Deep South Crescent Rolls bake from triangles of dough rolled up and curved into crescent shapes. The dough for both of these rolls can be mixed ahead and placed in the refrigerator until you're ready to shape and bake.

If you like the flavor of whole wheat, be sure to try Shredded Wheat Feather Rolls. Made from crumbled shredded wheat cereal, these rolls give you nutty whole wheat taste without using whole wheat flour.

## DEEP SOUTH CRESCENT ROLLS

1 package dry yeast
½ cup warm water (105° to 115°)
½ cup sugar
½ cup shortening
2 cups milk
7 cups all-purpose flour, divided
1½ teaspoons salt
½ teaspoon baking soda
½ teaspoon baking powder

Dissolve yeast in warm water; set aside.

Combine sugar, shortening, and milk in a medium saucepan; place over medium heat, stirring until shortening melts. Cool to 105° to 115°.

Combine milk mixture and yeast mixture in a large mixing bowl; mix well. Add 5 cups flour; stir well. Cover and let rise in a warm place (85°), free from drafts, 2 hours or until doubled in bulk.

Combine remaining 2 cups flour, salt, baking soda, and baking powder; mix

well. Punch dough down, and stir in flour mixture. Knead dough until smooth and elastic (about 8 to 10 minutes). Place in a well-greased bowl, turning to grease top. Cover and refrigerate until needed.

Punch dough down, and divide into fourths. Roll each fourth into a circle about 12 inches in diameter and ¼-inch thick; cut into 10 wedges. Roll each wedge tightly, beginning at wide end.

Place rolls on greased baking sheets, point side down; curve into crescent shape. Cover and let rise in a warm place (85°), free from drafts, 1½ hours or until doubled in bulk. Bake at 400° for 10 minutes or until lightly browned. Yield: about 3 dozen.

*Elizabeth M. Haney,*
*Dublin, Virginia.*

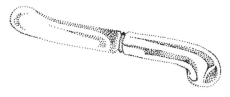

## SPEEDY YEAST ROLLS

4½ cups all-purpose flour, divided
3 tablespoons sugar
½ teaspoon baking soda
1 teaspoon salt
2 packages dry yeast
1¼ cups buttermilk
½ cup water
½ cup butter or margarine
Melted butter or margarine

Combine 1½ cups flour, sugar, baking soda, salt, and yeast in a large mixing bowl; set aside.

Combine buttermilk, water, and ½ cup butter in a small saucepan; heat to 120° to 130°, stirring well. Add to flour mixture. Beat at medium speed of electric mixer 4 minutes. Gradually add remaining flour, mixing well.

Turn dough out on a floured surface, and knead until smooth and elastic (about 5 to 8 minutes). Place in a greased bowl, turning to grease top. Cover and let rise in a warm place (85°), free from drafts, about 30 minutes or until doubled in bulk.

Punch dough down, and shape into 1½ inch balls. Place on greased cookie sheets; cover and let rise in a warm place (85°), free from drafts, 30 minutes or until doubled in bulk. Bake at 400° for 15 to 20 minutes. Brush with melted butter. Yield: about 2 dozen.

*Carol Forcum,*
*Marion, Illinois.*

## SHREDDED WHEAT FEATHER ROLLS

2 packages dry yeast
½ cup warm water (105° to 115°)
⅔ cup milk, scalded
½ cup butter or margarine
2 tablespoons sugar
1½ teaspoons salt
2 eggs, beaten
4 cups all-purpose flour, divided
1½ cups (about 4) shredded whole wheat cereal biscuits, crumbled

Dissolve yeast in warm water; set aside.

Combine scalded milk, butter, sugar, and salt in a large mixing bowl; stir until sugar and salt are dissolved. Cool to 105° to 115°.

Add yeast mixture and eggs to milk mixture; mix well. Stir in 2 cups flour. Add remaining flour and shredded wheat; beat at medium speed of electric mixer 1 minute, scraping sides of bowl with a spatula. Cover and let rise in a warm place (85°), free from drafts, 1 hour or until doubled in bulk.

Punch dough down. Shape into ¾-inch balls; place 3 balls in each cup of well-greased muffin pans. Cover and let rise in a warm place (85°), free from drafts, 45 minutes or until doubled in bulk. Bake at 375° for 18 to 20 minutes. Yield: 1½ dozen. *Judy Cunningham,*
*Roanoke, Virginia.*

## REFRIGERATOR YEAST ROLLS

1 package dry yeast
¼ cup warm water (105 to 115°)
¼ cup shortening
¼ cup sugar
1 egg, slightly beaten
1 cup warm water (105° to 115°)
1 to 1½ teaspoons salt
4 cups all-purpose flour

Dissolve yeast in ¼ cup warm water; set aside. Cream shortening; gradually add sugar, and beat until light and fluffy. Stir in egg, 1 cup warm water, and yeast mixture; beat until smooth. Stir in salt and flour to make a soft dough.

Place dough in a well-greased bowl, turning to grease top. Cover and refrigerate 24 hours.

Lightly grease muffin pans. Shape dough into 1-inch balls; place 3 balls in each muffin cup. Cover and let rise in a warm place (85°), free from drafts, 1 hour or until doubled in bulk. Bake at 400° for 12 to 15 minutes or until brown. Yield: 1½ dozen. *Rena C. Nixon,*
*Mount Airy, North Carolina.*

## PARKER HOUSE REFRIGERATOR ROLLS

2 packages dry yeast
1 cup warm water (105° to 115°)
½ cup sugar
1½ teaspoons salt
⅔ cup shortening
1 cup water
2 eggs, beaten
6 cups all-purpose flour
Melted butter or margarine

Dissolve yeast in 1 cup warm water; set aside.

Combine sugar, salt, shortening, and 1 cup water in a small saucepan; heat, stirring often, until shortening melts. Cool to 105° to 115°. Combine yeast mixture, shortening mixture, and eggs in a large mixing bowl. Gradually stir in flour.

Turn dough out onto a floured surface, and knead until smooth and elastic (5 to 8 minutes). Place in a well-greased bowl, turning to grease top; cover and refrigerate 1½ hours.

Punch dough down; turn out onto a floured surface. Roll out to ¼-inch thickness. Cut into 2½-inch circles, and brush with melted butter. Make a crease across each circle, and fold one half over. Gently press edges to seal. Place on greased cookie sheets, and let rise in a warm place (85°), free from drafts, 1 hour or until doubled in bulk. Bake at 400° for 15 minutes or until golden brown. Brush with melted butter. Yield: about 3 dozen.

*Mrs. Michael A. Cohen,*
*Havre de Grace, Maryland.*

# Serve This Christmas Quiche Anytime

Leigh Ann Ball of Fort Lauderdale, Florida, says she doesn't reserve her Quiche Noël for holidays only. "Green pepper and red pimiento pieces decorate the top, and that makes it so pretty for Christmas parties," she says. "But I serve it anytime I want something quick and filling."

Her quiche combines the flavors of chicken, Cheddar cheese, onion, green pepper, and pimiento in a tasty dish suited for breakfast, a light lunch, or a late-night supper. "I can whip it up in no time," says Leigh Ann. "I serve it with a tossed salad or fresh fruit to make a full meal."

## QUICHE NOEL

Pastry for 9-inch deep-dish pie
¾ cup cubed cooked chicken
1 cup (4 ounces) shredded Cheddar
  cheese
¼ cup chopped green pepper
2 tablespoons chopped pimiento
6 eggs, beaten
1 cup half-and-half
1 tablespoon instant minced onion
½ to ¾ teaspoon seasoned salt
¼ teaspoon white pepper

Line a 9-inch quiche dish or piepan with pastry; trim excess pastry around edges. Prick bottom and sides of pastry with a fork. Bake at 400° for 3 minutes; remove from oven, and gently prick with a fork. Bake 5 minutes longer. Let cool on rack.

Sprinkle chicken, cheese, green pepper, and pimiento in prepared pastry shell. Combine remaining ingredients, beating well; pour into prepared pastry shell. Bake at 425° for 30 to 40 minutes or until set. Let stand 10 minutes before serving. Yield: one 9-inch quiche.

*Leigh Ann Ball,*
*Fort Lauderdale, Florida.*

# Warm Up With Chili

A bowl of spicy chili is one of the best warm-ups on a cold winter day. Many chili-lovers like to individualize the basic recipe—making it as fiery as they choose. A generous amount of chili powder goes into Texas-Style Chili, while Company Chili gets extra hotness from smoked sausage and spicy brown mustard.

If you're pushed for time, try Virginia Mathews' recipe for Easy Chili. It's simple to prepare, and you'll probably have most of the ingredients on hand. Serve it with a basket of crackers or chips for a delightfully satisfying winter meal.

## EASY CHILI

1 pound ground beef
1 onion, chopped
1 (8-ounce) can tomato sauce
1 cup water
½ cup chopped green pepper
1½ to 2 tablespoons chili powder
½ teaspoon salt
¼ teaspoon pepper
Dash of ground oregano
2 (16-ounce) cans kidney beans,
  undrained

Combine ground beef and onion in a Dutch oven; cook until beef is browned, stirring to crumble meat. Drain off pan drippings. Add remaining ingredients except kidney beans; cover and simmer 20 minutes. Stir in kidney beans; continue to cook, covered, 45 minutes. Remove cover, and cook an additional 15 minutes. Yield: 2 quarts.

*Virginia M. Mathews,*
*Jacksonville, Florida.*

## CHEESY CHILI

1 pound ground beef
1 medium onion, chopped
1 medium-size green pepper, chopped
1 (6-ounce) can button mushrooms,
  drained and halved
2 cloves garlic, minced
3 cups water
1 (16-ounce) can kidney beans, drained
2 (6-ounce) cans tomato paste
1 (16-ounce) can whole tomatoes,
  undrained and chopped
¼ to ½ cup diced ripe olives
1 hot pepper, diced
2 tablespoons chili powder
1½ tablespoons brown sugar
½ teaspoon salt
½ teaspoon garlic salt
¼ teaspoon ground cumin
¼ teaspoon pepper
Shredded Cheddar cheese

Combine ground beef, onion, green pepper, mushrooms, and garlic in a Dutch oven; cook until beef is browned, stirring to crumble meat. Drain off pan drippings. Add next 12 ingredients, mixing well. Cover and simmer 1½ hours. Sprinkle individual servings with cheese. Yield: 3 quarts. *Stephanie Creim,*
*Bellingham, Washington.*

## CHILI CON CARNE

1½ pounds boneless round steak, cut into
  ½-inch cubes
2 tablespoons vegetable oil
1 (15-ounce) can tomato sauce
1½ cups water
1 beef-flavored bouillon cube
2 tablespoons chili powder
2 teaspoons dried whole oregano
1 teaspoon salt
1 teaspoon ground cumin
1 teaspoon minced garlic
½ teaspoon hot sauce
2 tablespoons cornmeal
2 (16-ounce) cans kidney beans, undrained

Brown meat in oil in a Dutch oven. Add tomato sauce, 1½ cups water, and bouillon cube; cover and simmer 30 minutes. Add next 6 ingredients; cover and simmer 40 minutes, stirring occasionally. Stir in cornmeal and beans. Cover and simmer 30 minutes, adding additional water if necessary. Yield: about 2 quarts. *Charlie R. Hester, Austin, Texas.*

## TEXAS-STYLE CHILI

3 pounds ground chuck
1 pound hot bulk sausage
3 medium onions, chopped
4 cloves garlic, minced
¼ cup chili powder
2 tablespoons all-purpose flour
1 tablespoon sugar
1 tablespoon ground oregano
1 teaspoon salt
2 (28-ounce) cans whole tomatoes, undrained and chopped
3 (16-ounce) cans kidney beans, drained

Combine ground chuck, sausage, onion, and garlic in a Dutch oven; cook until meat is browned, stirring to crumble meat. Drain off pan drippings. Stir in next 6 ingredients. Cover and simmer 1 hour, stirring occasionally. Add beans, and simmer an additional 20 minutes. Yield: about 5 quarts.
*Faye Beard, Lipscomb, Alabama.*

## COMPANY CHILI

1 pound ground beef
1 pound hot smoked sausage, sliced
1 cup chopped onion
1 (28-ounce) can pinto beans, undrained
1 (28-ounce) can whole tomatoes, undrained and chopped
½ cup catsup
1 tablespoon chili powder
2 teaspoons brown sugar
1 teaspoon spicy brown mustard
½ teaspoon salt

Combine ground beef, sausage, and onion in a Dutch oven; cook until beef is browned, stirring to crumble meat. Drain off pan drippings.

Drain pinto beans, reserving liquid. Add liquid to Dutch oven; stir in remaining ingredients except beans. Cover and simmer 45 minutes. Stir in beans. Cook an additional 15 minutes. Yield: about 3 quarts. *Mary H. Gilliam, Cartersville, Virginia.*

*Tip: If soups, stews, or other foods are too salty, add 1 teaspoon of vinegar and 1 teaspoon of sugar and reheat.*

# Stir Up A Pumpkin Dessert

With this recipe, Mrs. Vernon Richardson of Orange Park, Florida, took first place honors at a Jacksonville cooking contest. You'll get the next blue ribbon when you serve this skillfully seasoned pumpkin dessert to your family and friends.

## PUMPKIN MOLD

1 (16-ounce) can pumpkin
½ cup water
2 envelopes unflavored gelatin
¼ cup water
¼ cup firmly packed brown sugar
1 cup super fine sugar
1½ teaspoons pumpkin pie spice
1 teaspoon brandy extract
1 tablespoon lemon juice
¼ teaspoon salt
1 cup whipping cream
2 tablespoons super fine sugar
2 egg whites
⅛ teaspoon cream of tartar
2 tablespoons super fine sugar
Brandy-Macadamia Sauce

Combine pumpkin and ½ cup water in container of an electric blender; process on medium speed 2 minutes. Soften gelatin in ¼ cup water. Combine pumpkin mixture, gelatin, brown sugar, and 1 cup super fine sugar in a saucepan; cook over low heat until gelatin dissolves, stirring occasionally. Remove from heat; let cool 5 minutes, stirring occasionally. Stir in pumpkin pie spice, brandy extract, lemon juice, and salt. Cool.

Beat whipping cream until foamy; gradually add 2 tablespoons super fine sugar, beating until soft peaks form. Fold whipped cream into pumpkin mixture. Beat egg whites (at room temperature) and cream of tartar until foamy. Gradually add 2 tablespoons super fine sugar, beating until soft peaks form. Fold into pumpkin mixture. Spoon into a lightly oiled 2-quart mold. Chill until firm. Unmold and serve with Brandy-Macadamia Sauce. Yield: 10 servings.

*Brandy-Macadamia Sauce:*

¼ cup firmly packed brown sugar
1½ teaspoons arrowroot
¼ teaspoon pumpkin pie spice
½ cup boiling water
1 tablespoon butter or margarine
2 tablespoons brandy extract
½ teaspoon vanilla extract
¼ cup chopped macadamia nuts

Combine brown sugar, arrowroot, and pumpkin pie spice in a small saucepan. Stir in water, mixing well; cook over medium heat, stirring constantly, until thickened and bubbly. Stir in remaining ingredients. Yield: about ⅔ cup. *Mrs. Vernon Richardson, Orange Park, Florida.*

# Baked Crabmeat At Its Best

William Phillips of Guntersville, Alabama, shares this outstanding recipe for Crabmeat Imperial. The crabmeat is enhanced by sautéed green pepper, celery, and pimiento, and is lightly seasoned to complement the fresh ocean taste. Phillips suggests baking and serving the mixture in baking shells or individual casseroles. A dollop of mayonnaise, pimiento strips, and a sliced olive top each attractive serving.

## CRABMEAT IMPERIAL

¼ cup chopped green pepper
¼ cup chopped celery
1 (2-ounce) jar chopped pimiento, drained
2 tablespoons butter or margarine
1 teaspoon Old Bay seasoning
1 teaspoon butter-flavored salt
2 teaspoons chopped fresh parsley
½ teaspoon prepared mustard
Dash of hot sauce
Dash of red pepper
1 egg, beaten
3 tablespoons mayonnaise
1 pound fresh crabmeat, drained and flaked
Mayonnaise
Pimiento strips (optional)
Sliced pimiento-stuffed olives (optional)

Sauté green pepper, celery, and pimiento in butter in a medium skillet until tender. Stir in next 6 ingredients. Combine egg and 3 tablespoons mayonnaise; stir in vegetable mixture. Gently stir in crabmeat. Spoon into four 6-ounce individual baking shells or dishes. Top each with a dollop of mayonnaise; garnish each with 2 pimiento strips and 1 olive slice, if desired. Bake at 375° for 15 minutes. Broil 5 inches from heat for 3 minutes. Yield: 4 servings. *William Phillips, Guntersville, Alabama.*

# Beverages With Spirit

When the calendar is turned to the holiday season, treat your guests to one of these smooth beverages for spirited sipping. Irish Cream Nog, enriched with eggs and thickened with whipping cream, gets its flavor from Irish cream liqueur and a dash of nutmeg.

### IRISH CREAM NOG

6 eggs
½ cup sugar
3 cups milk
1½ cups Irish cream liqueur
½ teaspoon ground nutmeg
½ cup whipping cream, whipped
Ground nutmeg

Beat eggs until foamy at medium speed of an electric mixer. Gradually add sugar, beating 5 minutes or until thick and lemon colored. Reduce speed to low; gradually add milk, liqueur, and ½ teaspoon nutmeg, beating until combined. Chill thoroughly. To serve, stir in whipped cream, and sprinkle with additional nutmeg. Yield: 2 quarts.

### CAFE CREAM

1 quart vanilla ice cream
1 cup cold coffee
½ cup brandy
½ cup Kahlúa or other coffee-flavored liqueur
Cracked ice

Combine half the first 4 ingredients in container of electric blender. Gradually add enough ice, processing until smooth, to make 3½ cups liquid. Repeat procedure with remaining ingredients. Serve over ice. Yield: 7 cups.
*Frances Ponder,*
*Cullman, Alabama.*

*Irish Cream Nog, a festive version of eggnog, gets its warmth from Irish cream liqueur.*

# From Our Kitchen To Yours

What's for dinner? You probably hear that question all the time, and sometimes you're caught without the answer. But don't panic. Here's help.

## About Meal Planning

**Plan Ahead**—Advance planning is especially important during the holidays, but you should always plan your meals at least one week in advance. Write down menus for each day including breakfast, lunch, and dinner or whatever combination of meals you're responsible for preparing. Also, post the menus on the refrigerator or kitchen bulletin board so the rest of the family can see what's for dinner.

After your meals are planned, make a market order for the groceries you'll need. Be sure to check recipes and supplies on hand before making the final marketing list.

**Plan With a Flair**—To get started planning your menus, choose a focus for each meal. Center the menus around a sandwich, meat, main-dish salad, or casserole. Then plan the accompaniments carefully. Don't match fried chicken with french-fried potatoes or stuffed pork chops with stuffed baked potatoes. As a rule of thumb, let variety be your guide. By serving a variety of foods prepared in a variety of ways, chances are you'll be providing nutritious as well as attractive meals.

Consider the color, flavor, texture, shape, and size of each part of a meal. Foods come in a multitude of colors, so be sure to include contrasting ones. Instead of serving fried chicken, creamed potatoes, and cauliflower—all white and beige, substitute brightly colored broccoli or carrots for the cauliflower. Colorful garnishes also help. Simple extras such as orange twists, parsley sprigs, or lemon wedges add sparkle to your dinner plates.

Don't repeat flavors. If you've put tomatoes in a salad, avoid serving a broiled tomato as a side dish. Be sure to introduce milder flavors before strong ones. If you want your entrée to be fully appreciated, don't serve a spicy, full-flavored appetizer—it tends to overpower the taste buds. Remember, plan only one highly seasoned or strong-flavored item for each meal.

Try combinations of foods with smooth and soft textures with those having crispy, crunchy ones. Serve at least one food with crunch at each meal. Some crisp foods are raw vegetables, some fruits, vegetables cooked just until crisp-tender, nuts, seeds, and crusty breads.

Temperature variations of foods in a meal are especially pleasing to the palate. Cold soups, chilled fruit, and vegetable salads provide welcome contrasts to hot entrées and side dishes. Always serve food at the proper temperature—serve hot foods hot and cold foods cold, not lukewarm.

Vary the shapes of food just as you would the color and texture. For example, meatballs, new potatoes, and brussels sprouts create a poor menu because of the repetitious shapes. Sliced meat loaf and green beans would make better partners for new potatoes. Don't include too many mixtures. For instance, don't serve beef stew, Waldorf salad, and peas and carrots.

**Consider Your Time**—When you're planning, always consider the time you have available. Don't overextend yourself. If time is limited, plan quick and easy dishes that can be prepared in minutes instead of hours. Plan to use leftovers, convenience foods, and the neighborhood deli. When you have time, cook in bulk and freeze serving-size amounts. With careful planning, you can prepare delicious, nutritious meals in a hurry.

## Some Other Tips

**Food Saver**—With a food processor or electric blender, you'll never again have to throw away those dried-out bread slices or leftover hot dog and hamburger buns. Just tear the bread into pieces and process in either appliance for a few seconds. Store the breadcrumbs in an airtight container, and freeze. Use the same procedure for stale crackers, and you'll always have a supply of cracker crumbs available.

**Party Preparation**—Before your next party, let time work for you by preparing as many things ahead as possible. Some casseroles, breads, cakes, sauces, and pies can be prepared in advance and frozen. Gelatin salads can usually be made one or two days before the party. Also, make ice cubes ahead of time and store in plastic bags in the freezer.

**Cooking for a Crowd**—Plan your menu so you can utilize several cooking appliances rather than just the oven. Don't forget to use the stove top, microwave, electric skillet, and toaster oven when you're preparing your holiday meals.

**Congealed Salad Making**—Ever been ready to pour your gelatin mixture into a mold to congeal, but were unsure of the size of your mold? Most gelatin molds do not have a size stamped on them. You can easily determine the capacity of a mold by measuring the number of cups of water it will hold.

# Soups To Start A Meal

What better way to start a dinner party than with an appetizer soup. Whether served formally at the table or offered in mugs on a tray in the living room, a warm soup will spark both appetites and your party.

A light way to begin an Oriental menu is with Egg Flower Soup; lacy strands of egg float alongside cubes of tofu in a base of chicken broth. When the weather turns cold, warm up your guests with Cheesy Anytime Soup or Cream of Broccoli Soup. Swedish Fruit Soup is made from dried fruit and brings a touch of spring or summer to winter tables.

## SWEDISH FRUIT SOUP

1¾ cups mixed dried fruit
½ cup golden raisins
1 (3-inch) stick cinnamon
4 cups water
2¼ cups unsweetened pineapple juice
½ cup red currant jelly
¼ cup sugar
2 tablespoons quick-cooking tapioca, uncooked
¼ teaspoon salt
1 medium orange, unpeeled, sliced, and seeded

Slice dried fruit in half. Combine dried fruit, raisins, cinnamon, and 4 cups water in a Dutch oven; stir well. Bring to a boil. Reduce heat; simmer, uncovered, 30 minutes or until fruit is tender.

Stir in remaining ingredients. Bring to a boil; reduce heat and simmer 15 minutes, stirring occasionally. Cover and chill 3 to 4 hours. Yield: 7 cups.
*Doris Garton,*
*Shenandoah, Virginia.*

*Tip: Placing a jar of jam, jelly, syrup, or honey in a pan of simmering water dissolves the sugar crystals on top.*

## SHRIMP-VEGETABLE BISQUE

1 pound zucchini, thinly sliced
1 cup thinly sliced carrot
½ cup chopped celery
½ cup sliced green onion
½ cup chicken broth
1¾ cups skim milk
½ cup water
1 (10¾-ounce) can cream of mushroom soup, undiluted
½ cup plain yogurt
1 (4½-ounce) can small shrimp, drained and rinsed
1 tablespoon dry white wine

Combine vegetables and chicken broth in a Dutch oven; cover and simmer 15 to 20 minutes or until vegetables are tender.

Spoon half of vegetable mixture into container of electric blender, and process until smooth. Repeat procedure with remaining mixture.

Return vegetable mixture to Dutch oven; stir in remaining ingredients. Cook over low heat, stirring constantly, until thoroughly heated. Yield: 10 cups.
*Marie Hayman,*
*Lake Worth, Florida.*

## EGG FLOWER SOUP

1½ tablespoons cornstarch
⅓ cup water
6 cups chicken broth
1 cup (8 ounces) cubed tofu (soy bean curd)
1 (2- x 1- x ⅛-inch) slice gingerroot
½ teaspoon sugar
⅛ teaspoon pepper
3 eggs, beaten
1 teaspoon sesame seed oil
1 green onion, minced

Combine cornstarch and water; stir well, and set aside.

Bring broth to a boil. Add tofu, gingerroot, sugar, and pepper; boil mixture 1 minute.

Stir in cornstarch mixture; boil 1 minute. Remove from heat. Slowly pour beaten egg into soup, stirring constantly. The egg forms lacy strands as it cooks. Remove gingerroot.

Stir in sesame seed oil, and sprinkle with onion. Serve immediately. Yield: about 7 cups.
*Sue-Sue Hartstern,*
*Louisville, Kentucky.*

## CREAM OF BROCCOLI SOUP

2 (10-ounce) packages frozen chopped
   broccoli
2 (10¾-ounce) cans cream of mushroom
   soup, undiluted
2⅔ cups milk
3 tablespoons butter or margarine
¼ to ½ teaspoon dried whole tarragon
Dash of pepper

Cook broccoli according to package
directions; drain well. Add remaining
ingredients, and cook over low heat
until thoroughly heated. Yield: about 8
cups.
*Mary Pappas,*
*Richmond, Virginia.*

## CHEESY ANYTIME SOUP

¼ cup butter or margarine
¼ cup plus 2 tablespoons all-purpose flour
2 (10¾-ounce) cans chicken broth,
   undiluted
2 cups milk
¼ teaspoon white pepper
2 tablespoons chopped pimiento
¼ cup plus 2 tablespoons dry white wine
½ teaspoon Worcestershire sauce
¼ teaspoon hot sauce
2 cups (8 ounces) shredded sharp Cheddar
   cheese

Melt butter in a heavy saucepan over
low heat; add flour, stirring until
smooth. Cook 1 minute, stirring constantly. Gradually add broth and milk;
cook over medium heat, stirring constantly, until thickened and bubbly. Stir
in pepper.
Add next 4 ingredients. Heat to boiling, stirring frequently. Remove from
heat; add cheese, and stir until cheese
melts. Serve immediately. Yield: about
5 cups.
*Jodie McCoy,*
*Tulsa, Oklahoma.*

# Spice Cakes–Rich With Tradition

Everyone remembers old-fashioned
spice cakes—rich with molasses and
warm with a fragrant blend of cinnamon, allspice, cloves, and nutmeg. We
found several versions of this classic
dessert among our readers' recipes, such
as Dark Spice Cake, shared by Mrs.
Lamar McMath of Jacksonville, Florida.
She mixes the batter with sour cream
and bakes it in a tube pan.

Cheryll Tuthill of Virginia Beach says
she added more seasonings to a basic
recipe to create her favorite layer cake,
Spice Cake With Caramel Frosting. She
also substituted molasses for some of
the sugar in the original recipe and
added white wine for richer flavor.

## DARK SPICE CAKE

1 cup butter or margarine, softened
1 cup sugar
6 eggs, separated
1 cup molasses
4 cups all-purpose flour
1 teaspoon salt
1 teaspoon ground allspice
1 teaspoon ground cinnamon
1 teaspoon ground cloves
1 teaspoon ground nutmeg
1 (8-ounce) carton commercial sour cream
1 teaspoon baking soda
Powdered sugar

Cream butter; gradually add sugar,
beating until light and fluffy. Add egg
yolks and molasses, beating well.
Combine flour, salt, and spices; mix
well. Combine sour cream and baking
soda; mix well. Add flour mixture to
creamed mixture alternately with sour
cream mixture, beginning and ending
with flour mixture.
Beat the egg whites (at room temperature) until stiff peaks form; gently
fold into batter.
Pour batter into a greased and
floured 10-inch tube pan. Bake at 300°
for 1 hour and 40 minutes or until a
wooden pick inserted in center comes
out clean. Cool in pan 10 minutes; remove from pan, and cool completely.
Sprinkle with powdered sugar. Yield:
one 10-inch cake.
*Mrs. E. Lamar McMath,*
*Jacksonville, Florida.*

## SPICE CAKE WITH CARAMEL FROSTING

2¼ cups all-purpose flour
1 cup sugar
1 tablespoon baking powder
1 teaspoon salt
1 teaspoon ground cinnamon
½ teaspoon ground nutmeg
¼ teaspoon ground allspice
¼ teaspoon ground cloves
½ cup shortening
1 tablespoon molasses
¾ cup dry white wine
1½ teaspoons vanilla extract
¼ cup milk
2 eggs
Caramel frosting (recipe follows)
½ cup finely chopped pecans

Combine first 8 ingredients in a large
mixing bowl; mix well. Add shortening,
molasses, wine, and vanilla; beat on
medium speed of electric mixer until ingredients are well blended. Add milk
and eggs, one at a time, beating well
after each addition. Beat mixture 2 minutes on medium speed of electric mixer.
Pour batter into 2 greased and
floured 9-inch round cakepans. Bake at
325° for 25 minutes or until a wooden
pick inserted in center comes out clean.
Cool in pans 10 minutes; remove from
pans, and cool completely. Spread caramel frosting between layers and on sides
of cake; add pecans to remaining frosting, and spread on top of cake. Yield:
one 2-layer cake.

*Caramel Frosting:*

½ cup butter or margarine
1 cup firmly packed brown sugar
3 to 4 tablespoons milk
3 cups sifted powdered sugar
1 teaspoon vanilla extract

Melt butter in a medium saucepan.
Add brown sugar, and cook 1 minute
over low heat. Stir in remaining ingredients, and beat until smooth, adding
more milk if necessary for proper
spreading consistency. (Frosting will be
thin.) Yield: enough for one 2-layer
cake.
*Cheryll Tuthill,*
*Virginia Beach, Virginia.*

*Tip: To keep cake layers from sticking
in pan, grease the bottom and sides of
pan and line bottom with waxed paper.
(Trace outline of pan on waxed paper
and cut out.) Pour batter in pan and
bake. Invert cake layer on rack to
cool; gently peel off waxed paper while
cake is still warm.*

# Appendices

## EQUIVALENT WEIGHTS AND MEASURES

| Food | Weight or Count | Measure or Yield |
|---|---|---|
| Apples | 1 pound (3 medium) | 3 cups sliced |
| Bacon | 8 slices cooked | ½ cup crumbled |
| Bananas | 1 pound (3 medium) | 2½ cups sliced, or about 2 cups mashed |
| Bread | 1 pound | 12 to 16 slices |
| | About 1½ slices | 1 cup soft crumbs |
| Butter or margarine | 1 pound | 2 cups |
| | ¼ - pound stick | ½ cup |
| Cabbage | 1 pound head | 4½ cups shredded |
| Candied fruit or peels | ½ pound | 1¼ cups cut |
| Carrots | 1 pound | 3 cups shredded |
| Cheese, American or Cheddar | 1 pound | About 4 cups shredded |
| cottage | 1 pound | 2 cups |
| cream | 3 - ounce package | 6 tablespoons |
| Chocolate morsels | 6 - ounce package | 1 cup |
| Cocoa | 1 pound | 4 cups |
| Coconut, flaked or shredded | 1 pound | 5 cups |
| Coffee | 1 pound | 80 tablespoons (40 cups perked) |
| Corn | 2 medium ears | 1 cup kernels |
| Cornmeal | 1 pound | 3 cups |
| Crab, in shell | 1 pound | ¾ to 1 cup flaked |
| Crackers, chocolate wafers | 19 wafers | 1 cup crumbs |
| graham crackers | 14 squares | 1 cup fine crumbs |
| saltine crackers | 28 crackers | 1 cup finely crushed |
| vanilla wafers | 22 wafers | 1 cup finely crushed |
| Cream, whipping | 1 cup (½ pint) | 2 cups whipped |
| Dates, pitted | 1 pound | 3 cups chopped |
| | 8 - ounce package | 1½ cups chopped |
| Eggs | 5 large | 1 cup |
| whites | 8 to 11 | 1 cup |
| yolks | 12 to 14 | 1 cup |
| Flour, all-purpose | 1 pound | 3½ cups |
| cake | 1 pound | 4¾ to 5 cups sifted |
| whole wheat | 1 pound | 3½ cups unsifted |
| Green pepper | 1 large | 1 cup diced |
| Lemon | 1 medium | 2 to 3 tablespoons juice; 2 teaspoons grated rind |
| Lettuce | 1 pound head | 6¼ cups torn |
| Lime | 1 medium | 1½ to 2 tablespoons juice |
| Macaroni | 4 ounces (1 cup) | 2¼ cups cooked |
| Marshmallows | 11 large | 1 cup |
| | 10 miniature | 1 large marshmallow |
| Marshmallows, miniature | ½ pound | 4½ cups |
| Milk | | |
| evaporated | 5.33 - ounce can | ⅔ cup |
| evaporated | 13 - ounce can | 1⅝ cups |
| sweetened condensed | 14 - ounce can | 1¼ cups |
| Mushrooms | 3 cups raw (8 ounces) | 1 cup sliced cooked |
| Nuts | | |
| almonds | 1 pound | 1 to 1¾ cups nutmeats |
| | 1 pound shelled | 3½ cups nutmeats |
| peanuts | 1 pound | 2¼ cups nutmeats |
| | 1 pound shelled | 3 cups |
| pecans | 1 pound | 2¼ cups nutmeats |
| | 1 pound shelled | 4 cups |
| walnuts | 1 pound | 1⅔ cups nutmeats |
| | 1 pound shelled | 4 cups |

| Food | Weight or Count | Measure or Yield |
|------|-----------------|------------------|
| Oats, quick-cooking | 1 cup | 1¾ cups cooked |
| Onion | 1 medium | ½ cup chopped |
| Orange | 1 medium | ⅓ cup juice and 2 tablespoons grated rind |
| Peaches | 4 medium | 2 cups sliced |
| Pears | 4 medium | 2 cups sliced |
| Potatoes, white | 3 medium | 2 cups cubed cooked or 1¾ cups mashed |
| sweet | 3 medium | 3 cups sliced |
| Raisins, seedless | 1 pound | 3 cups |
| Rice, long-grain | 1 cup | 3 to 4 cups cooked |
| pre-cooked | 1 cup | 2 cups cooked |
| Shrimp, raw in shell | 1½ pounds | 2 cups (¾ pound) cleaned, cooked |
| Spaghetti | 7 ounces | About 4 cups cooked |
| Strawberries | 1 quart | 4 cups sliced |
| Sugar, brown | 1 pound | 2⅓ cups firmly packed |
| powdered | 1 pound | 3½ cups unsifted |
| granulated | 1 pound | 2 cups |

## EQUIVALENT MEASUREMENTS

| | | | | | |
|---|---|---|---|---|---|
| 3 teaspoons ................. | 1 tablespoon | | 2 cups ................... | 1 pint (16 fluid ounces) |
| 4 tablespoons.............. | ¼ cup | | 4 cups ................... | 1 quart |
| 5⅓ tablespoons.............. | ⅓ cup | | 4 quarts ................. | 1 gallon |
| 8 tablespoons.............. | ½ cup | | ⅛ cup.................... | 2 tablespoons |
| 16 tablespoons.............. | 1 cup | | ⅓ cup.................... | 5 tablespoons plus 1 teaspoon |
| 2 tablespoons (liquid) ... | 1 ounce | | ⅔ cup.................... | 10 tablespoons plus 2 teaspoons |
| 1 cup........................ | 8 fluid ounces | | ¾ cup.................... | 12 tablespoons |

## HANDY SUBSTITUTIONS

| Ingredient Called For | Substitution |
|-----------------------|--------------|
| 1 cup self-rising flour | 1 cup all-purpose flour plus 1 teaspoon baking powder and ½ teaspoon salt |
| 1 cup cake flour | 1 cup sifted all-purpose flour minus 2 tablespoons |
| 1 cup all-purpose flour | 1 cup cake flour plus 2 tablespoons |
| 1 teaspoon baking powder | ½ teaspoon cream of tartar plus ¼ teaspoon soda |
| 1 tablespoon cornstarch or arrowroot | 2 tablespoons all-purpose flour |
| 1 tablespoon tapioca | 1½ tablespoons all-purpose flour |
| 2 large eggs | 3 small eggs |
| 1 egg | 2 egg yolks (for custard) |
| 1 egg | 2 egg yolks plus 1 tablespoon water (for cookies) |
| 1 cup commercial sour cream | 1 tablespoon lemon juice plus evaporated milk to equal 1 cup; or 3 tablespoons butter plus ⅞ cup sour milk |
| 1 cup yogurt | 1 cup buttermilk or sour milk |
| 1 cup sour milk or buttermilk | 1 tablespoon vinegar or lemon juice plus sweet milk to equal 1 cup |
| 1 cup fresh milk | ½ cup evaporated milk plus ½ cup water |
| 1 cup fresh milk | 3 to 5 tablespoons nonfat dry milk solids in 1 cup water |
| 1 cup honey | 1¼ cups sugar plus ¼ cup liquid |
| 1 (1-ounce) square unsweetened chocolate | 3 tablespoons cocoa plus 1 tablespoon butter or margarine |
| 1 tablespoon fresh herbs | 1 teaspoon dried herbs or ¼ teaspoon powdered herbs |
| ¼ cup chopped fresh parsley | 1 tablespoon dehydrated parsley |
| 1 teaspoon dry mustard | 1 tablespoon prepared mustard |
| 1 pound fresh mushrooms | 6 ounces canned mushrooms |

# METRIC MEASURE/CONVERSION CHART

### Approximate Conversion to Metric Measures

| When You Know . . . | Multiply by . . . | To Find . . . | Symbol |
|---|---|---|---|
| | **Mass (weight)** | | |
| ounces | 28 | grams | g |
| pounds | 0.45 | kilograms | kg |
| | **Volume** | | |
| teaspoons | 5 | milliliters | ml |
| tablespoons | 15 | milliliters | ml |
| fluid ounces | 30 | milliliters | ml |
| cups | 0.24 | liters | l |
| pints | 0.47 | liters | l |
| quarts | 0.95 | liters | l |
| gallons | 3.8 | liters | l |

# APPROXIMATE TEMPERATURE CONVERSIONS—FAHRENHEIT TO CELSIUS

| | Fahrenheit (°F) | Celsius (°C) |
|---|---|---|
| **Freezer** | | |
| coldest area | -10° | -23° |
| overall | 0° | -17° |
| **Water** | | |
| freezes | 32° | 0° |
| simmers | 115° | 46° |
| scalds | 130° | 55° |
| boils (sea level) | 212° | 100° |
| Soft Ball | 234° to 240° | 112° to 115° |
| Firm Ball | 242° to 248° | 116° to 120° |
| Hard Ball | 250° to 268° | 121° to 131° |
| Slow Oven | 275° to 300° | 135° to 148° |

Fahrenheit to Celsius: Subtract 32 • Multiply by 5 • Divide by 9
Celsius to Fahrenheit: Multiply by 9 • Divide by 5 • Add 32

# COOKING MEASURE EQUIVALENTS

| Metric Cup | Volume (Liquid) | Liquid Solids (Butter) | Fine Powder (Flour) | Granular (Sugar) | Grain (Rice) |
|---|---|---|---|---|---|
| 1 | 250 ml | 200 g | 140 g | 190 g | 150 g |
| ¾ | 188 ml | 150 g | 105 g | 143 g | 113 g |
| ⅔ | 167 ml | 133 g | 93 g | 127 g | 100 g |
| ½ | 125 ml | 100 g | 70 g | 95 g | 75 g |
| ⅓ | 83 ml | 67 g | 47 g | 63 g | 50 g |
| ¼ | 63 ml | 50 g | 35 g | 48 g | 38 g |
| ⅛ | 31 ml | 25 g | 18 g | 24 g | 19 g |

# TIMETABLE FOR ROASTING BEEF AND LAMB

| Kind and Cut | Approximate Weight | Internal Temperature | Approximate Total Cooking Times at 325°F. |
|---|---|---|---|
| | pounds | | hours |
| **Beef** | | | |
| Standing ribs* (10-inch ribs) ........................... | 4 | 140°F. (rare) | 1¾ |
| | | 160°F. (medium) | 2 |
| | | 170°F. (well done) | 2½ |
| | 6 | 140°F. (rare) | 2 |
| | | 160°F. (medium) | 2½ |
| | | 170°F. (well done) | 3½ |
| | 8 | 140°F. (rare) | 2½ |
| | | 160°F. (medium) | 3 |
| | | 170°F. (well done) | 4½ |
| Rolled ribs ...................................... | 4 | 140°F. (rare) | 2 |
| | | 160°F. (medium) | 2½ |
| | | 170°F. (well done) | 3 |
| | 6 | 140°F. (rare) | 3 |
| | | 160°F. (medium) | 3¼ |
| | | 170°F. (well done) | 4 |
| Rolled rump ..................................... | 5 | 140°F. (rare) | 2¼ |
| | | 160°F. (medium) | 3 |
| | | 170°F. (well done) | 3¼ |
| Sirloin tip ...................................... | 3 | 140°F. (rare) | 1½ |
| | | 160°F. (medium) | 2 |
| | | 170°F. (well done) | 2¼ |
| **Lamb** | | | |
| Leg ........................................ | 6 to 7 | 180°F. (well done) | 3¾ |
| Leg (half) .................................... | 3 to 4 | 180°F. (well done) | 2½ to 3 |
| Cushion shoulder ............................... | 5 | 180°F. (well done) | 3 |
| Rolled shoulder ................................ | 3 | 180°F. (well done) | 2½ |
| | 5 | 180°F. (well done) | 3 |

*Standing ribs (8-inch ribs) allow 30 minutes longer.

# TIMETABLE FOR ROASTING SMOKED PORK

| Cut | Approximate Weight | Internal Temperature | Approximate Cooking Times at 325°F. |
|---|---|---|---|
| | pounds | | minutes per pound |
| **Ham (cook-before-eating)** | | | |
| Whole.................................... | 10 to 14 | 160°F. | 18 to 20 |
| Half..................................... | 5 to 7 | 160°F. | 22 to 25 |
| Shank portion............................ | 3 to 4 | 160°F. | 35 to 40 |
| Butt portion............................. | 3 to 4 | 160°F. | 35 to 40 |
| **Ham (fully cooked)** | | | |
| Whole.................................... | 10 to 12 | 140°F. | 15 to 18 |
| Half..................................... | 5 to 7 | 140°F. | 18 to 24 |
| Loin..................................... | 3 to 5 | 160°F. | 25 to 30 |
| Picnic shoulder (cook-before-eating)............. | 5 to 8 | 170°F. | 30 to 35 |
| Picnic shoulder (fully cooked).................. | 5 to 8 | 140°F. | 25 to 30 |
| Shoulder roll (butt)........................ | 2 to 4 | 170°F. | 35 to 40 |
| Canadian-style bacon........................ | 2 to 4 | 160°F. | 35 to 40 |

# TIMETABLE FOR ROASTING FRESH PORK

| Cut | Approximate Weight | Internal Temperature | Approximate Cooking Times at 325°F. |
|---|---|---|---|
| | pounds | | minutes per pound |
| Loin | | | |
| Center .............................. | 3 to 5 | 170°F. | 30 to 35 |
| Half................................ | 5 to 7 | 170°F. | 35 to 40 |
| End................................ | 3 to 4 | 170°F. | 40 to 45 |
| Roll................................ | 3 to 5 | 170°F. | 35 to 40 |
| Boneless top ....................... | 2 to 4 | 170°F. | 30 to 35 |
| Crown................................ | 4 to 6 | 170°F. | 35 to 40 |
| Picnic shoulder | | | |
| Bone-in............................. | 5 to 8 | 170°F. | 30 to 35 |
| Rolled.............................. | 3 to 5 | 170°F. | 35 to 40 |
| Boston shoulder .................... | 4 to 6 | 170°F. | 40 to 45 |
| Leg (fresh ham) | | | |
| Whole (bone-in).................... | 12 to 16 | 170°F. | 22 to 26 |
| Whole (boneless)................... | 10 to 14 | 170°F. | 24 to 28 |
| Half (bone-in)..................... | 5 to 8 | 170°F. | 35 to 40 |
| Tenderloin........................... | ½ to 1 | 170°F. | 45 to 60 |
| Back ribs............................ | | cooked well done | 1½ to 2½ hours |
| Country-style ribs .................. | | cooked well done | 1½ to 2½ hours |
| Spareribs............................ | | cooked well done | 1½ to 2½ hours |
| Pork Loaf............................ | | cooked well done | 1¾ hours |

# TIMETABLE FOR ROASTING POULTRY

| Kind of Poultry | Ready-to-Cook Weight | Oven Temperature | Internal Temperature | Approximate Total Roasting Time |
|---|---|---|---|---|
| | pounds | | | hours |
| Chicken (unstuffed)* | 1½ to 2 | 400° | 185°F. | 1 |
| | 2 to 2½ | 375° | 185°F. | 1 to 1¼ |
| | 2½ to 3 | 375° | 185°F. | 1¼ to 1½ |
| | 3 to 4 | 375° | 185°F. | 1½ to 2 |
| | 4 to 5 | 375° | 185°F. | 2 to 2½ |
| Capon (unstuffed) | 4 to 7 | 325° | 185°F. | 2½ to 3 |
| Cornish Hen (stuffed) | 1 to 1½ | 375° | 185°F. | 1 to 1¼ |
| Duckling (unstuffed) | 3½ to 5½ | 325° | 190°F. | 2 to 3 |
| Goose (unstuffed) | 7 to 9 | 350° | 190°F. | 2½ to 3 |
| | 9 to 11 | 350° | 190°F. | 3 to 3½ |
| | 11 to 13 | 350° | 190°F. | 3½ to 4 |
| Turkey (stuffed)† | 4 to 8 | 325° | 185°F. | 3 to 3¾ |
| | 8 to 12 | 325° | 185°F. | 3¾ to 4½ |
| | 12 to 16 | 325° | 185°F. | 4½ to 5½ |
| | 16 to 20 | 325° | 185°F. | 5½ to 6½ |
| | 20 to 24 | 325° | 185°F. | 6½ to 7½ |

*Stuffed chickens require about 5 additional minutes per pound.
†Unstuffed turkeys require about 5 minutes less per pound.

# TIMETABLE FOR COOKING FISH AND SHELLFISH

| Method of Cooking | Product | Market Form | Approximate Weight or Thickness | Cooking Temperature | Approximate Total Cooking Times |
|---|---|---|---|---|---|
| Baking | Fish | Dressed | 3 to 4 lbs. | 350°F. | 40 to 60 min. |
| | | Pan-dressed | ½ to 1 lb. | 350°F. | 25 to 30 min. |
| | | Steaks | ½ to 1 in. | 350°F. | 25 to 35 min. |
| | | Fillets | | 350°F. | 25 to 35 min. |
| | Clams | Live | | 450°F. | 15 min. |
| | Lobster | Live | ¾ to 1 lb. | 400°F. | 15 to 20 min. |
| | | | 1 to ½ lb. | 400°F. | 20 to 25 min. |
| | Oysters | Live | | 450°F. | 15 min. |
| | | Shucked | | 400°F. | 10 min. |
| | Scallops | Shucked | | 350°F. | 25 to 30 min. |
| | Shrimp | Headless | | 350°F. | 20 to 25 min. |
| | Spiny lobster tails | Headless | 4 oz. | 450°F. | 20 to 25 min. |
| | | | 8 oz. | 450°F. | 25 to 30 min. |
| Broiling | Fish | Pan-dressed | ½ to 1 lb. | | 10 to 15 min. |
| | | Steaks | ½ to 1 in. | | 10 to 15 min. |
| | | Fillets | | | 10 to 15 min. |
| | Clams | Live | | | 5 to 8 min. |
| | Lobster | Live | ¾ to 1 lb. | | 10 to 12 min. |
| | | | 1 to 1½ lbs. | | 12 to 15 min. |
| | Oysters | Live | | | 5 min. |
| | | Shucked | | | 5 min. |
| | Scallops | Shucked | | | 8 to 10 min. |
| | Shrimp | Headless | | | 8 to 10 min. |
| | Spiny lobster tails | Headless | 4 oz. | | 8 to 10 min. |
| | | | 8 oz. | | 10 to 12 min. |
| Cooking in water | Fish | Pan-dressed | ½ to 1 lb. | Simmer | 10 min. |
| | | Steaks | ½ to 1 in. | Simmer | 10 min. |
| | | Fillets | | Simmer | 10 min. |
| | Crabs | Live | | Simmer | 15 min. |
| | Lobster | Live | ¾ to 1 lb. | Simmer | 10 to 15 min. |
| | | | 1 to 1½ lbs. | Simmer | 15 to 20 min. |
| | Scallops | Shucked | | Simmer | 4 to 5 min. |
| | Shrimp | Headless | | Simmer | 5 min. |
| | Spiny lobster tails | Headless | 4 oz. | Simmer | 10 min. |
| | | | 8 oz. | Simmer | 15 min. |
| Deep-fat frying | Fish | Pan-dressed | ½ to 1 lb. | 375°F. | 2 to 4 min. |
| | | Steaks | ½ to 1 in. | 375°F. | 2 to 4 min. |
| | | Fillets | | 375°F. | 1 to 4 min. |
| | Clams | Shucked | | 375°F. | 2 to 3 min. |
| | Crabs | Soft-shell | ¼ lb. | 375°F. | 3 to 4 min. |
| | Lobster | Live | ¾ to 1 lb. | 350°F. | 3 to 4 min. |
| | | | 1 to 1½ lbs. | 350°F. | 4 to 5 min. |
| | Oysters | Shucked | | 375°F. | 2 min. |
| | Scallops | Shucked | | 350°F. | 3 to 4 min. |
| | Shrimp | Headless | | 350°F. | 2 to 3 min. |
| | Spiny lobster tails | Headless | 4 oz. | 350°F. | 3 to 4 min. |
| | | | 8 oz. | 350°F. | 4 to 5 min. |

## CANNED FOOD GUIDE

| Can Size | Number of Cups | Number of Servings | Foods |
|---|---|---|---|
| 8-ounce | 1 cup | 2 servings | Fruits, Vegetables |
| 10½- to 12-ounce (picnic) | 1¼ cups | 3 servings | Condensed Soups, Fruits and Vegetables, Meats and Fish, Specialties |
| 12-ounce (vacuum) | 1½ cups | 3 to 4 servings | Vacuum-Packed Corn |
| 14- to 16-ounce (No. 300) | 1¾ cups | 3 to 4 servings | Pork and Beans, Meat Products, Cranberry Sauce |
| 16- to 17-ounce (No. 303) | 2 cups | 4 servings | Principal Size for Fruits and Vegetables, Some Meat Products |
| 1 pound, 4 ounce (No. 2) | 2½ cups | 5 servings | Juices, Pineapple, Apple Slices |
| 27- to 29-ounce (No. 2½) | 3½ cups | 7 servings | Fruits, Some Vegetables (Pumpkin, Sauerkraut, Greens, Tomatoes) |
| 46-ounce (No. 3 cyl.) | 5¾ cups | 10 to 12 servings | Fruit and Vegetable Juices |
| 6½-pound (No. 10) | 12 to 13 cups | 25 servings | Institutional Size for Fruits and Vegetables |

## VEGETABLE GUIDE

### Selecting and Storing Vegetables

1. Buy fresh vegetables in season that are crisp, bright in color, and free from decay.
2. Compare prices of fresh versus frozen or canned vegetables. For example, if you are buying tomatoes for soup, you may find that canned ones would be the most economical. Some vegetables will remain fresh for a day or so after picking; others, like corn, start losing their flavor as soon as they are picked.
3. Buy only that amount of vegetables which can be stored properly. Although most vegetables should be washed and dried before storing, potatoes, onions, and garlic should never be washed. Do not soak fresh vegetables; too much moisture increases the possibility of spoilage and decay. Store immediately in vegetable crisper of refrigerator, or wrap in plastic wrap or plastic bags, and refrigerate. Immediate storage helps vegetables retain freshness and nutritional value. To prevent browning of leaves keep head lettuce intact without removing core or leaves until ready to use.
4. Put frozen vegetables into the freezer as soon as possible after purchase. Follow package directions about thawing before cooking. If frozen packages have been broken, rewrap in moistureproof paper or aluminum foil.
5. Store canned foods in a cool, dry place. Discard any cans that are puffed at ends—usually an indication of spoilage.

| Amount to Buy | Servings per Pound or Unit | Amount to Buy | Servings per Pound or Unit |
|---|---|---|---|
| Artichokes | 1 | Green Pepper | ½ to 1 whole per serving |
| Asparagus | 3 or 4 | Greens | 4 or 5 |
| Beans, snap or green | 4 | Mushrooms | 4 |
| Beets, diced, without tops | 4 | Okra | 4 |
| Broccoli | 3 or 4 | Onions, cooked | 3 or 4 |
| Brussels Sprouts | 4 to 6 | Peas | ¾ pound per serving |
| Cabbage | | Potatoes | 2 or 3 |
| Cooked | 3 or 4 | Rhubarb | 4 or 5 |
| Raw, diced or shredded | 6 to 8 | Rutabaga | 2 or 3 |
| Carrots | | Spinach | |
| Cooked | 3 or 4 | Cooked | 3 |
| Raw, diced or shredded | 5 or 6 | Raw | 6 |
| Cauliflower | 3 or 4 | Squash, summer | 3 or 4 |
| Celery, raw | 8 to 10 | Squash, winter | 2 or 3 |
| Corn | 1 to 2 ears per serving | Sweet Potatoes | 3 |
| Cucumber | 1 regular for 2 to 3 servings | Tomatoes | 4 or 5 |
| Dry Beans, Peas, or Lentils | 10 or 11 | Turnip | 4 or 5 |
| Eggplant | 4 | | |

# WINE SELECTION GUIDE

| Type of Wine | Specific Wine | Serve With | Temperature | When to Serve |
|---|---|---|---|---|
| Appetizer | Sherry (dry), Vermouth (dry), Port | Appetizers, nuts, cheese | Chilled, room temperature, over ice | Before dinner |
| Table Wines (white) | Rhine, Chablis, Sauterne, Light Muscat, Sauterne, Riesling, White Chianti | Fish, seafood, poultry, cheese, lamb, veal, eggs, lighter foods, pork (except ham) | Chilled | With dinner, any time, with or without food |
| Table Wines (red) | Rosé | Curry, patio parties, Chinese food, any food | Slightly chilled | With dinner, any time, with or without food |
| | Claret | Game, Italian food, beef, Hawaiian food | Slightly chilled | With dinner |
| | Chianti | Red meat, cheese, Roasts, game, Italian food | Slightly chilled | With dinner |
| | Burgundy | Cheese, Italian food, game, ham, heartier foods, roasts, steaks | Slightly chilled | With dinner, any time, with or without food |
| Sparkling Wines | Champagne, dry | Appetizers, fish, seafood, poultry, main courses, desserts, cheese, any festive meal | Chilled | Any time, with or without food |
| | Sparkling Burgundy | Appetizers, main courses, roasts, game, desserts | Chilled | Any time |
| Dessert Wines | Port, Muscatel, Tokay, Champagne (sweet), Sherry (cream), Madeira (sweet), Sauterne, Marsala, Malaga | Desserts, fruit, nuts, cheeses, cakes, pastries | Cool room temperature | After dinner With dessert |

# WINE BUYING GUIDE

The following size bottles give you approximate servings based on 3- to 3½-ounce servings for dinner wines and champagne; 2- to 2½-ounce servings for appetizer and dessert wines.

| Size | Ounces | Dinner Wines and Champagne | Appetizer and Dessert Wines |
|---|---|---|---|
| Fifth (4/5 qt.) | 25.6 | 8 servings | 8 to 12 servings |
| Tenth (4/5 pt.) | 12.8 | 4 servings | 4 to 6 servings |
| Split (2/5 pt.) | 6.4 | 2 servings | 2 servings |
| Quart | 32.0 | 10 servings | 10 to 14 servings |
| Pint | 16.0 | 5 servings | 5 to 7 servings |
| ½ Gallon | 64.0 | 20 servings | 20 to 30 servings |
| Gallon | 128.0 | 40 servings | 40 to 60 servings |
| Magnum | 52.0 | 16 servings | |

# COOKING HINTS

| | |
|---|---|
| **Baking** | Unless otherwise specified, always preheat the oven at least 20 minutes before baking. |
| **Browning** | For best results in browning food in a skillet, dry the food first on paper towels. |
| **Measuring** | Always measure accurately.<br>Level dry ingredients with top of a cup or a knife edge or a spoon handle.<br>Measure liquids in a cup so that the fluid is level with the top of the measuring line.<br>Measure solid shortening by packing it firmly in a graduated measuring cup. |
| **Storing** | Milk cartons make splendid freezing containers for stocks, soups, etc. They also serve well for freezing fish or shrimp, foods that should be frozen in water. |
| **Baking Powder** | Always use double-acting baking powder. |
| **Breads and Cakes** | To test for doneness in baking a butter or margarine cake, insert a straw or wire cake tester into the center of the cake in at least two places. The tester should come out clean if the cake is done.<br>The cake should be lightly browned and should be beginning to shrink from the pan's sides.<br>If the cake is pressed with a finger in the center, it should come back into shape at once.<br>If cake tests done, remove from oven, invert cakepan for 5 minutes (or time specified in the instructions); then loosen the cake from the sides and bottom of the pan. Invert it onto a plate or cake rack and turn it right side up on another cake rack so that air may circulate around it. This prevents sogginess.<br>A sponge cake should be tested for doneness in the same manner as a butter cake, but keep the sponge cake inverted until it is thoroughly cold. Then run a knife around the sides and across the bottom and remove from pan. Trim off any hard edges.<br>To test bread made with fruit or nuts, thump the crust and if it sounds hollow, remove the bread from the oven and cool on a wire rack.<br>Bread cooked with fruit or nuts should be tested with a straw in the center. The straw should come out perfectly clean if the bread is done. |
| **Butter** | When a recipe says "greased pan," grease the pan with solid shortening or an oil, unless butter is specified.<br>Do not use whipped margarine in place of butter unless the recipe calls for melting the butter. |
| **Candies** | The weather is a big factor in candymaking. On a hot, humid day it is advisable to cook candy 2° higher than in cold, dry weather. |
| **Eggs** | Unused or extra egg whites may be frozen and used as needed. Make meringues or angel pies with the whites later. Egg whites freeze well and do not need to be defrosted.<br>When boiling eggs, add 1 teaspoon salt to the water. This prevents a cracked egg from draining into the water. |
| **Fruit** | A whole lemon heated in hot water for 5 minutes will yield 1 or 2 tablespoons more juice than an unheated lemon. |
| **Sauces** | When a sauce curdles, remove pan from heat and plunge into a pan of cold water to stop cooking process. Beat sauce vigorously or pour into a blender and beat.<br>When making a cream or white sauce, melt butter, add flour, and blend well. Remove from heat before adding warmed milk. It should never lump. |
| **Seafood** | For improved texture and flavor with canned shrimp, soak shrimp for 1 hour in ice water; drain.<br>One pound raw shrimp yields about 2 cups cooked and peeled shrimp. |
| **Vegetables** | Cooking such vegetables as green peppers and cucumbers briefly in boiling water makes them more digestible than raw vegetables.<br>All strings can be easily removed from string beans after washing if they are plunged into boiling water for 5 minutes. Drain in colander and string.<br>New potatoes should be cooked in boiling water. Old potatoes should start in cold water and be brought to a boil.<br>When vegetables or other foods scorch in cooking, immediately remove the pan's cover and the contents and plunge the saucepan into cold water for 20 to 30 minutes. Wash saucepan and return contents and resume cooking.<br>Rub hands with parsley to remove any odor. |

# Glossary

**à la King**—Food prepared in a creamy white sauce containing mushrooms and red and/or green peppers

**à la Mode**—Food served with ice cream

**al Dente**—The point in the cooking of pasta at which it is still fairly firm to the tooth; that is, very slightly undercooked

**Aspic**—A jellied meat juice or a liquid held together with gelatin

**au Gratin**—Food served crusted with breadcrumbs or shredded cheese

**au Jus**—Meat served in its own juice

**Bake**—To cook food in an oven by dry heat

**Barbecue**—To roast meat slowly over coals on a spit or framework, or in an oven, basting intermittently with a special sauce

**Baste**—To spoon pan liquid over meats while they are roasting to prevent surface from drying

**Beat**—To mix vigorously with a brisk motion with spoon, fork, egg beater, or electric mixer

**Béchamel**—A white sauce of butter, flour, cream (not milk), and seasonings

**Bisque**—A thick, creamy soup usually of shellfish, but sometimes made of pureed vegetables

**Blanch**—To dip briefly into boiling water

**Blend**—To stir 2 or more ingredients together until well mixed

**Blintz**—A cooked crêpe stuffed with cheese or other filling

**Boil**—To cook food in boiling water or liquid that is mostly water (at 212°) in which bubbles constantly rise to the surface and burst

**Boiling-water-bath canning method**—Used for processing acid foods, such as fruits, tomatoes, pickled vegetables, and sauerkraut. These acid foods are canned safely at boiling temperatures in a water-bath canner

**Borscht**—Soup containing beets and other vegetables, usually with a meat stock base

**Bouillabaisse**—A highly seasoned fish soup or chowder containing two or more kinds of fish

**Bouillon**—Clear soup made by boiling meat in water

**Bouquet Garni**—Herbs tied in cheesecloth which are cooked in a mixture and removed before serving

**Bourguignon**—Name applied to dishes containing Burgundy and often brasied onions and mushrooms

**Braise**—To cook slowly with liquid or steam in a covered utensil. Less-tender cuts of meat may be browned slowly on all sides in a small amount of shortening, seasoned, and water added

**Bread, to**—To coat with crumbs, usually in combination with egg or other binder

**Broil**—To cook by direct heat, either under the heat of a broiler, over hot coals, or between two hot surfaces

**Broth**—A thin soup, or a liquid in which meat, fish, or vegetables have been boiled

**Capers**—Buds from a Mediterranean plant, usually packed in brine and used as a condiment in dressings or sauces

**Caramelize**—To cook white sugar in a skillet over medium heat, stirring constantly, until sugar forms a golden-brown syrup

**Casserole**—An ovenproof baking dish, usually with a cover; also the food cooked inside it

**Charlotte**—A molded dessert containing gelatin, usually formed in a glass dish or a pan that is lined with ladyfingers or pieces of cake

**Chop**—A cut of meat usually attached to a rib

**Chop, to**—To cut into pieces, with a sharp knife or kitchen shears

**Clarified butter**—Butter that has been melted and chilled. The solid is then lifted away from the liquid and discarded. Clarification heightens the smoke point of butter. Clarified butter will stay fresh in the refrigerator for at least 2 months

**Coat**—To cover completely, as in "coat with flour"

**Cocktail**—An appetizer; either a beverage or a light, highly seasoned food, served before a meal

**Compote**—Mixed fruit, raw or cooked, usually served in "compote" dishes

**Condiments**—Seasonings that enhance the flavor of foods with which they are served

**Consommé**—Clear broth made from meat

**Cool**—To let food stand at room temperature until not warm to the touch

**Court Bouillon**—A highly seasoned broth made with water and meat, fish or vegetables, and seasonings

**Cream, to**—To blend together, as sugar and butter, until mixture takes on a smooth, cream-like texture

**Cream, whipped**—Cream that has been whipped until it is stiff

**Crème de Cacao**—A chocolate-flavored liqueur

**Crème de Café**—A coffee-flavored liqueur

**Crêpes**—Very thin pancakes

**Croquette**—Minced food, shaped like a ball, patty, cone, or log, bound with a heavy sauce, breaded and fried

**Croutons**—Cubes of bread, toasted or fried, served with soups or salads

**Cruller**—A doughnut of twisted shape, very light in texture

**Cube, to**—To cut into cube-shaped pieces

**Curacao**—Orange-flavored liqueur

**Cut in, to**—To incorporate by cutting or chopping motions, as in cutting shortening into flour for pastry

**Demitasse**—A small cup of coffee served after dinner

**Devil, to**—To prepare with hot seasoning or sauce

**Dice**—To cut into small cubes

**Dissolve**—To mix a dry substance with liquid until the dry substance becomes a part of the solution

**Dot**—To scatter small bits of butter over top of a food

**Dredge**—To coat with something, usually flour or sugar

**Filé**—Powder made of sassafras leaves used to season and thicken foods

**Fillet**—Boneless piece of meat or fish

**Flambé**—To flame, as in Crêpes Suzette or in some meat cookery, using alcohol as the burning agent; flame causes caramelization, enhancing flavor

**Flan**—In France, a filled pastry; in Spain, a custard

**Florentine**—A food containing, or placed upon, spinach

**Flour, to**—To coat with flour

**Fold**—To add a whipped ingredient, such as cream or egg white to another ingredient by gentle over and under movement

**Frappé**—A drink whipped with ice to make a thick, frosty consistency

**Fricassee**—A stew, usually of poultry or veal

**Fritter**—Vegetable or fruit dipped into, or combined with, batter and fried

**Fry**—To cook in hot shortening

**Garnish**—A decoration for a food or drink

**Glaze (To make a shiny surface)**—In meat preparation, a jelled broth applied to meat surface; in breads and pastries, a wash of egg or syrup; for doughnuts and cakes, a sugar preparation for coating

**Grate**—To obtain small particle of food by rubbing on a grater or shredder

**Grill**—To broil under or over a source of direct heat

**Grits**—Coarsely ground dried corn, served boiled, or boiled and then fried

**Gumbo**—Soup or stew made with okra

**Herb**—Aromatic plant used for seasoning and garnishing foods

**Hollandaise**—A sauce made of butter, egg, and lemon juice or vinegar

**Hominy**—Whole corn grains from which hull and germ are removed

**Jardiniere**—Vegetables in a savory sauce or soup

**Julienne**—Vegetables cut into thin strips or a soup containing such vegetables

**Kahlúa**—A coffee-flavored liqueur

**Kirsch**—A cherry-flavored liqueur

**Knead**—To work a food (usually dough) by hand, using a folding-back and pressing-forward motion

**Marinade**—A seasoned liquid in which food is soaked

**Marinate, to**—To soak food in a seasoned liquid

**Meringue**—A whole family of egg white-sugar preparations including pie topping, poached meringue used to top custard, crisp meringue dessert shells, and divinity candy

**Mince**—To chop into very fine pieces

**Mornay**—White sauce with egg, cream, and cheese added

**Mousse**—A molded dish based on meat or sweet whipped cream stiffened with egg white and/or gelatin (if mousse contains ice cream, it is called bombe)

**Panbroil**—To cook over direct heat in an uncovered skillet containing little or no shortening

**Panfry**—To cook in an uncovered skillet in small amount of shortening

**Parboil**—To partially cook in boiling water before final cooking

**Pasta**—A large family of flour paste products, such as spaghetti, macaroni, and noodles

**Pâté (French for paste)**—A paste made of liver or meat

**Petit Four**—A small cake, which has been frosted and decorated

**Pilau or pilaf**—A dish of the Middle East consisting of rice and meat or vegetables in a seasoned stock

**Poach**—To cook in liquid held below the boiling point

**Pot Liquor**—The liquid in which vegetables have been boiled

**Preheat**—To turn on oven so that desired temperature will be reached before food is inserted for baking

**Puree**—A thick sauce or paste made by forcing cooked food through a sieve

**Reduce**—To boil down, evaporating liquid from a cooked dish

**Remoulade**—A rich mayonnaise-based sauce containing anchovy paste, capers, herbs, and mustard

**Render**—To melt fat away from surrounding meat

**Rind**—Outer shell or peel of melon or fruit

**Roast, to**—To cook in oven by dry heat (usually applied to meats)

**Roux**—A mixture of butter and flour used to thicken gravies and sauces; it may be white or brown, if mixture is browned before liquid is added

**Sauté**—To fry food lightly over fairly high heat in a small amount of fat in a shallow, open pan

**Scald**—(1) To heat milk just below the boiling point (2) To dip certain foods into boiling water before freezing them (also called blanching)

**Scallop**—A bivalve mollusk of which only the muscle hinge is eaten; also to bake a food in a sauce topped with crumbs

**Score**—To cut shallow gashes on surface of food, as in scoring fat on ham before glazing

**Sear**—To brown surface of meat over high heat to seal in juices

**Set**—Term used to describe the consistency of gelatin when it has jelled enough to unmold

**Shred**—Break into thread-like or stringy pieces, usually by rubbing over the surface of a vegetable shredder

**Simmer**—To cook gently at a temperature below boiling point

**Skewer**—To fasten with wooden or metal pins or skewers

**Soak**—To immerse in water for a period of time

**Soufflé**—A spongy hot dish, made from a sweet or savory mixture (often milk or cheese), lightened by stiffly beaten egg whites

**Steam**—To cook food with steam either in a pressure cooker, on a platform in a covered pan, or in a special steamer

**Steam-pressure canning method**—Used for processing low-acid foods, such as meats, fish, poultry, and most vegetables. A temperature higher than boiling is required to can these foods safely. The food is processed in a steam-pressure canner at 10 pounds' pressure (240°) to ensure that all spoilage micro-organisms are destroyed

**Steep**—To let food stand in not quite boiling water until the flavor is extracted

**Stew**—A mixture of meat or fish and vegetables cooked by simmering in its own juices and liquid, such as water and/or wine

**Stir-fry**—To cook quickly in oil over high heat, using light tossing and stirring motions to preserve shape of food

**Stock**—The broth in which meat, poultry, fish, or vegetables has been cooked

**Syrupy**—Thickened to about the consistency of egg white

**Toast, to**—To brown by direct heat, as in a toaster or under broiler

**Torte**—A round cake, sometimes made with breadcrumbs instead of flour

**Tortilla**—A mexican flat bread made of corn or wheat flour

**Toss**—To mix together with light tossing motions, in order not to bruise delicate food, such as salad greens

**Triple Sec**—An orange-flavored liqueur

**Veal**—Flesh of a milk-fed calf up to 14 weeks of age

**Velouté**—White sauce made of flour, butter, and a chicken or veal stock, instead of milk

**Vinaigrette**—A cold sauce of oil and vinegar flavored with parsley, finely chopped onions and other seasonings; served with cold meats or vegetables

**Whip**—To beat rapidly to increase air and increase volume

**Wok**—A round bowl-shaped metal cooking utensil of Chinese origin used for stir-frying and steaming (with rack inserted) of foods

# Recipe Title Index

*An alphabetical listing of every recipe by exact title*

**330    Recipe Title Index**

# Month-by-Month Index

*An alphabetical listing within the month of every food article and accompanying recipes*

**Month-by-Month Index**     337

# General Recipe Index

*A listing of every recipe by food category and/or major ingredient*

**Mustard**
German Mustard, Hot, 298
Homemade Mustard, Zesty, 55
Sauce, Light Mustard, 178

**Noodles**
Casserole, Eggplant and Noodle, 230
Casserole, Sausage and Noodle, 123
Chili with Noodles, 57
Spinach Noodles, Chicken and, 19

**Oatmeal**
Bread, Oat-Molasses, 139
Cookies, Nutty Oatmeal-Chocolate
Chip, 185
Cookies, Oatmeal-Date, 109
Muffins, Oatmeal, 129, 210

**Okra**
Fried Okra, French-, 126
Medley, Mixed Vegetable, 126
Pilaf, Okra, 126
Plantation Okra, 126
Stewed Okra, Southern, 134

**Omelets**
Chicken Liver Omelet, 44
Mushroom Omelet, Rolled, 70
Rising Sun Omelet, 281
Vegetable Omelet, Golden, 123

**Onions**
Cheese Onion Bake, 32
Cheese Onions, Sherried, 32
Creole Onions, 32
Gravy, Fried Quail with Onion, 214
Green Onion Teasers, 42
Micro-Baked Onions, 32
Pie, Onion, 191
Rice, Seasoned Onion, 166
Sauce, Onion, 72
Stuffed Baked Onions, 32

**Oranges**
Beverages
Banana Flip, Orange-, 48
Citrus Cooler, 160
Grapefruit-Orange Refresher, 174
Magnolias, 196
Punch, Orange-Lime, 160
Punch, Orange-Mint, 121
Slush, Orange, 49
Spiced Nog, Orange, 48
Breads
Cranberry-Orange Coffee Cake, 283
Cream Cheese Bread, Orange-, 210
Nut Bread, Orange-, 75
Rolls, Orange, 17
Rolls, Orange Butter, 206
Desserts
Bars, Pineapple-Orange, 129
Brandied Orange Juice, Strawberries
with, 160
Cake, Williamsburg Orange, 23
Crêpes, Orange Dream, 183
Pears in Orange Sauce, Poached, 19
Pops, Orange-Banana, 129
Pudding, Orange, 111
Sherbet Ambrosia Cups, 159
Tapioca Crème, Orange-, 283
Dressing, Orange Blossom, 266
Frosting, Orange Cream, 14
Frosting, Orange-Cream Cheese, 16
Glazed Apples, Orange-, 51
Glazed Pork Chops, Orange-, 25
Glaze, Orange, 75, 206
Marmalade, Orange-Pineapple, 150

Marmalade, Peach-Orange, 150
Rice, Orange, 200
Salad, Cherry-Orange, 56
Salad, Lobster and Orange, 207
Salad, Mandarin Orange and
Pineapple, 266
Salad, Orange-Cauliflower, 266
Sauce, Carrots in Orange, 107
Sauce, Chicken Livers in Orange, 218
Sauce, French Toast with Orange, 47
Sauce, Orange, 47
Sweet Potatoes in Orange Cups, 272

**Oysters**
Barbecued Oysters, 247
Dressing, Oyster Bread, 251
Fresh Oysters, Preparing, 127
Fried Raw Oysters, 14
Johnny Reb, Oysters, 42
Pie, Turkey-and-Oyster, 267

**Pancakes**
Buttermilk Griddle Cakes, 22
Sauce, Peach-Blueberry Pancake, 177

**Pastas.** *See also* specific types.
Garden Pasta, 199
Manicotti, Spinach, 199
Minestrone, 4
Salad, Main-Dish Pasta, 199
Salad, Overnight Pasta, 276
Tetrazzini, Ham, 77
Vermicelli Vinaigrette Salad, 189

**Peaches**
Baked Peaches and Sausage, 50
Baked Peaches with Ginger, Oven-, 170
Bread, Peach, 170
Butter, Peach, 308
Cobbler, Fresh Peach, 139
Cobbler, Old-Fashioned Peach, 170
Compote, Berry-Peach, 133
Cream, Bavarian Peach, 171
Cream, Peach Almond, 108
Crêpes, Peach, 184
Curried Ham and Peaches, 60
Freeze, Creamy Peach, 144
Fuzz Buzz, 160
Ice Cream, Peach, 171
Marmalade, Peach-Orange, 150
Parfait, Peach, 166
Pie, Fresh Peach, 170
Preserves, Old-Fashioned Peach, 150
Salad, Frosted Peach, 145
Salad, Frozen Peach, 54
Sauce, Peach-Blueberry Pancake, 177

**Peanut Butter**
Candy Squares, Peanut Butter-
Chocolate, 56
Chicken, Peanut Butter-Marmalade, 30
Cookies, Peanut Butter, 56
Granola, Peanut Butter, 296
Muffins, Peanut Butter-Honey, 56
Sandwich, Peanut Butter Breakfast, 55
Shake, Peanut Butter, 48
Slice-and-Bakes, Peanut Butter, 185

**Peanuts**
Candied Popcorn and Peanuts, 295
Chicken with Peanuts, Oriental, 236
Ice Cream Pie, Peanutty, 56
Spicy Nuts, 161
Sugared Peanuts, 249

**Pears**
Cheesecake, Pear-Berry, 141
Cobbler, Best Ever Pear, 194
Pie, Double-Crust Pear, 194

Pineapple-Pear Delight, 54
Poached Pears in Orange Sauce, 19
Poached Pears in Wine, 194
Poached Pears, Lemon, 74
Preserves, Pear, 195
Red Wine, Pears in, 254
Stuffed with Cheese, Pears, 290
Tart, Pear, 304

**Peas**
Black-Eyed Peas, Marinated, 156
Black-Eyed Peas, Southern-Style, 107
English
Buttered Peas and Mushrooms, 204
Casserole Supreme, Pea, 281
Cauliflower, Peas and, 288
Salad, Marinated English Pea, 54
Soup, Peppery Pea, 271
Snow Pea Stir-Fry, Beef and, 98

**Pecans**
Bars, Pecan, 209
Bites, Cheesy Pecan, 248
Bread, Cherry Nut, 36
Cake, Praline Pound, 88
Cake with Praline Glaze, Pecan, 196
Cookies, Butter Pecan, 139
Cookies, Cherry Pecan, 136
Glazed Pecans, 136
Glaze, Praline, 196
Ice Cream, Pralines and Cream, 184
Loaf, Tasty Apricot-Nut, 10
Pie, Choco-Pecan, 86
Pie, Coffee Pecan, 74
Sauce, Butterscotch-Pecan, 212
Spicy Curried Nuts, 250
Sugar and Spice Pecans, 297
Sugared Pecans, 167
Waffles, Southern Chicken-Pecan, 231

**Peppermint**
Mousse, Peppermint Candy, 71

**Peppers**
Chile-Cheese Casserole, 90
Chile Dip, Hot, 248
Chile Pepper Quiche, 224
Chile Sauce, Green, 220
Chiles Rellenos (Stuffed Chiles), 220
Green
Beefed-Up Peppers, 186
Fried Pepper Strips, 208
Jelly, Unusual Green Pepper, 132
Spaghetti with Veal and
Peppers, 14
Stuffed Pepper Medley, 131
Stuffed Peppers, Spinach-, 180
Stuffed Peppers with Rice and
Ham, 131
Jalapeño-Cheese Spread, 248
Jalapeño Cornbread, Beefy, 142
Jalapeño Hominy, 51

**Persimmons**
Bread, Persimmon Date-Nut, 218

**Pies and Pastries**
Apple Pie Cake, 226
Apple Pie, Dutch, 273
Apple Pie, Old-Fashioned, 299
Apple Roll, 178
Blackberry Roll, 178
Black Bottom Pie, 53
Boysenberry Pie, 133
Brownie Pie, Crustless, 33
Buttermilk Lemon Pie, 23
Buttermilk Pie, 53
Caramel Ice Cream Pie, 181
Caramel Pie, Burnt, 53

**General Recipe Index**   353

# Notes

*SOUTHERN LIVING 1982 ANNUAL RECIPES*

*Southern Living®:*
   Foods Editor: Jean Wickstrom Liles
   Associate Foods Editor: Margaret Chason
   Assistant Foods Editors: Deborah Garrison, Susan Payne
   Registered Dietitians: Betsy Fannin, Susan M. McIntosh
   Test Kitchens Director: Lynn Lloyd
   Assistant Test Kitchens Director: Karen Parker
   Test Kitchens Staff: Diane Hogan, Laura Nestelroad,
      Peggy Smith, Fran Tyler
   Photo Stylist: Beverly Morrow
   Editorial Assistant: Catherine Garrison
   Production Manager: Clay Nordan
   Photographers: Charles Walton: cover, pages i, 27, 28,
      61, 62, 63, 64, 81, 116, 117, 152, 153, 154, 187, 188,
      221, 222, 255, 292, 293, 294; Jim Bathie: pages ii, iii,
      iv, 118, 256, 257, 258, 291; Jerome Drown: pages 82,
      115; Van Chaplin: page 151

Oxmoor House, Inc.:
   Manager, Editorial Projects: Ann H. Harvey
   Editor: Annette Thompson
   Editorial Assistant: Cecilia Robinson
   Production: Jerry Higdon, Joan Denman

   Designer: Carol Middleton
   Illustrator: Cindia Pickering

# A WELCOME AID FOR BUSY HOMEMAKERS

## Protect your favorite recipes from spills and splatters.

Get a clear view of your entire recipe behind a protective shield with this durable, acrylic cookbook stand. Your book sits firmly at an easy-to-read angle, open to your working recipe, safe from sticky fingers, mixing splatters and accidental spills. After cooking, the stand can be wiped clean with a damp sponge. A generous 16¾″ wide by 12″ high, this stand can accommodate most cookbooks.

Price and availability are subject to change without notice.

Send your order with a check or money order for $12.95 to: